# Fort Cumberland

## Volume 2 of 2

By Lannie Dietle

Published by: **The Allegany County Historical Society**
218 Washington Street,
Cumberland, Maryland 21502

Cover Design: Special thanks to Joan Rilling Johnston for photo and effects depicting the site of Fort Cumberland, and to McClarran and Williams Art Director Jen Rowe for an insightful design that places an early version of the British colors symbolically underneath the modern Cumberland skyline.

*This book is dedicated to my adorable wife Cheryl Dietle.*

*History is written for the most part from the outside. Truth often suffers distortion by reason of the point of view of the narrator, some pre-occupation of his judgment or fancy not only as to relative merits but even as to facts in their real relations.*

Major-General Joshua Lawrence Chamberlain, in "**The Passing of the Armies**", 1915.

# Table of Contents

# 10. 1758: Fort Duquesne is captured

### In 1758, Sharpe reports that the area this side of Fort Cumberland had been settled

A letter[829] Governor Sharpe wrote to his brother William Sharpe on January 1, 1758 references inhabitants in the following statement:

*I doubt not but this proposal of our Assembly's to give up at once by a Law Fort Cumberland & a Tract of Country on this side of it 60 Miles in Extent which was till lately well setled will be represented to the Ministry by the Earl of Loudoun in proper Colours & therefore I have already sent Mr Calvert Triplicates of a minute account of all my Transactions (relative to our Troops & their Disposition) & with the Assembly during the last & the preceeding Session that in case Lord Baltimore should be called upon he might be well prepared to give answers to any questions that may be asked & I hope to justify my Conduct.*

### Dinwiddie sails for England on January 12, 1758

The February 23, 1758 issue of the "**Maryland Gazette**" has an article titled *"Williamsburg"* that includes the statement, *"January 13. Yesterday the Honorable Robert Dinwiddie, Esq; our late Governor, sailed from York Town in the Baltimore, Capt. Cruikihanks, on his Return for England."*

### Governor Pownall has an idea for a central warehouse for Indian stores at Wills Creek

The lengthy January 15, 1758 *"Memorial stating the Nature of the Service in North America, 1755, and proposing a General Plan of Operations founded thereon, by Governor T. Pownall, enclosed in his Letter to Mr. Secretary Pitt"*[830] includes the following statement:

*That the several Colonies who have hitherto constantly raised monies for Indian affairs, as a private provincial service, should for the future appropriate such monies to this general fund.*

*That such Colonies as have never raised any monies for these services should for the future raise and appropriate to this fund such sums, under a quota in proportion to the benefit received, or the harm avoided by the barrier arising from this general alliance and administration of Indian affairs: and it becomes worthy of consideration whether the islands in the West Indies, their interest being inseparably connected with the continent, should not bear a certain proportion to the charge of the war.*

*Matters within ourselves being thus prepared and provided for;*

*The first step of our measures in this branch should be, establishing, by advice of people of the best authority and most knowledge of the affairs of each nation respectively, at proper places, general magazines for this service, at the most convenient entrepéts between marine and island navigation of carriage, whence lesser stores, respectively subordinate to these, might be best supplied within the Indian countries, or where is most convenient for the countries. As, for instance, one at Schenectady, or rather at Mount Johnson; one either at William's Ferry, on the Potomack, or at Fort Cumberland, on Will's*

---

[829] "**Correspondence of Governor Sharpe, 1757-1761**".
[830] "**History of William Pitt Earl of Chatham…**"

*Creek; one either somewhere on the Roanoak or James's River; one other at Fort Augusta, on the Savannah.*

*From these general magazines the several national or tribe stores shall be constantly supplied. These stores would be also public truck-houses, and the storekeeper be also a public truck-master. These to be fixed in each particular nation, in such places and in such number as hath been usual, or as will be best for the good of the service, at each of which there should also be a smith: the commissary appointed to the affairs of each nation, to command and superintend all the store-keepers, truck-masters, and smiths, and all the stores, and be constantly circuiting through these, living always at some one of them, and attending respectively at any of them, wheresoever he is commanded by the general agent, or the good of the service requires; also at all times, (unless in matters of a more public general import, when the general agent is to attend,) to negociate and transact all matters and business such nation may have to do with any other, or with any colony, and to interpret between the Indians he is appointed commissary to, and in general, within the powers of his instructions, to do all those things and matters as have been usually done by provincial agents and interpreters; that the store-keepers and smiths do keep constant journals, and make report to the commissary; that the commissaries keep a regular journal of these reports and of their own transactions, and report to the general agent, and he likewise to keep a journal, and record and report to the Commander in-chief.*

Whether anything came of this part of the plan is unknown to me.

### Samuel S. Welder receives a promissory note

Samuel Stansby Welder, who was eventually killed by Indians near Thomas Cresap's, received a promissory note from Bartholomew Hatton on February 3, 1758. Edward Dorsey, Welder's attorney, attended the Frederick County, Maryland court on June 17, 1760 in pursuit of payment.[831]

### Combat on Georges Creek early in February

The February 16, 1758 issue of the "**Maryland Gazette**" contains the following account of an event that happened earlier in the month:

*The Week before last, John Lane and Griffith Johnson, being out on a Scout, pretty far up on Patowmack, they came across the Tracks in the Snow of some Indians, which they followed and came up with on George's Creek, near Savage River, at Night; when the Indians, being Nine in Number, stopped and made a Fire, and Lane and Johnson Fired upon them, and knock'd down Two, but one of them got up again, and made off with the other Seven; Lane run in to scalp his Man, but whilst he was stooping down, his Backside being towards them, the Indians fired at him, and one Bullet went through the Crotch of his Breeches, making Two Holes in them, and he very narrowly escaped being serv'd as bad as, or worse than, being scalp'd; for the Bullet just graz'd —— and took off a small piece of the Skin. He finish'd scalping the Indian; and they both came off safe with the Scalp. This Mr. John Lane, is the same valiant Man, who was taken Prisoner by the Indians last November (after he and one Cox had kill'd Two of them) stripp'd Naked, Pinion'd, and had a Halter tied about his Neck, on which the Indians laid down when they went to Sleep, but cut himself loose with a broken Piece of Bottle which he had found on General Braddock's Road, and conceal'd under his Arm; and on his Return, dug up an Indian which they had buried, took away his Match-coat, and scalp'd him with a broken stone.*

---

[831] "**Colonial Records of the Upper Potomac**", Volume 6.

The story of Lane's escape from captivity is given in the December 8th and 15th, 1757 issues of the "**Maryland Gazette**". In the December 15th article, Lane's first name is given as *"Jacob"*.

## The French discover that Fort Cumberland is being strengthened

An English translation[832] of a February 13, 1758 letter the Marquis de Vaudreuil wrote to the Minister of France from Montreal includes the following statement:

*M. de Rocheblave, on his last reconnoitering trip, approached very near Fort Cumberland. He saw that the English had built, on the outside, two redoubts in which they had placed batteries of cannon; and that they were also building a fort, with the logs laid lengthwise, around the stockaded fort. In this fort, the English are in greater number than before, since they were in a position to send out 150 men to pursue one of our parties.*

Fort Cumberland is being converted to an earthworks type of fort, with the earth held in position with logs.

## Cresap petitions the government regarding October 1756 losses

Volume 31 of the "**Proceedings of the Council of Maryland, 1753-1761**" includes the following depositions, which were presented to the Council of Maryland on February 24, 1758:

*To his Excellency Horatio Sharpe Esq. Governor of Maryland.*

*The Petition of Col. Thomas Cresap of Frederick County.*

*Humbly sheweth*

*That in the year seventeen hundred and fifty six your Petitioner was obliged thro' Fear of the Indians to leave his dwelling Plantation in Frederick County at a place called the old Town about fourteen Miles to the Southward of Fort Cumberland that your Petitioner not being able to remove his Effects from his said House at the Time he was obliged to depart from it left in his dwelling House and Store house locked up and secured in the best manner he was able about one thousand Weight of Wheat Flour, five Bushels of Salt one Hogshead of Rum, about one thousand pounds of brown Sugar, about five Gallons of Melasses in a Stone Bottle, about one thousand Pounds of bar Lead, about sixty thousand Nails, a Cask of China Ware a Cask of Glass Ware, about two Dozen frying Pans, Carpenters Tools, Smith Tools Brass Kettles, and Plantation Utensils, and some Household Furniture as by an Affidavit made by your petitioner hereunto annexed may appear, the most valuable Part of which Effects your Petitioner buried in a Cellar of his House to prevent the same from being discovered by the Indians in Case they should break and enter his House, your Petitioner further sheweth that since his leaving his said House and Plantation Henry Enocks the elder and Henry Enocks the younger, Jacob Lane, and William Lockhart all of Frederick County in the Colony of Virginia have been concerned in taking and stealing from your petitioners said House some of his Effects as appears from the Depositions hereunto annexed taken before a Justice of Peace in Frederick County in Virginia, and your petitioner has Reason to apprehend that most of his Effects left by him at his said Dwelling House at the old Town have been taken and stolen by the said Henry Enock the elder, Henry Enock the younger Jacob Lane and William Lockhart or some of them, and your Petitioner further sheweth that he is advised that the said persons can't be prosecuted for the said Felony in Virginia as the same was committed in Maryland, and that as the said ffelons are resident in Virginia and cant be taken in Maryland, that your Petitioner can't prosecute them for the said Felony unless the Government of Virginia can be prevailed upon to send the said Felons into this*

---

[832] "**Wilderness chronicles of Northwestern Pennsylvania**", 1941.

*Province to receive their Tryal your Petitioner therefore humbly prays that your Excellency will be pleased to represent this Matter to the Government of Virginia and take such Steps to procure the said Felons to be sent into Frederick County in Maryland to receive their Trials for the same as to your Excellency shall seem proper, and your Petitioner as in Duty bound will ever pray &c.*

*Tho[s] Cresap.*

*This Day came before me William Cocks Gentleman one of his Majesty's Justices of the peace for the County of Frederick, and being sworn on the holy Evangelist deposeth and saith that some Time in October last this Deponent was with some others a hunting and came to the Plantation of Col: Thomas Cresap where this Deponent see Henry Hencock junior take from the said Cresap's plantation about two Bushels and a Half of Flour, and after taking the Flour he hunted about and took a large Jugg which this Deponent thinks had Melasses in, and a Cannister which had some Pepper in it and after that he the said Henry Enocks junior broke a Jugg which had some Sugar in it and William Lockard took the Sugar away, and further saith not.*

*Jacob Lean*

*Frederick County ss: The above Deposition sworn to before me. May 29: 1757..*

*H Cocks.*

*Frederick County in the Colony of Virginia (to wit.)*

*The Deposition of Richard Lane aged forty nine Years and upwards taken on the holy Evangelists of almighty God before Thomas Caton Gentleman a Justice of the peace for the said County the 10: Day of May 1757 deposeth and saith that he went up to Henry Enocks' plantation on Cape Capon sometime last Fall a hunting where he stayed for a considerable Time in Company with the said Henry Enocks his Son Henry Enocks jun[r] this Deponents Son Jacob Lane and William Lockhart and that when this Deponent first came to the said Henry Enock's House he saw there about three Pecks of Salt about a Bushel and a half of Flour which the said Henry Enocks sen[r] told this Deponent they had brought from Col. Thomas Cresap's House at the old Town, and that after a few Days he the said Henry Enocks sen[r] sent the said Henry Enocks jun: the said William Lockhart and this Dep[ts] Son Jacob Lane to the said Cresap's Plantation again, and after their Return to the said Henry Enock's House this Deponent saw them have a Jugg of Melasses which he heard the said Henry Enocks junior say he had taken from the said Cresaps' Plantation but did not steal it for the said William Lockhart had appraised the same at five Shillings, and that if the said Cresap would give him the said Henry Enocks junior half a Crown he might have the Jugg again, and this Deponent further saith that the said Henry Enocks junior Jacob Lane and William Lockhart likewise brought with them about half a Barrel of Meal, and this Deponent further saith that he heard the said Henry Enocks sen. say, our Lads (meaning as this Deponent understood, the said Henry Enocks junior William Lockhart and Jacob Lane) found a fine Kettle and did not bring it with them, upon which this Deponent asked Henry Enocks sen[r] if he would go to steal the Kettle, to which the said Henry Enocks sen: replied, if he (the said Henry Enocks had it till Hunting was over he should not care what the Devil went with it afterwards, and further this Deponent saith not.*

*Sworn before me Tho[s] Caton*

*May 10: 1757:*

*Frederick County in Maryland (to wit)*

*The Deposition of Friend Cox aged forty two Years and upwards taken on the holy Evangelists of Almighty God before Thomas Caton Gentleman a Justice of the Peace for the County aforesaid the 10<sup>th</sup> Day of May 1758.. deposeth and saith that he heard Jacob Lane say he had seen Henry Enocks junior break a large Jugg that was in a Hole in Col: Cresap's House at the old Town full of Sugar in order to get at a Kettle which was in the said Hole which the said Henry Enocks would have taken away but the said Lane cursed the said Henry Enocks and threatned to tell of it, and this Deponent further saith that he heard Henry Enocks senior Father to the aforesaid Henry Enocks jun: acknowledge that he had the said Kettle in his Possession, and this Deponent further saith that he saw a Jugg at the House of Henry Enocks senior, and heard Jacob Lane say that Henry Enocks junior had brought it from the said Cresap's House. and this Deponent further saith that he has often heard the said Jacob Lane say that he would tell Col: Cresap that Henry Enocks had taken his Goods, and further this Deponent saith not.*

*Sworn before me Tho<sup>s</sup> Caton*

*May 10th 1757*

*Frederick County in the Colony of Virginia to wit.*

*The Deposition of Davis Morgan aged thirty eight Years and upwards taken on the holy Evangelists of almighty God before Thomas Caton Gentleman a Justice of the Peace for the said County the 10<sup>th</sup> Day of May 1757.. deposeth and saith that he was at the Plantation of Col: Thomas Cresap called the old Town some Time last Fall in Company with Henry Enocks junior and William Lockhart and saw the said Henry Enocks have a brass Kettle which this Deponent imagined would hold about two Gallons and understood that the same was the Property of the said Cresap, and this Deponent further saith that he saw the said William Lockhart take a Parcel of Spoons out of a Cask which had been buried in the Ground but dug up again, and that this Deponent saw the said Henry Enocks receive the said Spoons from the said William Lockhart, put them into his Wallet, and carry them away and this Deponent further saith that he saw another large Kettle by the aforesaid Hole which this Deponent took carried into the Fort and left in a Shed, and that this Deponent told John Nichols where he had left it, that he might give an Account of the same to the said Cresap or any of his Family that should come that Way, and this Deponent further saith that Lawrence Ross and Robert Ross told this Deponent there was two Pounds of Powder and 12.. or 13.. lb.. of Musquet Balls hid in the Loft of their Father's House, and that if this Deponent would take the Trouble to move some Corn and look for it he should be welcome to it if he could find it, and this Deponent further saith that in looking for the said Powder and Lead he found sundry Looking Glass hid in the said House some of which he took and carried away, and that one Night when this Deponent was at the said Ross's House on the South Branch of Potowmack the said William Ross & his Sons the said Lawrence Ross and Robert Ross came there and brought an Iron Pot with them with a Bit broke out of the Edge which this Deponent had seen in the said Cresaps lower Fort sometime before which Pot the said Ross told this Deponent he had brought for him to cook in while he stayed there, and that the said Ross told this Deponent it was his Pot. and further this Deponent saith not.*

*May 10<sup>th</sup> 1757..*            *Sworn before me Tho<sup>s</sup> Caton*

*Frederick County in the Colony of Virginia (to wit)*

*The Deposition of James Cox aged nineteen Years or thereabouts taken on the holy Evangelists of almighty God before Thomas Caton Gentleman a justice of the Peace for the County aforesaid the 10<sup>th</sup> Day of May 1757.. deposeth and saith that he being at the House of Henry Enocks sen: on Cape Capon sometime last Fall saw a Jugg of Melasses in the said House which he heard Jacob Lane tell Henry*

*Enocks senior that his Son Henry Enocks junior from the Plantation of Col: Thomas Cresap called the Old Town, and further this Deponent saith not.*

*May 10<sup>th</sup> 1757..*                                                    *Sworn before me Tho: Caton*

*Frederick County in the Colony of Virginia to wit.*

*The Deposition of John Nichols aged forty eight years or thereabouts taken on the holy Evangelists of Almighty God before Thomas Caton Gentleman a Justice of the peace for the County aforesaid the 10<sup>th</sup> Day of May 1757.. deposeth and saith that sometime last Fall as this Deponent and several others had been up to Fort Cumberland they called at Col: Thomas Cresap's House at the old Town, and saw one David Morgan pick up a Kettle which lay by the said Cresap's Upper Fort, which he the said David Morgan said he would carry home, and mend his (the said David Morgan's) Kettle with and this Deponent further saith that some time after as he was going up towards the said Cresap's Plantation again he saw the said Morgan have several Looking Glasses which this Deponent imagined were brought from the said Cresap's Plantation, and this Deponent further saith that he has heard Jacob Lane say several Times that Henry Enock junior had broke a Jugg that was buried in a Hole in the said Cresaps' Plantation, in Order to get at a Kettle that was buried in the same Hole, and that the said Henry Enocks junior was going to take the same away but that the said Lane threatened to tell the said Cresap of it and this Deponent further saith that he saw an Ax at the House of Henry Enocks sen<sup>r</sup> on Cape Capon which this Deponent suspected the said Henry Enocks had stolen from the said Cresap's House, and on examining him about it the said Henry Enocks sen: told this Deponent that somebody had brought the same and hid it under his House, and this Deponent further saith that he heard the said Enocks say that Rogues made a practice of stealing Things and hiding them under his Floor. and further this Deponent saith not.*

*May 10th 1757..*                                                    *Sworn before me Tho: Caton.*

*Frederick County in the Colony of Virginia to wit*

*The Deposition of Isaac Thomas aged twenty one Years or thereabouts, taken on the holy Evangelists of Almighty God before Thomas Caton Gentleman a Justice of the peace for the County aforesaid the 10: Day of May 1757.. deposeth and saith that this Deponent and one Jacob Lane having been up at Fort Cumberland sometime last Fall called at the House of Col: Thomas Cresap at the old Town and laid in the said Cresap's Upper Fort one Night and the next Morning they went into a Cellar under a Shed of the said Cresap's House to look for some dried Beef for themselves to eat and found there four Bars of Lead which this Deponent imagines would weigh about a Pound each and that this Deponent took two of the same and the said Lane took the other two and carried them away and converted the same to their own Use, and this Deponent further saith that in a Discourse had between the said Jacob Lane and this Deponent the said Jacob Lane told this Deponent that he the said Jacob Lane William Lockhart and Henry Enocks junior had taken a Jugg of Melasses which the said Jacob Lane and James Cox was eating some of, and this Deponent eat some with them at the House of Henry Enocks sen. on Cape Capon, and that the said Lane at the same Time said there was a large Kettle in a Hole out of which they had taken the said Jugg and that the said Henry Enocks jun: broke a large Jugg that was full of Sugar in Order to get at the said Kettle, and was going to take the same away till the said Lane cursed him and threatned to tell if he did, and this Deponent further saith that when he was at the said Cresap's House he saw sundry Goods lying about the said House, to wit, Weeding Hoes, Frying Pans, and several Bars of Steel, and further this Deponent saith not.*

*Sworn before me Tho: Caton*

*May 10<sup>th</sup> 1757..*

*Ann Arundel County ss..*

*The Deposition of Col: Thomas Cresap aged about 66: years or thereabouts taken before me the Subscriber one of his Lordships Justices for Ann Arundel Court this twenty second Day of January 1758 who being sworn on the holy Evangels of Almighty God deposeth and saith that sometime in June 1756 he this Deponent was obliged to leave his Plantation at the old Town in Frederick County for Fear of the Indians and in his Dwelling House and Storehouse he left several Store Goods and Household Goods with some Provision, about the Quantity of one thousand Pounds of Wheat Flour, five Bushels of Salt, one Hogshead of Rum, about 1000: lb of brown Sugar and five Gallons of Melasses in a Stone Bottle Jugg, upwards of 1000 lb of Bar Lead, about sixty thousand Nails, a Cask containing sundry China Ware, one other containing drinking Glasses, two Doz: frying pans, all Sorts of Carpenters Tools and Smiths Tools, several Plantation Utensils and several brass Kettles; the greatest part of the several Goods before mentioned he this Deponent has great Reason to believe, was taken from out of his Houses on his Plantation af<sup>t</sup> by a certain Henry Enocks senior and junior by Reason several of the above mentioned Goods being proved to be in their Custody, and further this Deponent saith not:*

*Sworn to before me the Day and Year above.*

*Tho.. Jennings*

*It is the Advice of this Board that his Excellency be pleased to write to the President of Virginia and send him a Copy of the aforegoing Petition and Depositions for his Consideration, thereupon the following Letter being prepared was sent accordingly.*

*Annapolis the 24.. of February 1758.*

*Sir*

*At the Request of the Petitioner and by the Advice of the Council of this Province I take the Liberty to send you the Petition of one of our Frontier Inhabitants named Thomas Cresap wherein he represents that sundry Goods to a considerable Value have been stole from him as he is informed by some persons who live in Virginia and that this being the Case he cannot prosecute the supposed Offenders in Order to bring them to Justice, unless the Governm<sup>t</sup> of Virginia will have them apprehended and sent into Maryland where the Facts were committed. You will learn from the Depositions that are annexed to the Petition, who are the Persons accused, what Grounds there are for the Petitioners Suspicion, and also the Names of some Persons that will be called upon as Evidences; if you shall be of opinion that the former ought to be apprehended and delivered up to an Officer of this Governm<sup>t</sup> you will be pleased to give Orders for that Purpose and to intimate to me at what Time and Place one of our Sheriffs might be directed to attend and receive them. As our Provincial Court will sit the eleventh of April next I hope they can be brought hither before that Time and if you will be so kind as to give Orders that the Evidences attend the Tryal, Protections for them shall be delivered to the Sheriff that might be ordered to receive the prisoners*

*I am Sir, your most humble & most obedt Servant          Hor.. Sharpe*

*To the honbte John Blair Esq:*

*Ordered that the Clerk of the Provincial Court issue Protections for Jacob Lane Richard Lane, Friend Cox, David Morgan and William Lockhart, as Witnesses to the next provincial Court on Behalf of Thomas Cresap.*

## Lawsuits in Frederick County, Virginia

The records of the Frederick County, Virginia court reveal that Abraham Bird was being sued[833] by Nicholas Crist on March 8, 1758 for trespass, along with assault and battery, and Thomas Cresap was being sued by William Ross on March 10, 1758. On the same day, a lawsuit against Garrett Pendergrass was abated as a result of the death of the plaintiff, John Moore.

## Maryland troops at Fort Cumberland haven't been paid since October 8, 1757

A March 10, 1758 letter[834] that Governor Sharpe sent to Baltimore closes with the following statement:

*About 300 of the Men that were raised here last Summer continue at Fort Cumberland tho they have not received any Pay since the 8ᵗʰ of October & there are a few still at Fort Frederick, but as it cannot be conceived that they will be prevailed on to serve on such Conditions much longer I shall write to Colᵒ Stanwix & press him to send a Company or two of Regular Troops to Fort Cumberland as soon as possible unless he can give those that are there some assurance of being paid.*

A March 10, 1758 letter[835] that Governor Sharpe sent to Calvert via Captain Cunliff includes the following:

*Fort Cumberland is as yet garrisoned by some of the Troops that were raised for the more immediate Defence of this Province; they had some Reason to hope that the Earl of Loudoun would have given orders for their being paid from the 8ᵗʰ of Octʳ last out of the Contingent Fund as the Assembly would not make any Provision for their Support; but I am afraid they will now be disappointed in such their Expectations.*

Sharpe informed Pitt of the situation in a March 16, 1758 letter.[836]

## Jonathan Plumer is involved with a criminal trial

On page 68 of the 1759 Frederick County court docket book[837], in a section titled *"Tryall Criminal Dockett for the 3ʳᵈ Tuesday and Nineteenth day of June Anno Domini 1759"*, a record dated March 11, 1758 lists Jonathan Plummer in a matter connected with *"Jnᵒ Shelby & Phil Mason bail"*.

## John McDonald is appointed to appraise an estate

John McDonald was one of the men who was appointed[838] by the Augusta County court on March 16, 1758 to serve as an appraiser for the William Claypool estate. In 1761, a John McDonald appears on the Old Town Hundred list. The court record suggests he was living in Virginia in 1758.

---

[833] **"Colonial Records of the Upper Potomac"**, Volume 6.

[834] **"Correspondence of Governor Horatio Sharpe"**, Volume II, 1890.

[835] **"Correspondence of Governor Horatio Sharpe"**, Volume II, 1890.

[836] **"Correspondence of Governor Horatio Sharpe"**, Volume II, 1890.

[837] MSA No. C782-11

[838] **"Colonial Records of the Upper Potomac"**, Volume 6.

### Sharpe reports to Abercromby about the troop funding situation

A March 20, 1758 letter[839] that Governor Sharpe sent to Abercromby includes the following:

*When I found that the two Houses of Assembly would not agree on a Bill for the Support of our Forces I informed the Earl of Loudoun how matters stood & intreated him to order some other Troops to Fort Cumberland lest the Garrison that was then there should upon hearing that the Assembly would not support them disband themselves & the Fort with its Artillery be thereby abandoned to the Enemy. but as the winter was now far advanced & the Roads to Fort Cumberland become almost impracticable His Ldp was pleased to engage for the Payment of our Troops as long as they should continue to garrison that place & Col° Stanwix gave orders for their being supplied with as much Provision as they might stand in need of. Upon this Footing have our Men remained ever since the 8th of October last but I am afraid the Officers will not be able to keep them together much longer without Pay & the late Conduct & Resolutions of our Assembly forbid me to hope that they will appropriate any money to pay the Arrears that are now due to them...*

### Forbes requests that the road be mended between Conocheague Creek and Fort Cumberland

A March 21, 1758 letter from General Forbes to Governor Sharpe states, *"And you will be so good to give your orders, about the Road leading from Williams's Ferry, to Fort Cumberland, espetialy the Road from Colonel Cressop's to Fort Cumberland, which may be mended in some measure, by your people now at that Fort."*

### Forbes mentions Fraser at Wills Creek

Forbes' March 21, 1758 correspondence[840] to Sharpe also contains the statement:

*If it could possibly be contrived _____ some Intelligent person up to the Ohio, and Fort Duquesne, to get some Intelligence of the Enemys situation in those parts, I should make it very well worth his while perhaps Capt Dagworthy at Fort Cumberland, might find some such person to send. ... They say there is one Fraser at Wills's Creek who knows all the Ohio Indians perfectly well.*

Forbes sent a similar letter[841] to Governor Denny on March 20, 1758 that states:

*If it could possibly be contrived to find some Intelligent Person who would venture up to the Ohio, either as a Merchant or a Deserter, & would bring us Intelligence what was going on in those parts, I should certainly reward him handsomely. Perhaps such a one might be found in some of your Provincial Companies up a Fort Loudoun, &ca, &ca.*

### Blair responds to the correspondence about the burglaries at Cresap's

On March 25, 1758 John Blair replied to Sharpe's February 25, 1758 letter as follows:

*Your Excellency's Letter of the 25th of February with the Depositions taken on Col: Cresap's Complaint came to my Hands four Days ago. The Council being convened on Mr Secretary Pitts Letter of December 30th I laid yours' before them they were willing to have Justice done to Col: Cresap, but apprehended considerable Difficulties to get it done in time for a Trial in your Provincial Court on the 11th of April as they are at a great Distance from hence and no opportunity of sending a Writ soon, without the Charge*

---

[839] **"Correspondence of Governor Horatio Sharpe"**, Volume II, 1890.
[840] **"Correspondence of Governor Sharpe, 1757-1761"**, Volume 9.
[841] **"Minutes of the Provincial Council of Pennsylvania..."**, Volume 8.

*of an Express, and the Hazard of sending them in Time, and if apprehended they must be confined 'till I can advertise with Certainty when and where they may be delivered to an Officer that you shall send to receive them, and they were of Opinion that we could not bind the Witnesses to appear at your Court but that Col: Cresap must engage them to be willing to go. I have since advised with our Attorney General, and some other of our Lawyers, who on reading the Depositions I find are of opinion there is no Proof of their breaking the House; As much is lost, and what they took is but of little Worth it is probable it had been rifled before they came there, and they think he had better punish their Purses, for that they could not on those Depositions be convicted capitally, or that it would be too severe for the Offence, I hope Col: Cresap will reconsider it, and let me hear again how he thinks I may serve him in it, for I am desirous to do him Justice.*

## Teaching men to live without victuals

A March 27, 1758 letter[842] from Sharpe to St. Clair states:

*I am obliged to you for encouraging General Forbes to entertain a favourable opinion of me & of my Desires to forward the Service, but I am much afraid that it will not be in my power to confirm it. In short, I cannot promise him any men from this Province unless He or General Abercromby will engage to pay them & I have taken the Liberty to tell him as much in the Letter I have now sent. It is well Capt Dagworthy & the Rest of our Officers taught their men to live without Victuals last Summer; otherwise they may not have found it so easy a matter to keep them together 6 months without pay in the Winter. How much longer they will be contented to serve on this Footing I cannot tell, but lest Accidents should happen I hope some other Troops will be ordered to Fort Cumberland as soon as possible.*

## A reference to a road from Shippensburg via Fort Frederick

A March 29, 1758 letter from Sharpe to St. Clair includes the statement, *"...am informed that the Road which leads to Fort Cumberland from Shippensburg by Fort Frederick is near twenty miles shorter than the Road which goes by Williams's or the mouth of Conegochiegh."*

## Waggoners petition for a Maryland road to Fort Cumberland

The March 31, 1758 proceedings[843] of the Upper House of Maryland include the following:

*Read the Petition of several Waggoners in Frederick County praying an Allowance may be made for making a Waggon Road in this Province from Fort Frederick to Fort Cumberland referred to the Consideration of the Lower House and sent by Col: Tasker.*

## Washington has doubts about the feasibility of a road from Fort Frederick

An April 10, 1758 letter[844] that Washington wrote to General John Stanwix from Fort Loudon includes the following: *"In the next place, I am fully convinced there never can be a road made between Fort Frederic and Fort Cumberland, that will admit the transportation of carriages. For I have passed it with many others, who were of the same opinion ..."*

---

[842] **"The Pennsylvania German Society, Proceedings and Addresses..."**, Volume XXII, 1913.
[843] **"Archives of Maryland"**, Volume LV.
[844] **"The Writings of George Washington"**, Volume 2, Fitzpatrick, 1931.

## John Nicholas is sued in Frederick County, Virginia

The records of the Frederick County, Virginia court reveal that William Forman was summoned[845] on May 9, 1758 to act as a witness in Wendell Brown's lawsuit against John Nicholas. The lawsuit was over Nicholas's non-payment of a 1757 bill for four hogs that had a total weight of 420 pounds.

## The troops at Fort Cumberland are seven months without pay

A May 14, 1758 letter[846] that Governor Sharpe sent to Lord Baltimore includes the following:

*The Troops that were raised here last year continue still to garrison Fort Cumberland & Fort Frederick altho it is now 7 Months since they received any Pay; what will be now done with them I do not know but have reason to believe that when Brigadier Forbes & I meet on the Frontiers towards the End of this Month he will be prevailed on to take them into His Majesty's Pay as Rangers during the Campaign.*

## Forbes authorizes investigating a road from Raystown to the Youghiogheny

According to Hulbert's 1903 book "**The Old Glade (Forbes's) road**", Forbes wrote the following to Bouquet on May 20, 1758, *"By all means have the road reconnoitered from Rays town to the Yohageny."*

## A fort is tentatively planned for Raystown

The construction of a fort at Rays Town was still being contemplated in May of 1758. Bouquet's May 22, 1758 letter to Forbes has an outline of the numbered construction stages of the route from Lancaster to Rays Town. Stage four is listed as *"4 18 miles 1/2 way to Rays Town, where I shall have a stockade Erect'd"*, and stage five is listed as *"5 17 miles at Rays Town where we shall Build a Fort."*

## Forbes mentions an intent to build a fort at Raystown

A May 23, 1758 letter[847] Forbes wrote to Bouquet from Philadelphia includes the statement:

*I have told him that you was to push Col. Armstrongs and Burds Reg^mt forward towards Raestown in order to build the Fort and Store houses & have desired Washingtons Bat^n to be ready to join you after sending a reinforcement to Fort Cumberland.*

## Washington's regiment is to march to Fort Cumberland

A translation[848] of a May 25, 1758 letter that Bouquet wrote to General John Forbes from Carlisle contains the statement:

*I wrote to Sir John St. Clair to have Washington's regiment march to Fort Cumberland, and as soon as we are able to advance to Reas Town, 400 men of that corps will be employed in cutting the road of communication between these two posts, and will come to join us.*

*I do not know how much ammunition there is at Fort Cumberland, but I understand that there was a great deal used everywhere, and that there is a lack of bullets and lead. The difference in caliber of the*

---

[845] "**Colonial Records of the Upper Potomac**", Volume 6.

[846] "**Correspondence of Governor Horatio Sharpe**", Volume II, 1890.

[847] "**The Papers of Henry Bouquet**", Volume 1, 1972.

[848] "**The Papers of Col. Henry Bouquet**", 1940.

*provincials' guns is a great inconvenience, since they have no molds, and our bullets cannot be used in them.*

### Sharpe describes the Fort Cumberland Situation to St. Clair

A May 29, 1758 letter[849] that Governor Sharpe sent to St. Clair includes the following:

*I hope you have by this time received Instructions from the General relative to the Payment of the Troops that are in Garrison at Fort Cumberland & Fort Frederick & that have now served near 8 months without Pay, I cannot help being uneasy about them as it is owing to the Encouragement which I have given the Officers in Consequence of the Earl of Loudoun's & General Forbes's Letters that the men have kept together so long & unless the General will order Payment to be made for the Provisions which they have been supplied with very shortly the Person that has victualled them must be inevitably ruined.*

### Bouquet wants men for road cutting and garrisoning Fort Cumberland

A translation[850] of a May 30, 1758 letter that Bouquet wrote to General John Forbes from Carlisle contains the statement:

*Following your orders enabling me to make use of Washington's regiment, I had written to Sir John to have him send the entire regiment to Fort Cumberland, to leave the number necessary for its defence in the fort, and that I would send orders for the rest to join me, cutting the road from Cumberland to Reas Town on their march. This seems to me a still better arrangement. My express left 4 days ago, and I have not yet received any reply. I wrote again today to Sir John that if the 5 companies and that of the artificers intended for Shippensburg have not gone when he receives my letter, he should have them march to Fort Cumberland, according to my first directions.*

### A long day of writing

A May 31, 1758 letter[851] that St. Clair wrote to Sharpe from Winchester states:

*Your Letter of the 29th of this month I received this afternoon. When I wrote to you I did not imagine you cou'd either provide me with Provisions or Waggons, but before I take either the one or the other it is my duty to ask you. I am glad the Carabines &c are at Conegogee. The one half of the troops go to Shippensbourg and the other half to Fort Cumberland, so that 6 Compys march to morrow to the northward and so soon as I get your Arms for 400 more they shall take the same Route. And I shall prepare the other half as fast as possible to move to the Westward, but I do not think I shall abe able to put that division in motion till the 9th of the month. After that I shall be at your disposal*

*I hope to get an explicit answer about yr troops at fort Frederick & fort Cumberland; Genl fforbes wants that you and I shou'd settle it, if so we ought to begin to coin in time. I think of going towards the Pennsylvania forts so soon as I am done here, but I may receive orders to go by fort Cumberland. I have wrote Eleven hours this day and tired with that & Vexation*

---

[849] **"Correspondence of Governor Horatio Sharpe"**, Volume II, 1890.
[850] **"The Papers of Col. Henry Bouquet"**, 1940.
[851] **"Archives of Maryland"**, Volume 9.

## Some of Washington's and Byrd's troops will be at Fort Cumberland

A translation[852] of a June 3, 1758 letter that Bouquet wrote to General John Forbes from Carlisle contains the statement:

*For lack of provisions, as I suppose, Sir John is sending me at Fort Loudoun 5 of Washington's companies and a company of workmen. They are to arrive this evening, and will have to make bark shelters, Indian fashion, as there is not a tent to give them.*

*The rest of the regiment, with half of Bird's, will be at Fort Cumberland on the 16th of the present month.*

## Sharpe writes to St. Clair about payment and provisions for Fort Cumberland

A June 3, 1758 letter[853] that Governor Sharpe sent to St. Clair from Mr. Darnall's near Frederick Town states:

*Since the General leaves it entirely to you & me to settle & pay what is due to the Troops that are in Garrison at Fort Cumberland & Fort Frederick It is time I think you should know what Sum will be sufficient that you may proceed to coin as soon as you please for that purpose. By the inclosed Sketch or general Account you will see that there was due to our Troops the 8ᵗʰ of April last a Trifle more than £4536 Currency or £2835 Stᵍ & that the Agent Victualler's Account for supplying with Provisions from the 8ᵗʰ of Octʳ last to that time amounts to £2970. 15 Currency exclusive of a Hospital Account & the Expence of carrying Provisions from Fort Frederick to Fort Cumberland. There is likewise a considerable sum due to him for Victualling the several Parties of Indians that have been at those Forts since the Beginning of April 1757, but what the exact Sum is I do not as yet know. You have been already told that our Lower House of Assembly gave it as their opinion in October last that no Forces which should be placed as a Garrison in Fort Cumberland could contribute in any manner whatever to the Security of the Province, they Resolved also at the same time that they would neither pay nor victual any men that should be there after sent or ordered to garrison that place. When I sent the Earl of Loudoun Advice of the Assembly's having come to such a Resolution & intreated him to order some of His Majesty's regular Troops to march & take Possession of that place lest the Maryland Forces should hear that the Assembly had granted no money for their farther Support & should thereupon abandon it His Ldp was pleased to tell me that it was extreemly inconvenient to move the Troops at such a Distance at that Season of the year & that therefore if I would keep up the Maryland Forces or as many of them as might be necessary to garrison Fort Cumberland he would engage to pay them & to pay for the Provisions that might be delivered to them while they should continue in the Service as you will see by the inclosed Copy of His Ldp's Letter. In obedience to His Ldp's orders & to the orders of the Generals who succeeded him in the Command of His Majesty's Forces in America our Troops have been kept up till this time, most of them have remained constantly at Fort Cumberland & many of the Rest have been employed in convoying them Provisions, our Assembly have met twice since I received the Earl of Loudoun's Letter but all my Endeavours to prevail with them to grant a Sum of money to pay off the Arrears that were due to our Troops & to Mʳ Ross for Victualling them proved fruitless. It would be unnecessary to trouble you with a Detail of all that passed between the Assembly & me while they were sitting relative to our Troops but it might not perhaps be amiss to inform you that in an Address which the Lower House of Assembly presented me the 17ᵗʰ of April they spoke of the five Companies which were at that time & are still in Garrison at Fort Cumberland & Fort Frederick as Companies in the Service & Pay of this Province & said that they presumed it was the reasonable Dependance which those Soldiers had that the several Branches of the Legislature would soon agree upon a Bill for paying them that had prevented their*

---

852 **"The Papers of Col. Henry Bouquet"**, 1940.
853 **"Correspondence of Governor Horatio Sharpe"**, Volume II, 1890.

*disbanding themselves before that time. In case the General will fulfill the Earl of Loudoun's Engagement with respect to the Maryland Troops & will forthwith advance as much money as is due to them & to the Person by whom they have been victualled He might if he thinks proper allude to this Address in the Demand that I presume he will make on this Province & I am really of opinion that our Lower House of Assembly will think themselves in some Sort bound by these Declarations of theirs to repay at some future Session whatever Sum the General shall advance for the Payment of our Troops to the time that that Address was presented or to the End of their last Session; but concerning this Matter I shall communicate my Sentiments to you more fully when the General has given you an explicit answer & when I have the pleasure of seeing you after you can leave Winchester. The inclosed Extract of a Letter from Doctor Ross to M<sup>r</sup> Ridout will shew you that it is high time a fresh Supply of Provisions was sent to Fort Cumberland especially as you are about to reinforce that Garrison, As I have not desired Doctor Ross to send up any because I know that he is already too much endebted to the Frontier Inhabitants to be able to procure a quantity entirely on Credit, You will be pleased to give such orders for victualling the Troops at Fort Cumberland & to such Person as you shall think fit —*

### St. Claire receives junk carbines from Fort Cumberland

A June 3, 1758 letter[854] that St. Clair sent to Governor Sharpe from Winchester includes the following. *"I have received 17 Carbines from Fort Cumberland and Nothing else, whenever your Arms come here, I shall send Them to Frederick Town, they are good for Nothing."*

### Francis Fauquier becomes Governor of Virginia on June 7, 1758

The 1852 book "**The History of Virginia**" states:

*In the mean while, the affairs of the province had been materially benefited by a change of governors. Dinwiddie had sailed for England in January, 1758, leaving behind him a character for arrogance and avarice, which made his departure a source of congratulation rather than of regret. Lord Loudoun had been appointed to succeed him; but the pressure of his military duties detaining him at the north, John Blair, president of the council, acted as chief magistrate until the 7th of June, when he surrendered his authority into the hands of the newly commissioned governor, Francis Fauquier.*

### Preparing to march men from Fort Frederick to Fort Cumberland

A June 9, 1758 letter[855] that Governor Sharpe sent to Forbes from Conegochiegh includes the following: *"I have also given orders to those of our Troops that are at Fort Frederick to hold themselves in readiness to march to Fort Cumberland on the first Notice after the 15<sup>th</sup> Inst by which Day I expect two Companies of Militia will be here ready to take their Post."*

### The main army is to march through Pennsylvania

A June 11, 1758 letter[856] that Governor Sharpe sent to Calvert from Conegochiegh includes the following:

*The General seems inclined to take the Maryland Troops (which are now reduced to about 350 Men) into His Majesty's Pay as Rangers during the Campaign & I hope he will be prevailed on likewise to pay them the Arrears that have become due to them since the 8<sup>th</sup> of Oct<sup>r</sup> last in Expectation that the Assembly will*

---

[854] "**Correspondence of Governor Horatio Sharpe**", Volume II, 1890.

[855] "**Correspondence of Governor Horatio Sharpe**", Volume II, 1890.

[856] "**Correspondence of Governor Horatio Sharpe**", Volume II, 1890.

*reimburse him at their next Session. Those of the Men that are at Fort Frederick are to march towards Fort Cumberland about the 16ᵗʰ Inst. & I shall then garrison the former Place with two Companies of Militia which I have ordered out from the interior Part of this County for that Purpose. I find that the Army is to march thro Pensᵃ to Rays Town, & not by Fort Frederick as I expected.*

## Bring the wagons by the road we will open from Fort Cumberland

A translation[857] of a June 11, 1758 letter that Bouquet wrote to General John Forbes from Fort Loudoun contains the statement:

*After mentioning all these obstacles, which will – I hope – be without foundation, permit me to submit my ideas on the ways to overcome them.*

*1. I think that until I have taken post at Reas Town, it would be wise not to put all the troops on that road, but to hold them at Carlisle or Shippensburg within reach of Fort Cumberland, if it should be found by experience that this is better.*

*2. As for provisions, I think a very great number of wagons must be used at once as soon as we are established at Reas Town, in order to prepare stores there for the whole campaign in a short time.*

*And I would suggest that cattle and the flour transported by the wagons obtained in Virginia be sent by the road which we shall open from Fort Cumberland. ...*

*The provisions at Cumberland will last only to the 21st of this month. I shall take it on myself to have some sent through Sir John from Virginia, as it is impossible to send it by way of Reas Town without doubling the expense and the time lost.*

## How long will it take to cut a road from Fort Frederick to Fort Cumberland?

A June 13, 1758 letter[858] Bouquet wrote to Sharpe from *"Conigogegh"* states:

*As it will be of the greatest benefit to His Majesty's Service, to have a road of communication open from Each of the Provinces to Fort Cumberland. I am under the necessity of requesting of you, to have the straightest Road reconnoitred, leading from Fort Frederick to Fort Cumberland: Recommanding to those you appoint to mark it out to report the time that 500 men will take to cut it: any Expense you may be at shall be paid by Sir John Sᵗ Clair; as he will be the nearest to you, Please to send him the Report of it, that if found practicable, he may send Troops to work at it."*

A committee, which included Thomas Cresap of Oldtown, wrote a report that included the following statement regarding the condition of the existing road:

*Your committee have made an inquiry into the situation of the present wagon-road from Fort Frederick to Fort Cumberland, and are of the opinion that the distance by that road from one fort to the other is at least eighty miles, and find that the wagons which go from one fort to the other are obliged to pass the river Potomack twice, and that for one-third of the year, they can't pass without boats to set them over the river.*

---

[857] **"The Papers of Col. Henry Bouquet"**, 1940.
[858] **"Correspondence of Governor Horatio Sharpe"**, Volume II, 1890.

*Your committee have also made an inquiry into the condition of the ground where a road may be made most conveniently to go altogether on the north side of the Potowmack, which will not exceed the distance of sixty-to miles, at the expense of £250 current money...*

*Your committee are of the opinion that a road through Maryland will contribute much to less then the expense of carrying provision and warlike stores from Fort Frederick to Fort Cumberland, and will induce many people to travel and carry on a trade through the province, to and from the back country.*

## A plan for getting troops in place at Fort Cumberland to cut the road

A translation[859] of a June 14, 1758 letter that Bouquet wrote to General John Forbes from Fort Loudoun contains the statement:

*I have arrived from Conegogech, where I had an interview with Governor Sharpe, Sir John St. Clair, and Col. Washington. In it we planned the march of the rest of the Virginian troops, as soon as they are armed and provided with necessities.*

*Washington's 5 companies, Bird's second company of workmen, and the Light Horse, will leave Winchester for Fort Cumberland on the 24th of this month.*

*The 26th, all of Bird's regiment which is ready will follow by the same route. The rest will march as soon as possible, under the command of Lieut. Col. Mercer.*

*A company of Rangers, with 30 invalids from Washington's regiment, will remain at Winchester, with some small parties to cover the communication with Fort Cumberland.*

*Commissary Walker, after making arrangements with Mr. Hoops, has orders to provide for the subsistence of these troops on the road, and to send, besides, a six weeks' supply of provisions for 1800 men to Cumberland.*

*Part of this convoy will go with the troops; the rest will be escorted by one of Bird's companies.*

*30 barrels of powder 150 boxes of bullets and tools, sleeping-sacks, etc., will be sent with them from Winchester.*

*They have orders to begin immediately to open the communication as far as Reas Town, flanked by the Indians following Col. Bird.*

*The difficulties that I am afraid of encountering on the road through Reas Town, made me hear with pleasure one of Governor Sharpe's proposals, which is to open a communication from Fort Frederic to Fort Cumberland. The highway through Carlisle and Shippensburg is very good as far as Rawlins' house, 23 miles from Shippensburg. From there Sir John has had a good road cut as far as Fort Frederic, 12 miles away. It is about 42 miles in a straight line from there to Cumberland, of which 12 are already cut. 30 miles would remain to be opened, which could be done by five or six hundred men in 3 weeks.*

*By this, we could avoid crossing the Patomack, whose frequent floods stop all communication. The road is more than 20 miles shorter, and wagons could go there at all times from Pennsylvania.*

*At our request, Col. Sharpe has sent to reconnoiter the terrain and mark the route, and you will have a report of it very soon, in case the enterprise is found practicable and you approve it. The new recruits who will still be at Carlisle could be employed on this, and I am leaving tools at Fort Loudoun.*

---

[859] **"The Papers of Col. Henry Bouquet"**, 1940.

### Shelby is to set out tomorrow to blaze the road to Fort Cumberland

A June 14, 1758 letter[860] that Governor Sharpe sent to St. Clair from Fort Frederick states:

*This Day I send off the Camp Kettles &c. for Winchester & M᷃ Shelby setts off to Morrow in order to reconnoitre & blaze the Road from Fort Frederick to Fort Cumberland. Inclosed you have the account of 70 Blanketts sent by my order to Winchester which were delivered to Colo Byrd the 9ᵗʰ of this Inst. With the great Pains that Capt Bosomworth & Capt Pearis have taken 9 Indians out of 14 have been prevailed on to march to Fort Loudoun & continue the Campaign. There are about 20 Indians at Fort Cumberland which I am apprehensive may be for returning back to their own Country unless prevented. I have therefore with the Advice of Capt Bosomworth ordered Capt Pearis to that Fort who is in case they are for returning home to use his best Endeavours to carry them to Fort Loudoun, as this is interfering with Indian Affairs am doubtful how it may be taken a Line of Advice with regard to this matter will much oblige Sir &c*

### Shelby's orders

The June 15, 1758 orders[861] that Governor Sharpe gave to Captain Evan Shelby state:

*As it will be of the greatest Benefit to His Majesty's Service to keep open the Communication between Fort Frederick & Fort Cumberland you are hereby directed to reconnoitre & mark out as strait a Road as the Country will admit from this Place to Fort Cumberland taking particular notice of the several waters that are to be passed, the Soil on each Side of the Fords & where Bridges may be necessary; If any Rocks or marshy Land you are to report the same with the time that 500 men will take to cut the Road.*

### In case Forbes wants to open communication between Fort Frederick and Cumberland

A translation[862] of a June 16, 1758 letter that Bouquet wrote to General John Forbes from Fort Loudoun contains the statement:

*I am leaving Lieut. Basset here with tools in case you order the communication opened from Fort Frederic to Cumberland, supposing, however, that before deciding you will want to know what kind of roads I shall find in the direction of Reas Town.*

### Forbes hopes to be soon able to provide back pay

A June 20, 1758 letter[863] that Forbes sent to Governor Sharpe from Philadelphia includes the following statement:

*The Enclosed Letter from M᷃ Kilby, our Contractor for provisions, will show you I have taken the first opportunity of making D᷃ Ross easy as to what he has furnished, and I hope very soon to Enable you to make those Officers & Troops that were at F. Cumberland Easy as to the past, and I do myself Engage for the present pay, while they remain in the King's Service, during this Campaign.*

*I shall order Tents, Canteens &c. for them, and send them up as soon as possible.*

---

[860] "**Correspondence of Governor Horatio Sharpe**", Volume II, 1890.

[861] "**Correspondence of Governor Horatio Sharpe**", Volume II, 1890.

[862] "**The Papers of Col. Henry Bouquet**", 1940.

[863] "**Correspondence of Governor Horatio Sharpe**", Volume II, 1890.

*Colonel Bouquet & Sir John S. Clair Writes me of the Road you propose from Fort Frederick to Cumberland; If it is thought the most Eligible, you will be very obliging in giving a look to it, and your Directions to those Employed to make it. Any Advances of money for the present to Clear the by past pay or Expence of the Maryland Troops, must by no means diminish, or Interfere with our Claim for the same from the Province.*

### St. Clair receives a letter from Cresap

A June 22, 1758 letter[864] that St. Clair sent to Sharpe from Carlisle includes the statement, *"Last night I received a Letter from Old Cresop, in which he tells me that he had seen Leiu$^t$ Shelby and that a good road may be made in a fortnight upon this I have taken my measures to have a good many Troops at hand at Fort Loudon to assist in that work if necessary... I hope the Canteens & Kettles for Col$^o$ Byrds Regim$^t$ have been sent from Conogogee. I have received the Arms from it and they have sent me back the Hatchets by mistake Old Cresop looking upon them as Arms."*

### Shot and shell are forwarded for Fort Cumberland

A June 23, 1758 letter[865] that St. Claire sent to Governor Sharpe from Carlisle includes the following statement:

*I have this day sent Captain Jocelyn of the Royal American Regiment with 60 men to Fort Fredrick. I beg M$^r$ Ross may provide them with Provisions, they escort a Convoy of upwards of thirty Waggons loaded with Shott & Shells which I should be glad to send up to Fort Cumberland so that I must intreat of you to appoint some one or other to take charge of the Amunition and get forwarded with Battoes & Canoes to fort Cumberland for this Service and purchasing more Indian Corn & Oats I have sent you two hundred Pound & one hundred Pound of Virginea Currency for paying for Forrage that Colonel Procter may be able to collect at Shanado.*

### Sharpe discredits Cresap's report

A June 23, 1758 letter[866] that Sharpe sent to St. Clair includes the statement, *"What Col$^o$ Cresap has wrote concerning the Road I am apt to believe will have but little weight when I assure you that Capt Shelby had not at the time the Col$^o$ met him reconnoitred the least Part of the Road he undertook to lay out except Sidling Hill; it is now eight Days since he left this Place and no news of his Return..."*

### Captain Shelby submits his road report

A June 25, 1758 report[867] that Captain Shelby provided to Governor Sharpe at Fort Frederick states:

*In obedience to Your Excellency's Orders communicated to me the 15$^{th}$ Inst I have reconnoitred the Country that lies between this Place & Fort Cumberland & am of opinion that a good Road might be made between these two Forts by the following Rout, From Fort Cumberland to Evat's Creek 5 Miles over a good gravelly & level Soil, I think a good Road might be opened between these two places in two Days by 50 Men, the Distance from Evats Creek to a small Run called Flint Stone Run is 5 miles the Land is pretty Level & firm I am of opinion that 50 men might make this a good Road in two Days. From Flint*

---

[864] "**Archives of Maryland**", Volume 9.

[865] "**Correspondence of Governor Horatio Sharpe**", Volume II, 1890.

[866] "**Archives of Maryland**", Volume 9.

[867] "**Correspondence of Governor Horatio Sharpe**", Volume II, 1890.

*Stone Run to Town Creek is 6 miles a level gravelly Soil, there is heavy Timber on it for the Distance of about 3 miles. I suppose 50 Men would open this Road in five or six Days at the Distance of two or three Miles from Town Creek lies Middle Ridge & at about the same Distance from Middle Ridge on this Side is the Main Fork of Town Hill Creek the Soil is gravelly & I think 50 men might make a good Road from Town Creek to the main Fork of Town Hill Creek in 10 Days. from the main Fork of Town Hill Creek (where is a very good Ford which is never impassable unless after a very heavy Rain & then not more than for 24 hours at most) to the Beginning of the Descent of the Ragged mountain is about 6 miles, it is a Slaty firm Soil, as it is Sidling it will require a good Deal of Digging & I suppose 200 men may be employed 10 Days in making it a good Road. from this the Descent down the Ragged mountain for about a quarter of a mile is pretty steep it is a Slaty Soil not broken, 200 men would I believe make it a good Road in two Days by making one Traverse. At the Distance of 5 or 6 miles from this lies Sidling Hill Creek, the Land is pretty much covered with small Stones but is not Rocky & I think 200 men might make it a good Road in two Days. the Ford over this Creek is a very good one. from Sidling Hill Creek to Sidling Hill the Distance is about 7 miles firm & level Ground & I imagine 200 men would clear it in a Day. the Ascent up Sidling Hill is gradual the Descent on this Side pretty quick it is about a mile over, I suppose to make this mile a good Road would employ 200 men four Days. from the Foot of Sidling Hill to the Mouth of little Tonalloway Run the Distance is 7 miles over a gravelly Soil, I believe 100 men might make it a good Road in 2 Days. the Distance from little Tonalloway Run to Tonalloway Creek is two miles, here is already an old Waggon Road but it will require Widening & some Digging I suppose a hundred men would finish it in one Day. The Distance from Tonalloway Creek to Fort Frederick is 9 miles, near Licking Creek (which is about 3 miles from Fort Frederick) are some Rocky Points that ought to be blown (perhaps 7 or 8 Blasts will be enough to make the Road sufficiently wide for two Waggons to pass abreast. there must likewise be a Bridge thrown over Licking Creek which is about 80 yards wide & five Log Bridges ought to be made over as many small Gutts that intervene, I suppose it would require a hundred men about 17 Days to make these 9 miles a good Road. Upon the whole it is my opinion that a Road might be made between the two Forts which will not be 60 miles in Length & there will be no bad Pinches for Waggons to ascend nor any bad Fords...*

## Teagarden, Ross, and McCarty are paid for their services

Governor Horatio Sharpe's account[868] of *"disbursements for the western expedition against Fort Duquesne"* shows that William Teegarder was paid £3 for *"carrying Arms as p rec.ᵗ"* on June 26, 1758 and William Ross was paid £6 for the same service on June 28, 1758, and also shows that Adam M^cCarty was paid £1/10/0 on June 29, 1758 for *"assisting Capt. Shelby in laying out a new Road to F C"*.

## Tools are being forwarded

A June 27, 1758 letter[869] that St. Claire sent to Governor Sharpe from Carlisle includes the following:

*I hope by this time Captain Jocelyn has joined you, I shall make up his command to a hundred men, as soon as I can lay my hands on them; in the mean time I shall send you off three Companies of the Lower Counties with Major Wells of a hundred men each, I am not able to tell you if they can all march to morrow untill I see my next convoy up, I intend sending all the Shott and Shells by fort Frederick, for which purpose I beg you will get the Canoes on Pottomack collected, and as many made as possible. I shall pack off to morrow all the entrenching Tools I have at this place, which will be barely sufficient for*

---

[868] "**Archives of Maryland**", Volume LV.

[869] "**Correspondence of Governor Horatio Sharpe**", Volume II, 1890.

*your Service, but with a hundred & fifty good felling Axes some timber may be cut down. The second Engeneer on the Establishment shall attend you ...*

*I have no miners Tools here but shall order you two sets from Fort Loudon, and as soon as my head Miner comes up he shall be forwarded to you. I have wrote Col° Bouquet who is at Rays Town to abridge his work, as Fort Cumberland will serve for the grand Deposite, and to cut his road down to it, and to desire Col° Washington to cut back in order to meet you for which reason I hope Captn Shelby has blazed every part of the Road.*

*I shall order Major Wells to obey your Command and the inclosed Letter to Captain Jocelyn is to the same effect. ...*

## Construction of Fort Bedford commences on June 28, 1758

A translation[870] of a June 28, 1758 letter that Bouquet wrote to General John Forbes from the camp near Reas Town states:

*I arrived here the 24th with the Pennsylvania regiment and the detachment of Virginia troops. I received your letter of the 19th on the 25th of this month, and as I had only the same express to send you, I have kept him until the present time so that I could give you an account of the establishment of this post.*

*The road beyond Juniatta is very good, and all the woods are full of excellent forage. Since my arrival I have been almost constantly on horseback, searching with Captain Gordon for a terrain suitable for the proposed plan. We have searched without avail, and have found only high ground without water, or water in low and vulnerable places. Of the two inconveniences we finally chose the least and decided on the location which seemed least objectionable.*

*The fort intended to contain our stores will be on a height and will have a communication with a water supply which cannot be cut off.*

*Work was begun this morning, and will be pushed with all possible dispatch. From the very start I encountered a difficulty which I had foreseen, in that the Virginia troops do not wish to work without being paid. The Pennsylvanians have all offered voluntarily to work for a gill of rum a day. While awaiting your orders, I shall have the former mount guard, and employ the latter on the works.*

*If one wished to put it on the basis of paying the troops in America when they must work, the army would cost nearly four times as much, because no step can be taken without axe or spade in hand. If I had enough troops, I should send them to Fort Cumberland to remove the bad example they give But you will see by the enclosed report that I am weakened by the detachments left in the rear.*

*I am writing to Sir John to have them relieved as soon as he can, by the Americans, the Highlanders, or the companies from North Carolina, in order to enable me to push the construction of this post with the necessary diligence.*

*I have received all the convoys, and sent the wagons to Carlisle for another load.*

*Our Indians are behaving very well, scouting every day in the vicinity of the camp, and I always have hunters in the field. We have noticed no sign of the enemy, but I suppose that they will lose no time in coming to reconnoiter us.*

---

[870] **"The Papers of Col. Henry Bouquet"**, 1940.

*This morning I sent off Captain Johny and his Catawbas to the Ohio, and gave them Lieut. Chew of the Virginians, a very alert young man, with two other men. They have orders to try and take a prisoner, and to reconnoiter the enemy's forces.*

*Two other parties, each with 15 Cherokees and 15 of our men, under the command of Captain Clayton, Captain Ward, Lieut. Crawford, and Lieut. Blythe, are leaving tomorrow morning to reconnoiter the roads beyond the Alleghenies, with the instructions I reported in my last.*

*The post of Shingalamuch is not so easy to reconnoiter. It is 30 miles from here to Franks Town, and 70 from there across continuous mountains. The Indians do not seem inclined to make this journey; I shall see if I can persuade them to make it, and give them a couple of our men.*

*The approval which you were pleased to give what I have done is an ample reward for the troubles I may have had. With organized troops I should have lost less time, but these men have never been together, and everything seems new and difficult for them.*

*I hope that we shall not be obliged to reduce the rations to the rate fixed by General Abercrombie. These provincials have already been dissatisfied at no longer having as much food as they used to receive from their provinces, and if they were told of being cut down still more, it would put them in a very bad humor. The work and the brisk air of the mountains gives them an appetite which always makes them find the ration too small. From the beginning, I had put the officers on the footing of a single ration, before receiving the General's order communicated by Major Halkett.*

*I am very much obliged for the attention you have given my recommendation regarding Doctor Ross's debt. That will have a very good effect.*

*Since we are uncertain whether our proposed route will be practicable, wouldn't you find it expedient to send provisions to Cumberland for a month, instead of the 15 days for which Mr. Walker has contracted to supply the Virginia troops, after their arrival?*

*I am so busy with small details and so often interrupted that I can scarcely find a moment to write to you. If I forget something, you will pardon it, as well as the repetitions, for I do not have time to copy any letters.*

## Working on the road east of Fort Cumberland

A June 28, 1758 letter[871] that Governor Sharpe sent to St. Claire from Fort Frederick includes the following, *"I shall order Capt Dagworthy to begin to clear the new Road from Fort Cumberland to the Old Town Creek but he is too weak to spare many Men for that Service especially as he must immediately on the Arrival of the Canoes at the Old Town or the Flatts send down a strong Party to receive them & to convoy them to Fort Cumberland ... When Major Wells arrives I shall order him to clear the Road between the Old Town Creek & Sidling Hill. Mr Ross will be able upon the Credit of Mr Kilby's Letter to get money of his Friends to purchase Provisions for any Troops that may be ordered this way."*

## McCarty is to blaze the road to Town Hill Creek

A June 28, 1758 letter[872] that Governor Sharpe sent to Dagworthy from Fort Frederick states:

---

[871] **"Correspondence of Governor Horatio Sharpe"**, Volume II, 1890.

[872] **"Correspondence of Governor Horatio Sharpe"**, Volume II, 1890.

*With Monroe the Bearer of this comes one Adam M^cCarty who has my orders to apply to you for an Escort or covering Party & then to blaze a Road with the utmost Dispatch from Fort Cumberland to the Town Hill Creek, as soon as he shall make Report to you of his having so done. You are to have a good Road opened with the greatest Expedition & by way of Encouragement to the Party that you may order on this service to exert themselves. You are permitted to allow them a small quantity of Rum or other Spirit every Day, for which S^r John S^t Clair will order Payment to be made in about 8 Days you may expect 13 or 14 Canoes at the Flatts or (if the Water should be too low there) at the Old Town with the Kings Stores: As the Party that will be sent up with them as an Escort will be ordered to return hither immediately I must desire you to send down a strong Party to receive & guard them as soon as you shall be advised of their being arrived & I must leave it to you to get them to Fort Cumberland in the best manner & with the greatest Dispatch that you possibly can. I am told that in all Probability some Waggons which are ordered from Winchester to Fort Cumberland with Provisions &c will be there before the Canoes can get up, should this be the Case you will detain them a Day or two to fetch up the Stores with which the Canoes will be loaded but if this should not be the Case you are then to make up as many Teams as you can at the Fort & employ them in this Service & the owners of all the Waggons which shall be employed will be paid after the Rate of 15/ a Day for each by S^r J S^t Clair or me upon producing Your Certificates to shew that they have done the Service.*

Adam McCartney appears many times in this book, including in the 1761 Old Town Hundreds lists.


### A road repair crew was fired on sometime around June 15, 1758

A June 29, 1758 letter from Sharpe to Tasker states:

*I learn by a Letter from Capt Dagworthy that a Party of fifteen or Sixteen Indians about a fortnight ago fired upon six Men of a Party which had been ordered out under the Command of Ensign Beall to repair the Road between Fort Cumberland & the Old Town these men were it seems advanced about 150 yards before the Rest the Indians killed two of them & wounded two others. They would have scalped those they had killed but were prevented by Ensign Beall who immediately ran up with his Party & obliged them to retire.*


### Washington is to open the road as far as Rays Town

A translation[873] of a June 30, 1758 letter that Bouquet wrote to Sir John St. Clair from the camp near Reas Town contains the following statements:

*I have only 811 men to use, and besides using them as guards, I have to construct a fort and the army storehouses.*

*I am obliged to build shelters for the provisions and munitions in a hurry, which doubly delays the work I must do. ...*

*The communication through Fort Frederic to Cumberland will be shorter than through Reas Town, and since the general has approved it, not a moment should be lost in opening it.*

*I am sending orders to Colonel Washington to employ 300 men immediately for this purpose, including the Maryland troops which are with him, and to leave a sufficient garrison at Cumberland.*

*With the rest of the troops he is to open the road as far as Reas Town.*

---

[873] **"The Papers of Col. Henry Bouquet"**, 1940.

*If they need tools, as I suppose they do, you can supply them with some from the allotment arrived from England.*

*I left tools enough for about 200 men at Loudoun, and as we need them badly, especially axes, I beg you to have them sent to us, leaving at this fort only the number necessary to repair the roads. ...*

*I do not know if our Cherokees will always be so well disposed, but today they have done what I have never heard of any Indian doing before. That is working for us, and carrying a quantity of bark to roof our storehouses. Those who had gone with a party to Cumberland returned in one day, and report that the road is very level.*

### Captain Jocelyne is ordered to convoy the canoes up the Potomac

A July 1, 1758 letter[874] that Governor Sharpe wrote to Captain Jocelyne from Fort Frederick includes the statement:

*In a Letter which I received from S$^r$ John S$^t$ Clair a few Days ago he desires me to send a quantity of Bomb Shells & Shott that are here to Fort Cumberland in Canoes, the Canoes are now at Johnson's Landing within a mile of this Place & I have ordered the Shells &c. to be put on board, but as there are not Provincial Troops enough here to convoy them to Fort Cumberland or as far up Potowmack as the Canoes shall be able to go I must desire you to spare some men for that Service.*

### Jonathan Plumer is mentioned in court records

On page 20 of the 1759 Frederick County court docket book[875], in a section titled *"Continuances from August Court 1758 To March Court 1759"*, a record dated July 1, 1758 lists Jonathan Plummer in a matter that references the bail of Van Swearingon and Peter Butler. The same case is mentioned on page 78, in a section titled *"Continuances from August Court 1758 to June Court Anno 1759"*. The same case is mentioned on page 117, in a section titled *"Tryal Docketts for the third Tuesday and Twenty first day of August Anno, 1759"*.

### Washington proposes adopting Indian-style clothing

A July 3, 1758 letter[876] that Washington wrote to Bouquet from the *"Camp, near Fort Cumberland"* states:

*According to orders I marched from Winchester on the 24th ultimo, and arrived at this place yesterday, with five companies of the first Virginia regiment, and a company of artificers from the second, as you may observe by the enclosed returns. My march, in consequence of bad teams and bad roads, notwithstanding I had sent forward the artificers and a covering party three days before, was much delayed. As I cannot suppose you intended to send any part of my men upon the roads, till joined at this place by Colonel Byrd, I shall decline sending any on that service till he arrives, which I presume will be to-morrow.*

*There came twenty-eight wagons with me to this place, and I believe, if they were wanted, ten more might be had upon the South Branch, strong and good; but carrying-horses are certainly more eligible for the service to which we are destined. I have received a very scanty allowance of tents for the five companies,*

---

[874] **"Correspondence of Governor Horatio Sharpe"**, Volume II, 1890.
[875] MSA No. C782-11
[876] **"The Writings of George Washington..."**, Volume II, Sparks, 1834.

*namely, sixty-nine only. Out of these most of the officers must either be supplied, or lie uncovered. They will readily pay for what they receive, if required. No bell-tents were sent to us.*

*My men are very bare of regimental clothing, and I have no prospect of a supply. So far from regretting this want during the present campaign, if I were left to pursue my own inclinations, I would not only order the men to adopt the Indian dress, but cause the officers to do it also, and be the first to set the example myself. Nothing but the uncertainty of obtaining the general approbation causes me to hesitate a moment to leave my regimentals at this place, and proceed as light as any Indian in the woods. It is an unbecoming dress, I own, for an officer; but convenience, rather than show, I think, should be consulted. The reduction of bat-horses alone would be sufficient to recommend it; for nothing is more certain than that less baggage would be required, and the public benefited in proportion.*

## 60 wagon loads of musket balls will be sent to Fort Cumberland

A July 3, 1758 letter[877] that Governor Sharpe wrote to Virginia Governor Fauquier from Fort Frederick includes the statement:

*Col° Bouquet with Six Companies of your Troops & some of the Pens° Forces was opening a New Road from F. Lyttleton to Ray's Town & thence to the Forks of the Yogyogany which was likely to prove a very laborious & difficult Task. A small Detachment of the Royal American Regiment & two Companies of the Delaware Troops are come hither with Sixty Waggon Load of Musquet Ball & Artillery Stores, which are if it is possible to be sent to Fort Cumberland by water I sent off about Twenty Tun of them yesterday morning but am afraid the waters of Potowmack will be too much fallen before the Canoes return for them to make another Trip.*

## The fellows prick up their Ears like a Deer

A July 6, 1758 letter[878] that Robert Munford wrote to his uncle Colonel Theodoric Bland from Fort Cumberland includes the statement:

*I was permitted to walk every step of the Way to this humble Fort, to eat little, to lay hard, over Mountain, thro' Mud and Water, yet as merry & hearty as ever. Our Flankers & Sentrys pretend they saw the Enemy daily, but they never approached us. A Detachment is ordered off this moment to clear a Road thirty miles, and our Companies to cover the Working Party. We are in fine scalping ground I assure you, the guns pop about us, it you may see the fellows prick up their Ears like a Deer every moment.*

## Washington inquires about orders

A July 7, 1758 letter[879] that Washington wrote to Bouquet from a *"Camp near Fort Cumberland"* states:

*Colo. Byrd with 8 Companies of his Regim't arriv'd here yesterday, he left many sick Men behind him, as may be seen by the Inclos'd report; which, with the Company he Posted at Edwards's and Pearsalls, reduces our strength Considerably. I am a good deal at a loss therefore, to know how to Act for the best, since your last Orders for joining you at Rays Town Were not positive, and seem'd to be given on a supposition that Mr. Walker either cou'd not, or was not to supply us with Provisions here. Your doubts will in some measure be obviated when you see Mr. Walker's Letter to me on this head; and the returns of our Provisions; which I now send. If this therefore was your motive for desiring a Garrison to be left*

---

[877] "**Correspondence of Governor Horatio Sharpe**", Volume II, 1890.
[878] "**History of Cumberland...**", Lowdermilk, 1878.
[879] "**The Writings of George Washington**", Volume 2, Fitzpatrick, 1931.

*at this place, and for me to March on to Rays Town with the remainder of the Virginia Troops, you will, I presume, countermand our March to that place, for the following Reasons: first, because 300 Men may, I think, open the Communication to Rays Town with safety, and with much greater ease and convenience than if our whole Body Marches on, incumber'd with a number of Waggons. Secondly, it will, if the Army is oblig'd to take this Rout as I am told from all hands it certainly must, prevent the fatigues of a Counter march to Men and Horses, just going upon Service; thirdly, it will afford us an opportunity of lodging our Provisions and Stores here, while the Waggons may return for another Convoy, and save by that means the great expense of transporting them to there and back again, if we shou'd not be able to proceed from thence. And fourthly, Colo. Byrd Assures me that the Indians with him absolutely refuse to march any other Road than this they are acquainted with.*

*I was advis'd to hint these things to you, and wait the result of your answer before I put the whole in Motion. Whatever you direct under the Circumstances I shall execute with the greatest punctuality, and Expedition in my power. I enclose a return of the No. of Waggons now at this place, that you may be judge of the Expence.*

*Captn. Dagworthy telling me that Governor Sharpe is to open the Road to the Town Creek (which is within 15 Miles of this place) and as Maryland has near 200 Men here fit for Duty, I hope you will be of opinion that they are sufficiently strong to proceed on the Fort Frederick Road, without needing a reinforcement from us; especially if you will please to consider at the same time, that they are in a manner cover'd by the Troops at this place, and those which may be employ'd on the Road to Rays Town, on which I shall send a detachment to Work tomorrow.*

*I had wrote thus far when your Letter of yesterday came to hand; as we lye so contiguous, and can hear in so short a time from you, I shall only be preparing to obey your Orders; but shall not actually March till I hear from you again.*

*A pretty good stock of Liquor came up with the last convoy. We have no Hay at this place; 'twas Corn I call'd forage. We shall have Tools sufficient for opening the Road to Rays Town among the Artificers of Colo. Byrd's Regiment, and I enclose a list of what is here, belonging to Maryland, that you may be able to judge of their wants.*

*I am sorry to hear that the Cattawbas have so egregiously misbehav'd. When I write to Govr. Fauquier, which I expect may be in a few days; I shall touch on this subject. I am etc.*

### Daniel Pursley is paid for carrying artillery stores to Fort Cumberland

Governor Horatio Sharpe's account[880] of *"disbursements for the western expedition against Fort Duquesne"* shows that on July 8, 1758, £46/12/8 was paid to *"Dan.ˡ Pursley & other Battoemen for Carrying Artillery Stores to Fort Cum.ᵈ"*, and on July 10, 1758 £9/10/0 was paid *"To Geo Ross for a Horse that was shot Yesterday by Indians under Corporal Madden as he was going to Carlyle with a Lettʳ to Sʳ John St Clair"*.

### The musket balls reach Old Town

A July 8, 1758 letter[881] that Governor Sharpe wrote to St. Clair from Fort Frederick in the P.M. includes the statement:

---

880 "**Archives of Maryland**", Volume LV.
881 "**Correspondence of Governor Horatio Sharpe**", Volume II, 1890.

*Inclosed you have an Invoice of the Stores that I sent last Sunday to Fort Cumberland. The Canoes are just returned but the men say it will be impossible for them to make another Trip unless it should rain as the waters of Potowmack are fallen more than two Inches since they left this Place & they were obliged as they went up this time to drag their Canoes at many Places. They left the Convoy yesterday noon at the Old Town where the Stores were landed.*

A letter that Sharpe wrote to St. Claire at 10:00 a.m. on the same day includes the statement, *"The miners Tools came yesterday from Fort Loudoun but our miner is at Fort Cumberland."*

### Dagworthy is believed to be opening the road from Fort Cumberland to Town Creek

A July 9, 1758 letter[882] that Governor Sharpe wrote to St. Claire states:

*The inclosed which I have just received by Capt Ware will shew you that there is great Reason to hope that Capt Dagworthy with 300 Men is at this time opening a Road from Fort Cumberland to the Town Creek if I had now 150 good men here to reinforce Capt Jocelyne & Major Wells I think I could engage to have a good Road made from this place to Fort Cumberland by this Day Fortnight.*

### Fort Cumberland is believed to have 1,800 men

A July 9, 1758 letter[883] that Governor Sharpe wrote to Baltimore from Fort Frederick includes the following:

*I imagine that all the rest of the Virginia Forces except the six Companies that are with Colº Bouquet are by this time at Fort Cumberland; the New Levies as well as the old Regiment are very good Men. They are Commanded by Colº Washington & Colº Byrd a Gentleman of the Council, and amount I suppose to upwards of 1800 Effective men.*

### Washington begins the road to Raystown

A letter[884] Washington wrote to Bouquet from a *"Camp near Fort Cumberland"* on July 9, 1758 states:

*Your favour of yesterday was deliver'd me last Night. I immediately directed all your Orders to be executed. The Waggons (save those attending the Road Cutters) go of to day. Three Companies under Colo. Mercer proceed on the Rays Town Road, which we began to open Yesterday; they carry 6 days Provisions with them, and Orders to apply to you for more, if that don't suffice. Captn. Dagworthy and the Marylanders begin to open the Road to Morrow toward Fort Frederick; and are furnish'd with 10 days Provisions for that purpose; but an extraordinary Affair has happen'd in regard to their Provisions; I mean that having no Flour, notwithstanding 6000 lbs. and better, was included in a return which I sent you Sign'd by their Commissary, I have been oblig'd already to supply them with 2000 w't. of this Article, and shou'd be glad to know if they are entitled to any part of the Provisions laid in here by Mr. Walker for the use of the Virginia Troops; under the Circumstances they were; I was oblig'd to deliver out the above Flour, or see them starve, or desert, the latter they yet seem very Inclinable to do.*

*Maj. Lewis of the first Regiment attends you with 200 Men with whom I have Order'd Captns. Frazer and Walker to proceed to you. I am Sir with great regard, etc.*

---

[882] **"Correspondence of Governor Horatio Sharpe"**, Volume II, 1890.
[883] **"Correspondence of Governor Horatio Sharpe"**, Volume II, 1890.
[884] **"The Writings of George Washington"**, Volume 2, Fitzpatrick, 1931.

## Washington writes to Bouquet about various things

Another letter[885] Washington wrote to Bouquet from a *"Camp, near Fort Cumberland"* on July 9, 1758 states:

> *Colonel Byrd, with eight companies of his regiment, arrived here yesterday. He left many sick men behind, and, as he posted a company at Edwards's and Pearsall's, our strength is considerably reduced.*

> *Captain Dagworthy informed me, that Governor Sharpe is to open the road to Town Creek, within fifteen miles of this place, and, as Maryland has nearly two hundred men here fit for duty, I hope you will be of opinion, that they are sufficiently strong to proceed on the Fort Frederic road, without needing a reinforcement from us; especially if you will consider, that they are in a manner covered by the troops here, and by those to be employed on the road to Raystown, to which service I shall send a detachment to-morrow. We have no hay at this place; it was corn, which I called forage. We shall have tools enough to open the road to Raystown, among the artificers of Colonel Byrd's regiment.*

> *I am sorry to hear that the Catawbas have so egregiously misbehaved. When I write to Governor Fauquier, I shall touch on this subject.*

> *It gives me great pleasure to find, that you approve the dress I have put my men into. It is evident, that soldiers in that trim are better able to carry their provisions, are fitter for the active service we must engage in, less liable to sink under the fatigues of a march, and we thus get rid of much baggage, which would lengthen our line of march. These, and not whim or caprice, were my reasons for ordering this dress.*

## Origin of the name of Raystown

A July 10, 1758 letter[886] from Forbes to Pitt sheds light on the naming of Raystown, stating, *"I halt tomorrow and shall then proceed 100 miles further to Raestown, where I have now 1500 of the Provincialls, who are building some Storehouses and stockading a piece of Ground for our Ammunition and provisions. For in Raestown there is not one single house; The place having its name from one Rae, who designed to have made a plantation there several years ago ..."*

## Washington's troops begin their encampment at Fort Cumberland on July 2, 1758

A July 10, 1758 letter that Washington wrote to Governor Fauquier from the camp at Fort Cumberland includes the following statement, *"I Marchd from Winchester the 24th Ulto according to Orders, and Incampd at this place the 2d Instt; Colo. Byrd follow'd the 26th and arrivd here 4 days after me."*

## Sharpe mentions the road cutting activity between Raystown and Turkeyfoot

A July 10, 1758 letter Sharp sent to Calvert from Fort Frederick includes the following:

> *Colo. Bouquet having intimated to us while we staid a few Hours at Conegochiegh that he was afraid he should find it a very tedious & laborious Task to make the Road which the General had ordered him to open for the Army to march from Fort Lyttleton to the Forks of the Yogyogany by the way of Rays Town, by reason that the Road would pass over some very steep craggy Rocks...*

---

[885] **"The Writings of George Washington..."**, Volume II, Sparks, 1834.
[886] **"Monthly Bulletin of the Carnegie Library of Pittsburgh"**, Volume 14, 1909.

## The road is now a brush wood

On July 10, 1758, Bouquet wrote a letter to William Pitt that includes the statement, *"For were I to pursue Mr Braddock's route, I should save but little labour, as that road is now a brush wood, by the sprouts from the old stumps, which must be cut down and made proper for Carriages as well as any other passage that we must attempt."*

## The road from Cumberland will be open very soon

A translation[887] of a July 11, 1758 letter that Bouquet wrote to General John Forbes from the camp near Reas Town contains the following statements:

*It was with the greatest satisfaction that I just now received your letter of the 6th of this month, as I was very uneasy about having none since the 19th of June.*

*The change of route at such an advanced season seemed to me a hazardous measure, and although I proposed it to you, it was only in case this one was impracticable, asking you at the same time not to decide anything in that regard until I had reported to you on the state of the roads as far as Reas Town.*

*I am very pleased to learn that you did not allow yourself to be influenced in this matter. The roads are bad, but experience proves that they are practicable, and the communication with Cumberland is very good, not mountainous, and will be open very soon, as there are 300 men cutting from the other end, and 200 from this end to meet them.*

*All the letters I receive from Virginia are filled with nothing but the impossibility of finding a passage across Lawrell Hill, and the ease of going by Braddock's road. This is a matter of politics between one province and another, in which we have no part; and I have always avoided saying a word on this subject, as I am certain that we shall find a passage, and that — in that case — we should for many reasons prefer this route, if not for the whole army, at least for a large detachment. ...*

*From all the disinterested persons who have gone from here to Fort du Quesne, I learn that it is possible to have a wagon road across Lawrell Hill, and that on the other side there is nothing but some small mountains which cannot stop us, with forage and water all the way. The last resort is to follow the Indian Path, taking only pack horses, and sending the heavy baggage and the artillery by the other route, but I hope we shall not be reduced to that.*

*The Catawbas have left us like scoundrels, after bringing us one scalp, which was recognised by the Cherokees as an old scalp which they themselves gave them in the spring. I am omitting details until your arrival, but for the time being I have asked Col. Washington to write to the governor of Virginia, to make complaints about it to their tribe. Captain Jonny who commands them received only scorn at Cumberland and, I hope, at Winchester, which may prevent the same desertion among the others. ...*

*The Virginia troops are at Cumberland with provisions for three weeks. As soon as you are able to decide on your route from the reports I shall send you, it will be time to start them off.*

*I had 200 men sent here, but as soon as I receive reinforcements, I should like to send them to Cumberland. They seem to work grudgingly in another province, and if the two Pennsylvania battalions are filled, we can finish the whole job with them.*

*The fort progresses, in spite of the difficulties of digging in several places in the rock. We have storehouses ready for three Months' provisions, and more than a third of the stockades are in place.*

---

[887] **"The Papers of Col. Henry Bouquet"**, 1940.

*The location is good, and the water excellent. ...*

*The Indian reinforcement is agreeable news, especially at this time when it will no longer be necessary to let them grow rusty in idleness.*

*Mr. Glen is at Cumberland, and ready to come here as soon as he is sure of your arrival.*

*I am writing to him as well as to Col. Byrd, for them to try to send the new Indians here. I am afraid that they, like the 60 with Col. Byrd, will take it into their heads to be unwilling to take any other route than Braddock's, which they know.*

*If there is still time, I beg you to send orders to Gist to send the Little Carpenter (in case he arrives) straight to Reas Town by the Pennsylvania Road, for the reasons given above.*

*Bosomworth will go to Cumberland tomorrow to supply them, and to try to bring them here. He continues to manage his Indians very well. This evening five of them arrived, whom we had left at Loudoun, and then those that Captain Paris brought from Frederic.*

*I do not understand on what grounds Sir John is convinced that no road can be found beyond this place without dropping down to Braddock's. As the country we have to cross is absolutely unknown, except for the paths of the Indian Traders, who are not observant men, and whose reports are hardly reliable, we shall know the truth about it, when I must go there myself. The detour is not long, going to Cumberland by way of Reas Town, and whatever Lawrell Hill may be, you can in all safety follow your first plan and establish your storehouses here.*

## North Carolina companies join the road making effort

A July 12, 1758 letter[888] that Governor Sharpe wrote to Fauquier from Fort Frederick includes the following:

*The two Companies from N. Carolina consisting of 110 men came hither Yesterday from Winchester to assist in making a Road that the General has ordered to be laid out thro this Province to Fort Cumberland.*

## An Indian attack near Fort Cumberland

A letter[889] George Washington wrote to Bouquet from a *"Camp at Fort Cumberd"* on the night of July 13, 1758 includes the following:

*Abt. 4 Oclock this afternoon — after I had closed my letter to you — I received Information that two men were killed and a third taken prisoner on the Road about a mile from this place. I got the Indians to go, and sent a command of 50 men immediately to the spot, where they took the Track of six Indians and followed them till near dark, when the Indians returned, as did our party also.*

*They discovered that one of the men killed was a soldr. of the second regiment, and that the other two were herds going to our grass guards in the most careless, straggling, manner, contrary to repeated, and positive orders given to prevent small parties stragling from camp.*

*The mischief was done abt. 8 this morning — Our discovery of it too late to give us a chance to overtake the enemy — I thought it advisable, nevertheless, to give you Intelligence that the enemy are about, and*

---

[888] "**Correspondence of Governor Horatio Sharpe**", Volume II, 1890.
[889] "**The Writings of George Washington**", Worthington Chauncey Ford, Volume II, 1889.

*that I expect we shall be pester'd with their parties all this morn, haunting our camps, and watching our motions*

## Murder near Fort Cumberland, and inability to assist Dagworthy with tools

A July 13, 1758 letter[890] Washington wrote to Captain John Dagworthy from Fort Cumberland states:

*Your letter came to hand just as I was seeking a messenger to go to you, with an acc't of the murder of two People by a Party of the Enemy on the Road, a mile from this, — I dare say I need not recommend watchfulness to a Person so sensible of the necessity of it as you are — but I hope notwithstanding, that you will cause the greatest vigilance to be observed by all under your command, as we are certain the Enemy are about, and taken a Prisoner from Us.*

*It is not in my power to assist you with any of those Tools you ask for — I shall however acquaint Colo. Bouquet this night with y'r wants p'r express — I must entreat you not to suffer small Parties to straggle from you — from the signs we have seen the Enemy are not numerous — but this is no certain way of judging the danger.*

## An update on cutting the road

A translation[891] of a July 15, 1758 letter that Bouquet wrote to General John Forbes from a camp near Reas Town contains the following statements:

*Two men were scalped, the day before yesterday, and a third taken by 6 Indians, who were said to be Cherokees, in the party which met them near Cumberland. They were pursued in an attempt to recover the prisoner, the Indians going to station themselves in the passes. ...*

*Your orders were read to all the troops here, and sent to Fort Cumberland. ...*

*The 500 men on the road to Fort Cumberland are making little headway because of the swamps which they must bridge with causeways, but the road will be good and not mountainous. There about 20 miles cut.*

*There will be two log houses halfway, with bastions at the two opposite corners, flanking each other on the two sides of the road. They may serve as shelter for a detachment, and as a storehouse. This will mean a couple of days' work. ...*

*The 16 Indians whom Captain Paris had brought, left us yesterday like rascals, after having solemnly promised to take part in the campaign. Perhaps I wrong their leader, but I think he rather thought to put himself forward by bringing them under the lure of getting presents for their past services, instead of seeking to make them render new services. He is not a trustworthy man, in spite of the recommendations that may be given to you at Carlisle. (He left the day before yesterday to go to Cumberland with Bosomworth.)*

The log blockhouses were built on a tract of land (Book A-75 Page 292) along Evitts Creek and the east side of Wills Mountain that William Trent received a warrant for on May 31, 1762. Samuel Finley's

---

[890] A transcript is available in the 1893 book "**Valuable Collection of Autograph Letters and Documents...**" and the 1934 book "**The Writings of George Washington from the Original Manuscript Sources**". Bill Zapf identified the relevance of this letter to the road from Fort Frederick.

[891] "**The Papers of Col. Henry Bouquet**", 1940.

November 5, 1766 survey (Book C-70 Page 3) identifies Trent's property as, *"W^m Trents Land Called the Block houses"*.

## Washington sends out Indian war parties to harass the French

A letter[892] Washington wrote to Bouquet from a *"Camp at Fort Cumberland"* on July 16, 1758 states:

*I was favoured with yours of the 14th. Inst't, at 11 Oclock last Night, the Express who brought it, informs me, that he was twice fired at by six Indians, and oblig'd to abandon his Horse*

*There's three Parties gone from hence towards the Enemy's Country within these few days. The largest of them, (consisting of an Officer and 18 Cherokees,) March'd 3 days ago. I always send out some white people with the Indians, and will to day or to morrow, send an Officer and some alert white men, with another Party of Cherokees as you desire it; tho' I must confess, that I think these Scalping Parties of Indians we send out, will more effectually harass the Enemy (by keeping them under continual Alarms) than any Parties of white People can do; because small parties of ours are not equal to the undertaking, (not being so dexterous at skulking as Indians;) and large ones will be discover'd by their spies early enough to give the Enemy time to repel them by a superior Force; and at all events, there is a great probability of loosing many of our best men, and fatiguing others before the most essential Services are enter'd upon and am afraid not answer the propos'd end. ...*

*I shall direct the Officer that Marches towards the Enemy to be at particular pains in reconnoitring General Braddock's Road; tho I have had repeated accounts of it wanting such small repairs as can with ease be done as fast as the Army can March; it is impossible for me to send out any Men to repair it, as Colo. Mercer and Captn. Dagworthy got every Tool for that purpose I had. If we had Tools to go upon the Roads, the 2d. Company of Artificers wou'd no doubt be wanted here, but as it is, I imagine they will be better employed with you. ...*

*Since writing the above, the Warrior of the Party of Cherokees insisted on Marching Instantly, and that but one white Man shou'd go, they are gone, and I have given the white Man necessary Orders relative to the Road &c.*

## Washington writes to Halkett about clothing the regiment

A letter[893] Washington wrote to Major Francis Halkett from a *"Camp at Fort Cumberland"* on July 16, 1758 includes the following:

*It gives me a great deal of pleasure to find that I have in a great measure, anticipated the Generals Sentiments and Orders, in regard to dress. And reduction of Baggage; I am sensible that I have by this means lessen'd the appearance of the first Virginia Regiment, but I beg the General will think that, I have render'd them more fit for the active Service they are to engage in, by this means ...*

## Washington writes to Lieutenant Colonel Adam Stephen about regimental clothing

A letter[894] Washington wrote to Adam Stephen from the *"Camp at Fort Cumberland"* on July 16, 1758 includes the following:

---

[892] **"The Writings of George Washington"**, Volume 2, Fitzpatrick, 1931.

[893] **"The Writings of George Washington"**, Volume 2, Fitzpatrick, 1931.

[894] **"The Writings of George Washington"**, Volume 2, Fitzpatrick, 1931.

*The Quarter Master brings you all the stuff he has for Breech Clouts: if the quantity falls short you must purchase more, and charge the Publick with the cost (if he has not oppertunity of doing it himself while there).*

*I have directed the adjutant to transmit you a Copy of several Orders that I have Issued at this place for regulating the Mens dress; and beg that you will cause them to be punctually observ'd by that part of the first Regiment under your Command. It gives me great pleasure to find this Dress; or undress as you justly remark; so pleasing to Colo. Bouquet, and that therein I seem to have anticipated the Generals Orders. If my Orders shou'd be a little unintelligable in any Instance you will make the dress of the Officers and Soldiers of Maj. Lewis's Company a guide to come at my meaning; that we may, even in this trim, have some regard to uniformity.*

*Leaving all our Cloathing at once place is certainly right, and I shou'd be glad if you cou'd contrive yours here least you shou'd take some other Rout.*

### Joseph Tomlinson is paid for wagon services on the new road

Governor Horatio Sharpe's account[895] of *"disbursements for the western expedition against Fort Duquesne"* shows that Joseph Tomlinson was paid £9/15/0 on July 17, 1758 for his Waggon attending the Pennsylvania detachments under the Command of Major Wells on the New Road.

### The fort at Raystown is mentioned on July 17, 1758

An article in the October 7 to 10, 1758 issue of London's **"The General Evening Post"** provides an *"Extract of a letter from an officer in the expedition against Fort Du Quesne, dated at Fort Loudon, July 17, 1758"* includes the following statement, *"A strong fort is building at Ray's Town, and a large magazine."*

### Dagworthy is ordered to finish a bridge at Fort Cumberland

A July 19, 1758 letter[896] Washington wrote to Bouquet from a *"Camp near Fort Cumberland"* includes the following:

*You make me quite happy by your coinciding on opinion with me, relative to the propos'd Expedition. Captain Dagworthy's Party return'd hither yesterday in consequence of Orders from Sir Jno. St. Clair, forwarded by the Commanding Officer at Fort Frederick. I have directed him to finish a Bridge at this place, which I imagine he will effect by to morrow Night, with his Tools; I will next day send out a Party on General Braddock's Road, which I shall be able to reinforce when Colo. Mercer returns.*

### A bridge is completed at Fort Cumberland

A July 21, 1758 letter[897] George Washington wrote to Bouquet from a *"Camp near Fort Cumberland"* includes the following:

*We have got the bridge finished at this place, and to-morrow Major Peachy, with three hundred men, proceed to open General Braddock's road. I shall direct their going to George's Creek, ten miles advanced. By that time I may possibly hear from you. If they go farther, it may be requisite to reinforce*

---

[895] **"Archives of Maryland"**, Volume LV.

[896] **"The Writings of George Washington"**, Volume 2, Fitzpatrick, 1931.

[897] **"The Writings of George Washington"**, Worthington Chauncey Ford, Volume II, 1889.

*the party. But this matter, I suppose, will be ordered according to the route determined on by the General, for it will be needless to open a road that no use is made of.*

The bridge was most likely across Wills Creek.

### Needing covers for gun locks

A July 21, 1758 letter[898] George Washington wrote to Major Francis Halket from Fort Cumberland includes the following:

*It is morally impossible to get at this place, covers for our Gun Locks having nothing but Neats Hydes to make them of; and an insufficiency of those to answer the purpose. The Commissaries ask 18/ a piece for them; pray give me your advice in this case.*

### The Virginians agitate against a new road through Pennsylvania

On July 23, 1758, James Young, commissary of musters and paymaster general, wrote a letter to Richard Peters that includes the statement, *"The Virginians are making great interest that our Rout may be by Cumberland, but I hope they will not succeed."*

### Barton mentions fortifications and encampments at Rays Town

In his July 24, 1758 journal entry, Thomas Barton mentions the fort at Rays Town, along with storehouses and some breastworks surrounding two encampments.

### Peachy is working on Braddock's road

A July 25, 1758 letter[899] George Washington wrote to Bouquet from the *"Camp, near Fort Cumberland"* includes the following:

*Major Peachy, who Commands the Working Party on Genl. Braddocks Road, writes me, that he finds little repairs wanting; I shall however Order him to Night, to proceed as far as Savage River and then Return, as his Party is rather too Weak to adventure it further.*

*All the Indian Parties that went out, are now return'd (save one, consisting of three only) without making any discoveries.*

### Cattle are moved to Cresap's planation

A July 25, 1758 letter[900] Washington wrote to Bouquet from the *"Camp at Fort Cumberland"* states:

*I wrote you by Colo. Stephen, since which I have been favour'd with your kind and agreable Letter of Yesterday.*

*We have advice that our Second Convoy of Seventy odd Waggons (contents you were informd of in my last) will be at the South Branch to day, where I expect they will be joind by some Waggons with Forage — the number I cant ascertain — and all proceed to this place immediately. On Friday I shall look for them.*

---

[898] "**The Writings of George Washington**", Volume 2, Fitzpatrick, 1931.

[899] "**The Writings of George Washington**", Volume 2, Fitzpatrick, 1931.

[900] Lowdermilk provides a different version of this letter.

*I shall most chearfully proceed to Work on any Road; pursue any Rout; or enter upon any Service that the General or yourself can think me qualified for, or usefully employd In; and shall never have a Will of my own where a point of Duty is requird at my hands: but since you desire me to speake, permit me to observe this; that after having examind all the Guides, and been convincd by them, and every other Person who has knowledge of that Country, that a Road comparable to General Braddocks (or indeed fit for any Service at all, even for Carrying Horses) cannot be made; I own, I say, after this, I shoud sollicit that Rout with less warmth — not because difficulties appear in it, but because I shoud much doubt giving Satisfaction in the Executive Part. I dont know what reports your Reconnoitring Parties have given, but I have been told on all hands that if any thing is expected there, disappointments will ensue, for nothing can be taken that way without destroying of Our Carrying Horses, so extreame bad the Hills are.*

*I shoud be extreme glad of one hours conference with you, and that after the General arrives; I coud then much readier determine; or — I think I coud then demonstrate the advantages of pushing out a Body of light Troops on this Quarter. I shoud make a trip to Rays Town with great pleasure, if my absence here coud be dispensd with a day or two; and that you can now be a judge of.*

*We shall need no Provisions from you. this Second Convoy added to what we have, will furnish us with a tolerable good Stock.*

*If Major Levingston, or any other Officer at this place draws more than one Ration it is contrary to Orders publishd here — and to my knowledge, and ought to be attributed to the Commissary, whose fault chiefly it must be for delivering it.*

*We have been obligd for the sake of Our Cattle to remove our Grass Guard to Cresaps — 15 Miles from hence. there the Provisions is Slaughterd, and servd out to the Guard, and to the Troop of Light Horse —(also at that place) — it is therefore necessary that Mr Dow, or some other attendant of the Commissary's (or Agent Victualler's) shoud be present and see to the Issuing of it.*

*There were two Commissaries at this place, besides a numerous Train of Butchers, Herds, &ca; so immensely lazy that I was under a necessity of ordering some of them to attend the Guard to keep them out of Mischief. The Commissaries lookd upon the Cattle to be at the Kings risque, were therefore easy what went with them — & in short, gave themselves no trouble on that Score till I made one of them attend, to Number them Night & Morning.*

*I send you a Return of the two Regiments, and the Maryland Troops, at this place. at the bottom of each return is notified the Number of Tents each Corps has receivd, and have by them. from thence you may judge of our Wants — many of the Officers, as I once before observd to you, are in the same Condition with the private Centinals in regard to Tents.*

*Kelly and Stalnaker (two Guides) are on the Road with Majr Peachy — all the rest at this place I have directed to attend You.*

*It woud be extreme inconvenient to me at this time, to Garrison the Block House on Rays Town Road — having such large Detachments already out — and the Camp Duty very hard.*

With the cavalry stationed at Cresap's plantation, the place was, temporarily at least, a military camp. On September 21, 1758 while at Fort Cumberland Joseph Galbreath indicated[901] that 50 sheep and 60 beef cattle had been pastured at Cresaps for two months, commencing on July 15, 1758, and were kept there for the benefit of George Washington's forces.

---

[901] "**Colonial Records of the Upper Potomac**", Volume 6.

## Dagworthy is ordered to march to Raystown

A July 28, 1758 letter[902] Washington wrote to Bouquet from the *"Camp at Fort Cumberland"* includes the following:

*I have given Captn. Dagworthy Orders to March to Rays Town so soon as he can draw in his Grass Guard. Inclos'd is a return of the Tents wanting to compleat the first Regiment and I have desir'd Colo. Byrd to send one for the 2d. Regiment also.*

*I will agreeable to your direction's, send the Waggons back to Winchester, having receiv'd no Orders to the Contrary from the General or Sir John.*

*Forty Six of Colo. Byrds Indians have left this for their Nation; 16 Only remain. I was greatly surpris'd to hear of a Report spread, and believ'd in your Camp, that a Party of Delawares Were come into this place; there never has been the least distant cause for such a report.*

## Appropriations are made for paying the troops and Dr. Ross

A July 29, 1758 letter[903] that Governor Sharpe wrote to Kilby from Fort Frederick states:

*Since I was favoured with Your Letter dated the 19ᵗʰ of June the Receit of which I am now to acknowledge, I have taken an Opportunity to see General Forbes at Carlyle & to acquaint him in a more full & particular manner than I could well do by writing with the present State & Circumstances of the Officers & Men that compose the Maryland Forces, with the late Conduct of our Assembly relative to those Troops, with the Encouragement which the Officers have at times receiv'd from General Stanwix & Myself in Consequence of the Earl of Loudoun's Letters, with the Encouragement & Instructions that Doctor Ross hath also received from us, & in pursuance whereof he has continued to Victual our Troops as well as the Friendly Indians that have since the Beginning of April 1757 been at Fort Cumberland or any other Place on the Frontiers of this Province. I likewise took the Liberty to communicate to His Excellency the Contents of your Letter with which he seemed to be well satisfied, but with respect to the Sum which you proposed to allow for the Hospital, Indians & Transportation of Provisions to Fort Cumberland His Excellency has been pleased to enlarge it. The General has already advanced our Troops by the hand of Sʳ John Sᵗ Clair the sum of £1890 Currency in part of the Pay that is due to them, this he is willing to make up £2400 & he has accordingly desired me to draw on Mʳ Joshua Howell for the Remainder being £510 Currency, which Sum I understood from the General & conclude from your Letter that Mʳ Howell has received your Instructions to pay. Besides this & over & above the £2976. 15 Currency (or the Value thereof in Bills of Exchange) which you impowered me to draw for by your Letter of the 19ᵗʰ of Iune, the General has desired me as I have already hinted to draw on Mʳ Howell for the Sum of £800 stg towards defraying the Expence of transporting Provisions to Fort Cumberland & other Contingencies; which several Drafts for £510 Currency; £2976. 15 Currency (or the Value thereof in Bills), & £850 Stg will I expect be in a few Days presented by D. Ross, who is going to Philᵃ for that purpose & to receive M. Howell's Directions with respect to the Form that must be observed by him in making out his Accounts in case our Assembly should continue averse to paying him but indeed I am not without hopes that they will when they meet again & when I communicate to them a Letter which the General has lately wrote to me & wherein he makes a Demand on our Assembly for the Sums which he & you have been prevailed with to advance on the Credit of the Province for the purposes abovementioned; I am not I say without hopes that they will pursue different measures from those they have lately taken & that they will before Christmas next Raise & appropriate a Sum of Money to repay*

---

[902] "**The Writings of George Washington**", Volume 2, Fitzpatrick, 1931.
[903] "**Correspondence of Governor Horatio Sharpe**", Volume II, 1890.

*you what shall have been so advanced & for such other purposes as it might be recommended to them to provide for. It remains only for me to return you Thanks in behalf of our Officers & M$^r$ Ross for relieving them in some measure out of the Difficulties wherein they were involved & to assure you that I am &c.*

*Copies of sundry orders drawn by Governor Sharpe on M$^r$ Joshua Howell of Phila$^a$ dated at F$^t$ Fred$^k$ the 29$^{th}$ Iuly 1758.*

*Sir*

*Be pleased to pay to Doctor David Ross or order the sum of £2976. 15. Currency or the Value thereof in Bills of Excha. agreeable to the Instructions which you have received from Christopher Kilby Esq. who by his Letter to me dated the 19$^{th}$ of June last hath agreed to advance the said Sum of £2976. 15. Maryland Currency towards paying him the said D$^r$ David Ross for Victualling the Maryland Forces from the 8$^{th}$ Day of Oct$^r$ to the 8$^{th}$ Day of May last, I am &c.*

*Sir*

*At Ten Days Sight Be pleased to pay to D$^r$ David Ross or Order for the Use of the officers of the Maryland Forces the Sum of £4.510 Maryland Currency agreeable to the Instructions which you have received or may receive from Christ Kilby Esq. the same being to be advanced the said officers towards paying their respective Companies & agreeable to the orders of Brigadier General Forbes. I am*

*Sir*

*Be pleased to pay to Doctor David Ross the sum of £850 stg. or the Value thereof in Current Money agreeable to the Instructions which you may have received from Christopher Kilby Esq. the same being to be advanced by him at the Desire of Brigadier General Forbes towards defraying the Expence of Transporting Provisions to Fort Cumberland & other Contingencies — I am &c*

## Washington writes to Bouquet on August 2, 1758 about the road for Forbes' campaign

Volume 2 of Sparks' 1833 book "**The Writings of George Washington**" indicates that George Washington wrote a letter to Colonel Bouquet on August 2, 1758 that includes the following:

*Camp Near Fort Cumberland, 2d. August. 1758.*

*Sir; — The matters of which we spoke relative to the roads, have since our parting, been the subject of my closest reflection, and so far am I from altering my opinion, that the more time and attention I bestow, the more I am confirmed in it, and the reasons for taking Braddock's road appear in a stronger point of view. To enumerate the whole of these reasons would be tedious, and to you who have become so much master of the subject, unnecessary. I shall therefore, briefly mention a few only which I think so obvious in themselves, that they must effectually remove objections.*

*Several years ago the Virginians and Pennsylvanians commenced a trade with the Indians settled on the Ohio, and, to obviate the many inconveniences of a bad road, they, after reiterated and ineffectual efforts to discover where a good one might be made, employed for the purpose several of the most intelligent Indians, who, in the course of many years' hunting, had acquired a perfect knowledge of these mountains. The Indians, having taken the greatest pains to gain the rewards offered for this discovery, declared, that the path leading from Will's Creek was infinitely preferable to any, that could be made at any other place. Time and experience so clearly demonstrated this truth, that the Pennsylvania traders commonly carried out their goods by Will's Creek. Therefore, the Ohio Company, in 1753, at a considerable expense, opened the road. In 1754 the troops, whom I had the honor to command, greatly repaired it, as far as*

*Gist's plantation;*[904] *and, in 1755, it was widened and completed by General Braddock to within six miles of Fort Duquesne.*

## A Virginian's view of the situation

An August 4, 1758 letter[905] that Robert Munford wrote to his uncle Colonel Theodoric Bland from a *"Camp Near Fort Cumberland"* states:

*If 'tis honorable to be in the service of one's country, 'tis a reputation gain'd by the most cruel hardships you can imagine, occasioned more by a real anxiety for its welfare, than by what the poor carcase suffers. Every officer seems discontented in camp, happy on command, so deep is the interest of our country implanted in the minds of all. Sometimes the army wears a gloomy, then a joyous, aspect, just as the news either confirms our stay here, or our departure. The General with the small pox in one, the flux in the other, division of our forces, and no provision ready, are indeed excuses for our being here at present; yet all might have been prevented. A few hearty prayers are every moment offered up for those self-interested Pennsylvanians who endeavor to prevail on our General to cut a road for their convenience, from Raystown to Fort Duquesne, that a trifling good to particulars, should retard what would conduce to the general welfare! 'Tis a set of dirty Dutchmen, they say, that keeps us here! It would be impertinent to condemn, yet I must [think] our leaders too deliberate at this important juncture, when all are warm for action, all breathing revenge against an enemy that have even dared to scalp our men before our eyes. The amusement we have in the meantime is only following the brave dogs over the mountains for some miles, and our sole satisfaction sufficient fatigue to make us sleep sound. An old scoundrel has intimated to the General that the Virginians have bribed the guides; for 'tis practicable to go the new road, contrary to their report. We have lost all our Indians by the assistance of a man, the [aforesaid] old dog, who interposed through some dirty views he has of superseding Mr. Atkins. Thus are our officers in a manner ruined by persons whose souls scorn a thought that tends not immediately to their own advantage. I'm sorry to live upon my country, when I've so small a prospect of repaying her by any service. We shall march to Raystown shortly, thence to the Fort if permitted. I shall embrace the next opportunity of writing you our transactions, and am as always, dear sir, your most Aff'te nephew, &c*

## Washington reports on the wagon convoy

An August 6, 1758 letter[906] Washington wrote to Bouquet from the *"Camp at Fort Cumberland"* includes the following:

*I have repair'd the Road over the Mountain, at this place as Sir John St. Clair desir'd. I had also sent the Second Company of Artificers to make Bridges on the Rays Town Road according to your Orders, transmitted me thro' by Colo. Stephen; twas yesterday before I cou'd get them in: and to day they March. Nineteen Waggon's came here Yesterday Loaded with Musket Ball from Fort Frederick; 18 more left their loads at the old Town, and are gone back, the first 19 Waggons, and an Escort are gone to bring up their Loads, and will be here to day. I can't send you a return of the Contents having receiv'd none.*

*The Waggoners are constantly applying for Grain to give their Horses. I shou'd be glad if you wou'd direct how I am to act in this Case.*

---

[904] Using the shortest present-day route, it is about 64 miles from Cumberland to Gist's.

[905] **"History of Cumberland…"**, Lowdermilk, 1878.

[906] **"The Writings of George Washington"**, Volume 2, Fitzpatrick, 1931.

*Inclos'd is a Return of Provision's wanting to serve Us till our next Convoy arrives from Winchester, We have not above 5 days Flour upon hand, I shall therefore send the Waggons to Rays Town to Morrow for this Article, &ca., after they return from the old Town.*

*Twelve Tents was the number I return'd for, and they are safe arriv'd.*

## Washington sent out a detachment to waylay French parties on the road

An August 7, 1758 letter[907] Washington wrote to Bouquet from the *"Camp at Fort Cumberland"* states:

*Captn. Waggoner and 50 Men with 19 Waggons wait upon you for Provision's agreeable to a return sent you yesterday.*

*A Letter which I have just received from Mr. Walker, tells me, that the Convoy may be expected at Pearsall's the 15th. Inst., and desires that the Escort (already consising of 75 Men) may be augmented, as the Waggons and Cattle will cover a long space of Ground.*

*Pray what will you have done with these Waggons when they come up? and those now going to Ray's Town, when they Return with Provision's?*

*I was this Inst't favour'd with your's pr. Express; I am not surprized to hear the Enemy are about, but have really been astonished at the calm that has prevail'd so long. I shall this moment send out a Party to way lay the Road; I anticipated this Order, by requesting leave to do it in a Letter I wrote to you yesterday.*

*Inclos'd is a return of the Shott &ca. that have been brought to this place since my arrival here.*

## Forbes writes about Washington's resistance to the new road

On August 9, 1758, Forbes wrote a letter to Bouquet that stated *"By a very unguarded letter of Col. Washington that accidentally fell into my hands, I am now at the bottom of their scheme against this new road, a scheme that I think was a shame for any officer to be concerned in, but more of this at meeting."* On September 4, 1758, Forbes wrote *"Therefore would consult G. Washington, although perhaps not follow his advice, as his Behavior about the roads, c."*

## Sending Corn from Fort Cumberland

An August 13, 1758 letter[908] Washington wrote to Sir John St. Clair from the *"Camp at Fort Cumberland"* states:

*Your favour of the 9th. I was honour'd with the 11th.: 39 Waggons are loaded with Stores according to your Orders. 8 other Waggons contain 160 Bushels of Indian Corn which with 94 deliver'd to the 47 Waggoners returning to you (two Bushels to each) and 18 more to the Maryland Waggon Master, takes all the Grain we have, save about 60 Bushel reserv'd for the light Horse; Captn. Stewart telling me it was your orders he shou'd have grain.*

*The Maryland Waggons under Mr. Long, will go with an Escort (intended to reinforce that with the Convoy from Winchester) to Pearsalls for the Grain at that place with which they shall proceed to Rays Town when that Convoy does, according to Order.*

---

[907] "**The Writings of George Washington**", Volume 2, Fitzpatrick, 1931.
[908] "**The Writings of George Washington**", Volume 2, Fitzpatrick, 1931.

*We have neither Grindstones or Intrenching Tools at this place.*

*I offer you my sincere congratulation's upon your safe return from Loyalhanning; and upon the discovery of a good Road which I hear you have made ...*

## Washington reports to Bouquet

An August 13, 1758 letter[909] Washington wrote to Bouquet from the *"Camp Fort Cumberland"* states:

*The Waggons met with all possible dispatch in loading, but being assur'd that the Horses were not able to return till today, I did not Order them of sooner.*

*My Soldiers Cloathing, unluckily, are sent to this place. If I march that way I shall take them along, with those of that part of the Regiment now with me. Since we are like to make so late a Campaigne of it.*

*I sent Orders to Captn. Stewart to detach half his Troop under an Officer to you. They are not yet arriv'd from the Grass Guard 15 Miles of.*

*I wish with all my Soul you may continue to find little difficulty in opening your Road. I am certain if you find much, you will not have time for any other Service this Campaigne.*

*I detach'd Captn. McKenzie with 4 Officers and 75 Rank and file to way-lay the Road at the great Crossing; from him a Sergeant and four active Woodsmen of my Regiment is to proceed to Fort Duquesne so that I am in great hopes we shall be able to get some Intelligence of the strength of the Enemy at that place.*

*I cou'd wish most sincerely, that our Accounts from the No. Ward were clearer, and more favourable than they appear to be. If you have any Intelligence from Ticonderago, I shou'd be extreme thankful for the acct. We have expected hourly, to hear that Louisburg is in Our hands, pray Heaven we may not be disappointed at last.*

*I transmitted your request of Cattle to Mr. Walker pr. Express. No Tools are yet arriv'd from Fort Frederick, nor have we any Minors at this place. There were one or two pretty good one's in my own Company, and where that Company is you best can tell.*

## Can Sharpe cover Fort Cumberland so the Virginians can accompany Forbes?

An August 16, 1758 letter[910] that Forbes wrote to Governor Sharpe from Shippensburg includes the following:

*... our new road advancing apace, so that in a few days I hope to have our advanced post on the other side of Laurell Hill pretty well advanced towards the Enemy.*

*My Gripes[911] obliges me to make use of another Hand writing than my own which I know you have goodness enough to excuse ...*

---

[909] "**The Writings of George Washington**", Volume 2, Fitzpatrick, 1931.

[910] "**Correspondence of Governor Horatio Sharpe**", Volume II, 1890.

[911] When I was growing up, *"grip"* was understood as being an antiquated word for influenza. I think that here it is being used to describe Forbes' illness.

*Quere if I should march strait out, could you take the Garrison of Fort Cumberland under the protection of your Militia for a fortnight or so, in order that I might strengthen myself with all the Virginians that I shall other ways be obliged to leave there.*

### The Fort at Raystown is mentioned on August 16, 1758

Joseph Shippen wrote a letter to Richard Peters dated *"Camp at Rays Town 16 Augt 1758"* which states, *"We have a good stockade fort built here with several convenient & large Store Houses. Our Camps are all secured with a good Breastwork & a small Ditch on the outside."* The fort was named by December 28, 1758.

### Finney is marching to Fort Cumberland with about 26 men

An August 17, 1758 letter[912] that Governor Sharpe wrote to Forbes from Fort Frederick includes the following:

*It is with Concern but my Duty obliges me to acquaint you that should the Militia be ordered to Fort Cumberland I do not believe they would march & am apt to think you will be of my opinion when I assure Your Excellency that for several Days together there has been no more than 9 or 10 men doing Duty in this Garrison & am very apprehensive that many more will not come up even as far as this. Ensign Finney of the Pensilvᵃ Forces marched hence this morning for Fort Cumberland with about 26 men one half Invalids they were left Sick here when Major Wells marched for Rays Town*

### Bouquet wants strong parties out

An August 17, 1758 letter[913] Bouquet wrote to Washington includes the following:

*As it is highly necessary to keep the enemy in doubt about our roads, the General desires that you continue sending strong parties along, with orders to reconnoitre where the junction of the two roads could be made. I hear by Kelly, who is gone from Loy: H. — to the Salt Lick, that it is about 16 miles across from that post to the end of Chestnut Ridge, where this path goes; and the woods so open that without cutting, carrying horses may easily go through, all pretty level.*

### Washington responds to Bouquet's letter

An August 18, 1758 letter[914] Washington wrote to Bouquet from the *"Camp at Fort Cumberland"* states:

*I am favour'd with yours of Yesterday, intimating the probability of my proceeding with a body of Troops on G— B— R—d and desiring my retaining for that purpose a Months Provisions at this place, a thing which I shou'd be extreme fond of, but as I cannot possibly know what quantity of Provisions may be necessary for that time, without knowing the Number of Men I may probably March with, and when it is likely I may leave this, I hope you will be pleas'd to give me the necessary Information on this head. As also how this place is to be Garrisoned, and what Provision's and stores shou'd be left in it.*

*I have talk'd a good deal with Kelly upon the Nature of the Intervening Ground from the New R—d to B—s, and from what he says, I apprehend it impracticable to effect a junction with the Troops on the new R—d till we advance near the Salt Lick which is no great distance from F—D—Q and how far it may be*

---

[912] "**Correspondence of Governor Horatio Sharpe**", Volume II, 1890.
[913] "**The Writings of George Washington**", Volume 2, Fitzpatrick, 1931.
[914] "**The Writings of George Washington**", Volume 2, Fitzpatrick, 1931.

*advisable to send a small Body of Troops so near the Enemy, at so great a distance from the Army without any kind of Tools (which is certainly our Case) for repairing the Roads, or throwing up any kind of Defence in case of need, I shall not presume to say, but I cannot help observing, that all the Guides and Indians are to be drawn from hence, and that the greatest part of my Regiment is on the other Road; so that I have but few remaining with me of the first Regiment, and 8 Companies of the Second only; whose Officers and Men can be suppos'd to know little of the Service, and less of the Country, and near, or I believe quite a fifth of them Sick; I thought it incumbent on me to mention these things, that you might know our Condition; at the same time I beg leave to assure you, that nothing will give me greater pleasure than to proceed with any number of Men, that the General or you shall think proper to Order.*

*With Regard to keeping out a Succession of strong Parties on his R—d from the Troops here, I must beg leave to remark that we have not so much as one Carrying Horse to take Provision's out upon, being under a necessity t'other day of pressing 5 Horses from some Country-men, (that came to Camp upon Business) before I cou'd equip Captn. McKenzie's Party for a 14 days March. That we have not an Oz. of Salt Provision's of any kind here, and that it is impossible to preserve the Fresh (especially as we have no Salt) by any other Means than Barbacuing it in the Ind'n manner; in doing which it looses near a half; so that a Party who receives 10 days Provision's will be obliged to live on little better than 5 days' allowance of meat kind, a thing Impracticable. A great many of Colo. Byrd's Men are, as I before remark'd very sickly, the rest become low spirited and dejected; of Course the greatest share of that Service must fall upon the 4 Comp'ns of the 1st. Regt. This Sickness, and depression of Spirits, cannot arise I conceive from the Situation of Our Camp, which is undoubtedly the most healthy (and best Air'd) of any in this Vicinity; but is caus'd I apprehend by the change in their way of living (most of them till now having lived in ease and Affluence), and by the Limestone Water and Air. The Soldrs. of the 1st. Regt. like those of the 2d; wou'd be sickly, were it not owing to some such Causes as these.*

*Captn. McKenzies Party is not yet Return'd,*[915] *I will advertise you of his discoveries if any are made by him.*

*We have Reason to believe that Parties of the Enemy are likewise at this place, about us, a waggoner being shott at yesterday afternoon, and his horse kill'd under him abt. 3 Miles from this place.*

*We have no Indian Goods of any kind here. It gives me great pleasure to hear that the General is getting better, and expected soon at Rays Town. Colo. Byrd joins me in his Compliments to you.*

## Washington reports to Bouquet

An August 19, 1758 letter[916] Washington wrote to Bouquet from the *"Camp at Fort Cumberland"* states:

*This afternoon the Party Commanded by Captn. McKenzie returning without being able to discover any thing of the Enemy's Motion's, they waylaid the Road for several days near the great Crossing and intended to have advanc'd quite to that Post, had not their Provision's entirely spoil'd, notwithstanding every method, and the utmost pains for its preservation was taken.*

*Some of their advanc'd Sentries had nearly kill'd a small Party of 3 Cherokee Indian's, returning from War. This small Party went from hence upwards of Six Weeks ago and this is the 4th. day since they left*

---

[915] This is from Washington's letter book copy. Another version of the letter includes the following, *"The convoy from Winchester has been detained much longer than was expected. Mr. Walker desired a party to reinforce the escort at Pearsalls (30 miles distant), the 15th Inst. which was accordingly sent; but I have since been informed that the waggons did not leave Winchester till a few days ago."*

[916] **"The Writings of George Washington"**, Volume 2, Fitzpatrick, 1931.

*Fort Duquesne, the Environs of which they long watch'd and at length was oblig'd to Cross the Ohio where they kill'd two Squaws whose Scalps they brought in here.*

*They say there are a good many Women and Children on that side the River, but very few Men, either French or Indians at the Fort.*

*Captn. McKenzie says there is no signs of the Enemy's having been in General Braddocks Road, so far as he proceeded on it; Sergeant Scott and 4 privates of his Party went on to Fort Duquesne; so soon as they return will transmit you any Intelligence they may procure.*

*I shou'd be extremely glad to receive some Bacon or Salt Prov'n of some kind, without which it will be Impossible for any Party I can send out to answer the propos'd end.*

*The Convoy from Winchester was yesterday at the No. River (five days March for them, from hence) so that we can not expect them in less than 5 or 6 days, especially as they have lost their Horses.*

*This Moment an Oficer came in to inform me, that Captn. Beale and a Party of abt. 90 Marylanders were escorting some store Waggons, and wou'd be in immediately, I shall forward them to you to Morrow, agreeable to Sir Jno. St. Clairs Order's.*

## Washington wonders if he will remain in command after Sharpe arrives

An August 21, 1758 letter[917] that Washington wrote to Bouquet from the *"Camp, at Fort Cumberland"* states:

*Twenty-five Catawbas came here this evening, and the convoy may be expected the day after to-morrow, as it was at Pearsall's last night.*

*Governor Sharpe may be expected here in a day or two. I am at a loss to know how he ranks, and whether he is entitled to the command. In the British army his rank is that of lieutenant-colonel only, but what it maybe as a governor, in his own province, I really do not know, nor whether he has any out of the troops of his province. I should, therefore, be glad of your advice, being unwilling to dispute the point with him wrongfully, or to give up the command, if I have a right to it.*

Bouquet provided the following reply[918] on August 23, 1758, *"The Governors in America have no command of the troops even of their own Province as soon as they are joined with any other of his Majesty's forces, unless they have a commission from the Commander — in-chief for that purpose. I have commanded the forces at Philadelphia and at Charles Town. Tho' the Governor was Captain General in his Province, and was entirely independent from them. Governor Sharpe will not expect to have the command as governor; and as Lieut. Col. he can not, and would not, I suppose, choose to serve in that rank. Therefore, you are very right in keeping it."*

## Sharpe thinks he can bring 250 men to temporarily hold down the fort

An August 21, 1758 letter[919] that Governor Sharpe wrote to Forbes from Fort Frederick includes the following:

*In Consequence of the Quere proposed in Your Letter of the 16th Inst I sent an Officer immediately down the country to try the Disposition of the Militia who writes me that about 250 Voluntiers have offered*

---

[917] "**The Writings of George Washington...**", Volume II, Sparks, 1834.
[918] "**The Writings of George Washington**", Volume 2, Fitzpatrick, 1931.
[919] "**Correspondence of Governor Horatio Sharpe**", Volume II, 1890.

*their Service to go with me & take possession of Fort Cumberland for 3 weeks or a month. If approved of I propose to be there on Friday or Saturday next come Sen'night or any time after that Your Excellency shall appoint. It will necessary for me to have Your Excellency's order to the Commissary for supplying the Officers & Men with Provision likewise a power to purchase some Salt Vinegar & Pepper & to give each man a Jill of Rum a Day. As it will not be in my power to keep these People together after the Expiration of the time agreed upon I am well satisfied Your Excellency will order us Relief accordingly...*

## Sharpe is to delay the departure to Fort Cumberland

An August 23, 1758 letter[920] that Forbes wrote to Governor Sharpe from Shippensburg reveals that there has been a great deal of confusion over payments (some of the confusion related to his illness), and then states:

*I Thank you for yours of the 21st and I am very much Obliged to you, for your offer of taking care of Ft Cumberland which will be a great help to me; but I do not think that I shall want your People before the Week after next, altho' my new Road is quite ready the length of Laurel ridge, & I have sent to take post on the other Side of it, from whence it is all good to the Ohio. But I Expect a great meeting of the Indians, when they must Determine Friends or Foes: I Fancy they'll Choose the Last, as they are now Scalping within a mile of this, and I have only 50 men with me, but I Expect 200 Highlanders this Night, so if possible shall Endeavor to way lay them, but this does not look as if they were Courting a Peace.*

The letter has a postscript that states, *"I shall Write to you soon when your people will be wanted at Cumberland..."*

## The convoy from Winchester has arrived

An August 24, 1758 letter[921] Washington wrote to Bouquet from the *"Camp at Fort Cumberland"* states:

*Your favour of the 21st. Inst't accompanied by the 20 Pack Horses with about 3000 w't of Salt Pork came safe to hand, as likewise did your Letter of the 23d. The General's happy recovery, affords me vast satisfaction; and I am glad the New Road turns out so much to your liking.*

*The Convoy from Winchester arriv'd here the 23d. Inst't they set out with 468 Beeves, 9 were kill'd on the Road, and 411 deliver'd here the rest were lost on the Road, but as their Officer sent immediately back after them, we are in hopes the greatest part of them will be found.*

*As only 26,000 W't of Flour came up; (which is not quite a Month's Provision's for the Troops here) I have according to your Orders detain'd it, and likewise 90 Beeves, the rest sets out early to morrow morning for Rays Town, as does all the Forage except 60 Bushels of Corn. '*

*When the Convoy got within 6 Miles of this garrison 3 Cuttawba men and 2 Squaws (contrary to the advice of the Officers) set on before the Convoy for this Camp, and soon after were fir'd upon by about 10 or 12 of the Enemy; who kill'd Captn. Bullen, and Captn. French, and wounded one of the Squaws; the loss we sustain by the death of these two Indians is at this juncture very considerable, as they were remarkable for their bravery, and attachment to Our Interest; particularly poor Bullen whom (and the other) we buried with Military Honours. The Rest of the Cuttawbas, and what Nottoways and Tuscarora's that are here set out to morrow with the Waggon's for Rays Town.*

---

[920] **"Correspondence of Governor Horatio Sharpe"**, Volume II, 1890.
[921] **"The Writings of George Washington"**, Volume 2, Fitzpatrick, 1931.

*As we had Intelligence of several Parties of the Enemy being about, I detach'd Parties different way's in hopes of coming up with them, or cutting of their Retreat, but without any Effect. at the sametime, I reinforced the Convoy w't 50 Men.*

*There are several Waggons which came up here with the Flour, that I am at a loss what to do with.*

*Sergeant Scot (mention'd in a late Letter) return'd this day; he, when within two Miles of Fort Duquesne, unfortunately came upon a few fresh Tracks making Inwards which he follow'd, apprehending they were just at hand, till his Provisions were expended, and was thereby oblig'd to Return without making any discoveries worth mentioning. I am glad Mr. Chew and Mr. Allen has been able to give you accts. so agreeable.*

*Captn. Woodward of the first Regiment 3 Subs and 75 Rank and File Marches tomorrow with 12 days Prov'ns to way lay the Road in the same manner that Captn. McKenzie did.*

*Inclos'd is an exact Account of Our Strength at this place.*

### Sharpe hopes to be able to perform as promised to garrison Fort Cumberland
An August 24, 1758 letter[922] that Governor Sharpe wrote to Forbes from Fort Frederick goes into detail to explain the confused funding situation, and then states:

*I shall endeavour to get the Voluntiers that I expect to march with me to Fort Cumberland hither the 1ˢᵗ of Sept' or on any other Day that you may think fit to appoint but notwithstanding the Report the Officer has made me & the hopes he has given me that the men will make no Difficulty of marching I am afraid many of them will be dissuaded or discouraged by the members of our Assembly or their Instruments who are I understand extremely busy below & leave no Stone unturned that may hinder any men from marching to serve on the Frontiers under my Command. ... I hope I shall yet be able to perform as much as I have ever promised, I mean if You can leave Rays Town within this Fortnight & can proceed to Fort Du Quesne before the Beginning of Oct' when I must necessarily meet the Assembly I hope to be able to get men enough to garrison not only this Place but Fort Cumberland...*

### Washington reports to Bouquet from Fort Cumberland
An August 28, 1758 letter[923] Washington wrote to Bouquet from the *"Camp at Fort Cumberland"* includes the following:

*All the waggons at this place fit for service, come to you under the Escort Ordered for Mr. Hoops.*

*Any Troops not of Virgina, shall be forwarded to you according to Order; and I could wish most sincerely that our Rout was fixt that we might be in motion; for we are all of us most heartily tir'd and sick of Inactivity. Colo. Byrd in particular is really ill.*

*A letter which Colo. Byrd recd. from the Genl. of the 19ᵗʰ Inst: gives room to imagine that the Destination of the Virg'a Troops will be fix't on so soon as he arrives at Rays Town, as he there expresses a desire of Colo. Byrd and I there immediately.*

*Frazer having left this with the Convoy must be with you e'er now. I am very glad to hear that your artillery pass the Allegany with so much ease.*

---

[922] **"Correspondence of Governor Horatio Sharpe"**, Volume II, 1890.
[923] **"The Writings of George Washington"**, Volume 2, Fitzpatrick, 1931.

## An explanation of why the Maryland troops are needed at Fort Cumberland

An August 28, 1758 letter[924] that Governor Sharpe wrote to Calvert from Fort Frederick includes the following statement:

*As the General has been obliged to leave 700 Men on the Frontiers of Pens[a] to garrison the Stoccades that have been built in that Province & is very unwilling to weaken himself more by leaving a Garrison at Fort Cumberland if it could possibly be avoided I have at his Request promised to go up with 200 or 250 Volunteers from the Militia of this County & to garrison that Post untill the Affair is decided, I shall contrive to be there just before the Rear of the Army moves from Raes Town so that the Virginians which are at present at Fort Cumberland may join the Army either at Rays Town or very soon after the General leaves that Place. I cannot tell exactly how long I shall be detained at Fort Cumberland because it will depend on the Quickness of the Generals motions, but he has promised to send back a sufficient Number of Men to relieve the Volunteers that I am to carry up so soon as he has had a Decisive Action be the Event of it what it will.*

## Forbes reports the death of Captain Bullen

On August 28, 1758, General Forbes wrote a letter[925] to Richard Peters from Shippensburg that includes the following statement:

*Col[o] Byrd writes me from Fort Cumberland that a large party of Enemy Indians have been in that neighbourhood, and that Cap[t] Bullen and Cap[t] French who had just brought 50[926] Catawbas to our assistance, coming from Winchester, would go before the party when they come near Fort Cumberland, by which means they were attacked by 9 Indians, killed, and scalped within a mile of the Fort. This is a very great loss, as Bullen had proved himself a sincere friend to us.*

The death of Captain Bullen is also mentioned in Thomas Barton's August 25, 1758 journal entry. Barton reports that he heard the news by express, indicates that Bullen's father was Irish and Bullen referred to himself as *"The Irishman"*, and reports that the Delawares who killed Bullen tricked him by saying they were friendly Cherokees.

The September 14, 1758 issue of the "**Maryland Gazette**" includes the following on the topic:

*We are also informed, that his Excellency our Governor marched from Fort Frederick for Fort Cumberland last Thursday, with upwards of 200 Volunteers from the Militia of Frederick County, who have engaged to Garrison Fort Cumberland for a few Weeks, that the Virginia Troops which were there, under the Command of Col.-Washington, may join the Rear of the Army: That Capt. Bullen, a Catawba Indian, and a sincere Friend to the English, was lately killed by a party of the Enemy as he was crossing Patowmack, a few Miles on this Side Fort Cumberland; And that Yesterday su'nnight one William Beard, and another Man, were pursued by Four Enemy Indians as they were coming down from Fort Cumberland; which Indians are supposed to belong to a Party of about a Hundred, that are said to have lately come down to Fort Duquesne from the Western Lakes.*

---

[924] "**Correspondence of Governor Horatio Sharpe**", Volume II, 1890.

[925] "**The Pennsylvania magazine of history and biography**", Volume 33, 1909.

[926] This may read *"60"*.

## Baker and Ross are paid for contributions to the western expedition

Governor Horatio Sharpe's account[927] of *"disbursements for the western expedition against Fort Duquesne"* shows that on August 30, 1758 Isaac Baker was paid £4/10/0 for his Waggon's Attendance on the New Road, and £6 for liquor delivered to the parties that made the road from Pawlins's to Fort Frederick, and David Ross was paid £4/19/9 for provisions delivered to the battoemen who carried stores to Fort Cumberland.

## Washington writes a gloomy letter

A September 1, 1758 letter[928] that Washington wrote to Robison (Speaker of the Virginia House of Burgesses) from Fort Cumberland states:

*We are still encamped here, very sickly and quite dispirited at the prospect before us.*

*That appearance of glory which we had once in view, that hope, that laudable ambition of serving our country, and meriting its applause, are now no more; all is dwindled into ease, sloth, and fatal inactivity. In a word all is lost, if the ways of men in power, like certain ways of Providence, are not inscrutable. But we, who view the actions of great men at a distance, can only form conjectures agreeably to a limited perception; and being ignorant of the comprehensive schemes which may be in contemplation, might mistake egregiously in judging of things from appearances, or by the lump. Yet every fool will have his notions — will prattle and talk away; and why may not I? We seem then in my opinion to act under the guidance of an evil genius. The conduct of our leaders, if not actuated by superior orders is tempered with something I do not care to give a name to. Nothing now but a miracle can bring this campaign to a happy issue.*

## A report on the ammunition stored at Fort Cumberland

On September 2, 1758 Fort Major James Livingston prepared a *"Return of Ammunition in the Stores at Fort Cumberland"*[929] for George Washington, reporting 503 Round Shot, 70 Grape Shot, 5400 Swan Shot, 460 Grenades, 38 Barrels Powder, and 360 Boxes Musquet Balls.

## Washington reveals that his road opinions are related to trade rivalry with Pennsylvania

A September 2, 1758 letter[930] that Washington wrote to Governor Fauquier from Fort Cumberland includes the following:

*Your favour of the 17th Ulto I had the honor to receive the 30th following. If you are surpriz'd to find us Still Incamp'd at this place I shall only remark that your Surprise cannot well exceed my own. ...*

*In the conference I had with Colo. Bouquet ... I did among other things to avert the resolve of opening a new Road, represent the great Expence the Coloney of Virg'a had been at to support the War ... and after this demonstrated very clearly the time it wou'd take us to proceed on the old Road; and at how much easier expence, even if we were oblig'd to get all our provisions and Stores from Pensylvania; and no occasion for this surely. In fine I urg'd every thing then I could do now ... but urg'd in vain, the Pensylvanians whose*

---

[927] **"Archives of Maryland"**, Volume LV.

[928] **"History of Cumberland..."**, Lowdermilk, 1878.

[929] Library of Congress.

[930] **"The Writings of George Washington"**, Volume 2, Fitzpatrick, 1931.

*Interest present and future it was to conduct the Expedition thro' their Government, and along that way, because it secures their Frontiers at present, and the Trade hereafter ...*

## Washington requests 100 wagons to be sent to Fort Cumberland with flour and corn

A September 2, 1758 letter[931] Washington wrote *"To Mr. Thomas Walker or person acting in his place"* from the *"Camp at Fort Cumberland"* states:

*Colonel Bouquet desires 100 Waggons, if possible, may be Engag'd in Virginia; and that as many of them as can, may be sent to this place loaded with Flour, and the remainder with Indian Corn (Oats I suppose will do) where they will receive further Orders.*

*I beg you will, therefore, use your utmost diligence to Comply with this request; and let me know also, immediately, how far you think you shall be able to comply with it; first in regard to the No. of Waggons, next the q'ty of Flour and Corn; and lastly, what time you think they may be got to this place. Such Waggon's as cannot get Loads, must come up empty.*

*You must not expect an Escort from hence; I shall certainly be March'd before you can need one. You must therefore apply to His Lordship [Fairfax] who I flatter myself will Order you one from the Militia, or from Captn. Rutherfords Rangers, if they can be spar'd.*

## Washington writes to Bouquet, hoping to march with packhorses instead of wagons

A September 2, 1758 letter[932] Washington wrote to Bouquet from the *"Camp at Fort Cumberland"* discusses the advantages of marching with packhorses, and then includes the following:

*The Sick most certainly must go to the General Hospital, for we can neither afford Surgeons nor Medicenes from the Regiments to be left for their benefit and many are not in a Condition to move.*

*I have wrote to Mr. Walker, or person acting in his place for the Waggons you desire: they cou'd easily have been had on timely notice but now I cannot promise; in case he succeeds I have desir'd him to apply to Lord Fairfax for an Escort of the Militia, but I cannot promise he will get one. ...*

*I have heard nothing yet from Captn. Woodward's Party; on Wednesday last Sergeant Scot with five men went out once more to try their Success at Fort Duquesne. I can answer for his good endeavours, but it is not more tedious than dangerous bringing a Prisoner such a Distance.*

*Colo. Byrd is very ill but desires nevertheless that his Complem'ts may be made to you.*

## The target date for Sharpe's forces to be at Fort Cumberland is September 10th or 12th

A September 3, 1758 letter[933] that Forbes wrote to Governor Sharpe from Shippensburg includes the following statement:

*I propose leaving this to morrow morning in a kind of Horse litter, being so weakened by my distemper that I neither can ride nor bear the roughness of my slopwaggon However I hope a few days will make a great change.*

---

[931] "**The Writings of George Washington**", Volume 2, Fitzpatrick, 1931.

[932] "**The Writings of George Washington**", Volume 2, Fitzpatrick, 1931.

[933] "**Correspondence of Governor Horatio Sharpe**", Volume II, 1890.

*I have wrote to Col° Bouquet of your kind agreement of Garrisoning Fort Cumberland for the first month of my absence, and that 250 of your men would be there by the 10th or 12th Instant, ordering the Commissary to furnish them with provisions and a Gill of spirits each p day during their stay in that service, If there be any thing more wanted let me know, or if when there, you find any other thing necessary you will be so good as to order it, as the Commissary shall have directions to do whatever you require.*

### How will Sharpe identify friendly Indians?

A September 4, 1758 letter[934] that Governor Sharpe wrote to Forbes from Fort Frederick includes the following statement:

*you may depend on my being at Fort Cumberland with 200 men at least the 8th or 9th Inst. I suppose the Virginians or most of them will have received Orders to march to Rays Town as soon as they shall be relieved, but I should be obliged to you for ordering the Surgeon or his Mate at least to remain with us. ... it is not improbable that some of the Southern Indians or of these Delawares or perhaps some of the Enemy Indians may come to Fort Cumberland while I have the Command there & desire to be admitted into the Fort I should be obliged to you for letting me know what Signal our Friend Indians are to make.*

### Washington's invalids to stay at Fort Cumberland

A translation[935] of a September 4, 1758 letter that Bouquet wrote to General John Forbes contains the following statement concerning Colonel Washington:

*I have made the necessary arrangements for Colonel Wash's march. I shall give you a detailed report on your arrival. He needs 28 wagons, 210 pack horses, 50 oxen, and he will have 100 cartridges, 6 weeks' provisions, tools for entrenching himself, etc. His march can be covered by a corps of 500 men, who will go one or three days ahead of him from our advance post to ??? and will help him to make his entrenchment. His invalids will stay at Cumberland, where they will be sent a surgeon, drugs, and some equipment, since we have no way of lodging them here. They have no more than 12 days' supply of flour.*

### Thomas Barton writes about the blockhouses

Reverend Thomas Barton's journal entry[936] for September 6, 1758 mentions the blockhouses between Raystown and Fort Cumberland and estimates that they are about 14 miles from Raystown. He describes them as being located near three springs and flanking one another, each one having bastions. He reports that they had been built by Major Lewis for the defense of road cutting personnel.

### Thomas Barton describes the fort

Reverend Thomas Barton's journal entry[937] for September 7, 1758 describes the Ohio Company storehouse as a large building located on a hill on the Virginia side of the Potomac River, approximately 400 yards south-southwest from Fort Cumberland. He reports that the storehouse was then being used as a hospital and was guarded by thirty men.

---

[934] **"Correspondence of Governor Horatio Sharpe"**, Volume II, 1890.
[935] **"The Papers of Col. Henry Bouquet"**, 1940.
[936] **"The Pennsylvania Magazine of History and Biography"** 95 (1971).
[937] **"The Pennsylvania Magazine of History and Biography"** 95 (1971).

Barton's journal entry provides a description of Fort Cumberland 20 days before a gunpowder explosion. He states that the fort was originally a 100-foot square stockade built of excessively light timber and had four bastions. He states that the fort had recently been reinforced with a 12-foot-tall, 20-foot-thick earthen-filled reinforcement constructed with squared logs that protected nearly three sides of the fortification. He also describes an associated dry ditch that was unfinished at the time. Based on subsequent descriptions of the fort, this seems to be something that was added to protect the sides of the fort that were not protected by the ravelin described in Adam Stephen's December 9,1756 letter.

Barton also indicates that the fort had ten embrasures that were each armed with a four-pounder cannon. Like other observers before him, Barton describes Fort Cumberland as being poorly situated, because of surrounding hills. Barton reports that the fort could be attacked by cannon fire from the hill where the Ohio Company storehouse is located, and from a hill that is located about 300 yards northwest of Fort Cumberland.

Barton also reports that there were several fine fenced in vegetable gardens on the banks of the river, about 40 yards from the fort. His journal entry ends with the description of the pyramidal-topped square post monument with an inscribed lead plate that is described below.

## A British map that was captured at the Battle of Monongehela

The next set of images are from a British map that was made before Braddock's expedition, and captured by the French at Braddock's defeat.[938] It bears an inscription in French that states, *"Found in the military cache of General Braddock along with plans and instructions. 10th July 1755. Captain Dumas."*[939] The roads to Rort Duquesne are shown, along with a road to Virginia that crosses Wills Creek.

An inscription in English is difficult to read. As best I can make out this inscription, it states, *"South gate weak. 2 twelves here. 2 nines on the others. Barracks for 750 men. Guns stored on the southeast casemate, southeast angle. Five houses for Indian traders. Trail lead to Du Quesne. Portage of scow not 25 yards. Hilly Ground and marshy. 2 Field pieces. Two howitzers. Two cohorn."* A cohorn is a mortar, and fires in a high arching trajectory. A casemate is a small room with firing ports that is built into the thick wall of a fort. The reference to barracks for 750 men is remarkable. It's hard to imagine how extensive the barracks had to be to house that many men.

The drawing appears to use solid lines to illustrate the 20-foot-thick earthworks that Barton describes, and appears to use dashed lines to illustrate the dry ditch that Barton describes. The main face of the 20-foot-thick revelin is oriented toward the hill located northwest of the fort. Several hills are identified where cannon can be advantageously located to fire on the fort. These hills are easily matched to local topography. The drawing was probably modified by the French to show the revelin, dry ditch, and earthen reinforcements based on the reports of French spies.

---

[938] Map provided by Robert L. Bantz.
[939] Translation provided by Ben Press.

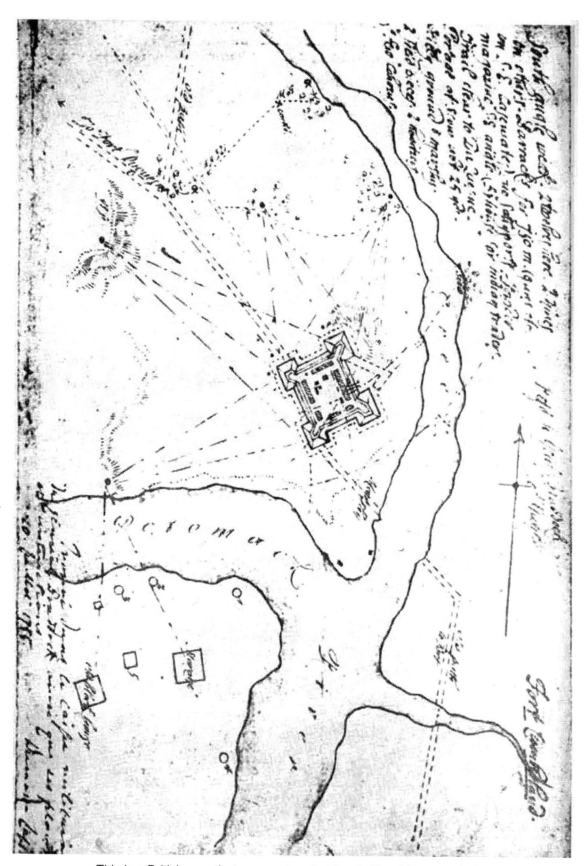

This is a British map that was captured at the Battle of Monongahela.

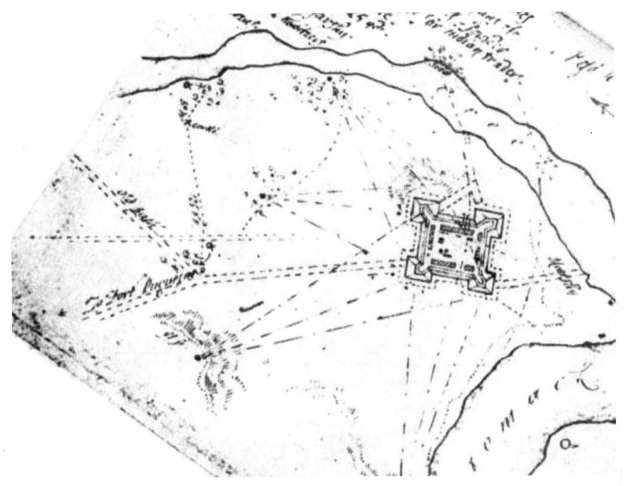

This is a portion of the captured British map, oriented so that north is at the top.

This is another portion of the captured British map, oriented so that north is at the top. The five houses are numbered, and the new store and block house are labeled. The drawing shows that the blockhouse and new store are vulnerable to close range cannon fire from the Maryland side of the river.

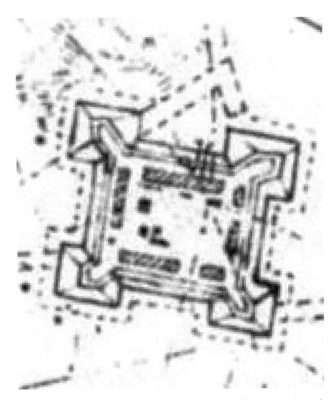

Unlike drawings 122/38 and 122/39, the guard houses are not illustrated as forming the west curtain.

## A soldier's memorial at Fort Cumberland in 1758, regarding November 1756 service

According to J. Thomas Scharf's 1882 book "**History of Western Maryland**", the April 1788 issue of the "**Columbian Magazine**" includes the following letter:

*To the Editor of the Columbian Magazine:*

*Sir, — The following is an extract from the journal of an officer on Gen. Forbes expedition against Fort Du Quesoe (now Fort Pitt) in the year 1758:*

*"About one hundred yards from Fort Cumberland is a large square post with a pyramidical top, having a plate of lead with the following inscription nailed on one side of it, viz.:*

*To The Memory of Sergeant William Shaw, Sergeant Timothy Shaw, Jeremiah Poor And James Cope, Soldiers Of The 1st Virginia Regiment; This Monument Is Erected, To Testify the Love And Esteem Paid Them by Their Officers For Their Courage And Gallant Behaviour, Nov. 1756. They went with 11 Catawbas To Gain Intelligence; And In The First Encounter With The Enemy Met With The Success Their Courage Deserved — Incited By this Advantage, and Fired with Noble Ambition to Distinguish Themselves, They Engaged A Party Of The Enemy, Hard By Fort Duquesne, And Fell Gloriously, Fighting Bravely, Being Greatly Overpowered By Superior Numbers.*

*In Premium Virtutis Erigendum Curavit*

*Adamus Stephen."*

*. . . Some of these men afterwards returned, and are now officers in the Virginia service. B.*

This description of the pyramidal-topped square post monument with an inscribed lead plate is part of Barton's journal entry for September 7, 1758. The description of the monument is also included on page 267 of Lowdermilk's 1878 book "**History of Cumberland**".

### Only three days of flour remain at Fort Cumberland

A September 9, 1758 letter[940] Washington wrote to Lieutenant Colonel George Mercer from the *"Camp at Fort Cumberland"* states:

> *I this moment receiv'd notice from the Commissary, that only three day's Flour remain upon hand for the Troops at this Incampment. Mr. Hoops is wrote to on the occasion, and I must beg the favour of you to facilitate any measures he shall propose to supply us in time; by affording an Escort &ca. Not knowing how soon we may be order'd to join you, I can't tell how much Provisions is wanted; possibly, ten days will serve till, the Generals pleasure be known. We have no Waggon's at this place, otherwise I wou'd have given you no trouble in this affair.*

### Sharpe writes from Fort Cumberland

A September 12, 1758 letter[941] that Governor Sharpe wrote to Forbes from Fort Cumberland states:

> *I have just time to acquaint You of my Arrival here & that unless you are pleased to send me an order by the Bearer Ensign Murdock for supplying the Men with Rum as mentioned in my former Letters it will not be in my Power to keep them together, I must likewise desire the favour of you to order M$^r$ Adam Hoop to send us an immediate Supply of Flour & Beef.*

### Washington was ordered to join Mercer at Raystown

A September 14, 1758 letter[942] that Bouquet wrote to Colonel Mercer from the *"Camp at Loyal Hannon"* incudes the statement, *"Please to Send immediately an Express in the night well escorted to Cumberland, Col Washington has order to join you at Reas Town"*.

### Fort Cumberland supply inventory, September 15, 1758

A September 15, 1758 document written by Commissary Galbraith is titled, *"A Return of Provisions in Store at Fort Cumberland for the use of His Majesty's Troops"*. The return lists ten bags of flour, 3,277 barrels of flour, 2,000 pounds of pork, 5,000 puns of bacon, seven tierces[943] of Rice, and zero cattle. This is difficult to reconcile with contemporaneous letters. Imagine the storehouse space required to house 3,277 barrels of flour.

### Provisions are to be sent to Fort Cumberland on September 17, 1758

A September 16, 1758 letter[944] that Francis Halkett wrote to Governor Sharpe from the *"Camp at Reastown"* states:

---

[940] "**The Writings of George Washington**", Volume 2, Fitzpatrick, 1931.

[941] "**Correspondence of Governor Horatio Sharpe**", Volume II, 1890.

[942] "**The Papers of Col. Henry Bouquet**", 1940.

[943] A tierce is a certain size of cask having a diameter of about 20.5-inches.

[944] "**Correspondence of Governor Horatio Sharpe**", Volume II, 1890.

*This evening Colonel Washington arrived, who surprises the General extreamly by the account that he gives of the great scarcity of provisions at Fort Cumberland after having wrote to Colonel Bouquet so fully upon that subject, how ever the General (who is greatly fatigued from the business that his just coming to Reastown has oblidg'd him to go through) has order'd me to inform you, that he will send off a Convoy of provisions to morrow, the particulars of which M* S* Clair will inform you of, at the same time the bearer carryes order for all the Virginians to be ready to march immediately upon the arrival of Colonel Washington, who sets out for that purpose to morrow morning, which will deminish the Consumpsion of Provisions at Fort Cumberland very considerably, and make it a very easy matter to support you for the future as your numbers will be so much diminish'd.*

*Three days ago Commissary Clerk wrote to M* Rutherford at Winchester, to supply your people with spirits, and all the other necessarys that you desir'd, which letter I hope will be in good time to answer your expectations*

## Surprise that Rutherford has not supplied Fort Cumberland

A September 16, 1758 letter[945] that James Sinclair wrote to Governor Sharpe from the *"Camp at Rays town"* includes the following:

*I am desired by General Forbes to acquaint you that he is in the greatest concern to find M* Rutherford, to whom the suplying of fort Cumberland was entirely intrusted, has not yet furnished the necessary Suplys, as the General had given such directions for that purpose, as he thought could not fail of doing it effectualy before your arrival. There was an Express sent off yesterday to M* Rutherford from M* Hoops constituent at this place, to hasten things as much as possible and order him up immediately from Winchester, in the mean time, if you will be so good as let the General know your wants, they shall be suplyed from hence as well as possible, notwithstanding the great difficulties wely under with regard to Carriages.*

## Two hogsheads of liquor to be sent to Fort Cumberland

On September 16, 1758, General Forbes wrote a letter[946] to Governor Sharpe from Raestown that includes the following statement:

*I received your letter from Fort Cumberland at Juniata last night, and that I might answer it more exactly brought your officer on here this day, where I now find there has a transport gone from here this morning for Fort Cumberland with provisions which will serve in the meantime untill Mr Rutherford arrives; what I was to do with regard to spirits I could not well say, imagining they could be bought as reasonable and cheap at Fort Cumberland as they could be sent from this, but now being informed of the contrary I have ordered two hogsheads to be sent off directly, which will give me time to look about me for a day or two and draw Breath, being at this present moment in bed wearied like a dog.*

The letter includes a postscript that states:

*If spirits can be purchased reasonable at Fort Cumberland, I dont see why we should be obliged to send them from this. Mr St Clair is just now come in and informs me that the transport of provisions above mentioned, did not proceed as I have said — However as there is an Express gone to Winchester to Mr. Rutherford to hasten him up, I hope you will be able to make a shift untill that he arrives or that I can*

---

[945] **"Correspondence of Governor Horatio Sharpe"**, Volume II, 1890.
[946] **"The Pennsylvania magazine of history and biography"**, Volume 33, 1909.

*send you a fresh supply, which shall be the first thing I shall take care of when any comes to this place, and that expect tomorrow or the day after*

## Washington is to temporarily leave 100 men at Fort Cumberland

A September 17, 1758 letter that Bouquet wrote to Forbes includes the statement, *"I wrote Colonel Washington to march to Raystown, leaving 100 men at Cumberland, until the arrival of the Maryland militia. This reinforcement was necessary to protect our convoys on the communication"*.

## Sharpe reports that the volunteers will want to leave the fort by October 10

A September 20, 1758 letter[947] that Governor Sharpe wrote to Forbes includes the following:

*I earnestly request the favour of a Line from you before the 10th of next month at which time the Voluntiers under my Command (amounting in all to 215 men officers included) will be for returning home.*

## A September 27, 1758 explosion at Fort Cumberland

The October 4, 1758 minutes[948] of the Virginia House of Burgesses includes the following:

*A Message from the Governor was delivered by Mr. Walthoe.*

*Mr. Speaker,*

*The Governor has commanded me to deliver to your House, several Letters his Honor received last night, by Express from Colonel Washington, and Lieutenant Smith, giving an Account of the late Engagement with the French near Fort Du Quesne, and of the blowing up one of our Magazines at Fort Cumberland.*

The October 5, 1758 issue of the "**Maryland Gazette**" describes a September 27, 1758 explosion at Fort Cumberland as follows:

*We hear from Fort Cumberland, that on Wednesday the 27th of last month, as Captain Sprigg and Mr. Luckett were searching the inward Magazine for Tent Cloaths, to make better Provision for the Sick, it blew up, and set the Fort on Fire in several Places, particularly in Two, very near the grand Magazine, the Door of which was bust open: But by the Activity and Resolution of the Garrison, the Fire was happily extinguished, and the Place saved, with Loss of the Two unfortunate Gentlemen, and the Stores that were in the Magazine.*

*Last Tuesday ended the Election in Frederick County, having lasted six Days, when Capt. Henry Wright Crabb, Mr. Edward Dorsey, Capt. Joseph Chapline, and Col. Thomas Cresap, were declared duly Elected.*

*His Excellency, our Governor, we hear, is not expected Home from Fort Cumberland, 'till the 20th Instant.*

The referenced *"grand magazine"* may have been the one in the northwest bastion. The phrase *"inward Magazine"* tells us that the explosition occurred in one of the storehouses inside the fort. The fact that the door of the grand magazine was blown open by the explosion is a strong clue that the grand magazine in the northwest bastion was not underground.

---

[947] "**Correspondence of Governor Horatio Sharpe**", Volume II, 1890.
[948] "**Journals of the House of Burgesses of Virginia 1758-1761**", 1908.

## Sharpe reports that the Virginians have 20 men fit for duty at Fort Cumberland

An undated 1758 letter[949] that Governor Sharpe wrote to Forbes from Fort Cumberland states:

*Since my last I have had the Misfortune to lose Capt Spriggs & M[r] Luckett my Adjutant by the blowing up of the lesser Magazine, the Fire it occasioned was soon got the better of & no Loss sustained except the Stores therein lodged & what they were I can give Your Excellency no Account not having received any of the Stores left here. Your Excellency will I persuade Myself excuse my not being more particular when I assure you it was not in my power to obtain from Major Levingston any Acco[t] whatever of the Stores left here. As the time for which the Voluntiers engaged to garrison this place is near expiring I think it my Duty to acquaint you that Lieut[t] Hays of the Virg[a] Forces (to whom I shall leave the Command of this place has 20 men fit for Duty 47 upon the Recovery & 49 sick.*

## The Virginians complain that the Marylanders have taken some of their horses

A September 30, 1758 letter[950] that Major Halkett wrote to Governor Sharpe from the *"Camp at Reastown"* includes the following:

*The General ... approves greatly of every thing you say regarding the sick at Fort Cumberland, but as it would be attended with great inconveniency to make a Detachment from this place just now for the Garrisoning of Fort Cumberland, he is in hopes you will be able to detain the Militia now with you till the tenth of October against [which] time he will take care to provide for its security, and in a few days he will take an opportunity to write you very fully in answer to your letter.*

*The Virginians make a Complaint of some of your people haveing taken up some of their horses, as stray horses, & detaind them, altho some of their Bass men were sent over to demand them, the General therefore begs that you will be so good to examine into it, and put it to Rights, and as they have sent a party over to Receive them that you will order them to be deliver'd*

*The General desires that you will inform Lieutenant Haze of the Virginians, that it is his orders, he remain at Fort Cumberland with all the sick & recover'd men under his Command till further orders.*

## Halkett requests ammunition be forwarded from Fort Cumberland

On October 2, 1758 Francis Halkett wrote a letter from the *"Camp at Reastown"* to Governor Sharpe, who was then at Fort Cumberland. The letter states:

*About this time we expect their will be a number of the Shannondo Waggons arriving at Fort Cumberland with provisions from Winchester; the General therefore begs that you will be so good as to engage as many of them as possible upon the same terms as the Pennsylvania waggons, to go upon our Expedition, and that you will take the opportunity of their coming here, to send over all the Buck shott at Fort Cumberland, seven Boxes containing two hundred weight each, were lodged in the new store under the hill, which was sent from Fort Frederick along with the shelles. Six hundred weight was likewise lodged in store that was blown up, if any of that remains undistroyed, you will send it also, and provided the carriages can be ready time enough they may take the benefite of the officer and thirty men sent from the Second Virginia Regiment for horses, to escort them — if this party marched before that the waggons can be got Ready they must be escorted by the Recoverd men of the Virginia Regiments.*

---

[949] **"Correspondence of Governor Horatio Sharpe"**, Volume II, 1890.
[950] **"Correspondence of Governor Horatio Sharpe"**, Volume II, 1890.

*If their are any spair wheels or carriages for Howitzers be pleased to send them likewise in some of the empty Waggons, Captain Hay having brought no spair ones with the Train, and we may come to have occasion for them.*

The letter includes a postscript that states:

*Upon shewing this letter to the General, he has alter'd that part of it, for the Recoverd men of the Virginians to escort the Waggons, provided the officer & 30 men be Returnd with the Horses, and desires that you will favour him with a few lines to inform him of the number you can engage, and he will order a party from this Camp to march to Fort Cumberlan to Escort them hither...*

Sharpe apparently replied to one or both of the above two letters with an undated letter[951] that states:

*The Shannando Waggons being 41 in number are just arrived with 28 Days Flour, a necessary Supply not having more than 5 Days Flour & 25 of Bacon in Store & but three Steers that I have ordered to be kept for the use of the Sick nor is there any Likelyhood of any further Supplies coming from Winchester for this place. There are as I am informed some spare Howitzer Wheels in an outward Store house the Key whereof was not delivered to me however shall order it to be opened & take out such Carriages or Wheels as may be therein the Buck Shot left in the lesser Magazine were all destroyed the Rest shall be sent with the Waggons which only wait for Convoy. I am extremely sorry that the Virginians should have troubled Your Excellency with Complaints ag[st] my people for having taken up some of their Stray Horses & detained them altho some of their Batt Men were sent to demand them as it obliges me to take up too much of Y[r] time in giving it an Answer, the first part of their Charge is true having promised the Hunters a Reward of 5[s] for every Horse they should bring in & I can assure Your Excellency they lost no time in making their Demand & I did myself order an Officer to see them delivered up which I am well assur'd was done for I saw them taken away by their Batt Men, it is likewise true that part of the latter Charge may be just but no further than this the Reverend M. Barkley who was here at the time that two of his Horses were brought in after being lost for some considerable time refused paying the Reward upon which I ordered them to be detained until he thought proper to comply which he did a short time after. Upon the strictest Enquiry I cannot find that anything has happened wherein my People were any ways concerned except my ordering a sick man to be put on one of the stray Horses to give him an Airing for half a quarter of a mile w[ch] gave one of their Batt Men great offence & furnished him with an occasion as appears by all the standersby of being very insolent & abusive for which one of the Militia struck him with a Bridle the Bit whereof did him some harm.*

## Washington's opinion on which road Forbes should follow is disdained by some

On October 3, 1758, Colonel John Armstrong[952] wrote a letter to Richard Peters that includes the statement, *"The Virginians are much chagrined at the opening of the road through this government, and Colonel Washington has been a good deal sanguine and obstinate upon the occasion."*

---

[951] "**Correspondence of Governor Horatio Sharpe**", Volume II, 1890.

[952] John Armstrong had a military post at Kickenapaulin's during Forbes' campaign, and describes the place in a July 26, 1758 letter, stating, "*some of the Ground Cleared some time ago by the Indians*". In an August 8, 1758 letter, Bouquet mentions Armstrong's post, and states, "*I shall march to Loyal Hannon before the road is open from Kickeny Pawlins.*" In an August 15, 1758 letter, Col. Stevens writes that the post at Kickeny Paulins has been reinforced. In an August 16, 1758 letter, Saint Clair wrote, "*A small retrencht is picked out at Kikeny Pawlings.*" Thomas Barton's August 18, 1758 journal entry locates Armstrong's post at Quemahoning Creek. In an August 23, 1758 letter, Bouquet wrote, "*Col. Armstrong is to command at Kickeny Pawlins and along the Communication from the Gap of the Allegheny to the foot of Lawrell Hill*". According to the March 11, 1975 issue of the "**Somerset Daily American**", Armstrong's fortification at Kickenapaulin's was then still faintly discernible when the water of the Quemahoning Reservoir was low.

## Thank you for taking care of our good Fort Cumberland

An October 5, 1758 letter[953] that Forbes wrote to Governor Sharpe from *"Raes Camp"* states:

*I am this moment favourd with yours and am very much obliged to you, for the Care you have taken of our good Fort Cumberland, this will be deliverd you by M' Clerk, whom I had sent over on purpose to settle matters with regard to provisions &c, So whatever you have wanted or may want he will settle with you as you shall please to direct, as to the Virginia complaint I thought it frivilous and triffling from the begining, you can easily see I was obligd to take notice of it, on purpose to please. I shall send of an Escort tomorrow for the Waggons, but if the Escort of Coll° Byrds Reg' is not yet come away, they may Stay and Come along with the Waggons, or Escort them till they meet the Party I send off tomorrow. As there will be some empty waggons, I shall expect the Spare wheel Carriage that Major Halket wrote about. As I understand you have some Garden Stuff such as Cabbage &c. I beg you will be so good as ord' some to be sent over here by the Waggons.*

## Wagons are discovered in a large storehouse at Fort Cumberland

An October 6, 1758 letter[954] that Governor Sharpe wrote to Halkett from Fort Cumberland states:

*This is to acknowledge the Receit of Your Letters bearing Date the 30th of Sept' & the 2d Inst as well as to acquaint you that there are no spare Carriages or Wheels for Hobitzers or Cannon but there are in an out Store House about fifteen or sixteen compleat Military Waggons. I must desire the favour of you to pay my Respects to the General & to acquaint him that the Militia are resolved to march on Monday Morning next nor will the General I flatter myself be surprized thereat when he is acquainted of their being now taken sick Day after Day & no able Person left here to take care of them.*

Imagine how big a storehouse would have to be to hold 15 or 16 wagons.

## Plumer and Cresap are mentioned in court records

On page 26 of the 1759 Frederick County court docket book[955], in a section titled *"Continuances from August Court 1758 To March Court 1759"*, a record dated October 6, 1758 lists Michael Hubbly and Jonathan Plumer in a matter that references *"Thomas Cresap bail"*. The same case is listed on page 82, in a section titled *"Continuences from August Court 1758 to June Court Anno 1759"*; this listing references *"Cash Tho' Cresap Bail"*. The same case is listed on page 164, in a section titled *"Tryal Docketts to the third Tuesday & Twentyeth Day of November Annoque Domini 1759"*. The same case is also listed on page 12 of a surviving fragment of the 1760 Frederick County Maryland court docket book[956], in a section titled, *"Tryal Dockett for the third Tuesday and eighteenth Day of March Annoguo Domini 1760"*.

## Wheels are belatedly found at Fort Cumberland

An October 8, 1758 letter[957] that Governor Sharpe wrote to Forbes from Fort Cumberland includes the statement, *"I am sorry this place did not afford Your Excellency a better Supply of Carriages or Wheels & those sent were not discovered untill the Party had marched."*

[953] **"Correspondence of Governor Horatio Sharpe"**, Volume II, 1890.
[954] **"Correspondence of Governor Horatio Sharpe"**, Volume II, 1890.
[955] MSA No. C782-11
[956] MSA No. C782-11
[957] **"Correspondence of Governor Horatio Sharpe"**, Volume II, 1890.

## I have nothing to expect from Maryland

An October 22, 1758 letter[958] Forbes wrote to the Provincial Council of Pennsylvania from *"Raystown Camp"* includes the following:

> *I have received no Answer from you relating to Fort Duquesne, if it should please God to grant Success; but whether that Fort is taken or not, the Forts of Loyal Hannon, Cumberland, Raystown, Juniata, Littleton, Loudoun, Frederick, Shippensburgh, and Carlisle, ought to be Garrisoned, beside those on the other Side of the Susquehannah. I have wrote to Mr. Fouquiere to know what assistance I may have from the Colony of Virginia, which I do not expect will be very great, not even to Garrison Fort Cumberland, their Frontiers are so extensive that Augusta County will require Two Hundred Men to Garrison its Forts; Winchester, with the south Branch of Potomack, Three Hundred Men more, to which Colonel Washington's Regiment will not amount at the End of the Campaign. I have nothing to expect from Maryland, as I am told they have abandoned Fort Cumberland and Fort Frederick.*

## Washington describes the explosion to Governor Fauquier

An October 30, 1758 letter[959] George Washington wrote to Governor Fauquier from the *"Camp, at Loyal Hanna"* includes the statement, *"Governor Sharpe in person commanded a garrison of militia, (from his province,) at Fort Cumberland, when the magazine was blown up, and had, I believe, his storekeeper included in the blast."*

## Sharpe describes the explosion to Baltimore

A November 3, 1758 letter Governor Sharpe wrote to Lord Baltimore from Annapolis also describes the September 27, 1758 gunpowder explosion at Fort Cumberland:

> *On Arrival at Fort Cumberland the Virginians evacuated it & encamped but they did not march towards Raes Town till late in Septr the 27th of that month I had the misfortune to lose one of our Militia Captains & a Young Gentleman that I had appointed Adjutant by the following Accident; Some of the People who were sick being in great want of Bedding the abovementioned Gentlemen went into a Store Room for some old Tents &c. which had been heretofore left there by the Virginia Troops, it happened that among a great many other Stores which had been deposited in this Place there were three or four Barrells or Parts of Barrells of Powder & some useless Arms some of which were probably loaded, while the Gentln were pulling out the Tents I imagine that one of the Firelocks must have fallen down & gone off otherwise I cannot account for the unhappy Accident. All that we know for certain is that the Store was blown up the Captain & Adjutant killed & the Fort in an Instant set on fire in several Places particularly in one a very few Yards only from the grand Magazine of Powder, the Door of which was burst open. When the Virginians marched they left more than a hundred Men sick in the Hospital, these dying very fast sometimes three or four in a Day & many of the Militia being taken ill they begun to be uneasy & I foresaw that it would not be in my Power to keep them there a Day longer than they had engaged to remain with me when they first went up, I perceived likewise that I could not do the General much Service by continuing there until that time as I was well informed tha S^r J S^t Clair could not before the Middle of Octr return to Raes Town with the Waggons which he had gone down the Country to collect & in which the General expected to receive his last Supply of Provisions, however as the General appeared more sanguine in his Expectations than I thought he had reason to be I stayed at Fort Cumberland until the 10^th of Oct^r when about 50 of the Virginians who had been left in the Hospital being pretty well recovered*

---

[958] **"Minutes of the Provincial Council of Pennsylvania..."**, Volume 8.

[959] **"The Writings of George Washington"**, Worthington Chauncey Ford, Volume II, 1889.

*& able to do Duty I resigned up the Fort to their Commanding Officer having first wrote to the General & obtained his Approbation ...*

### Jenny Frazer is at Raystown in November 1758

The Frazer's were at Raystown by November 4, 1758. Frederick Post's November 4, 1758 journal entry states, in regard to some Cherokees visiting *"Rays-town"*, *"Pesquitomen, finding Jenny Frazer here, who had been their prisoner and escaped, spoke to her a little rashly."* Post's November 5 journal entry states, *"Pesquitomen, before we went from hence, made it up with Jenny Frazer, and they parted good friends..."* Kenny's May 28, 1759 journal entry states, *"I have been setting Pisquetims raisors this morning; he says he is yᵉ brother of Shingas yᵉ Beaver ..."* and his June 26, 1759 journal entry states, *"Shingas is come & his brother Pisquiton, but yᵉ Beaver King, their brother is not returnd yet ..."* *"Pesquitomen"*, *"Pisquetims"* and *"Pisquiton"* may be phonetically spelled variations of the same name.

### Washington continues to agitate for the use of Braddock's road

A letter[960] George Washington wrote to General Forbes from Chestnut Ridge on November 16, 1758 includes the following:

> *The keeping Fort Duquesne (if we should be fortunate enough to take it) in its present situation, will be attended with great advantages to the middle colonies; and I do not know so effectual a way of doing it, as by the communication of Fort Cumberland and General Braddock's road, which is, in the first place, good, and in the next, fresh; affording good food if the weather keeps open, which is more than a road can do as much used as this has been.*

### Colonel Cresap is involved in a Virginia lawsuit

On November 17, 1758 John Daugherty was summoned by the Frederick County, Virginia court to answer a suit by Thomas Cresap over an £10/4/2 debt.

### Fort Cumberland is ordered to disarm a group of Cherokees

A fragmented transcript of a letter[961] General Forbes wrote to Colonel Burd from *"New Camp, 20 miles west of Loyal Hannon, November 19ᵗʰ, 1758"* includes the following:

> *He has often told us in public that his nation were going to make war against the Virginians and His Majesty s subjects. I therefore thought him a good pledge in our hands to prevent that, and consequently the whole of them were indulged in every extravagant, avaricious demand they made; but seeing that those who have thus deserted and abandoned us, with all the aggravating circumstances attending their desertion, now preludes to what we may expect from them. I therefore desire, that upon receipt of this, you will instantly dispatch an express to the commanding officer at Raystown, who is to send one to Winchester and Fort Cumberland, in case that he, the Carpenter[962] and his followers, should have already past Raystown, and notice ought to be sent to Fort London likewise with my orders, which are that having under the cloak of friendship robbed us these several months, but now having discovered themselves our private enemies, and having turned the arms, put in their hands by us, against his Majesty's subjects, which the former parties have already done, that, therefore prudence and self preservation obliged us, to require of them the returning of their arms and ammunition directly, as likewise the horses that were*

---

[960] **"The Writings of George Washington"**, Worthington Chauncey Ford, Volume II, 1889.

[961] **"Letters and papers relating chiefly to the provincial history of Pennsylvania"**, 1855.

[962] The Cherokee Chief.

*furnished them to accompany us to war; that as their blankets, shirts, silver truck, &c., are not of that consequence, therefore the peremptory stripping of them need not ...*

*... fellow subjects of the parts of Virginia borough, where no doubt they would commit all sorts of outrage, so that it will be necessary to send a sufficient escort along with them, allowing of them a sufficiency of provisions and no more, so that the Cherokee nation may see plainly they will have nothing to complain of but the baseness and perfidy of those, whom they have sent amongst us as friends for these seven months past. The garrison of Fort Cumberland is strong enough to compel them to deliver up their arms, so let a copy of this my letter be sent to the commanding officer, who is to make use of all the fair means in his power before he takes their arms from them. At Raystown they are to do the same. ...*

*Mr. Smith the interpreter ought to be sent after them to serve to explain matters, and to prevent as far as can be, the bad consequences of their going home through Virginia and North Carolina, armed, for which purpose this letter is wrote, as Virginia has always suffered.*

## Fort Duquesne is captured on November 25, 1758, and renamed Pittsbourgh

Forbes took possession of the ruins of Fort Duquesne on November 25, 1758. From there, he wrote a letter dated *"Pittsbourgh 27th Novemr 1758."* to William Pitt that includes the following statement:[963]

*I have used the freedom of giving your name to Fort Du Quesne, as I hope it was in some measure the being actuated by your spirits that now makes us Masters of the place.*

The capture of Fort Duquesne is described in the following December 14, 1758 letter from Governor Sharpe to Lord Baltimore:

*It is with great pleasure I inform Your Ldp that Lt Colo Dagworthy is just arrived here from the Army commanded by General Forbes & brings us the agreeable Account of His Excellencys having on the 25th of last Month taken Possession of Fort Du Quesne which the Enemy had abandoned two Days before. A Virginia Lad who made his Escape from them as they were going off says that about Half the Garrison (which consisted of 500 men commanded by Monsr Desligneris) went down the Ohio in Battoes carrying the Artillery & all their Stores with them & that the Rest having first set fire to all the Houses in & without the Fort marched towards Venango which is about 60 Miles to the Northwd of Fort Du Quesne & where they have a small Stoccado Fort. They had it seems been some time in great Want of Provisions, (which was probably owing to the Loss they suffered last Summer at Frontenac) their Indians had all left them, they perceived that General Forbes was approaching with upwards of 3000 Men who were within two Days March of the Fort when they abandoned it & happily for us the Weather continued extreemly favourable.*

*The first Intelligence the General received of the Enemys being gone off was from some Friendly Indians who had been on a Scout & returned to his Camp on the Evening of the 24th Orders were immediately issued for Lt Colo Dagworthy to march next Morning at Break of Day with a hundred Men to reconnoitre & if the Indian's Intelligence was true to take Possession of the Fort. He had scarcely left the Camp when he met Capt Pearisone of our Officers who had been sent out the Night before with a small Party to make Discoveries & by him he was assured of the Truth of what the Indians had before told the General. The inclosed Plan or Draft which Colo Dagworthy has at my Desire sketch't out from his Memory will shew Your Ldp what Works the French had made & in what Condition they left them. & the other inclosed Paper will inform Your Ldp how the General has disposed of the Provincial Troops that served on this Expedition. Besides the 200 Provincials who are destined to garrison Fort Du Quesne this winter Colo*

---

[963] Forbes' letter is published in the March 14, 1907 issue of "**The Nation**".

*Dagworthy left most of the Highlanders & Royal Americans there but he supposes that they are by this time coming in with the General (who was in a very ill State of Health) & that all the Regulars will be sent down among the Inhabitants for Winter Quarters. As soon almost as our Troops arrived at Fort Du Quesne four or five Indians appeared on the other Side of the Ohio & desired to be fetched over & introduced to the General which they were the next Day on the 27th they were dismissed with an Answer to the Message they had brought from their respective Towns & Mr Croghan the Deputy Agent for Indian Affairs with an Interpreter was ordered to accompany them Colo Dagworthy does not know what passed between the General & those Indians but he says it was expected that all the Indians on the Ohio will immediately come in & sue for Peace. In my Letter of the 8th Inst I told Your Ldp there was a Report that the French had only retired to another Fort which they had built about 20 miles lower down the Ohio but I learn from Colo Dagworthy that there is no such Fort & that those of the Enemy that fell down the River were seen more than 30 Miles below Fort Du Quesne by the four Indians abovementioned. Your Ldp will perceive by the Orders which the General gave out the 29th of Novemr that he has sent a hundred of the Maryland Soldiers to Garrison Fort Cumberland expecting I presume that our Assembly will at least agree to support that Number, but if he has proceeded on this Supposition I am much afraid he will be disappointed & that Fort Cumberland will be soon evacuated, for the Gentlemen of the Lower House are still determined to adhere to their Assesment Bill, which I am told will be now offered to the Upper House in two or three Days. The General having thought fit to leave it to me to dispose of the Rest of the Maryland Forces I have ordered them to repair to this Place where they will be ready to be disbanded if no Supplies are granted or to receive their Arrears of Pay & be cloathed if the Assembly shall be prevailed on to raise Money at this time for that purpose.*

This letter indicates that the French lost their Indian allies prior to the arrival of Forbes due to lack of provisions. With all the atrocities the French and their Indian allies committed against civilians during the preceding four years, it's not too surprising that the French made sure they were already well away from Fort Duquesne when Forbes arrived with his overwhelming force.

## A summary of the Forbes expedition

This brief summary of the Forbes expedition is from the 1913 book "**A History of the United States: A century of colonial history, 1660-1760**":

*The command of the Duquesne expedition was given to Brigadier General John Forbes, who had begun life as a physician, but had now been in the military service for some years. He had twelve hundred Highlanders besides colonial troops from Pennsylvania and the colonies to the southward, numbering in all about six thousand men. His leading subordinate was Lieutenant Colonel Henry Bouquet, a Swiss from Canton Berne. Contrary to Washington's advice, Forbes decided to proceed through Pennsylvania, Braddock's road being circuitous and overgrown with brush. He advanced by short stages, everywhere fortifying as he went. This slow rate of progression turned out to be in favor of his success, for the Indian allies of the French, disgusted at having nothing to do, deserted their employers. What made most in Forbes's favor, however, was a treaty of peace, which the Pennsylvanians were able to make with the Delaware and Shawanoe Indians who had been attacking the frontier settlements for several years. During the whole campaign Forbes was so ill that he had to be carried in a litter. The command of the advance fell to Bouquet. Unfortunately he permitted one of his subordinates, Major Grant, to reconnoitre out of supporting distance from the main body. This detachment was set upon by the French and Indians and badly defeated. So slow was Forbes's advance that November found the army still at some distance from the fort and a decision was reached to stop further progress for the year. Information then came to Forbes that the French were in a critical condition. With twenty-five hundred men he now pushed rapidly forward, Washington being in command of his right wing. When they reached the vicinity of the fort, explosions were heard and a reconnoissance showed that the French had blown up their defenses and abandoned their stronghold (November 24, 1758). In this way the French possession of western Pennsylvania came to a close.*

### Maryland troops are ordered to Fort Cumberland in late November

A December 14, 1758 letter[964] that Governor Sharpe wrote to Baltimore includes the following statement:

*Your Ldp will perceive by the Orders which the General gave out the 29ᵗʰ of Novemʳ that he has sent a hundred of the Maryland Soldiers to Garrison Fort Cumberland expecting I presume that our Assembly will at least agree to support that Number. but if he has proceeded on this Supposition I am much afraid he will be disappointed & that Fort Cumberland will be soon evacuated, for the Gentlemen of the Lower House are still determined to adhere to their Assesment Bill, which I am told will be now offered to the Upper House in two or three Days.*

Sharpe wrote a letter to Bouquet from Annapolis on December 30, 1758 that includes the following statement:

*...I embrace the Opportunity to congratulate Your Excellency on the Success of His Majestys Forces under Your Command ... Colº Dagworthy informs me that before he left the Camp at Loyalhannon[965] he ordered 100 of the best men that were in the Maryland Troops to march & garrison Fort Cumberland till Your Excellency's pleasure should be farther signified, & Capt Beall[966] having brought all the Rest of the Men hither...*

### The men at Fort Pitt are in pitiful condition in December 1758

Washington wrote a letter[967] to Governor Fauquier from Loyal Hanna on December 2, 1758 that includes the statement:

*The general has in his letters told you what garrison he proposed to leave at Fort Du Quesne, but the want of provisions rendered it impossible to leave more than two hundred men in all; and these must I fear abandon the place or perish. Our men left there are in such a miserable condition, having hardly rags to cover their nakedness, and exposed to the inclemency of the weather in this rigorous season, that sickness, death, and desertion, if they are not speedily supplied, must destroy them.*

### Logstown was rebuilt by the French

Frederick Post's journal entry[968] for December 2, 1758 states, *"I, with my companion, Kekiuscund's son, came to Logs Town, situated on a hill. On the east is a great piece of low land, where the Old Log's Town used to stand. In the New Log's Town, the French have built about thirty houses for the Indians."*

---

[964] **"Correspondence of Governor Horatio Sharpe"**, Volume II, 1890.

[965] Fort Ligonier. According to William C. Reichel's study of Moravian missionary John Heckewelder's papers, published in Volume 1 of the 1876 **"Transactions of the Moravian Historical Society"**, Loyalhanna is *"corrupted from Laweel-hánne, signifying, the middle stream."*

[966] This seems to most likely be a reference to Captain Alexander Beall.

[967] **"Washington and the Generals of the American Revolution"**, Volume 1, 1848.

[968] **"The Wilderness Trail..."**, Volume 1.

## Condition of the road between Fort Cumberland and Cresap's

The December 15, 1758 proceedings of the Lower House of the Maryland Assembly prove that the road was adequate between Cresap's and Fort Cumberland, stating, *"From Col. Cresap's to Fort Cumberland wants no clearing 15 Miles"*.

## Fort Bedford was named by December 28, 1758

The 1916 book "**Report of the Commission to locate the site of the frontier forts of Pennsylvania**", quotes the December 28, 1758 entry in the second journal of Christian Frederick Post as follows, *"The general sent Mr. Hays express, to fort Bedford and commanded him to see if the place for encampment, under the Allegheny mountain was prepared; as also to take care that refreshments should be at hand, at his coming."* This shows that the fort had already received its name.

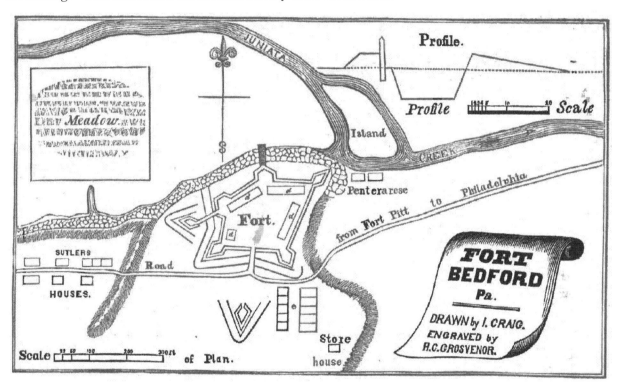

This plan of Fort Bedford is from the April 1843 issue of the "**American Pioneer**" and identifies two buildings labeled *"Penterarese"* (Pendergrass). It is *copied from a copy furnished to the honorable Richard Biddle, from the British Museum, to which institution it was presented by George the Fourth."*

## A birth near Fort Cumberland in 1758

While not documentary evidence, Volume 3 of "**The Hesperian**" (1839) states:

> *Peter and Andrew Anderson, from above Wheeling, came at the same time. Peter married a daughter of old Mr. Coleman. He was born in the year 1758, near Fort Cumberland, in Maryland, and moved with his father, west of the Mountains, and settled on Buffalo creek, near the present town of West Liberty,[969] Virginia, in the year 1770, when only twelve years old.*

---

[969] The 1833 book "**A History of the Valley of Virginia**" states, *"In the month of October, 1787, the town of West Liberty, in the county of Ohio, was established. Sixty acres of land was laid off into lots and streets by Reuben Foreman and Providence Mounts."* As recorded in Volume 12 of the 1823 book "**The statutes at large: being a collection of**

### The cost of carrying goods from Fort Cumberland to Redstone during the war

In a response to the April 15, 1772 "**Report of the Lords Commissioners for Trade and Plantations, on the Petition of the Honorable Thomas Walpole and his Associates, for a Grant of Lands on the River Ohio, in North America**", Benjamin Franklin wrote a point by point reply[970] that contains the following reference to the cost of hauling merchandise to Redstone Creek during the French and Indian war:

*As we have only hitherto generally stated the small expense of carriage between the waters of Potomac and those of the Ohio, we shall now endeavour to show how very ill founded the lords of trade and plantations are in the fifth paragraph of their report, viz. That the lands in question "are out of all advantageous intercourse with this kingdom." In order, however, that a proper opinion may be formed on this important article, we shall take the liberty of stating the particular expense of carriage, even during the last French war, (when there was no back carriage from Ohio to Alexandria) as it will be found, it was even then only about a halfpenny per pound, as will appear from the following account, the truth of which we shall fully ascertain, viz.*

*From Alexandria to Fort Cumberland, by water, per hundred weight*      *1s. 7d.*

*From Fort Cumberland to Red Stone Creek, at fourteen dollars per*

*wagon load; each wagon carrying fifteen hundred weight*      *4 2*

     *5s. 9d.*

*Note. The distance was then seventy miles, but by a new wagon road, lately made, it is now but forty miles — a saving, of course, of above one half the 5s. 9d. is at present experienced.*

*If it is considered that this rate of carriage was in time of war, and when there were no inhabitants on the Ohio, we cannot doubt but every intelligent mind will be satisfied, that it is now much less than is daily paid in London for the carriage of coarse woolens, cutlery, iron ware, etc., from several counties in England.*

---

all the laws of Virginia", the town of West Liberty was established by *"An act to establish a town at the court house in the county of Ohio"*, which passed November 29, 1787. West Liberty, West Virginia, is located at Latitude 40.168118°, Longitude -80.596948°, not far from the state line and Washington County, Pennsylvania. This Providence Mounts is the son of the miller Colonel Providence Mounts, an early resident of the present-day Connellsville, Pennsylvania area. For more information on these two men, see the fourth edition of the book "**In Search of the Turkey Foot Road**".

[970] "**The Complete Works of Benjamin Franklin**", Volume 5.

# 11. 1759: Burd departs for Redstone

### Isaac Baker's residence

The January 8, 1759 journal entry[971] of trader James Kenny mentions *"Isaac Baker's on Conogocheque"*.

### A description of Fort Frederick

Kenny's January 9, 1759 journal entry provides the following description of Fort Frederick:

*Set off this morning passed ye wagons & came to Fort Frederick where is a village of little houses, about 18 I think, without $y^e$ Fort it being constructed of good stonework & high, only one large gate to $y^e$ South & $y^e$ King's Storehouse fronting it on $y^e$ North. In $y^e$ Fort a row of Barracks on $y^e$ East & West sides, & great space in $y^e$ middle. I met my partner S. L., who had put up at James Long's, $y^e$ farthest house of $y^e$ village from $y^e$ fort, but $y^e$ best usage.*

### Fort Cumberland is losing men to desertion due to a lack of pay

A January 9, 1759 letter[972] Richard Pearis wrote to Forbes from Fort Cumberland includes the following:

*I think it my Duty to let you know that I never had the Complement of Men at this Fort agreeable to your Orders, the most I could get here was Ninety Rank and File, and out of them you'l see by the Return how Many is Deserted since my last. Notwithstanding all I can do with them and have Done, without Money verry soon to Pay them I don't expect there will be in a Short time any Body to Garrisson this Fort but Officers, we have given them Shoes and other things but all wont do.*

### An accused horse embezzler from Fort Cumberland

The January 16, 1759 journal entry[973] of Colonel John Armstrong includes the statement, *"Received William Darling Waggoner sent Prisoner by Capt Pearis for embezzing the Kings Horses. Confin'd him in the Goal in the Fort"*. The January 20, 1759 journal entry includes the statement, *"Came from $F^t$ Cumberland $Cap^t$ Pearis & Liut Gorril Presided at a Court of Inquiry, on Darling the Waggoner, for embezzling 2 of the Kings Horses."*

A January 20, 1759 document[974] titled *"At a Court of Inquiry held by Order of Coll Bouquet, at Fort Bedford"* states:

*Was examined William Darling, confin'd by Captn. Pearis, on Suspicion of embezling two of His Majesty's Horses.*

*$Capt^n$ Pearis informs the Court, that one Varnell (who had accompnied the Prisoner from Fort Cumberland home) had inform'd him $Cap^t$ Pearis that the Prisoner had bragg'd to him of the fine Hawl he had made in his Trip to $F^t$ Cumberland having, as he said, got a Mare worth ten Pounds & a Horse*

---

[971] **"The Pennsylvania Magazine of History and Biography"**, Volume 37, 1913.

[972] **"The Papers of Henry Bouquet"**, Volume III, 1976.

[973] **"The papers of Col. Henry Bouquet"**, 1941

[974] **"The Papers of Henry Bouquet"**, Volume III, 1976.

*worth about five. And that the said Darling in coming back brought the Mare part of the Way, in order to dispose of her, but would not bring her so far as Cumberland, lest she should be own'd & taken from him. That upon this information he, Capt^n Pearis, sent for the Prisoner, and tax'd him with carrying off the King's Horses. And as the Prisoner could not give a Satisfactory Account, for being in Possession of them Capt^n Pearis order'd him to be confin'd 'till he procur'd Bail for his appearing in eight Days, & producing the two Horses.*

*The Prisoner being ask^d, by the Court, what right he had to take the Mare out of the Fort says, that he claim'd her, as his Brother's Property, and on that Claim obtained Leave to take her away, being ask'd if he attempted to send her back, or acquaint the Commanding Officer at F^t Cumberland of his mistake, answers, not 'till he was sent for, which Capt^n Pearis says, was more than three Weeks after taking her away*

*The Prisoner says also that he gave 25 Shillings for her to a Soldier of the 2^d Virginia Regim^t And as to the Horse, he says, he took his from Jo: Goolding, & Dan^l M^cFall, out of Pitty, that he might not Suffer by hunger. The Prisoner informs the Court that Varnell had a parcell of Tires, &c: conceal'd under his Bed, which he believes belong to the King's Waggons at Fort Cumberland.*

Ourry was President of the inquiry. The document has the following endorsement:

*January the 22^d The said Darling was releas'd from the Guard; being bail'd by John Cockendall, in a Bond of two hundred Pounds Sterling for his appearance at Hamshire Court the 17^th of March next insuing*

## Bouquet writes to the men at Fort Cumberland about their pay

A January 22, 1759 letter[975] Bouquet wrote *"To the Soldiers of the Maryland Forces in garrison at Fort Cumberland"* from Fort Bedford states:

*As it is represented to me by Cap^t Rich^d Pearis that you have received no Pay for a considerable Time, by which deficiency you are reduced to such distress that you think of abandonning the Fort if not relieved in a Short time.*

*I have there upon thought proper to let you know that the money lately voted by your Province as a gratification for your past good services, Shall be punctually paid to you, according to the Intentions of the Government, without any deduction for the advances you may have received from time to time, which advances are to be Stopped afterwards when you receive your full Pay: and in order to enable you to wait a few days for your Share of the above Gratification, I have impowred Cap^t Pearis to advance 20 Sh. to Each man, which Shall be deducted from y^e Said Gratification.*

*And whereas the Settling of your arrears and pay requires Some time; I do expect from your Fidelity, honour, and duty, that you Shall wait patiently untill the 15^th of March next by which time, and perhaps sooner, I hope to See all your affairs Settled to your satisfaction;*

*I place such Confidence in you that I make no doubt of your ready Compliance to my desire, and I think you too wise to loose by a precipitate and rash Step, the fruit of all your Labours, your reputation, and your Money.*

---

[975] **"The Papers of Col. Henry Bouquet"**, 1940.

*I propose to set out to morrow for the settlements where I Shall represent in the Strongest terms to the General your Situation, and the Justice of your demands, and Shall inform Capt Pearis of the Success of my sollicitations in your favour.*

*It has been reported to me that one Balsar Kern a Soldier Should have Spread among you false Reports from me. That I had offered him ten Pistoles to Enlist in the R. A. R. and other infamous Insinuations tending to dispirit the Garrison, and make you take wrong and pernicious measures: I therefore have thought it necessary to inform you myself that I never did Speak to, or even Saw the Said Balsar Kern, who has basely and maliciously contrived the above falshood to bad Purposes: Therefore I have given Strict orders to Cap^t Pearis have the Said Balsar Kern tried by a Court Martial, and punished with the utmost severity of the Law against Such Seditious discourses.*

*I recommand you again to have Patience, till you hear from Me, which will be in a Short time, and to continue to do your duty in Such a manner as to inforce my Recommandations in your behalf and you may depend upon my utmost Endeavours to See you righted in your Pretensions.*

### Sending horses to Fort Cumberland to haul hay

The January 22, 1759 journal entry[976] of Colonel John Armstrong includes the statement, *"Sent to F^t Cumberland 10 Carcasses of Pork and a Q^r Cask of Wiskey by the return'd S^o Branch Wagons ... Sat out this Morning for F^t Cumberland, Cap^n Pearis & L^t Gorril. Sent two Horses to Ft Cumberland to help to hawl some hay hither"*.

### A sergeant and 14 men desert Fort Cumberland

A January 23, 1759 letter[977] Captain Richard Pearis wrote to Bouquet from Fort Cumberland states:

*I am sorry I have to inform you that on the twenty first Ins^t at Night Deserted from here Serj^t Fill and fourteen Men with Him Notwithstanding the Promises they Made to me, agreeable to your Orders I Read your letter to those Remaining, they all Return you hearty thanks for your kind Proposals, and Care for them, and says they will do their Duty with Spirit agreeable to your Request untill the 15^th of March, I beleave if those that Deserted on the twenty first, had not been gon before I Came home they would not gon. tomorrow Morning I send Ensign Love with the Coppy of your letter after those that are gon hopeing that it will have the Desired Effect on them to Return. I also send a copy to Governor Sharpe with a list of the Deserted in hopes he will send some of them Back in Case they go to Annopolis, Balser Kern shall be tryed to morrow the Rest of the men Appears to be Much Displeased with him for his false seditious Reports.*

### Bouquet writes that the garrison intends to abandon the fort for lack of pay

A translation of a January 23, 1759 letter[978] Bouquet wrote to Forbes from Fort Bedford includes the following:

*Captain Pearis arrived here yesterday from Cumberland, and told me that the garrison had resolved to abandon the fort, as they no longer wished to serve without receiving their pay. With a great deal of trouble he made them promise to stay until he had spoken to me.*

---

[976] **"The papers of Col. Henry Bouquet"**, 1941
[977] **"The papers of Col. Henry Bouquet"**, 1941
[978] **"The Papers of Henry Bouquet"**, Volume III, 1976.

*He informed me that the province of Maryland had voted £1500 to be distributed as extra pay to their troops, on the refusal of the Council to pass the bill for their pay and arrears.*

*The soldiers who are at Fort Frederic have received their share of this extra pay, and Lieutenant Colonel Dagworthy must have the rest for the troops which are at Cumberland, but he has not written a word since his departure, and the soldiers make very insolent remarks regarding him and this money.*

*In the hope that the province will finally provide their pay, or the government if they default, I thought it my duty to prevent the complete desertion of these men by the only means which lay in my power, which was to write them the enclosed letter, which I hope you will approve under the existing circumstances. Pearis believes that they will make no difficulty about remaining on that footing until March 15th, a sufficient time to make a decision regarding them. I shall learn their decision by express.*

*The number of horses and wagons stolen during the campaign is so great that I have no doubt you will order search warrants in the three provinces. These rogues will betray one another, and punishing them will prevent similar crimes in another campaign.*

*Captain Pearis sent me a prisoner, a Virginia farmer, who stole two horses. I had him examined by a court of inquiry, and released under bail of 200 pounds Sterling.*

## The smallpox is bad at Fort Cumberland

The January 24, 1759 journal entry[979] of trader James Kenny, written somewhere in the *Conogocheque-*Fort Frederick area, states. *"This day came here about a dozen of y$^e$ soldiers from Cumberland, deserted; y$^e$ Small Pox is very bad there."*

## Money and people problems at Fort Cumberland

A January 31, 1759 letter[980] Captain Richard Pearis wrote to Captain Lewis Ourry from Fort Cumberland states:

*Since I have Wrote my sentiments to Coll: Bouquet and you, I am informed by M$^r$ Love that Coll: Dagworthy sent 100 pounds of the Present Money to M$^r$ Riley who is now Deceased to bring here for the Men at this Garrison, I Cant see the Reason why he Did not send the whole without he Intends to Defraud them out it, as the Men says, for I think he has no Right to make any storages. Also, I have Just heard by M$^r$ Love that Coll Dagworthy gave privit Orders Orders to M$^r$ Lenox unknown to me who he new was to Command untill he Came, to let aney of the Men have furloughs that wanted them which he has don without my leave Notwithstanding the Generalls orders for 100 men to be kept here, this I would beg you would aquaint Coll: Bouquet with or enclose this to him, Am Quite tired of this Command without Matters were Carried on in a more Juster manner then has Been*

## Flour and meal are in transit to Pittsburgh via Fort Cumberland

A February 3, 1759 letter[981] Ourry wrote to Forbes from Fort Bedford includes the following:

*And I am told that a great Number of Horses, with Flour, & Indian Meal are moving to Pitsburgh by Bradock's Road: I know that upwards of 80 have already pass'd by Fort Cumberland in the Space of a Week. Meanwhile I have given all possible encouragement to the Country People that brought Provisions*

---

[979] **"The Pennsylvania Magazine of History and Biography"**, Volume 37, 1913.
[980] **"The papers of Col. Henry Bouquet"**, 1941
[981] **"The Papers of Henry Bouquet"**, Volume III, 1976.

*or Liquors here, to go up, and, from those that could not be prevail'd upon, I have bought. Liquors, grain, Cattle, &c. (as may be seen at the back of the Return:) to pay for which, & keep up my Credit, or rather that of the Army, I have been put to all Sorts of shifts; most of the People I have to deal with, living in a part of the Country, where I have no Conections.*

*The Weather here has been very Severe lately, and those who have gone up to Pitsburgh, or even Ligonier, have earned their Bread very dearly. The Snow, they tell me, is now near three feet deep on the Allegehany.*

## A court martial at Fort Cumberland for desertion

A February 5, 1759 document[982] that is titled, *"A Court Martial Held at Fort Cumberland the fifth Day of Feb^ry 1759"* lists Lieutenant Linn as President, lists Lieutenant Gorroll and Ensign Mearns as members, and states:

*To try Such Prisoners as Shal be Brought Before them Jn° Ragon Corp^l confine^d By Cap^t Rich^d Pearis for Goeing from the Garrison Seven Miles Without Leave threatning to Desert if he Could Gett Any Good fellow to Goe w^th Him & Insulting Ens^n Love*

*The Prisoner being Examin^d Confeses he went to Isaac Colliers without Leave*

*Geo: Tecter of Cap^t Alex^r Bealls Comp^y Being Examin^d Says that this Morning in y^e Hospital he heard the Prisoner Say that if he had but a Good Fellow w^th him he Soon would Goe of for He had No Right to Doe Duty in this Place without pay*

*Ens^n Love Proves to the Court that he Saw the Prisoner on the Parade & Knowing him to be Confin^d Ordered him to y^e Inside of y^e Guard Room & Said it was a fine Usage on these words y^e Prisoner Dam^d him & the Usage too and the Prisoner Confesses he Expressed the Words*

*The Prisoner in His Defence Says that he thought he had No Right to Ask Leave to Goe Abroad he Serving without Pay The Nature of the Prisoners Crime being Such that y^e Court Judges thot they have Not a Right to Pass Sentance on Such Crime it Being of too henious a Nature*

> *W^m LINN*

> *A True Copy of the proceeding of the Court*

## Pearis writes to Bouquet about the court martial

A February 5, 1759 letter[983] Captain Richard Pearis wrote to Bouquet from Fort Cumberland states:

*I send you Inclosed the Proceedings of a Court Martial held to try Corpo: Ragon of Coll: Dagworthys Company where in You'l see what insulting Mutenus behavour Rains amongst the Men of this Garrison Notwithstanding y^e Money I have paid them Agreeable to your Orders, and the Promises made by them. I have sent the above Ragon Prisoner to Fort Bedford untill your Pleasure is known, knowing him to be a Soer of Muteney amongst the Rest. I Also send you a Return of what Horses loaded with flower has passd for Pitsburg since my last many more yet following, According to Your Order I sent to William Rosses, who was Accused by Creasep for Concealing some of his Majestys Horses where Ensign Mearns found three two of which appeares to belong to the Virginia Officers and one to his Majesty Ross says he*

---

[982] **"The papers of Col. Henry Bouquet"**, 1941
[983] **"The papers of Col. Henry Bouquet"**, 1941

*took them, up in the Woods, also Ross informes on one Eves and one Plum who lives at Cresaps that they have Conceald ten or twelve of his Majestys Horses, Cresaps Servant Man Confirms what Ross says, only he says ther is but seven of them Belongs to the King I have sent an officer to bring both Men and Horses in Case they are taken, would be glad Be Glad to Receive Your Orders how to Proceed, Nothing else Extraordinary*

### Renting a house at Cumberland in 1759

The February 7, 1759 journal entry[984] of trader James Kenny, written well-east of Fort Cumberland, states, *"Samuel set off to get Tho⁵ Kenton[985] and packhorses to carry yᵉ goods to Pittsburg, having received letters to that purpose last night & we have taken a lease of a house at Cumberland."*

### Daniel Pursel is involved in a Virginia lawsuit

Jacob Hite was being sued[986] in the Frederick County, Virginia Court by Daniel Pursel on February 8, 1759.

### 196 packhorses headed west from Fort Cumberland

A February 9, 1759 letter[987] Ourry wrote to Bouquet from Fort Bedford includes the following:

*Captain Pearis, who has sent me two Loads of Hay, acquaints me that Several Horses have been found, conceal'd by divers Persons, who, as soon as detected, discover others, which he has sent an Officer to take up And he asks my Opinion, what he is to do with them. I told him I would write to receive your Directions on that head. But in the meantime thought he would do well to make them produce the Horses immediately and give Bond for their appearance at the next Court; and to make what Discoveries he could by taking Depositions of all Informers ...*

*The Horses gone by Bradocks Road, have met with some obstacle or other, for tho' 196 had passed by Fort Cumberland between the 23d of January & the 5ᵗʰ Insᵗ not one was arrived at Pittsburgh the 3ᵈ as Col Mercer informs me. But a Suttler who left that Place the 3ᵈ at Night tells me that Intelligence was just brought to the Colonel, of upward of 200 Horses being within 20 Miles, and that he sent out a Party to meet them. So I make no doubt of their being arrived now. The 196 that I know of, were loaded as Pʳ inclosed Return.*

### Samuel Stansby Welder and Thomas Cresap are involved in a court case

On page 49 of the 1759 Frederick County court docket book[988], in a section titled *"Original Writs to the third Tuesday of March 1759"*, a record dated February 10, 1759 lists Samuel Stansby Welder in a matter concerning £6-16 Virginia currency of the Value of £?:10 Maryland currency. The record mentions *"Thomas Cresap...for Costs"*.

---

[984] **"The Pennsylvania Magazine of History and Biography"**, Volume 37, 1913.

[985] Kinton Knob, at the north end of Wills Mountain, is said to be named for the Indian trader Thomas Kinton, who settled near there. The Fort Bedford Museum has a 1751 document *"Rec'd of Thomas Kinton towards his old debt Eighty-one pounds fifteen shillings to Jeremiah Warden."* that lists various items, including cloth, women's thimbles, a hoghead, beads, lace, gunflints, and *"5 thousand white and 5 thousand black wampum."* (Information on the document was provided by Suzanne L. Smith Trussell.) Although not documentary evidence, Charles A. Hanna's 1911 book **"The Wilderness Trail"** reports that Thomas Kinton was *"at Pickawillany in February, 1751"*.

[986] **"Colonial Records of the Upper Potomac"**, Volume 6.

[987] **"The Papers of Henry Bouquet"**, Volume III, 1976.

[988] MSA No. C782-11.

A February 13, 1759 record on page 16 of a surviving fragment of a 1760 Frederick County Maryland court docket book[989], included in a section titled, *"Tryal Dockett for the third Tuesday and eighteenth Day of March Annoguo Domini 1760"*, lists Sam Stansby Weldor and Barth Hatton, apparently as adversaries, and mentions *"Tho$^s$ Cresap ___ for Cash"* in another column. I don't know if this is the same matter referenced above.

### Bouquet has an extremely low opinion of Sir John St. Claire

A translation of a February 14, 1759 letter[990] Bouquet wrote to Forbes from York includes the following:

*Sir John's maneuvers do not surprise me. ...*

*He has spread his underhand defamations too long. It is time to snatch away the mask and reveal the man as he is. It is a service rendered to the public to expose the reefs hidden under the water, on which there is constant danger of being wrecked. ...*

*It would be tiresome to follow his tracks from the beginning of the campaign. I shall say only that from the very first he showed signs of what was to be expected.*

*At Carlisle I had had all the meadows appraised; they are very numerous and very fine. I had marked those which were to be used for grazing, and those which were to be mowed. I sent him these lists with those from Shippensburg. However, I had not been away fifteen days before all these meadows were laid waste under his eyes without one wagonload of hay having been cut.*

*All the abandoned meadows on the frontier could have supplied considerable stores, and the grass was left to rot there until September when you went to Fort Loudoun and had the remains saved.*

*A hundred wagonloads of hay could have been made in Cresap's meadows, fifteen miles from Cumberland, and he never thought of it. It was excusable for us to ignore these resources, but should they escape the attention of a quartermaster general who had made a campaign in these parts, and whose duty obliged him to be informed?*

### The road westward from Fort Frederick toward Cresap's

The February 14, 1759 journal entry[991] of trader James Kenny tells of his journey westward toward Cresaps from Thomas Mills' residence, which was about four miles from Fort Frederick:

*Lodged at Mills; last night it thundered, rained & lightened. Before morning fell a Snow about ankle deep & y$^e$ bushes all covered with it. I crossed Liking Creek, being very high, early this morning & kept along a path until I came into y$^e$ road. Having no company I set out alone but could not go much out of a walk. Some miles distant I missed y$^e$ old road & keeping y$^e$ new, which was not finished I came to a gut by y$^e$ river, which was very high with back water, and the bridge over it not finished. I sounded it at y$^e$ fording with a long pole I cut, & found it so high I concluded to head it, led my horse up a steep hill above it & then along it some distance I found y$^e$ old Road. In crossing big Chinnalawas my horse blundered, and y$^e$ water got into one of my boot-tops. About noon sat down by a tree & fed myself & horse, y$^e$ wind being high & blowing snow showers. I came to Sidling Hill, it is very steep & high & only a foot path along it & a smart creek runs close at y$^e$ foot so that in case a man should stumble off y$^e$ path, unless he could be caught by some sapling or bush could not stop until he went into y$^e$ creek. My horse lame & y$^e$*

---

[989] MSA No. C782-11.
[990] **"The Papers of Henry Bouquet"**, Volume III, 1976.
[991] **"The Pennsylvania Magazine of History and Biography"**, Volume 37, 1913.

*snow balling his feet made his passing something doubtful, but I lead him along & got safe across, but in swimming yᵉ creek yᵉ water got into my boots & saddle-bags. I emptied yᵉ bags & walked until I was warm. Some miles further on met some packhorses from Pittsburgh; yᵉ men told me it was 19 miles to Col Cressap's & I must swim yᵉ creek. It being late, and about 4 or 5 miles further, I began to look for a lodging place, which I found under yᵉ side of a great mountain in a hollow stump. After I cleared yᵉ snow out & made a floor of bark & a great fire at yᵉ door, I lodged with more comfort than I expected & slept some.*

## Kenny reaches Cresap's

The February 15, 1759 journal entry[992] of trader James Kenny states:

*After feeding my horse & refreshing myself proceeded, but took yᵉ advantage of yᵉ old town creek so as not to swim it. Being very cold I walked turn about & rode until I came to Cressap's, where I stayed & put my horse to hay that night, as I heard yᵉ wagons had not yet crossed yᵉ river. Was very kindly used by yᵉ Colonel.*

## Ejecting two drunken women from the rented house at Cumberland

Kenny's February 16, 1759 journal entry[993] states, *"Got to Cumberland about noon, it being about 15 miles from Cressaps. Delivered John St. Clair's letter to yᵉ Commandant, who said they would assist us all they could. He came with me to our rented house, got it cleared of two drunken women, and a soldier that helped to clean yᵉ house, making too big a fire in yᵉ hearth, yᵉ chimney being very foul, it took fire which cleaned it well, without damage. It proved a timely warning to me before yᵉ goods came."*

## Lieutenant Linn is temporarily in command at Fort Cumberland

Kenny's February 17, 1759 journal entry[994] at Fort Cumberland states, *"I walked up yᵉ river with Lieutenant Linn, who commanded in Capᵗ Paris's absence & wrote to my employer."* This seems to be an allusion to a path or road along the river.

## Ourry proposes a canoe at Collier's place

A February 17, 1759 letter[995] Ourry wrote to Bouquet from Fort Bedford includes the following:

*I have been obliged to assist the Country People coming back from Pittsburg, who, besides suffering extreamly by the Cold, were quite out of Provisions, & Forrage, not being able to proceed, & some drowning their Horses by attempting the Fords. Those that return'd by Bradocks Road, were greatly distress'd, having nobody to relieve them, and the Potomawk impassible. I have desired Capᵗ Pearis to supply them with Provisions; and, least they should be discouraged by such retardement as such Freshes might again occasion, I have beg'd of Captn Davis to allow our Canoe builders to go to Fᵗ Cumberland, there to make a Canoe for the Conveniency of Passengers, & to carry over Loads, & Swim the Horses, at a Place about Seven Miles below Fᵗ Cumberland, where one Collier, a Smith who lives there might be allow'd a Ration a Day, for taking care of the Canoe and Carrying Passengers over: and who might be*

---

[992] **"The Pennsylvania Magazine of History and Biography"**, Volume 37, 1913.
[993] **"The Pennsylvania Magazine of History and Biography"**, Volume 37, 1913.
[994] **"The Pennsylvania Magazine of History and Biography"**, Volume 37, 1913.
[995] **"The Papers of Henry Bouquet"**, Volume III, 1976.

*of use in repairing an old Flat, which is near there, and could, if in Order, carry over Waggons, or Horses with Loads more expeditiously, when large Quantities.*

*Your particular Directions on that Head, would be agreable to Capt$^n$ Pearis, who, in the Mean time, will get the Canoe made out of Hand, as the River is sometimes impassable for loaded Horses, & Waggons, three Weeks or a Month at a time.*

## The rain is impacting the waggoners' profit margins

Kenny's February 18, 1759 journal entry[996] at Fort Cumberland states:

*Being y$^e$ first day of y$^e$ week, y$^e$ wagons came this afternoon. I received y$^e$ goods according to y$^e$ invoices, y$^e$ officers & many spectators by. The wagoners complain much of their bargain being cut down by y$^e$ rains, I sent for a quart of liquor to y$^e$ Commissary & gave it to those that tarried all night, they being wet. One of them had an invoice of y$^e$ most of his load which they had weighed at home, as he said by a pair of stilliards that on one side weighed 112 lbs. to y$^e$ hundred, by which that weight overrun ours, but I told him I believed they had a wrong notion of y$^e$ stilliards & I cast up their invoice allowing only to be 100$^{lb}$ to each Hundred & it fell somewhat short of our weight, however, I missed nothing.*

## Drying out some wet items

Kenny's February 19, 1759 journal entry[997] at Fort Cumberland states, *"Opened some things that had received some wet & put them in a position for drying. Being asked to dine with y$^e$ officers I went, but did not tarry long. Rain much of y$^e$ night."*

## Magnus Tate visits Fort Cumberland in 1759

Kenny's February 20, 1759 journal entry[998], written from Fort Cumberland states, *"Lodged here. Last night Magnus Tate came from Pittsburgh, being an old Acquaintence in Youghland & Isaac Baker came back & lodged in y$^e$ Fort. I sent a long letter with him to my employer."*

## The bridge over Wills Creek was mended on February 20, 1759

Kenny's February 21, 1759 journal entry[999] states, *"The end next y$^e$ fort of y$^e$ Bridge over Wills's Creek fell by y$^e$ flood washing y$^e$ bank away, was mended today"*

## Finding Kenny's wayward horse

Kenny's February 23, 1759 journal entry[1000] at Fort Cumberland states:

*My horse missing this morning, & after hunting this side of y$^e$ creek & over y$^e$ bridge in vain, I found his track over y$^e$ Ford below y$^e$ bridge & followed it along up y$^e$ hill, and about one mile from y$^e$ fort toward home, another track with it. They left y$^e$ road toward y$^e$ river & I lost it, but took a course about a mile*

[996] **"The Pennsylvania Magazine of History and Biography"**, Volume 37, 1913.

[997] **"The Pennsylvania Magazine of History and Biography"**, Volume 37, 1913.

[998] **"The Pennsylvania Magazine of History and Biography"**, Volume 37, 1913.

[999] **"The Pennsylvania Magazine of History and Biography"**, Volume 37, 1913.

[1000] **"The Pennsylvania Magazine of History and Biography"**, Volume 37, 1913.

*further down toward y^e river, where I came upon him & a mare of y^e Captains lying down in y^e woods; brought both back.*

### Providing firewood

Kenny's February 24, 1759 journal entry[1001] at Fort Cumberland states, *"Capt Paris spent awhile with me, & I provided some firewood y^e rest of y^e day."*

### The Captain's wife is present at Fort Cumberland in 1759

Kenny's February 25, 1759 journal entry[1002], written from Fort Cumberland, states, *"Being asked I went to dine at y^e Captain's; being my countryman I presented him with y^e little book wrote by y^e New England man & ye paper y^e was printed in Philadelphia in regard to gaining y^e Indians to our interest, & I gave his wife some of my dried Apples. Was persuaded by y^e Captain to draw some provisions & not buy bread which is so dear, although our biscuits had come."*

### Kenny sends his horse and a letter back east

Kenny's February 26, 1759 journal entry[1003] from Fort Cumberland states:

> *As my oats was almost exhausted & y^e officers persuading me that my horse would in all probability be stolen from me, especially if I took him to Pittsburgh, I sent him off by a Dutch baker that was going home to Conestoga, in Pensilvania, to be left at W^m Joliff in Hopewell, with a letter.*

### Brury Cox was living about five miles below Cresap in 1759

A February 26, 1759 letter[1004] that Lieutenant Lewis Ourry wrote to Bouquet from Fort Bedford includes the following:

> *Since my last to you of the 24^th Cur^t I have receiv'd two Let^rs from Capt^n Pearis, who informs me that Numbers of People returning from Pittsburgh have been greatly distress'd having suffer'd much hardship, through cold & hunger, & sustain'd great losses by the Death, & loss of their Horses, Starved & Stray'd. Some that took up Six brought back but one, some two. Several Men in Swimming their Horses, nearly lost their Lives. He has assisted them, & got the Flatt afloat, which, it seems, is of great Service. He recommends building another, about 5 Miles below Cressaps, at one Bruery Cox, as being between 30 & 40 Miles nearer from Winchester than the other Road, by that means he thinks the People from those parts would be encouraged to carry up Provisions. He has recover'd 8 or 10 Horses which I have sent for.*

> *He acquaints me also that he has receiv'd Directions from S^r John S^tClair, to receive in his Stores a Quantity of Indian Goods 'till they can be transported to Pittsburgh. They are arrived there.*

---

[1001] "**The Pennsylvania Magazine of History and Biography**", Volume 37, 1913.
[1002] "**The Pennsylvania Magazine of History and Biography**", Volume 37, 1913.
[1003] "**The Pennsylvania Magazine of History and Biography**", Volume 37, 1913.
[1004] This reference was found by Francis Bridges.

## Reinforcements from Raystown arrive at Fort Cumberland

Kenny's February 27, 1759 journal entry[1005], written from Fort Cumberland, states, *"Came here today Lieut. Scott with a reinforcement of about 20 men from Raystown. He is a young man from Bucks County, also two of my former scholars who were born in $y^e$ Valley & another acquaintance from $y^e$ same place, all seeming glad to see me."*

## Maryland forces at Fort Cumberland reduced to one fourth their original number

A March 1, 1759 letter[1006] Bouquet wrote to General Amherst from Philadelphia includes the following:

*The 100 men of Maryl. Troops lefft at Cumberland for the Garrison of that Fort are reduced by desertion to 25, and in a short time I am afraid that Post will be abandonned. These Troops having no Pay nor any certainty of receiving any.[1007]*

## Kenny goes fishing then becomes ill

Kenny's March 2, 1759 journal entry[1008] from Fort Cumberland states, *"Caught a mess of Trout & Fall fish just below $y^e$ house in $y^e$ River, and ye Captain dined with me."*

Kenny's March 4, 1759 journal entry from Fort Cumberland states, *"Being asked to dine at ye Captains I excused myself being indisposed. Snowed some this morning."*

## The remaining men at Fort Cumberland will leave if they aren't paid by the 15th

A March 4, 1759 letter[1009] Pearis wrote to Bouquet from Fort Cumberland includes states:

*You have the Monthly Returns by $M^r$ Ourry, who I have sent them to, as I am informed you are gon to Philadelphia, I Beg leave to trouble you, to Indeavour to have my Indians Accounts Setled, which is in the hands of $Cap^t$ Bozmouth, as I cant attend myself. I hope you would think it two troublesome to see them adjusted and Setled.*

*The Men left in this Garrison wates Impatient untill the fifteenth of March when they will all abanden the Fort without their pay, there is maney of them at Fort Frederick that left this is Willing to Return on hearing of their Money being Come, I hope at least you'l order the Present money here that I may be able to stop what I advanced by Your Order You'l see by the Return that there is Maney of them Deserted sence I advanced to them and purhaps may Receive the whole money Below*

## Amherst hopes to settle the issue of troops at Fort Cumberland with the governor

A March 5, 1759 letter[1010] Amherst wrote to Bouquet from New York includes the following:

---

[1005] "**The Pennsylvania Magazine of History and Biography**", Volume 37, 1913.

[1006] "**The papers of Col. Henry Bouquet**", 1940.

[1007] The version of this letter that is included in "**The Papers of Henry Bouquet**", Volume III, 1976 states, *"The 100 men Lefft at Cumberland of the Maryland Troops are reduced by desertion to 25, and in a Short time I expect that Fort will be abandonned; The men having neither Pay nor certainty of receiving any".*

[1008] "**The Pennsylvania Magazine of History and Biography**", Volume 37, 1913.

[1009] "**The papers of Col. Henry Bouquet**", 1941.

[1010] "**The papers of Col. Henry Bouquet**", 1940.

*I should directly apply to the Governor of Maryland in regard to the Troops which are supposed to garrison Fort Cumberland but he will doubtless be on the road for Philadelphia where I hope we shall be able to settle that and many other material affairs*

### Cold weather and a visit by traders returning from Pittsburgh

Kenny's March 6, 1759 journal entry[1011] from Fort Cumberland states, *"Very cold, I keep close at the house but cannot keep warm enough."*

Kenny's March 7, 1759 journal entry states, *"Very Cold; as I dined today, ye Doctor called & took a share."*

Kenny's March 8, 1759 journal entry states, *"Some of Geo: Clark's company that had been at Pittsburgh with goods & liquors, called here today, they say they suffered much from yᵉ Cold."*

### The garrison at Fort Cumberland is reduced to a few men

A March 11, 1759 letter[1012] Bouquet wrote to Amherst from Philadelphia includes the following:

*By a Letter received this day I hear that the Garrison of Fort Cumberland being reduced to a few men, an officer and 20 men were to march from Bedford for the guard of the stores; agreeable to the order I had sent upon Expectation of what has happened.*

### Burn Fort Pitt and retreat to Ligonier or Fort Cumberland if attacked

A synopsis[1013] of a March 13, 1759 letter Bouquet wrote to Amherst from Philadelphia includes the statement, *"The disaffection of the Ohio Indians confirmed; the difficulty of ascertaining the strength of the French in these parts. The weakness of the new fort at Pittsburgh. If attacked the garrison to burn it and fall back on Ligonier or Fort Cumberland. The state of the garrisons of Ligonier, Bedford, Cumberland, &c."* The portions of the letter[1014] that reference Fort Cumberland state:

*The new Fort at Pittsburgh having been first calculated for 200 men being very small, crowded with Barraks, and not tenable against artillery, Col. Mercer had orders in case of an attack to make no Capitulation. But if he could not succeed in attempting to spike or destroy the Canon of the Ennemy, in that case to burn the Fort in the night, destroy his Provisions & ammunition, and return in his Battos over the Monongehela, and make the best of his Way to Ligonier, or if prevented to Fort Cumberland. ...*

*The Garrison at Bedford is now reduced to about 80 men after the Detachment send to Cumberland and as the Hospital general is there and a quantity of stores, that Post requires more men...*

*The necessity of reinforcing Cumberland, Bedford and Ligonier are evident, but there are no Provincial Troops to Send The few Scattered in the Provinces wᵗʰ or without furlough I shall endeavour to collect by an advertisenᵗ but having been 5 months without Pay or Cloathing they will not be very fit for duty Such is in general the present state of the frontiers...*

*and in order to quicken the transport of provisions I would propose to make use of the two Roads & station the Waggons all along the Communication, Each Brigade within a day of one another So that they*

---

[1011] **"The Pennsylvania Magazine of History and Biography"**, Volume 37, 1913.
[1012] **"The papers of Col. Henry Bouquet"**, 1940.
[1013] **"Sessional Papers of the Dominion of Canada"**, Volume 23, 1890.
[1014] **"The papers of Col. Henry Bouquet"**, 1940.

*should never exceed the limit of their stations and to make use at the same time of the Potomack to form Magasines at Fort Cumberland, from whence they could be transported by Waggons and Pack Horses to the Monongehela the distance being about 70 miles.*

## A former student makes a pot pie for Kenny

Kenny's March 13, 1759 journal entry[1015] from Fort Cumberland states, *"One of my old scholars being a soldier came & made me a pot-pie of part of half a quarter of Venison I bought & some of my beef."*

## Lightfoot left the packhorses at Siding Hill

Kenny's March 14, 1759 journal entry[1016] states, *"My friend Samuel Lightfoot came this evening; he left ye pack-horses at Sidling Hill, of which I am very glad."* This may be a reference to a local place known as Sidling hill, that is located about a mile above the beginning point of Thomas Prather's September 30, 1747 *"The Choice"* survey.

## Civilians at Fort Cumberland in 1759

Kenny's March 15, 1759 journal entry[1017] indicates that other civilians were present at Fort Cumberland, stating, *"Employed Adam M$^c$Carty, and old trader, & Jn$^o$ Slater to help pack y$^e$ goods & one Campbell helped me to bend y$^e$ lead."* Lead was bent into a *"U"* shape for loading onto packhorses.

## Pasture four miles from Fort Cumberland

Kenny's March 16, 1759 journal entry[1018], written from Fort Cumberland, states, *"It rained almost all this day, but we packed y$^e$ goods in y$^e$ house, y$^e$ packhorses lie about four miles down y$^e$ river on y$^e$ far side, at a place called y$^e$ Swan ponds, where there is pasture."* The name *"Swan ponds"* is a reference to an early Virginia tract surveyed for Thomas Lord Fairfax by James Genn in the late 1740s.[1019] The tract was located with a horseshoe bend of the Potomac River, opposite to the Maryland *"Pleasant Valley"* tract. The approximate center of the tract is at Latitude 39.617384°, Longitude -78.743531°. The pasture suggests the presence of a farm.

## A civilian lad at Fort Cumberland in 1759

Kenny's March 17, 1759 journal entry[1020], written from Fort Cumberland, states, *"We sent a lad two days since after a man who had engaged Samuel to come with 12 packhorses but y$^e$ lad has brought a letter from his Son, that y$^e$ father was gone to Winchester & he knew nothing more concerning y$^e$ affair — y$^e$ river so high that y$^e$ packhorses cannot get over."*

## Pearis borrows money to pay the troops at Fort Cumberland

A March 17, 1759 letter[1021] Captain Richard Pearis sent to Bouquet from Fort Cumberland states:

---

[1015] "**The Pennsylvania Magazine of History and Biography**", Volume 37, 1913.

[1016] "**The Pennsylvania Magazine of History and Biography**", Volume 37, 1913.

[1017] "**The Pennsylvania Magazine of History and Biography**", Volume 37, 1913.

[1018] "**The Pennsylvania Magazine of History and Biography**", Volume 37, 1913.

[1019] The survey reference was provided by Francis Bridges.

[1020] "**The Pennsylvania Magazine of History and Biography**", Volume 37, 1913.

[1021] "**The papers of Col. Henry Bouquet**", 1941

*With great satisfaction I Receiv'd your favour this Day & Read part of your Letter to the men in this Garrison indeavouring to let them kno the maney Disapoointments you Laboured Under in Regard to the setling their affairs, which I have made them sensible of, and are Quite Satisfied untill your farther Orders is known, on the 15ᵗʰ I was Obliged to Confine 13 of the Men and on the 16ᵗʰ they Petitioned me for Releasment which I Granted on Promising they would stay till Your Letter Came. I this day Borrowed forty Pounds from Coll: Cresap to give them, which I belieave will satisfie them untill I Receive further Orders if soon. They blame Coll: Dagworthy greatly for keeping their Present Money from them as they have Never Receiv'd one farthing of it yet I hope youl take care to Order it here that I may be able to make Stopages for what I have advanced for them*

*If the Men had got that Present money when Granted by the Province, I am Confident the cheafest Part of them would abeen here yet*

*Inclosed you have a Return of the strength of the Garrison. I am sorry to hear Geneˡ Forbes state of health. I will use all Proper means to Continue the Men untill I Receive further Orders.*

### Three young friends try to desert from Fort Cumberland

Kenny's March 18, 1759 journal entry[1022] from Fort Cumberland states:

*We cross'd yᵉ river in a little canoe (that yᵉ Maryland soldiers had made to desert in but were stop'd) & Samuel went down to see how they fared, there being three young men Friends in yᵉ company Viz. Joseph Wright, Jnᵒ· Mickle & James Hammond from York County.*

### Packhorses leave Fort Cumberland, but Kenny stays

Kenny's March 19, 1759 journal entry[1023] from Fort Cumberland states:

*Having loads enough ready packed for yᵉ 34 horses employed, we projected to go down with yᵉ canoe & ferry over yᵉ goods & swim yᵉ horses, which was executed, so got yᵉ horses loaded about 2 of yᵉ clock. Thoˢ Kenton came whilst loading, but as he must return to Philadelphia, was rejected from coming after us. Set off about 2, I went about a mile to convey them but must tarry to receive yᵉ goods to come by James Long from Frederick & remain until yᵉ packhorses return to take them a second trip, it being concluded to take them this time no further than to a certain place on yᵉ Monongahela where Samuel is to proceed & get a bateau or two, to come from Pittsburgh there & receive them.*

### Samuel returns to Fort Cumberland for a tarp

Kenny's March 20, 1759 journal entry[1024] from Fort Cumberland states:

*Last night Samuel returned here having forgot somethings and stayed 'till morning, yᵉ horses going but about 4 miles distant yesterday. It rained in yᵉ night & some this morning; Samuel set off again and carried a tarpaulin they had forgot.*

---

[1022] **"The Pennsylvania Magazine of History and Biography"**, Volume 37, 1913.
[1023] **"The Pennsylvania Magazine of History and Biography"**, Volume 37, 1913.
[1024] **"The Pennsylvania Magazine of History and Biography"**, Volume 37, 1913.

### Arguing against using heathen names for the month

Kenny's March 22, 1759 journal entry[1025] from Fort Cumberland states:

*This morning Lieut. Linn called to see me, & having borrow'd Barcleys Apology of me before, he found how much we were against excess, & calling y$^e$ days & months by y$^e$ Heathen names, & strove to vindicate both, arguing that y$^e$ use of many things that we counted excess helped to promote trade & augmented y$^e$ Revenues of y$^e$ Crown; but upon telling him that such excesses was a means to deprive y$^e$ subjects of an Heavenly King would be no means of gaining a blessing, & on reasoning some concerning y$^e$ names of y$^e$ months & days he gave out & went away.*

### A civilian is flogged at Fort Cumberland in 1759

Kenny's March 23, 1759 journal entry[1026] from Fort Cumberland states, "*Jn$^o$ Slater, although he is no soldier, received 250 stripes this day & was drumm'd out over y$^e$ bridge not to be seen here any more after six days time, upon ye penalty of receiving 500, for carrying off some old Copper hoops & old mountings of guns, which I hear he says he bought of a man that brought them from Pittsburgh.*"

### Six horses lost from the packhorse train

Kenny's March 24, 1759 journal entry[1027] from Fort Cumberland states:

*Returned, Joseph Wright one of our packhorse men in quest of six of y$^e$ horses that stray'd from y$^e$ company y$^e$ 22$^d$ at night about 34 miles from here, they being within about 8 miles of y$^e$ first crossing of y$^e$ Youghogany. Having exhausted most of their foreage they have he says, divided 5 of y$^e$ lost horses's loads, leaving one load of Lead & carried y$^e$ rest along — fell some snow today.*

### George Clark's hired man is looking for missing horses

Kenny's March 25, 1759 journal entry[1028] from Fort Cumberland states:

*We wait for Adam McCarty & a man of Geo. Clark's that went out to seek two horses of Clark's & a load of skins that was left near y$^e$ first crossing of y$^e$ Youghogany who promised y$^e$ young man that is to come, to look for our horses as they have not returned here.*

### The horses are still missing

Kenny's March 26, 1759 journal entry[1029] from Fort Cumberland states:

*We went up Wills's Creek along Braddocks old road to where it comes through y$^e$ mountain but could see nothing of y$^e$ horse tracks. M$^c$Carty & y$^e$ other man returned with their load of skins, but have no account of their own horses nor ours; they say that y$^e$ snow that fell on y$^e$ 24$^{th}$ is very deep out about y$^e$ Little Meadows & the mountains.*

---

[1025] "**The Pennsylvania Magazine of History and Biography**", Volume 37, 1913.

[1026] "**The Pennsylvania Magazine of History and Biography**", Volume 37, 1913.

[1027] "**The Pennsylvania Magazine of History and Biography**", Volume 37, 1913.

[1028] "**The Pennsylvania Magazine of History and Biography**", Volume 37, 1913.

[1029] "**The Pennsylvania Magazine of History and Biography**", Volume 37, 1913.

### The creeks are too high for hunting the horses

Kenny's March 27, 1759 journal entry[1030] from Fort Cumberland states, *"I engaged Adam McCarty to go back with Joseph Wright tomorrow to hunt our horses, but as it rained much in y$^e$ night & this morning, they judged y$^e$ creeks to be too high."*

### Walking up along the river

Kenny's March 28, 1759 journal entry[1031] from Fort Cumberland states:

> We took a walk near two miles up y$^e$ river & it beginning to rain, turned up y$^e$ mountains above y$^e$ river & went across into y$^e$ road that goes to Pittsburgh & so returned, but no sign of y$^e$ horse tracks coming this way; it thunderd & is exceeding warm, y$^e$ creeks too high.

This journal entry may be a clue that there was path up along the river. Two miles along the river would would reach a point that coincides with Route 220. There the terrain would have conveniently allowed one to turn generally north toward Braddock's road.

### Various houses and individuals along the river at Fort Cumberland in 1759

Kenny's March 29, 1759 journal entry[1032] from Fort Cumberland states:

> It has continued to rain all y$^e$ night & this day & night to about 12 of y$^e$ clock it also snowed some. The river rose from about dark until midnight y$^e$ matter of 4 feet. I was under some concern of mind relateing to y$^e$ goods that are on their way coming from Frederick & the people out toward Pittsburgh, their being so much rain & y$^e$ river very high so that y$^e$ most of y$^e$ bridges on Wills' Creek is swept off. I could not sleep until near 12 of y$^e$ clock, when I heard Adam McCarty, Jn$^o$ Trotter & Slater and their wives talking & busy out of doors, they moving into an out house higher up on y$^e$ bank, y$^e$ river having overflowed into their houses, but not having y$^e$ good nature to acquaint their neighbours. I being suspicious got up & opening y$^e$ door, saw y$^e$ water coming in at y$^e$ gate before y$^e$ door, made haste & got my clothes on, & my boots, & aroused y$^e$ young man that came back after y$^e$ horses, who was asleep, lighted a candle & got all y$^e$ goods that lay on y$^e$ lower floor, upon y$^e$ loft, only some lead & y$^e$ cask of biscuit, which we put on y$^e$ top of an empty cask; put my bed & blankets up stairs & laid our chest on y$^e$ bedsteads with some other things. By this time y$^e$ water came in at y$^e$ door of y$^e$ house, we waded out about middle leg deep and went to y$^e$ house where was about half of our powder that was left. I went in & set y$^e$ kegs on y$^e$ top of some coal that lay high up, & so we got to a house where y$^e$ water did not reach & tarried until morning with several others that I called up.

In addition to describing several houses, and three men living outside of the fort with their wives, this passage mentions the presence of more than one bridge across Wills Creek. The letter also reveals that John Slater remained in the immediate area of the fort, despite being threatened with 500 lashes if he was seen in those parts.

---

[1030] "**The Pennsylvania Magazine of History and Biography**", Volume 37, 1913.

[1031] "**The Pennsylvania Magazine of History and Biography**", Volume 37, 1913.

[1032] "**The Pennsylvania Magazine of History and Biography**", Volume 37, 1913.

## The floodwater abates

Kenny's March 30, 1759 journal entry[1033] from Fort Cumberland states, *"The river rose suddenly & fell as quickly; about ten today yᵉ water abated out of yᵉ house, doing us no damage save carring off some firewood out of yᵉ yard."*

## A bridge over Wills Creek is thought to be flood proof

A March 31, 1759 document[1034] that was prepared by Captain Richard Pearis at Fort Cumberland states:

*A Return of the Dementions of a Brid to be made over Will's Creek supposed to be sufficient to stand any flood. With the Dementions of the two Connewe's already made for the use of his Majesty's Service at this Garrison. ...*

*If it's thought Proper to be ordered made by these Dementions I think it will stand any Flood & will be of the utmost Service for Carrag's passing for Pittsburg both from Virginia & Maryᵈ and in purticular this Garrison as Timber is very inconvenient to be got any other place then by Crossing Will's Creek, some People on their Return from Pittsburg has been oblige to stay here this 4 Days on Acount of the Creek being so high and Rapped that yᵉ Connew Coud not Cross and likely to stay severall days longer without Swimming their horses, one hose was Drowned Yester Day attempting to swim it*

The length of the proposed bridge was 270 feet. There were to be six 12 by 24 stone-filled pillars having a height of 20 feet and having the shape of Isosceles triangles. The large canoe was 29 feet long, two-and-one-half feet wide, and one foot seven inches deep. The small canoe was 20 feet long, one foot nine inches wide, and one foot five inches deep.

## A canoe is overturned by a tree drifting in the current

Kenny's April 1, 1759 journal entry[1035] from Fort Cumberland states:

*Got a horse of Lieutenant Jamˢ Gorrell to carry yᵉ men over yᵉ creeks & carry their provision & blankets & sent them off this afternoon as yᵉ weather seems pretty fair-like, to hunt yᵉ horses. This evening came William Clemmens, one of yᵉ canoe men that James Long sent with our goods & informed me that on yᵉ 29ᵗʰ of last month, at night, yᵉ river rising so high and yᵉ canoe lay in a gut by one of Cressap's Bottoms & they fastened it with a long rope, as yᵉ Rain was so constant and went to Cressap's themselves & tarried that night. The back water surrounding yᵉ Bottom made an island, that they had to wade out from yᵉ Bottom where yᵉ canoe lay. Next day as they went to see it with a canoe of Cressap's they found in overset, by reason of some trees driving down with yᵉ current. Two of yᵉ small bales, yᵉ cask of shot lies in yᵉ gut & may be got out, and 2 saddles, 12 tin kettles, yᵉ Gridiron & more lies in yᵉ Bottom there yet.*

## Searching in the water for lost goods

Kenny's April 2, 1759 journal entry[1036] from Fort Cumberland states:

*Upon this account I let yᵉ man have some provisions as they were out, & was for returning home & carrying what of yᵉ goods they had found back to James Longs, so I borrowed a creature & went down to yᵉ canoe & helped to search yᵉ gut but all was found that lay in it before I came. One of yᵉ men that I*

---

[1033] "**The Pennsylvania Magazine of History and Biography**", Volume 37, 1913.

[1034] "**The papers of Col. Henry Bouquet**", 1941

[1035] "**The Pennsylvania Magazine of History and Biography**", Volume 37, 1913.

[1036] "**The Pennsylvania Magazine of History and Biography**", Volume 37, 1913.

*sent off from Cressap's to stay by what was found whilst I dined striped before I got there & waided through yᵉ gut & found sundry things. I charged them to put yᵉ things they had found to dry, & search diligently for yᵉ rest, for they were liable to suffer yᵉ damage of what was not found. I took particular account of what they had found & let them know what was missing, so about dark returned to Cressap's & stayed all night. The young man that had been sent to look up yᵉ horses had returned & followed me to Cressap's as I had ordered, having found four of yᵉ horses, for I was in yᵉ mind to stay some days to help look for yᵉ goods, notwithstanding I did not reccon it should be my employer's loss.*

### Cutting up hide for ropes
Kenny's April 3, 1759 journal entry[1037] from Fort Cumberland states:

*Returned home & made ready to set off yᵉ next day to look up yᵉ other two horses, as we had horses now to ride. Cut up a hide we had in soak for ropes & put them to stretch & dry. I had in view of taking four loads of lead, but declined as I judged it would hinder us to hunt yᵉ horses.*

### Lodging at the Little Meadows
Kenny's April 4, 1759 journal entry[1038] states:

*Employed Adam MᶜCarty to go with us, & not much pasture being here we took yᵉ 4 horses with us making yᵉ 4ᵗʰ one to carry our blankets & provisions, searched each side of yᵉ rode & lodged at yᵉ Little Meadows.*

### Finding a human skull in a swamp
Kenny's April 5, 1759 journal entry[1039] states:

*We searched up & down yᵉ Meadows this morning & I walked as far as yᵉ Little Youghagany, taking another course back, but no late signs of horses. About noon we set off to yᵉ place yᵉ horses had strayed from McCarty taking off yᵉ Road on one side & I on yᵉ other looking for tracks & dung as we went, letting yᵉ young man keep yᵉ road; very intricate place I pass'd through, up hills and down deep Vales, & runs with swamps yᵉ young man stop'd until we overtook him & so we proceed'd to yᵉ place our party lay yᵉ night yᵉ horses left them. I found a man's skull with yᵉ teeth in yᵉ upper jaw, lying in a swamp. I called yᵉ place Golgotha.*

### One of Clark's horses is found
Kenny's April 6, 1759 journal entry[1040] states:

*This morning found a horse of Geo. Clark's that was left some miles from here in yᵉ Winter he failing with a load of skins; 10ˢ being bid for taking him up. I told MᶜCarty to bring him along & get yᵉ 10ˢ; so we brought him & on this side of George's creek, coming on yᵉ tracks of yᵉ horses coming down. Returned to Cumberland in yᵉ night.*

---

[1037] **"The Pennsylvania Magazine of History and Biography"**, Volume 37, 1913.
[1038] **"The Pennsylvania Magazine of History and Biography"**, Volume 37, 1913.
[1039] **"The Pennsylvania Magazine of History and Biography"**, Volume 37, 1913.
[1040] **"The Pennsylvania Magazine of History and Biography"**, Volume 37, 1913.

## Money appropriated for building a road between Fort Frederick and Fort Cumberland

The minutes[1041] of the General Assembly of Maryland for April 7, 1759 include the following:

*Resolved also, That out of the said Supplies, shall be appropriated the following Sums, viz.[1] ...*

*A Sum not exceeding Two Hundred and Fifty Pounds, for clearing a Road from Fort Frederick to Fort Cumberland, thro' this Province, for his Majesty's Service, agreeable to the Report of a Committee appointed last Session to enquire into the Utility of such a Road.*

## Sending men six miles up Wills Creek to look for lost horses

Kenny's April 7, 1759 journal entry[1042] from Fort Cumberland states:

*Being informed by Cap[t] Paris that y[e] goods was to come to day, such as were saved with y[e] canoe, I tarried at home & cut up a hide into ropes, having another cut & drying, in order to have these goods made into loads against y[e] packhorses return & sent McCarty & Joseph Wright up Wills's creek about six miles, to look y[e] two horses as y[e] other four that we found made that way, but they brought no intelligence of them. Y[e] Canoe came before they return'd & had found all y[e] goods only 1 of y[e] 4 small bales, y[e] 2 casks of Tobacco & a large cask with sundries, 1 keg of Pipes, my saddle & 3 Pounds of Tobacco, 1 Shirt &c.; y[e] saddles being y[e] most damaged of any y[e] rest I took them into my care, letting them have a receipt according as they seemed to deserve.*

## Sending off Joseph Wright with four horses

Kenny's April 8, 1759 journal entry[1043] from Fort Cumberland states:

*Had busy work in sending Joseph Wright off with y[e] 4 horses that was found of y[e] strays, with y[e] remainder of y[e] Bar Lead, y[e] Hatchets & about 100 cwt. of Shot, each horse having about 150 lb. for a load. Ordered him to proceed until he met y[e] packhorses & hide his loads there & return with them, with y[e] same horses & when he was gone had y blankets all of y[e] large Bale that was wet to spread out, likewise y[e] contents of three of y[e] small bales, it being a warm day.*

## Drunken fighting at Fort Cumberland

Kenny's April 9, 1759 journal entry[1044] from Fort Cumberland states:

*M[c]Carty & I packed up goods to day, made 9½ loads up, in order to have them ready when y[e] horses returns which I expect now soon, as I heard that Samuel was got to Pittsburgh this day week in order to get a bateau up to receive y[e] goods that went out. Here has been odious work to day amongst y[e] soldiers with drunkenness & fighting & y[e] women also. Some officers being come to 'list y[e] Marylanders into y[e] Royal Americans & as I believe sent some men with liquor before them, they 'listed I heard nine of them to day. Thunder & rain this night.*

---

[1041] **"Proceedings and Acts of the General Assembly, 1758-1761"**.

[1042] **"The Pennsylvania Magazine of History and Biography"**, Volume 37, 1913.

[1043] **"The Pennsylvania Magazine of History and Biography"**, Volume 37, 1913.

[1044] **"The Pennsylvania Magazine of History and Biography"**, Volume 37, 1913.

### Finishing packing the goods

Kenny's April 10, 1759 journal entry[1045] from Fort Cumberland states:

*Adam M<sup>c</sup>Carty & I finished packing y<sup>e</sup> goods this evening & I paid him for two days packing 6<sup>s</sup> & for three days hunting y<sup>e</sup> horses 6<sup>s</sup>. I think I can pack better now than him, for I shewed him methods that he prefered to his own.*

*This evening returned & came 31 of y<sup>e</sup> packhorses, leaving 2 by y<sup>e</sup> way, viz. 1 of James Hammon's roan, & 1 of young Jacob Bales gray, that gave out. Received a letter from S. L. dated y<sup>e</sup> 6 inst. at y<sup>e</sup> mouth of Redstone creek, on y<sup>e</sup> Monongahela.*

### A driver has an injured leg

Kenny's April 13, 1759 journal entry[1046] from Fort Cumberland states:

*One of y<sup>e</sup> drivers having gotten some hurt on his leg & is inflamed, he insists for this days rest & thinks he can proceed tomorrow on y<sup>e</sup> journey out again, & y<sup>e</sup> drivers generally insisting that some more of y<sup>e</sup> horses are like to fail, having no food but y<sup>e</sup> young grass, I allowed them to tarry this day.*

### Another wife at Fort Cumberland in 1759

Kenny's April 14, 1759 journal entry[1047] from Fort Cumberland states:

*As we had y<sup>e</sup> loads out & ready to set off this morning, it began to rain & continues dull & cloudy so we stopt going. I let Cap<sup>t</sup> Paris's wife have one of y<sup>e</sup> little Brass Kettles, which weighed 2½<sup>lb</sup>, I likewise, let Ross's wife have one of y<sup>e</sup> least tin kettles, as we buy milk from her.*

### Sending off to Cresap's for sugar

Kenny's April 15, 1759 journal entry[1048] from Fort Cumberland states:

*This being a good day I sent off ye horses with all y<sup>e</sup> goods only 2 kegs of Pipes & 19 packsaddles; sent to Cressap's for 6<sup>lb</sup> of Sugar as Samuel ordered to get some at any rate. Richard Cocks's mare gave out about noon.*

Kenny's April 16, 1759 journal entry from Fort Cumberland states:

*This morning returned y<sup>e</sup> man from Cressap's & brought me only 4<sup>lbs</sup> of Sugar. Today is very wet & our drivers will ly by.*

### George French is involved in a slander lawsuit

On page 101 of the 1759 Frederick County court docket book[1049], in a section titled *"Original Writs to June Court Anno 1759"*, an April 16 record lists George French and George Lambert in connection with a case of slander. The same case is referenced on page 132, in a section titled, *"Imparlances from June Court Anno Domini 1759 To August Courts"*. The same case is also listed in a surviving fragment of the 1760

---

[1045] **"The Pennsylvania Magazine of History and Biography"**, Volume 37, 1913.

[1046] **"The Pennsylvania Magazine of History and Biography"**, Volume 37, 1913.

[1047] **"The Pennsylvania Magazine of History and Biography"**, Volume 37, 1913.

[1048] **"The Pennsylvania Magazine of History and Biography"**, Volume 37, 1913.

[1049] MSA No. C782-11

Frederick County Maryland court docket book[1050], in a section titled, *"Tryal Dockett for the third Tuesday and eighteenth Day of March Annoguo Domini 1760"*. A George French later appears in the 1783 Old Town and Skipton hundreds lists.

### Waiting for the milk cows

Kenny's April 17, 1759 journal entry[1051] from Fort Cumberland states:

*With some considerable impatience I wait here for Adam M^cCarty returning with some milch cows he went to buy, one of which I sent money for & am to have my choice when they come. We heard by some that came here from Ray's Town, that y^e Indians have killed & taken some by Loyalhannan.*

### Kenny mentions Collier's place

Kenny's April 18, 1759 journal entry states:

*After having stayed until today, I went down as far as Coliers this morning to enquire after McCarty, but no account of him I returned & got y^e Captain's wife to engage to take y^e cow if he brought one, & pay us y^e money, so I set off about 2 p. m. after y^e packhorses & walked y^e most of y^e way, so kept on until I got to y^e Little Meadows, some time about y^e middle of y^e night & made a fire, so stayed until morning.*

The location of Collier's place is identified on the 1755 manuscript map "**Mr. Armstrong's rough draft of the country to the west of Susquehanna**", which locates him on a Warriors path from the north, and a path to Fort Cumberland. John Jacob's book on the life of Michael Cresap states, *"Elizabeth, the youngest daughter of Colonel Thomas Cresap, was married to a Mr. Isaac Collier, from Pennsylvania, who was rather a dissipated character."* A Collier Run joins the Potomac River southeast of Cumberland at Latitude 39.566862°, Longitude -78.725042°, about seven miles west of Oldtown.

### Fauquier writes to Sharpe about paying Walker for provisions left at Fort Cumberland

On April 18, 1759, Fauquier wrote a letter[1052] to Sharpe from Williamsburgh that states:

*I am informed by M^r Thomas Walker who was commissary for the Virginia Forces that when Fort Cumberland was Evacuated, and the Troops of Maryland took possession of it there were some provisions left belonging to this Colony, which by agreement were to be paid for by Maryland or to be replaced. M^r Walker is now going for Maryland to Settle that acc^t and I beg the Favour of you to appoint some Body to adjust that affair with him.*

### Wolves destroy some of the ropes at Bear Camp

Kenny's April 19, 1759 journal entry[1053] states:

*In y^e morning it rained, but I set off & over took y^e company in about four miles farther, so they got loaded & proceeded to y^e Great Bear Camps within Seven miles of y^e Big Youghogany. Four loads of Lead being left there; y^e Wolves having destroyed y^e ropes we were obliged to encamp there.*

---

[1050] MSA No. C782-11

[1051] "**The Pennsylvania Magazine of History and Biography**", Volume 37, 1913.

[1052] "**Correspondence of Governor Sharpe, 1757-1761**".

[1053] "**The Pennsylvania Magazine of History and Biography**", Volume 37, 1913.

## Crossing the Youghiogheny River

Kenny's April 20, 1759 journal entry[1054] states:

*It Rained a good deal in y<sup>e</sup> night & this morning, but abating awhile we got up y<sup>e</sup> horses & loaded them, covering each load. It rained smartly whilst we were loading, but I was for getting over y<sup>e</sup> Big Youghogany least it should rise too high for us; but we got over safe, one blanket falling off as we crossed & it floating down about 40 perches one of y<sup>e</sup> drivers Thomas Mercer stripped all off & waided up to his armpits & brought it out, & so we encamped near y<sup>e</sup> river upon a little creek-side, as there was no more good pasture until we go to y<sup>e</sup> Great Meadows. This evening James Hammons & John Mickle killed a bear, which is good eating.*

## Reaching the Great Meadows

Kenny's April 21, 1759 journal entry[1055] states:

*Proceeded to y<sup>e</sup> Great Meadows. Three of y<sup>e</sup> creatures gave out about ½ of y<sup>e</sup> way, but I tarried behind & brought them along. Put two loads on my own horse, so got them all to y<sup>e</sup> Meadows, where is good pasture. One of them belonging to William Underwood died in y<sup>e</sup> night; he could not swallow grass when he chewed it, but put it out.*

This is where Kenny leaves the environs of Fort Cumberland and travels on to Pittsburgh, hearing of many Indian depredations.

## What to do with the Maryland officers remaining at Fort Cumberland?

An April 26, 1759 letter[1056] Bouquet wrote to Stanwix from York Town includes the following:

*Falfe has got twenty men at Fort Cumberland which he brought yesterday, he would have inlisted the 14 remaining, had not some of their officers interfeared.*

*Col. Byrd had Sent one of his officers to that Post who offered £10= Bounty, but Ralfe had been before hand with him, and he did not get one Cap<sup>t</sup> Pearis who goes down, was very assistant, I promised & paid him 30/. Curr<sup>y</sup> for Each man, for his trouble and supposed Expences on that Occasion.*

*I think he would be able to raise 50, or 60 more in Maryland, If you thought proper to make an agreement with him; There are four officers of the Marylanders remaining at Cumberland, who having been ordered there with 100 men by Brig<sup>r</sup> Forbes, desires your Orders for their Conduct: The men being near all gone, they can be of no further service there, as their Province does not Seem disposed to pay them.*

At least two different versions of this letter exist. For another version see "**The Papers of Col. Henry Bouquet**", 1940, Series 21652.

## Sharpe replies to Fauquier about paying Walker

On May 18, 1759, Sharpe wrote a letter[1057] to Fauquier that includes the following:

---

[1054] "**The Pennsylvania Magazine of History and Biography**", Volume 37, 1913.
[1055] "**The Pennsylvania Magazine of History and Biography**", Volume 37, 1913.
[1056] "**The Papers of Henry Bouquet**", Volume III, 1976.
[1057] "**Correspondence of Governor Sharpe, 1757-1761**".

*At the same time I do myself the honour to acknowledge the Receit of Your Lett' by M' Walker in Compliance, with which I have wrote to D' Ross who had the Care of Victualling our Troops at Fort Cumberland & have desired him to account w^th M' Walker for the Provisions that were left there when the Virg^a Troops evacuated that post in April 1757 & which were afterwards served out to the Maryland Provincials & I hope these Gentl^n will settle the Affair to the Satisfaction of all Parties —*

### A man is scalped and a boy taken prisoner near Fort Cumberland

A May 27, 1759 letter[1058] Adam Stephen sent to Bouquet from Bedford includes the statement:

*The Loss of another Convoy ruins the Advance Post. Be Pleasd to order Some Virginians from Winchester to Fort Cumberland, a Man was Scalpd & a Boy taken at that place the night before last, and fifty of the Enemy Could burn the place.*

The reference to a man and a boy indicates the presence of civilians in the environs of Fort Cumberland. The letter includes a postscript that states, *"Some of the Enemy has been as low as Cressops"*.

### Only 13 men guarding Fort Cumberland in dangerous times

George Croghan's May 29, 1759 journal entry[1059] states:

*Captain M^cKinney set off for Philadephia. An Express from Fort Cumberland says that a Man was Killed there and a Boy taken Prisoner by the Indians a few days agoe, and that they were seen every day about the Fort and the Sentrys were fired on every Night by them the officer that Commands there has but Twelve Men so that he dares not trust a Man out and the Stores are all full of Kings Stores.*

### Fort Cumberland is in danger in the June 4 timeframe

The minutes[1060] from a Virginia *"...Council held June 13, 1759"* includes the following synopsis of a letter that the Governor communicated to the Board: *"A Letter from Col. Byrd, dated Winchester June 4^th informing that Fort Cumberland is in Danger, the Indians appearing before it every Day — that he had sent Captain McKenzie there with Fifty Men..."*

### A lawsuit against Cresap is abated

The Frederick County, Virginia case of William Ross versus Thomas Cresap was abated on June 7, 1759 because William Ross was deceased.

### Samuel Plum is involved in litigation

Samuel Plum was being sued by Stephen West in the Frederick County, Maryland court on June 19, 1759.

### Ross is being prosecuted for allegedly stealing two steers from Thomas Cresap

On page 55 of the 1759 Frederick County, Maryland court docket book[1061], in a section titled *"Tryall Criminal Dockett for June Court Anno 1759"*, a record exists for a case of Lordship versus William Ross

---

[1058] "The papers of Col. Henry Bouquet", 1941

[1059] "The Pennsylvania Magazine of History and Biography", October, 1947.

[1060] "Executive journals of the Council of colonial Virginia", Volume 6.

[1061] MSA No. C782-11

states *"Prosm[t] for stealing two Steers the property of Co[ll] Cresap"*. On page 56, in a list related to Recognizances for the *"June Court Anno 1759"*, William Ross is listed with an £25 bond *"for his apps to Ans[r]"*, and this bond is somehow associated with *"March Court 1757"*. In connection with the same case, Evan Shelby and George Ross are listed with discharged £12-10 bonds *"for W[m] Ross's apps to Ans[r]"*; John Slater and Jon[n] Plumer are listed with £15 bonds *"for Mary Slaters apps to Test a W[m] Ross."*; Jon[n] Plumer is listed with a £20 bond *"for W[m] Youngs apps to Test a W[m] Ross"*; and Jon[n] Plumer, Samuel Plumb, Phil Mason, Elis Plumb, and Samuel Dow are listed with £20 bonds *"for their apps to Test a W[m] Ross"*. Samuel Plumb appears on the 1761 Old Town Hundred list.

### Report of an impending attack on Fort Pitt or Ligonier

A letter[1062] Croghan wrote to Bouquet from Pittsburgh on the evening of July 11, 1759 states:

> *Inclosed you have the Intelligence I received yesterday, and just now arrived two Indians from Priskisle, sent to me with the following Account by a Six Nation Indian, which I employed some time agoe to watch the motions of the Enemy there.*

> *They say that Eight days agoe a large Party of French, and Indians arrived at Priskisle with a quantity of Provissions, and Horses, that the French and Indians said there would be eight Hundred Indians when they all came together, they cannot tell how many was then there but think there could not be less than Seven Hundred French, and Indians, that when the whole was collected at Venango, they were to attack either this Post, or Ligonier, but those Indians say they think they will attack this Post, they have either Eight or ten Pieces of Cannon two of which I take to be twelve Pounders and the rest Six Pounders by the description these two Indians give of their size, they further say that on their way here they met ten principal Men and Warriors going after the Indians to endeavour to turn them back over the Lakes as all the Nations there are determined to be at Peace with the English*

### Livingston arrives at Fort Bedford

A July 12, 1759 letter[1063] Major John Tulleken sent to General John Stanwix from Fort Bedford includes the statement, *"...I had likewise sent an express to Col. Bird of the Virginians to desire he would push on, imagineing from the intelligence I than had that he was at Fort Cumberland..."* and includes the statement, *"Major Livingston arrived here yesterday from Fort Cumberland and by him I received Captain M[c]Kenzies letter, I inclose you his return of Stores &c at Fort Cumberland."*

### About 50 acres of hay can be mowed near Fort Cumberland

A July 13, 1759 letter[1064] Major John Tulleken sent to Bouquet from the *"Camp at Fort Bedford"* includes the statement:

> *I inclosed in the letter directed to the General or you, I sent you Major Livingston account of stores at F. Cumberland*

> *You will be greatly disappointed if you expect wee have cutt much Hay at this place, or if you expect to find any Grass here. But Maj[r] Livingstone tells me that there is above Fifty acres you may cutt within a few miles of Fort Cumberland if necessary.*

---

[1062] **"The Papers of Henry Bouquet"**, Volume III, 1976.
[1063] **"The papers of Col. Henry Bouquet"**, 1941
[1064] **"The papers of Col. Henry Bouquet"**, 1941

This indicates the presence of at least one farm near Fort Cumberland — it may be a reference to Thomas Cresap's place.

### Burd has no tools to open Braddock's road

A July 13, 1759 postscript[1065] to a letter Bouquet wrote to Major John Tulleken includes the following:

*After writing the above the General received a Letter from Col. Byrd, Informing him that he had no Tools to open Braddocks Road & build the Post at Red Stone Creek, and that his two artificers Comp$^s$ being only half full, he thought it would be best to march that Way himself with his whole Corps, which he judged the more advisable as the Small Pox was broke amongst his men.*

*The General has wrote to him in answer that he approved his Plan, and that he was to proceed in consequence with the whole to Red Stone Creek*

*But if upon your application he had already passed Fort Cumberland to go to Bedford In this case he was to abandon the Plan at Red Stone Creek & proceed directly to Ligonier.*

### A letter references opening the communication with Fort Pitt

A July 22, 1759[1066] letter[1067] Major John Tulleken wrote to Bouquet from the *"Camp at Fort Bedford"* includes the statement:

*Col. Byrd left all the Waggons and Cattle he had at Fort Cumberland, but did not leave any body to escort them here, so that I must weaken my self very much in sending a Captain and Fifty men for them which I intend dooing however tomorrow, nor do I imagine that this detachment will be able to return here with the Waggons in less than Ten days, as they will have new roads to cutt in many places the old road being here and there impassable. ...*

*As to opening the Communication between Ft. Cumberland and Pittsburgh it would certainly be of infinite service and is much to be wish'd for; Col. Byrd had received your orders on that head, but ... Col. Byrd not thinking one hundred men sufficient for that end, and likewise imagining as things then stood that you would want all his people this way he has done nothing in it, and hopes the General will approve of his measures.*

### Requesting Dr. Walker to put 500 horses into service from Fort Cumberland

A July 23, 1759 letter[1068] Bouquet wrote to Thomas Rutherford and Dr. Thomas Walker from Fort Chambers states:

*Being informed by M$^r$ Hoops that You and M$^r$ Walker could procure a good Number of Pack Horses to carry Provisions and forrage for the army to the Westward: I would have been glad to know on what Terms. But as I make no doubt, but that they will be reasonable, I desire you would immediately contract for 200, without waiting for an answer from me, and if the Conditions are agreeable to the General, you*

---

[1065] **"The Papers of Col. Henry Bouquet"**, 1940.

[1066] The date of the letter was determined from a synopsis in the **"Sessional Papers of the Dominion of Canada"**, Volume 23, 1890, that states, *""Necessity of sending an escort to Fort Cumberland for waggons and cattle. ... A communication between Cumberland and Pittsburg would be of infinite service. Byrd has done nothing about it, for reasons given."*

[1067] **"The papers of Col. Henry Bouquet"**, 1941.

[1068] **"The Papers of Col. Henry Bouquet"**, 1940.

*will receive orders for 300 more as five hundred are wanted to carry from Fort Cumberland to the mouth of Red Stone Creek.*

*The Horses must be appraised, and will be paid for if taken or Killed by the Enemy.*

*They must be Strong, and One driver for Six Horses, Great Care is to be taken that The Saddles, Pads, or whatever your People make use of, don't hurt the Backs of their Horses; and as paying by the day is attended with many Inconveniencees and delays — I desire you would Contract to carry by the hundred Gross Weight, Either to Red Stone Creek or by Fort Bedford to Ligonier; The Distances are as follows*

*from Fort Cumberland to Red Stone Creek 72 Miles*

*From d° to Fort Bedford 30 miles*

*From Bedford to Ligonier 50 miles*

*We pay 16 Shillings for the Hundred to Capt<sup>n</sup> Callender and Barnabas Hughes from Fort Bedford to Ligonier.*

*They must be divided in Brigades of 100 Horses under the Care of a diligent Horsemaster. Escorts shall be furnished.*

*As this service requires the greatest expedition I beg you will loose no time in raising the first 200 Horses on the best Conditions you can; Let me Know at Bedford what money you may want, and where you can receive it.*

*You will please to buy Strong Baggs, and load the Horses w<sup>th</sup> Flour.*

## A proposal to open a road from Fort Cumberland to Pittsburgh

A July 26, 1759 letter[1069] Major John Tulleken wrote to General John Stanwix from the *"Camp at Fort Bedford"* includes the statement, *"I send you this by M<sup>r</sup> Finnie a gentleman from Virginia who comes to make proposals to you for opening a road to Pittsburgh from Cumberland. Upon enquiry I find he is head sutler to the Virginia Regim<sup>t</sup> but a man of substance and one you may put faith in, and a person of some interest in that Province."*

## A proposal to use men from Fort Cumberland to escort supplies

A July 29, 1759 letter[1070] Colonel Adam Stephen wrote to Bouquet from Fort Ligonier includes the statement, *"I sent up Tarr and Rosin for the Battoes; and if the roads are not much infested — I would beg Leave to recommend Redstone Ck. as a copious channel for Supplies. Two hundred men at Fort Cumberland to escort in Small parties Occasionally, will in my Opinion exceed your Excellencys expectation."*

## Gordon wants people to bring their produce to Fort Cumberland

An August 1, 1759 letter[1071] Captain Harry Gordon wrote to Bouquet from Pittsburgh includes the statement:

---

[1069] "**The papers of Col. Henry Bouquet**", 1941.

[1070] "**The papers of Col. Henry Bouquet**", 1941.

[1071] "**The Papers of Col. Henry Bouquet**", 1941.

*After all I return to my former Opinion that without the Communication is opened to Red Stone Creek to bring this Seasons Crop from the South Branch and the frontiers of Virginia you will have the Greatest Difficulty in laying in a Winters Stock for this Garrison, therefore I think as soon as the Virginia Artificers get up here, they ought to be sent up the Mononghela one of them to fix a Post, and the other to open the Communication to Fort Cumberland, where the people ought to have orders to bring their Produce forthwith. They will doe it chearfully if that Post is fixt and it will be of good Effect as it will remove the Notions of Partiality, which tho' ill grounded, they seem to have.*

## Bouquet approves Stephens' plan to use the Cumberland road to supply Pittsburgh

An August 2, 1759 letter[1072] Bouquet wrote to Colonel Adam Stephens from Bedford states:

*The General has received your Letters and approves the measures you have taken to Supply Pittsburgh, as well as releaseing the officer who was under arrest.*

*Your notion of the advantages of Cumberland road will I hope be justified by the success, But as the Country People would not dare to venture without at least small escorts, a Garrison of 200 men should be stationed there to file of to Pittsburgh in small escorts, And I write to Col. Byrd to know what number he could spare of his Regm$^t$ for that Station; As the Pennsilvanians are already spread all along the communication from Carlisle, keep all the little Forts, and furnish all the escorts below, It would appear hard to them to be obliged to furnish again the whole at Fort Gumberland.*

*As soon as you wee see the carriages of all kinds in proper order, I shall have the pleasure to join you, and wee may then proceed together to the Ohio.*

On the same day, Bouquet wrote a letter[1073] to Captain Harry Gordon that includes the statement, *"The harvest being now over we can expect more assistance from the Province of Pensilv$^a$ & Cumberland Road being opened may be of service to us."*

## 500 sheep and 64 wagons at Fort Cumberland

An August 2, 1759 letter[1074] Alexander Finnie wrote to Tulleken from Fort Cumberland states:

*I herewith Send you the return of yours from Winchester but from what I understand there is no apearenc of our being Joined by the Partey from that Quarter without loosing too much time I have this Day brock Ground with the working Partey with a Guard of twelf men & a Sargant in order to have one Days Start of the waggons who will March tomorrow if you think it Neasary to Send any more men now to Join us you ar the best Judge we have in all with us 64 waggons about 500 sheep Sum catle how they all belong to I know not Pray Send off the bearer as he is one of our nessary hands*

In your mental image of Fort Cumberland, reserve a spot for five or six hundred head of cattle or sheep, large numbers of pack horses, and significant numbers of wagons and wagon horses.

---

[1072] **"The Papers of Col. Henry Bouquet"**, 1940.

[1073] **"The Papers of Col. Henry Bouquet"**, 1940.

[1074] **"The Papers of Col. Henry Bouquet"**, 1941.

### Cattle are to be appraised at Fort Cumberland and escorts are to be provided

An August 3, 1759 letter[1075] Bouquet wrote to the *"Officer commanding at Fort Cumberland"* from Fort Bedford states:

> *It is General Stanwix's order that you See all the Cattle coming from Virginia for The Use of His Majestie's Forces to The Westward, Justly Estimated, by One Man Appointed by You in behalf of The Crown, and one Appointed by The Contractors; And that you do Certifie the amount of The whole*

> *You are also to direct all kind of Provisions coming from Virginia or Maryland to take Braddock's Road, and give them Escorts from your Garrison*

### Rutherford is asked to purchase 200 horses and put them in service

An August 3, 1759 letter[1076] Bouquet wrote to Thomas Rutherford from Fort Bedford states:

> *As you represent that Pack Horses can not be hired on any Terms in Virginia; The General desires that you purchase forthwith two hundred of them; They must be divided in two Brigades; You are to appoint a Horse master to Each, with the same Pay as a Waggonmaster, and one Driver for Each Six Horses.*

> *In fitting them out you will please to take the greatest Care, that their saddles, or any thing in lieu thereof fits Each Horse exactly, as the whole depends upon preserving their Backs.*

> *They are to be loaded with flour and forrage and proceed by Cumberland to Pittsburgh by Braddocks Road, taking an Escort at Cumberland.*

> *The Bags must be strong, and the Horse masters are to be answerable for them, & bring them back They must be provided with some Thread to mend them on the Road.*

> *I Send you inclosed twelve Bills of Exchange for £ 2000=Pensilv<sup>a</sup> Currency or £ 1244-8-10 1/2 St, for which please to Send me a Receipt.*

> *M<sup>r</sup> Clark writes you to send to Fort Cumberland the 250 Beeves you had orders to send to Carlisle, as it will save Time. He will require you also to purchase the hundred more with 200 sheep*

> *The whole to proceed by Braddocks Road after they have been received and valued by a Commissary at Fort Cumberland.*

> *You will inform M<sup>r</sup> Clark of the time they are to be at that Post, that he may have People ready to appraise them.*

> *I desire you will Send as much Indian Corn and oats you can forward either to Rays Town or Pittsburgh; Let me know what money you will want for it, & you shall be regularly supplied.*

> *If the 200 Horses above mentioned do good services, I will Send you orders for more.*

### Finnie's petition states that he commenced road repairs on August 4

The November 7, 1759 minutes[1077] of the Virginia House of Burgesses includes the following:

---

[1075] **"The Papers of Col. Henry Bouquet"**, 1940.
[1076] **"The Papers of Col. Henry Bouquet"**, 1940.
[1077] **"Journals of the House of Burgesses of Virginia 1758-1761"**, 1908.

*A Petition of Alexander Finnie was presented to the House and read, setting forth, That when he arrived at Fort Cumberland, on the twentieth of July, he found that the Virginia Regiment had marched for Pittsburg by the Pennsylvania Road, and that there had been no Attempt made to clear the Road opened by General Braddock: That the Petitioner went immediately to Rays Town, and from thence to Fort Lyttleton, where he met with General Stanwix, and having convinced him of the great Advantages that would arise to the Publick by opening the said Road, as by that Means the Forces and Garisons over the Allegheny Mountains would, with the greatest Ease, be plentifully supplied with Provisions and Necessaries, which by Experience he had found could not be done from Pennsylvania, on Account of the great Distance and bad Roads that the Pennsylvanians have to encounter with; he gave the Petitioner Leave to undertake this Work, and gave him an Order to the Quarter-Master General for Tools, Ammunition and Provision, and ordered a Number of Men to cover the working Party: That the Petitioner hired, at his own Expence, thirty Workmen on the South Branch, at the Prices mentioned in a Schedule to his Petition annexed, and was at other Expences as appears by the same Schedule. That he began the said Work the fourth Day of August, and finished on the twentieth, when he arrived at Pittsburg with 60 Provision Waggons, 500 Sheep, and 70 Head of Cattle, and at that Time the Garison had not eight Days Provision. That there have been great Quantities of Provisions and Goods sent from this Colony since, and Contracts made for much more, and for the Convenience and Security of Traders and others, Store Houses are built by the General at the Little Crossing, Great Meadows, and Red Stone Creek; and praying that the House will make him a suitable Allowance for his Expences and Trouble as they shall think he deserves.*

*Ordered, That the said Petition be referred to M* Attorney, M* Waller, M* Richard Henry Lee, and M* Washington; That they do examine into the Allegations thereof, and report the same, with their Opinion thereupon, to the House.*

The November 9, 1759 minutes[1078] of the Virginia House of Burgesses includes the following:

*M* Attorney reported. That the Committee to whom the Petition of Alexander Finnie was referred had had the same under their Consideration, and examined divers Witnesses as to the Facts in the said Petition alledged, and had agreed upon a Report, and come to a Resolution thereupon, which he read in his Place, and afterwards delivered in at the Table, where they were again twice read, and agreed to by the House. as follow:*

*It appears to this Committee that the said Alexander Finnie obtained Leave from General Stanwix to clear the Road in the said Petitioned mentioned, which he performed in such a Manner as to admit of the Passage of a considerable Number of Waggons in the publick Service; and that by an Account, with an Affidavit at the Foot of it, to the said Petition annexed, it appears he expended the Sum of £169. 13 in that Service.*

*It further appears that the said Alexander Finnie opened a Subscription, in Order to obtain Money to defray the Expence of that Work, which, with his own Subscription of £30, amounted to about £70, but how much of the said Subscription hath been collected doth not appear.*

*Resolved, That the said Alexander Finnie ought to be allowed the Sum of £100 current Money, to be paid by the Publick, as a full Satisfaction for his Services aforefaid.*

---

[1078] **"Journals of the House of Burgesses of Virginia 1758-1761"**, 1908.

## Matters of transportation and supply

An August 10, 1759 letter[1079] Colonel George Mercer wrote to Bouquet states:

*I saw your Letter to Cap$^t$ Gunn, where the General is pleased to order, Me to march up Braddock's Road, and the Comanding officer there to consult with Me in opening or repairing it. No Advice or Assistance I can afford, shall be wanting to forward & compleat this Service.*

*As every Person who has served his Majesty among these Mountains, well knows the Difficulty attending the Carriage of Provisions &c, I think it my Duty to obviate any that lies in my Power. In 1754 I comanded a Working Party which opened a Road from Gist's Plantation to the Mouth of Red Stone Creek, at least within 3 or 4 Miles of it. Were this Road repaired, and I am certain it woud easily be done, as I do not now recollect being obliged to lay down a Bridge the whole Way, and the Provision carried to the Mouth of Red Stone, it might from thence be conveyed in Battoes of any Size, to Pitsburg, down the Monongahela and woud save at least 30 or 35 Miles Land Carriage, as it is not more than 70 or 75 Miles from Fort Cumberland to the Mouth of Red Stone.*

*Shoud the General please to order this Comunication to the Waters of the Ohio to be opened, I can venture to affirm that by the last of November any Quantity of Flour & Forage might be laid in at Pitsburg, as many of the principal Farmers of this County have applied to Me to purchase for the Army, & woud have contracted for considerable Quantities.*

*An Exaction of 2 ½ P C$^t$ which one Bealor a Waggon Master imposed on the People for paying Them their Money, has hurt the Service much: and discouraged the Farmers from hiring their Waggons again, but not withstanding that, I am sure 20 or 30 Waggons at least might be imediately contracted for that woud, willingly, go between Winchester & Fort Cumberland as long as the Roads continued good, which We may reasonably suppose will be till the Middle of November. Many, from these Parts, that are already out with the Army, if discharged woud cheerfully undertake this Service, while others again might be engag'd to ply between Cumberland & Red Stone; Or shoud it be thought better to transport the Provision on Pack Horses, I am certain 3, or 400, exclusive of the 200 already procured by M$^r$ Rutherford, might be purchased in this and the adjacent Counties at a short Warning. I woud not venture to mention these Things upon Report. I know they may be effected, and it will be a great Saving to his Majesty as the Rout I have mentioned is not more than 150 Miles Land Carriage, which does not much exceed the Distance from Bedford to Pitsburg, without considering the Goodness of the Roads.*

*There might too now be purchased here a great Number, of Hogs, Bullocks & Sheep. I woud not presume Sir to dictate to the General or you; I thought it my Duty to mention these Facts, as a sure Method I had conceived of forwarding the Service, and I hope I shall not be thought impertinent in informing him of Them.*

*No Doubt the Comanding Officer will advise the General of his March, & what occasioned it to be delayed so long*

*I hope Sir you do Me the Justice to assure the General, that the Orders he has or may hereafter please to give Me, as far as I have Authority as a Volunteer, shall be executed with the greatest Punctuality, to the best of my Knowledge. Ignorance may betray Me into an Error, but Negligence never will.*

---

[1079] **"The Papers of Col. Henry Bouquet"**, 1941.

### 100 men march from Fort Bedford

An August 10, 1759 letter[1080] Bouquet wrote to Colonel William Byrd from Fort Bedford includes the statement, *"You will see by the two Inclosed what men we have left: 100, of them march to Day with about 300 Pack Horses, and 100 more must be Sent to Cumberland: You will Judge of the impossibility to Send any reinforcement for the present".*

### Catawba Indians are marching via Fort Cumberland

An August 12, 1759 letter[1081] Colonel George Mercer wrote to General John Stanwix from Winchester contains the following passage about Catawba Indians:

*I thought it my Duty to give you the earliest Intelligence of their Arrival and Resolution to join your Excellency with all possible Dispatch. As they have insisted upon my attending Them, I will take Care they lose no Time on the March, but if you woud please to send any Person to Cumberland to meet with Them, & take Them off my Hands, I shall cheerfully resign the Comand, as they are generally excessivily troublesome to all concerned. I expect they will be at Cumberland on Thursday, and woud be glad you woud please to direct Me whether I must proceed to Raes Town, or up General Braddock's Road agreeable to your former Order. If it is possible to get myself quit of Them, I will go up Braddock's Road unless your Excellency is pleased to direct Me farther on this Head, they are 62 in Number, and picked Warriors.*

### Gordon requests a post at the Great Crossing

An August 15, 1759 letter[1082] Captain Harry Gordon wrote to Bouquet from Pittsburgh includes the statement, *"A Flat must be built soon at the great Crossing of the Yoghiogeni on the Cumberland Road and a small Post for 30 Men made there."*

### John McDonald is replaced as constable

The Augusta County court replaced[1083] *"John McDonall"* with Francis McBride as constable on August 16, 1759. In 1761, a John McDonald appears on the Old Town Hundred list. The court record suggests he may have moved away from Augusta County by August 16, 1759.

### Opening the road to Monongahela

An August 22, 1759 letter[1084] Bouquet wrote to Captain Harry Gordon from Fort Bedford includes the statement:

*Col. Burd marches himself with Col° Shippen, & Cresap to open the Road from the great meadows to The Mononghehela, where They are to Build Store Houses and a little Stockadoe, and I beg you will send them some good Carpenters (2 or 3) to direct the Work. I will Send them Nails for Shingles, locks & hinges*

---

[1080] **"The Papers of Col. Henry Bouquet"**, 1940.

[1081] **"The Papers of Col. Henry Bouquet"**, 1941.

[1082] **"The Papers of Col. Henry Bouquet"**, 1941.

[1083] **"Colonial Records of the Upper Potomac"**, Volume 6.

[1084] **"The Papers of Col. Henry Bouquet"**, 1941.

*Col⁰ Burd will Send you an Express to inform you of what he wants, the place where he builds, and the time your Carpenters Should be there in a Batteau.*

## Why Burd was sent to Redstone

An August 22, 1759 letter[1085] Bouquet wrote to Stanwix from Ford Bedford explains the reason for going to Redstone as follows:

*as you was pleased to Authorize me to take the most conducive measures towards hastening the formation of the Magazine at Pittsburgh; I contracted Yesterday wᵗʰ Mʳ Ramsey, a Substantial Merchant of Virginia, to deliver One Thousand Barrels of Merchantable Flour upon the Monongohela, at 36 sh. Virgᵃ Currenʸ for the 112ˡᵇ Vizᵗ 50,000 ˡᵇ on or before the beginning of 8ᵇᵉʳ and every fortnight after the Same quantity to the above amount, under the penalty of £61000 Sterˡ*

*In consideration whereof, I engaged to advance him £1000 Virgᵃ Money, which I beg Mʳ Barrow would Send me in a in a Bill upon Col⁰ Hunter, in favor of George Mercer Esqʳ in the same form as the £800 Sterᵍ he received here I have also Contracted with another Merchant Mʳ Graham to deliver at the Same place 600 Bushells of fine Salt at 22 Sh. Virgᵃ money the Bushell, under the Penalty of £500;*

*These two Contracts are Advantageous as the Carriage alone of the Salt from Carlisle to Pittsburgh would amount to near £3: pʳ Bushell, besides the Saving So many Waggons for other purposes. We can Sell our Salt at Carlisle as this new Communication will be more expeditious than to go all the way by Land from Cumberland, I Send Col⁰ Burd, at his request with a hundred & odd men of his Battalion with Cressap to open that Road from the great Meadows, and build The Store houses, & Stokadoes upon the Monongohela; I give him Cattle, 100 of the Virgᵃ Horses wᵗʰ flour, Tools, Liquor, Ammunition &ᶜ and desire Captⁿ Gordon to Send him from Pittsburgh two or three head Carpenters to direct the Work.*

*Lieuᵗ Col⁰ Mercer will have nothing further to do than to provide forrage & Waggons to transport it.*

## The storehouses at Fort Cumberland are in bad repair

An August 22, 1759 letter[1086] Mercer sent to Bouquet from Fort Cumberland states:

*I have examined all the Store Houses here to Day and find Them much out of Repair, they have by Appearance been torn up for Fire wood. I have ordered Mʳ Livingston to have Them repaired as as possible, but find he can do Nothing till he has Assistance from You. Twill require 6 Carpenters at least for that Purpose with all necessary Tools, as there are none in Store here. It is necessary to have 2 of these 6 Sawyers. Nails locks & Hinges will be wantᵍ also, these I shall send from Winchester, as I know you have none with you. the Tools for the Sawyers and Carpenters I imagine you have.*

*I am told the Pack Horses are to set out from Winchʳ to Day, I have desired Majʳ Livingston when they arrive here to stop Them for your Orders.*

*I have set the Smith here to make the Hinges & Staples for the Store house, on the Monongahela, with old Iron I found in this Fort.*

*You will receive the Return of Provision here inclosed.*

*Since I left you I have recollected that Expresses to or from the General may want Forage, as well as the King's Waggons coming from Pitsburg for Loads here; & I have directed Livingston to furnish Them,*

---

[1085] **"The Papers of Henry Bouquet"**, Volume III, 1976.
[1086] **"The Papers of Col. Henry Bouquet"**, 1941.

*unless you contradict the Order by the Return of the Express. I have told him at the same Time to charge the Forage at the Price We receive it, on the Back of their Certificates.*

*M' Livingston will want a Waggon here to draw logs for sawing the Plank, & making Boards, it will be necessary but for a short Time.*

*As I know my Presence will be necessary at Winchester, I shall endeavor to leave this to Night.*

*You may depend I shall use the utmost Diligence in complying with the Generals Orders & Expectations.*

## Sutlers waggoners retire to Fort Cumberland from Pittsburg

An August 23, 1759 letter[1087] Mercer wrote to Colonel Byrd from Pittsburgh states:

*Two days ago a Waggoner was Kill'd and Scalped near this place, this Morning three Indians Fired upon another Waggoner three Miles upon the road to Legonier Kill'd His Horse, & Carried off some more Horses, from a Convoy of Empty Waggons Escorted by an Officer & Twenty Five Men, and I have Just now received Information that some Waggons have been found upon the road to Cumberland with the Traces Cutt, and a Good many Indian Tracts about the place, which Tracts, were found Tending down to Legonier.*

*From these Circumstances, it is Evident, that a party of the Enemy is about us, and that Convoys are not safe, without good Escorts, as a great many Delawares, and Other Indians, have moved off within These few days, it is as likely to be some Villains of that Tribe as french Indians from Over the Lake.*

The letter includes a postscript that states:

*A party was prepared to go to Cumberland with such of the Kings and Sutlers Waggons, as were unfit for the Service, but finding some were to be detain'd the Sutlers Waggoners went out of Camp without my Knowledge.*

## Burd is to repair the storehouse at Fort Cumberland

An August 26, 1759 letter[1088] Bouquet wrote to George Mercer from Fort Bedford includes the following:

*The Store house at Fort Cumberland will be repaired by Col° Burd's Artificers. He is to march to morrow with 200 Men to open the Road by Gist to Redstone Creek and build there the Store houses: So you may direct Every body that Way: and for Some time the Convoys will have Small Escortes at Cumberland.*

*The Second Brigade of 100 Pack horses must be loaded with Oates or Corn, at any Rate, and proceed directly to Pittsburgh.*

*If any Horse was hurt'd they must be left at Cumberland till they are well again. Your directions for forrage at Cumberland are very proper. M' Finnie who will deliver you this is of opinion that we could have flour, Corn, & oats at Cumberland and Mononghehela, for the prices fixed in a paper that he is to give you. I beg you will consider that matter, and determine what you think right, by the Information you will have from the Country people, our want of forrage is of So destructive a Consequence that if money can procure it, I beg you will give great Encouragemt as far as the first of Novem', and then we shall only want Corn for the Indians, and feed Some Horses to Carry on the Works in Winter.*

---

[1087] **"The Papers of Henry Bouquet"**, Volume III, 1976.
[1088] **"The Papers of Col. Henry Bouquet"**, 1940.

## Letters from Bouquet about supplies

An August 28, 1759 letter[1089] Bouquet wrote to Adam Hoops from Fort Bedford concerning supplying Pittsburgh includes the statement, *"I did not see the Bullocks Sent by Rutherford as they proceeded from Cumberland, where they were estimated at 300 ¼ with one another, and reduced to 21 C, besides what will be lost on the way."*

An August 28, 1759 letter[1090] Bouquet wrote to Daniel Clark from Fort Bedford includes the statement, *"Cumberland, Bedford, and other Small Posts are to be Supplied by the Contractors"*.

## Mercer writes to Bouquet about supplies

An August 28, 1759 letter[1091] Colonel George Mercer wrote to Bouquet from Winchester includes the following:

*I mentioned to you before Sir that I thought the Price of the Oats too small here; and those People who take Pains always to find out the Market of Pennsylv^a as much as their own, especially when We are obliged to have Recourse to Them have assured Me, that you have advertised 2/ p Bushel for Oats delivered to M^r Barr in Lancaster, and they expect an extraordinary Premium for going up to Fort Cumberland; so that I really am of Opinion that We cant get any delivered there for less than 4/ p Bushel.*
*...*

*The first Question they ask Me, is, if I will give them any hard Cash? I do not know, say they, how that might tempt Me. I believe with some Gold, and a little higher Price, I coud contract for a Quantity of Oats delivered at Fort Cumberland in October...*

*One hundred of Rutherfords Pack Horses (the first Brigade) march this Day loaded with Flour, they are good Horses a very well equiped. The other Brigade is as good, and will march on Thursday with Flour; as you did not till now order any Forage to be laid in here. If you chuse now that shoud be done, the 2^d Brigade may return after leaving the Flour at Fort Cumberland Please to inform Me imediately.*

*M^r Rutherford has purchased 200 Sheep as you before directed which will be sent off imediately, the rest shall be bought up as soon as possible.*

*M^r Finnie told Me you gave him Orders to tell Me to endeavor to get Workmen here to go to Cumberland. I have set up Advertisements for that Purpose already, but fear I shall get none on this Side the Ridge, as this is the most extravagant Place on the Continent for Tradesmen. If I dont get them soon 1 will send Advertisements down the Country*

*I shall set about opening the Road to Cumberland to morrow with 7 Soldiers, all that are fit for Duty out of 28, and they just coming out of the Small Pox are very weak, so that I believe I shall be obliged to be at some trifling Expence to the Country People before I get it compleated, tho it may easily be repaired, and made an exceeding good Road. ...*

*I shall send the Nails &c for the Store Houses at Monongahela and Cumberland so soon as they come up.*

---

[1089] **"The Papers of Col. Henry Bouquet"**, 1941.

[1090] **"The Papers of Col. Henry Bouquet"**, 1941.

[1091] **"The Papers of Col. Henry Bouquet"**, 1941.

### The packhorses are headed to Fort Cumberland

An August 30, 1759 letter[1092] Colonel George Mercer wrote to Bouquet from Winchester includes the following:

*As, I before mentioned, We had no Notice of buying Forage the $^{2d}$ Brigade of Pack Horses will set out to morrow for Cumberland, they may leave their Loads there, and return again to this Place by the Time we can purchase the Forage which shall be done now without any Delay. Tho the Planters have yet none of their Forage threshed, yet Money will make Them do it. as you order it shall be done at any Rate I shall do the best I can, & take the cheapest Method, but as I wrote you before it must be an extraordinary Price that will drive Them out of their comon Road. When they know the Advantage of the Trade We can make Them sell for less, indeed upon our own Terms.*

*Pray Sir have you determined to open the Road to Red Stone by Gists, or the Way that was before proposed some Miles above it? ...*

*We make a tolerable Progress on our Road to Cresaps, I have got many of the County People to assist Me. it will be an exceeding good Road...*

### Thomas Cresap is listed in a Frederick County court record

On page 164 of the 1759 Frederick County court docket book[1093], in a section titled *"Tryal Docketts to the third Tuesday & Twentyeth Day of November 1759"*, an August 31 record lists Thomas Cresap, and his adversary appears to be Frederick Garrisson. The same case is listed on page 11 of a surviving fragment of the 1760 Frederick County Maryland court docket book[1094], in a section titled, *"Tryal Dockett for the third Tuesday and eighteenth Day of March Annoguo Domini 1760"*.

### A communication by river to Pittsburg

Burd's journal[1095] states, *"Ordered, in August, 1759, to march with 200 men of my battalion to the mouth of Redstone cr., where it empties itself into the river Monongahela, to cut a road somewhere from Gen. Braddock's road to that place as I shall judge best, and on my arrival there to erect a fort in order to open a communication by the river Monongahela to Pittsburg, for the more easy transportation of provisions, &c., from the provinces of Virginia and Maryland. Sent forward the detachment under the command of Lieut. Col. Shippen, leaving one officer and thirty men to bring our five wagons."*

### Pack horses loaded with flour arrive at Fort Cumberland

A September 1, 1759 letter[1096] Bouquet wrote to Stanwix from Fort Bedford includes the following statements:

*The 100 first Pack Horses from Virginia arrived yesterday at Fort Cumberland with flour, Col. Byrd takes 40 of them to feed his People, & Send you 60 & the rest is to load forrage for Pittsburgh as the article chieffly wanted ...*

---

[1092] **"The Papers of Col. Henry Bouquet"**, 1941.

[1093] MSA No. C782-11

[1094] MSA No. C782-11

[1095] **"Historical Collections of the State of Pennsylvania"**, Sherman Day, 1843.

[1096] **"The Papers of Henry Bouquet"**, Volume IV, 1978.

*Lieut Colonel Mercer has engaged a good many People to bring forrage to Cumberland, and some to carry Indian Goods to Pittsburgh. ...*

## Bouquet reports that Burd and Shippen are gone to Fort Cumberland

A September 1, 1759 letter[1097] Bouquet wrote to Edward Shippen from Fort Bedford includes the following statement:

*Colonel Burd & Col Shippen are gone to Fort Cumberland, to open a new Road to the Mouth of Red Stone Creek, and build Storehouses upon The Mononghehela; being at last obliged to have recourse to Virginia to avoid the Impending Ruin of the Army.*

## Forage for the lame horses at Fort Cumberland

A September 1, 1759 letter[1098] Bouquet wrote to Colonel James Burd from Fort Bedford includes the following:

*I hope you arrived Safe tho' I have heard nothing from you by two Expresses from Cumberland. Notwithstanding my Orders of the 3ᵈ August to load the Pack Horses with forrage & flour, I hear that they are only loaded with the last Article, and must desire you to take as many of them as You will want with flour, and Send all the rest back to Winchester to load forrage, leaving orders that Some unload at Cumberland, for our lame Horses (if no other forrage is expected there) some others must carry you Oats to the Mononghehela, and the rest proceed to Pittsburgh with forrage also.*

*I beg you would write to Lieutᵗ Colᵒ: Mercer for what you may want, and as the Artificers are Scarce & very dear at Winchester, I wish you could get the Storehouses repaired without their Assistance. Mercer writes me that he wants a Ship Carpenter to Cork the Scows upon Patowmack. Unless you can Spare him one we have none here.*

## Horses to be sent from Fort Cumberland to Winchester, cattle to go by Braddock's road

A September 1, 1759 letter[1099] Bouquet wrote to George Mercer from Fort Bedford includes the following:

*I write to Colᵗ Burd at Fᵗ Cumbᵈ to send back part of Said Horses to Winchester to be loaded with forrage, And I am obliged to send my own Horses to Cumberland with Forrage for his Teams*

*I remember to have said to Mᵗ Graham to see where he could get Beeves if wanted but I do not remember to have given him any order to buy them, Notwithstanding, he may send by Braddock's Road what he has already bought, but I beg you will tell him to buy no more 'till he has Orders for it, and to send me the accᵗ of what he sends up. ...*

*I refer you to the Lettᵗ: I desired Colᵗ Burd to write you in regard to Artificers for F Cumberland, and if he has a Ship-Carpenter, he will send him to you. we have none here.*

*He is to open the Road by Gist, and not the Way proposed by Cressup.*

---

[1097] "**The Pennsylvania Magazine of History and Biography**", Volume 33, 1909.
[1098] "**The Papers of Col. Henry Bouquet**", 1940.
[1099] "**The Papers of Col. Henry Bouquet**", 1940.

## Twelve carpenters at Fort Cumberland

A September 2, 1759 letter[1100] James Burd wrote to Mercer from Fort Cumberland states:

*I have this Moment (just as I was going to march) received a Letter from Col° Bouquet wherein he acquaints me with the Difficulty you have in getting Carpenters & likewise that you are in Want of a Ship Carpenter. I am very glad that I have it in my Power to supply you with both; I leave here eleven Carpenters for the Works & I send you by the Pack Horses a Ship Carpenter*

*Of M' Sweringhams Brigade of Horses only 99 arrived here, forty of which I take with me loaded with Flour & eight to follow me with Forage that comes from Bedford in two of Col° Bouquets Waggons; one I am obliged to send Express to Bedford, and fifty I send back to Winchester to be loaded with forage, the flour of these sent back I have put in Store here; The other hundred Horses with these fifty Col° Bouquet desires may be loaded with forage & sent forward to Pittsburg, leaving what may be necessary at Col° Cressap's for fifty two of the Kings Waggon Horses that are there at Pasture, & what I may want at Red Stone Creek, concerning which I have given Major Levingston Directions. I am very glad to see such a good Brigade of Horses. I shall be glad to hear from you in the mean time*

## Burd updates Bouquet

A September 2, 1759 letter[1101] James Burd wrote to Bouquet from Fort Cumberland states:

*I this moment received your Favour just as I was going to march from hence dated 1ˢᵗ Curr'. You observe that two Expresses left this since my Arrival & you had not heard from me, its true, permit me to give my Reasons when the first left this, I could not write things were in such a Situation here that I could form no Judgement of Matters, the second Express when past this place between twelve & one in the Morning. I hope these reasons will excuse me to you.*

*I have disposed of the Brigade of 99 horses since Receipt of Yours in the following Manner, viz' 40 I take with me loaded with Flour, 8 follows me with Oats from your Waggons when they arrive, & one I am obliged to send with this Letter to you (as there is not a horse to be hired here for any Money) and fifty I send back to Winchester to be loaded with Oats, and to proceed to Pittsburg with the other hundred as you direct.*

*I have wrote Col° Mercer of Virginia upon this Head signifying to him your pleasure, but instead of sending the Forage here for our 52 Waggon horses have desired him to order it to be left at Col° Cressap's, where the Horses are. I have supplyed all the Wants of Carpenters here out of the Troops, I have left 11 Carpenters at this Place, & I send Lt Col° Mercer a Ship Carpenter by the Return of the Pack horses.*

*I have given Major Levingston Directions about the making up of the Hay for your Waggons & sending them back loaded directly I have likewise directed him about the Stores &c. of this place and have acquainted him that I carry eighteen Days Provisions with me that he may forward more to me if there should be Occasion, that is, if the River should prove too low for Battoeing.*

*I am sorry at your disappointment of Forage, but let us hope for the best. We unfortunate enough to have seven Men deserted from us last Night and they have carried off two of my Waggon Horses, however I will supply their place out of the Team that was in my Broken Waggon. I march directly, & beg to remain with great Regard.*

---

[1100] "**The Papers of Henry Bouquet**", Volume IV, 1978.
[1101] "**The Papers of Henry Bouquet**", Volume IV, 1978.

## Horses are gone to Fort Cumberland

A September 3, 1759 letter[1102] Bouquet wrote to Captain John Hambright from Fort Bedford includes the following cryptic statement, *"I Sent 28 Horses to Fort Loudoun which I beg you would See, and bring with you Such as might be fit for immediate use 52 more are gone to Fort Cumberland to recruit, I never Saw Such a destruction."*

## The road is too bad to send wagons to Fort Cumberland

A September 4, 1759 letter[1103] Bouquet wrote to Major Livingston from Bedford states:

*The Road being too bad to Send my Waggons to Fort Cumberland, 12 Pack Horses are carrying Oates for Colonel Burd, which you will please to Send him with the Pack Horses he left behind for that purpose, Sending back our 12 Pack Horses here, with the Baggs*

*The rest of the Oates you will Order to The Waggon master Donaldson Keeping Some for The Team we Send you:*

*The broken Waggon is to come back, with the Horses & geers left by Colonel Burd. When the Pack Horses come from Virginia you will order one of the Brigades of 100 to proceed to Pittsburgh w^th forrage: and the other to carry forrage & flour to Red Stone Creek for the Troops with Colonel Burd.*

*I Shall be Obliged to you when the Weather will permit to get Hay made in Ropes to be brought here.*

*Let me know what Quantity of flour & Baggs were left by the first Brigade of Pack Horses, which flour must not be consumed by the Garrison (unless you Should want it) But must go to Red Stone Creek: The garrison at Cumberland must be Supplied by the Contractors, who are to find Themselves the Carriages.*

*I hope you'l dispatch your necessary Reparations of Stores, and Send as soon as possible the Artificers to join their Corps.*

On the same day, Bouquet sent a letter[1104] to Colonel Burd from Bedford that states:

*I had yesterday the favour of your Letter which gave me the more Pleasure, as I meet with difficultis, and obstructions from all sides, But you never knew any where the service was concerned: The Weather is a great misfortune, and am afraid will hurt your People.*

*It was not possible to send Waggons loaded by that Road till the Rain is over; Therefore I have sent 12 Pack Horses loaded with forrage to Cumberland, to load & Send you the Horses you left behind: and I have given the following directions to Major Livingston.*

*That when the Pack Horses come from Virginia he is to Send 100 loaded with forrage to Pittsburgh and all the rest to you with flour and forrage and your artificers as Soon as possible. He has a new Waggon & 2 Horses for Express.*

*I heard last night that Hambright was detained at Lancaster for want of oats to load his fine Brigade. But I have sent an Express to hurry him to Carlisle, where I hope he can be loaded.*

*He has engaged upwards of 80 Drivers which will enable us to give you back your men.*

---

[1102] "**The Papers of Col. Henry Bouquet**", 1941.
[1103] "**The Papers of Col. Henry Bouquet**", 1940.
[1104] "**The Pennsylvania Magazine of History and Biography**", Volume 33, 1909.

*There is upwards of 50 Waggons upon the Road loaded with forrage, and I have a mind to employ the 30 new Waggons from Hambright to carry between Cumberland & Redstone Creek, The distance will be shorter, The Road they Say better and the grass certainly So; But of this I Shall be glad to have your sentiment; and to know for certain what sort of Road you will find.*

*I desired the General to Send a Batteau to meet you and reconnoitre the navigation of the Mononghehela, by which you will have a free Communication with Pittsburgh.*

*My best Compliments to Col. Shippen, M<sup>r</sup> Jones is to go to Cumberland, and to join you with the first Convoy I have advanced him money for his men.*

## Colonel Burd's forces are on the march westward of Fort Cumberland

A September 5, 1759 letter[1105] Colonel James Burd wrote to Bouquet from the *"Camp at Martines 10 miles from Fort"* states:

*I have only gott thus farr upon my march, we have had a prodigeous heavy Constant Rain for those three days past which makes it very difficult to gett our Wagons along, however you may depend no time will be lost, from Cumberland hence is hilly road & stonny & we have Crossed in this little distance I think 14 or 15 Creeks so farr as I have March'd there is not one single Bridge repaired neither can I observe any thing done on the road by M<sup>r</sup> Fenny and I am told theres very little done before me but I shall Suspend my Judgement untill I see it*

*I have lost 17 men by Desertion since I left Cumberland A great many of them old troops of the best men in my Battallion.*

*I have sent Advertisements to Virginia & Maryland & as Capt. Vanbiber is on his March from Pitsburg to Cumberland his Reinforcement will make that Garrison very strong I have desired Capt<sup>n</sup> Paris to send one Officer & twenty, or twenty five men, down the Pottomack to try if some of these fellows could not be Catch taken lurking about these Remote places*

*I shall take particular notice of this road in order that I may be able to render you a just Account of it on which you may Rely; what I have gon over I think may be made a tollerable road with a little pains, but I can't say what Inconvenience may Arrise from the Number of Creeks, I immagine they must be often impassible they are very stormy but not large, there is fine food on this road & I think Cattle & horses must raither Improve than fall away if any care is taken of them that goes by this Communication so farr I have seen*

*I have had a Vyolent fever for some days past but I'm in hopes I shall gett the better off it by the Assistance of Jesuits Bark*

*I don't know wheither I mentioned to you in my last that the Virginia Pack horses are the best we have ever had in the service but the Horse Mast<sup>r</sup> Complains very much of the badness of the sadles he says they will Ruin all their backs which will be a very great pity*

The letter contains the following postscript:

*Since writing the above I have Rece<sup>d</sup> A letter from Cap<sup>t</sup> Paris from Fort Cumberland acquainting me that he is in great distress for want of meat for his Garrison I gott 4 bullocks that had been lost from the drove that went up to Pitsburg & I sent Capt<sup>n</sup> Paris 3 of them the 4<sup>th</sup> being killed*

---

[1105] **"The Papers of Col. Henry Bouquet"**, 1941.

*This goes to Cumberland by Lieut West on his March from Pitsburg*

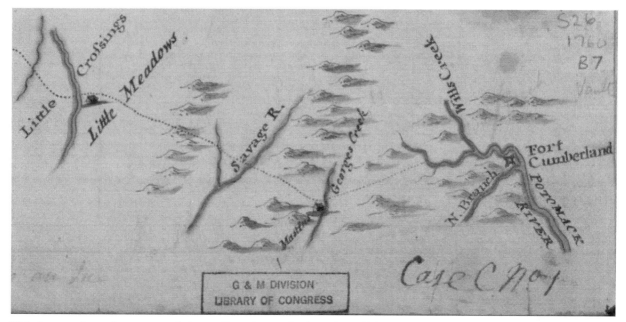

This is a portion of a manuscript map that shows the location of Martin's plantation (*"Mastlins"*), on Georges Creek, and also shows a house at the Little Crossings. A portion of the map not included here shows the location of Fort Burd, on the Monongahela River, near Redstone Creek. The presence of this fort helps to date the map.

## Rutherford commits to supplying Fort Cumberland

A September 6, 1759 letter[1106] Thomas Rutherford wrote to Bouquet from Winchester includes the statement, *"Nothing in my power Shall be wanting to assist Col° Mercer in Sending out Forrage, I have rote the Comanding officer at F. Cumberland to acqua[^l] Me when they Are in Want of Provisions & I shall Supply them."*

## Repairing Fort Cumberland, and making hay four miles below the fort

A September 6, 1759 letter[1107] Livingston wrote to Bouquet from Cumberland states:

*I rece[^d] you[^rs] with the 15 pack Horses loaded which 8 I Sent off this day that will Come up with Colo[^l] Burd this night he only left Georges Creek this morning Slow marching Since Sunday 4: oClock only: 11 miles.*

*as to the rest of the oats Shall Send part too Donaldson according to you[^r] Dirictions*

*The broken Waggon Shall be returnd but have only two horses as Colo[^l] Burd took two from the Said waggon he having lost two which render the Waggon unservicable Since as to the hay I have twisted two waggon Load for you[^r] use and as you[^r] waggons Cant Come think it may be brought one pack horses the hay up the river I Shall have a waggon road finish'd this week but Waggons must be got I'mediatly to bring it down as the river is likely to rise. I have them Still at Hay Cutting and making 4 miles below this fort as to the repairs of the fort it is been pushd one with as much precipitation as the Tools and*

---

[1106] **"The Papers of Col. Henry Bouquet"**, 1941.
[1107] **"The Papers of Col. Henry Bouquet"**, 1941.

*artificers would alow 2 Store houses Made recepetable for Provision Stores and Forrage as to any artificiers belonging to Colo^l Burd Theirs none but what belongs to the Low^r Countys vs 12 Carpenters & 1 Smith which Colo^l Burds allowance for them is a pisterin p day with an allowance of: 1: Gill of rum Gaties mowers at 3: Including their pay and 1: Gill of rum. Hay makers 1: Gill the Sawers by the feet all other Labrours a Gill of Liquor as to you^r Directions in regard to the pack horses from Virginia Shall be punctualy obeserv'd the hay Shall be all rept as Soon as possible I return only 4 Bags out of twelfe it being imposible for me to get any bags hear that would Contain Above 3 Bushels and them not fit for Service*

## The improved condition of Braddock's road

The September 27, 1759 issue of the "**Maryland Gazette**" contains an article titled, *"Williamsburg, September 7"* that includes the following:

*By the Direction of General Stanwix, and the care and Assiduity of Major Finnie, General Braddock's Road is cleared and completely finished, so that Waggons or any other carriages can go with Safety from Fort Cumberland to Pittsburg. The Advantages to this Colony have been already found to the Amount of 4000 l. for Provisions ordered for Subsistance of the Garrison there.*

*As the Communication is now opened, it is expected that the Inhabitants of this Colony will be able to supply the Army with Provisions, as the Roads are much better and nearer than from Pennsylvania. For their Encouragement, we can acquaint them, that the General has appointed Col. George Mercer, a Deputy-Quarter-Master, who will pay ready Money for all Sorts of Provisions and Forage that shall be carried to Fort Cumberland, or Red-Stone creek, where Storehouses are now building; and those who proceed to Pittsburg, will have an Allowance made them, according to the Distance: Since the Road has been opened Col. Bouquet has contracted at Fredericksburg and Augusta for large Quantities. — A very large Stone Fort is now building at Pittsburg, the Expence of which is estimated at 50,000 l.*

*A new Road is projected from Winchester to Fort Cumberland by Cresap's, which will reduce the Distance to less than 60 Miles.*

## Asking for instructions regarding deserters

A September 7, 1759 letter[1108] Captain Richard Pearis wrote to Bouquet from Fort Cumberland states:

*Last Night I Rec^d a letter from Coll. Burd wherin he mentions 17 Men being deserted from him since He left this & desires that I would send 20 or 25 Men with L^t West to Scour the woods about Potomack in order to find them if Possible I have offer'd the men to M^r West but he says it is to no purpose to go out without he goes to Susquehannah or perhaps over, therefore I think Proppor not to let the Men go so far without your Orders thereon I have therefore sent M^r West to You in order to Receive Your instructions I have just now heard from Coll. Mercer he is Expected as far as Crissops this Night I have just now sent an Officer & 20 Men to Clear the Roads as far as Ashby's Fort, have also sent another Party clearing the Road to Crissops meddow they are in great want of Axes. I hear of no Provision coming from Virginia*

## Burd reports that Braddock's road needs improvement

A letter[1109] Colonel Burd wrote to Bouquet from *"Camp at the Little Meadows, Sept. 7^th, 1759"* states:

---

[1108] "**The Papers of Col. Henry Bouquet**", 1941.
[1109] "**Letters and Papers Relating Chiefly to the Provincial History of Pennsylvania**", 1855.

*I came to this ground last night, where late in the evening I had the pleasure to receive your favors of the 4th instant. It is very lucky you did not attempt to send your wagons to Fort Cumberland, as they certainly could not get along that road; after so much rain it must be a perfect swamp. I last night received a horseload of the oats you were so good to send to Cumberland.*

*The road from my last encampment to this is really excessively bad; the Alleghany Hill is by no means the worst of it; there are two hills extremely bad and long. From Martin's place to this they esteem it eleven miles, and I think it very bad for wagons. There has been nothing done upon it by Finney. If the road is all along as I have found it hither, I think wagons can carry one-third more on the other roads than this, and with more ease to the horses; and I would strongly advise that a party from Fort Cumberland may be ordered upon this road from thence to Guest's; I'll answer[1110] from thence to the mouth of Redstone Creek, The commanding officer of the party should not hurry, but make the road good, and take time. It seems to me that Mr. Braddock was in a hurry to get along, and so did not allow time to make the road as it ought or easily could be made. It is not more than ten feet wide, and carried right up every hill almost without a turn, and the hills almost perpendicular; however, if the officer who is sent on it from Cumberland has any understanding and regard for the service, he may make it a good communication, as it is very capable of improvement; and I know I could make it a good road for the part of the country, but as it now stands it is too bad. You know Mr. Avery weighed the loads of my wagons, and they were 12 cwt. I found they could not get along even with this moderate load; and I took out about 14 cwt. and loaded upon the officers' horses, and at the hill I put six soldiers to each wagon to hoist them up. I hope to march from hence twelve miles to-day; if I make out this march I will be very happy at night.*

*I observe you have some thought of sending the three wagons this way. I hope they will do very well after the road is mended; as the hills must be turned up by winding, and not left as they are now, straight up. The stones must be thrown out of the road, all new bridges, and old ones tossed on one side, and I think the road should be widened; but this might be dispensed with.*

*I am very glad the General will find a conveyance[1111] to meet me at the Monongahela. I will immediately upon my arrival ascertain the situation of the water, and then we can proceed accordingly with the transportation from Cumberland. The weather has been very severe upon my people, and not a little so upon myself, as I have had a fever; but now we are all in good spirits and no complaints.*

### Part of the First Battalion of Pennsylvania is left at Fort Cumberland as an escort

A September 7, 1759 letter[1112] Bouquet wrote to Stanwix from Fort Bedford includes the statement:

*In Consequence of your orders of the 2ᵈ Insᵗ the first Battlⁿ of Pennsylvanias march to morrow for Ligonier. The Second consisting of 200 is gone to Redstone Creek, and part is left at Cumberland to Escort the pack Horses, and Waggons coming from Virginia as the Country people will not go without, I will Order up three of the Companies left on the Communication with Carlisle, the Three others to take care of the Roads & keep them in repair.*

### Beef and forage

A September 8, 1759 letter[1113] Stanwix wrote to Bouquet from *"Pittsbro"* includes the following:

---

[1110] He apparently means that he will be responsible for the condition of that part of the route.

[1111] In one transcript of this letter, the word is *"Battoe"*

[1112] **"The Papers of Henry Bouquet"**, Volume IV, 1978.

[1113] **"The Papers of Henry Bouquet"**, Volume IV, 1978.

*we get the 215 beeves from Cumberland but they are very small things nothing equal to what we got the other way.*

*L$^t$ Dow sends you a return of Flower & Forrage here w$^{ch}$ youl find in no proportion equal to your calculation but hope it will rise soon to it.*

*Col: Mercer's engaging to send farmers w$^{th}$ Forrage to Cumberland is right for we shall want it from all quarters*

## Fort Cumberland was under-provisioned in September of 1759

A September 8, 1759 letter[1114] Colonel George Mercer wrote to Bouquet from Winchester includes the following:

*I have altered the Prices of all the Articles except Rye 6$^d$ p Bushel. This I am in Hopes will engage the Planters to exert Themselves. I was Yesterday at the Court of this County, where I harangued Them so much that most of the principal Ones have promised to send what they have imediately to Fort Cumberland, and some will even go farther. If they comply with their Words which I have no Reason to doubt, We shall have a considerable Quantity of Forage at Cumberland by the first of October. I know Nothing of the Order to M$^r$ Rutherford concerning it, therefore had every Thing to do after the Receipt of your Lre, The Pack Horses returned unexpected, but I hope We can load Them imediately. Col$^o$ Burd writes, you ordered the second Brigade to be loaded with Forage too, but it had gone off two Days before that Letter came to Hand, and was ordered to return after leaving their Loads at Fort Cumberland, for Forage. The Col$^o$ writes also that he is much pleased with the Appearance of the Pack Horses. ...*

*I just now got a Letter from Cap$^t$ Pearis at Fort Cumberland acquainting Me they had no Provision at that Garrison. M$^r$ Rutherford had prepared it for Them in Consequence of your Order, but this is the first Notice We have had of their Wants. they shall be imediately supplied. ...*

*I shall be on the S$^o$ Branch from Sunday next till Wednesday or Thursday sending all the Forage I can get there to Cumberland or the Red Stone.*

*We go on with the Road from hence to Cumberland tolerably, considering the Number We have to work I have been up with Them twice or thrice. I was obliged to employ an old experienced Waggoner, to attend Them, & direct how they ought to be repaired, as I could not be with Them myself.*

## A letter about paying for supplies for the Indians between Cumberland and Winchester

A September 10, 1759 letter[1115] Bouquet wrote to Mercer from Bedford includes the following:

*As much as Possible engage your People to deliver their forrage at Red Stone Creek, or Pittsburgh, the rest at Cumberland. ...*

*The Certificates for Provisions given to The Indians between Cumberland & Winchester must be paid either by The Province or The Crown, Settle that Point as you will think right.*

*There has been no Occasion for Escorts for a long while, but if your People want any, There are 200 Men at Fort Cumberland, intended for that Service, and upon Your Application They will furnish any Number you may Judge Necessary for Each Convoy.*

---

[1114] **"The Papers of Col. Henry Bouquet"**, 1941.

[1115] **"The Papers of Col. Henry Bouquet"**, 1940.

## Fort Cumberland is to be supplied by contractors

A September 10, 1759 letter[1116] Bouquet wrote to Thomas Rutherford from Bedford states:

*In my Letter of the 3ᵈ August, I desired you to load the Pack Horses with flour & forrage, and it was a great disapointment to me that the last article was forgotten.*

*Col. Burd who Saw the first Brigade at Cumberland wrote me that the Horses were good, but the Horse Master complained that the Saddles were so bad that they would ruin them; You may remember how particular I was in my Instructions to you on that Subject, he have sent 300 Horses this Way by that Same fault, & unless you rectify that neglect we can expect no service of your 200.*

*I am glad you have contracted for 1000 Bushells of forrage to be delivered at Pittsburgh, I wish you could send more there.*

*Send the Sheep when they are ready; Col. Mercer will order Escorts for your Convoys from Cumberland. I shall be obliged to you to give him any assistance in your Power.*

*The Garrison of Cumberland is now 200 strong, and as that Post is to be Supplied intirely by the Contractors, you will please to charge all the Carriages for the Provisions they will want to Mᵣ Hoops, and not employ our Pack Horses for that service.*

*I write to him to Send you positive orders and money.*

*Please to Send me as soon as possible the account of the 200 Horses; I have sent a sadler to Fort Cumberland to help to repair the Sadles. I hope they will set out without delay compleatly equipped; 100 with forrage for Pittsburgh, the rest (one half loaded With forrage, the other half with flour) for Red Stone Creek; The Whole are to continue afterwards to carry between that & Cumberland, allowing them proper Rest.*

## Instructions for the commander at Fort Cumberland

September 10, 1759 instructions[1117] sent from Fort Bedford to Captain Woodward, commanding officer at Fort Cumberland, state:

*In Answer to a Letter of this Day's Date to Colonel Bouquet, I am desired to inform you that Mᵣ Rutherford being acquainted with the Scarcity of Provisions at Fort Cumberlᵈ will immidiately Supply that Garrison, it is Pity he was not informed of your Stock some time before it was so low.*

*I am Surpriz'd you could not get a Horse to Send with the Express, two went from hence, to be Stationed at Fort Cumberland for that purpose.*

*The two Hundred Pack Horses carrying from Winchester to Your Garrison are to be disposed of in the following manner.*

*The first 100, loaded with Forrage, are to proceed to Pittsburgh, under Escort of an Officer & twenty Men of your Garrison (none of them to be of Colˡ Burd's Battaalion) Pennsylvanians)*

*The Second 100 partly loaded with Forrage & partly Flour, to go to Redstone Creek Escorted by Captⁿ Pearis & his Company*

---

[1116] **"The Papers of Col. Henry Bouquet"**, 1940.
[1117] **"The Papers of Col. Henry Bouquet"**, 1940.

*The Bullocks also coming from Winchester to be forwarded to Pittsburgh and Escorted by an Officer & 25 Men.*

*And as Lieu$^t$ Jones of the 2$^d$ Batt. Pennsylvania, is to join his Corps at Red Stone Creek, with his Party of 25 Men, you will Order him with the next Convoy that goes that Road, after Capt$^n$ Pearis.*

*In general you are to furnish Small Escorts to any Considerable Convoy going either to Pittsburgh or Redstone Creek, in Case they apply for it, or you Judge it necessary*

*Any Application from Liut$^t$ Col$^l$ George Mercer, for Men to Escort Convoys, or any Duty relating to the Service, is to be Complied w$^{th}$*

*When the Pack Horses return from Pittsburgh or Red Stone Creek, They are to be put into Pasture to recruit, and allowed a reasonable time to get Strength, and in that time the Saddles, Baggs, &c are to be refitted, the Horses Shod and every thing prepared for their next Trips,*

*And their loads to be either flour or forrage, every Bag to be weighed, and not to exceed 150, or 160, according to the strength of the Horses, who are for the rest of the Campaigne, to Carry to Red Stone Creek only.*

*And in Case you should be relieved, this is to be delivered to the Commanding Officer that Succeeds you, for his Instruction.*

*P. S. You will from time to time inform M$^r$ Rutherford of the Strength of your Garrison, and the Quantity of provisions in Store before you find your Magazine too low.*

*As soon as you have a Sufficiency of Forrage, you will Order 6 Quarts of Oats per Day to the Horses under the Care of Donnaldson, and have an Eye over them.*

## Burd identifies the location of Braddock's grave

Two of Col. J. Burd's 1759 journal entries[1118] state:

*10 Sept. Saw Col. Washington's fort, which was called Fort Necessity. It is a small circular stockade, with a small house in the centre; on the outside there is a small ditch goes round it about 8 yards from the stockade. It is situate in a narrow part of the meadows commanded by three points of woods. There is a small run of water just by it. We saw two iron swivels.*

*11 Sept. Marched this morning; 2 miles from hence we found Gen. Braddock's grave, about 20 yards from a little hollow in which there was a small stream of water, and over it a bridge. We soon got to Laurel hill; it had an easy ascent on this side, but on the other side very steep. At the foot of the hill we found the path that went to Dunlop's place, that Col. Shippen and Capt. Gordon travelled last winter, and about a quarter of a mile from this we saw the big rock so called. From hence we marched to Dunbar's camp, — miles, which is situated in a very stony hollow, surrounded by hills, and commanded on all sides; the worst chosen piece of ground for an encampment I ever saw. Here we saw vast quantities of cannon-ball, musket bullets, broken shells, and immense destruction of powder, wagons, &c. Reconnoitred all the camp, and attempted to find the cannon and mortars, but could not discover them, although we dug a great many holes, where stores had been buried, and concluded the French had carried them off. We continued our march and got to Guest's place; here we found a fine country.*

---

[1118] **"Historical Collections of the State of Pennsylvania"**, Sherman Day, 1843.

### Blythe will be assigned to Cumberland

A September 11, 1759 letter[1119] Bouquet wrote to Stanwix from Fort Bedford includes the following:

*The remainder of the 2ᵈ Pennsylvᵃ Battalⁿ being only 180, are all gone to Red Stone Creek having left part of them at Cumberland to escort. ...*

*Cumberland being now a place of great resort we must Send a Deputy Commissary there, and I will Station also Mʳ Blythe from Fort Loudoun at that Post to take care of the forrage, and to load & direct the Virgᵃ Pack Horses. ...*

### Rutherford is to supply Fort Cumberland

A September 11, 1759 letter[1120] Bouquet wrote to Adam Hoops from Bedford includes the following statement regarding Rutherford, *"Please also to Send him Orders to Supply The Garrison of Fort Cumberland, where we have now 200 Men; you know that Post is to be Supplied by the Contractors Carriage & all."*

### The William Ross will is probated

On September 11, 1759 William Ross's will[1121] was in probate in the Hampshire County, Virginia Court, with Arminella Ross serving as the executrix.

### Reaching the Great Meadows on the return trip from Pittsburgh

Kenny's September 12, 1759 journal entry[1122] states, *"This day we stop'd by yᵉ Great Meadows & I followed yᵉ King's wagons."*

### Hoops instructs Walker about supplying Fort Cumberland

A September 13, 1759 letter[1123] Sinclair wrote to Bouquet from Carlisle includes the statement, *"Mʳ Hoops desires me to inform you, he has given Instructions to Mʳ Walker about supplying the Garrison at Fort Cumberland, and that 500 of the Sheep you ordered are ready to send off."*

### Cattle were sent to Fort Cumberland

A September 13, 1759 letter[1124] Mercer wrote to Bouquet from Fort Pleasant includes the following:

*I have been here three Days, and do not know that I ever was more perplexed, the People have been so hard to please. I have been to every little Fort, and Plantation for 10 or 15 Miles round. The Inhabitants have at last consented to exert Themselves and I shall have more than 1000 or 1500 Bushels of Forage out at Red Stone so soon as their Horses return from Pitsburg, wᶜʰ will be in 8 or 10 Days. I was obliged in Order to effect this to give a Price for it delivered here, as I found by riding about that many had perhaps 6 or 8 Bushels only, which it was not worth their while to carry all the Way to Fort Cumberland. I have contracted with Persons to carry any Quantity, up to Red Stone, under 4000 Bushels, that may be*

---

[1119] **"The Papers of Col. Henry Bouquet"**, 1941.

[1120] **"The Papers of Col. Henry Bouquet"**, 1941.

[1121] **"Colonial Records of the Upper Potomac"**, Volume 6,

[1122] **"The Pennsylvania Magazine of History and Biography"**, Volume 37, 1913.

[1123] **"The Papers of Henry Bouquet"**, Volume IV, 1978.

[1124] **"The Papers of Col. Henry Bouquet"**, 1941.

*delivered, here; so that this Scheme will both forward the Service and oblige every one who has even 2 Bushels of Forage to sell. I have given an extraordinary Price too here, the it saves Money to the Crown, for as I allowed 4/ p Bushel for Oats delivered at Cumberland, and found it woud not suit many to do that I made a Price for it delivered here — 2/6 p Bushel and allow; 22/ C<sup>t</sup> Carriage to Red Stone from hence which pleases them all very much, and saves Money to the Public 1/3 p c<sup>t</sup> for I calculate 3 ½ Bushels of Oats to weigh 102 lb it woud cost delivered at Cumberland 14/ here its delivered for 8/9. the Difference is then 5/3 which added to the 18/ allowed for Carriage from Fort Cumberland makes 23/3 and I only give 22/. I am certain this Scheme will bring Us some Forage.*

*Tis absolutely necessary to have a Scow on the Potomack but I will still strive to find out one of the old Ones. Maj<sup>r</sup> Livingston writes Me Col<sup>o</sup> Burd's Ship Carpenter was sent from Fort Cumberland the 3<sup>d</sup> Instant, & as I have heard nothing of him yet, suppose he has deserted.*

*I have sent 12 Cattle to Fort Cumberland, and will take Care to have a separate Account kept for that Garrison. 12 more shall be sent to Col<sup>o</sup> Burd imediately. Maj<sup>r</sup> Livingston has wrote Me he has sent him eight Horses loaded with Forage. The rest shall be loaded as you direct...*

## Bouquet writes about supplies for Burd, and the lack of tools to repair Braddock's road

A September 13, 1759 letter[1125] Bouquet wrote to Colonel Burd states:

*Fort Bedford 13<sup>th</sup> September 1759*

*Dear Sir,*

*I received your favours of the 5th & 7<sup>th</sup> Instant and hope you have got to your ground by this time, The weather having been remarkably fine.*

*I wrote to Cumberland to send you flour & forrage, by the first Pack Horses from Virginia, but wish you had taken more with you. Col. Mercer is desired to send you 12 Beeves, Capt. Woodward is to inform you by express of the time those supplies will set off from Cumberland.*

*Had we Tools and proper People to employ, the reparation of Braddocks Road would be very necessary; for want of those two things, I am afraid we shall do nothing Cap<sup>t</sup> Pearis has orders to join you with his Company, taking the Pack Horses under his Escort, and Lieut. Jones is to follow with the next Convoy to you.*

*We have had an account from St. Lawrence that Gen'l Wolff attacked the lines the 31<sup>st</sup> July with all the Granadiers & 200 R. A. but was repulsed with loss of 400 men partly wounded. People begin to think that he will not succeed, But will ruin the Country in his Retreat. I hope better, he has beat the Canadians & Indians everywhere, killed great numbers, & got 500 Prisoners.*

*No news from Europe, Callendar is arrived with his new Horses, But Hambright is yet at Lancaster.*

*I am my Dear Sir*

*Your most obed<sup>t</sup> hble serv<sup>t</sup>*

*Henry Bouquet*

*Col. Armstrong marched with his Batt<sup>n</sup> the 8<sup>th</sup> for Ligonier.*

---

[1125] **"The Pennsylvania Magazine of History and Biography"**, Volume 33, 1909.

*For fear of exposing you to want, if the Pack Horses should not return in time from Winchester, I send orders to Capt Woodward to send you directly ten of Donaldson's Horses with 150ʷ of flour each and six Beeves under an Escort of a Lieut. & 16 men and as soon as the Pack Horses arrive to order 36 to proceed to you with____ & 18 with forrage, the rest to go to Pittsburgh.*

*H.B.*

### Reaching the Great Crossing on the return trip from Pittsburgh

Kenny's September 13, 1759 journal entry[1126] states:

*Came to yᵉ Upper Crossing of Youghʸ yᵉ wagoners insisting that their teams would not be able to hold out to yᵉ next good pasture, which is by little Youghʸ, I agreed to tary here tomorrow, it being good pasture & hunting ground.*

### Meeting people from the South Branch at the upper crossing of the Youghiogheny River

Kenny's September 14, 1759 journal entry, written from the upper crossing of the Youghiogheny River on his return trip from Pittsburgh, states:

*We lay by here today & being a fine one I opened such of yᵉ skins as I judged wanted air, uncovering yᵉ wagons & turning yᵉ rest of yᵉ bundles to yᵉ Sun, promising yᵉ wagoners a quart of Rum at Cumberland if I could get any there for helping me. yᵉ South Branch of Pottomock people are in droves along yᵉ road, going to Pittsburgh, some with flour & some with corn oats butter cheese &c. The day I overtook yᵉ wagons, I met Col. Burdᵃ of Pennᵃ & a party with wagons & pack-horses going to yᵉ mouth of Redstone Creek to build some storehouses, in order to have yᵉ carriage on this road to go from thence down yᵉ Monongahela to Pittsburgh, old Cressap being their pilot. Here came one Sthalmaker, going out with flour from yᵉ Branch to whom my deceased friend Samuel Lightfoot had lent his old Horse & 20s. of Cash last winter. The man came to me & owned both,[1127] but had neither at present, so I ordered him to pay yᵉ money to & leave yᵉ horse with Wᵐ Joliff, near Winchester. Derr that was lost with us in yᵉ woods, lost his pocket book a little way from here this morning as he set along yᵉ road & being found by Sthalmaker he delivered it to me to keep for Derr, having 32/6ᵈ of Cash in & many papers that I did not look into; next night he lost his horse. I let yᵉ wagoners have 1 quart Rum bought on yᵉ road, cost 5/.*

This letter indicates that farming continued on the South Branch in 1759.

### Hoops promises that Fort Cumberland will be kept supplied

A September 15, 1759 letter[1128] Adam Hoops sent to Bouquet from Carlisle includes the following:

*I am favour'd with yours of the 11ᵗʰ Currᵗ I have order'd Mʳ Rutherford to keep the Garison at Fort Cumberland well Supplyed, and to observe any Instructions he may receive from you relative to the purchasing of Beeves Sheep &cᵃ & that I should furnish him with money for those uses I shall not commission him to buy any more Beeves as we Will be able to supply you with a Sufficient Number of Pennsylvania Cattle.*

*As I am sure yᵉ sheep from Rutherford will goe by Fort Cumberland, If you think it Necessary that any of them should be sent to Bedford Juniata & those other Small Posts, the best way would be to acquaint the*

---

[1126] "**The Pennsylvania Magazine of History and Biography**", Volume 37, 1913.
[1127] Acknowledged both debts.
[1128] "**The Papers of Col. Henry Bouquet**", 1941.

*Command$^r$ Officer at Fort Cumberland of the Number to be Sent forward to Pittsburgh that Load, & the Residue as you please to dispose of them.*

## Meeting a civilian on the road, delivering liquor to Redstone

Kenny's September 15, 1759 journal entry[1129] states, *"We came to the little Yough$^y$ met a man going with liquor to Redstone, also a small party of soldiers with some bullocks."*

## A request to send invalids to Fort Cumberland

A September 16, 1759 letter[1130] Colonel Adam Stephen wrote to Bouquet from Ligonier includes the statement, *"I have Sent down some Invalids to the General Hospital and will be obligd to you to have them ordered for Fort Cumberland, to be sent from that to Winchester, as soon as they are refreshed a little."*

## Stanwix wants to talk to Bouquet about repairing Fort Cumberland

A September 16, 1759 letter[1131] General John Stanwix wrote to Bouquet from Pittsburgh includes the following, *"Your ordering Commissary read to come to Bedford is quite right & to appoint one at Cumberland, want to talk with you about repairing that Fort at least the Store rooms w$^{ch}$ I am told are not bad."*

## Reaching Georges Creek, with little food left

Kenny's September 16, 1759 journal entry[1132] states, *"We came to George's Creek within about 12 miles of Cumberland. It rained y$^e$ most of y$^e$ way. I only brought about 5 lb. bread from Pittsburgh & two Neats Tongues, which were exhausted by y$^e$ time I over took y$^e$ wagons."*

## Smallpox at Fort Cumberland in September 1759

Kenny's September 17, 1759 journal entry states, *"It rained most of y$^e$ night, but had a good day & came into Cumberland; got y$^e$ skins unloaded into a store without lock or key, having no other to get, y$^e$ house we had before, being a Hospital for y$^e$ smallpox y$^e$ Store House is ye Ordinance Store under y$^e$ care of Major Livingstone."*

## Woodward is commanding at Fort Cumberland

A synopsis of a September 18, 1759 letter written from Bedford states, *"Instructions to Captain Woodward, commanding at Fort Cumberland."*

## One of Kenny's horses has been impressed into the King's service

Kenny's September 18, 1759 journal entry[1133] states:

*Being a fine day I had most of y$^e$ skins opened & those that were not in need of opening had y$^e$ bundles out to air, y$^e$ skirts of some being wet with y$^e$ rain & many wet in y$^e$ foldings, which needed to be sun'd,*

---

[1129] **"The Pennsylvania Magazine of History and Biography"**, Volume 37, 1913.

[1130] **"The Papers of Col. Henry Bouquet"**, 1941.

[1131] **"The Papers of Henry Bouquet"**, Volume VI, 1978.

[1132] **"The Pennsylvania Magazine of History and Biography"**, Volume 37, 1913.

[1133] **"The Pennsylvania Magazine of History and Biography"**, Volume 37, 1913.

*so Capt. Woodward command', let me have four Camp Color men[1134] to help. Employed Adam M'Carty & Jn° Slater to make y° skins up into bundles. The horse that was left here of ours is sent to Bedford & entered into y° King's service.*

### Mercer is short on cash for supplies

A September 19, 1759 letter[1135] Mercer wrote to Stanwix from Winchester includes the statement, *"I stand engaged for more Money than I have now on Hand for Forage and Carriage, besides the Necessaries I am obliged to procure for the Store Houses &c at Monongahela & Cumberland by Col° Bouquets Order, and Forage is daily coming in."*

### Paying for biscuits with rum

Kenny's September 19, 1759 journal entry[1136] states:

*Began at y° opening & worming such bundles as were not opened yesterday, & making up fit for wagon carriage. I was obliged to give y° wagoners 1 quart Rum for letting me have bisquet on y° road, my provisions being out.*

### Making up loads for the packhorses

Kenny's September 20, 1759 journal entry[1137] states, *"Came Jn° Trotter about noon to help to make y° skins up & Jn° Mickle with two hands more & 12 horses, so we got loads made ready for them."*

### The Virginia packhorses leave supplies for Fort Bedford at Fort Cumberland

A September 21, 1759 letter[1138] Bouquet wrote to General Stanwix from Fort Bedford includes the following:

*I have been equally disappointed by the Virg° Pack Horses, which being loaded the first Trip with very coarse Meal, in lieu of flour lefft their Loads at Cumberland for the subsistance of the Garrison; The Contractors having neglected to send any Provisions to that Post, which they are to Supply at their own Expence. These Pack Horses having been sent back to load Forrage at Winchester, are not yet Returned, but will be I hope on the Road, Tho' it is not possible in the present Condition of our Waggons to form a Magazine at Pittsburgh.*

*We have Carriages enough, to Subsist the Troops there during the Campaign, and lay in Six Months provisions for a Thousand Men.*

*We Shall have fifty compleat new Waggons in the service and when they are wore out, The 100 Waggon Horses, we have here and at Cumberland will be able again to go up;*

---

[1134] William Duane's 1810 book, **A Military Dictionary...**" gives the following definition: *"Camp-Color Men Soldiers under the immediate command and direction of the quarter-master of a regiment. Their business is to assist in marking out the lines of an encampment, &c. to carry the camp colors to the field on days of exercise, and fix them occasionally for the purpose of enabling the troops to take up correct points in marching, &c. So that in this respect they frequently, indeed almost always, act as guides, or what the French call Jalonneurs. They are likewise employed in the trenches, and in all fatigue duties."*

[1135] **"The Papers of Henry Bouquet"**, Volume VI, 1978.

[1136] **"The Pennsylvania Magazine of History and Biography"**, Volume 37, 1913.

[1137] **"The Pennsylvania Magazine of History and Biography"**, Volume 37, 1913.

[1138] **"The Papers of Henry Bouquet"**, Volume VI, 1978.

*The immense Number of Waggons employed for Tools, Implem[ts] Hospitals Cloathing and Baggage have retarded the Provisions which I hope for the future will be the only Article to carry.*

## If possible, send flour, not meal

A September 21, 1759 letter[1139] Bouquet sent to George Mercer from Bedford includes the following:

*I desire that <u>Flour</u> and not <u>Meal</u> be Sent to Pittsburgh, and Redstone Creek: and such is the Contract with if Ramsay, But by the Return from Cumberland it seems that the Pack Horses were loaded with <u>Meal</u>; (having just now inquired of the Commissary, he Says it was <u>Coarse Meal</u>) If <u>Flour</u> cannot be had, in that Case we must take what we can get, rather than to loose the Short remainder of the Season.*

*As we have no other Carriage to depend upon but the 200 Pack Horses, I beg you will not receive at Fort Cumberland, much more flour or forrage, than you judge you can get Carriages for this Year, as a Magazine there would be of no use.*

*I Send to that Fort Lieu[t] Blythe of the Pennsylv[a] Reg[t] an Industrious, intelligent, and Active Man, to whom you will please to direct every thing and give your Orders to forward you Convoys.*

*The General begins to be Impatient reciving nothing from your Frontiers, I hope they will soon Answer his expectation.*

*You will please to Aply to the Commanding Officer at Cumberland for Escorts to M[r] Ramsay & M[r] Graham's Convoys, as we promised to them tho' it is now unnecessary, but we must not be deficient in any respect.*

*I Should be glad to receive M[r] Rutherford's Account of the Pack horses, and Know the Number of Beeves bought by M[r] Graham, which I hope are gone to Pittsburgh: You will remember that the Garrison at Cumberland and Col: Burd's 200 Men at Redstone Creek, are to be Supplied from Virginia.*

## A livestock-related update

A September 22, 1759 letter[1140] Captain Woodward wrote to Bouquet from Fort Cumberland states:

*I have just rec[d] thirty nine horses, thirty nine baggs, And thirty eight Pack saddles. the Saddles are much out of order & upon Enquiry, I find the Saddler has nothing to repair them with, I have therefore sent them that he may supply himself. the Drivers complain much of being out Longer from home than they were informd they shoud be, & that they are in want of every Necessary, besides their horses having sore backs, &. much fatigu[d] which is indeed very true. however I have orderd them to a Pasture, till farther Orders. A man just now came here to inform Me that 113 sheep were upon the road and twenty horses loaded with flour. the sheep and horses are now at Coll[o] Cressaps where they wait for Orders but as two hund[d] horses are expected from Winchester in two or three days at farthest: If You think proper they had better stay there that the whole may go up together.*

## Burd mentions Nemacolin's creek, near present-day Brownsville

According to Volume 2 of the 1896 book **"The frontier forts of western Pennsylvania"**, Burd's September 22, 1759 journal entry states:

---

[1139] **"The Papers of Col. Henry Bouquet"**, 1940.

[1140] **"The Papers of Col. Henry Bouquet"**, 1941.

*This morning I went the River Monongahela, reconnoitered Redstone, &c, and concluded upon the place for the post,[1141] being a hill in the fork of the River Monongahela and Nemocollin's Creek, the best situation I could find, and returned in the evening to the camp.*

This letter helps to document the fact that Nemacolin lived near Brownsville long enough for a creek to be, at least temporarily, named for him.

## Making plans for the first half of 1760

A September 22, 1759 letter[1142] Bouquet wrote to Adam Hoops from Bedford includes the following statement:

*You may Now take your Measures to purchase in proper time a Sufficient Quantity of large Pennsylv<sup>a</sup> Beeves and Virg<sup>a</sup> Hogs to Salt at Pittsburgh, Ligonier, Cumberland &c<sup>t</sup> for the Winter Stock.*

*You may Suppose the Garrison at Pittsburgh to consist of thirteen hundred Men, two hundred & fifty at Ligonier, one hundred at Cumberland, as many at Bedford, besides 25 at Redstone Creek upon the Mononghehela*

*They must have Provisions to the 1<sup>st</sup> of July 1760*

*The General has given the Necessary Orders for the building of Vatts, and Barrells for the Salt Meat*

## Paying Livingston for wagon transportation

Kenny's September 22, 1759 journal entry[1143] from Fort Cumberland states:

*Finished bundling & weighing y<sup>e</sup> skins, y<sup>e</sup> whole weight being 39<sup>lb</sup> less here than at Pittsburgh, weighing there 9025<sup>lb</sup>, & here 8986<sup>lb</sup>. I paid Major Livingstone & Capt Battle y<sup>e</sup> sum of £115. 9. 8. for y<sup>e</sup> carriage here stoping 20/ for y<sup>e</sup> carriage of 11 Bearskins being rotten.*

Kenny's September 23, 1759 journal entry states:

*I set off to seek for wagons, and came that night to Piersalls Fort, on y<sup>e</sup> South Branch of Pottomack, where I heard that Richard Vernon failed in getting me wagons. I was well satisfied for I expect to get them cheaper myself — I stayed here this night.*

Here we temporarily part ways with Kenny until he heads back toward Fort Cumberland.

## A reference to contractors supplying Fort Cumberland

A September 24, 1759 letter[1144] Stanwix wrote to Bouquet from Pittsburgh includes the statement, *"tis true the Contractors should supply Fort Cumberland but they will still depend on us."*

---

[1141] The site of the fort is believed to be at or near Nemacolin Castle, in Brownsville.
[1142] **"The Papers of Col. Henry Bouquet"**, 1941.
[1143] **"The Pennsylvania Magazine of History and Biography"**, Volume 37, 1913.
[1144] **"The Papers of Henry Bouquet"**, Volume IV, 1978.

## Burd camps at the mouth of Nemacolin's Creek

A letter[1145] that Burd sent to Bouquet is addressed, *"Camp at the mouth of Nemocallings Creek on the Manongehelo one mile above the mouth of Redstone Creek 25ᵗʰ Septem. 1759"*. It includes the statement, *"I ... believe the People in Virginia intends to Starve me and all my People I have been these three days past on Allowance of half a pound of flour p man officers & soldiers and at this allowance I have but two days more I can't Conceive the meaning of this, if they can't supply my small detauchment surely they put us to unesessary trouble in oppening This Communication, the flour last sent me was scandalously spoilt some of it could not be eat, it takes two of the bullocks to Weight one of those I brought from Bedford. I have just eight bullocks left."*

## Fort Cumberland needs medicine

A September 25, 1759 letter[1146] Captain Woodward wrote to Bouquet from Fort Cumberland states:

*I receivd Your Favor by Lieuᵗ Blyth, and think myself extreamly happy in meeting with Your Approbation for what I have done. You may Depend Sir, upon My Utmost and constant Endeavors in persevering to do evry thing which shall be conducive to his Majestys Service Pr Your Desires. the two hundᵈ pack-horses are not Yet Arrived, tho I momently expect them, they shall be divided And Escorted conformable to Your Orders.*

*The Doctor (who .is the Bearer of this) waits upon You, to inform You of the State of His Sick, and Medicines, at this Place. the Latter he is almost out of, & the former are daily increasing. If You Sir judge it proper to order Dʳ Bass to let him have a few Medicines it woud be of Infinite Service to this Garrison.*

## The road from Cumberland to Red Stone is in bad order

A synopsis[1147] of a September 27, 1759 letter William Ramsay wrote to Bouquet from Winchester includes the statement, *"That he is using his best endeavours to get flour forwarded, but the dry weather delays the grinding. Hopes in four or five days to send off 60,000 or 70,000 weight. Is told that the road from Cumberland to Red Stone Creek is in bad order, &c."* The portion of the letter[1148] concerning the road states, *"I am inform'd little or nothing has been done to the road from Cumberland to Redstone Creek & that it is in bad order, besides where the Flour is now to be deliver'd, is ten Miles further than the place first intended, this makes a very considerable odds in the Waggonage by burthening a hard contract, as I am now convinc'd this is..."*

## Assurance of providing supplies for Burd's garrison and Fort Cumberland

A synopsis of a September 28, 1759 letter Mercer wrote to Bouquet from Winchester includes the statement:

*Shall take care to supply Burd's garrison at Fort Cumberland, but William Hoops changes his orders so often that it is impossible to guess what is to be done, and details are given to show his variable orders. The dry weather, as stated by Ramsay, prevents the grinding of flour. The quality and quantity of flour that Ramsay will send.*

The parts of this extremely long letter[1149] that relate to Fort Cumberland state:

---

[1145] "**The Papers of Col. Henry Bouquet**", 1941.

[1146] "**The Papers of Col. Henry Bouquet**", 1941.

[1147] "**Sessional Papers of the Dominion of Canada**", Volume 23, 1890.

[1148] "**The Papers of Col. Henry Bouquet**", 1941.

[1149] "**The Papers of Col. Henry Bouquet**", 1941.

*I shall take Care to supply Col° Burd, & the Garrison at Cumberland properly; tho M$^r$ Hoops changes his Orders so often, that I am obliged to do every Thing myself, as it is impossible for anyone to guess what he ought to do, where he is concerned...*

*I mentioned, to M$^r$ Ramsay, the Complaint of the Comissary at Cumb$^d$ and he has assured Me, his Flour shall be as good, as ever was, or can be made, in Virginia. I had before warned him of it, upon receiving a Letter from Major Livingston, which informed Me of the Inspectors Report, and he writes, at the same Time, that neither Officer or Soldier in that Garrison, had ever complained of it. I have taken some Pains, to examine it here in Bread, as I am not a Judge of the Looks of it, and it really makes as good, white, sweet, and light Bread, as ever I saw eat in any Camp. ...*

*I shall take Care Sir, not to Lay in too large a Magazine of Forage at Cumberland. They are sending out from the Branch but that is to go all the Way to Red Stone. ...*

*The Indian Goods I mentioned to you were sent off, but the Waggon I hear is broke between this and Cumberland, which will delay Them some Time longer. ...*

*I cant get Flour or Forage from Maryland delivered at Cumberland even. You see by the inclused from Mr Gary a principal Merchant there, the Reason why the latter cant be purchased; and I am assured by one Williams an active industrious Gent in that Province, that they get 30/ p Cent for their Flour delivered at Bedford, which is not above 15 or 20 miles farther than Cumberland from Them. Indeed I am told they will take that Rout, as soon as the cold Weather sets in, which they know will destroy their Roads, more than ours.*

*A Person in Augusta offered Me 60 Pack Horses, but tho I had no Authority to buy Them, I have endeavored to make them as useful as possible to the Service; and have engaged him to load them with Oats from his own House, & drive Them thro the Woods to Cumberland. He woud not go farther with them, as he intends, if I do not buy Them, to carry Then to Pennsylv$^a$ for Sale, and it will not be much out of his Way, to call at Cumberland. They will set out the 10$^{th}$ Day of October, & will be at Cumberland by the 20$^{th}$ at farthest, with 300 Bushels of Oats. So soon as they set out, he will come by this Town himself, to receive my Answer. He says the Horses are very fit for the Service, and that he can make Them up 100 in six or eight Days Notice. ...*

*I have been in the Country these four or five Days past, for Beeves &c for Col° Burd, & Cumberland, and did not receive your Letters till my Return Yesterday. I shall have 100 good Beeves at Cumberland by the 10$^{th}$ of next Month, for Col° Burd & that Garrison. ...*

## Juggling horses, assuaging bruised feelings

A September 29, 1759 letter[1150] Bouquet wrote to Captain Woodward from Bedford states:

*I am Sorry Cap$^t$ Ourry's Letter of the 27$^{th}$ did give you any uneasiness, it was not his Intention nor mine, being fully Satisfied of your Conduct in every Respect.*

*You have misunderstood that Letter; I meant that Cap$^t$ Pearis Should have marched with the first Convoy, that is with the 15 Waggon Horses, & Beeves sent to Col. Burd, as his Compny was wanted there, and not L$^t$ Jones who was ordered to march after him, and finding upon my last another pretense for not marching himself, I thought it time to end those delays, in ordering Capt Pearis[1151]*

---

[1150] "**The Papers of Col. Henry Bouquet**", 1940 and "**The Papers of Henry Bouquet**", Volume IV, 1978.

[1151] There is a great deal of fairly angry material stricken out in the letter after this, which is not included here.

*Please to desire M[r] Blyth to send us to morrow all the Waggon Horses you have at Pasture; and if Col Burd sends back the fifteen you sent him They are to be Kept in the best Pasture till further directions are sent about them.*

*Donaldson and his drivers are to come with the said Horses, and if they want assistance you will please to give them some men to help in driving the Horses.*

*They must have some forrage with them and their saddles, saggins &[c.]*

## Burd's letter mentions Nemacolin's Creek, and the desperate lack of food at Redstone

James Burd wrote a letter[1152] to General Stanwix that is dated *"Camp at the mouth of Nemoraling's Creek, on the Monongahela, about one mile above the mouth of Redstone Creek, Sept. 30th, 1759"* that states:

*I have cut the road from Guest's, and came to this ground the twenty-third inst. I would have wrote your excellency ere now, but have been hourly expecting the arrival of a batteau at Pittsburgh. I think this will be a very fine post, it is situated upon a hill in the fork of the river and creek, commands both, and is not commanded by anything; the hill is almost fifty yards from the river, and joins the creek. I have kept the people constantly employed on the works[1153] since my arrival, although we have been for eight days past upon the small allowance of one pound of beef and half a pound of flour per man a day, and this day we begin upon one pound of beef, not having one ounce of flour left, and only three bullocks, I am therefore obliged to give over working till I receive some supplies. I have expected Captain Pearis with a quantity of provisions for some time, and know nothing of the reason of the delay. I wrote five days ago on this subject, and shall find an express to Cumberland this day. I shall measure the road from Guest's thither, and make a return of it; I compute the distance seven miles. Enclosed is a return of the troops under my command.*

Burd sent a somewhat similar letter to Bouquet the same day. Burd was in the process of building a fort that became known as Burd's fort. Volume XII, page 347, of the **"Pennsylvania Archives"** (1856) mentions this letter, then states, *"Nemoralling's Creek above mentioned or Nemocalling's Creek as it is called in the Pioneer,[1154] is now Dunlap's Creek, and empties into the Red Stone."* Dunlap Creek actually empties directly into the Monongahela River at Brownsville.

Burd's September 30, 1759 letter[1155] to Bouquet, written from the *"Camp at Monongehela"*, states:

*I wrote you the 25th Curr[t] since which I have not been favour'd with any from you*

*I am sorry to be under the Nesessity of inform[g] you of my want of Provisions, the Troops here have been for eight days past, upon the allowance of One pound of Beaff and half a pound of flour, & this day we begin the allowance of One pound of Beaff, Only, not having one ounce of flour left, & but three Bullocks; I know nothing of any Supplys being on the road not having heard from Cumberland since the 14th Curr[t], I can't Conceive what is become of Capt[n] Paris, I have this day wrote to Capt[n] Woodward upon this subject*

[1152] **"Letters and Papers Relating Chiefly to the Provincial History of Pennsylvania"**, 1855.
[1153] Colonel Joseph Shippen described Fort Burd as follows, *"The curtain 97-1/2 feet, the flank 16, the faces of the Bastions 30 feet, a ditch between the bastions 24 feet wide and opposite the faces 12 feet, the log house for a magazine and to contain the women and children 39 feet square, a gate 6 feet wide and 8 high, and a drawbridge…"*
[1154] Volume 2, page 60, **"The American Pioneer: A Monthly Periodical…"**, 1843.
[1155] **"The Papers of Col. Henry Bouquet"**, 1941.

*I have keep't the People Constantly upon the works Since my Arrivall, but now I am obliged to give over working, very much Contrary to my Inclination you will believe, but I hope I will soon Receive supplys; at present I have but five days as the allowance of One pound of Beaff*

*No Battoes Arrived here yet, I send to Pitsburg this day*

## Beef cattle to be sent to Fort Cumberland

A September 30, 1759 letter[1156] Thomas Rutherford wrote to Bouquet from Winchester includes the statement, *"I shall send from here the 6th of next Month 100 Beeves for Fort Cumberland, and the Mouth of Red Stone Creek"*.

## Fort Cumberland fails to supply Burd's forces

A September 30, 1759 letter[1157] Bouquet wrote to Burd from Bedford states:

*Your letter of the 25th received last night surprised & vexed me beyond Expression; after giving such strict charge to Lt. Col. Mercer to subsist you & repeated orders to the Commanding officer at Cumberland to forward Provisions with the utmost diligence, Could I imagine that they would let you starve? It is hard to have nobody to depend upon; Those Pack Horses you sent back to be loaded with forrage are not come back yet; and that was the Province to subsist the whole army.*

*I hope your Beeves have saved your Lives, with what Deers you could kill, till the Convoy gone from Cumberland reaches you: There is 41 Waggons from Winchester loaded with flour, and the Pack Horses going to your Post; I wish you had sent to Pittsburgh for supplies, it would have been easier. I had beg'd of the Genl. to send a Battoe to meet you, But with other Things was forgotten. I am sorry to my Soul of your cruel situation, reproaching myself to have trusted to any Body but myself the Care of your subsistence, But I did not then expect to have been so long detained here.*

*Hambright's Brigade arrived at last yesterday with at least 20 Horses lost & 9 Drivers. They will require 3 or four days rest, & when I see them on their Way forward, I shall proceed myself to Pittsburgh.*

*Ourry sends you the things you want which we were obliged to get done in a hurry not to detain this Express. I hope the nails & other things from Winchester will be sent to you. But to make sure you could write for some to Cap Gordon and replace them to him, when you arrive. You will have oats for your Horses, If you find the River navigable, Please to write to the General to send you the Battoes to take what flour and salt will come to you.*

*I am glad you could find such a pretty situation for your Post. Give it a shorter name than the wild one of the Creek.*

*If I don't go to Niagara (as I hear I am ordered by Gen. A) I will pay you a visit, if you have not joined us when I am at Pittsburgh*

*Provost Smith is expected at Philad^a having defeated the Philistins compleatly*

*There is some Church Squabble stirred up by one M'clanigan, supported by Mr Rob & Party. No better news from Quebec. It is generally expected we shall miscarry there.*

---

[1156] **"The Papers of Henry Bouquet"**, Volume IV, 1978.

[1157] **"The Pennsylvania Magazine of History and Biography"**, Volume 33, 1909.

*Nothing from Europe.*

*Mrs Sterling is gone. The departure was so lamentable that Pat writes me he was sent for to moderate the grieff.*

*Farewell my dear Sir, my kind Compliments to Col. Shippen.*

> *I am Dear Sir*
>
> *Your most devoted hble Servant*
>
> *Henry Bouquet.*

*On His Majesty's Service To COLONEL BURD upon the Monongahela To be forwarded from Fort Cumberland by another man & Horse to Colonel Burd.*

## Bouquet writes a detailed letter to George Mercer

An October 1, 1759 letter[1158] Bouquet wrote to George Mercer from Bedford includes the following:

*The disappointment of the Pack Horses was attended with a fatal Consequence, the starving of Col. Burd's Party who never received any Provisions from Virginia Except 10 Horse loads I Sent him upon the King's Waggon Horses and he has been without Flour from the 27th September and reduced to 8 Small Beeves for 250 Men. A little Convoy went to him yesterday, But I am terribly afraid of the Consequences — which I could not forsee having not received your short Letter with the reasons of the delay of the Pack Horses and Expecting they would go up every day.*

*These Pack Horses are after this Trip to be employed to Carry between Fort Cumberland & Red Stone Creek whatever Flour or Forrage you can get ready for them, giving your directions thereupon to Lieut Blythe.*

*I am much Obliged to You for your trouble about the Sadles &Cta Please to See that the drivers be engaged to Serve during the Campaigne, having none to replace them.*

*The 39 Horses returned to Cumberland were so much hurt by their Sadies, that they are not yet able to go up: I desire Mr Blyth to load the best with forrage for Col: Byrd: to proceed, with the 50 loaded with Flour: The other will go when recruited either with Flour or forrage; as you will direct. ...*

*Having neither Tools nor Men, I cannot get Braddock's Road repaired now: Had not Mr Finnie declared it to be extremely good, I would have desired Col. Burd to repair it.*

*As we are Circumstanced the only thing I See is that you engage every Waggoner to take an Ax, a Spade, or a Pick ax: and with the assistance of their Escort, remove Such difficulties as could stop them, you may allow them for the use of Said Tools or pay them, upon receipt if they leave them at Red Stone Creek. ...*

*Please to send Col; Burd the Nails &cta wanted and to take Care of his Subsistence; He should have besides the 50 Pack Horses loaded with Flour 20 Beeves, out of the 100 you prepare to send to Pittsburgh.*

*I have Spoken to Captn Callender of the 60 Pack Horses and he desired me to tell you that if the Men who Offers them, will make them 100, and give him notice of the day he will be at Fort Cumberland, he Shall meet him there, and if they cannot agree they will Each Choose a man to fix the Prices, and He will take*

---

[1158] **"The Papers of Col. Henry Bouquet"**, 1940.

*them: But they Should have saggings and drivers. We have 14,000 Bushells of dry forrage here & at Ligonier, and it comes in, in such plenty from Pennsylv^a & Maryland that we can hardly Stow it. ...*

## Cumberland can have some nails out of cask no. 1

An October 4, 1759 letter[1159] Mercer wrote to Burd from Winchester includes the statement, *"As I imagine they will want some Nails at Cumberland, I have Wrote Them that they may take one of the Casks of 8^d & some 10^d out of the Cask N° 1 which I have desired Them to inform you of, shoud they be necessary."*

## Flour and forage arrive at Fort Cumberland

An October 6, 1759 letter[1160] Captain Thomas Woodward wrote to Captain Lewis Ourry from Fort Cumberland states:

*You will be pleasd to inform Coll Bouquett that two Brigades are this day arriv'd from Virg^a the One consisting of 87 horse-loads of Forrage and the other 45 horse-loads of Flour. M^r Blyth will inform You the exact Quantity. they shall be disposed of in the following Manner. Viz: 18 horses loaded with Forrage, to Coll° Burd, And 36 loaded with Flour and 80[1161] loaded with Forrage sent to Pittsburgh, for in all there is 134 horses but One of their loads they lost by the way. I shall also send up four more beeves to Coll° Burd and 17 horse loads more of Flour exclusive of what I mentioned before, from those horses that returnd some time from Redstone Creek.*

The letter has two postscripts. The first postscript states, *"If You have any Employ for a very good blacksmith I shoud be glad to know as I can recomend one to You You woud much oblige me in the Loan of a Jack Plane"*. The second postscript states, *"Thu Bearer's going off directly M^r Blyth defers writing to You Till Monday when he will send an Exact picture of the Quantity as he is now weighing it out"*

## Kenny describes Cock's residence and returns to Fort Cumberland

Kenny's October 7, 1759 journal entry states, *"Set off from Pews & reached Cocks' on Potomack. I lay on a damp earthen floor, on some corn fodder, y^e house being unchinked or daubed & no door; had my horse in their orchard."*

Kenny's October 8, 1759 journal entry[1162] from Fort Cumberland states, *"Set off in ye morning a heavy fog being along y^e river; got one foot a little wet crossing y^e river; came to Cumberland that evening turned out my horse in y^e Bottom."*

## John Slater's wife was at Fort Cumberland in 1759

Kenny's October 9, 1759 journal entry, written from Fort Cumberland, states:

*Taken with a strong fever & cold fits. Put up with Tho^s & Alex^r Blair, two moderate young men and y^e Commissaries having no nourishment, only cold water & wine, I sent for Capt Battle, being chief in command & delivered what money I had to him, being more than £29, also my saddlebags with y^e books & papers. He sent to Bedford for sugar, tea & chocolate for me, y^e Doctor persuaided me to take some medicine & I took a vomit & got Jn° Slaters wife to tend me. Here I lay on y^e boards, only some Bearskins*

---

[1159] **"The Papers of Henry Bouquet"**, Volume IV, 1978.
[1160] **"The Papers of Col. Henry Bouquet"**, 1941.
[1161] This quantity is conveyed by a footnote to the letter.
[1162] **"The Pennsylvania Magazine of History and Biography"**, Volume 37, 1913.

*under me y^e space of two weeks. I moved down to Jn° Slater's where his wife attended me & I lay some better, where I took sundry things of y^e Doctor, which under Providential mercy I believe afforded much help. While sick my horse was taken & rode by Capt Wright to Pittsburgh & y^e man that I hired y^e creature of at Pittsburgh coming here & his creature being lost then, made me pay what he said it was valued £5, however, I found both creatures since I recovered my sickness in some degree. I paid Slater's for my lodging & nursing £1.7/; y^e Commissary's lad for tending me there 5/; y^e Commissary for a hide 12/; McCarties people for milk 7/; a Sutler for liquor £1.1. 6.; M^cCarty & Slater for overhauling y^e load of skins that was left so as to have y^e account of them separate 5/. My friend Jessie Pew, from Hopewell, came to see me whilst I was bad, but now my brother Charles came from home, to see whether I was dead as he had heard.*

### Callender is waiting to purchase more horses at Fort Cumberland

An October 9, 1759 letter[1163] Ourry wrote to Bouquet from Fort Bedford includes the statement, *"Capt^n Callender only waits the arrival of the Horses at F Cumberland to go and purchase them, tho' he has bought twenty or thirty since you went away, & he expects some more up daily."*

### Packhorses and cattle coming to Fort Cumberland

An October 9, 1759 letter[1164] Colonel George Mercer wrote to Bouquet from Winchester includes the following:

*As I found M^r Hoops was not willing any Body shoud have the smallest Share of his Profits, I have advised M^r Graham to quit his Bargain in Regard to the rest of the Cattle, as I had not Money sufficient to advance for Them. He will therefore only take out one Drove of 100, 60 of which at least are fit for Pittsburg, as M^r Hoops says none sent there must weigh less than 400. all of 60 will do this, and some be very near 500. Those that will not do for Pittsburg which I have desired the Kings Comissary at Cumberland to judge of, I have desired Cap^t Woodward to answer for himself & Col° Burd at Red Stone, in general those I believe will weigh 350, which are large enough for driving so short a Distance.*

*As it is very troublesome &. expensive to be sending Cattle every Week up, I have, exclusive of those of M^r Graham's, sent 98 to Cap^t Woodward from which and the Remainder of M^r Grahams I have desired him to supply Col° Burd.*

*The Person who spoke to Me about the Pack Horses has called upon Me this Day about Them, but not having heard from you I coud give him no Answer but he will drive them on to Cumberland with their Loads of Oats, they are to set out to morrow. ...*

*The Pack Horses from Fort Cumberland are not yet come down, nor do I know what you woud chuse to have Them loaded with, when they do come here, or from Fort Cumberland. I coud provide a Load of what you'd rather have, by the Time they returned from Pittsburg & Red Stone if I knew in Time what you woud have them to be loaded with. ...*

---

[1163] **"The Papers of Henry Bouquet"**, Volume IV, 1978.
[1164] **"The Papers of Col. Henry Bouquet"**, 1941.

### No word from Fort Cumberland

An October 11, 1759 letter[1165] Ourry wrote to Bouquet from Fort Bedford includes the statement, *"My Surprise encreases, at not hearing from Fort Cumberland."*

### A request for orders concerning the provisioning of Fort Cumberland

An October 12, 1759 letter[1166] Doctor Thomas Walker wrote to Bouquet from Winchester includes the following:

*To my Great Consern & no less Surprise I am Informed the Forces at Redstone Creek have Suffered for want of provisions which were expected from this place I Can Venture to assure you their was No Orders given to Me or any other person here, that I Know of, to Provide for them before the 26ᵗʰ of September, and as Soon as Such Orders were Given provisions were Provided & Sent With the greatest dispatch, and you May depend If Colᵒ Mercer or any other person Residing here is Authorised to Order provisions for that or the Garrison at Fort Cumberland there will be No danger of Want, but So long as we Are to Receive our Instructions from persons distant from this place there will be always Danger of Disappointments as Such Instructions are liable to Delays, and Sometimes by having Matters of Greater importance to Mannage Small things Are Neglected by the distant persons Wheras if he was present Applcation Could be Made to him if he should be otherwise engaged*

*I find the weight of Our Beef Cattle is Not agreeable to Expectation but I Assure you they are as Good as Can be gathered on so Short Notice as is gennerly given and had I Longer Warning It Would Not be in My power to purchase so large Cattle as are Commonly in pensilvania Nor is our Flour so good as that Made their With which I Acquainted the General & Contractors last May: the Reasons May Not So Readily appear to you as they do to persons Who have long Resided in Virginia I therefore beg leave to Mention Some few. Our Staple is Tobaco the Mannage Ment of that engrosses M the greatest part of Our time, the Flour Made in the upper parts of the Colony was Chiefly Consumed Among the Farmers who Are So frugal as to eat the Midlings Mixed With the Flour gennerly, and Many use the Shorts in the Same Manner that It was found uneces for the Millers to go to the Expence of Merchant Boutting Cloths at that time and Most of them use those by then provided, but if Such Flour as Our Mills Can make will be exceptable you May depend on any Quantity this Country Can afford If you will Give Me timely Notice the present Crop of Wheat being so great that I make No Doubt of purchasing Two Hundred Thousand Between this & the Spring and if It is thought Convenient to encourage the Carriage by Water up Potomack to Fort Cumberland the expence Will be Much lessned and a large quantity transported thithur then we Shall be able to get up by any other Means*

*As the Season for Providing Beef and Transporting Flour Conveniantly is Near expiring I have Sent an express to Mʳ Hoops for Orders what quantity to lay in at Fort Cumberland & the Mouth of Redstone Creek for those Garrisons, Whose Return I expect on the 15ᵗʰ and Colᵒ Mercer informes Me if It should So happen that I Do Not Receive Orders from Mʳ Hoops he will under take to give Such Instructions as he thinks Necessary and has Already Ordered Me to purchase about Sixty Thousand Wᵗ of Flour for that purpose*

*A large Quantity of Pork Good Pork May be purchased & Sent to Pittsburgh or any of the Garrisons between this place and that about the Middle or last of December ...*

---

[1165] **"The Papers of Henry Bouquet"**, Volume IV, 1978.
[1166] **"The Papers of Col. Henry Bouquet"**, 1941.

## Rutherford's cattle are refused at Fort Cumberland due to their size

An October 14, 1759 letter[1167] Colonel George Mercer wrote to Bouquet from Winchester includes the following:

*I have never received your Answer to my Letter of the 28th Ult° How it has miscarried I cannot guess, as Mʳ Turner assures Me you wrote, & sent off an Express with it to Cumberland, while he was with you. I have been at a Loss how to answer many People whose Business depended upon your Orders. Among others the Owner of the Pack Horses I mentioned to you, has been twice with Me concerning Them. I have, till I coud receive your Directions, engaged him to make a second Trip with Them to Cumberland, farther he woud not go, unless he sold the Horses.*

*Mʳ Walker is just come up, and writes the General very fully concerning his Business.*

*Mʳ Turner to my great Surprize informed Me of the Scarcity of Provision at Red Stone Creek; I can not attribute it to any Thing but the Carelessness & Indolence of the Drivers, who have no Doubt loitered away their Time between this and Cumberland, as I assure you Sir since I first was ordered to supply Them, Provision has always been sent up in due Time, and Plenty of it. It must have been delayed somewhere. From hence it was duly dispatched. But as I soon saw the Inconvenience attending the Driving such small & frequent Droves I have sent Capᵗ Woodward 120 or 130 to go up as he thinks proper, and as Provision cant be a Drug, I have desired Mʳ Walker imediately to provide for Them to the first of May. The Flour is already engaged.*

*I have, you know Sir, frequently complained of Mʳ Hoops, who often directs his Agents here, in such a Manner, as entirely contradicts your Orders. Mʳ Walker says he will mention that Subject, to the General himself. The very next Letter Rutherford had from him, after you had directed the Garrisons, at Red Stone & Cumberland to be provided from hence, & 1000 Sheep to be sent up, expressly forbids him buying any more Cattle or Flour till he sends him farther Orders as he can be supplyed in Pennsylvᵃ, and as the Season for Sheep was over tells him he is to buy no more of Them, as they woud not answer. At this Time the Garrison at Red Stone is supplyed without any Authority from Mʳ Hoops. ...*

*When I had wrote so far, Mʳ Rutherford informs Me some of his Cattle have been refused by the Comissary at Cumberland which requires his Attendance there, so that he will be Bearer of this to you; it will save the Expence of a second Messenger. ...*

The letter has the following postscript:

*Mʳ Rutherford says his Cattle are refused upon Account of their Size. As this Country does not abound in large Cattle, if such as have been sent will not answer, We can not furnish the Troops at all. All the Drove was in exceeding good Order very fat I think and certainly if they weigh but 200ᶫᵇ and are fat, they are better than poor ones that will weigh 400ᶫᵇ True small Cattle will not answer Driving so well the Expense I mean, but for the Garrison at Cumberland which is so near Us, I do not think they can be too small provided they are fat, & exceed 2 or 3 Years old. It is impossible in this Country where the Generality of our Cattle are small, to get a Drove entirely of large Ones, for the Farmers will not allow their Herds to be picked, as the best must serve to help off the Meaner Ones. I examined the Cattle before they were sent off, and did not imagine any woud be refused at Cumberland as I assure you they were all very fat; and as they were collected in a Hurry I thought them a very good Drove; and that some woud answer for Pittsburgh, which I desired the King's Comissary to pick out.*

---

[1167] "**The Papers of Col. Henry Bouquet**", 1941.

## A herd of cattle arrive at Fort Cumberland

An October 15, 1759 letter[1168] Ourry wrote to Bouquet from Fort Bedford includes the following statement:

*By a Lett* I reed Yesterday from Cap* Woodward, I find that 138 head of Cattle are arrived at F Cumberland from M* Rutherford. 60 of which he Escorts to Pittsburgh, with two Wagons of Tools, & one of Indian goods the private property of Mesr Lemmon & Buch of Winchester 40 Beeves he sends to Col. Burd, and 38 are for the Garrison of F Cumberland.*

## Some wagon horses are unfit for hauling

An October 16, 1759 letter[1169] Ourry wrote to Bouquet from Fort Bedford includes the following statements:

*I have this Day call'd 24 of our Waggon Horses, from those return'd from F Cumberland who will not be fit to hawl this Year, but may carry Loads to Ligonier without being quite ruin'd, and I shall send them up in two Days with Forrage. ...*

*I will immediately set the Bakers to Work agreeable to your Regulation and recommend it to the Commanding Officer at F* Cumberland. ...*

*L* Col* Mercer has wrote to M* Blyth to get a Bridge made over Will's Creek & a Flatt, but there are neither Materials nor Artificers fit for that undertaking at Fort Cumberland. ...*

## Kenny leaves Fort Cumberland for home

Kenny's October 17, 1759 journal entry[1170] from Fort Cumberland states, *"So we got ready on y* 17th 11mo & set off from Cumberland, came to one Plumbs & stayed all night."* His journal entry for the 18th states *"Crossed Potomack, being very high, so that y* water got in our boots & came to Enoch's, stayed all night."* The journal ends with a November 8, 1759 entry that states, *"My mother joyful to see me."*

## Walker is to lay in provisions at Cumberland

An October 18, 1759 letter[1171] Adam Hoops sent to Bouquet from Carlisle includes the following statement:

*Doctor Walker is to lay in provisions at Cumberland, and Red Stone Creek; sufficient for those Garrissons, till the first of June next, and at the other Small Garrisons the Clerks can Oversee the Salting of Beef and Pork.*

## A proposed bridge at the Little Crossing

An October 20, 1759 letter[1172] Colonel James Burd wrote to General John Stanwix from the *"Camp at Monongahelo"* includes the following:

*I shall send off the party to day to the Great Crossing of Youghyogane to build the Flat &ca there, think if it is Aggreable to the Gen* if two Small houses was built there to flank each other they would be Quite Sufficient, one for a small party and the other for any Stores that may at any time be at that place, I shall send Col: Shippen to the Crossing to give the Nesessary direction.*

---

[1168] "**The Papers of Henry Bouquet**", Volume IV, 1978.

[1169] "**The Papers of Henry Bouquet**", Volume IV, 1978.

[1170] "**The Pennsylvania Magazine of History and Biography**", Volume 37, 1913.

[1171] "**The Papers of Col. Henry Bouquet**", 1941.

[1172] "**The Papers of Col. Henry Bouquet**", 1941.

*As to the Little Crossing I am of Opinion that a Bridge would be best over it, and as it is but 25 miles from Fort Cumberland I would begg leave to propose to have a strong party ordered from Ft. Cumberland with propper Nesessarys to finish the Bridge, but if the Gen<sup>l</sup> should not approve of this I shall with pleasure Receive your orders Concerning it*

*I shall send to the Great Crossing one ship Carpenter & two Sawyrs more which will forward the work, it will take them some time to gett to the Ground as it is 50 miles from hence ...*

## Ramsay complains of having his flour inspected at Fort Cumberland

An October 22, 1759 letter[1173] Colonel George Mercer wrote to Fort Cumberland Assistant Commissary Joseph Galbraith from Winchester includes the following:

*I have Just been apply'd to, by M<sup>r</sup> Ramsey Contractor for Flour from this Collony, who thinks it a hardship to have his Waggons stopped at Cumberland for the Inspection of his flour, without having any Allowance made for it. As M<sup>r</sup> Ramsay will be Obliged to Employ a Number of Waggons in this Service, it must be a very Considerable loss to him to have Every one of them Delayed a Day, or Perhaps two, w<sup>ch</sup> must be the Case when any Number goes together, to have his flour Examined at Fort Cumberland. He is far from expecting it to Pass without any Inspection, but he Chuses that Should be at the Place of Delivery RedStone Creek, as it can be Done there without y<sup>e</sup> waggons lossing any time. I was Present when the Contract was made & am Certain there was no Such thing mentioned, and he has Insisted that I Shall Urge that Part of it. Concerning the Delay of his Waggons, which I must think from the Nature of the Bargain have no Right to be Stopped any where 'till they Come to RedStone Creek. He is just sending off 50 Waggons loaded with Flour & if they are Stopped only one Day at Cumberland which it will Certainly Require to Examine all their Loads, it must be a Certain Expence of at Least £ 30 Which the hire of these waggons cost him Daily, upon the Whole I am of Opinion that we have no Right to Delay his Waggons at all, or to inspect his Flour at Fort Cumberland, and unless You have Possitive Orders to the Contrary as his is a Contract for Delivery of So much Flour at RedStone Creek, I Desire You will not give him Reason to apply to me with a Second Complaint, but forward his waggons on to RedStone Creek Where he expects & is willing it Should be Examined at the Delivery. I Do not Mention this to You as a General Rule for Your Conduct, 'tis only in Regard to M<sup>r</sup> Ramsays contract that I would not have you interfere, unless you have Received Possitive orders to the Contrary. I am Certain he never had the least hint given him that his Flour Should be Inspected — at Cumberland — & I Dare Say you must be Convinced it will be a Considerable Loss to him to have his waggons Delayed there and he is Willing to Run the Risque of it's going to RedStone. ...*

## A memorandum about the cattle refused at Fort Cumberland

A memorandum[1174] written by Alexander Blair, Manager for the Contractors at Fort Cumberland, and left with Mr. Read at Fort Bedford on October 24, 1759, states:

*Upon M<sup>r</sup> Thomas Ruthorfords bringing back the Cattle that was Condemned by Jos: Galbraith Assisstant Commiss<sup>ry</sup> at Fort Cumberland who having reviewed the Cattle told M<sup>r</sup> Rutherford that some of them would not Pass the Inspection, directly Rutherford Came to me the Subscriber telling me that the Cattle were all Passed Demanding a Receipt for them which I gave him, and I afterwards hearing that two of the Cattle were not Passed, went and Demanded my Receipt to Alter it, upon which M<sup>r</sup> Rutherford told me he had got the Receipt and I might make my best of the Cattle for he would have nothing to say to*

---

1173 **"The Papers of Col. Henry Bouquet"**, 1941.
1174 **"The Papers of Col. Henry Bouquet"**, 1941.

*them. I then went to Cap' Battell of the New Castle Troops then Commanding Officer to See if he would have me righted he told me he would have nothing to say to us.*

## Building a bridge at the Little Crossing

An October 24, 1759 letter[1175] Bouquet wrote to Burd[1176] from Pittsburgh states:

*Pittsburgh 24ʰ October 1759*

*Dear Sir*

*I arrived here the 15ᵗʰ and was since upon the new Road opened from the three Redoubts to this Place which has proved a heavy and difficult Work. I returned yesterday and the General ordered me to answer your Letter of the 18ᵗʰ*

*He approves of the two small Houses you propose to build at the Crossing of Yioghiogheny, and desires when the flatt and Houses are finished that you would order a carefull Sergeant and ten men to keep that Post. They must have a couple of falling axes and a Padlock for the Stores. As there is neither men nor Tools at Fort Cumberland or Bedford you must be so good to take the charge of getting the Bridge built upon the little crossing and to order the Loggs to be covered with good fascines[1177] and Earth and secured by strong Pins. As soon as your own Post is finished, the General desires you to march with the remainder of your detachment to Pittsburgh, leaving a diligent officer and 20 or 25 men at Burd's Fort. The officer must give Certificates for all Provisions, Forrage &c, that will be sent there from Virgᵃ and Maryland and inform the General or me thereof that Battos may be sent to bring them down. He will give a Regular Invoice of Each article sent here, to prevent neglect and Confusion: Some allowance will be made to him in Consideration of his Care. I shall be extremely glad to see you here and remain, my Dear Sir*

*Your most obedt Hble Servt*

*Henry Bouquet*

*They say Quebec is fallen, Wolff killed, Montacalm and 2 more generals killed. 500 lost on our side. 1600 on the French.*

## Directions about procuring beef for the two crossings

An October 25, 1759 letter[1178] Bouquet wrote to Burd from Pittsburgh includes the statement:

*To prevent any future deficiency of provision at your Post, Please to send orders to Messrs Walker and Rutherfurd for the quantity of Beeves that you may want at your Post & the two crossings of the Yioghiogheny and stop the flour you will have occasion for from the Convoys passing at your Post*

---

[1175] "**The Pennsylvania Magazine of History and Biography**", Volume 33, 1909.

[1176] A synopsis of an October 24, 1759 letter Bouquet wrote to Burd from Pittsburgh that is published in the "**Sessional Papers of the Dominion of Canada**", Volume 23, 1890, contains enough matching detail to prove that the recipient of the letter was Burd, stating, *"The General approves of the two small houses to be built at the crossing of the Yioghiogheny; a sergeant and 10 men to be left at that post. He is to get the bridge built at the little crossing, Fort Cumberland. He is to leave a lieutenant and 35 men at his post, and take the rest of his detachment to Pittsburgh."*

[1177] Bundles of brush used to hold earth in place.

[1178] "**The Pennsylvania Magazine of History and Biography**", Volume 33, 1909.

## Bouquet saves Burd's men at Redstone from starvation

An October 25, 1759 letter[1179] Bouquet wrote to Thomas Walker from Pittsburgh includes the following:

*Col. Mercer having agreed w$^{th}$ Col. Burd in August last to supply him upon the Mononghehela w$^{th}$ Provisions from Virginia, can tell you by what accidents they were not forwarded. Itis certain that these Troops would have been starved, had I not Sent them some Beeves, and two small Convoys of flour upon the King's Horses. ...*

*The Garrison at Fort Cumberland is to be interely supplied by M$^r$ Hoops on his Agents for account of the Contractors, who are to pay all Charges of Carriages for Provisions to that Place.*

*We Shall want no more Beeves from Virg$^a$ this year, (excepted for Redstone Creek & Cumberland) as the Pensilv$^a$ Cattle are fitter for salting on account of their size.*

## Bouquet is the source of the cattle size requirement

An October 25, 1759 letter[1180] Bouquet wrote to Colonel George Mercer from Pittsburgh includes the following:

*You may remember that I contracted wth M$^r$ Ramsay for <u>merchantable flour</u>, and not Meal. Nevertheless to prevent the fatal Consequences of a disapointment, I desired the King's Commissary at Fort Cumberland to receive Meal if good of the Kind rather than be deprived of So great a supply depended upon for the subsistance of the Troops, But he writes that the first Convoy was so bad that he could not receive it, even for Meal. Add the disapointm$^t$ in point of quantity & time, & you may imagine what I must think of M$^r$ Ramsay: I hope he will be more punctual to his Engagement, as we depend absolutely upon it, and cannot at this distance repair such a breach.*

*As to the Beeves, Experience plainly Shews that the largest are the best for driving and salting, and for that reason I fixed the lowest Weight of those to be bought from M$^r$ Graham to 400 $^{lb}$ Each, Therefore those sent by Rutherford being So deficient in that Respect were justly rejected: and as you observe that Virg$^a$ can not afford large Cattle; There is no Occasion to buy any more this year in that Province, except what may be wanted at <u>Burd's Fort</u> on the Mononghehela , & Cumberland.*

*If M$^r$ Ramsay Send all his flour there will be no occasion for any more this year; But forrage may be sent to the first of January: so you may recall your advertisements and settle the Accounts accordingly.*

*The pack Horses are to be loaded with forrage at Cumberland for <u>Burd's Fort</u>, (Redstone Creek) and if the salt loaded by M$^r$ Graham, is not in Barrils, I beg you will take Care that it may be well Secured from Rain, or damp.*

*This article is so material, that if we had the misfortune to be disapointed in receiving of it either in time, quality, or quantity, it would be our utter Ruin and destruction: Therefore I recommand it in the strongest manner to your most particular care.*

## A disgruntled wagon master

An October 27, 1759 letter[1181] written by Colonel George Mercer to General John Stanwix from Winchester includes the following:

---

[1179] "**The Papers of Col. Henry Bouquet**", 1940.

[1180] "**The Papers of Col. Henry Bouquet**", 1940.

[1181] "**The Papers of Col. Henry Bouquet**", 1941.

*On the 18th late in the Night arrived Mr Graham's Waggon Master here with two Waggons, and upon my not receiving him very civily after such a Disappointment, he went off and has left Me to transact Mr Graham's Business for him. I have got about 200 Bushels of the Salt up to Cumberland, and shall send it up as fast as possible till Mr Graham can come down himself. As Mr Graham's Waggon Master I believe never stirred for a Waggon, Mr Ramsay has engaged all that I know of, so that I am now under a Necessity of employing Pack Horses to take it up, as the only Method left. No Man ever had fairer Promises than I have concerning these Horses, but yet I dare not say they will come.*

*After all these Disappointments I am afraid to propose any Thing from Virginia tho I believe were the Thing to continue the People woud know more of the Matter by the next Season. This Affair has come upon Them so unexpectedly, that few are prepared for it. But as Mr Walker a Gentleman well acquainted with the Business who has been employed since the Comencemt of the War in victualling the Troops, has given Me Assurances that he will at a Certain Price contract for the victualling 1000 Men at Cumberland Red Stone & Pittsburg, and as he offers & I am sure can give undoubted Security for what he promises I have desired him to write your Excellency upon the Subject which he says he will do now very fully. I am certain no one knows better what may be had from this Country, and as he is very cautious & diligent I am sure he woud not promise more than he woud perform, for which himself proposes to give a Bond in any Penalty you shall fix. I know the principal Gent of this Country have so good an Opinion of him that he coud get Security if required for £ 50,000*

*I have sent up several People to Pittsburg with Cheese Butter &c which I make no Doubt woud be acceptable. Those who have returned from thence, on that Business, have expressed the utmost Satisfaction, & all the Gratitude they were capable of, for the good Treatment & Reception they met with. If the Waggons were not chiefly engaged to Mr Ramsay & myself for Carriage of Flour &c to Cumberland I do not believe there would be Butter Cheese or Apples Potatoes &c left in the County. The Receipt of the ready Cash here, to which they have not been accustomed for some Time past, is of particular Service, & very acceptable to Them. ...*

## A treaty is concluded at Pittsburgh on October 27, 1759

An article in the November 22, 1759 issue of the "**Maryland Gazette**" states:

*From Pittsburg our Advices, of the 28th of October, are as follow, viz.*

*"that every Thing goes extremely well there; fine Weather, Plenty of Provisions; and the Works growing to Admiration, under the direction of the indefatigable General. That on the 27th ult. The Treaties with the Indians were concluded, to the mutual Satisfaction of all Parties Concerned: That they have engaged formally to deliver up all the Prisoners; and one Nation alone gave the General 41 Sticks, being the Number of their Captives; and they promise, that exept those that may die, we shall see them all."*

## Taking forage from Fort Cumberland to Fort Burd

An October 28, 1759 letter[1182] Bouquet wrote to Colonel George Mercer from Pittsburgh includes the following:

*The Pack Horses as I wrote you before are to be constantly loaded with forrage at Fort Cumberland, where I make no doubt you have by this time a Sufficient magazine ready for them: They are to go to Burds Fort on the Monongahela ...*

---

[1182] "**The Papers of Col. Henry Bouquet**", 1940.

*I Send you Copy of the Commissary's Letter at Fort Cumberland, by which you will observe that he has made no difficulty to receive Meal for flour, and only objected to what was not receivable as such. I hope M$^r$ Ramsay will see himself what he Sends to prevent any further disapointment.*

### Galbraith defends inspecting Ramsay's flour

An October 28, 1759 letter[1183] Joseph Galbraith wrote to Colonel George Mercer from Fort Cumberland states:

*I Received yours by M$^r$ Nevill, with 40 head of Beef Cattle which have Passed Inspection, and are Estimated at 300$^{lb}$ Each, of Nett Beef.*

*I am Sorry any Complaint Should be made by M$^r$ Ramsay to you in Regard to my Stopping his Waggons at this place. I am affraid this Affair has been misrepresented to You as I can Prove by the Officers in this Garrison I have Never Delayed his Waggons above 2 or three hours, and in Case he sends 50 at once I shall Dispatch them in Less then half a Day. M$^r$ Ramsays Projection of having his waggons w$^{th}$ Flour Examined at Red Stone Creek will not Answer, as that would be bringing an Additional Expence on the Crown by Employing another Person to Act in Behalf of the King at RedStone Creek, Whilst one Stationed here can Inspect all the Provisions Destined for this place, Red Stone Creek & Pittsburgh Sent from Virginia. Besides it is Certainly better for M$^r$ Ramsay to have his Flour Inspected here then at at Red Stone as the Carriage will be more Expensive I Dare Say M$^r$ Ramsay's Notion of Letting the waggons Pass my Post without Inspection is founded on a Scheme of the Troops at RedStone Creek being in Necessity for Bread Whilst those at Pittsburgh were in the Same Delimma, therefore would take any Stuff Rather then Starve, as has already been the Case at Red Stone Creek where the Troops were obliged to Eat Meal (Instead of Flour) of which Even the Contractor's Clerks have Complained as not being Sufficient. I have Inclosed you a Copy of my Instructions by w$^{ch}$ you will See I have Acted only agreeable to them, and Can by no means Suffer Provisions of any kind not Sufficient to Pass this Place Destined for the Army under Command of General Stanwix. If you find any Clause in my Instructions which will allow one to Dispence with the Inspection of M$^r$ Ramsays Flour I Pray the favour you will Let me know it: As to M$^r$ Ramseys making Complaints against me a Second or third time whilst I do my Duty to the best of my Power, I Shall not give myself any uneasine about it as Col$^o$ Bouquet sent me here in a great Measure to see that M$^r$ Ramsay fullfilled his Contract, as allso the other Gentlemen who Sends Provisions here for the Troops*

*The Meal of Ramsays which I Refused was not Realy fit for any Soldiers to Eat; When the King Pays Such an Extravagent Price for their Provisions they Ought to have the Best or Such as is good.*

### Burd writes about the supplies needed at the big and little crossings

An October 29, 1759 letter[1184] Colonel James Burd wrote to Bouquet from the *"Camp at Monongehelo"* includes the statement, *"I shall give M$^r$ Rutherford Derections about the supply's Nesessary for this Garrison and the Two Crossings, I have press'd the People at Cumberland to take care that the building of the Flatt &$^{ca}$ should not be stop't for want of Provisions"*.

---

[1183] **"The Papers of Col. Henry Bouquet"**, 1941.
[1184] **"The Papers of Col. Henry Bouquet"**, 1941.

### It's okay to receive meal of the sound and good kind

An October 29, 1759 letter[1185] Bouquet wrote to Ourry from Pittsburgh includes the following:

*We will have no more Cattle from Virginia this Year, Therefore give directions accordingly to Cumberland: They are only to send the necessar number to feed Col. Burd's People & go no further being Sufficiently provided*

*Desire M' Read to give orders to his Deputy at Cumberland to receive Meal in lieu of flour, provided it be sound & good of the Kind, as otherwise we would be entirely disapointed from that Quarter. ...*

### Flour sent to a party at the Great Crossings

An October 31, 1759 letter[1186] Ourry wrote to Bouquet from Fort Bedford includes the following:

*Besides what M' Blythe has sent up last Week, as appears by his enclos'd Return, He informs me that the 29th he forwarded 24 Horse Loads of Flour & 54 Beef Cattle, destin'd, as he says, for a Party at the great Crossings of Yochiogeni, Red Stone Creek & Pittsburgh.*

*Ramsay continues Sending Such Stuff, as the King's Commissary cannot pass; and endeavours to persuade Col' Mercer, that it is not to be inspected at F' Cumberland, but at Red Stone Creek (where you know there is no King's Com'')*

*It seems the Country People carry up good Flour, which proves that it can be had. And, if I remember right, the Contract expressly says Flour / not Meal.*

*M' Blyth having applied to me for Cash to pay Artificers, Pack Horse Drivers &c: I have sent him £30 of the Virginia Money I mention'd to you.*

### Reed writes to Bouquet about the coarse meal

A November 2, 1759 letter[1187] Reed wrote to Bouquet from Fort Bedford includes the statement, *"Inclosed you have a letter from Col° Mercer A. D. Q. M. G. to my Assistant at Fort Cumberland and his Answer thereto, and I hope his Conduct will not be disagreeable to you, the Coarseness of the Meal is only Complained of."*

### Virginian forces are ordered to Fort Cumberland

A November 4, 1759 letter[1188] Bouquet wrote to Captain Ourry from Pittsburg includes the statement:

*Our Circumstances do not allow to make difficulties about receiving Meal for flour at Cumberland. Therefore you will desire M' Read to send Positive to His deputy there, to receive all the Meal sent by M'Ramsay provided it be sound, & good of the Kind.*

*I hope after so many repeated orders that They will send no more Beeves from Virginia for Pittsburgh and to prevent it effectually, M' Read is to send orders to His Deputy, to receive no other Beeves this Campaign than what will be necessary to Subsist Col. James Burd's detachment; but none at all for*

---

[1185] **"The Papers of Henry Bouquet"**, Volume IV, 1978.

[1186] **"The Papers of Henry Bouquet"**, Volume IV, 1978.

[1187] **"The Papers of Henry Bouquet"**, Volume IV, 1978.

[1188] **"The Papers of Henry Bouquet"**, Volume IV, 1978.

*Pittsburgh: — and for the flour forrage, and all kind of Provisions they are not to go farther than Burd's Fort at Red Stone Creek as we allow no higher Price here than there.*

*Part of the Virginia Reg.^t will be ordered to Fort Cumberland and Col. William Byrd sends orders to M^r Walker to lay in Provisions for them. I have nothing to do with it and what I mention here is exclusive of Said Orders, and Confined to Pittsburgh & the Communication.*

## Ourry implements Bouquet's instructions

A November 4, 1759 letter[1189] Ourry wrote to Bouquet from Fort Bedford includes the following:

*Cap.^t Callender is return'd with 156 fresh good Horses 105 go off today with Forrage, he assures me he will make them 400 this Week. No acc.^t of those that were to come to Cumberland …*

*I have wrote to M.^r Blyth to send you no more Virg.^a Cattle.*

*And told M.^r Read to write to his Dep.^y to receive Meal at F Cumberland. …*

## Walker proposes victualing Pittsburgh, Redstone, and Fort Cumberland

A November 5, 1759 letter[1190] Doctor Thomas Walker wrote to Bouquet from Winchester includes the statement:

*Your favour of y.^e 25^th of October I received yesterday & you may depend will forward Provisions Sufficient for the Garrisons at Fort Cumberland and Redstone Creek also the twenty five Thousand Pounds of Pork ordered for Pittsburgh by M.^r Hoops.*

*I shall use my best endeavours to Forward Forage to Redstone Creek between this & the first of January next, though am Doubtfull but little can be sent as the winter is just comeing on and no food for the Horses betwen that Post and Fort Cumberland Ad to that the Badness of the Road, you may depend I will not purchase more than I can send*

*I will prepare a copy of my payments to send the next time I write. Had I known you desired one I would have Stayed M.^r Rutherford untill I could have prepard one to send by him*

*I am greatly concerned to hear of the many disappointments from Virginia, but am not discouraged from Contracting to feed one thousand men at Pittsburgh Redstone and Cumberland by the Ration if it Should be thought convenient by the General to provide for them in that manner; & if I undertake will give Bond With sufficient security for the performance of my undertaking. As the winter is now begining I would not prepare for so great an undertaking before next May but will wait on the General when & Where he shall think proper to appoint, in order to treat about it …*

Walker wrote a similar letter[1191] to General John Stanwix the same day. That letter includes the statement:

*I am much concerned at the Disappointments you have met with from Virginia, though am not sensible any of them have in any Respect been Oweing to me and if It is agreeable to Your Excellency I will Contract to Vicctual One Thousand men at Pittsburgh Redstone Creek & Cumberland by the Ration*

---

[1189] **"The Papers of Henry Bouquet"**, Volume IV, 1978.

[1190] **"The Papers of Col. Henry Bouquet"**, 1941.

[1191] **"The Papers of Col. Henry Bouquet"**, 1941.

*Commenceing from Next May If I engage am willing to give Sufficiant security for the Performance of my engagement.*

## M^c^Gearry is late coming to Fort Cumberland

A November 7, 1759 letter[1192] Captain Robert Callender wrote to Bouquet from Fort Bedford states:

*I ariv^d^ here on Thursday last with one Hundred and fifty five Horses and Since have Loaded from here three Hundred, and Shall to Morrow or next Day Send Send on upwards of an Hundred more, As the Man is not yet come from Virgenea to Fort Cumberland whom Col Messer Mention'd in his Letter wou'd be there the Sixteenth of the last Month, I desire y^r^ Instructions in Case he comes. y^u^ May depend on my doing every thing in My power for the Benefit of the Service...*

A November 17, 1759 letter (included below) reveals that the referenced man was Edward M^c^Gearry.

## Frazier continues his trade at Fort Bedford

A November 13, 1759 letter[1193] Ourry wrote to Bouquet from Fort Bedford includes the following statements:

*All the Artificers, except three Smiths, & as many Wheelwrights, & one Saddler, and some Carpenters have been discharg'd Some time. I have wrote to M^r^ Blythe to send me the Saddler from fort Cumberland that I may discharge the two together. This week I shall dismiss the Carpenters except two, having compleated all the Stores, & Granaries, & finish'd the necessary House & put the Guns under Cover, and perfected my Waggon-Bridge. I have also a Stock of Boards, seasoning against they may be wanted. In a little time we may discharge the Blacksmiths also, as I have set up a Smith, who is now at Work for himself in the Gunsmiths new House. And Frazer has built himself a Shop, intending to Work at his Trade.
...*

*Much of my time has lately been taken up in detecting Horse Stealers. The Man I mention'd to you sometime ago, going down with the King's & Callender's Horses, has now a Sore back.*

*I have just recover'd a Mare that had been carried off from Fort Cumberland as M^r^ Blyth Can Inform you.*

*Inclos'd you have the Minutes of two successive Courts of Inquiry, the first, at Capt^n^ Blagg's request, on my confining his Man, in Order to have him sent to Ligonier, the Second at mine to find out who was accessary to his Escape. Had I time, I could enlarge much on the Subject, but I shall only say that Capt^n^ Blag, on his Way to Fort Cumberland, overtook the Man ...*

## Read writes to Bouquet about Rutherford

A November 15, 1759 letter[1194] John Read wrote to Bouquet from Fort Bedford states:

*I received a Letter from M^r^ Galbraith Assistant Commissary at Fort Cumberland wherein he Expresses his concern for having so little to do, as Provisions Comes so Slow from Virginia; by his last Return there is but 1839^lb^ meal and 8 Beeves, and the Issuings P Diem amounts to 200 Rations.*

---

[1192] **"The Papers of Col. Henry Bouquet"**, 1941.
[1193] **"The Papers of Henry Bouquet"**, Volume IV, 1978.
[1194] **"The Papers of Col. Henry Bouquet"**, 1941.

*He has heard that M͏ʳ Rutherford has told some illnatured Stories to the General and You of his delaying Waggons and Refusal of some Beef Cattle; and that M͏ʳ Galbraith had been Retained by M͏ʳ Hoops to Refuse Provisions Coming from Virginia & to strike a dam on the Supplies from Virginia.*

*I Expect this will meet you at Fort Cumberland And on Inquirey you will be able to Judge of M͏ʳ Galbraiths Conduct if he has Erred it is in favour of the Troops, upon the whole I have Reason to believe he has Acted Agreeable to his Instructions which you was Pleased to Approve of. I should be the last that would Excuse him, if he has not acted up to the trust Reposed in him as it is the Security the Kings Forces have for being Provided with good Provisions Agreeable to Contract.*

The letter includes a postscript that states, *"Inclosed you have a Copy of amend͏ᵐ Relative to M͏ʳ Rutherfords behaviour to the Contractors Manager at F͏ᵗ Cumberland".*

## A man absconds with a horse, and rides it to Fort Cumberland

A November 18, 1759 letter[1195] Major Edward Ward wrote to Bouquet from Fort Bedford includes the following:

*I should be Averest to make complaints but am Obliged through M͏ʳ Grimeses The contractor's ill usage, to acquaint you That he took A Mare belonging to a Wagginor from Stonney Creek and ride Said Mare to this Garrison and from hence, to Cumberland, has Not returned heir Since his arrival there which is Some days ago.*

*Said Mare I Hired from this poor Man from the foot of Loral hill to Stonney creek My horse being tired. I depend on your Seeing this Poor Man don Justice. Captain Ourry has Entered the Wagginor's Name and Place of Aboad.*

## Robert Callender purchases horses at Fort Cumberland

A November 19, 1759 letter[1196] Captain Robert Callender wrote to Bouquet from Fort Cumberland states:

*I am to inform you that on the 17͏ᵗʰ Ins͏ᵗ I arrived at this Garrison With a Disgn to See you upon My Arrival I Met With Edward M͏ᶜGearry With a Brigaid of About 70 Horses who told Me his reason for Not being here Sooner was he had Not received Orders from Colonel Mercer So that he Could Not Cum Sooner & as I find the Horses fat and fit for the Service I have purchast Said Horses, Not With An intent to put them Upon the Crown but with An intent to keep them According to Contract Without you Should think proper to keep them in behalf of the Crown I Should have Weated here to have Seen You but M͏ʳ Reason Bell informs Me You Will Not be here in less then ten or twelve Days So that My business will Not Admit of My Staying any Longer if there Should be Occasion to Send this Brigaid Any More to Red Stone Creek I Should be Glad to No that I Might Send Sum Old hand to take Care of them.*

*Sir as I have been Alreadey to borrow Money and Know Oblig'd to borrow to pay M͏ᶜGearry, I Should be Extreamly Oblig'd to you if you Would Send Me a Draf for a thousand pownds as Our receipts for Carriages at this Time Amounts to between Nine & ten thousand pownds Exclusif of the loss of Horses and other Detainments I hop you will pardon Me for Disobaying your letter as it Was Cap͏ᵗ Ourrys Oppinion that we Should be Oblig'd to purchas More the roads being So bad if you Should Make Any halt at this Garrison & Should have Any instructions for M͏ʳ Hughs or Me upon intellegence of the Same Should imedeatly weat of you at that place.*

---

[1195] **"The Papers of Col. Henry Bouquet"**, 1941.

[1196] **"The Papers of Col. Henry Bouquet"**, 1941.

The letter has a postscript that states, *"I have Allso left With M<sup>r</sup> Blyth a Bundle of Money for you Which Cap<sup>t</sup> Ourry Sent by Me".*

## Blyth forwards salt and forage

A November 19, 1759 letter[1197] William Blyth wrote to Bouquet from Fort Cumberland includes the statement:

*I Reced your favour of the 9<sup>th</sup> Ins<sup>t</sup> and have done Every thing in my Power to forward the Convoys of Salt & Forage with all Expedition. Since the 12<sup>th</sup> Ins<sup>t</sup> I have sent out 97 horses loaded with salt & 73 Loaded with Forage for Red Stone Creek, upon the Receipt of yours I Wrote to Col° Mercer a very Pressing Letter to forward with all Possible Speed, forage and Salt, and mad bold to Inclose him a Copy of yours to me, at the same time I also wrote to his assistant on the South Branch M<sup>r</sup> Steenberger to the Same Import, but has as yet Rece<sup>d</sup> no answer.*

## Bouquet is heading to Fort Cumberland

A November 19, 1759 letter[1198] Bouquet wrote to General John Stanwix from Fort Burd includes the following:

*We arrived here the 16<sup>th</sup> The Water being so low that our Empty Battoes run aground twenty times, the River is now high enough, had we Provisions to Send down, But except Nine Waggons that came in last night, and five that are expected to day (having Sent back the Horses of the first to bring them up,) The rest of Ramsay's Waggons have given out, upon the Road and were obliged to carry the flour upon their Horses to the House at the Crossing.*

*The first have been 18 days from Cumberland and they Say that it is not possible for this year to bring up more Carriages; Pack Horses only can go in the Winter:*

*This day arrived 42 ½ Bush salt upon Pack Horses, which I Send down with what flour, is in store.*

*Col. Byrd can have no dependence upon the Waggons returning from this Post, as most of them leave them here taking only their Horses back.*

*We have lost again here some of the few Horses we had left, which distresses us greatly There are Thieves everywhere, and I expect great havock among yours when the Troops are ordered down.*

*I Set out to morrow for Fort Cumberland to forward the salt upon Pack Horses.*

*I bought twelve Barrils flour from some Country People; who have promised to bring more*

*The Snow is very deep upon the Mountains, tho' there has been no frost yet here.*

*The Fort is the prettiest thing of the kind I ever saw, and finished with the utmost nicety: ...*

## Callander's house has been lost to fire

A November 21, 1759 letter[1199] Blyth wrote to Bouquet from Fort Cumberland states:

---

[1197] **"The Papers of Henry Bouquet"**, Volume IV, 1978.
[1198] **"The Papers of Col. Henry Bouquet"**, 1940.
[1199] **"The Papers of Henry Bouquet"**, Volume IV, 1978.

*Last Night we received the Unhappy news that poor Cap.<sup>t</sup> Callander has met with a most Mellancholly Accident his House in Carlisle and all he had together with all his Papers are Burnt to Ashes, having only the Comfort that his wife & Children Excaped the Conflagration, and am Sorry to hear you are a Sufferer allso, as Everything you Left there is gone allso. I am apprehensive Cap.<sup>t</sup> Ourry's Letters will inform you more Particularly of this affair.*

## Enough storehouses repaired at Fort Cumberland

A November 26, 1759 letter[1200] Bouquet wrote to Stanwix from Cumberland states:

*after the constant disapointments we have met with from Virg.<sup>a</sup> I could expect but little from that Province But even that little has failed, for I find here neither salt forrage, or flour nor do I hear anything of M.<sup>r</sup> Mercer or his Contractors: I Shall loose no time in repairing that breach:*

*M.<sup>r</sup> Graham had sent here 149 Bushells of salt to which have been added 57 Bushells bought here from D.<sup>r</sup> Ross. The whole is gone to Fort Burd and tho' the Weather has been very wett I hope you will receive the greatest Part of it.*

*I have sent this morning for 50 Bushells more lefft upon the Road from Winchester, which I hope to forward in three days, having horses ready for it.*

*There was about 300 Bushells at Bedford The half has been sent up, Tbe rest goes upon Pack Horses in three days; If that quantity Should arrive safe it would be enough. But I Shall not trust to uncertainty's. I have ordered 200 Bushells that are at Fort Loudoun in Pens.<sup>a</sup> to be sent for & forwarded Immediately besides what Chance may Send us from Winchester and to prevent accidents every Bagg Shall be covered w.<sup>th</sup> a Blankett, and the Horse masters will have Waggon Cloath & likes to build a Shade every night to Keep it free from the damp.*

*These Blanketts will serve for the Troops at Pittsburgh and if the Hospitall Blanketts are not sufficient I have directed Cap.<sup>t</sup> Ourry to buy as many more at Bedford as will be wanted.*

*He is also to forward the 500 Heads of large Cattle, bought by M.<sup>r</sup> Hoops for the Winter stock which w.<sup>th</sup> what you may have lefft and the Hogs to be sent from Virg.<sup>a</sup> will be over and above what you may want.*

*We have bought Horses collected strays & Impressed whatever was able to carry a Load to the Mononghehela, and tho' late, I hope the Troops will not suffer But after this fatal Experience of the Virg.<sup>a</sup> Promises and ressources any man who could trust them, deserves to be served as we are.*

*one Hundred Horses are gone up from hence with forrage & with what has been Sent lately to Ligonier I suppose you will have a sufficient quantity.*

*Cap.<sup>t</sup> Callendar has had the Misfortune to have his House at Carlisle burnt to the ground with every thing in it except his Wife & Children and by that accident, I have lost all the Papers and Receipts concerning the public Service to the End of July which I had left there, besides my Bagage & private Papers.*

*His Partner M.<sup>r</sup> B. Hughes is come here to have £1200 Pens.<sup>a</sup> Currency to pay his drivers & the last Horses they bought to carry the Salt, gone from hence and Cap.<sup>t</sup> Ourry wants £400 for his Department, as I have no Credit upon Pens.<sup>a</sup> I beg you would please to order a bill of £1000 sterling upon Nelson to be Sent to Cap.<sup>t</sup> Ourry for those Waggons The Warrant and Receipts to be drawn in my name.*

---

[1200] "**The Papers of Henry Bouquet**", Volume IV, 1978.

*The Roads are so bad that I was obliged to abandon my Waggon & Baggage, in the Woods loading the best upon the Horses nothing but Pack Horses can go this way at present; The flatt was finished but the Bridge being a great Work will not be done for two days*

*I expect every moment to hear from M*^r^ *Graham & Mercer, and as soon as I see the Salt forwarded, I Shall proceed to Winchester to finish if I can forever with all those worthy Gentlemen*

*There will be a Sufficient quantity of Storehouses repaired here to answer all the Purposes of the next Campaigns & I got a flatt build to cross the River & back.*

*The Remainder of the Second Bat*^n^ *Recr*^ts^ *are marched to Bedford, where they are to Stay till they receive your further orders;*

*Inclosed you have two Courts of Inquiry concerning the extraordinary Proceeding of Cap*^t^ *Blagg's and I have discovered the 13 Was carried down by Cap*^t^ *M*^c^*Neal, he had before sent five to Virg*^a^ *which were sold for his account wether his property or not I do not know your orders will come to me sooner by Bedford than by the Road.*

*There is about 50 Barrells of M*^r^ *Ramsays flour in the stores at the great Crossing, where the Virg*^a^ *Reg*^t^ *may be Supplied if they come down*


## Disappointment from Virginia

A November 27, 1759 letter[1201] Bouquet wrote to Captain Ourry from Cumberland states:

*I arrived last Night after a long & tedious march, having left part of our Baggage with the Waggon on the Road, and brought the best upon the Horses back.*

*I rec'd. your Letters of the 13*^th^ *17*^th^ *& 20*^th^ *& 24*^th^ *Inst*^t^ *which I Shall now answer.*

*I find this Post contrary to Expectation without forrage and not a grain of Salt. I cannot & I believe nobody can account for Lieut*^t^ *Col. Mercer's extraordinary Conduct, nor what he has done of the large Sums he has received. I am afraid to look in the Bottom of all this: I hear nothing of him, nor of our Contractors but See plainly that we can have no dependence upon Such People.*

*Therefore must do everything from Bedford. You'l please to load The first Horses of Callenders & Hughes fit for service, with all the salt left at Bedford, without keeping an Ounce of it. These Horses must be Chosen among the best as They are to proceed to Pittsburgh.*

*The Salt is to be put in strong Bags, about two Bushells & a half in Each, and the Drivers provided with Thread & Needles to repair them. Each bag is to be Covered with a Blankett, and you will Employ for that Use The Hospital Blanketts, but if they were not Sufficient you'l Buy as many as you'l want from M*^r^ *Hughes: Said Blanketts are to be left at Pittsburgh for the use of the Garrison and Besides the Blanketts the Horsemaster must be provided w*^th^ *one or two Waggon Cloths to Cover his Bags at Night when he cannot reach the Houses, and have two Axes to build a little Shade to keep the Salt from the Ground. Please to give the same directions for the Salt that might be forwarded from Ligonier.*

*You will also Send me one hundred of the Hospitall Blanketts here (if you have them) for the same use. But if you have not so many left. Buy as many new ones as will make them fifty only for this Post, and send also a Waggon Cloth with them. We send you two horses to fetch them.*

---

[1201] **"The Papers of Henry Bouquet"**, Volume IV, 1978.

*I cannot Promise you the Team you wanted with Hay, Keeping every Horse here to forward the expected Salt. But if you must have Hay for The General, Let me know it; In the mean time we Shall muster all your Horses, and if I can Spare that Team you will have it. There is I think Some salt at Littleton, and 11 Tierces and five Barrells at Loudoun*

*I beg you will take the most Expeditious method by yourself or Sinclair to get that Salt to Bedford and forward it at any Rate to Pittsburgh in the same manner as the rest.*

*You must'nt think of Sending any more Waggons to Ligonier, nothing but Pack Horses can be depended upon: so much for Salt*

*You are not to Salt any Meat at Bedford the Pork being Sufficient for that Garrison But some of the last Salt must be be left at Ligonier w<sup>th</sup> a Sufficient number of Beeves to serve the Garrison of 100 men to the first of July next, and some more for the Use of Passengers &c<sup>a</sup> The same for 30 men at Stoney Creek M<sup>r</sup> Hoops must provide for the other Posts below Bedford.*

*Tho the General has ordered 100 Bullocks P<sup>r</sup> week, this is only to be understood for the five or 600 Heads bought by M<sup>r</sup> Hoops for Salting. But he is not to send any more than that Number, as they had a great number besides at Pittsburgh.*

*Send me if you can a Return of the Quantity of flour, forrage & salt, received at Ligonier and Pittsburgh Since the 12<sup>th</sup> Ins<sup>t</sup> that I left it;*

*They had then 650 Barrells of flour at Pittsburgh, and no forrage: and at Ligonier about 90,000<sup>lb</sup> of flour, forrage uncertain. And you will keep the Pack Horses going with Salt, flour, & forrage, as long as they can*

*Those which are able, are to proceed to Pittsburgh I need not repeat that Salt is the first thing to be forwarded.*

*You may now Send the Cattle up, as we have forwarded 200 Bushells of Salt from hence, and about 50 more will go in two days, besides what you have & will forward from Bedford.*

*I write to The General to send you a Bill for a 1000 £ ster<sup>g</sup> out of which you will pay £1200 Pennsyiv<sup>a</sup> Currency to Mes<sup>rs</sup> Callender and Hughes and keep the remainder in your hands. The receipts must be made for me, as I shall be charged with the whole Sum.*

*I send you the Receipt for the money you have sent me Besides what you have discovered of Capt<sup>n</sup> Blagg and Capt" M<sup>c</sup>Neals dealings, I found out that the last had before Sent five Horses to Virginia which were sold for his Acc<sup>t</sup>*

*The Wine I thought to have at Bedford was left and went in Poor Callender's House.*

*I am undone If my Papers are destroyed, having all my receipts there before August, besides my private Papers & Baggage.*

*Please to send to Carlisle what Baggage I left in your Room, except my Gun, that I would have here if An Oppertunity Offers. I recommend to your Protection my two Pupps either to leave them in Your hands or send them down.*

*I shall not leave this Place till I have made Somthing of Virg<sup>a</sup> and heard what you can do on your side to save Our People at Pittsburgh: Send the inclosed with all dispatch to The General.*

*Farewell my Dear Ourry this is hard Work when we had reason to expect to have nothing else to do*

The letter has the following postscript:

*Col: Burd's Batt^n (200 Men) march to Bedford, as they have no Tents please to lodge them, in the Barracks & Hospital and to receive all The King's & Stray'd Horses they have*

## A new bridge at the Little Crossings

A November 27, 1759 letter[1202] Bouquet wrote to Captain Richard Pearis from Fort Cumberland states:

*You are to march to morrow Morning with Your Company to the Bridge now making over The little Crossing of The Youghyogeny with four days Provision for your Party, Cutting and clearing away all The Trees & other incumberances that you may find on the Road from hence to that place and Cut a New Road round such places as the Waggons can't pass. You will find A Tree with Three Nothes upon it about A quarter of a Mile on this side the little Crossing from which Tree you will open a New Road to the Bridge along the Valley, and from the other side of the Bridge you will cut as good a Road as you can into The Present one,*

*At the present Crossing you'l find a Bridge out of Repair You'l cutt new Loggs and make it Sufficient.*

*You are to Join Ensign Duffields Party and work upon the Bridge until it is quite Compleated, after which you are to march your whole Detachment to Fort Bedford and there wait for further Orders, when you have finished the Bridge you will find at the Great Crossing the Sillards all the Tools and what Provisions, &^ca you have not occasion for and take The Sergiants Receipt for the same. You take with you three Bullocks, and you'l send to the great Crossing for what flour you may want for your Detachment, and you will give each Man of your Detachment one Jill of Rum p^r day and keep a Regular Accompt of those that work & send it to Col^o James Burd who will pay them, you are to pin down every Logg upon the Bridge (but you need) not) Cover them with Fasheens & Earth are formerly directed*

A December 12, 1759 letter included below indicates that the recommended new road was not cut.

## Flour Inspection reports at Fort Cumberland

A November 27, 1759 *"Report[1203] of the Inspection made of a Quantity of Flour for the Use of His Majestys Troops, being Part of M^r Walkers Contract"* concerning *"9 Baggs of Meal"* at Fort Cumberland states, *"It is the Opinion of the following Officers Order'd by Colonel Bouquet to Inspect the Said Meal That it is Course, Damaged & not fitt for Use Given under our Hands at Fort Cumberland the 27^th of Novem^r 1759"*. The report is signed by Captain Levi Trump, Captain H^n Vanbebber, Lieutenant George Speake, Lieutenant C. Graydon, Lieutenant George M^cKnight, and Ensign Ryves Holt. The meal weighed 956 pounds.

The same men signed a November 27, 1759 *"Report[1204] of the Inspection made of a Quantity of Flour for the Use Majesty's Troops, being Part of Ramsay's Contract"* concerning *"10 Baggs of Meal"* and *"30 Baggs of Course Meal"* at Fort Cumberland states, *"It is the Opinion of the following Officers Order'd by Colonel Bouquet to Inspect the said Meal That it is Sound & Good in its Kind. Given under our Hands at Fort Cumberland the 27^th of Novem^r 1759"*. The ten bags of meal weighed 2,274 pounds, and the 30 bags of course meal weighed 6,604 pounds. Bouquet was at the fort in this timeframe.

---

[1202] **"The Papers of Col. Henry Bouquet"**, 1940.
[1203] **"The Papers of Col. Henry Bouquet"**, 1941.
[1204] **"The Papers of Col. Henry Bouquet"**, 1941.

### John Nicholls is appointed to serve the Old Town Hundred

On November 27, 1759, according to Volume 6 of "**Colonial Records of the Upper Potomac**", the Frederick County, Maryland court appointed John Nicholls to serve the Old Town Hundred above 15 Mile Creek, possibly as a constable.

### Mercer recommends a bridge over Wills Creek

A November 28, 1759 letter[1205] Colonel George Mercer wrote to Bouquet from Winchester includes the following:

*I received yours of the 9th Instant on my Return from Williamsburg, where not only my Business, but a most violent Cold I had taken, detained Me many Days longer than I expected; which made Me determine not to halt by the Way tho if a very bad Cold, & constant Fevers woud have apologized for a Delay, I really had those Arguments to plead in my Defence.*

*I am sorry Sir to find you have Cause to complain of the Contracts from hence not being complyed with tho I observe Mr Galbreath is not satisfied with The just Right he has, or rather the General and you have, to find Fault, therefore has chose in Order to help the lame Dog over the Style, to urge & assist absolute and notorious Falsities Sorry shoud I be, and much ashamed Sir, had I ever given you Cause to suspect the Truth of any Thing I affirmed, but here I shall insist that about 40 very honest Men may be called upon to convince you that I have not asserted a Falsity; but I will not take up more of your Time tho on this Subject, till I have the Pleasure of seeing You.*

*My Accounts shall be as clear as possible against you come down, indeed I never allow Them to be other ways, they are always ready & fit for Inspection but it is impossible to close Them, as my Customers are so dispersed thro the Country.*

*The Horses and Waggons being impressed for Mr Graham's Salt, has put an entire Stop to every Thing, as the Report imediately spread, but as he expects to get all his Salt, I am in Hopes they'll fall to Work directly.*

*You no Doubt Sir will see that a Bridge or Boat must be built over Wills's Creek. I am so well acquainted with that Stream, that I assure you 'tis not fordable in Winter, but very seldom and unless some Thing is done there it will entirely stop our Comunication to Red Stone &c. this Winter. I have been obliged to send to Norfolk for Oakum & Tar for repairing our Scows. The Ship Carpenter you sent, or ordered to be sent, Me in the Sumer has never yet appeared; but as I make no Doubt there are some in Colo Bird's Virginians I think it will be best to stop them at Cumberland till I send Tar & Oakum for the One at Patterson's Creek. They may take the other two over Poto at Cox's and Cacapchon near Enocks's in their way down; as I shall leave a necessary Supply of Tar and Oakum with each of Them. ...*

The letter includes the following postscript, *"As Cox who lives on the Poto refuses to take Care of the Ferry Boat woud it not be proper to leave two or three of the Soldiers there for that purpose?"*

### Bouquet's puppies are well

Two November 30, 1759 letters[1206] Captain Ourry wrote to Bouquet from Fort Bedford describe how he is complying with Bouquet's instructions. One includes a postscript that states, *"Mr Hughes desires that you will leave Directions to F Cumberland for the disposal of their Horses when they Return from Redstone*

---

[1205] "**The Papers of Col. Henry Bouquet**", 1941.
[1206] "**The Papers of Henry Bouquet**", Volume IV, 1978.

*Creek."* The other accompanied the delivery of Bouquet's gun to Fort Cumberland, and includes a postscript that states, *"The two Puppies are very well Pray let me know by the Return of the Express when you leave F Cumberland, & where I may direct to you next."*

## Wheeling and dealing in flour

A December 3, 1759 letter[1207] John Read wrote to Bouquet from Fort Bedford includes the following:

*I was Honoured with yours dated at Fort Cumberland the 27th Ultimo and am glad Mr Galbraiths Conduct is agreeable to you.*

*When I was at Fort Cumberland Mr Galbraith Shewed me Samples of Flour brought there by Country People independent of Walker or Graham which was as good as I could wish to have.*

*Mr Ramsay Complains by Mr Heath that Rutherford has hurt his Contract, by taking Coarse Meal such as he Refused, the People that Sell Meal to the two Contractors Ramsay & Walker, Say they will not make their Meal finer for the one as the other will take it as it is; So they have Agreed to hurt one anothers Contracts which brings their Colonys Supply to discredit.*

## Blyth writes to Bouquet

A December 4, 1759 letter[1208] Lieutenant William Blyth wrote to Bouquet from Fort Cumberland states:

*Inclosed you have a Return of My Last Weeks Transactions as also a Return of Forage Received Passed by & Sent forwards from this Garrison Since My Arrival Calculated to the best of My Power to give you all the Insight into this affair I Possibly could & am Possitive that it is an Exact Acco[t] of all the Forage Came this way, but am not Sure on whose Acco[t] Some of it was Brought whether on the Kings or Private Property*

*Last Night Part of Cap[t] Callenders brigade of Horses which he bought of Mr Geary Arriv'd here about 50 in Number & in a poor Shatter'd Condition the remainder being 18 are I believe lost or Dead, to day I Intend sending them 3 or 4 Miles on the road to Bedford Whether I am Sending em to Cap[t] Callender As I Don't find one of them fit to return to Red Stone.*

*I Assure you I begin to Dispair of Lewis Moors 24 Horses which I have Detained in Order to Rest them a few Days being able to return to Red Stone as the Weather Setts in so very severe however shall attemp[t] it. I Spoke to Mr Graham According to your Desire Puting him in mind of Paying for the Mare, he Says he wont Pay for her before he hears from Major Ward What She was appraiz'd at & Expects to Deduct of that the Value of her Work Since apprized.*

*Colonel George Mercer has wrote me to Know how we stand in Regard to Provisions, I take the Liberty to Begg the favour you would Acquaint him our Stock is 36 Beef Cattle and 11244# of Meal Exclusive of Ramseys According to the Commissary's Returns Yesterday Morning.*

*You May Depend on My Assiduity & Industery both to obay all your Orders & Endeavour by all Possibillity to get up the Salt of Mr Grahams.*

---

[1207] **"The Papers of Col. Henry Bouquet"**, 1941.
[1208] **"The Papers of Col. Henry Bouquet"**, 1941.

The letter includes a postscript that states, *"Sir this Morning About Six aClock an Express Arrived from Bedford, No Letters for You Colonel Burd of the Virginians Will be here this day about two aClock the lower counteys have recived Orders to hold themselves in Rediness to March."*

A December 5, 1759 letter[1209] Lieutenant William Blyth wrote to Bouquet from Fort Cumberland states:

*I am to inform you, that on the Arrival of Colonel Byrd I was obliged by his orders to furnish him with Ten of the Best Horses we had Belonging to the King, to go as far Cresaps, and I Intend they shall bring back a Load of Salt Each when they Return.*

*I am doing my best Endeavours to get up this Salt, and have Been Necessitated to Empress 8 Pack Horses, and the Horses of 2 Waggons, Carrying up Forage from the South Branch from SteenBergens Which I have sent Down for a Load of Salt to Cresaps, after they Return I Shall Reload them wit the Salt of M<sup>r</sup> Grahams here and to Proceed Red Stone Creek.*

## Failure to provide forage and wagons

A December 10, 1759 letter[1210] Richard Graham wrote to Bouquet from Fort Cumberland states:

*The people on the Branch has disapointed us in Bringing the Forage they Sold me, as also in the Horses, Which has oblig'd us to Stop a Brigade of eight Horses Load with Forage from the Branch for Redstone & thirteen Horses Load with Brandy &c which with what others we have already dispatch'd takes up the quantity Salt, excep't Forty eight Bushells, which I expect to procure Horses for, tomorrow or next day Without Using any of the Kings Horses. As M<sup>r</sup> Blyth thought these Twenty-five you ordered to go to Weak We have used none Since you left this, only a Brigade under the Caro of M<sup>r</sup> Moore to bring up 123 Bush<sup>s</sup> from Cock's here, 44 Bush<sup>s</sup> of which I must forw<sup>d</sup> with 4 Bush<sup>s</sup> here which makes out as above the 500 B<sup>s</sup> which with Walter's Brigad from Winchester of 100 B compleats the 600 Bush<sup>s</sup> the overplus being 79 B<sup>s</sup> must be left here without you think proper to send me New orders to empress on the Branch, in the mean I shall Stop 18 or 20 more Horses thats coming up with Brandy to take out the 48 Bush<sup>ls</sup> as I believe that Article cannot be much wanted, there being above Two hundred Horses pass'd Col<sup>n</sup> Cresap's Load chiefly with it, since you went down Captain Parris is just come in from the Little Crossings Four of my Beeves that was lost has been found & kill'd there, which I hope you will take into your Acc<sup>t</sup> what is found of them & kill'd here Shall look to M<sup>r</sup> Hoops for We have got three in here to day, four more is still wanting*

The letter has a postscript that states:

*I have a Waggon here and a Team very good Horses Should be glad to have them in His Majestys Service either here or elsewhere. The Soldiers Stationed at this place are Cutting Stockades for the New Fort, Which the Waggon might be taking to the place, for if the Woods getts on Fire which they Seldom miss theer work will all be Burnt*

## Reporting troubles at Fort Cumberland

A December 11, 1759 letter[1211] William Blyth wrote to Bouquet from Fort Cumberland states:

*I am to inform you that by order of Col<sup>o</sup> Byrd, as he marched down, Ensign Vass of his Regiment is appointed to take charge of all the Kings Stores at this place, and therefore imagines I have no further Business here, and request you will send me orders whether I shall march to Fort Loudon, where I*

---

[1209] **"The Papers of Col. Henry Bouquet"**, 1941.

[1210] **"The Papers of Col. Henry Bouquet"**, 1941.

[1211] **"The Papers of Col. Henry Bouquet"**, 1941.

*understand I am to be stationed this Winter. You will please let me know what I shall do with the money you left with me to pay for the Butter Cheese &^c that was taken into the Kings Store at Redstone Creek, as no one has applied to me for payment as yet nor perhaps will not before I go. I expect that M^r Graham will deliver the Last of his Salt, at this Garrison to night I have pressed two or three small Brigades of packhorses loaden with Forage for Redstone, and loaded them with Salt. The Forage I have kept at this place*

*The remainder of the Salt that is here I cant tell in what manner it will be carried up as the Kings horses are not able to carry a Load. I shall send the weakest of the horses to Cressops and what are able shall send down to Winchester*

*Since the affair of pressing these Brigades, there have several past by at a distance being afraid of being pressed had they come to the Fort therefore I think it will, be difficult getting horses at this place to carry up the remainder of the Salt this Season.*

*The Ship Carpenter that you agreed with at This place to build a flatt is gone with the rest of the Companies of the Lower Counties and would not stay on any account. The two Sawyers are getting of plank M^r Ourry has sent me nothing of the materials that is wanting for the Flatt but some Oakum Not one of the Virginians that are stationed here understand any thing of building a Flatt. I do not remember the materials that are necessary for it otherwise should have let you known agreable to your orders, having sent the memorandum that I had from the Ship Carpenter to M^r Ourry*

*I do not think any thing will be done further about the Flatt unless you send a Ship Carpenter from below w^th what materials he thinks will be necessary*

*I wrote you yesterday of the same import as this but have made bold to trouble you again lest the other should, have miscarried as I sent it by a Countryman*

## The horses at Fort Cumberland are in sorry shape

A December 12, 1759 letter[1212] William Blyth wrote from Fort Cumberland states:

*About 7 o'clock this morning I received yours of the 10^th. I could wish that Col^o Bouquet had received my Letter before this Express came from you wherein I have mentioned the true State of the two Virginia Brigades of Packhorses according to the best of my Judgment and the account we have of the Roads. It is also the opinion of M^r Lewis Moore that there is not above four or five horses belonging to the two Brigades here which would be able to carry a Load up. M^r Swaringham is not come in yet he is with a number of weak horses on the Road near the little Crossings I have sent forage to him to Enable him to come down.*

*This I have concluded that all the horses shall go down to Cressops where they shall have plenty of Forage and wait your answer, if they must proceed to Redstone with Salt I will take the best of them, there is still some Salt at Cox's and a quantity of Flower which I proposed to bring to this Garrison by the strongest of the horses before I sent them down*

*Please to acquaint Col^o Bouquet that I should be glad to have an answer to my Letter of the 11^th Instant if they are come to hand, as also please acquaint him that M^r Blair is not at this place, by order of M^r Hoops he is gone settle his accounts with him the sixth Instant and informed me, he would not be gone above ten days and shall acquaint him at his return of the Colonels orders*

---

[1212] **"The Papers of Col. Henry Bouquet"**, 1941.

*You also desire that I should make you a return of all the Salt received here and sent forwards to Redstone the which I shall endeavour to do the next opportunity.*

*I have informed Major Levingston of your desire for him to send down the Vouchers for the application of the £ 20 as also to acquaint you what time he was employed here as forage Master which I expect he will do by first opportunity which he informs me will be in two days as there is an Express to go down to Major Stuart to acquaint him of some Recruits that are enlisted for him here*

*Agreeable to your orders in regard of the weak horses, if they are able to march they shall all go down except twelve which shall be left at Col° Cressops which I suppose was a second consideration of Col° Boquets as he wrote me from Cressops that fifty of the weak ones should be left there.*

*Please give my compliments to Col° Bouquet*

## Bridge work west of Fort Cumberland

A December 12, 1759[1213] letter Captain Richard Pearis wrote to Bouquet from Fort Cumberland states:

*Agreeable to Your orders I have finished the Bridge Clear'd & Cut the Road on both sides thirty feet wide I did not cut the road the way you mark'd as I found Washington's road much the best & measured both the old & New roads and find the New to be nigher than the old by fifteen chains I have also renewed & made good every Bridge between the little Crossings and this Place, Cut round all Places where Waggons could not easily pass, have measured the road from the Bridge to this Place & markd it & find the distance to 23 1/8 Miles I was obliged to get more Liquor for the Men as M*<sup></sup>* Duffield deliver'd me but three Gallons. I have sent all the Tools to the Great Crossings but 12 Axes one Spade one Shovel & one Grubbing hoe which I have deliverd at Cumberland with the Horses & Geers &.*

*I have Inlisted Ten or Twelve Men & expect a great many more, should be glad you would be Pleased to order an Officer to Receive them from me at Carlisle as my Bussiness requiors me to return from there if discharged from that place.*

## Mercer provides instructions to Graham

A December 14, 1759[1214] letter Colonel George Mercer wrote to Richard Graham from Winchester states:

*Yours of the 12ᵗʰ Instant by Express was just now delivered Me. Col° Bouquet is not a little surprized at M*<sup></sup>* Livingston's presuming to interfere with those Horses he had so positively ordered to be impressed. The Col° tho has **again** given the necessary Directions on that Head, and expects you will yet see your Salt forwarded to Red Stone. What you have at Cumberland more than the 600 Bushels must be left there for the Use of the Garrison.*

*If any more of the Proprietors of the impressed Horses shoud refuse to proceed with Them, their Horses must be taken, & Soldiers chose out to drive Them and the Col° now sends Orders to have any impressed for that Service that come to Cumberland except those from the S° Branch, as they were Concerned in some Contracts for the King, to these he has given a Protection if loaded with any Comodity for the King's Use.*

*Waters having taken the Small Pox has prevented his Brigade being with you, tho all the Salt is already gone off from hence, & I expect his Horses in to Day to set out for Red Stone. Bill too with his Brigade*

---

[1213] "**The Papers of Col. Henry Bouquet**", 1941.
[1214] "**The Papers of Col. Henry Bouquet**", 1941.

will set off next week. If there is not a sufficient Quantity of Forage at Cumberland, to forward the Salt, Col° Bouquet desires you will provide it.

So soon as you get out all the Salt you must repair to this Place with your Certificates that your Accounts maybe settled, and you must take Care to note how each Load has been carried out whether upon Horses of the King, those that have been impressed & from whom, or such as you have contracted with.

Col° Bouquet has ordered Me to acquaint you that you shall be paid for those Beeves of yours found, when you produce proper Vouchers for Them, and that he has no Occasion for any Waggons for the public Works, therefore desires you may dispose of yours as you can.

## Horses are to be used to transport salt

A December 14, 1759 letter[1215] Bouquet wrote to Lieutenant William Blythe from Winchester states:

I have your Letters of the 10$^{th}$ & 12$^{th}$ Instant in which I see that Col. Byrd had given orders to Ens$^n$ Wass to take Charge of the stores at Fort Cumberland. In consequence thereof you will please to take an Inventory of all kinds of stores in the said Fort leaving a Copy thereof to Ens$^n$ Wass, and sending me another Signed by him and you.

The People of the S$^{th}$ Branch being concerned in some Contracts for Forrage & other Provisions for the use of the Army, I have given them a Protection for their Horses, which are not to be Impressed; But any other Horses going up, and chiefly those loaded with Liquor, are to be Impressed to carry the remainder of the salt, except 79 Bushels which being over and above the 600 contracted for must be lefft at Fort Cumberland for the use of the Garrison.

Besides the Horses loaded with salt some must be loaded with Forage to enable the rest to make their Trip: and if you have not a Sufficient quantity in store for that purpose, M$^r$ Graham must provide it from the S$^{th}$ Branch

All the King's Horses branded are to be sent to Col. Cresap who will keep 50 of the weakest of them to be wintered there. I write to him on that subject and you will Please to give him the £ 112-5-6 Virg$^a$ Money I lefft you, to buy forage &$^c$ for Said Horses The two Horse Masters, with all the Drivers and the remainder of the King's are to proceed from Cressap to Winchester, where L$^t$ Col. Mercer will dispose of them.

And all the Strays, and Horses not branded are to be Sent by soldiers to Cap$^t$ Ourry at Bedford to be wintered at Fort Loudoun; except such as would not be able to perform that Journey, which must be Sent to Cresap, and be Part of his 50. He is to provide People to attend said Horses during the Winter, and not keep any of the Drivers.

Col. Byrd lefft at Cumberland the only Boatbuilders he had, Therefore if they cannot build the Flatt, It must be laid aSide for this Winter; and in that Case consult with Col. Cresap if the old Flatt sunck at Colyers could not be got up to Cumberland, to make Shifft w$^{th}$ some repairs till the spring.

When you have sent the Horses to their respective Quarters, and taken the above Inventory of the stores with M$^r$ Wass you will go to Bedford where you are to Settle your Accounts with Cap$^t$ Ourry charging your Pay to the 31$^{st}$ Inst$^t$ and then proceed to Fort Loudoun.

---

[1215] **"The Papers of Col. Henry Bouquet"**, 1940.

## The King's horses are moved to Cresap's place

A December 17, 1759 letter[1216] Lieutenant William Blyth wrote to Bouquet from *"Colonel Cresseps"* states:

*This Morning about Nine aClock I Received your favour of the fourteenth Ins[t] & Shall Punctually Observe all your Orders there in to the best of My Knowledge, about three aClock this Day I Set owt for Colonel Cresseps to Dispose of the Kings Horses in the best Manner I Could, as all that could be collected of the two Virginia Brigaids are assembled at this place Under the Direction of M[r] Lewis Moor & Thomas Swearingen & Shall Agreeable to your Direction Dispose of them before I leave this place.*

*You Also Desire I Should pay to Colonel Cresep the Hundred & Twelve pownds Virginia currency. Sir I am to Inform you that Sundry Bills which I did Not think of whilst you wore here have came in Since, The which Makes Me unable to produce that sum in that Specia. I think I Shall be able to give him this Day Nintey or a hundred pounds of it & I Shall Acc[t] with M[r] Ourry Aggreeable to your orders for the remainder of the Cash received of you Sir I Shall with My return of the Stores a Copy of the receipt from Colonel Cressep for the Cash delivered him.*

*Sir there is Nothing Surprises Me More then Seeing a letter from you Reflecting on Major Levingston Conduct in Not impressing Horses Or otherwise forwarding his Majestys Service. I assure you Sir & upon My Honour there could Not be a Man More Ascedious for the good of the Service then Major Levingston was And to the best of My Knowledge Shew'd No parsiality to any Person Whatsoever as for M[r] Grahams Letter I think it is Malishous and Without any Foundation & Sir I think I have as good a right to Know these things as any Person Whatsoever & Sir had there been any Such thing Transacted there I Should have Acquented you of it. I think Sir in Sum Measure it is a reflection upon Me, that a think of that Kind Should be done & there who had the Charge*

*Sir You Also Mention y[t] M[r] Graham Will Find Forage for the pack Horses Carrying out this Salt please to give Me leave to tell You that it dos Not appear to Me that Ever M[r] Graham Will find Forage to Carrey out this Salt.*

*For this reason he has Made Several Attempts or at least Said So, that he had purchast Several parsels of Forage, but I Could Never See it yet, this fur I Know that he press'd Me at this Garrison to take 14 Horses Belonging to poor people which had been up at red Stone Creek to go about fifteen Miles for Corn Which he Said he had readey to go for I Assure you Sir they return'd Without it as there was None there for M[r] Graham. in Short I think this Sir that if M[r] Graham had Continued at Winchester & Never Appear'd in the Contry about the Cariage of the Salt but Endavour'd to get it to Fort Cumberland it Might I think have been, or would have been at Pittsburgh Before Know*

*Please to Excuse heast & the Imperfectness of this letter*

## Certificate of Mr. Graham against Mr. Livingston, Fort Major at Cumberland

Amongst Bouquet's papers is a December 19, 1759 certificate[1217] that was prepared at Fort Cumberland and signed by Richard Pearis and Rachford Duffield. The certificate states:

*This is to Certifie That we the Subscribers were present and heard Major Livingston Tell M[r] Rich[d] Graham that he the Said Graham was very much to blame for bring back Macraes Horses, And that Said Graham might depend on <u>Suffering</u> for it to which Said Graham Answer'd that he tho't it was agreeable*

---

[1216] **"The Papers of Col. Henry Bouquet"**, 1941.
[1217] **"The Papers of Col. Henry Bouquet"**, 1941.

*to all the Gentlemen here at the time as they were all present when the thing was propos'd on which we the subscribers heard Maj[r] Livingston reply that it was not agreeable to him, and further added that he would not Suffer another Horse that was coming up the Road, to be impress'd to Carry Salt let the consequence be what it would. And he the Said Livingston further Said that Col[o] Bouquet would not take nor Suffer to be taken the Horses that were coming up for that Service, with many oth[r] things to the same purpose Still blameing Said Graham, to the highest degree for offering to proceed in that Manner*

## Addressing the Virginia accounts

A December 20, 1759 letter[1218] Bouquet wrote to Stanwix from Winchester includes the following:

*I was detained here much longer than I exxpected to and have finished at last our accounts wth Virg[a] Except a few, who have yet their Horses in the Service; I have paid all what was clearly due. But referred all their Losses to your further Consideration I take all the Vouchers with me, to enable you to make them what allowance you may think proper for the Same.*

*You will see by the Inclosed Accounts the amount of the total Expence, and what money remains in D[r] Walker's & L[t] Col. Mercer's Hands to pay the ballance, due in Virg[a] that Province when settled. M[r] Ramsay being not able to comply with His Contract I have given no good security to deliver at Fort Burd & for about £800 he remains debtor, for which he has engaged to deliver at Fort Burd a quantity of flour Part of Which is actualy at Cumberland, & Part in store at the great Crossing; We must therefore for the future have our Sole dependance for Bread from Pensilv[a] _____ Fort Cumberland; The Remainder will follow by degrees, having agreed with Several People to take Loads of it. But I am afraid it will be a difficulty to get it if the River is frozen*

## Ordinance stores at Fort Cumberland

Amongst Bouquet's papers is a December 22, 1759 *"Return[1219] of the different Species of Ordinance Stores"* at Fort Cumberland. The return includes 10 Pieces of Cannon, 107 Muskets fit for Service, 142 Muskets out of Repair, 46 Broken Muskets, 150 Cannon Shott, 100 Paper Cartridges for Cannon, 26 Barrels of Powder, 349 Boxes of Musket Ball, 28 Keggs of Fusee Ball, 1 Powder Barrels w[th] Pistol Ball, 4 Boxes of hand Granadoes, 4,000 Flints, 60 Bayonets, 80 Cartouch Boxes, 205 Gun Screws, 28 Tents, 18 Falling Axes, 3 Broad Axes, 2 Hand Hatchets, 2 Whip Saws, 2 Hand Saws, 3 Whip Saw Files, 7 Hand Saw Files, 4 Augers, 5 Chizzles, 1 Plain Irons, 3 Drawing Knives, 6 Scythes, 25 Bill Hooks, 8 Pick Axes, 7 Shovels, 2 Spades, 2 Iron Wedges, 1 Claw hammers, 1 Barrels of Single Tens, 70 Pounds of Double Tens, 15 Waggons Compleat, 13 Wheelbarrow Bottoms, 77 Wheelbarrow Wheels, 33 Park Pickquets, 62 Copper hoops, 1 Twenty eight pound weights, 1 Fourteen pound weights, 1 nine pound Weights, 1 Four pound Weights, 1 Two pound Weights, 1 One pound Weights, 150 Pounds of Oakum, 1 Four pound, Copper powder measures.

## Graham presents his certificate to Bouquet

A December 23, 1759 letter[1220] Richard Graham wrote to Bouquet from Fort Cumberland states:

*I have got receipts down from Fort Burd for about four hundred Bush[s] Salt, which with two Brigades I expect up from Winchester, Thirty King's Horses & ab[t] Twenty other's that is to Sett of from hence the 26th Ins[t] will about compleat the Quantity. There is Several Waggons come up from Winchest[r] Since I*

---

[1218] **"The Papers of Henry Bouquet"**, Volume IV, 1978.
[1219] **"The Papers of Col. Henry Bouquet"**, 1941.
[1220] **"The Papers of Col. Henry Bouquet"**, 1941.

*Wrote you last, So that there will be near Three hundred Bushells here, which I hope you will take for next Season.*

*As I understand by Mess$^{rs}$ Blyth & Vass that Maj$^r$ Livingston got Letters from them that they did not hear him Say any thing against taking Horses, have got a Certificate from the Gentlemen that was present a Copy of which you have inclos'd, for as I am a Stranger to you no doubt the Maj$^{rs}$ representations to you would readily make you believe that I had represented the thing to Col$^n$ Mercer wrong.*

### John Frazier was living at Fort Bedford in 1759

Frederick Post's December 30, 1759 journal entry documents John Frazier living at Bedford for some time, stating, *"...I...came late to Bedford; where I took my old lodging with Mr. Frazier."*

Although not documentary evidence, Chapter XXVII of the 1884 book "**History of Bedford, Somerset and Fulton Counties**" describes John Frazier's inn at Fort Bedford:

*When the Virginians, under Washington and Burd, marched from Fort Cumberland northward to join other detachments of Forbes' army at Raystown, Fraser and wife accompanied them, and on their arrival at this point, a small log cabin was built on the right bank of the Raystown branch, just below the present iron bridge, where meals were cooked for officers. The place finally became known as Fraser's Inn. Their son William, whose birth occurred in 1759, was, it is claimed, the first white child born within the present limits of Bedford county. Fraser became one of the most prominent men in the region surrounding Fort Bedford. As shown in a chapter relating to the first settlement of the three counties, he was present at Fort Pitt, in 1768, during a grand council meeting held between the representatives of the province and the chiefs of the Six Nations and other tribes, and with Capt. William Thompson (also a resident of Bedford in, 1768) was chosen as a messenger to visit and warn off the trespassing settlers located west of the Alleghenies. When Bedford county was organized he was appointed one of its first justices of the peace, and served as such until his death, which occurred before the beginning of the revolutionary war. Subsequently his widow married Capt. Richard Dunlap. She was the mother of children by both husbands, and thus became the ancestor of the Frasers of Schellsburg and the Williamses of Napier, Rainsburg and Everett. She died in 1815, in Colerain township. Capt. Dunlap, her second husband, was killed in a fight with the Indians near Frankstown in 1781.*

### A 1759 description of the cause of the war

While not documentary evidence, the 1759 book "**The Continuation of Mr. Rapin's History of England...**" states, *"The Pennsylvanians ... opened the design of the Ohio company to the Indians, whom he spirited up to call the French in to their assistance."*

### Fort Cumberland list of horses lost in service during 1759

Amongst Bouquet's papers is a Fort Cumberland list[1221] of horses that were either killed, died in service, lost in service, or captured by the enemy during 1759. The grand total of the losses was 235 horses.

### Martin's is illustrated at Georges Creek on a period map

A early manuscript map at the Library of Congress (G3821.S26 1760 .B7) titled *"Case C N° 1"*, from the Peter Force map collection, illustrates Fort Cumberland and Fort Burd, and illustrates *"Mastlins"* house

---

[1221] "**The Papers of Col. Henry Bouquet**", 1941.

(Martin's plantation) where Braddock's road crosses Georges Creek, and illustrates another house where Braddock's road crosses the Youghiogheny River. According to the Library of Congress, Fort Burd was established in 1759, which helps to date the map.

# 12. 1760: Lord Calvert approves a manor

### Preparations for the Western Department in 1760

Amongst the Bouquet papers[1222] is a numbered list that is titled, *"Necessary Preparations for the Western Department in 1760"*. The items specific to Fort Cumberland are:

*1. Form a Magazine of flour at the mouth of Conegogegue to be carried by Water to Fort Cumberland: Fix a Price for merchantable Flour, and good Meal, The Barrills to be well hooped.*

*2. Provide a number of Oxen Teams for the Service, with able drivers to be stationed at Bedford or Cumberland. ...*

*10. Repair the Roads, & determine whether to repair Braddocs or open a new one, in this case Send to reconnoitre*

*11. Establish Farmers at Bedford, Ligonier, Wetherhold, Cumberland, Crossing, Guest, F<sup>t</sup> Burd, and Pittsburgh to raise oats, Indian Corn, Wheat, and Rye &<sup>c</sup> a Power vested in the Command<sup>g</sup> officer to grant such Lands. ...*

### Livingston reports on salt deliveries

A January 9, 1760 letter[1223] Major James Livingston sent to Bouquet from Fort Cumberland states:

*I Having this Opportunity to Acquant you that on My way to this Fort the 24<sup>th</sup> Ult. I met Near Col<sup>o</sup> Crissaps M<sup>r</sup> Graham Goeing to Crissaps to hold His Christmas. I asked him if he had Seen Any Pack Horses Goeing upwards (with Liq<sup>rs</sup> he Told me he had & Gave the Serjeant Orders to Stop them. I desired the said Graham to Return & see the Horses Loaded His Answer was, the Serjeant had Orders to Load them. When I Arrived I Enquired if Such a Brigade had Pass'd the Fort was told they Had not. Upon which I sent Out a Party & Found them five Miles below this, Encamped in the Woods Who Brought them to this Fort with Eighteen Horses, Two of which was Unfit to Go Out, Where I loaded them with 1,635<sup>lb</sup> of Salt As Appeared by their Receipts from Fort Burd the 9<sup>th</sup> Ins<sup>t</sup>.*

*This Day Cap<sup>t</sup> Moore Seets off with his Brigade of the Kings Pack Horses Consisting of Forty Horses, & Carrys As Near as Can be Conjecherd 6,000<sup>lb</sup> of Grahams Salt Cumputed to 100 Bushells at Sixty Pounds p Bushell. By Computation the Quantity the first Brigade Carried was 27 ¼ Bushells Total of Salt Carried forward is 127 ¼ Bushells Remaining in Store Forty four Baggs Suppos'd to Contain four Bushells in Each Bagg Makeing in the Whole 176 Bushells*

*The Quality of Forrage Rec<sup>d</sup> Out of the Kings Store for the Use of the Two Brigades of Pack horses Carrying of Grahams Salt is thirty Seven Bushells of Corn, and Ninty Bushells of Oats, with 1,300<sup>lb</sup> of Hay for said Horses they Also Drue One Hundred & thirty four Rations of Provisions for the Horse Drivers This I send you in Case Graham Wants To Settle with you before all his Salt is sent forward As I Dont Expect there Can be Any More Sent Out till the beginning of March*

---

1222 **"The papers of Col. Henry Bouquet"**, 1940.
1223 **"The Papers of Col. Henry Bouquet"**, 1941.

## Two Kegs of whiskey for Fort Cumberland

A January 13, 1760 letter[1224] Captain Ourry sent to Bouquet from Fort Bedford includes the statement:

*Major Livingston has applied to me for Liquor to give to the People employ'd about the Garrison, Horses &c: I wrote him that I thought Fort Cumberland was to be intirely Supplied from Virginia but he tells me that Liquor is not in their Contract. So, I have Sent him two Keggs of Whiskey, with Caution to be very Sparing, for that I should not send any more soon.*

*He informs me that Capt[n] Moore, Sat off the 10th Ins[t] with 40 Horses loaded with Salt, and 12 with Forrage, for Red Stone.*

## Packhorse matters

A January 25, 1760 letter[1225] Colonel George Mercer wrote to Bouquet from Winchester includes the statement:

*I expect to be able to bring you a compleat Settlement of all the Accounts, except for Grahm's Salt, which has been sent by so many different Hands, that I despair making a Conclusion of that Matter. M[r] Walker too is very bad with the Rheumatism at Home, but Rutherford I think can do his Business.*

*Moore I expect is by this at Cumberland on his Return. He went out with 45 or 50 of our Pack Horses with Salt. I have sent him Orders upon his Arrival at Cresap's to discharge all his Men for 25 Days when they are to meet him there again by which Time the Horses will be sufficiently recruited and able to go another Trip. As We have great Plenty of Forage at Cumberland, the Horses can very well carry out a Load every Month which will greatly defray the Expence of Pasturage.*

## Cultivated land near Fort Cumberland in 1760

Volume II of the 1810 book "**Laws of the Commonwealth of Pennsylvania: May 24, 1781-Sept. 3, 1790**" references a court case *"Ross's lessee, v. Cutshall"* that took place at Bedford, Pennsylvania in October 1806, stating:

*The plaintiff claimed under a warrant of the 1st of February, 1760, from lord Baltimore to David Ross, "for 500 acres of vacant land, in Frederick county, Maryland, between Little Meadow and Buck[1226] on Potomac river, above Fort Cumberland, partially cultivated.*

## Samuel Welder becomes the administrator of the Christopher Gist estate

On February 5, 1760 Samuel Stansby Welder was appointed[1227] by the Frederick County, Virginia court to be the administrator of the Christopher Gist estate. Thomas Rutherford was one of the individuals who was appointed to be an appraiser of the estate.

---

[1224] "**The Papers of Henry Bouquet**", Volume IV, 1978.

[1225] "**The Papers of Col. Henry Bouquet**", 1941.

[1226] This may be a reference to David Ross's interestingly named May 3, 1762 survey *"Buck Lodge"*, where the Allegany Fairgrounds are located.

[1227] "**Colonial Records of the Upper Potomac**", Volume 6.

## Few provisions are available at Fort Cumberland
A February 21, 1760 letter[1228] Adam Hoops wrote to Bouquet from Carlisle includes the statement, *"I find they have but a small quantity of Provisions at Fort Cumberland & Redstone Creek."*

## Country people at Fort Cumberland
A March 1, 1760 letter[1229] Colonel George Mercer wrote to Bouquet from Winchester includes the following:

*A few Days ago I rcced a Lre from the Comissary at Red Stone, acquiainting Me, that Garrison would be out of Flour, in 14 Days from the Date of his Letter, which Time had expired before it came to Hand. I dispatched an Express imediately to Cumberland to desire Maj* Livingston woud do the best he coud, to supply Them, till I coud send off the Pack Horses, and I am told he impressed 19 Horses belonging to some Country People, and sent Them off imediately loaded with Flour. I had before ordered Moore out the 25th Ult° with the 50 Horses at Cresaps, to take up the Remainder of Graham's Salt, and the Lre just arrivings I met him here, I ordered him off Imediately, to load with Salt at Cumberland, and carry it to the Great Crossing, there to change it for a load of Flour, & after leaving it, at Red Stone, to return & take up the Salt, as this Supply of Flour woud last that Garrison till the Middle of May or June. He set out with his Men from hence the 21st Feb* and I hope is a considerable Part of his Way to Mononahela by this, As we have Plenty of Forage at Cumb* Moore says the Horses perform better now then in the Sumer M* Walker is not yet come up, the Town & Country round Us being much infested with the Small Pox which has now become very fatal. ...*

*As We may expect moderate Weather now, I think Col° Byrd's Regiment coud not be so well employed as in repairing the Roads between this and Cumberland. If the General would please to write the Gov* about it I am certain he woud order Them imediately upon that Service.*

The reference to country people indicates the presence of civilians at Fort Cumberland.

## A few hogs dropped off at Fort Cumberland
A March 10, 1760 letter[1230] Ourry wrote to Hoops from Fort Bedford includes the statement, *"Since writing my first of this Day's Dated have received 39 Hogs from Virginia, 8 were left at F* Cumberland and 2 or 3 Drowned on the way."*

## Samuel Plum is selling rum and cider in 1760
According to an £2/3/3 bill that is reproduced in Volume 6 of **"Colonial Records of the Upper Potomac"**, Samuel Plum sold rum and cider to William Philips on March 11 and 13, 1760. Later, in 1763, Plum would apply for a license to run an ordinary. The bill, which was proven on September 26, 1766, also includes a March 10, 1760 charge for *"Sundry Expenses"*.

[1228] **"The Papers of Col. Henry Bouquet"**, 1941.
[1229] **"The Papers of Col. Henry Bouquet"**, 1941.
[1230] **"The Papers of Henry Bouquet"**, Volume IV, 1978.

### New watercraft on the Potomac

A March 14, 1760 letter[1231] Captain Evan Shelby wrote to Bouquet from Frederick Town includes the following postscript:

*Sir there is two or three New Battos and Severall New Connoss made on partomack River since you was there so that I beleive if ther was work for them that they wood go on very Briskly and Severall mor talk of Bilding Battos if they were Shuer of work to doo this Sumer by Watter from frederick to Cumberland.*

### Hogs have been sent to Bedford and Cumberland

A March 14, 1760 letter[1232] Hoops wrote to Bouquet from Carlisle passes Ourry's March 10 information along with the statement, *"M<sup>r</sup> Walker has at Last sent some few Hoggs to Bedford, and Cumberland; But I am not informed of any going to red stone..."*

### Cresap sues Welder

Samuel Stansby Welder was sued[1233] by Thomas Cresap for 313-1/4 pounds of tobacco and £23/18/9 on March 18, 1760. Thomas Cresap received a promissory note from William Ives for £8/16/3 on November 12, 1756, for which unpaid debt Cresap sued Ives in the Frederick County, Maryland Court on June 19, 1759. Welder had been Ives' manucaptor in the Cresap versus Ives case, and was sued over Ives' failure to pay Cresap.

### Flour at Fort Cumberland will be transported west

An April 6, 1760 letter[1234] Captain Ourry sent to Bouquet from Fort Bedford includes the statement:

*I observe that you have agreed with a Virginian for 50000<sup>lb</sup> of Flour to be delivered at F. Burd by the 15 of May I don't know if I have done right, but I thought Store no Sore, Therefore have Contracted with a Marylander to deliver 50000<sup>lb</sup> at Fort Pitt, by the 30 of August, at Such Price as shall be allow'd to others. And 50000 more, if required, by the 30 of October.*

*10000 of the above Flour is actually at F Cumberland, and 10000 more wdl be there in 10 Days, brought by Water, and as soon as the Season will permit, the Waggons will begin to transport it. I fear no Disappointment from this Man who the better to enable him to perform his Contract, is to receive at Carlisle, 20 Sh<sup>t</sup> on Acc<sup>t</sup> for every C<sup>t</sup> lodged at Fort Cumberland. the remainder to be paid on delivery of the whole at Fort Pitt by me, or any other Manager.*

### Welder writes a promissory note to Thomas Prather

On April 10, 1760 Thomas Prather received a promissory note from Samuel Stansby Welder. The Frederick County, Maryland court issued a summons to Welder, requiring him to appear before the court in November 1761 in order to answer Thomas Prather – evidently for defaulting on the debt.[1235]

---

[1231] **"The Papers of Col. Henry Bouquet"**, 1941.
[1232] **"The Papers of Henry Bouquet"**, Volume IV, 1978.
[1233] **"Colonial Records of the Upper Potomac"**, Volume 6.
[1234] **"The Papers of Henry Bouquet"**, Volume IV, 1978.
[1235] **"Colonial Records of the Upper Potomac"**, Volume 6.

## A proposal for a military road that would finally be cut 19 years later

An April 26, 1760 letter[1236] Bouquet wrote to Stanwix from Philadelphia states:

*As it is probable that the War can not last much longer on this Continent; and consequently that no Provincial Troops will be raised hereafter; All Publick Works requiring great number of Hands Should if possible be executed this Campaign.*

*On that supposition I beg leave to lay before you my sentiment concerning the communications w^th the Ohio: We have at present two Roads to Fort Pitt; the cotinual repairs of which will require every year a number of men, who can hardly be Spared from the Garrison of that Post, and these Roads being extended out of the settlements, will soon become impracticable by the Severity of Winters in those Mountains, as it is not to be expected that the Provinces will repair them.*

*But if the two Roads were reduced to one, the Repairs would be reduced to one half: What is to be considered in that Case is which Road Should have the preference? not to disoblige either of the three Provinces, or obstruct their Trade? To avoid giving any Jalousie, and for many other Reasons I am of opinion that neither the Virginia, nor the Pensilvania Road ought to be chosen, But a new one opened in such a manner as to serve equally these three Provinces.*

*By the actual surveys of both Roads, It appears that Pittsburgh lies about 60 miles to the Northward of Fort Cumberland, & about 30 to the Northward of Bedford.*

*The distance from Lancaster to Pittsburgh by the Pensilvania Road is 245 Miles.*

*If that Road in Stead of going thro' Carlisle was directed thro' York Town, Fort Frederic, and Fort Cumberland, the Distance to Pittsburgh would be about the same, and you have no mountains as far as Cumberland excepted the S^th Mountains, which are very Inconsiderable & you miss intirely Seydeling Hill, & Rays Hill, as I observed in coming down the Patowmack that this River makes large Gaps in these two Mountains, and leaves a space of about 100 yards from the highest Water Mark to the foot of the Hills, where the Road would Pass.*

*There is not above 50 miles of that Road to cut to Fort Cumberland; Sir John S^t Clair having two Years ago made a considerable Progress in it, when the Troops employed there, were recalled by Gen^l Forbes, who thought the season too far advanced to finish it.*

*Besides the advantages of being equally convenient to the three Provinces, (beginning in Pensilvania, & going thro' Maryland and Virginia) this Road coast the Patowmack, and would afford an opportunity of making use of the navigation of that River, and running as far as Fort Cumberland thro' a settled Country, the Inhabitants could be obliged by Law to keep it in Repair, which can never be the Case with the Road to Bedford, the Land being too barren to be ever settled.*

*Now as the Course of Braddock's Road runs S^th West, in stead of N. W. from Fort Cumberland making the distance to Pittsburgh about 125 miles of a bad Road, with many Creeks and Rivers to cross; It is thought that a better and Shorter Road could be found in a direct Course N. W. beginning along Will's Creek, and avoiding the Waters of the Mononghehela and Yioghiogheny, (excepted the North Branch of this last), and passing near Gist's Plantation within a few miles of the last Crossing of the Yioghiogheny, where a Short Communication could be opened to make use of that River when navigable in the Spring & Fall, and continue the Straight Road till it Should intersect the Pensilvania Road, somewhere between the three Redouts & Pittsburgh.*

---

[1236] **"The Papers of Henry Bouquet"**, Volume IV, 1978.

*The Shortest distance from Fort Cumberland to the last Crossing of the Yioghiogheny is about 60 miles, & from thence to Pittsburgh about 40 d*[1237] *The Land Carriage would be reduced to those 60 miles, to the great advantage of that Communication.*

*If you Should think that this Road would answer the End of reducing the Communications to one common to three Provinces concerned. The Country beyond Fort Cumberland must be explored, and the Course blazed before the Leaves and Weeds are too thick: and Cap* Shelby Seems the properest Person to be employed, having already a knowledge of that part of the Country.*

*I can answer that this Road would be better and shorter as far as Fort Cumberland having seen it myself: But I can only guess at the rest by the general Face of the Country where I observed that the Allegheny and Lawrell Hills are not so high as where the Pens* Road crosses these Mountains.*

*Braddock's Road could still be used to go to Fort Burd on the Mononghehela, and the Pensilvania Road remain open to the People who would Chuse to go that Way*

Charles Clinton and Providence Mounts cut such a road in 1779, as described later in this book. It avoided crossing the Youghiogheny River, terminated on Braddock's road, near Hunker, Pennsylvania, and saved 20 to 25 miles over Braddock's road.

### Sharpe proposes that the proprietor's manor be located west of Fort Cumberland
A May 4, 1760 letter[1238] written to Calvert by Sharpe includes the statement:

*The Surveyor of Frederick County assures me that neither he nor either of his Assistants know or can hear of any Parcel of tolerable Land in the Inhabited Parts of the County which contains the quantity of 5000 Acres & is not already taken up by some Person or other, so that I am afraid it will not be possible to have another Mannour laid out & reserved there unless a Tract of good Land shall be discovered large enough for that Purpose beyond Fort Cumberland & His Ldp chooses to have a Mannour laid out in that distant Part of the Province.*

This letter reveals something of the extent of private land ownership east of Fort Cumberland in 1760.

### Colonel Byrd writes about Fort Cumberland
The following is a May 8, 1760 letter[1239] from William Byrd to Lieutenant Jethro Sumner of the Virginia Regiment:

*By the Honble William Byrd Esq. Colo of the Virginia Regiment and Commander In Chief of the Virginia Forces.*

*You are (with Sergeant Nash) to proceed with all convenient Expedition to Fort Cumberland, on your arrival there you are to Pay the Detachment of my Regiment in that Garrison two Months Pay for which you will take Receits.*

*You are to be extremely diligent in getting the Men taught the new Exercise, and have them out at Drill at least twice every Day, you are not to suffer any of them to work or do any other Duty besides that of the Garrison and learning their Exercise without my Orders.*

---

[1237] *"Ditto"*
[1238] **"Correspondence of Governor Sharpe, 1757-1761"**
[1239] **"The Colonial Records of North Carolina"**, Volume 6.

*Given under my Hand at Winchester this 8th Day of May 1760*

A postscript to this letter states, *"I shall send you all necessarys for the Men very Soon"*

## Colonel Byrd is ordered to Fort Cumberland

A May 28, 1760 letter[1240] General Robert Monckton wrote to Bouquet from Philadelphia states:

*The Express Sent to Pittsburgh not returning at the Usual Time, leaves me in Doubt as to the Situation of our Affairs that way.*

*I must therefore desire that you will not lose any Time in proceeding, immediately on the receipt of this letter, with The Four Companys of The R. A. R. to Fort Bedford, upon Your Arrival there, I desire you will directly Detach One Hundred Men, with Officers in proportion, to Fort Legonier, but in Case either that post, or Pittsburgh, should require Immediate Aid, I beg you will not fail to March with all The Troops you can Collect by Forced Marches, & without Baggage, to the Relief of Both, or Either, of Those Garrisons, As I am very Anxious about Legonier, there being a great many Ordnance Stores there, I would not have the party Intended for the reinforcement of that post Halt a Single Day, & if you see it is necessary to proceed there, with the whole 4 Companys, by Forced Marches, Your Baggage may very Easily follow You under the Care of a Small Escort.*

*I shall leave this place on Monday, & should be Glad to receive in my way up, any Intelligence that comes to your Hands I have Orderd Colonel Byrd to proceed without Delay to Fort Cumberland, from whence you will hear from Him on Your March, as you wall please to Open all letters directed for me, from any of The Posts beyond Carlisle.*

## Settlers are pushed to and fro

The May 29, 1760 issue of the "**Maryland Gazette**" includes the following:

*We hear that may Families who left the Western parts of this Province some Years since, on Account of the Indians, and went to settle in Carolina, are now by the Indians forced from thence, and return'd and returning to this Province again.*

## Colonel Byrd ordered from Fort Cumberland to Fort Bedford

A June 8, 1760 letter[1241] Gates wrote to Bouquet from Carlisle includes the statement, *"Byrd is Orderd to March His Men from Cumberland, to Bedford, & to Encamp there until further Orders..."*

## Joseph Mounts obtains land on Braddocks Road

A rectangular 100-acre tract named *"Good Will"* was surveyed for Joseph Tomlinson on June 8, 1760 by John Murdock and examined and passed on September 30, 1761 and patented to him (Frederick County Patent Certificate 1680, MSA S1197 1745). The tract began *"at a bounded wild Cherry tree standing on the North side of Braddocks Road and on the East side of the Little Meadows..."*

---

[1240] "**The Papers of Henry Bouquet**", Volume IV, 1978.
[1241] "**The Papers of Henry Bouquet**", Volume IV, 1978.

## Thomas Cresap is involved in two lawsuits

On June 17, 1760 Thomas Cresap was being sued[1242] by Frederick Garrison in the Frederick County, Maryland court, and James Livenston was being sued by Thomas Cresap.

## Lord Calvert approves a manor west of Fort Cumberland

A long letter[1243] Sharpe wrote to Calvert on July 7, 1760 includes the following:

*I conclude from what you say of His Ldp's Desire to have the best Land secured that is to be found in Frederick County that if a Quantity of vacant Land cannot be found on this Side Fort Cumberland he would have some secured beyond that Place & that if a large Tract is not to be found altogether, he would have so many smaller Tracts secured as will make up the Numbers of Acres he ordered to be laid out & reserved by way of a mannour & shall therefore give the Surveyor of that County Orders to proceed accordingly.*

## Thomas Cresap makes an offer to Bouquet

A July 24, 1760 letter[1244] Thomas Cresap wrote to Bouquet from Old Town states:

*At the Request of several of the Members of the Ohio Company, of which I myself am one, I take the Freedom of Acquainting your Honour, that they are inclined to let you be a Partaker of the Grant, which his Majesty has been graciously pleased to give them of Five Hundred Thousand Acres of Land, lying on & adjacent to the South Side of the River Ohio, on the same Terms and Conditions as they themselves are under, each Members Share of said Land being Twenty Five Thousand Acres.*

*If your Honour should approve of becoming a Member of said Company, I should be glad to receive a Letter from You, that I might acquaint the Gentlemen (several of whom are of his Majestys Council in Virginia) with your Determination*

The letter includes the following postscript:

*The Company proposes so soon as the Wars are ended, to settle the Land with Germans & Switzers, which they shall send for, and encourage.*

## Turner gives Welder power of attorney

According to the records of the Frederick County, Virginia court, Morris Turner gave Samuel Stansby Welder power of attorney on August 7, 1760.[1245] The purpose of this assignment isn't known. On the same day, Daniel Pursley was beng sued in the Frederick County, Virginia court by John Hardin. [1246]

---

[1242] "**Colonial Records of the Upper Potomac**", Volume 6.

[1243] "**Correspondence of Governor Sharpe, 1757-1761**", Volume 9.

[1244] "**The papers of Col. Henry Bouquet**", 1941.

[1245] "**Colonial Records of the Upper Potomac**", Volume 6.

[1246] "**Colonial Records of the Upper Potomac**", Volume 6.

## Thomas Cresap obtains lot no. 62 on the South Branch of the Potomac River

*The 1939 book*[1247] ***"Early Records Hampshire County Virginia"*** *records the following for August 8, 1760, "MURPHEW, Hugh of Hampshire Co. to Thomas Cresap of Frederick, Md. Lot No. 62 on So. Branch; rec. 3-10-1762. Wit.: Sam Dew."*

## Isaac Collier purchases Hart's Delight

Blacksmith Isaac Collier purchased the Hart's Delight tract from Thomas Cresap on August 8, 1760.[1248] The witnesses were Sarah and Ruth Cresap and Jarvis Hougham. Cresap surveyed this 85-acre Maryland tract on May 31, 1745 and patented it on June 25, 1759 (Patented Certificate 1848). The property includes the mouth of Collier Run and is located across the Potomac River from the mouth of Patterson Creek.

## Thomas Cresap describes the size of his farm in a threatening August 30, 1760 letter

On August 30, 1760 Thomas Cresap wrote the following letter[1249] from Old Town to Thomas Walker:

*The answer given me by Mr. Hoops, to my account, pasturage of cattle in 1758, greatly surprises me. He tells me the account is out of time, the charge is exorbitant, and that he don't believe that the pasturage was had. It is very extraordinary that a man of his forbearance should be cut out of his money. As to the rate charged, it is the same paid me daily, and as to the number of cattle and sheep charged, it is not a fourth part of what were pastured that year by me, Mr. Galbraith only signing a certificate for those last taken away, without allowing anything for what were killed the whole summer for the garrison at Fort Cumberland. As I always looked on you as a gentleman of an established good character, I cannot think you will agree to an act of injustice. Therefore hope you will order the payment of this account and prevent my giving you any trouble, that on its not being discharged I must, in justice to myself, do, and which would be very disagreeable to me. At the time the cattle were brought to my plantation, there was above 60 acres of meadow fit to mow, as good as ever scythe was put into, besides 60 acres of exceeding good pasture, and they had the full swing of the whole plantation. If I am obliged to make use of any means to right myself, which may not be agreeable to you, hope you will excuse me, as I choose rather to seek justice in Virginia than in Pennsylvania. I am, sir, your most humble servant. Thomas Cresap.*

The letter provides a peek at the size of one of the better-known farms in the area in 1758 and shows that it was used in support of provisioning Fort Cumberland. Cresap's attitude in this letter, which include a veiled threat, is best interpreted in the light of the difficult wartime experiences Cresap had recently been through, and the many contributions he made to the war effort. Cresap ended up suing Walker, as detailed later herein.

## Thomas Cresap serves on a Virginia jury.

On September 3, 1760 Thomas Cresap served[1250] on a jury in Frederick County, Virginia, which is hard to explain unless he was then living on one of his Virginia properties. This can't be Colonel Cresap's son Thomas, because that son was killed in 1756.

---

[1247] This book was identified by John DeVault.

[1248] "**Colonial Records of the Upper Potomac**", Volumes 4 & 6.

[1249] A transcript of the letter is provided in Volume 1 of the 1812 book "**Chronicles of the Scotch-Irish Settlement in Virginia**".

[1250] "**Colonial Records of the Upper Potomac**", Volume 6.

## A 1760 decision to repair the Wills Creek storehouse

On October 17, 1760, the committee of the Ohio Company passed a resolution to repair the Wills Creek storehouse that states:

*Resolved that the Companys Storehouse at Wills Creek be repaired and put into good Order, that the Treasurer write to Col° Cresap to furnish plank and Scantlin from his Saw Mill for that purpose and that Col°. George Mercer be Desired and empowered to agree with Workman to undertake the same taking Bond and Security for the performances and that the charge thereof be paid by the Treasurer on the Companys Account.*

The presence of a sawmill in the area in 1760 is initially surprising but shows the enterprising nature of Thomas Cresap. This seems likely to be the same sawmill that was mentioned in 1756.

## Frederick Ice proves an October 1760 bill before a magistrate

Frederick Ice appeared before magistrate Benjamin Kuykendall of Hampshire County on February 15, 1762 to prove a delinquent bill from October 1760 that was made out to Daniel Shybly.[1251] One of the items on the bill was using his horses to fetch Shybly's merchandise from John Nichol's place.

## Local appointments by the Frederick County, Maryland court

On November 18, 1760 the Frederick County, Maryland court appointed[1252] Issac Collier to be the road overseer between Nicholl's Neck and 15 Mile Creek, and appointed Providence Mounts as the constable of the Old Town Hundred. On the same day, an agreement was apparently reached in Samuel Stansby Welder's lawsuit against William Wells regarding the estate of Christopher Gist.

## A few Virginians are to be left at Fort Cumberland

A November 29, 1760 letter[1253] Bouquet wrote to Monckton from Fort Pitt includes the statement, *"The Virginians exceeding 300 R & F. are going down, and out of them Lt. Col. Stephen is to leave a few at Fort Cumberland."*

## Welder is sued in his capacity of administrator of Gist's estate

In his capacity as administrator of the estate of Christopher Gist, Samuel Stansby Welder was sued by Henry Reynolds, William Brown, Thomas Clark and Henry Baker in the Frederick County, Virginia court on December 3, 1760.[1254] The issue at hand was a large debt owed by Christopher Gist: £259/6/0.

## Frederick Ice is a chain carrier on a local survey

Frederick Ice was one of the chain carriers on a December 4, 1760 survey that was performed by John Moffett on Green Spring Run. The survey adjoined properties of Daniel Cresap and a Polson.[1255] This suggests that the Frederick Ice associated with the north branch of the Potomac Rive was no longer a captive of the Indians.

---

[1251] **"Colonial Records of the Upper Potomac"**, Volume 6.

[1252] **"Colonial Records of the Upper Potomac"**, Volume 6.

[1253] **"Collections of the Massachusetts Historical Society"**, Volume IX, 1871.

[1254] **"Colonial Records of the Upper Potomac"**, Volume 6.

[1255] **"Colonial Records of the Upper Potomac"**, Volume 6.

## Welder sues in his capacity of administrator

In his capacity as administrator of the estate of Christopher Gist, Samuel Stansby Welder sued Robert Stewart in the Frederick County, Virginia court on December 5, 1760.[1256] On the same day, Michael Murphy was sued by Thomas Cresap.

## Two cabins on the Cresap's Kindness survey

David Ross's December 14, 1760 survey[1257] for Cresap's Kindness mentions the presence of two old houses, stating, *"About Ten acres of Cleared ground whereon, is Two Old houses, ___ one about 16 feet by 12, the other about 12 feet Square Cover'd with Long Shingles"*. This 1,415-acre property is located within the Mexico Farms loop of the Potomac River. The presence of two old houses in 1760 is harmonious with early settlement activity.

## A falling out between Major Stewart and Joseph Galbraith

A December 23, 1760 letter[1258] Joseph Galbraith wrote to Bouquet from Venango states:

*I am Sorry to Inform You that Major Stewart of the Virginia Regiment has fallen out with me Beyond all Hopes of Reconciliation Altho' I have made all the Concessions in my Power. As I have always Acted on the Rules of Justice & Honesty I think it very hard to be Accused in the Manner I am; Your Honour thought Proper to Employ me Last year to Inspect the Provisions bro[t] from Virginia to Cumberland In the Execution of which if I was not too Severe I was not any thing Lenitive I don't Know that Major Stewart would be mean Enough to owe me Spite on that Acco[t] but Whatever it is he has Certainly Conceived an Irreconcilable Hatred to me. 'Tis True, I Scorn to Lye, I have been Times a Little negligent in my Bussiness but do Sincerely promise to do so no more. Major Stewart has Left me Pretty near thirty Pound Sterlings worth of Returns to Pay for, which is more than all my wages.*

*D[r] Sir out of your wonted Good Nature please to write to the Command[G] officer here to Sign those Vouchers Remaing & please to Consider I have Told you the naked Truth as I am Assured a Gentleman of Your Penetration would Soon find it out*

*As Major Stewart Intends me all the Mischief he Possibly Can I must Implore Your Intercession, & Suffer me not a Young fellow with a family Depending to be Ruined, which I am Sensible he will do if in His Power. this is the first time I Ever was a Supplicant and hope you will forgive the unwillfull Errors of Your most Obed[t] Serv[t] JO[S] GALBRAITH*

## Monckton recommends that the Virginia troops garrison Fort Cumberland

A synopsis[1259] of a December 25, 1760 letter Monckton wrote to Bouquet from Philadelphia includes the statement, *"Leaves the distribution of troops to himself, but thinks the Virginians should garrison Forts Burd and Cumberland..."*

---

[1256] **"Colonial Records of the Upper Potomac"**, Volume 6.

[1257] Frederick County Patent No. 1013, identified by Suzanne Trussell.

[1258] **"The papers of Col. Henry Bouquet"**, 1941.

[1259] **"Sessional Papers of the Dominion of Canada"**, Volume 23, 1890.

### A 1760 description of the cause of the war

Although not documentary evidence, the 1760 edition of Smollett's "**Continuation of the Complete History of England...**" states:

> ...*they sent one Mr. Gist to make a clandestine survey of the country, as far as the falls of the river Ohio; and... his conduct alarmed both the French and Indians. The erection of this company was equally disagreeable to the separate traders of Virginia and Pennsylvania, who saw themselves on the eve of being deprived of a valuable branch of traffic, by the exclusive charter of a monopoly; and therefore employed their emissaries to foment the jealousy of the Indians.*

This interpretation overlooks the fact that the French were on the move against British trade more than a year before Gist's first tour of the Ohio country, which began on October 31, 1750.

# 13. 1761: Bouquet's proclamation

**Fort Cumberland is reported as having double log and earth construction**

Volume 32 of the "**Archives of Maryland**" includes the *"Proceedings of the Council of Maryland, 1761-1769"*. In undated official correspondence to the Crown that is located between 1761 and 1762 documents, the following is written, *"...the other Called Fort Cumberland is 75 miles Farther Westward, this is Built with double Logs and Earth, I believe there are at Present a few Soldiers there sent from the Garrison at Pittsburg."* This confirms Barton's description of earthen ramparts and suggests a military presence at Fort Cumberland in the circa 1761 timeframe.

The *"double Logs and Earth"* statement, combined with Barton's description of 12-foot-tall 20-foot-thick earthen ramparts made with squared logs, indicates a robust structure that is much more substantial than the original stockade fort. The purpose of such construction was to offer a defense against direct fire weapons; i.e. cannon. It offered virtually no protection against the indirect fire of mortars.

The one description of such ramparts that I have seen, an educational video, depicted horizontally laid squared timber walls that were tied together with cross-ties to resist the lateral force imposed by the earthen fill. The original vertically oriented stockade puncheons would be of questionable value in resisting such force.

**Bouquet helps to resolve a quarrel**

A January 6, 1761 letter[1260] Lieutenant Jethro Sumner[1261] of the Virginia Regiment wrote to Bouquet from Fort Cumberland states:

> *Major Stewart having inform'd me of the extreme genteel Manner in which you have been Pleased to act in that precipetate and unlucky affair, which happen'd between Maj' Heatcat and I, I embrace the earliest Opport' to beg you will Accept of my unfeign'd thanks for that Obligation which has impronted indelible marks of esteem in a heart replete with the most genuine Sentiments of Gratitude, to you; Some agrevating expressions, & apparonly contemptuous Behaviour kindled a Passion under the and Influence of which I might have Dropt something enconsistent w'th Decorum and Politeness, But — however I will only trouble you with begging you will be perswaded with how much Deference I am Sir y' Most Ob' most hum' Serv'*
> *JETHRO SUMNER*

**Virginians being sent to garrison Fort Cumberland in 1761**

A January 14, 1761 letter[1262] Colonel Henry Bouquet wrote to General Robert Monkton from Fort Pitt includes the following statement:

---

[1260] "**The papers of Col. Henry Bouquet**", 1941.

[1261] Although not documentary evidence, the 1860 book "**The pictorial field-book of the revolution**" states, *"Although the name of General Jethro Sumner does not appear very conspicuous in the general histories of the War for Independence, his services in the Southern campaigns were well appreciated by his peers and compatriots in the field. He was a native of Virginia, and as early as 1760 his merits caused him to be appointed a paymaster in the provincial army of that state, and commander of Fort Cumberland. In 1776, he lived in North Carolina, was appointed colonel of a regiment of Continental troops, and joined the army at the North, under Washington. ..."*

[1262] "**Michigan Historical Collections**", Volume 19, 1911 reprint of an 1892 book.

*As soon as the first Division of Vaughan's appear I shall march down the Virginians who will Garrison Fort Burd & Cumberland.[1263]*

## Colonel Bouquet writes to Major Livingston on January 24, 1761

A January 24, 1761 letter Bouquet wrote to Major James Livingston from Fort Pitt states:

*I received your Returns for December, you will please to continue to send them regularly every Month dated the 24th and order the man sent by Capt. Hay to take Charge of the Artillery stores Tools &c to give you his Returns of the same date to be transmitted to me, or the Commandg officer at this Post.*

*Major Stewart will deliver to you two Prisoners George Kerr, and Philip Stone, confined for Debts; You will deliver them both to the Sheriff, who will be sent to receive them at Fort Cumberland to be tried by the Civil Law, But you are not to Keep them Prisoners longer than thirty days from the time they arrive at Fort Cumberland, and if within that time a Sheriff is not sent for them, you will set them both at Liberty.*

*Creditors are to provide for the subsistence of those who are not to draw the King's Ration.*

## The Virginians marched to Fort Cumberland in January 1761

A January 26, 1761 letter[1264] Bouquet wrote to Monckton from Fort Pitt includes the statement, *"The last Division of Col. Vaughen's arrived here yesterday having released the Ports on the Communication below. Major Stewart with the Detachment of Virgª Troops is marched for Winchester, by Bedford & Cumberland."*

## Stewart's regiment is in dire need of replacement shoes and clothing

A February 5, 1761 letter[1265] to Bouquet that was written from the *"Camp at Fort Cumberland"* by Major Robert Stewart includes the following:

*I arriv'd here yesterday after a very fatigueing March in which the want of Clothes particularly Shoes (there being none to be got at any of the Posts) renderd the inclemency of the Weather doubly severe upon my Detachment, many of them are frost bitten and most of them quite lame, which for a few Days disables me from prosecuting my March to Winchester.*

*On my arrival here I Discharg'd the Pack horses & Inclose You the Horse Masters Rect for them, I have Deliver'd your Letter and the 2 Suttlers to Majr Levingston, I have likewise agreeable to your Orders brought Lt Sumner from Bedford and have in the strongest Terms I could represented to him the manifold inconveniencies that would inevitably result from his making a serious affair of what pass'd between Majr Heathcut & him, of wch he is so much persuaded, that he has determin'd to write to you & him upon that Subject.*

---

[1263] In Volume IX of the 1871 book "**Collections of the Massachusetts Historical Society**", this sentence is given as, *"As soon as the first Division of Vaughans' appears, the Virginians will march to Winchester leaving garrisons at Fort Burd & Cumberland."*

[1264] "**Collections of the Massachusetts Historical Society**", Volume IX, 1871.

[1265] "**The papers of Col. Henry Bouquet**", 1941.

### What to do with the prisoner who escaped from Fort Cumberland?

A February 12, 1761 letter[1266] that was written by Lieutenant Chichester Fortescue Garstin to Bouquet from Fort Bedford states:

> *Late last Night was brought in to this Fort Philip Stone late Prisoner at Fort Cumberland he made his escape out of Said fort but being persued taken and brought in here I have Confin^d him and beg to know your orders Concerning him the Said stone say^s he was marched down prisoner from Fort Pitt by your Order*

### Wheeling and dealing in cattle, which had to be fed with corn from Fort Cumberland

A February 21, 1761 letter[1267] that was written by Colonel Adam Stephen to Bouquet from Winchester states:

> *I have sent you up my Crop of Stallfed Cattle, expecting they will be very Acceptable to you & the Gentlemen of the Garrisons under your Command.*
>
> *They will cost me extreanly high in driving at this Season; besides the risk of losing Some, I am Obligd to load about twenty horses with Corn from Fort Cumberland, to keep them in tolerable heart in passing the mountains.*
>
> *I could have sold them very well at this place, but I knew you would be in need of fresh Beef, and my Chief intention was to let you, sir, See the fruits of my Farm; & what you might justly Expect from yours, so far Superiour to mine.*
>
> *I can Engage that the Same person who supplys me, will furnish you with any Numb^r of Cattle from the Southard;*
>
> *Expecting the Virg^a Regiment will soon be broke all my Views are turned towards farming & trade, hoping Your Concurrence & assistance in any scheme which wall Raise the Value of our Lands in the Back parts:*
>
> *My present design is to find a market for the produce of them, and to Establish flour & Hemp our Staple Commodities.*
>
> *I shall lose considerably by sending up my Cattle unless you allow me a great price, as the Hides and Tallow of so fine Cattle are very valuable. I understand Beef is now 5½^d neat m Philadelpha, so that by the time mine would reach that it will be at 6^d*
>
> *It is with pleasure that I assure you of the great Esteem & affection of all our Officers who have been under your Command, You possess their Hearts*

### The identity of one of the casualties on Patterson Creek

According to Volume 6 of "**Colonial Records of the Upper Potomac**", the February 28, 1761 petition of Benjamin Parker says that Indians killed his only brother George at Coxes Fort, which was located on Patterson Creek.

---

[1266] "**The papers of Col. Henry Bouquet**", 1941.
[1267] "**The papers of Col. Henry Bouquet**", 1941.

### Daniel Cresap and Evan Shelby are involved in a court matter

In a section titled, *"Tryal Dockett for November Court Ano Dom 1761"*, page 94 of The Frederick County, Maryland court book[1268] "**Doquetts Anno 1761**" includes a February 28 record for the case of *"Jnᵒ B. Murrow & Danˡ Cresap"* versus Evan Shelby that references *"Geo Ross bail"*. Page 30 of the same book includes a March 6 record that mentions Captain Evan Shelby and somehow relates to George Ross's bail. On page 68 of the same book, a section titled, *"Tryal Docquett to the third Tuesday and Eighteenth day of August Anno Domini 1761"* includes a record dated March 6 that mentions Evan Shelby and Jnᵒ Bapt. Morrow, apparently as adversaries. A section titled, *"Judicial Docquet"* in the Maryland book "**Frederick County Four Docquets For 1764**" contains a record no. 61 dated March 12 for the case of Evan Shelby versus *"George Ross Bail of John Morian"*. A section titled, *"Imparlances to June Court Anno Domini 1764"* in the same book includes a record no. 2 dated March 12 for a matter involving Evan Shelby regarding *"Geo Ross bail Jnᵒ Morreau"*. These records appear to have a common thread back to the case that involved Daniel Cresap.

### Neal Oqullion is involved in a court case

In a section titled, *"Original Writs returnable to the third Tuesday and sixteenth day of Juno Anno Dom 1761"*, page 51 of The Frederick County, Maryland court book[1269] "***Doquetts Anno 1761***" includes a case record dated March 25 that mentions Neal Oqullion and George Stout, apparently as adversaries. What appears to be same case is referenced in a section titled, *"Original Writs returnable to the third Tuesday And Eighteenth day of August Anno 1761"* on page 77 of the same book.

### Maryland refuses to raise men to garrison Fort Cumberland

Regarding the April 13, 1761 meeting of the General Assembly of Maryland, the book "**A History of the General Assembly of Maryland, 1635-1904**" states, *"By a vote of 31 to 4, the House refused to raise a hundred men to Garrison Fort Cumberland, Red-Stone Creek, and the Crossings."*

### Neal Oqullion posts a recognizance bond

In a section titled, *"Recognizances Respecting to August Court Anno Dom 1761"*, page 64 of The Frederick County, Maryland court book[1270] "**Doquetts Anno 1761**" a includes the £30 bond of Neal Oqullion, apparently obtained by T. Prather on April 20, *"for Neal Oqulliions app to Ansʳ"*. The bond is also mentioned on page 91, in a section titled, *"Recognizances respected to Novemʳ Court Anno Dom 1761"*.

### 13 lots with houses on Patterson's Creek

John Moffett's survey of the Patterson Creek Manor was completed on April 27, 1761. William H. Rice's study of this survey, which is reported in Volume 6 of "**Colonial Records of the Upper Potomac**", reveals that the first 13 of the 31 lots were claimed. Of these claimed lots, only the plat of lot one didn't include a house. The number of houses is surprising, considering the devastation along Patterson Creek in the 1750s.

---

[1268] MSA No. C782-11.
[1269] MSA No. C782-11.
[1270] MSA No. C782-11.

### Ice receives a warrant for land on the North Branch

Frederick Ice received a warrant for a tract of Virginia land at Burcham's bottom on May 2, 1761. The tract was located on the North Branch of the Potomac River, about ten miles upstream from Fort Cumberland.[1271] In 1762, Ice assigned the property to Major James Livingston, who in turn had it surveyed on June 5, 1762. John Nicholas, Jr. was one of the chain carriers on that survey, and on quite a few other surveys that were performed in the region. The marker for the survey was Adam McCarty. Rice's book[1272] seems to indicate that the assignment to Livingston was witnessed by Thomas Spencer and John Nicholas.

The phrase *"Burcham's bottom"* seems to be a reference to an early settler. In Volume 5 of **"Colonial Records of the Upper Potomac"**, William H. Rice opines that the property was probably claimed by Roger Burkham at one time. The tract was originally surveyed by Guy Broadwater as North Branch Lot No. 7, which was originally surveyed for John Gladden, who sold it to someone named Champ who then sold it to Frederick Ice.

On September 13, 1768, Enoch Innis, acting with power of attorney from James Livingston, sold the property to Marylander Daniel Cresap.

### Maryland once again votes against troops for Fort Cumberland in 1761

Volume 56 of the Maryland **"Proceedings and Acts of the General Assembly, 1758-1761"** records that on May 1, 1761, *"On Motion, the Question was put, That One Hundred Men be raised, for the Garrisoning of Fort Cumberland, Red-Stone-Creek, and the Crossings. Resolved in the Negative."*

### Herman Husband is involved in court matters

In a section titled, *"Original Writs returnable to the third Tuesday and sixteenth day of Juno Anno Dom 1761"*, page 56 of The Frederick County, Maryland court book[1273] **"Doquetts Anno 1761"** includes a case record dated May 22 that mentions Herman Husband and James Perry as adversaries. In a section titled, *"Imparlance Dockett to August Court Anno Domini 1761"*, page 71 of same book includes a May 23 record that mentions Herman Husband and Ben Swoope as adversaries. In a section titled, *"Continuances to November Court 1761"*, page 96 of the same book also mentions this matter, and references, *"Jnᵒ Williams bail."* In a section titled, *"Continuances to March Court Anno 1762"* in the Frederick County court book[1274] **"Dockett's Anno 1762"**, a record dated May 23 lists Hermon Husbands and Benj Swoope as adversaries, and mentions *"Jnᵒ Williams bail"*.

Husband would later show up in what is now Somerset County, Pennsylvania as an early settler.

### John Long is involved in a court matter

The Frederick County, Maryland court book[1275] *"Doquetts Anno 1761"* includes a May 26 record that mentions John Long and is somehow related to *"Jaˢ Graham bail."* I'm not sure if this is a reference to the John Adam Long who was captured by Indians.

---

[1271] **"Colonial Records of the Upper Potomac"**, Volume 6.

[1272] **"Colonial Records of the Upper Potomac"**, Volume 6.

[1273] MSA No. C782-11.

[1274] MSA No. C782-11

[1275] MSA No. C782-11.

### Thomas Cresap asks Bouquet to be a candidate for county representative

A May 27, 1761 letter[1276] Thomas Cresap wrote to Bouquet from Old Town states:

*I make bold by this opportunity to give You the trouble of a Line, which I hope you will excuse the freedom of; We are soon to have an Election for four New Members to represent the People of this County, and if it will be agreeable to You to stand as a Candidate for one of them, my Interest is at your Service, and make no doubt it will be sufficient, as it has allways enabled me to Carry one Gentleman whom I recommended.*

*I return You thanks for Your last favour, which enabled me to receive the Ballance due me for Wintering the Kings Horses*

### Frazier bills Mary Wood

The Hampshire County, Virginia estate record for Mrs. Mary Wood indicates that she was billed by John Frazier in May of the year 1761 for plowing.[1277] One charge was for four acres of plowing, and the other charge was for plowing a field that belonged to a Cornwell.

### Local men involved in a Virginia survey for Adam McCarty

John Nicholas, Jr. and *"Minor"* Johnson were chain carriers for John Moffett's June 4, 1761 survey[1278] for Adam McCarty, who appears on the 1761 Old Town Hundred list. The correct spelling for the name written as *"Minor"* is probably *"Maynard"*. The property was in Virginia at the head of Byrd's Run, a tributary of the North Branch of the Potomac River. Adam McCarty assigned the property to Samuel Plum in 1763.

### Property surveyed for John Nicholas, Sr.

Another survey[1279] dated June 4, 1761 was performed by John Moffett for Marylander John Nicholas, Sr. The property was situated on the North Branch opposite from an island that was located 1.5-miles downstream from the *"New Store"* tract. John Nicholas, Jr. was one of the chain carriers on that survey, and for another survey dated June 4, 1761 that Moffett performed on the north fork of Plum Run for George Williams.

### Nehemiah Martin serves as a chain carrier

Nehemiah Martin and Michael Martin served as chain carriers on a June 6, 1761 survey[1280] John Moffett performed for John Smith. The 40-acre tract was located on the north branch of the Potomac River, adjoining the property of John Parker, who was no longer living at the time of the survey. Nehemiah Martin appears on the 1761 Old Town Hundred list.

---

[1276] **"The papers of Col. Henry Bouquet"**, 1941.
[1277] **"Colonial Records of the Upper Potomac"**, Volume 6.
[1278] **"Colonial Records of the Upper Potomac"**, Volume 6.
[1279] **"Colonial Records of the Upper Potomac"**, Volume 6.
[1280] **"Colonial Records of the Upper Potomac"**, Volume 6.

### Hamlin leases property on Patterson Creek
The 1939 book "**Early Records Hampshire County Virginia**" records the following for June 8, 1761, "*HAMLIN, Joseph of Hampshire Co. to Henry Bagley of Hampshire Co. (lease and release) 50 a. on Patterson's Creek rec. 6-9-1761.*" Joseph Hamlin was on Lot No. 11 of Patterson's Creek in 1749.

### Estate appraisals by Cresap, Walker, and Williams
On June 16, 1761, Thomas Cresap was being sued[1281] by Michael Hubley in Frederick County, Maryland for the bail of Jonathan Plummer. On the same day, John Walker, Daniel Cresap, and Richard Williams completed the estate appraisals of Mr. & Mrs. Remembrance Williams. [1282]

### Jonathan Plummer is sued by Thomas Cresap
Jonathan Plummer, a cordwainer (shoemaker) by occupation, was being sued[1283] by Thomas Cresap on June 17, 1761 over failure to pay the promissory note Plummer signed on July 23, 1757. The same day, Thomas Cresap sold[1284] a portion of a tract named "*Dispute*" to Providence Mounts. The tract was located about two-miles downstream from the mouth of Evitts Creek.

### Nulla Bona
In a section titled, "*Judicial Writs to the third Tuesday and Eighteenth day of August Anno 1761*", page 73 of The Frederick County, Maryland court book[1285] "**Doquetts Anno 1761**" includes a June 18th record that mentions Thomas Cresap, and bears the words "*Nulla Bona*", which means there are no goods for the sheriff to seize.

### Trading between Pittsburg and Fort Cumberland
A June 20, 1761 letter[1286] that Abraham Mitchel wrote to Bouquet from Philadelphia states that Edmund Moran "*is now at Pittsburg, or in its Neighbourhood, with a Cargo of Goods & intends trading between Fort Cumberland & those Parts*".

### A complex Indian situation
A June 30, 1761 letter[1287] Bouquet wrote to Monckton from Fort Pitt includes the following:

*By the inclosed copys of the repeated Intelligences I have from Detroit, you will see the sudden Revolution happened in our Indian Affairs: I did give very little credit to the first advices, but upon the following Letter just received I have taken the necessary measures to prevent a Surprise ...*

*I beg you will please to send me your orders concerning the Presents which cannot be avoided to be given to the Delaware & Shawanese if agreeable to their engagements, they deliver their Captives and as the ammunition at Bedford & Cumberland may be wanted here, How you chuse to have it brought up, as we have no Carriages, and cannot afford Escorts, without neglecting the Works — I would think this a proper*

[1281] "**Colonial Records of the Upper Potomac**", Volume 6.
[1282] "**Colonial Records of the Upper Potomac**", Volume 6.
[1283] "**Colonial Records of the Upper Potomac**", Volume 6.
[1284] "**Colonial Records of the Upper Potomac**", Volume 6.
[1285] MSA No. C782-11.
[1286] "**The papers of Col. Henry Bouquet**", 1941.
[1287] "**Collections of the Massachusetts Historical Society**", Volume IX, 1871.

*opportunity to get more Troops of Pensilvania, inlisted for the time you will think necessary, and not only for a few months, one half of which they always contrive to loose by affected delays.*

*In this critical circumstance, you may be certain that should I receive your Leave to go down, I would not quit this Post till the Storm is blown over*

### Jonathan Plumer is involved with Ninian Hamilton in a court matter

In a section titled, *"Judicial Writs to the third Tuesday and Eighteenth day of August Anno 1761"*, page 75 of The Frederick County, Maryland court book[1288] **"Doquetts Anno 1761"** includes a July 6 record that mentions Jonathan Plumer and Ninian Hamilton and includes the word *"Enquiry"*.

### Bouquet requests supplies and ammunition for Fort Pitt

A July 27, 1761 letter[1289] Bouquet wrote to General Monckton from Fort Pitt includes the following:

*A Serjeant of the Pensilvanians is not less guilty. He broke open & robbed a Store, deserted with another man stealing Two Horses, was arrested near Fort Cumberland, made his Escape, came back here when he kept himself concealed several days in the Woods, persuaded five or six young Soldiers to desert w^th him, was discovered, all his companions secured, himself alone got off. He was taken again at Juniatta & is secured here.*

*Whatever turn our Indian affairs may take. It is almost certain that we shall be quiet for some time; when, if you thought it proper, some Stores & ammunition could be sent up from Bedford & Cumberland. The difficulty is to get carriages. The Country People being frightened don't come up as usual.*

### Bouquet is robbed of a large sum of money

A July 31, 1761 order[1290] Bouquet wrote at midnight and sent out to various posts from Fort Pitt states:

*I having been robed two hours ago of a Large Sum of Paper money, you are hereby required to arrest any person going down the Country, & Search them carefully. And not let any one proceed till you have Informed me of their Names & sent me their Passes. Officers are excepted from this order which is to be copied at Each Post upon the Communication & forwarded with the utmost diligence to Bedford from whence Cap^t Ourry will send it by Express to Fort Cumberland.*

### Nathanial Tomlinson is involved in a court matter

In a section titled, *"Original Writs returnable to the third Tuesday And Eighteenth day of August Anno 1761"*, page 85 of The Frederick County, Maryland court book[1291] **"Doquetts Anno 1761"** includes an August 3 record that mentions *"Nat Tomlinson"*.

### John Long is involved in a court matter

In a section titled, *"Judicial Writs to the third Tuesday and Eighteenth day of August Anno 1761"*, page 75 of The Frederick County, Maryland court book[1292] **"Doquetts Anno 1761"** includes an August 5 record that

---

[1288] MSA No. C782-11.

[1289] **"Collections of the Massachusetts Historical Society"**, Volume IX, 1871.

[1290] **"The Papers of Col. Henry Bouquet"**, 1940.

[1291] MSA No. C782-11.

[1292] MSA No. C782-11.

mentions Benj Martin and John Long, apparently as adversaries. I'm not sure if this is a reference to the John Adam Long who was captured by Indians.

## Oqullion and Welder are involved in court matters

In a section titled, *"Original Writs returnable to November Court Anno 1761"*, page 114 of The Frederick County, Maryland court book[1293] **"Doquetts Anno 1761"** has an August 10th record that names Neal Oqullion and page 110 has a record that is apparently from August 24 that also names Neal Oquillion. Page 111 has a record that names Sam Stans Weldor.

## Purchasing provisions from neighbors in 1761

A September 2, 1761 letter[1294] Major James Livingston wrote to Bouquet from Fort Cumberland includes the statement:

> *I am sorry I had not opportunity of sending before now, but hope you will excuse the Delay; as I have no Meat nor Forrage in the Store, I have no Opportunity of making any Return of either of them; the Garrison has been supplyed with fresh Provisions which I have purchas'd of the Neighbours by Order for a long time past; I am glad to hear of your Success in finding your Money and Papers, I used my Endeavours by stopping every suspected Person even by your Order, and shall be always proud to fulfil what lies in my Power to your Advantage ...*

The reference to neighbors indicates that settlers were living in the general vicinity of the fort in 1761.

## Henry Bouquet's 1761 proclamation against settling west of the Allegheny Mountain

The following proclamation[1295] was issued by Colonel Bouquet on October 30, 1761:

> *Proclamation by Henry Bouquet, Esqr., Colonel of Foot and Commanding at Fort Pitt and Dependencies.*

> *Whereas by a Treaty held at East Town[1296] in the year 1758, and since ratified by His Majesty's Ministers, the Country to the West of the Allegany Mountains is allowed to the Indians for their Hunting Ground, and as it is of the Highest Importance to his Majesty's service, the preservation of the peace and a good understanding with the Indians, to avoid giving them any just cause of Complaint, this is therefore to forbid any of His Majesty's subjects to Settle or Hunt to the West of the Allegany Mountains on any Pretence Whatsoever, unless such Persons have obtained leave in Writing from the General or the Governor of their Provinces Respectively and produce the same to the Commanding Officer at Fort Pitt.*

> *And all the officers and non commissioned officers commanding at the several Posts erected in that part of the Country for the Protection of the Trade, are hereby ordered to seize or cause to be seized any of His Majesty's Subjects who without the above Authority should pretend after the Publication hereof to settle or Hunt upon the said Lands, and send them with their Horses and Effects to Fort Pitt, there to be Try'd and Punished according to the nature of their Offence by the Sentence of a Court Martial.*

> *Given under my Hand at Fort Pitt this Thirtieth day of October 1761.*

---

[1293] MSA No. C782-11.
[1294] **"The papers of Col. Henry Bouquet"**, 1942.
[1295] **"Report on Canadian Archives"**, 1889.
[1296] I believe this is a reference to Easton.

Bouquet was criticized for stating that he would subject civilians to court martial. In an April 1, 1762 letter to Amherst, Bouquet revealed that part of the objective of the proclamation was to frustrate the settlement plans of the Ohio Company.

### Thomas Cresap and Richard Graham are involved in a court matter

In a section titled, *"Judicial Writs Returnable to the third Tuesday, and Seventeenth day of November Anno Domini 1761"*, page 105 of The Frederick County, Maryland court book[1297] **"Doquetts Anno 1761"** includes an October 30 record that mentions Thomas Cresap and Richard Graham as adversaries.

### Bouquet sends the proclamation to Fort Cumberland for posting

On October 31, 1761, Bouquet wrote a letter[1298] to James Livingston from Fort Pitt, stating:

> *Having had repeated Complaints from the Indians, that the white People do make a Practice to hunt on this Side the Allegheny Mountains; & that even some of them have made settlements upon the Said Lands, which are reserved hitherto for the Indians hunting-ground; I have thought fit to issue the inclosed Proclamation to be published and posted up at Fort Cumberland, and you will please to Inform the Country People thereof, that they Do not expose themselves to certain punishment for their Trespasses & disobedience of orders.*

Bouquet's copy of the letter is endorsed as follows, *"Substance of a Letter wrote to M<sup>r</sup> Livingston Fort Cumberland with a Proclamation dated 30<sup>th</sup> October 1761."*

### Tomlinson is appointed as constable of the Old Town Hundred

On November 17, 1761 the Frederick County, Maryland court appointed[1299] Aaron Moore to be the road overseer between 15 Mile Creek and Nichol's Neck. On the same day, Joseph Tomlinson was appointed to be the Old Town Hundred constable.

On the same day, the court reviewed Thomas Cresap's lawsuit against Richard Graham which involved a debt represented by a November 3, 1761 bill. The bill had been signed by S. S. Welder, Daniel Cresap, James Prather, and Isaac Collier.[1300] Also reviewed was the case of James Marshall versus Daniel Cresap and John Baptist Munrow.[1301]

### Various individuals are involved in court matters

In a section titled, *"Imparlances to November Court Anno Domini 1761"*, page 98 of The Frederick County, Maryland court book[1302] **"Doquetts Anno 1761"** includes a record that mentions Neal Oqullion and Thomas Crampkin as adversaries. The record also mentions *"Tho<sup>s</sup> Dickason & Geo Wade Jun<sup>r</sup> bail"*. The case is also listed in **"Dockett's Anno 1762"** in a section titled *"Continuances to March Court Anno 1762"* and is dated June 22, along with another June 22 record that mentions Jn° Wade.

---

[1297] MSA No. C782-11.

[1298] **"The Papers of Col. Henry Bouquet"**, 1940.

[1299] **"Colonial Records of the Upper Potomac"**, Volume 6.

[1300] **"Colonial Records of the Upper Potomac"**, Volume 6.

[1301] **"Colonial Records of the Upper Potomac"**, Volume 6.

[1302] MSA No. C782-11.

In a section titled, *"Original Writs returnable to November Court Anno 1761"*, page 106 of the "**Doquetts Anno 1761**" includes a record that names Joseph Tomlinson, and page 108 includes another record that names Nat Tomlinson.

### John Walker obtains land in Virginia

"**Dyers Index to Land Grants in West Virginia**", Volume 2 (1896) lists two 1761 grants to John Walker in Hampshire County, Virginia on the North Branch of the Potomac River. One grant was for 150 acres and the other was for 200 acres. The grants are recorded on pages 63 and 64 of Grant Book 1. The same book mentions a 1775 grant to John Walker for 33 acres on the North Branch of the Potomac River.

### The Old Town Hundred list from 1761

The 1761 Old Town Hundred list, which identifies the taxables in the area, was prepared by Constable Providence Mounts and attested by Sheriff Samuel Beale. The names on the list are:

*Francis Spencer; Wm. Spurgeon; Abraham Teagarden;[1303] Jno. Spurgeon; Joseph Mounts; James Spurgeon Jur.; Frederick Dunfield; Jno. Morris; John Castell; John McDonald; Adam MacCarte; Thos. Spencer; John Slater; Edmd. Martin; Saml. Plump; John Nickols Junr.; Edward Anderson; John Nichols Senr.; Providence Mounts; Saml. Beale Sherr.; John Trotter; Isaac Colyer; Nehemiah Martin; Aron Moore; Thomas Cresap; George Wade; Philip Mason; Samuel Welder; Daniel Puriel; James Winters; Timothy Sweet; Solomon Terpen; Andrews Hendricks; John Connel; Casper Everly; James Spirgeon Senr.; James Craptree; Andrew Linn; Nathan Friggs; Richard Morris*

Of these men, some stayed in the environs of Fort Cumberland for at least a few years. Joseph Mounts bought a tract above Fort Cumberland, and by 1783 had a mill on it. Adam McCarty had land surveyed on a tributary of Patterson Creek in 1762 and served as a marker on another Virginia survey the same year. A Thomas Spencer served as a messenger from Fort Cumberland in 1763. A Samuel Plum obtained a Virginia property from Adam McCarty in 1763, received a Maryland license for selling liquor near Evitts Creek in 1763, and sold supplies to Mason and Dixon in 1767. It's not always easy to distinguish the father from the son, but a John Nichole is on Andrew Bruce's 1778 Oath of Fidelity list and a John Nichells appears on the 1783 Cumberland Hundred list; both are probably John Nikols, Junior. Providence Mounts moved to the Connellsville, Pennsylvania area and in 1779 helped to cut the northern part a military road from Fort Cumberland. Samuel Beale is sometimes difficult to study in the early records, because a Senior and Junior are listed. A John Trotter appears on the 1783 Wills Town and Sandy Creek hundreds lists and appears in Deakins' list of settlers westward of Fort Cumberland. Isaac Collier Junior and Senior appear on Barrett's 1778 Oath of Fidelity list, and in 1783 Isaac Collier deeded local property to what may be two of his children. A Nehemiah Martin is on Barrett's 1778 Oath of Fidelity list. Thomas Cresap is a well-known local resident. Samuel Welder was killed by Indians in 1763. *"Daniel Puriel"* may be a transcription error for Daniel Pursel, who appears on Barrett's 1778 Oath of Fidelity list, and who evidently appears on the 1772 taxables list of Brothersvalley Township, Bedford County, Pennsylvania as Daniel Pursley. (The surname is spelled various ways in early records, including *"Puzzley"*.) An Andrew Hendrix appears on the 1772 taxables list of Brothersvalley Township and is one of my ancestors. Casper Everly was being sued by the estate of Samuel Welder in 1764, but I don't know where he was living then. James Crabtree was appointed to serve as the constable for the Old Town Hundred.in November 1763, but left Maryland

---

[1303] A bond signed by an Abraham Teagarden on October 8, 1750 indicates that he was then a Frederick County, Virginia blacksmith. ("**Colonial Records of the Upper Potomac**", Volume 5.)

by March 1764. Richard Morris was appointed to be the constable for the Old Town Hundred in March 1764, replacing Crabtree.

# 14. 1762: Indians request supplies

## Joseph Tomlinson was improving the Wills Town tract in 1762

The original Wills Town tract extended into what is now Pennsylvania and was later truncated by the Mason-Dixon line. Joseph Tomlinson was already making improvements on the Wills Town tract in 1762 and had a rental agreement with John Henthorn in the 1765 to 1767 timeframe. Volume 2, page 377 of the "**Pennsylvania Archives**", third series includes an entry recorded in Land Office Caveat Book 3 on January 20, 1767. The entry states, "*Joseph Tumbleston Caveats an acceptance of a Survey made by Cap't Finley on applications Nos. 902, 903 & 1773, Obtained by a John Hinthorn on a Part of Wills Town on Wills Creek S'd Lands being Imp't on by Said Tunbleston & held under Maryland Patent since the Year Sixty-two & Said Hinthorn Paying Said Tumbleston Yearly Rent this two years past for s'd Land.*" According to Volume 2, page 201, in the legal action of Joseph Tomlinson or Tunbleston against John Henthorn, Henthorn lost his right to the property because "*upon Doctor Ross's securing the Land Henthorn agreed to give the Whole purchase up to Tomlinson and to rent the Improvements he had made upon the place of Tomlinson for four years paying a bushel of Indian Corn a Year Rent.*" This passage shows that John Hinthorn was one of the settlers living near Fort Cumberland in the 1765 to 1767 timeframe.

## Joseph Tomlinson obtains a warrant for other property west of Fort Cumberland in 1762

The book "**Proceedings of the Council of Maryland, 1761-1769**" includes the minutes from an April 2, 1771 board meeting, which include the following:

*The Petition of Joseph Thomlinson of Frederick County was read setting forth that in the year 1762 he obtained a warrant out of his Lordship's Land Office in order to secure about 100 acres of Land to the westward of Fort Cumberland, which by reason of the war he could not get executed that ever since he has been deprived the Benefit thereof by reason of a Rescue being laid for his Lordship's use. The Board are of opinion that he ought to be redressed agreeable to Prayer, his warrant being prior to any Reserve made in that part of the Province.*

## The Virginians at Fort Cumberland are to be discharged

A January 7, 1762 letter[1304] Colonel Adam Stephen wrote to Bouquet from Fort Chiswell includes the statement, "*I am Commanded to march down the Virg$^a$ Regiment to the Inhabitants in order to be disbanded; and am ordered to request you, to have the men relieved at Fort Burd & Cumberland that they may be marched down to Winchester & there receive their Arrears of Pay, and be discharged.*"

## What to do with the stores at the crossing?

A January 30, 1762 letter[1305] Major James Livingston sent to Bouquet from Fort Cumberland states, "*As I have rec$^d$ an Express from Virginia for the Troops to march down, I desire to know what I must do with the Stores at the Crossings, whether I shall move them down to Cumberland or no, and if I may expect any Men here; in regard to the Mens Arms would be glad to hear if I shall take them into the Store at this Post. No news but the River Potomack is to be made navigable by Subscription of Virginia and Maryland, I shall*

---

[1304] "**The papers of Col. Henry Bouquet**", 1942.

[1305] "**The papers of Col. Henry Bouquet**", 1942.

*send you the Proposals so soon as I have Opportunity to send to Winchester, inclosed are the Return of Artillery Stores and State of the Garrison".*

## McDonald has men at the Crossings and Cumberland

A February 6, 1762 letter[1306] Bouquet sent to Sergeant McDonald from Fort Pitt states:

*I received yesterday a letter from Co<sup>ll</sup> Stephen acquainting me that your Regiment was ordered to the Settlements to be disbanded And desiring I would relieve your Post the Crossings and Cumberland that those men might march to Winchester to be settled with and Discharg'd.*

*As I cannot relieve you at Present, It is my Orders, that you remain with your Detachment as well as the others at your respective Posts till you are relieved, which shall be done as soon as Possible, and in order to make your men easy I do answer for their Pay for all time they shall Continue in the Kings service, but as it may be necessary to have their Accounts Settled you may either go your Self to Winchester, or send a trusty man with the Accounts of the Whole Detachment at Fort Burd and the Crossing, to have them Settled and Paid, I send the same order to Fort Cumberland, in case you go Yourself, you will leave the Command with your Corporal.*

## Fort Pitt cannot relieve the men at the Crossings and Fort Cumberland

A February 6, 1762 letter[1307] Bouquet sent to Jeffrey Amhurst from Fort Pitt states:

*I received last night a Letter from Coll. Stephen, who commands the Virginia Regim<sup>t</sup> dated Fort Chiswell January 7<sup>th</sup> He acquainting me that he had orders to march that Regiment to the Inhabitants to be disbanded, and to desire me to have the Detachments they lefft at Red Stone Creek, The Crossing of Yioghiogheny and Fort Cumberland, relieved, that those men might repair as soon as possible to Winchester, to be discharged, that is Two Serjeants, Two Corporals, and twenty Seven Private of that Regiment.*

*I Send orders to those Garrisons to Stand fast, till they are relieved, and I answer for their Pay, while they Stay at those Posts, in case their Province Should not pay them.*

*The present Situation of this Fort & Garrison making it impossible for me to relieve those three Posts, I Shall wait for your His Excellency Sir Jeffery Amherst Excellencys Orders.*

## Fort Cumberland receives a brass four-pounder cannon

A February 6, 1762 letter[1308] Bouquet wrote from Fort Pitt to Major Livingston at Fort Cumberland states:

*I received last night your Letter and returns of the 30<sup>th</sup> January.*

*As to the Garrisons at the Crossings and Fort Cumberland It is my positive order that they stand fast at those posts, till they are relieved And I so answer for their pay for all the time they shall Continue there in case the province of Virginia should not pay them.*

*I have sent the same order to Redstone Creek and Inform'd the General of it*

---

[1306] **"The papers of Col. Henry Bouquet"**, 1940.
[1307] **"The papers of Col. Henry Bouquet"**, 1940.
[1308] **"The papers of Col. Henry Bouquet"**, 1940.

*Please to let me know if the Twenty Barrils of powder return'd in your stores are in good Order of what size and if the powder is fitt for service. And who sent you the Brass 4ᶜᵉ you mention.*

*The Indians Complain bitterly that notwithstanding my My orders against hunting a Number of White Men have been out the Whole season and Distroyed a Great quantity of game; As that Infamous Practice will Occasion some disturbance I recommend to you to endeavour to seize some of those Villains that a satisfactory Example May be made of them.*

## A 1762 scheme to make the Potomac more navigable

An advertisement in the February 11, 1762 issue of the "**Maryland Gazette**" includes the following text:

*To the PUBLIC.*

*The Opening of the River Patowmack, and making it passable for Small Craft, from Fort Cumberland at Wills's Creek to the Great Falls, will be of the greatest Advantage to Virginia and Maryland, by facilitating Commerce with the Back Inhabitants, who will not then have more than 20 miles Land Carriage to a Harbour, where ships of great Burthen load annually; whereas at present many have 150; and what will perhaps be considered of still greater Importance, is the easy Communication it will afford the Inhabitants of these Colonies with the Waters of the Ohio.*

*The whole Land Carriage from Alexandria, or George Town, to Pittsburgh, will then be short of 90 miles; whereas the Pennsylvanians (who at present monopolize the very lucrative skin and Fur Trades) from their nearest Sea Port have at least 300: a Circumstance which must necessarily force that gainful trade into this Channel, should this very useful Work be effected; and that it may, is the unanimous Opinion of the best Judges, and at a moderate expense, compared with the extraordinary Conveniencies, and Advantages which must result from it.*

*That an Affair of such general Utility may be carried into Execution, it is proposed to solicit the Public for their Contributions, by the Way of Subscription.*

*Col. George Mercer and Col. Thomas Prather are appointed Treasurers, to whom all Sums subscribed are to be made payable; it being thought most expedient to deposit the Money raised in the Hands of one Person in each Colony. By this Means it may at all Times be more readily known what Sum is in Stock, and those employed on the Work may know to whom they are to apply for Payment; and also that Suits may be commenced in their Names, for any Sum subscribed and not duly paid: Thay are to give Bond and Security to the Managers, for the faithful Discharge of that Trust.*

*As it will be necessary for the Managers frequently to meet, to consult of the properest Methods of applying the Money raised; it was judged most suitable to make Choice of those who live convenient, as they can more readily attend when required, and have the greatest Opportunity from their Situation to be acquainted with the Nature of the Undertaking. The following Gentlemen are therefore appointed: In Virginia, George Mercer, Jacob Hite, William Ramsay, John Carlyle, John Hite, Joseph Watson, James Keith, James Hamilton, John Hough, John Patterson, and Abraham Hite. In Maryland, The Reverend Thomas Bacon, Dr. David Ross, Christopher Lowndes, Thomas Cresap, Benjamin Chambers, Jonathan Hagar, Thomas Prather, John Cary, Caspar Shoaff, Robert Peter, and Evan Shelby; any Eight of whom shall be a sufficient Number to proceed on Business.*

*The Managers and Gentlemen who are so obliging as to take in Subscriptions, are to receive the Sums subscribed, and pay them to the Treasurers, or transmit them an Account of what they have received by the last Monday in May next, when a general Meeting of the Managers is desired at Frederick-Town on Manockasy, in Maryland, and if a sufficient Sum is paid in to enable them to proceed on the Design,*

*Notice will be immediately given in the Virginia, Maryland, and Pennsylvania Gazettes, and a Day and Place appointed for Undertakers to meet the Managers, and give in their Proposals.*

*Some Skilful Gentlemen have agreed to view the Great-Falls in the Spring, and if they should Report the opening or passing of them practicable (which is now generally believed) it is proposed that whatever Balance remains in the Treasurers Hands after completing the first Design, shall be appropriated to that Purpose; but if this should be found too great an Undertaking, then to be disposed of as the Managers shall judge most conducive to the mutual Advantage of the two Colonies.*

*The Amount of Money paid the Treasurer, the Sums expended, and the Progress made in the Works, will be published from Time to Time in the several Gazettes, that the Contributors may be satisfie their Generosity is not abused.*

> *February 4, 1762.*

## The Virginians depart from Fort Cumberland

A synopsis[1309] of a February 12, 1762 letter Bouquet wrote to General Amherst from Philadelphia includes the statement, "*The Virginians have left Fort Burd and Cumberland; a few men will be sent.*"

## A cannon and swivel guns are found at Pearsal's fort

A February 14, 1762 letter[1310] Major James Livingston wrote to Bouquet from Fort Cumberland states:

*I received both your Favours, one on the 13th Instant late at Night, the other early this Morning; as to the Men I shall follow your Orders; and the Powder as I was informed by the Cooper of the Train was the best on the Communication, and I believe it still to be the same, except 2 Barrels which the late Springs rose on in the Magazine; if I had empty half Barrels, I could readily get Horses to send them to Red Stone, as Pack Horses are frequently going up, Serjeant McDonnald could readily convey them to me, and by the Coopers Assistance I could get them back to Red Stone; You wrote to know the Size, the whole is what you commonly call Barrels.*

*As to the Hunters, I have taken all the Pains I could to detect some of them, but to no purpose, for as they perceive the Proclamation to be so severe, they shun coming near the Fort, and cross the River 6 or 8 Miles from this Garrison*

*As to the Estimation of the Expence of the River, I believe it will not be settled, till the Survey of the River is made; the Brass Gun I mentioned in my last Return, I found at a Fort called Pearsals Fort, on the South Branch, with a Quantity of Grape Shot, and 4 Swivels, which they told me belong'd to the Ohio Company; as to the Cannon she was at this Fort when Gen^l Bradock came here, and for some years after, she seems to me to be a Spanish Piece, and is a Gun fit for Service, only a Piece of her Britch is broke off.*

## Providing liquor to Indians is prohibited

On March 1, 1762, Bouquet issued a general order to various posts, including Fort Cumberland, prohibiting individuals from giving, selling, or carrying liquor to Indians.

---

[1309] "**Sessional Papers of the Dominion of Canada**", Volume 23, 1890.
[1310] "**The papers of Col. Henry Bouquet**", 1942.

## A list of the men of the Virginia Regiment from 1762

The 1833 book "**Collections of the Virginia Historical and Philosophical Society**" includes the text of a paper in the possession of the editor of that book that was labeled *"For Mr. James Cocke, An Account of the Year's Pay paid the Officers of the Virginia regiment, 1762."* The content of the paper follows:

*A Account of Cash paid the Officers of the Virginia Regiment for their presents, allowed by Act of Assembly, Disbanded March 1, 1762.*

Lieutenant-Colonel Adam Stephen, £319 7 6
Major Andrew Lewis, - - - 273 15 o
Captains Robert Stewart, - 182 10 o
Mordecai Buckner, - 182 10 o
Thomas Bullitt, - - 182 10 o
Nathaniel Gist - - 182 10 o
John Blagg, - - - 182 10 o
Lieutenants John Lawson, - - 91 05 o
John Cameron, - - 91 05 o
Thomas Gist, - - 91 05 o
Reuben Voss, - - 91 05 o
George Weedon, - - 91 05 o
Walter Cunningham, - 91 05 o
Alexander Minzie, - 91 05 o
David Kennedy, - - 91 05 o
Joseph Fent, - - 91 05 o
Jethro Sumner, - - 91 05 o
William Daingerfield, - 91 05 o
Robert Johnston, - - 91 05 o
John Sallard, - - 91 05 o
Larkin Chew, - - 91 05 o
William Hughes, - - 91 05 o
Alexander Boyd, - - 91 05 o
William Fleming, - - 91 05 o
William Cocke, - - 91 05 o
Ensigns Barton Lucas, - - 73 00 o
Alexander McClannahan, 73 00 o
George McKnight, - 73 00 o
David Long,- - - 73 00 o
John Seayers, - - 73 00 o
Henry Timberlake, - 73 00 o
Surgeon John Stuart, - - 182 10 o
Captain John McNeill, - - 182 10 o
£3.951 02 6

*Col⁰ Wm. Byrd, Credit given him in his Acc', Virginia Ledger, £547 00.*
*Capt. Henry Woodward. Paid by the Treasurer, £182, 10.*
*Lieut. Leonard Price, Credit given him in his Acc', Virginia Ledger, £91, 05.*
*Lieutenant Charles Smith, paid by the Treasurer, £91, 05.*
*1762, Sept.—Lieut. William Woodford, Paid by Alexʳ Boyd, Pay Mʳ, after deducting his account with the Country—Balance, £84, 8, 11.*

## Job Pearsal sells property on the South Branch

The 1939 book "**Early Records Hampshire County Virginia**" records the following for March 10, 1762, "*PEARSAL, Job (w. Bithia) of Hampshire Co. to Bryan Bruen, Merchant, of Winchester, Frederick Co. (mortgage) 323 a. on South Branch; rec. 3-11-1762. Wit.: Sam Dew.*" The following is also recorded for the same day, "*POULSON, Anderson (POWELSON) Hampshire Co. to William Dopson Hampshire Co (lease and rel.) 200 a. on North Branch; rec. 3-11-1762. Wit.: Sam Dew.*"

## Oqullion is involved in a Frederick County lawsuit

Neal Oqullion was being sued[1311] by George Stout in the Frederick County, Maryland Court on March 16, 1762.

## A payment for hauling flour to Fort Cumberland in March of 1762

A section of the 1775 book "**Votes and Proceedings of the House of Representatives of the Province of Pennsylvania. Beginning the Fourteenth Day of October, 1758.**" titled "*The Commissioners appointed by Act of Assembly for disposing of the Hundred Thousand Pounds for the King's Use, for Cash paid Sundries, as per their Orders on the Trustees of the General Land Office*" records a payment for March 23, 1762 services as follows, "*Thomas Moor, for Carriage of Flour to Fort Cumberland.*"

## Bouquet mentions Thomas Cresap in a negative light

A synopsis[1312] of an April 1, 1762 letter Bouquet wrote to Amherst from Fort Pitt includes the statement, "*His reason for preventing outlaws from settling on Indian lands. His further reason was to frustrate the bubble scheme of Colonel Cresup to settle the Ohio. The attempt to bribe him (Bouquet) to go into the scheme. His attempt to prevent a scandalous breach of Treaty.*"

The bribe was contained in the July 24, 1760 letter Thomas Cresap wrote to Bouquet, inviting him to participate in the Ohio Company. The April 1, 1762 letter contains the following:

*I have avoided troubling you with a minute account of all the triffling Events that occur daily here, in which number I must class Fauquier's Letter to me, as I thought it intirely groundless, and expected that my answer would have been fully satisfactory to him.*

*as I know of no legal Title People can have to settle Indian Lands, but what must be derived from the Powers given by the Crown to the Comander in Chief, or the Governors of Provinces, I imagined to have obviated all Cavils by the Exceptions I had made.*

*Neither could I think that the Lieut. Governor of Virginia after desiring me to explain my Intentions in issuing that order, Should complain to you, before he had received that Explanation, For certainly his Letter to me in that Case was an unnecessary trouble to himself, and his Express a useless Expence to the Publick. I take the Liberty to inclose a Copy of the answer I made him at that time*

*I never had any design to obstruct any man's Just Rights, or give uneasiness to anybody, and much less to a respectable Colony. After having found every other method insufficient I thought the fear of Punishment would deter the outlaws, who were the only Persons I had in view, from their vile practices, but tho' some are since fallen in my hands, they have suffered no other molestation than to be expelled from their Improvements, and have their Hutts burnt, and they seem at last disgusted from making new*

---

[1311] "**Colonial Records of the Upper Potomac**", Volume 6.
[1312] "**Sessional Papers of the Dominion of Canada**", Volume 23, 1890.

*attemts, as they know, that tho' I overlook many things, I never do forgive a breach of orders in this departm*<sup></sup>

*I had yet another reason to make my Intentions publickly known at that time, and which I thought best not to communicate to Fauquier. I had been repeatedly informed, that one Coll. Cresap, who is concerned in one of the Ohio Companies (the favorite Scheme of Virginia) was proposing by way of Subscription to Several familys to remove from the frontiers of that Colony & Mariland, to form settlements on the Ohio: I foresaw that those poor People would be ruined by that bubble, and I was the more induced to credit that Report, from an offer made me by that same Gentleman of a share or 25,000 Acres of those Lands, which did not tempt me.*

*In preventing in the district intrusted to me a scandalous breach of a recent Treaty, by the measure complained of, I can not at least be Charged with interested Views, or having exerted the little Power vested in me, to the oppressions of the subject, or the Indian.*

*As an officer serving without Prospect of a higher Rank in the Army, There is no object, of ambition for me in this Country; and as a man I must have convinced every Individual who has been concerned in this department, of my disinterestedness in never receiving the most triffling acknowledgment from any man in it.*

*No Trader or settler ever paid me a shilling for their Licences, nor other People for the Plantations I was authorized by Gen[l] Monckton to grant along the Communication, and at Red Stone Creek, for the support of this Post; and I have constantly observed the same Rule with the Indians, in accepting no Presents from them.*

*Divested of all motives of ambition, and without private views of Interest, I flattered myself to be free of any Imputation of Partiality or Injustice, and having heard of no Complaints from either of the two other Provinces, I must ascribe this proceeding to the misfortune I had in the Campaign of 1758, to be obliged to differ in opinion with some Persons of Virg[a] about Roads & Provisions, and I am afraid I remain still obnoxious to them, which can only increase my desire of being removed from this Command, if it was consistent with your Pleasure.*

*The Obliging manner in which you are pleased to mention that affair to me, and so very different from M[r] Fauquier's behavior, required with my most grateful acknowledgments, that I should clear myself of an odious Imputation, the Effect of a groundless Jealousys and the greediness of ingrossing those Lands, and tho' from the distance of my station, I may be obliged to act sometimes without orders to the best of my Judgment, It shall be my constant endeavour not to incur your disaprobation, or disoblige any of the Provinces. ...*

## McDonald mentions desertion at Fort Cumberland

An April 1, 1762 letter[1313] Sergeant Angus McDonald wrote to Bouquet from Fort Burd includes the statement, *"I am afraid I Shall be left alone for my men dos not pay me the same Respect they use to do and I am afraid to Correct them for Should they disart I should loose all they owe me I am informed some of the men at Cumberland is gone."*

---

[1313] **"The papers of Col. Henry Bouquet"**, 1942.

### Thomas Gist is rewarded for bravery

Christopher Gist's sons Thomas and Nathaniel are listed as members of the Virginia Regiment. A month after the list was written, Thomas Gist was rewarded for bravery in Grant's action at Fort Duquesne on September 11, 1758. Volume 3 of the book "**Legislative Journals of the Council of Colonial Virginia...**" records the following for April 3, 1762:

> *A Message from the House of Burgesses by M<sup>r</sup> Pendleton that they had pass'd a Resolve that the sum of one Hundred Pounds be paid by the public to Lieutenant Thomas Gist as a Reward for his Bravery as an Officer in the late Virginia Regiment and as Recompense for a Wound he received in Colonel Grants Engagement, and the Hardships he underwent during a Years Captivity by the Indians, to which they desired the Concurrence of the Council.*
>
> *Which Resolve was read and agreed to.*[1314]

The April 7, 1762 minutes indicate that the Governor gave his assent the resolve.

### The location of John Nicholl's house is identified

David Ross's April 3, 1762 survey for the 425-acre White Oak Level tract (Frederick County, Maryland Patent No. 5111) includes the following statement:

---

[1314] The following is an account of Grant's action from the "**Pennsylvania Gazette**":
*Annapolis, October 5th, 1758.*

*We are informed by a letter from Frederick county, that on Monday, the 11th of September, Major Grant, of the Highland regiment, marched from our camp on the waters of the Kiskiminitas, with 37 officers and 805 privates, taken from the different regiments that compose the Western Army, on an expedition against Fort Duquesne.*

*The third day after their march, they arrived within eleven miles of Fort Duquesne, and halted till three o'clock in the afternoon; then marched within two miles of Fort Duquesne, and left their baggage there, guarded by a captain, two subalterns, and fifty men, and marched with the rest of the troops, and arrived at eleven o'clock at night upon a hill, a quarter of a mile from the Fort. Major Grant sent two officers and fifty men to the Fort, to attack all the Indians, &c., they should find lying out of the Fort; they saw none, nor were they challenged by the centries. As they returned, they set fire to a large store house, which was put out as soon as they left it. At break of day, Major Lewis was sent with 400 men, (royal Americans and Virginians,) to lie in ambush a mile and a half from the main body, on the path on which they left their baggage, imagining the French would send to attack the baggage guard and seize it. Four hundred men were posted along the hill facing the Fort, to cover the retreat of Capt. M'Donald's company, who marched with drums beating toward the Fort, in order to draw a party out of the Fort, as Maj. Grant had some reason to believe there were not above 200 men in the Fort, including Indians; but as soon as they heard the drums, they sallied out in great numbers, both French and Indians, and fell upon Captain M'Donald, and two columns that were posted lower on the hill to receive them. The Highlanders exposed themselves without any cover, and were shot down in great numbers, and soon forced to retreat. The Carolinians, Marylanders, and Lower Countrymen, concealing themselves behind trees and the brush, made a good defence; but were overpowered by numbers, and not being supported, were obliged to follow the rest. Major Grant exposed himself in the thickest of the fire, and endeavored to rally his men, but all to no purpose, as they were by this time flanked on all sides. Maj. Lewis and his party came up and engaged, but were soon obliged to give way, the enemy having the hill of him, and flanking him every way. A number were drove into the Ohio, most of whom were drowned. Major Grant retreated to the baggage, where Captain Bullet was posted with fifty men, and again endeavored to rally the flying soldiers, by entreating them in the most pathetic manner to stand by him, but all in vain, as the enemy were close at their heels. As soon as the enemy came up to Capt. Bullet, he attacked them very furiously for some time, but not being supported, and most of his men killed, was obliged to give way. However, his attacking them stopped the pursuit, so as to give many an opportunity of escaping. The enemy followed Major Grant, and at last separated them, and Captain Bullet was obliged to make off. He imagines the major must be taken, as he was surrounded on all sides, but the enemy would not kill him, and often called to him to surrender. The French gave quarters to all that would accept it.*

*Beginning at two bounded White Oaks standing on the Potomac River side about half a mile below the mouth of Everts Creek and about 3 quarters of a mile above John Nicholl's house, formerly bounded for a tract of land laid out for Thomas Bladen. Esq.*[1315]

This reference indicates that John Nicholas Senior or Junior had a house on the Butter and Cheese tract.

The 425-acre White Oak Level survey that was performed for David Ross on April 3, 1762 was for the same area that was covered by the smaller 300-acre Pleasant Valley survey that was performed for Thomas Bladen on June 1, 1745. James Prather and Daniel Cresap served as chain bearers on the 1745 survey. During litigation over the property, James Prather and Aaron Moore, who were acting as chain bearers during the April 3, 1762 survey, provided depositions indicating that Major Livingston of Fort Cumberland sent soldiers, who attempted to stop the White Oak Level survey by cutting the surveying chain.[1316] Aaron Moore appears on the 1761 Old Town Hundred list.

### Thomas Hutchins requests that Fredrick Ice be taken to Fort Pitt

Thomas Hutchins' 1762 journal[1317] includes the following from an April trip westward from Fort Pitt:

*The 7th Set out for Mohickon John's where I arriv'd the 19th. at 12 o'Clock after a very disagreeable March Occasioned by bad Weather; I made him and his Tribe acquainted by a Belt of Wampum that the Commander in Chief Insisted on his taking to Fort Pitt Edward Long and John Hague both deserters from the Kings Troops; And likewise one Frederick Ice who was taken Prisoner during the War and now is very troublesome to the Traders Passing and Repassing —*

*Mohickon John ... says that as Frederick Ice had Sundry times Stole Horses and Bells from travellers passing by his House for which himself and his People were blamed, One of his Young Men Tomhawk'd him —*

### Eyre identifies the location of Braddock's grave

Colonel Eyre's journal[1318] of a trip to Pittsburgh includes the following from April 5, 1762:

*After I got on the East Side of this Hill, I fell in with General Braddocks Road. The 5th came to the great Crossings. The Road all the Way very bad both wet and rocky, and very much out of Repair, particularly the Bridges, and Numbers of fallen Trees across the Road. The Country thro' which I came this Day much worse than that of yesterday, and more mountainous. The great Meadows as they are calld, seem'd to me to be not more than thirty or forty Acres, made famous by the Loss that Col.° Washington sustain'd, when he was attack'd in his Fort by the French and Indians. This Place is about one Mile nearer to Fort Cumberland than where General Braddock was buried. This Distance between General Braddocks Grave and the Crossings is nineteen or twenty Miles.*

### Three deserters are deposed at Fort Cumberland

An April 6, 1762 letter[1319] Major James Livingston wrote to Bouquet from Cumberland states:

---

[1315] This patent description was found as a result of the research of Francis Bridges and Steve Colby.

[1316] The information in this paragraph was found in Volume 6 of **"Colonial Records of The Upper Potomac"** by Francis Bridges.

[1317] **"The papers of Sir William Johnson"**, Volume X, 1951.

[1318] **"The Western Pennsylvania Historical Magazine"**, Volume 27, 1944.

[1319] **"The papers of Col. Henry Bouquet"**, 1942.

*Since my writing and inclosing the Returns to you Three Men deserted from this Place, and went to Winchester but were sent back again by Col° Stephens, at their Return I examined them, and a Justice being come up into these Parts, he took the Depositions of Two of them, by which it will appear that one Burny Ryley was the chief Instigator of their Desertion, and is to be sent in Irons to Fort Pitt by Col° Stephens Order, I have inclosed the Two Depositions to be Evidences against him: he is the Man who has been so often encouraged by the General and You, for raising Grain at Fort Burd ...*

## Eyre describes the state of Fort Cumberland on April 7-8, 1762

Colonel Eyre's journal[1320] of a trip to Pittsburgh includes the following from April 1762:

*The 6th pass'd the little Meadows which is call'd by some twenty two, by others twenty three Miles from Fort Cumberland, and the 7th reach'd Fort Cumberland which is reckon'd to be between forty two and forty four Miles from the great Crossings. All the Road from these Crossings, what is called Yonogeny to Cumberland is very bad, and I think next to impassable with any Waggons. The Road very hilly, Rocky, and wet, occasioned by Variety of Springs every where in the Mountains. In Short all the Road from Red Stone to Fort Cumberland is very bad. The Allegheny or Apalachian Mountains are very broad here, very near sixty Miles over. I found Fort Cumberland going to Ruin. The Side of it next the Hill would have been pretty strong, if it had not been for a Magazine of Powder, that blew up by Accident in the Fort which damag'd the two Curtains. These Sides were never finish'd; the other Sides are pretty open. There are ten Iron Four Pounders, and one Brass one, in pretty good Repair, twenty Barrels of Powder and three hundred and thirty or upwards, Boxes of small Musket Ball, some old Arms and nine good Wall Pieces that was never us'd. There are a vast Number of Artillery Waggons taken to Pieces in some Out Houses, and I believe a good Deal of small Cannon Ball, as likewise a great Number Hand Granades. The Ohio Company is building a Storehouse on the opposite Side of the River from the Fort. The 8th staid there and the 9th got to Fort Bedford. The Road very level the whole Way, chiefly between Hills, but in wet Weather, I fancy its extremely deep particularly near the Block House. Tho' this Road runs thro' a Valley, I never saw worse Ground in general, for so much as I observd the whole Way.*

It is simply incredible that repairs to two curtains damaged by the September 27, 1758 explosion had not been completed by April of 1762. It appears that the fort lay in a vulnerable state until around June 10, 1763, when repairs were finally made with the help of refugees.

## Eyre describes the condition of the roads

An April 10, 1762 letter[1321] Colonel William Eyre sent to Bouquet from Raystown includes the statement:

*I arrived here Yesterday Afternoon from F. Cumberland, and found the Road between that Place, & this, but very indifferent: I think it's about 36 Miles Distant.*

*The Road between that Post, & Fort Burd, is very Bad, Except 15 or 16 Miles on this Side of Red-Stone Creek, the rest of the Road I found Exceedingly out of repair: all the difference I can observe, between the Road by Red-Stone to Cumberland, And that between this Place & Fᵗ Pitt is that the former, May be made passable for Waggons, as it's in General more Level, & the Bottom hard, tho in many places Wet & very Stony. I fell into Gen. Bradocks Road on this Side of the Laurel Hill & came all the Rest of the way upon that Road to Fort Cumberland*

---

[1320] **"The Western Pennsylvania Historical Magazine"**, Volume 27, 1944.
[1321] **"The papers of Col. Henry Bouquet"**, 1942.

## Two deserters are returned to Fort Cumberland

An April 10, 1762 letter[1322] Bouquet sent to Sergeant Angus McDonald from Fort Pitt includes the statement:

*By the Evidences sent me from Fort Cumberland, it appears that Riley has been Guilty of inducing those Men to desert, you Will therefore send him a Prisoner to this Fort, the Deserters from Fort Cumberland have been all sent back to that Post*

## Fort Cumberland sends a few blankets and a tent westward

An April 24, 1762 letter[1323] Sergeant Angus McDonald sent to Bouquet from Fort Burd includes the statement, *"Immediatly Colᵒ Eyre Sent from fort Cumberland 4 Blanketts and a tent which I Shall Send by the first Conveyance"*.

## The Virginia residence of George Williams is identified

David Ross's May 2, 1762 survey of the 420-acre Buck Lodge tract (Frederick County, Maryland Patent No. 680) includes the following description:

*Beginning at a bound White Oak standing about two perches from the Potomack opposite the place where George Williams now lives on the Virginia side and formerly Benjamin Rogers and about one hundred perches above the lower end of a bottom and two or three miles above the mouth of Wills Creek formerly bounded for Thomas Bladen*[1324]

As stated previously, Benjamin Rogers and his entire family were reported as either being killed or kidnapped in 1755, during the French and Indian war. **"Dyers Index to Land Grants in West Virginia"**, Volume 2 (1896) lists a 218-acre 1762 grant to George Williams on the North Branch of the Potomac that is recorded in Grant Book 1, page 151.

## The pay for Fort Burd is waiting at Fort Cumberland

A May 15, 1762 letter[1325] Sergeant Angus McDonald sent to Bouquet from Fort Burd states:

*I Recived an account from below that our pay is lodged at fort Cumberland where is an officer Come to pay off those posts as I have no trusty Body that I Can send I hope it will not be disagreeable to your honour if I go myself. I likeways Recived orders to list any of my party that is willing to serve and to give ten pounds Bounty to Each man but Shall not Do any thing Concerning it till I have your Directions in that affair as I am ordered to Get your leave before I mention it to my Men*

## Bladen's paperwork is handed in late, on May 16, 1762

Volume 3 of the book **"Reports of Cases Decided in the High Court of Chancery of Maryland ..."** includes a detailed summary of a conflict between Thomas Bladen and David Ross concerning lands in Western Maryland that begins as follows:

*Ross v. Bladen.—The Judges of the Land Office to the Chancellor.—May it please your Excellency.— There having been a dispute in the Land Office of an uncommon and extraordinary nature, in which*

[1322] "**The papers of Col. Henry Bouquet**", 1942.

[1323] "**The papers of Col. Henry Bouquet**", 1942.

[1324] This patent description was found as a result of Steve Colby's research.

[1325] "**The papers of Col. Henry Bouquet**", 1942.

*Thomas Bladen, Esq. and Doctor David Ross are the persons concerned, we take the liberty, in pursuance of his Lordship's instructions, by which we are directed, in difficult and unprecedented cases, to desire your Excellency's advice and assistance, (Land Ho. Assis. 232, 234,) to submit to your Excellency, as Chancellor, a state of the case or matter depending before us together with our opinion, hoping you will be pleased to favour us with your Excellency's sentiments thereon.*

*On the 16th day of January, 1761, Doctor David Ross applied to us in usual form for warrants under the proclamation to resurvey, and be allowed the pre-emption of the following tracts of land, Wills's Town, Buck Lodge, Sugar Bottom, Turkey Flight, Prized, Lawrence, and Bigg Bottom, containing 2,254 acres, but as no certificates for those lands appeared to be returned or lodged in the office, which is essential to the issuing of a warrant under the proclamation, Mr. Ross petitioned for, and obtained special warrants to affect the lands aforesaid, having, as your Excellency knows is usual, first paid the agent caution money for the same.*

*On the 16th day of May following, the undermentioned certificates were returned into the office, signed by Mr. Thomas Cressap, who was deputy surveyor of the county at the times these certificates respectively bear date, viz: Wills's Town, surveyed in June, 1745, Buck Lodge, and Sugar Bottom, in June, 1746, Turkey Flight, and Prized, in August, 1746, and Lawrence and Bigg Bottom in November, 1746, containing in the whole 2,254 acres; surveyed, as is set forth in the said certificates, for Thomas Bladen, Esq. As the land described in these certificates appeared to be the same tracts for which Doctor Ross had, as we have already observed, obtained special warrants, we thought it our duty to forbid patent issuing to Mr. Bladen till we could examine the records and inquire how it had happened, that those certificates had lain so long dormant. ...*

Ross's 1762 Wills Town survey is Frederick County Patented Certificate 5196. Page 837 of Frederick County Maryland Deed Book J indicates that David Ross sold the Wills Town tract to Joseph Tomlinson for 274 pounds in October 1764. The tract is described as *"1,125 Acres Located In A Fork Of Wills Creek On The West Side Of Said Creek About 3 Miles From Fort Cumberland..."* The mileage statement refers to the beginning point of the survey.

## McDonald has leave to go to Fort Cumberland to get the pay for Fort Burd

A May 17, 1762 letter[1326] Bouquet wrote to Sergeant Angus McDonald from Fort Pitt states:

*I received this morning your Letter of the 15ᵗʰ and you have my Leave to go to Fort Cumberland to receive the Pay due to your Men, who I hope are now convinced that a good soldier will always find it his own advantage to do Stricly his duty.*

*The listing your men again being a Regimental Concern, I would not Chuse to interfere in it but As it is required I Would give my Opinion. It is not by any means to list them again; They never were discharged & have been continued in Pay by the Province Therefore have no Right to Bounty: & it would be A precedent of bad Consequence to the Service: But that they may Enjoy the advantages given to others I do recommend them to Coll. Stephen for a gratification, which if they receive they are to look upon as a Reward for their Past Services and not as a due for future ones.*

*Therefore you are not to mention any Bounty to them, or give them the least Room to think that they are free, till you receive further orders for the Purpose from the Comanding Officer of your Regiment.*

---

[1326] **"The papers of Col. Henry Bouquet"**, 1940.

*You will return to your Post as soon as possible, & as there is some Powder to come from Fort Cumberland to Redstone, if it be ready & Major Livingston can get horses you will come back with it & lodge it Securely in your stores w^th a Centry to it (with only his Sword or bayonet & no firelock for fear of accidents) When you Shall inform me of its being at Fort Burd, I Will Send the Barge from hence to bring it here.*

## Sneaking prohibited rum past Fort Cumberland

A May 24, 1762 letter[1327] Bouquet wrote to Sir Jeffery Amherst from Fort Pitt includes the following statement:

*The Salutary Effects of the prohibitions of Rum are Sensibly felt; Your orders have been well obeid, a Country man sent back from Fort Cumberland with his Cargo of Liquors, passed that Fort & other Posts in the Night and arrived safe here, where being detected, 17 kegs of Rum he had buried, have been Seized. I released the man & his horses, keeping the Rum in the Kings stores till you are pleased to order how it is to be dispose of. The Court of Inquiry being long, I only inclose the Carrier's own declaration.*

## Livingston forwards powder from Fort Cumberland in May of 1762

A May 28, 1762 letter[1328] Major James Livingston wrote to Bouquet from Cumberland states:

*I have sent you the Returns, and 24 Caggs of Powder; there was one Barrel so bad, which is left here, that the Conductor and Cooper thought it not worth sending; another Barrel also is left here fit for Service for the use of this Garrison; I have rode a great Way to procure Horses and Caggs, as there were none here, to bring the Powder up, but could not accomplish my Purpose as all the People are very busy about their Corn, till one William Walker came to this Post from Bedford with Flour, with whom I have agreed at 22^s/. p^r Cagg to carry it to Fort Burd, which amounts to £ 14,, 8,, 0 Penn^a Currency, which I hope you will discharge, I have given him an Order for that Sum; No News here, the Virginians are ordered to Fredericksburg to be the General Rendezvous, as they cannot be supplied at Winchester, 22^s / 6^d being paid p hund for Flour; Col^o Mercer is gone to Philad^a for Cloathing for the Regiment, with Orders for 6^s/. Sterl^g p^r yard for the private Men. Perhaps you may conjecture the Carriage to be high, but I could by no means help it.*

A May 28, 1762 postscript lists expenses associated with the gunpower shipment, including the cost of the kegs, the cost of *"Thread to sew the Covering"*, and the cost of *"Carriage of the 24 Caggs"*, and states, *"This day the Pack horses set off with the Powder."*

## Local chain carriers used on a Knobley Mountain survey

On June 5, 1762, Frederick Ice and John Nicholas, Jr. were chain carriers for John Moffett during a survey for Adam McCarty on Rodgers Run, a tributary of Patterson Creek on Knobley Mountain.[1329] The tract adjoined a property of an O'Neal.

---

[1327] "**The papers of Col. Henry Bouquet**", 1940.

[1328] "**The papers of Col. Henry Bouquet**", 1942.

[1329] "**Colonial Records of the Upper Potomac**", Volume 6.

## Cresap writes Sharpe about an Indian problem

On June 11, 1762, Thomas Cresap sent a letter[1330] to Governor Sharpe of Maryland that states:

*I have thought proper to acquaint you that there came to my House in the Last of April Last past Ten warrior Indians of this six nations who were going to war against the Cherokees and who also had a pass Setting forth that they had Been in actual service under General Johnston and requesting the Inhabitants through which they Pass to furnish them with Provision agreeable to the Treaty of Lancaster & in Consiquence of my former Instructions from Governors Ogle & Bladen my family supplyed them with Provisions the time they stayed at my Plantation which was three Days; They informed me that three hundred men of their nation would be along this way at the time that Corn would be waist high, who likewise designed to war against the Cherokees and as they always have and suppose always will make this their way Backwards and forwards & Commonly a Stage for some Days which is no small Inconvenience and Expence to me as they will have Provision either by fair or foul means which unless I can get some Retaliation or Satisfaction for (as it would be very Unreasonable I should Bare intirely such a burthen and Expence) shall Endeavour to protect my private property either by force or otherwise, I therefore recommend the Circumstances I am likely to fall under to your wise Consideration before I am compeld (as I in all Likelyhood may be) to enter into them that I may not be Culpable should the Indians Resentment be drawn on this Province thereby, I hope you will give me your Candid advice how to proceed in the above matter if Requisate and whether to let them have Provisions they Demanding it or Protect my Right by force as nothing is more Certain then that they will Endeavour to take it by force if Denyed them otherwise. I was just now in formed by two Gentlemen from Virginia that the Cherokees had Lately Robed one Cap Cristy a trader from Augusta County in Virginia to the Value of Fifteen hundred Pounds in goods and Killed one of his men. This is all we have meterial from those parts and not any thing worth mentioning*

Following this letter, the minutes of the Council of Maryland from a Friday in July of 1762 include the following:[1331]

*Ordered that the Clerk send the following Answer thereto.*

*Sir*

*I am ordered by the Governor and Council to acquaint you that as Soon as the Governor receives an Answer to your Letter of the 11th June last sent him a Copy whereof he has transmitted to his Excellency General Amherst, he will write you fully in Relation to the Subject Matter contained therein*

## Israel Christie is murdered and robbed on his return from the Cherokee nation

A June 13, 1762 letter[1332] Major James Livingston wrote to Bouquet from Fort Cumberland states:

*M<sup>r</sup> Greenfield Just Informs Me that he saw a Gentileman of Credit in Winchester from Augusta County in Virginia that Inform'd him that Cap<sup>tn</sup> Israil Christy: had been to the Cheerokee Nation with Goods and in their Return home was Overtoke by a party of the Cherokees: who Toke their Goods and Other Mirchandiz to the Value of £ 1500: allso kill'd One of his Men*

The letter includes a postscript that states, *"Inclosed you have the News Pappers"*.

---

[1330] **"Archives of Maryland"**, Volume 32.
[1331] **"Archives of Maryland"**, Volume 32.
[1332] **"The papers of Col. Henry Bouquet"**, 1942.

## Improvements at the Great Crossings

A June 17, 1762 letter[1333] written by Sergeant Angus McDonald to Bouquet from Fort Cumberland includes the statement:

*The Bearer Tho$^s$ Crafts is one of the men stiationed at the great Crossings and wants to have your promis that he shall not Be turned away before he makes any more Improvements at that stage they have got Corn growing and will, in a little time make that post Very usefull for travelers: they give Every Body satisfaction that goes the Road*

## A June, 25 1762 letter concerning deserters and transport of ammunition

A June 25, 1762 letter[1334] written by Major James Livingston to Bouquet from Fort Cumberland states:

*Inclosed you have the state of this Garrison, as to the Artilery there is no Alteration since Last Return; My party has Returnd from Winchester which I sent for one John Jones who is a Diserter from the Royal American Regiment & who is Inlisted into the Virginia Regiment but they Coud not get him unless they paid the Bounty which he Receivd from the Virginians it being Ten pounds. I shall set out Tomorrow morning for Winchester with two Deserters from the Virginians & shall then Enquire into the Matter Relative to the other & shell pay wha is Allowd by Act of Parlemint which is Twenty Shillings Ster$^g$ I shall be glad youd inform me what sum you woud Allow for the Carraige of, Two Boxes of Ball from this to Redstone as several has Applyd to me to Carry the same*

## Governor Sharpe writes to Amherst about Cresap's letter

Governor Sharpe wrote the following letter[1335] to Amherst on June 26, 1762:

*Inclosed I send your Excellency a Copy of a Letter which I received a few Days ago from a person who lives in the Western part of this Province about fifteen miles from Fort Cumberland. Not knowing but the Cherokees as I am told was once the case may take offence at their Enemies being supplied with Provisions & Necessaries by our Frontier Inhabitants while going to the Cherokee Country with hostile Intentions & may revenge themselves on such of our People I should not take the Liberty till I could know your Excellency's Desire to give Mr. Cresap any Instructions relative to the Subject on which he writes to me. Had I power to order payment for what such Indians may on their passage thro this Province be furnished with, but in fact I have no such power & have very little reason to think the Assembly would satisfy Mr. Cresap or any other person who might supply them with provisions, for when upon receiving a similar Letter from the Frontier some years ago my predecessor in the Governm$^t$ gave orders for these Indians being furnished with necessary provisions on their passage thro our Frontier Settlements and recommending it to the Assembly to reimburse the persons who had victualled such Indians he could not prevail on the Assembly to pay any Regard to his recommendation.*

## 'Indian Fields" is resurveyed

The *"Indian Fields"* tract was resurveyed by John Murdock on June 26, 1762, increasing the acreage from 250 to 510. Thomas Cresap received a patent for the resurvey on October 8, 1762.[1336]

---

[1333] **"The papers of Col. Henry Bouquet"**, 1942.

[1334] **"The papers of Col. Henry Bouquet"**, 1942.

[1335] **"Correspondence of Governor Sharpe, 1761-1771"**.

[1336] Frederick County Patented Certificate 3533, MSA S1197-3952.

### Kenny reports that Killbuck tried to kill Thomas Cresap during the late war

Kenny's July 15, 1762 journal entry[1337] states:

> *I hear that Killbuck had been threatening Old Co¹ Cressop, & that in yᵉ War time he says he lay many Days on a Hill Oposite his house waiting to Kill yᵉ Old Co¹, upon hearing of which Old Cressep has sent Killbuck a Chellange that he wou'd fight him, each to take a Gun. This letter coming now a few days since has frightened Killbuck from going to yᵉ Treaty.*

Here, even as Thomas Cresap enters his golden years, he is clearly not a man to be trifled with.

### Messengers are overtaken, and captured or killed

A synopsis of a July 27, 1762 letter written to Bouquet from Cumberland states, "*Major Livingston to the same. Will observe instructions about provisions. Asks him to write Col. Sephen (sic) for militia to assist to garrison this fort. Is sure that the two expresses sent on the 9ᵗʰ are killed or taken, as the pistol lent to one of them was found at Cresap's.*"

### Letters to Bouquet from Enoch Innis, his father-in-law Thomas Cresap, and Livingston

A July 27, 1762 letter[1338] written by Major James Livingston to Bouquet from Old Town includes the following:

> *I Received your favour the 23ᵈ instᵗ wherein you desire me to enquire into the terrm for Wintering Horses, Oxen & Cows of Colᵒ Cresap, He will Winter the Cattle at 1/ p head & as to Horses it is according as they are fed with Grain but the Colᵒ and you will not differ.*

A July 27, 1762 letter[1339] written by Thomas Cresap to Henry Bouquet from Old Town states:

> *Majʳ Livingston informed me that you were desirous I shoud Winter you some Cows & Horses & woud be glad to Knew On what Tirms, Your Cows Shan't exceed ten shillings p head & the horses agreable to the Quantʸ of Provinder you shall think fitt to Order them which Shall be as Cheap as Can be Offorded & all Possible Cars taken of them*
>
> *I am under a Necessity of Troubleing you: Requesting some further Favours in regard to sundry Persons at your Post Indebted to me on whome No Process of Law Can be served & by whone I am greatly sufferer in Perticular one Jonathan Plumer for whome I became spetial Bail some time before he left these parts which Debt & Costs I have since been obliged to pay Amounting to About Fifteen Pounds besides which he is indebted to me by Bonds to the Amount of Five hundred Pounds & Never Likely to get one Farthing unless through your Assistance*
>
> *I shoud be glad to Knew Whither a sheriff from this woud be Allowd to Bring him by a Writ from that Post or by what Means or Process he may be Compelld to Discharge his Debt Allso there is one William Shearer whose Bond I have inclosed & woud esteem it a singular Kindness if you woud order him to Discharge it & a Receipt from any Person whome you shall order to Receive it Shall be a Discharge for the whole or any Part thereof from me*

---

[1337] "**The Pennsylvania Magazine of History and Biography…**", Volume 37, 1913.
[1338] "**The Papers of Col. Henry Bouquet**", 1942.
[1339] "**The Papers of Col. Henry Bouquet**", 1942.

*I have sent you all so inclosed the Original Pattens of your Lands which Perhaps may be of Service some time or other*

A postscript to Cresap's letter states, *"Mr Innis who is a sone in Law of mine writes to you in Regard to a Debt Due him from a soulder in your Rege^t^ Your doing him any favour therein woud Lay a further obligation on Sir who am as Above".*

References to Jonathan Plumer are included elsewhere in this book.

A July 27, 1762 letter[1340] from Enoch Innis to Henry Bouquet states:

*Through the Intercession of Coll° Cresap I have made Bold to request your favour in Regard to a Debt due me from one John Coulton who was a Serg^t^ of the Granediers in your Regim^t^ It was a debt Contracted by him at Vinango in Ap^l^ 1761 with one John Woods to whome I become his Security of which I made No Scruple as I Knew that at the time I Left Pittsb^g^ for Vinango Which was in Dec^r^ 1760 his Credit was good for five times that Sum & was generally Lookd upon to be an Honest Industrous Person but on my Return to Pittsburgh from Vinango found that through his Misbehavior, had became not worth one farthing so was Obliged to Pay the Debt for which they had Obtaind his Note of Hand & took an Order on the back payable to me which was all the Sattisfaction I Cou'd at that time get as he was in Confinement I as I was Obliged to Come Immediatly down Left the Note with M^r^ Philip Rice with an order to pay it to him on whose Producing the Vote to the Drawer he took a Pen & drew it Along his Name with an Intent I Suppose to Race it Out but wou'd Not Discharge it Wou'd you therefore think Prosper to have it Stop'd out of his Pay or order him to Discharge It ...*

This letter is potentially relevant to the subject of this book because it may place Enoch Innis in the Ohio Valley in some merchant capacity. From the date shared by all three letters, one can reasonably suspect that they were sent to Bouquet together.

### Amherst replies to Sharpe's June 26, 1762 letter about Cresap's concern

The August 12, 1762 minutes of the Council of Maryland include the following July 4, 1762 letter[1341] General Amherst wrote to Governor Sharpe:

*Last Night I had the favour of your Letter of the 26^th^ June, Enclosing a Copy of One you had received from an Inhabitant of the Western part of your Province, in regard to Furnishing Provisions to Parties of Indians, belonging to the Six Nations, going to War against the Cherokees.*

*I have been Informed that some Parties do Intend to go against the Southern Indians, Bordering on the French and Spanish Settlements; but as your Province have done Nothing for the King's Service I should Imagine, on your Application to the Assembly, they would at least make Provision for Enabling the Inhabitants of their own Province, to Supply such Friendly Indians as Pass and Repass, with Common Necessaries, that they may Pursue their Intended Plan of Distressing the Enemy; but if they obstinately Refuse to lend the least Assistance towards the Security and Safety of their own People, they must be Answerable for the Consequences; for it is most Unreasonable to Imagine, that the Province of Maryland, should, in the midst of an Expensive, tho' Just and Necessary, War, Remain Idle Spectators, without giving the least Assistance, whilst the other Colonies are Exerting themselves with a becoming Spirit to Enable His Majesty to Reduce His Enemies so as to bring about a Lasting and an Honourable Peace.*

---

[1340] **"The Papers of Col. Henry Bouquet"**, 1942.

[1341] **"Archives of Maryland"**, Volume 32.

Immediately after this letter, the council minutes include the following:

*The following Answer being prepared is ordered to be sent by the Clerk of this Board to Col: Cresap.*

*Sir*

*The Governor having received an answer to the Letter he some time ago sent to S* Jeffery Amherst with a Copy of yours to Himself dated 11ᵗʰ of June last orders me to Inform you that the General was apprized of the Intention of some Parties of the Six Nation Indians to go and make War on Indians to the Southward and that he had no doubt but the Inhabitants of these Colonies as the Parties should Pass and repass would supply them with such Provisions as they should stand in need of presuming the Assemblies of the respective Provinces will satisfy such Persons as may be under a necessity of doing so, In consequence therefore of the General's Letter the Governor recommends it to you to furnish such Parties of Friendly Indians as may call at your House with necessary Provisions and if, when the Assembly meets you will Produce a proper Account of what you may furnish he will recommend it to the Assembly to make Provision for your Reimbursement which His Excellency Flatters himself they will readily do especially as being a Member yourself you can make the Gentlemen of the Lower House sensible that the steps you shall have taken were absolutely necessary to prevent the Indians committing Depredations on the Frontier Inhabitants and Disturbing the Peace of the Province.*

*I am your Humble Servant*

*John Ross.*

## Indians request to be supplied at Cresap's, advised to go by Fort Cumberland instead

The book "**Proceedings of the Council of Maryland, 1761-1769**" includes the following:

*His Excellency lays before this Board the following Letter*

*Philadelphia 2d October 1762.*

*Sir*

*The six Nations having taken a Resolution to continue the War against their old Enemies the Cherokees, their Chiefs requested of me at the Treaty lately held with a large body of them and the Western Indians, that I should open a Store for the Accommodation of their Warriors at Harris's Ferry, and that I would forward their Request to you, to have another opened at Cressap's on Potomack.*

*Conformable therefore to my Promise, I sent you an Extract of What passed between us on that Occasion, together with their Belt; and as they will expect an answer from you with all convenient Speed, I think if you would be pleased to send it under Cover to Sir William Johnson, he would take the first opportunity of conveying it to the Six Nations.*

*You will observe by the Extract that the Warriors intended to go through the settled part of Cumberland County, and through the very Country in which they had committed so many cruel Outrages, but that they altered their Design on my representing to them the Dangers of taking such a Route.*

*I am with the Greatest Respect*

*Sir your most Obedient & most*

*Humble servant*

*Governor Sharpe   James Hamilton*

*Extract from the Treaty held with the Indians at Lancaster in the Month of August 1762.*

*The Governor's Answer to the Six Nations.*

*Brethren*

*By the relation you gave me at Easton in 1758, when you was relating the Causes of the War, it appears that you were of Opinion, One of the principal reasons, which made you join the French against us, was owing in a great Measure to the ill treatment your Warriors met with in Virginia, in those places, where your War hath passed through the settled part of that Colony, and you have now desired me to write to the Governor of Virginia that as there are settlers on your War Path, whereby it is stopped, he would cause it to be opened, now Brethren, I must acquaint you, that all the way from Harris's Ferry to Patomack, the white People are settled very thick; so that should your Warriors now use that Path, frequent differences between them and the Inhabitants might probably arise, by means whereof, the Peace so lately established between us may be endangered and I must desire you for this reason to use your best Interest with your Warriors, in case they are determined to go to War, that they would pursue the old War Path from Shamokin, which lies along the foot of the Allegheney Hills, & which is the nearest way they can go to their Enemies Country.*

*A Belt*

*Brethren*

*By this Belt you desire a trading House may be erected on Potomack at Daniel Cressap's House, and that he may have the Care of it for the Supply of your Warriors, and that I will send your request to the Governor of Maryland.*

*Brethren*

*Your Belt and all you said upon it shall be carefully sent to Governor Sharpe.*

*Deogwanda the Onondago Chief's Answer to the Governor.*

*Brother Onas.*

*I mentioned to you the other day my desire, that there should be a Store House kept at John Harris's and that he might have the Care of the Store for the Warriors.*

*I desired at the same time, that the Road might be opened for the Warriors to pass through the back Settlements to the Southern Indians, you know we are, and always have been at War with them, and I shall now begin to strike them. You told me in answer that you thought it best that that Road should be stopt up, least any differences should arise between your People and our Warriors, and desired if any Warriors did go to War, they would take the Old Road, that led to the Southward under the Mountains; and I now tell you, that as you desired that Road should be stopt, it shall be so; and I will take the old Road.*

*Extract from the Treaty held by the Indians at Lancaster in the Month of August 1762.*

*Brother Onas,*

*I will also acquaint you of another Trading place which is the place they call Potomack in Maryland One Daniel Cressap has sent me word by my Warriors this Spring, and he tells me that if the Governor would order him to keep a Store there, he would Provide every thing for the Warriors; for his Father used to maintain all the Indian Warriors that passed and repassed that way, he Likewise tells me if the Governor would let him know what he must do, and if he should be allowed to do this, he would provide for the Warriors, We now desire that he may be the Person appointed to receive Messages, and that you would acquaint the Governor of Maryland with this, that the Warriors may pass and repass that way without any Molestation.*

*A Belt of 7 Rows.*

*Ordered that the following Letter be sent to Sir William Johnson*

*Annapolis 25th of November 1762.*

*Sir*

*Governor Hamilton having lately sent me an Extract of a Speech that was made to him by the Six Nations at the Lancaster Treaty last Summer, by which I observe they desire One Daniel Cresap of this Province may be ordered to keep a Store house on Potomack near the Road their Warriors pass on their Expeditions against the Southern Indians, I take the Liberty to send you a Copy of the Extract and to desire your Opinion of their Intention in making such applications for if they ask no more than that Daniel Cresap may be permitted to trade with and sell their Parties as they shall pass & repass Such Articles as they may want, he is at Liberty to do so without any Special License from me, there being no Law to restrain such Trade, but if what they want is that the abovementioned Person may be impowered to Supply their Parties gratis or at the Expence of the Province with such goods as they may apply for, I cannot take upon myself to give him orders to that Effect and am much afraid that the Assembly should I recommend the Matter to them would not subject their Constituents to such an Expence. However to prevent any Disputes between such Parties of Indians and the Inhabitants in Case they should want Provisions as they pass through this Province, I have recommended it to Mr Thomas Cresap the Father of the Person abovementioned, who lives about fifteen miles on this side Fort Cumberland to furnish with necessary Provisions such Indian Warriors as may apply to him, and I have Promised to lay his Accounts before the Assembly for Payment hoping they will not object to making him Satisfaction, though at the same time I wish those Indians when they go to the Southward could be prevailed on to take their Rout (which in my opinion is equally convenient to them) by the Way of Fort Cumberland, where I understand One of the King's Officers still resides in the Character of Fort Major, and is I Presume authorized and enabled to receive and entertain Such Friendly Indians as may at times take Occasion to call at that Place. As I shall decline returning any Answer to the Indians Request till you shall be pleased to communicate to me whether I may then take the Liberty to Address my Answer to you or by what other means I may convey it to them*

*I am Sir with great Regard your hble Servt*

*H. Sharpe*

## Joseph Tomlinson is involved in a court matter

In a section titled, *"Imparlances to March Court Anno 1762"*, page 13 of the Frederick County book **"Dockett's Anno 1762"**, a record dated October 24 lists Joseph Tomlinson and Dan Carroll as adversaries. Another October 24 record lists Jn° Murphy and Neal Oquillion as adversaries.

## A 1762 tour from Fort Cumberland

In 1762, Thomas Hutchins, who was named as the Geographer General of the United States in 1781, created a manuscript map titled *"A tour from Fort Cumberland north westward round part of the lakes Erie, Huron and Michigan, including part of the rivers St. Joseph, the Wabash[1342] and Miamis, with a sketch of the road from thence by the Lower Shawanoe Town to Fort Pitt. 1762"*.

## Neal Oqullion is involved in a court matter

In a section titled, *"Criminal Writs returnable the third Tuesday & Sixteenth day of March in the 11th year of his Lordships Dominion &c Anno 1762"* in the Frederick County court book[1343] **"Dockett's Anno 1762"**, a November 6 record on page one lists Neal Oqullion. In a section titled *"Recognizances respecting to March Court Anno Dom 1762"*, Neal Oquillion is listed with an £30 bond that was apparently served by T. Prather on April 20, 1761.

## A reward is offered for deserters delivered to Fort Cumberland

A November 10, 1762 letter[1344] Bouquet sent to James McGill from Fort Pitt includes the following statement:

> *... I Send you here annexed a List of those who have deserted since the 24th of May last for every one of which delivered to the officers Commanding at Fort Cumberland or Fort Bedford I promise a Reward of Five Pounds Current money of Pensilvania besides an allowance for reasonable Charges incurred in bringing them to the Said Posts to be paid upon the Receipt of one of those officers.*

## A slave transaction in Hampshire County

The 1939 book[1345] **"Early Records Hampshire County Virginia"** records the following for November 19, 1762, *"GREGG, Robert of Patterson Creek (see Gragg) to Power Hazell of Hampshire Co. (bill of sale) One negro child; rec. 5-11-1763. Wit.: Samuel Poe, Thomas Bull."*

---

[1342] The Wabash is a river in Indiana that forms part of the border with Illinois and flows into the Ohio River. According to a historical marker in Mascouten Park, in West Lafayette, Indiana, the river was called the *"Wah-bah-shik-ki"* by the Miami Indians.

[1343] MSA No. C782-11

[1344] **"The papers of Col. Henry Bouquet"**, 1940.

[1345] This book was identified by John DeVault.

# 15. 1763: One war ends and another begins

### Livingston has gone a long time without pay

In a January 10, 1763 request[1346] for orders that was written from New York, Bouquet asked Amherst about paying the staff of the Department of Fort Pitt, including, *"one Fort Maj$^r$ at Fort Cumberland, Maj$^r$ Levingston whose pay is due from the 24$^{th}$ Decem$^r$ 1760."* To this question, Amherst replied on January 11, 1763 as follows, *"The ... Fort Major at Fort Cumberland ... come properly within the D. Q.M. General's Department & ought to be paid by him ..."*

Another of Bouquet's January 10, 1763 questions was, *"How to Garrison Fort Cumberland, Fort Burd and the Crossing of Yohiogheny to replace the Virginia troops at those* Posts." To this question, Amherst replied on January 11, 1763 as follows, *"I Must Suppose that the Virginia Troops will not be Withdrawn from those Posts."*

### Five men sent to Fort Cumberland to guard the magazines

A translation of a February 8, 1763 letter[1347] Ecuyer sent from Fort Pitt includes the statement, *"As the regiment of Virginia is disbanded, I have been obliged to send a Corporal and four men to Fort Cumberland to guard the magazines of the king."* Another translation[1348] of this text states the task as, *"... to guard the King's Storehouse..."*

### The treaty of Paris is signed on February 10, 1763, ending the Seven Years War

After the victory of Britain over France and Spain, the Seven Years War (known to Americans as the French and Indian War) concluded with the signing of the Treaty of Paris on February 10, 1763. The portion concerning North America states:

*VII. In order to re-establish peace on solid and durable foundations, and to remove for ever all subject of dispute with regard to the limits of the British and French territories on the continent of America; it is agreed, that, for the future, the confines between the dominions of his Britannick Majesty and those of his Most Christian Majesty, in that part of the world, shall be fixed irrevocably by a line drawn along the middle of the River Mississippi, from its source to the river Iberville, and from thence, by a line drawn along the middle of this river, and the lakes Maurepas and Pontchartrain to the sea; and for this purpose, the Most Christian King cedes in full right, and guaranties to his Britannick Majesty the river and port of the Mobile, and every thing which he possesses, or ought to possess, on the left side of the river Mississippi, except the town of New Orleans and the island in which it is situated, which shall remain to France, provided that the navigation of the river Mississippi shall be equally free, as well to the subjects of Great Britain as to those of France, in its whole breadth and length, from its source to the sea, and expressly that part which is between the said island of New Orleans and the right bank of that river, as well as the passage both in and out of its mouth: It is farther stipulated, that the vessels belonging to the subjects of either nation shall not be stopped, visited, or subjected to the payment of any duty whatsoever.*

---

[1346] **"The papers of Col. Henry Bouquet"**, 1940.

[1347] **"The papers of Col. Henry Bouquet"**, 1940.

[1348] **"The papers of Col. Henry Bouquet"**, 1942.

*The stipulations inserted in the IVth article, in favour of the inhabitants of Canada shall also take place with regard to the inhabitants of the countries ceded by this article.*

As this quote reveals, France ceded an enormous amount of North America to Great Britain.

### The Virginians at Fort Cumberland are disbanded

A February 12, 1763 letter[1349] Bouquet sent to Jeffrey Amherst from Philadelphia includes the following:

*The Virginians who garrisoned Fort Burd & Cumberland being disbanded have quitted those posts. Capt Ecuyer will send a few men to take Care of the Stores.*

### Cresap leases Virginia land to William Haggard

The 1939 book "**Early Records Hampshire County Virginia**" records the following for February 15, 1763, *"CRESAP, Thomas of Frederick Co., Md. to William Haggard of Hampshire Co. (lease) 100 a. on So. Branch; rec. 5-10-1763. Wit.: Enoch Innis, Teter Ebrod, Sarah Innis."*

### William Young leases property from Thomas Cresap

The 1939 book "**Early Records Hampshire County Virginia**" records the following for March 10, 1763, *"CRESAP, Thomas of Frederick Co., Maryland to William Young of Hampshire Co. (lease) 337 a. on So. Branch; rec. 5-10-1763. Wit.: William Biggerstaff, Michael Cresap, Sarah Innis, Enoch Innis."* This was a ten year lease agreement for a Virginia property located along the Potomac River just upstream from Town Creek.[1350] William Young was assessed for the tract in 1782, and was living on the tract when he purchased it from Thomas Cresap on June 23, 1784.[1351] William Young is mentioned later in this chapter as a recipient of reward money for a scalp taken at Thomas Cresap's residence.

### The Ohio Company advertises Wills Creek property for sale and lease in 1763

An advertisement published in the "**Maryland Gazette**" from February 17 to April 7, 1763 offers a *"Number of Lots for a Town at Fort Cumberland"* for sale *"on Friday the 15th of April next"*. The advertisement also offered Ohio Company property in Virginia for lease, and in so doing provides a detailed 1763 description of two Ohio Company storehouses at the site of present-day Ridgeley, West Virginia. The March 31, 1763 advertisement states:

*At the repeated Solicitations of several Persons, the OHIO Company have agreed to lay off a Number of LOTS for a TOWN at Fort Cumberland, near the Mouth of Wills's Creek, on Patowmack River, in the Province of Maryland; and that each Purchaser may have an Opportunity of attending, and choosing the Lots he may judge most convenient, they will be SOLD to the Highest BIDDERS on Friday the 15th of April next.*

*Any one who will consult the Maps must see that Fort Cumberland, from its natural Situation and Contiguity to that very extensive and fertile Country on the Ohio and its Waters, must be the Key to all that valuable Settlement; it being the highest and most convenient Landing-place for the Inhabitants on the other side of the Allegheny Mountains, on all the river Patowmack, which affords a Water-carriage, that with a very inconsiderable Expense, might be rendered safe, certain, and easy, at all Seasons of the*

---

[1349] "**The papers of Col. Henry Bouquet**", 1940.
[1350] "**Colonial Records of the Upper Potomac**", Volume 4.
[1351] "**Colonial Records of the Upper Potomac**", Volume 4.

*Year, from the Great Falls to the Spot now proposed for a Town. It is about 75 Miles Land-Carriage to the Monongahela, which is navigable to the Ohio for flat-bottomed Boats or Battoes; and not more than 65 Miles to the Yauyougaine, where the Road, as it is at present cleared to Pittsburg, crosses; to which Place the Indians frequently, before the war, brought up their Battoes loaded with Skins: And all who are acquainted with the Country agree that a very good Waggon Road may be made to that very Spot, or even a few Miles lower down the River, which would reduce the Distance from thence to Fort Cumberland at least 15 Miles. 'The Land-Carriage from Pimmett's Warehouse, at the Little Falls, which is the highest Tide-Water of Patowmack, to the Great Falls, does not exceed 12 Miles; and the Manufactures of Great-Britain may be transported by the Patowmack to the Ohio, and it's Produce or Furs remitted through the same Channel, with only 90 Miles Land-Carriage at the most.*

*Fort Cumberland is about one 115 Miles from Pittsburg, 30 from Fort Bedford, 60 from Winchester, Land-Carriage, good Waggon-Roads, and 100 Miles Water-Carriage from the Mouth of Conococheague Creek in Maryland.*

*The Day the LOTS are Sold the OHIO Company will LET to the highest Bidder, for a Term of Years, Two very good Store-Houses, opposite to Fort Cumberland, in Virginia, one 45 by 25, with a Counting-Room and Lodging-Room at one End, the other 44 x 20, with proper Conveniences for a Family to live in, two Stories high each, besides Garrets[1352], with good dry Cellars fit for storing Skins, the whole Size of the Houses; and a Kitchen, Stable for 12 Horses, Meat-House and Dairy; there are Two good Battoes, which will be given to the Person who rents the Houses. The whole entirely new, and will be compleately finished, and fit to enter upon immediately; and the Person who takes the Store-Houses, may also have a Lease, for a Term of Years, of so much Land adjacent to them as he choses. Any one desirous to treat privately for the Store-houses, &c. before the Day of Sale, or the Town Lots, may know the Terms by applying to the Subscriber, who will attend at Fort Cumberland on the 15th Day of April before-mentioned, to deliver the Purchasers Deeds for their Lots. There is great Plenty of good Timber and Lime-Stone on the Lands, on each Side of the River; and the Company are building a Saw and Grist Mill, within a Mile of the Spot Proposed for the Town. GEORGE MERCER.*

The reason that the Ohio Company storehouses were described as being *"entirely new"* in 1763 is explained by a 1767 Ohio Company report that states:

*A fort was built, at this Place, by his Majesty's troops, called Fort Cumberland & the Company's Store Houses which cost Them a large sum, not only constantly used while necessary for the Troops, but when they abandoned Them and returned to the Fort, were pulled down to build Barracks, and the Timber for above a Mile round cut down and destroyed...*

Acquiring timber for construction was labor-intensive, and therefore, it was expedient for the military to repurpose the material used to build the original Ohio Company storehouses. As reported below, at one of the replacement buildings was also known as the New Store but seems to have been built at a different location than the original new store.

### *Memorial of the Ohio Company to the General Assembly of Virginia*
The November 20, 1778 *"Memorial of the Ohio Company"*, written to *"the honourable the General Assembly of Virginia"* provides more information on Ohio Company losses due to the surrender of Trent's fort, and the occupation of their land at Wills Creek by British military forces:

---

[1352] A garret is an attic.

*They also imported, from London, twenty new Swivel Guns, with a Quantity of suitable Ball, small-arms, Blunderbusses, Tools, and other Military Stores, prepared Materials, and were erecting a Fort, on the Spot where Fort pit now stands, under the Direction of Captain William Trent, the Company's Agent; when about seven hundred French and Indians, commanded by a regular officer, with several pieces of Cannon, came down the River in Battoes, and landing within a small Distance, drove away Your Memorialists' Workmen and People, took possession of the place, and built their Fort Du Quesne there.*

*That upon this Occasion, and by the french and Indian War which followed, Your Memorialists were not only prevented from proceeding further in the Execution of their plan, but sustained very great Losses, to the amount of _____ pounds, in their Materials, Tools, Stores, Horses, and other Effects in that Country, and even in their Houses and property upon Potomack River; which were wantonly destroyed by our own Troops, and the Lands the Company had purchased near Fort Cumberland entirely pillaged of Timber, for the public buildings, and for Beef, Pork & flour-Barrels; without Your Memorialists ever being able to obtain the least Satisfaction or Redress. And THAT the Nature of the Trade Your Memorialists were engaged in was such, that they were obliged to give large Credits to the Indian-Traders, most of whom were killed, captivated, or ruined in the Course of the War, and the Debts due to Your Memorialists thereby lost.*

Here, the Ohio Company claims they were erecting a fort under the direction of their agent William Trent, when Trent's forces were ejected by the French. Trent, however, was in the pay of Virginia at the time, as the commander of a company of Virginia forces, with a commission from Dinwiddie. Is this an obfuscation by the Ohio Company, or indicative of a certain blurring of lines between the government of Virginia and the Ohio Company? Perhaps both.

## A reply regarding the request for providing Indian supplies at Cresap's

The book "**Proceedings of the Council of Maryland, 1761-1769**" includes the following:

*At a Council held at the City of Annapolis on 28th March 1763*

*Present*

*His Excellency Horatio Sharpe Esquire Governor.*

*Benjamin Tasker Stephen Bordley John Ridout Esquires*

*His Excellency is pleased to lay before this Board the following Letter to him from Sir William Johnson*

*Johnson Hall January the 4th 1763.*

*Sir*

*Your favour of the 25th of November, I did not receive untill about three days ago, but hope this will proceed with greater Expedition. I am of Opinion that the Indians' Expectations in requesting Daniel Cresap were that he should supply them Gratis at the Expence of the Province, which they had been too much encouraged to hope for from the treatment they had been accustomed to by the French who found their interest in so doing, as it weakened our Interest with the Six Nations, and enabled them to carry on the War with vigour against the Cherokees, which at the same time that it gratified their inclination disabled them from affording us assistance.*

*The like Demand is made in Pensilvania, and I cannot but think that some Selfish People may have set them upon making such a request to serve their private interest at the expence of the Publick as otherwise I am of Opinion they would scarcely have made application for that purpose.*

*I am very sensible of the opposition with such a proposal must meet with from the House of Assembly, but hope they will allow Cresap for the Expences he may be at in Conformity to your directions, after which he can, and I suppose will keep goods for them at his own Expence, in case he thinks it necessary and beneficial.*

*At the request of Lieutenant Governor Fauquier for that purpose to me, my Deputy Agent desired at a meeting lately held at Onondaga that the Indians would take the Old Back Path in going to War against the Southern Indians, which they Promised to take into Consideration, But their passing by Fort Cumberland will be of no service to them as Sir Jeffery Amherst does not chuse to allow the Indians supplies in these parts, & I presume the Officer Commanding there is likewise restricted in the Same Manner.*

*I cannot but observe to you that I am Confident the shewing the Indians in general some favor, and bestowing a few Presents as yet Occasionally on them will greatly contribute to stifle many rising Jealousy's and suspicions now amongst them concerning Us, and that our disapproving or discourageing their prosecuting the War against the Southern Indians however reasonable, would greatly inflame them at present, and give them reason to think we had formed some of those projects which the French reasonably told them we should not fail to put in practice on the reduction of Canada.*

*Whatever Answer you shall think necessary to return the Indians, shall be Communicated to them on being transmitted to me, and you may at all times command my Sentiments on matters relative to the good of the Province, or your Own Satisfaction As*

> *I am with great Esteem*
>
> *Sir      Your most Obedient & Most humb<sup>le</sup> Servant*
>
> *Will: Johnson*

### Samuel Plum receives a license for selling liquor

In March of 1763, Samuel Plum, who is also mentioned elsewhere herein, made the following successful request to the Frederick County, Maryland court: [1353]

*Whereas there is no licenced ordinary or public house kept between Fort Frederick and the upper limits of this province on Potomac River, which is not only disadvantageous to travelers but also very inconvenient and pernicious to the back inhabitants inasmuch as travelers are often stopped by high waters and obliged to trouble housekeepers for necessaries who are not able to supply such needs gratis or even for money so that many often suffer and your petitioner residing on the wagon road near Evertts Creek a place much used for encamping by pack horse men and cattle drivers most humbly craves license for the vending and selling of liquors.*

Plum's petition makes it clear that there was enough traffic on the wagon road to warrant the request for a commercial license. From the reference to *"Evertts Creek"*, it appears that in 1763, Samuel Plum was still living on the Pleasant Valley tract he had moved to in 1759.

---

[1353] Information provided by Francis Bridges.

### An April 20, 1763 letter requests leave to work some fields near Fort Burd

An April 20, 1763[1354] letter[1355] Sergeant Angus McDonald wrote to Bouquet from Fort Cumberland states:

*while I was Commanding at fort Burd I Clear^d Some ground[1356] and was at Considerable Trouble and Expence in Improving it, I had two fields the one where your Lettle house Stands the other up the River about one mile, when I saw you last your honour told me you would give me the little house untill it was wanted for the Kings use.*

*Honoured Sir as I have no other Depenance at this time I should be for Ever obliged to you if you will Send me a permitt to Settle there before it is two Late to plant Corn if you Cannot Put me in Some Better Business I am Commonly at fort Cumerland where a line from your honour will be of Infinnit Service*

### A survey for James Spurgeon

*"James Spirgeon Senr"* and *"James Spurgeon Jur"* are two of the individuals named on the 1761 Old Town Hundreds list. The 300-acre Spurgeons Choice tract (Frederick County Patent Certificate 4510, MSA S1197 4934) was surveyed for James Spurgeon on April 26, 1763 and patented to him on September 29, 1764. The survey reads, ...*"I have Carefully Surveyd and Laid out for and in the name of him the said James Spurgeon all that Track of Land called Spurgeons Choice Lying & being in Frederick County afs Beginning at a bounded black Walnut Tree Standing on the point of a Little hill on the East side of a Small path that Leads from Spurgeons up the old town creek..."* The survey was performed by John Murdock.

### Cresap sues Walter Drenning over a debt to Hugh Parker

According to Volume 1 of the 1912 book "**Chronicles of the Scotch-Irish Settlement in Virginia**", the April 1763 records of the Augusta County Virginia court include the case of, *"Cresap vs. Drenning. — Walter Drenning, of Prince George's County. Maryland, trader, to Hugh Parker of Lancaster County, Pennsylvania, 1740."* For the same month and year, the book also states, *"Cresap vs. Drenning. — Walter Drinen's note to William Griffiths, 1742. Walter Drenning, of Prince George's County, Maryland, trader. Bond to Hugh Parker, of Lancaster County, Pennsylvania, dated 18th December, 1740."*

---

[1354] In the "**Fort Cumberland: The Missing Years**", this date was incorrectly stated to be April 20, 1761.

[1355] "**The Papers of Col. Henry Bouquet**", 1942.

[1356] In his book "**The Monongahela of old...**", James Veech states, *"The land just above Bridgeport, on the river, embracing some three or four hundred acres, was, in early times, the subject of long and angry controversies—from 1769 to 1785 — between adverse claimants under 'military permits.' It was well named, in the official survey, which one of the parties procured of it under a Pennsylvania location, 'Bone of Contention.' One Angus M'Donald claimed it, or part of it, under a military permit from Col. Bouquet, dated April 26th, 1763, and a settlement on it. In March, 1770, he sold his claim to Captain Luke Collins, describing the land as 'at a place called Fort Burd, to include the field cleared by me where the sawpit was above the mouth of Dunlap's creek.' Collins conveyed it to Captain Michael Cresap (of Logan's speech celebrity) on the 13th of April, 1772, 'at half past nine in the morning,' — describing it as situate between 'Point Lookout and John Martin's, land,' — recently owned, we believe, by the late Mrs. John S. Krepps. Cresap's executors, in June, 1781, conveyed to one William Schooly, an old Brownsville merchant, who conveyed to Rees Cadwallader. The adverse claimants were Henry Shryock and William Shearer, assignee of George Andrew. Their claim reached further southward towards the creek, and further up the river, covering the John Martin land. They sold out to Robert Adams and Thomas Sham. Although they had the oldest permit (in 1762) their title seems to have been overcome by the settlement and official location and survey of their adversary. One Robert Thorn seems also to have been a claimant of part of the land, but Collins bought him out. This protracted controversy involved many curious questions, and called up many ancient recollections."* The heirs of Angus McDonald are listed as owning a 500-acre property named Glenco in the 1783 Skipton hundred list.

## John Greenfield is involved in Virginia property transactions

The 1939 book "**Early Records Hampshire County Virginia**" records the following for May 3, 1763, "*GREENFIELD, John (w. Mary) of Frederick Co. to John Royce of Frederick Co. (lease and release) 149 a., Spreen Gap (Spring Gap) Mt.; rec. 5-10-1763. Wit.: Thom. Dent, Germ. Keyes, Bryan Bruen, Geo. Hoge, Tho. Rutherford.*" Also recorded for that month is, "*GREENFIELD, John (w. Mary) of Frederick Co. to John Royce of Frederick Co. (lease and release) 23 a., Hampshire Co.; rec. 5-10-1763. Wit.: Thom. Dent, Germ. Keyes, Bryan Bruen, Tho. Rutherford.*"

## The beginning of the siege of Detroit

The 1860 book "**Diary of the Siege of Detroit in the War with Pontiac**" contains entries regarding Fort Detroit, including the famous event where Pontiac attempted to take the fort by subterfuge, but was prevented from doing so by Major Gladwin. An entry regarding May 9, 1763 includes the statement, "*After having thus put all the English without the Fort to death...*" The entry regarding the next day states:

*On Tuesday the 10th, very early in the Morning, the Savages began to fire on the Fort, and Vessels which lay opposite to the east and west Sides of the Fort. About 8 o'Clock the Indians called a Parley and ceased firing, and half an Hour after, the Waindotes Chiefs came into the Fort, on their way to a Council where they were called by the Tawas and promised us to endeavour to soliciate and persuade the Tawas from committing further Hostilities. After drinking a Glass of Rum they went off at three o'Clock that Afternoon. Several of the Inhabitants and four Chiefs of the Tawas, Waindotes and Chippawas and Pottawattomes came and acquainted us, that most of all the Inhabitants were assembled at a Frenchmans House about a Mile from the Fort, where the Savages proposed to hold a Council, and desiring Captain Campbell and another Officer to go with them to that Council, where they hoped with their Presence and Assistance further Hostilities would cease, assuring us at the same Time that come what would, that Capt. Campbell and the other Officers that went with him, should return whenever they pleased. This Promise was assertained by the French as well as the Indian Chief, whereupon Captain Campbell and Lieutenant McDougal went off escorted by a Number of the Inhabitants and the four Chiefs, they first promised to be answerable for their returning y*^e^ *Night.*

*When they arrived at the House already mentioned they found the French and Indians assembled, and after counceling a long while, the Waindotes were prevailed on to sing the War Song, and this being done, it was next resolved that Captain Campbell and Lieutenant McDougall should be detained Prisoners, but would be indulged to lodge in a French House till a French Commandant arrived from the Ilenoes, that next Day five Indians and as many Canadians would be dispatched to acquaint the Commanding Officer of the Ilonies that Detroit was in their Possession and require of him to send an Officer to Command, to whom Captain Cample and Lieutenant McDougall should be delivered. As for Major Gladwin he was summoned to give up the Fort and two Vessels, &c., the Troops to ground their Arms, and they would allow as many Battoes and as much Provision as they judged requisite for us to go to Niagara: That if these Proposals were not accepted of, they were a thousand Men, and storm the Fort at all events, and in that Case every Soul of us should be put to the Torture. The Major returned for Answer, that as soon as the two Officers they had detained were permitted to come into the Fort, he would after consulting them give a positive Answer to their Demand, but could do nothing without obtaining their Opinion.*

## An Indian letter pertaining to the request for supplies

A letter three Indian captains sent to *"Brother Tokeryhogan"* from Oldtown on May 15, 1763 includes the statement:

*At a Treaty held at Philadelphia in 1762, We desired we might be furnished with Provisions, Powder, Lead, Paint, Tobacco and a few Knives, as We Pass through the Frontiers of this Province, to and from War, and requested these Necessaries might be delivered to us by Colo Thomas Cresap, or his Son Daniel, at this place, which is in our Road as we go and come, this was promised to us by the great men at the said Treaty, and we doubted not not their performance of that Promise; but now we are come here we find nothing but what said Cresap has given us on his own Account viz<sup>t</sup> some victuals, a few Knives and some Tobacco, therefor We desire our request may be complied with, which will prevent our taking any thing from the Poor Inhabitants.*

## Families living near the site of Somerfield in May 1763

The Indian trader James Kenny's journal entry for May 30, 1763 includes the statement, *"Lay in y<sup>e</sup> Woods between Dunbars Camp & y<sup>e</sup> Great Meadows"*, after being near Fort Burd earlier in the day. He was traveling east, toward Fort Cumberland. His May, 31 1763 journal entry indicates that three families were already living at the crossing of the Youghiogheny River, including Captain Speers:

*Came to ye Upper crossing of Youhiogheny where there is three familys living, Virginians, I lodged at a House of Cap<sup>t</sup> Spears[1357], his Brother being there, two of his Children & a Negro; a Man that lived on y<sup>e</sup> West side of y<sup>e</sup> Creek set off Directly to Paterson's Creek to get Speer to Send up Horses to Carry them away. Two Women & some Children being by themselves on that side y<sup>e</sup> Creek Stayed there & one of them Loaded a Gun I heard to stand in her defence if y<sup>e</sup> Indians Should come.*

The next day, Kenny arrived at Georges Creek. Based on this, and the reference to Captain Spears, the *"Upper crossing of Youhiogheny"* is clearly what was more commonly called the Great Crossings, at Somerfield,[1358] Pennsylvania, near Addison.

## Mynord Johnson's residence is mentioned in a 1763 survey

David Ross's May 31, 1763 survey of the 50-acre Johnsons Fancy tract (Frederick County, Maryland Patent No. 2213) includes the following statement:

---

[1357] As shown by the 1939 W.P.A. Addison Township *"survey warrant"* map, a man named Jacob Spears had a tract of land (Order No. 3078, April 11, 1768) where Braddock's road crossed the Youghiogheny River. Volume II, Chapter 4 of the 1906 book "**The History of Bedford and Somerset Counties…**" states, *"Jacob Spear received a warrant for a survey that bore the date of April 19, 1769, just sixteen days after the opening of the land office. It was surveyed in 1770. Spear afterwards sold this land to Philip D. Smyth, who platted the town now known as Somerfield on a part of it."* Uria Brown's 1816 journal, which is reproduced in Volume X of the 1915 "Maryland Historical Magazine", describes lodging at *"Phillip Smyth's Sine of General Jackson"* as follows, *"My Land Lord Phillip Smyth is a proud Empty Ignorant Rich Dutchman, Lives in a big wooden House with a Stone Chimney in each end, the house kept prodigeously Dirty; the Living for man & horse is as good & looks as well as any of their Taverns, Inns or Hotels, he is situated Just on the East Side of the big Crossings of Youghagany River in Somerset County, owns about 250 Acres of Land which he says that would sell for $50 pr Acre Just like a Top; he has Laid out a Town Just on the Bank of the River & directly on the Turnpike road which he calls Smyth-field and is now disposing of Lots some of them he says sells at $250 which is for ¼ of an Acre & fronting on the road (Baltimoreans Looke, Land Selling in the Middle of the Allegany Mountains @$1000 pr Acre) at this intended Town…"*

[1358] According to the February 1963 issue of the "**Laurel Messenger**", the now submerged town of Somerfield was founded by Philip Smyth in 1818 as the town of Smythfield. The town is identified as Smithfield on the 1817 Melish map of Fayette County, Pennsylvania.

*Beginning at five bounded White Oak standing on the North side of the sloop of the hill between Jennings Run and Braddocks Road about three miles on the North side of said road and near where Mynord Johnson is now setting[1359]*

The correct spelling for the first name is probably *"Maynard"*.

## News of the beginning of Pontiac's war is received at Fort Pitt

A May 31, 1763 letter[1360] from Fort Pitt includes the statement:

*There is most melancholy News here. The Indians have broken out in divers places, and have murdered Col. C. and his Family. An Indian has brought a War belt to Tusquerora, who says that Detroit was invested, and St. Dusky cut off. All Levy's goods are stopped at Tusquerora by the Indians; and last night eight or ten men were killed at Beaver Creek. We hear of scalping every Hour. Messrs. Cray and Allison's Horses, twenty-five, loaded with Skins, are all taken.*

The 1920 book "**History of Colonel Henry Bouquet and the western frontiers of Pennsylvania: 1747-1764**" includes the following transcript:

*Copy of Intelligence Brought to Fort Pitt by Mr. Colhoun June 1st 1763*

*Tuskarawas May 27 th 1763, at 11 o'Clock at Night King Beaver with Shingas Wheyondohela, Winginum, Daniel and William Anderson, Chiefs of the Delawares came and Delivered me the following Intelligence by a string of Wampum*

*Brother*

*Out of Regard to You and the Friendship that formerly subsisted between our Grandfathers and the English, which has lately been renewed by us. We come now to Inform you with what news we have heard, which you may depend upon is True.*

*Brother*

*All the English at Detroit were kild Ten Days ago, and not one left alive. At Sandusky all the white People there were kild five days ago, being nineteen in number, except the Officer who Commanded is taken prisoner and one boy who made his Escape which we have not heard of. At the mouth of the Twightwee River Hugh Crawford with one Boy was taken Prisoner, and six men Kild. At the Salt Licks we heard to Day, their was kil'd five white Men, five days ago. We have likewise seen a Number of Tracks On the road between this an Sandusky not far off, which we are sure is a Party coming to Cutt you, and your People off. But we have sent a man to watch their motion, and request you may think of Nothing you have Here; But Make the Best of your way to some Place of safety; as we would not Desire to see you kild in our Town. Be Careful to avoid the Road, and every Part where Indians Resort. Brother what goods and other Effects you have here, you nede not be uneasy about them we Assure you we will take Care and keep them safe for six Months, Perhaps by that Time we may see You, or send you word what to expect from us further. And we know there is one white man that belongs to you at Gueyahoga, do not be concerned for him, we shall take care to send him safe Home.*

*Brother*

---

[1359] This patent description was found as a result of Steve Colby's research.
[1360] "**Events in Indian History**", Wimer, 1841.

*We desire you to tell George Croghan, and all your great Men, that They must not aske us any thing aboute this News, or what has happend as we are not at all Concern'd in it. The Nations that have taken up the Hatchet against you, are the Ottawas and Chepawas. And when you first went to speak with these People, you did not Consult us upon it, Therefore desire you may not expect that we are to account for any Mischief they do. And what you want to know aboute this News you must learn by the same Road you first went. But if you will speak with us, you must send one or two men only, and we will hear Them*

*Brother*

*We thought Your King had made Peace with us and all the Western Nations of Indians; for our Parts we join'd it heartly, And desired to hold it allways Good, and you may Depend upon it we will take care not to be readily Cheated or drawn into a war again. But as we are seated on the Road between you and those Nations, who have taken up the Hatchet against you, we desire you will send no Warriors this way till we are Removed from this, which we will do as soon as we conveniently can, when we shall permit You to Pass without taking Notice, Till then we desire the Warriors may go, by the first Road You went.*

*Give a string of Wampum*

*The following is what Mr. Colhoun learnd on his way to Fort Pitt, from one of Three Indians, who were sent by the Aforesaid Chiefs to Conduct him safe Here (viz Daniel who is before mentioned as one of the above Chiefs) That Detroit was not really taken, but had been attack'd by the Indians four days before the Messenger who brought the news left it, which Mr. Colhoun immagines must have been from About the 13th to the 17th of May, and that the Indians had not then mett with much success. But strongly persisted in Carrying on the Attack, and Said they were determined not to give over, till they took it. And that The English had sent out three Belts, and the French two, desiring Them to Desist, which they Refused*

*Mr. Colhoun further says that when him and his Party (14 in number) were seting out from Tuskarawas, the Indians refused to let them bring their Arms, telling them that the three Indians that were going along with them, were sufficient to Conduct them safe But that the next day passing Beaver Creek, they were fired upon by a Party of Indians, and their Guides immediately disappeared without interfering for them, and he is Convinced that they were led by these Guides knowingly to this Party to be Cutt off, from which himself with three of his People, have only Escaped*

*Having lost his way and faling in upon the Road leading to Venango, aboute 20 miles above this Post, He saw a number of Indians Tracks that had gone that way*

The update provided by the Indian Daniel was correct. Detroit had been invested but was not taken.

## A June 1, 1763 journal entry documents a house on Georges Creek

James Kenny's June 1, 1763 journal entry describes staying at a house on Georges Creek. The journal entry states:

*Came this Day to George's Creek on yᵉ East Side yᵉ Allegheny Mountains. I seen an Indian run across through yᵉ Alders & Thickets a Head of us, (having an old Man with me from yᵉ Crossing) or Else some Bay or brown Creature must have deceived me much, as what I seen appears Straight in yᵉ Shape a Man & not over 10 or 12 Yards off. This night it was so Cold at yᵉ House by George's Creek we thot there was frost.*

## Building the new storehouse and repairing the old in 1763

The June 2, 1763 journal entry of James Kenny states:

> *Came only 12 Miles to Fort Cumberland, my little Beast having given out, so that I walked a Great part y<sup>e</sup> Road. I swaped it for a large Strong Horse, but not in very good order with one Martin, a Carpenter, who was undertaking of Building y<sup>e</sup> New Store House & repairing y<sup>e</sup> Old. I drew a Bill on ye Commissioners for £14,13.0. I was to Give to Boot,[1361] he sold y<sup>e</sup> Horse for a year.*

This entry tells us that the new store was still under construction in June of 1763. The identity of Mr. Martin is unknown.

## Indians acting suspiciously at Fort Pitt on June 2, 1763

The August 2, 1763 edition of the "**The London Chronicle**" contains the following article:

*Extract of a letter from Fort Pitt, June 2.*

*Thursday last just opposite the Fort, at dark arrived a number of Delaware Indians, with 15 horse-loads of skins and furs. Very early next morning they came over the river, and delt them all off, not seeming to care much what they took for them. Their indifference, and uncommon dispatch in trading, gave us some jealousies how they came by them. Just before they set off, I was standing with Mr. Alexander M<sup>c</sup>Kee on the bank of the river, when one of them came up and told him to go away, and that he must not stay more than four days these, with some other suspicious words, made us imagine they intended some mischief, and immediately after they told Mr. M<sup>c</sup>Kee, they set off. Next morning we found that all the Indians that lay up the river, a few miles above us, and planted corn, left their towns that very night, and took everything with them, which convinced us that they either intended, or knew of some mischief intended us. Sunday morning some people belonging to Col. Clapham arrived at the Fort, and informed us that the Colonel and four of his people were killed by the Wolf, and some other Delawares; the Colonel has since been brought down and buried here; he had been tomohawked and scalped. Two women were treated in such a manner that it would be indecent to mention it. Sunday night the enemy killed two of the soldiers at the Saw Mill, and on Thursday Burnt it. Monday a man hired with Alison and company, came to a party sent down to bury the dead, and informed them that he was driving 25 horse-loads of skins and furs, belonging to the said company, in company with Alexander M<sup>c</sup>Clure, Thomas Calhoon, and brother, and several others, amounting in all to fourteen, who were fired upon by a party of Indians, as they were crossing Beaver Creek, and several killed. Calhoon, and two of his men, have arrived since, but we have no account of the rest.*

*The whole garrison have been very alert in putting every thing in the best order since the first alarm; We have destroyed the Upper and Lower Towns, laying them level with the ground, and by to-morrow night we shall be in a good posture of defense. Every morning, an hour before day, the whole garrison are at alarm posts. Ten days ago, at Beaver Creek, the Indians killed on Patrick Dunn, and a man of Major Smallman's; also tow other men, Captain Callender's people are all killed, and the goods taken. There is no account of Captain Welsh, or Capt. Prentice, but it is feared they are likewise killed. Mr. Crawford is made prisoner, and his people are all murdered. Our small posts, I am afraid, are gone. Detroit was attacked four days without intermission. The French sent the Indians two belts, and the English three, to desist, but they determined to continue the attack, and were fighting, when the Indian, who brought this account to the Delawares, came away. We sent two men with an express to Venango in the night, but before they got a mile on their journey they were fired upon, and returned, one of them wounded.*

---

[1361] Meaning that, in addition to giving Martin the worn-out horse, a monetary payment was required.

## An Indian priest sends his wife and cattle to Fort Cumberland

A synopsis[1362] of a June 2, 1763 letter Captain Ecuyer wrote in French to Bouquet from Fort Pitt includes the statement, *"Hopes the Indian priest will send a good party; he send word he was bringing a party when he had sent his wife and cattle to Fort Cumberland."* An English translation[1363] of the letter contains the following reference to Fort Cumberland:

*This will inform you, of the arrival of Mr. Colhoon[1364] at this post with a speech[1365] from the Delawares. I will continue my last letter. The 31st I sent two settlers to Venango, but they could not get through. A mile and a half away they were attacked, and obliged to return; one of the two slightly wounded in the leg. Two young men arrived yesterday from Fort Burd, and went back with orders for the Sergeant to induce all the settlers to join me here with 600#[1366] of powder and 1,000# of lead which a merchant sent there, a few days ago; they should come either by water or through the woods. I hope to reap some advantage from the Indian Peter[1367]; he send word that he would come with a party as soon as he has sent his wife and his cattle to Fort Cumberland.*

## The Fort Burd garrison is reportedly retreating to Fort Cumberland

The June 5, 1763 journal entry[1368] of S. Ecuyer, Commandant at Fort Pitt, contains the following:

*5th, 2 o'clock at night one Benjamin Sutton came in, who says he left Redstone (or Fort Burd) two days ago and found that place evacuated, and saw a number of shoe tracks going towards Fort Cumberland which he supposes was the garrison, that there was with him there a white man named Hicks and an Indian named Kecois, who would have burnt the fort had he not persuaded them from it, that Hicks told him that an Indian war had broken out and that he would kill the white people wherever he found them...*

## Welder witnesses a deed several weeks before he is murdered

On June 7, 1763, about five weeks before his murder, Samuel Stansby Welder witnessed a deed documenting Marylander Isaac Baker's sale of property on Warm Spring Run, Virginia to Virginian Joshua Baker.[1369] The other witnesses were John Humphries and John Cole.

## The Indians complain of not receiving free goods at Old Town

The minutes[1370] of a meeting of the Council of Maryland on June 7, 1763 records the following correspondence, which indicates Thomas Cresap was no longer keeping a store in 1763:

*May it please your Excellency Old Town May 1763.*

*On Saturday the 14th instant a Party of between 70 and 80 of the Six Nation Indian Warriors, came here, with a pass from Capt Ourry and Col⁰ Croghan, and a Letter from the latter, desiring me to give those Indians a Pass, After I had read the Letter and put it my Pocket they asked me for some Powder, Lead,*

---

[1362] The synopses of correspondence in this chapter are from Volume 23 of the "**Sessional Papers...**" and the "**Report on Canadian Archives**".

[1363] "**The papers of Col. Henry Bouquet**", 1942.

[1364] In "**Fort Pitt and letters from the frontier**", Darlington, 1892, this is translated as *"Calhoun"*.

[1365] In "**Fort Pitt and letters from the frontier**", Darlington, 1892, this is translated as *"harangue.*

[1366] In "**Fort Pitt and letters from the frontier**", Darlington, 1892, this is given as *"100 lbs."*

[1367] In "**Fort Pitt and letters from the frontier**", Darlington, 1892, this is translated as *"Indian's Peltry"*.

[1368] "**Fort Pitt and letters from the frontier**", Darlington, 1892.

[1369] "**Colonial Records of the Upper Potomac**", Volume 6.

[1370] "**Proceedings of the Council of Maryland, 1761-1769**", Volume 32.

*Knives, Halfthicks, Paint, and Tobacco, I told them I had none, at which they seemed to look very angry, and after discoursing among themselves in their own Language, they said Mr Croghan had told them, that he had wrote to me, in that Letter, to give them the several things above mentioned, I answered I had no goods at all, they still doubting my telling them true, I sent for an Interpreter, (Mr John Walker) to interpret the Letter to them, a Copy of which is inclosed, These Indians say that some time last Summer, at a Treaty with their Brother Onas (the Governor of Pensylvania) at Philadelphia, they desired him to acquaint their Brother Toheryhogan, meaning your Excellency) that it was their request, you would order them to be furnished, as before mentioned, with Victuals and the goods mentioned above, and that their Brother Onas, and the great men, did then promise they would Communicate this their request to your Excellency, which they find has not been Complied with, therefore they desired me to write to you in their behalfs, which at their request I did, and now inclose it, and they Expect on their return some thing will be here for them, as they are vastly poor and naked, I find by their discourse, that as I formerly when I kept Store here, before the War, used to give them a few necessaries as they passed and repassed, and not keeping any Store now nor giving them any thing now except Victuals, some evil minded Persons has informed them that I was Paid for every thing I gave them, therefore they expect it, as usual, As to any hope that I can have of the Assembly Paying me for any thing I give them it is but small, when they have so often refused, If I cannot be paid here, I will apply at Home (as I intend there) where I doubt not I shall have Justice*

*I am*

*Your Excellencys Most Obedient Servt*

*Thomas Cresap.*

P. S. *This is the fourth Company since Christmas Last, that has been here, and daily expect more.*

*Belfield May the 5th 1763.*

*Dear Sir*

*The Bearers of this letter desired I would Recommend them to you as they are going to War against their Natural Enemies the Southern Indians that you would give them a Pass to go through Virginia, and Recommend them to the Peoples Hospitality, And as the War between the Northern and Southern Indians May Imploy[1371] those restless Savages against each other if the province would allow them some little Provisions as they Pass and Cross their Frontiers I am of Opinion it would answer a good End.*

*To conclude with my Compliments to you & yours*

*Geo: Croghan.*

*To Colo Thomas Cresap, at the Old Town*

*Old Town Frederick County May 15ᵗʰ 1763*

*Brother Tokeryhogan.*

---

[1371] Croghan is implying that the war between tribes will keep the Indians occupied, which would render the settlements safer — and therefore it would be beneficial to supply the Indians of the Six Nations with provisions to assist them in their forays against the southern Indians.

*At a Treaty held at Philadelphia in 1762, We desired we might be furnished with Provisions, Powder, Lead, Paint, Tobacco and a few Knives, as We Pass through the Frontiers of this Province, to and from War, and requested these Necessaries might be delivered to us by Colo Thomas Cresap, or his Son Daniel, at this place, which is in our Road as we go and come, this was promised to us by the great men at the said Treaty, and we doubted not their performance of that Promise; but now we are come here we find nothing but what said Cresap has given us on his own Account vizt some victuals, a few Knives and some Tobacco, Therefore We desire our request may be complyed with, which will prevent our taking any thing from the Poor Inhabitants.*

*Teowagawy*

*Cuttowygo*

*Tuthehaya.*

*This Certifies that the above Letter was wrote at the Request of the above three Capts the former of whom has made his Mark hereto.*

*his*

*John W Walker*

*Mark*

*To His Excellency Horatio Sharpe Esqr Governor of Maryland S. S. Welder.*

*Sir*

*The inclosed is a Copy of a Message the Governor sent the Six Nations of Indians in March 1762 which in case the party of Indians at whose Instance you wrote to his Excellency the 17. Day of May last should call on you when they return from the Southward you are desired to deliver them that they may be able to judge of the Governor good Intentions towards them*

*I am your hide Serv*^t^ *John Ross.*

*To Col*^o^ *Thomas Cresap.*

*Brethren of the Six Nations.*

*The Governor of Pennsylvania having sent me a Belt which you gave him for the Governor of Maryland at the Treaty you held with him last Summer at Lancaster and having also Signifyed to me that at the time you delivered such Belt You told him that One Daniel Cresap who lives on Potomack in this Province had sent you word by some of your Warriors last Spring that if I would order him to keep a Store there he would provide every thing for the Warriors who should pass and repass that way and that you desired he might be allowed to do so and to receive any Messages and that your Warriors may pass and repass thro this Province without Molestation I have thereupon wrote to Mr Cresap recommending it to him to Supply any of Your Warriors that may have occasion to pass or repass thro this Province and Near his House with such provisions as they may want for which he will I expect be paid by Your Brethren the Inhabitants of this Province and I have also recommended it to him in case any of your People shall choose to trade with him to procure and keep at his House such Goods as he supposes they may want and be willing to purchase, as the Inhabitants of this Province have always retained a true regard for their Brethren of the Six Nations tho by Reason of our being at so great a Distance, and almost Surrounded by*

*Virginia and Pennsylvania there has not been much Intercourse between you and Us You may be assured that your Warriors will not meet with any Molestation or Interruption as they pass or repass thro this Province while they themselves behave peaceably and as Brethren which I hope they will always do.*

*Horatio Sharpe*

*Annapolis in Maryland 28ᵗʰ of March 1763.*

## A garrison and suttlers from Fort Burd arrive at Fort Cumberland on June 9, 1763

A synopsis of a June 9, 1763 letter written to Bouquet from Fort Bedford by Ourry includes the following, *"The garrison of Fort Burd, with the settlers and goods, has arrived safely at Fort Cumberland. ... Major Livingstones' post is defensible and he has formed two companies of militia. ..."* A transcript of the letter has been found, indicating that the word *"settlers"* should have been *"suttlers"*. The letter includes the following statement:

*The Inhabitants of the Town are very hearty. The Settlers that have fled from their Plantations are the most wavering. I am obliged to harangue often and not without Effect, as I know what way to take them, and many having known me long have some confidence in me.*

*We live entirely on fresh Beef to save our own Salt Pork. I kill no Sheep neither because I can keep them in the Fort easily in case of a Blockade. And I have order'd a quantity of Biscuit to be baked for Scouting Parties, etc. as well as to have Some to eat in the Fort, still we could get an Oven up in case we should be shut up.*

*Tho' I take all these precautions, and many others, I am of opinion the Indians will not Attack this Post, nor indeed commit any Hostilities (at least yet awhile) on this Side of the Mountains, which I suppose they look upon as the Limits tho' I may be out in my Politicks, and therefore prepare for them.*

*The Garrison of Fort Burd, with the Suttlers, are arrived Safe at F. Cumberᶫᵈ, with a quantity of Goods belonging to Capⁿ Shelby.*

*The Serjᵗ threw four Casks of Powder in the Monongehella & buried 900 Ibs of Lead.*

*Majʳ Livingston also informs me that his Fort is now deffencible, that he has formed two Companies of Militia, but that he is crowded like me with Women and Children, that he can be plentifully Supplied with fresh Meat, but is scarce of Flour. Yesterday I sent him upwards of 1800 Ibs. of Flour, by Some Horses that are gone for Indian Corn.*

*I am Sending a party to meet a Drove of Cattle, I expect from Colᶫ Cresap belonging to Captⁿ Callender, intended for Detroit.*

## Fort Cumberland is crowded with country people who are repairing the fort

A June 10, 1763 letter that Ourry wrote to Amherst from Fort Bedford includes the following statement:

*Major Livingston, Fort Major of Fort Cumberland, has been joined by about 60 or 70 of the Country People, formed in two Companies of Militia by whose Assistance he has Stockaded a Part of the old Fort so as to make it deffencible, but he writes that he is, like me, crowded with Women & Children. He says he can be Supplied with plenty of Meat, but is Short of Flour. I sent him directly upwards of 1800ᶫᵇ He has also his Scouting Parties, and the whole Communication is apprised of the distinguishing Badge of our Warriours, by which they may know them from real Indians, vizᵗ a white garter tyed round their Heads to prevent false allarms.*

*The Small Garrison from Fort Burd is Safe arrived at Fort Burd Cumberland.*

## Livingston purchases gun flints
A manuscript document shows that Major Livingston purchased 3,000 gun flints from Samuel Postlethwaite & Company on June 10, 1763.

## Powder is needed at Fort Cumberland in June 1763
A synopsis of a June 1763 letter Captain Lewis Ourry wrote to Bouquet from Bedford includes the following, *"Fort Cumberland being strengthened, but powder wanted."* A June 14, 1763 letter[1372] Bouquet wrote to Ourry from Philadelphia includes the statement, *"As soon as you receive Powder you will send some to F: Cumberland, well escorted; till then Major Levingston must collect what necessary assistance he can get from the nearest Settlement and Winchester."*

## A June 16, 1763 advertisement describes the proposed town at Wills Creek
A June 16, 1763 advertisement in the **"Maryland Gazette"** includes the statement, *"THE OHIO Company have ordered 300 Half-Acre LOTS to be laid off for a TOWN, to be called Charlottsburg, on Patomack River, in the Province of Maryland, near Fort Cumberland; and an equal Number of Out Lotts, contiguous to the Town, will be annexed to it."*

## Fort Cumberland sends reinforcements to Fort Pitt
A June 16, 1763 letter[1373] Captain Ecuyer wrote to Bouquet from Fort Pitt includes the following:

*A man has arrived here who has assured me that Fort Burd is abandoned; I suppose they have retreated to Fort Cumberland. ... Captain Ourry sends me word that a party of nearly thirty men from his garrison will be here soon. As soon as I see them I will have a party ready to sustain them. ...*

## Eleven people killed near Fort Bedford on June 17, 1763
The September 30, 1763 **"Return of persons killed or taken by Indians in the Department of Fort Pitt"** states, *"James Clark, and Peter Vanest Killed and Scalped"* near Fort Bedford on June 17, 1763, and also states, *"Christopher Diven, his Father, Wife and 6 Children Viz' 5 Sons & 1 Daughter Killed"* near Fort Bedford on June 18, 1763.

## A biological attack on the Indians
William Trent's June 20, 1763 journal entry at Fort Pitt describes a discussion between Indians and the British, and includes the statement, *"Out of our regard to them we gave them two Blankets and an Handkerchief out of the Small Pox Hospital."*

## A June 21, 1763 letter describes attacks on settlements near Fort Bedford
The 1763 **"The London Chronicle"**, Volume 14, quotes from a June 21, 1763 letter written from Winchester, Virginia:

---

[1372] **"Papers of Col. Henry Bouquet"**, 1940.
[1373] **"Fort Pitt and Letters from the Frontier"**, 1892.

*Last night I reached this place, I have been at Fort Cumberland several days, but the Indians having killed nine people, and burnt several houses near Fort Bedford, made me think it prudent to remove from those parts, from which, I suppose, near 500 families have run away within this week. I assure you it was a most melancholy flight, to see such numbers of poor people, who had abandoned their settlements in such consternation and hurry, that they had hardly any thing with them but their children. And what is still worse, I dare say there is not money enough amongst the whole families to maintain a fifth part of them till the fall; and none of the poor creatures can get a hovel to shelter them from the weather, but lie about scattered in the woods.*

### The siege of Fort Pitt begins in June 1763

The August 2, 1763 edition of the "**The London Chronicle**" contains the following article:

*Extract of a letter from Philadelphia, dated Thursday, June 23, 1763.*

*By an express just now from Fort Pitt, we learn, that the Indians are continually about that place; that out of 120 traders, but two or three escaped; that Fort Detroit was attacked three or four days, but the enemy was beat off, St. Dusky was taken, with much goods, and all the people killed; several other small forts are taken; and it is said about 60 men, escorting provisions from Niagara to Detroit, were also cut off. About 30 of our inhabitants near Fort Bedford, are all cut off, and several houses burnt; so that now it is out of all doubt, it is a general insurrection among all the Indians.*

### Murder and abduction near Fort Bedford in late June 1763

The September 30, 1763 "**Return of persons killed or taken by Indians in the Department of Fort Pitt**" states, *"James Beaty Taken"* near Fort Bedford on June 28, 1763, and states, *"William Lyon, Andrew Enochs and Thomas Guilding, killed & Scalped"* near Fort Bedford on June 30, 1763.

### A reference to the intent to form a town at the mouth of Wills Creek in 1763

The June 1763 issue of "**The Monthly Chronologer**" includes an article concerning the possibility of having a town at Fort Cumberland:

*They write from Philadelphia, that the Ohio company have agreed to lay out a number of lots for a town at Fort Cumberland, near the mouth of Will's creek, on Potowmack river, in the province of Maryland. Fort Cumberland, from its natural situation and contiguity to the extensive and fertile country on the Ohio and its waters, must be the key to all that valuable settlement; it being the highest and most convenient landing-place for the inhabitants on the other side the Allegheny mountains, on all the river Potowmack, which affords a water carriage that with very inconsiderable expense, might be rendered safe, certain, and easy, at all seasons of the year, from the great falls to the spot now proposed for a town.*

George Mercer's 1763 field notes for the Charlottesburg survey mention a wagon road to Pittsburg, Wills Creek, the Potomac River, a main street, a cleared field, a garden, the bridge ford on Wills Creek, a storehouse for artillery wagons, the new storehouse, the north bastion of Fort Cumberland, Braddock's wagon road, the powder magazine of the fort, a chimney, and a location where some mills are to be built. The original document is available online as part of the Darlington Digital Collection, and the notes are published in Lois Mulkearn's 1954 book "**George Mercer papers relating to the Ohio Company of Virginia**".

The town of Charlottesburg did not become reality. According to Mulkearn, General Amherst gave a military order to George Mercer forbidding the lots to be sold.

### A July 3, 1763 report on Pontiac's war from Paxton

The August 23-25, 1763 edition of the "**The London Chronicle**" contains the following extract of a July 3, 1763 letter:

*Extract of a letter from Paxton, July 3.*

*Three Indians came down the river late last night, with intelligence. They bring an account of two nations, the Senecas and Cayugas, declaring war against the English, and joining the Indians to the westward; and that the accounts they have from Ohio are, that they have destroyed all the forts there, except Fort Pitt; that they expect to do that in a little time; and afterwards to march in a large body to the west branch of Susquehanna, and from thence to come by water, in a body of 900 men, to attack Fort Augusta, which they likewise expect to reduce; and then to march with that body down the country.*

### Bouquet writes that several British forts are taken, and Fort Pitt was attacked

On July 3, 1763, Colonel Bouquet wrote the following letter to Governor Hamilton, from Carlisle:

*Sir: — I am sorry to acquaint you that our posts at Presque Isle, Le Boeuf and Venango, are cut off, and the garrison massacred, except one officer and seven men, who have escaped from Le Boeuf. Fort Pitt was briskly attacked the 23d June — had only a few men killed and wounded; and dispersed the enemy. Fort Ligonier has likewise stood a vigorous attack, by means of some men who reinforced that small garrison from the militia of Bedford. The Indians expect a strong reinforcement to make new attempts on these two posts.*

*If the measures I had the honor to recommend to you in my letters of yesterday, are not immediately put into execution, I foresee the ruin of the part of the province on this side of the Susquehanna; and as York county would be covered by Cumberland, I think they ought to join in assisting to build some posts, and saving the harvest. It would not be less necessary to send immediately arms and ammunition to be distributed to the inhabitants to defend their reapers.*

### Aaron Wallace is abducted near Fort Bedford on July 3, 1763

The September 30, 1763 "**Return of persons killed or taken by Indians in the Department of Fort Pitt**" states, *"Aaron Wallace, Taken NB Return'd the Next Day"* near Fort Bedford on July 3, 1763.

### Delivering flour to Fort Cumberland, and then musket balls to Fort Bedford

A July 4, 1763 agreement[1374] Bouquet made with John McCullough at Carlisle states:

*Agreed this day w$^{th}$ M$^r$ John M$^c$Cullough to receive from 21 to 29 Horse Loads of fresh flour at Fort Cumberland on the 14$^{th}$ Instant and there to load his Horses w$^{th}$ Muskett Balls for Fort Bedford.*

### Henry Rowe and William Anderson were killed near Fort Cumberland on July 4, 1763

The September 30, 1763 "**Return of persons killed or taken by Indians in the Department of Fort Pitt**" states, *"Henry Rowe, & W$^m$ Anderson Killed and Scalped"* *"Ten Miles above Fort Cumberland"* on July

---

[1374] "**The papers of Col. Henry Bouquet**", 1940.

4, 1763. This may indicate that there was more than one William Anderson, because there are subsequent records of a William Anderson living in the environs of Fort Cumberland. According to Volume 6 of **"Colonial Records of the Upper Potomac"**, this incident was reported in a July 4, 1763 letter Lewis Ourry wrote to Bouquet from Fort Bedford.

### A letter intimating settlers between Fort Frederick and Fort Cumberland in 1763

On July 5, 1763, Horatio Sharpe sent a letter to Doctor Henry Heinzman at Fort Frederick that includes the following statement:

> *Should the Indians Commit any Murders or Acts of hostility within your County between Fort Cumberland and Fort Frederick I desire you will immediately send Colo Prather Notice thereof that he may give such orders to any part of the Militia under his Command as he shall think Expedient to prevent farther hostilities and to preserve the frontier Inhabitants in security and quiet, and in the mean time you are to take such Measures as you shall think best for the defence of the Fort and Protection of that Neighbourhood.*

Colonel Thomas Prather was the Commander in Chief of the Militia of Frederick County.

### Thomas Cresap's fort is filled with refugees

According to Volume 10 of the **"Ohio Archæological and Historical Quarterly"** (1901), an assistance request letter Colonel Cresap wrote to Governor Sharpe on July 10, 1763 includes the statement, *"his fort was filled with distressed families who had fled to his stockade for safety, and they were all in hourly danger of being butchered, unless relief was afforded."*

### The fort at Presque Isle is captured

The following letter[1375] was written from Fort Detroit on July 10, 1763:

*Fort Detroit 10th July 1763*

*Sir*

*I am sorry to have to acquaint you of my misfortune. On the 20th June at day break I was surrounded at my Post at Presqu Isle by about two hundred Indians a quarter of an hour after they began to Fire on the Block House and continued all that day very smartly. Likewise Fire arrows were thrown into the Roof of the Block house and Bastions. I received my greatest hurt from the Two Hills, the one ascending from the Lake the other from the bottom, they having made holes in the night to secure themselves. Notwithstanding two or three did their endeavor to get in the French were killed which made them cease fireing some hours, at which time they was employed in digging of passes through the earth in order to get at the bottom of the house. 21st They commenced fireing as hot as ever and also with Fire Arrows which set the house a second time on fire, the same day the Barrels of water I had provided was spent in extinguishing said Fires and found it impossible to get at a well which was sunk on the Parade, therefore was obliged to sink one in the house by hard labour, whilst we were digging to get at the well we were again set on fire but got it extinguished by throwing of some shingles from the roof at the same time they had approached as far as the Commanding Officers room on the parade they set it on fire and communicated it to the rushes round the Fort. We continued our fireing till midnight when one of them who spoke French informed me it was in vain to pretend to hold out for they could now set fire to the house when they*

---

[1375] **"History of Colonel Henry Bouquet and the western frontiers of Pennsylvania: 1747-1764"**, 1920.

*pleased if I would not surrender; we may expect no quarters, finding they had made their approaches aforesaid. That they could set me on fire above and below. My men being fatigued to the greatest extremity and not being able to extinguishing such fireing and resist their numbers, I asked them in English if there was any amongst them which understood that language, an Englishman then called up to me, that if I ceased my fireing he would speak with me, he told me they were of the Urin Nation that had ben compelled to take up arms by the Ottawas against Detroit, that there was part of other Nations with him, that they only wanted the house and that they would have now soon, that I might have liberty to go with my Garrison where I pleased. I desired them to leave off their fireing and I would give them an answer in the morning eariry. After considering my situation and of the impossibility of holding out any longer I sent out two soldiers as if to treat with them that they may find out their disposition and how they had made their approaches, and to give me a signal if they found what I imagined to be true finding if it be so and the vessel Hovering Between the two points all the while I was engaged could give me no assistance. I came out with my people they then took us prisoners, myself and four soldiers and a woman was brought to the Wiandotte Town, the rest of my garrison was taken by the other Nations. I was delivered up to Detroit with one soldier and a woman, the other two they killed at their town; the night I arrived there I was delivered up to Fort Detroit the 9th instant.*

*I am sir your most humble Servant*

*John Christie*

*P S All the Forts beyond this have met with the same fate. Captain Campbell, Lieut Tammet and Ensign Holmes is killed, the rest of the gentlemen is prisoners*

### Henry Horshaw is beheaded near Fort Bedford on July 12, 1763

The September 30, 1763 "**Return of persons killed or taken by Indians in the Department of Fort Pitt**" states, *"Henry Horshaw, Stabbed and Beheaded"* near Fort Bedford on July 12, 1763.and states, *"John Wade Killed" "Near Coll. Cresaps, Maryland"* on July 13, 1763.

### Bouquet writes that he is going to try to infect the Indians with smallpox

Amherst wrote a letter to Bouquet that includes the statement:

*Could it not be contrived to send them the Small Pox amongst those disaffected tribes of Indians? We must on this occasion use every stratagem in our power to reduce them.*

On July 13, 1763, Bouquet wrote a letter[1376] to Amherst from Carlisle that included the following statement in a postscript:

*I will try to inoculate the bastards with some blankets that may fall in their hands, and take care not to get the disease myself.*

*As it is pity to expose good men against them I wish we would make use of the Spanish Method to hunt them with English Dogs, suported by Rangers and Some Light Horse, who would I think effectualy extirpate or remove that Vermin.*

Regarding these letters, in his book "**The conspiracy of Pontiac…**" Francis Parkman states:

---

[1376] "**The papers of Col. Henry Bouquet**", 1940.

*We hear nothing more of it; but, in the following spring, Gershom Hicks, who had been among the Indians, reported at Fort Pitt that the small-pox had been raging for some time among them, and that sixty or eighty Mingoes and Delawares, besides some Shawanoes, had died of it.*

Bouquet's July 13, 1763 letter to Amherst also includes the following:

*There being considerable Magazines of Stores at Ligonier, Bedford & Cumberland & no Dependence to be had on the Inhabit<sup>s</sup> who will all desert those Posts, each cannot have less than thirty Men ... The Women, Children & all useless Hands may be escorted down with the Waggons & Packhorses, by the Militia, who will quit F: Pitt, & the Soldiers sent to reinforce Bedford & Cumberland ...*

## Four children scalped on the South Branch on July 14, 1763

The September 30, 1763 "**Return of persons killed or taken by Indians in the Department of Fort Pitt**" states, *"two Boys, Viz<sup>t</sup> Collins & Sullivan, Killed and Scalped"* and *"Two Girls, named Delong Scalped"* *"On South Branch Potowmack"* on July 14, 1763.

## An attack at Oldtown in mid-July 1763

On July 15, 1763, Thomas Cresap wrote the following letter[1377] to Governor Sharpe:

*Old Town July 15 1763*

*May it Please your Excellency I take this opportunity in the highth of Confusion to acquaint you with our unhappy & most wretched situation at this time being in Hourly Expectation of being massacred by our Barberous & Inhumane Enemy the Indians we having been three days successively Attacked by them Viz. the 13, 14 & this Instant on the 13th as 6 men were shocking some wheat in the field 5 Indians fired on them as they came to do it & others running to their assistance. On the 14th Indians crep up to & fired on about 16 men who were sitting & walking under a Tree at the Entrance of my Lane about 100 yards from my House but on being fired at by the white men who much wounded some of them they Immediatly Runn off & were followed by the white men about a mile all which way was great quantity of Blood on the Ground the white men got 3 of their Bundles containing sundry Indian Implements & Goods about 3 hours after several gunns were fired in the woods on which a party went in Quest of them & found 3 Beaves killd by them, the Indians wounded one man at their first fire tho but slightly. On this Instant as Mr. Saml Wilder was going to a house of his about 300 yards Distant from mine with men[1378] & several women the Indians Rushed on them from a Rising Ground but they perceiving their coming Run towards my House hollowing which being heard by those at my house they Run to their assistance & met them & the Indians at the Entrance of my lane on which the Indians Immediatly fired on them to the amount of 18 or Twenty & Killd Mr. Wilder. The party of white men returned their fire & Killd one of them dead on the spot & wounded severall of the others as appeared by Considerable Quantity of Blood strewed on the Ground as they Run off which they Immediatly did & by their leaving behind them 3 Gunns one pistole & sundry other Emplements of warr &c. &c.*

*I have inclosed a List of the Desolate men women & Children who have fled to my House which is Inclosed by a small stockade for safety by which you see what a number of poor Souls destitute of Every necessary of Life are here penned up & likely to be Butchered without Immediate Relief & Assistance & can Expect*

---

[1377] "**Correspondence of Governor Horatio Sharpe**", Volume 14.

[1378] This is given as *"4 men"* in the "**Annual Report Of The President Of The Maryland Historical Society**", 1850.

*none unless from the Province to which they Belong. I shall submitt to your wiser Judgment the Best & most Effectual method for such Relief & shall conclude with hoping we shall have it in time.*

*I am Honnourable Sir*

*Your most Obed' Serv'*

*Tho' Cresap*

*P.S. Those Indians who attacked us this day are part of that Body which went to the southward by this way in Spring which is known by one of the Guns we now got from them.*

An article in the July 21, 1763 "**Maryland Gazette**" that summarizes this letter begins with the statement, *"We have the Pleasure of acquainting our Readers, That Col. Cresap, and his Family, were not cut off by the Indians a few Days ago; but if he has not speed Relief, it is feared he will be soon."*

## Houses along Wills Creek north of the Narrows in July 1763

On July 16, 1763, at one o'clock in the morning, James Livingston wrote to Colonel Bouquet from Fort Cumberland about recent Indian depredations. The letter[1379] describes the Warriors path and private residences that were located along Wills Creek:

*A Party was this day up the River and returned just now. When Mr Tomlinson informs me, that he came to Jos Mounts house and found a Hog killed and laid upon a Shelf in the house, bleeding fresh, by which he conjectures, they had not been gone more than half an hour and we tracked them from thence along the old Warrior roads that leads up Wills Creek towards Bedford, soon after I perceived a great Smoke coming through the Gap of Wills Creek, which makes me conjecture they have burnt all the houses upon the Creek, but have not had time to be satisfied of it, as night drew on ...*

This is the earliest known reference to houses located along Wills Creek, above Cumberland. The letter also reveals that there was more than one Indian path along Wills Creek, north of Fort Cumberland. The letter also indicates that Joseph Mounts was already living along the Potomac River, above Fort Cumberland on July 16, 1763. The portion of this letter that precedes the above quote states:

*I just now received a melancholy account from Coll Cresaps, which is as follows. That on the 13th Instant the Indians fired upon Six men, shocking wheat in Col Cresaps field and killed one man, but was prevented scalping him by one man firing on them as they run up. On the 14th 5 Indians fired upon 16 men as they were sitting, standing and lying under a large tree at the End of Col Cresaps Lane about 100 yards from his House and wounded one man, but on being fired at by the white men, who wounded one or more of them, as appears by the great Quantity of Blood found on their Tracts, they immediately ran off, and were pursued but could not overtake them Some time after several guns were fired in the Woods adjacent, on which a Party went in quest of them and found three Beeves just killed. On the 15th about 10 o'clock in the morning as Mr Welder was going to a house of his about 300 yards distant from Colonel Cresaps with three men and several women the Indians to the amount of 20 or upwards rushed on them from a rising ground, but on being perceived by the white Party, they ran back hollowing, which being heard by them at the house, they immediately ran to their assistance and met them and the Indians at the end of Col Cresaps Lane about 100 yards from the Colonels house as mentioned before, on which the Indians instantly fired on them and killed Mr Welder, the Party of white men returned their fire, killed one of them dead on the Spot and wounded several more (as appears by the great Quantity of Blood left in the Field and on the Track. The Colonel expects daily to be further distrest and is in much want of*

---

[1379] "**History of Colonel Henry Bouquet and the western frontiers of Pennsylvania: 1747-1764**", 1920.

*assistance. The Indians are gone towards the Cove below Bedford, and it is suspected they are the party that went to the Southward some time ago, as we have got 2 Rifles and one smooth bore, which Col Cresaps Son thinks belongs to those who went there, with a great many other Implements, which they were obliged to leave behind them. The Indians were very bold and daring for some time, and one more so in particular who cut Mr Welder in the Back and divided his ribs from the Back Bone, after he was shot down, but we prevented his being scalped. Col Cresaps youngest Son scalped the Indian, all this was done within 100 yards of the Colonels Gate. The other Person killed was one Wade, the Person wounded was Richard Morris.*

John Minor elaborated on this event in a September 24, 1800 affidavit regarding Captain Michael Cresap that was witnessed by Evan Gwynn, as follows, *"...report says (which I believe) that he shot an Indian with a pistol while he (the Indian) was attempting to scalp a Mr. Welder that the Indians had killed at Old Town many years before Dunmore's war, and while Cresap was a youth."*

In his 1833 book, "**History of the Valley of Virginia**", Samuel Kercheval states, *"At the Rev. Mr. Jacob's present residence, on North Branch, a man by the name of Wade was killed."* Rev. John J. Jacob married Michael Cresap's widow and added the brick addition to Cresap's stone house in Oldtown. The book puts Rev. Jacob's residence in Hampshire County, Virginia.

This photo from Robert Bruce's 1916 book **"The National road; most historic thoroughfare in the United States..."** was taken looking northwest through the Narrows from Lover's Leap. It shows the farmland where James Livingston described houses in a July 16, 1763 letter.

## Fredericktown contributes to the support of Cresap's fort

A letter from Frederick that is published in the July 19, 1763 issue of the "**Maryland Gazette**" references Thomas and Michael Cresap as follows:

*On Sunday afternoon we had the pleasure of seeing Mr. Michael Cresap arrive in town with mokosins on his legs, taken from an Indian whom he killed and scalped, being one of those who had shot down Mr. Wilder, the circumstances of whose much-lamented murder and the success of Col. Cresap's family you no doubt have received from other hands. Money has been cheerfully contributed in our town towards the support of the men to be added to Col. Cresap's present force, as we look upon the preservation of the Old Town to be of great importance to us, and a proper check to the progress of the savages; but notwithstanding our present efforts to keep the enemy at a distance, and thereby shelter the whole province...*

### Orders to transport musket balls from Fort Cumberland to Fort Bedford

In a July 19, 1763 letter Bouquet wrote to Captain Robertson from Fort Loudoun, he asked Robertson to bring his detachment to Fort Cumberland, and then escort thirty, or possibly more, horses to Fort Bedford that Livingston will provide. Each of the horses were to carry 150 pounds of musket balls.

### Robertson's Light Infantry to be at Fort Cumberland as an escort

A synopsis of a July 20, 1763 letter Lewis Ourry wrote to Colonel Bouquet from Fort Loudoun states, *"Capt. Robertson's Light Infantry to be at Fort Cumberland to escort waggons. Hopes the State militia will be left to guard crops. Arrangements as to provisions, &c. Croghan's men to be dismissed if the Province does not provide their pay."*

### Lemuel Barritt's rangers sign up at Fort Cumberland for a two-month tour

A 1763 document states, *"Ye 26 of July 1763 att fort Cumberland we ye suscribers whos names are hereby subscribed ...to be lawfully inListed in a company of Rangers under ye command of Capt. Leumel Barett for to march to fort pitt for ye space of two months if Required..."*[1380] On their march to relieve Fort Pitt, they became engaged in fierce combat at Bushy Run, as described below.

### Enoch Innis reports that he was living at Fort Cumberland in 1763

As stated above, Lemuel Barritt's Rangers signed up at Fort Cumberland on July 26, 1763. A December 20, 1768 deposition by Enoch Innis, written in Cumberland, states, *"This day came Enoch Innis an Inhabitant of the Colony of Virginia before me one of his Majestys Justices of the peace for the County & Made _____ that he was a Resident & Inhabitant in Fort Cumberland in the Province Maryland at the Time Cap$^t$ Lemuel Barret engaged a Certain Tho$^s$ Sympson to Joyn him & others as Volunteers in an Expedition _____ for the Relief of Fort Pitt ... and was also an Inhabitant & Resident of Said Fort Cumberland at the Return of Said Barrat & Sympson after Said Expedition & that to the Knowledge of him the Deponent the Said Sympson was not any time Confined from, or Obstructed in his Business By Reason or Means of a wound he Rec$^d$ in Said Expedition".*

### A July 26, 1763 letter from Fort Cumberland requests reinforcements

On July 26, 1763, James Livingston wrote the following letter[1381] from Fort Cumberland:

*Sir*

*Cap$^t$ Field is here with Cap$^t$ Stanton and two more; and have sent the Bearer Thomas Spencer to acquaint you that this Garrison is quite destitute of men, therefore if you could send us a Company of Militia it*

---

[1380] In his book, **"The Monongahela of old..."**, James Veech states, *"Capt. Lemuel Barrett held the land where Bridgeport now is, under a 'military permit from the commander at Fort Pitt, in 1763, for the purpose of cultivating lands within the custom limits of the garrison then called Fort Burd.' He was a Marylander. In 1783 he conveyed his title to Rees Cadwallader, the town proprietor."*

[1381] The letter was identified by Nayano Taylor-Neumann (New York Public Library digital collection).

would be of infinite Service, as Col° Bouquet cannot spare one Man. Cap' Robinson of the 77th, &c Cap' Murray of the R Highlanders with their Companies left this the 23d Instant with 29 Horses loaded with Musket Ball.

Col.° Bouquet leaves Bedford this day or tomorrow with an Escort of 700 Horses with Ammunition & Provision for the Relief of Pitts, to which place God send him safe, but am afraid that he is too weak. If you can spare a Company, to be stationed at the New Store or here, it will be of great Importance, as they may way lay the Savages at Ice's Place,[1382] for not 2 day's pass, but Parties of them march to &c from the South Branch. I have not Ten men here that I can trust to, therefore must rely on you for Assistances, until we hear what will become of Col.° Bouquet. My two Expresses that I sent to Pitt the 9th Instant are both gone; as the Pistol I lent to one of them was left by the Party that attacked Cresaps Fort. I was attacked the 19th about 11 oClock at night, but did no harm, only scared half of the Garrison, they fired 10 or 12 Guns & went off. James Weir is gone to Bedford to enlist with the Penn° Rangers.

Give me Leave to conclude

Your most obed.' hum.' Servant

Cumberland                                   James Livingston

July 26. 1763

PS

Col: Bouquet have with him between 5 and 600 Menies have his Complements to you and all his old acquaintences. Please do send up some flour with the men, as none can be got here. Cattle we have plenty of.

## A request for militia to help to garrison Fort Cumberland

A July 27, 1763 letter[1383] Livingston sent to Bouquet from Fort Cumberland states:

I have just time to inform you that I have received your Instructions in regard to Provisions, which I shall observe.

As to any News I refer you to the Bearers, Cap^ts Field & Stanton.

If you think proper, write to Col° Stephen for one Company of Militia to assist garrison this Fort, I am almost sure it will be complyed with, as he is chief Commander of all the Militia in the Northern Neck of Virginia. I have wrote to him on the same head

I have nothing more, but wish you all the Prosperity, & may Heavens guard yourself and Party safe to your intended Post.

As for the two Expresses I sent the 9th Instant, I am sure they are killed or taken, as the Pistol I lent to one of them is now here, & was found at Col° Cresaps when Mr. Welder was killed.

---

[1382] This is most likely a reference to Frederick Ice, who had a tract of 391-acres where the Allegany Ballistics Laboratory is now located. The passage suggests that the antecedent to the Winchester Road was then in service. (Information on the Frenderick Ice tract was provided by Francis Bridges.)
[1383] **"The Papers of Col. Henry Bouquet"**, 1942.

**The 'Pennsylvania Gazette' describes the mid-July 1763 attacks at Colonel Cresap's**
The July 28, 1763 issue of "**The Pennsylvania Gazette**" contains the following account:

*GOD Save the KING. Extract of a Letter from Cumberland, in Frederick County, Maryland, dated July 16, 1763, One o'Clock in the Morning.*

*"Just now I received a melancholy Account from Colonel Cresap, which is as follows, viz. That on the 13th Instant the Indians fired upon six Men shucking Wheat in the Colonel Field, and killed one Man, but were prevented from scalping him, by another firing upon them as they ran up. On the 14th five Indians fired upon fifteen Men, as they were sitting, standing and lying under a large Tree, at the End of Col. Cresaps lane, about 100 Yards from his House, and wounded one Man, but on being fired at by the white Men, who wounded one or more of them, as appeared by the great Quantity of Blood found on their Tracks, they immediately ran off, and were pursued, but could not be overtaken. Some Time after several Guns were fired in the Woods adjacent, on which a Party went in Quest of them, and found three Beeves just killed. On the 15th, about Ten o'Clock in the Morning, as Mr. Welder was going to a House of his, about 300 Yards distant from Mr. Cresap, with three Men, and several Women, the Indians, to the Amount of 20, or upwards, rushed on them from a riding Ground, but on being perceived by the white Party they ran back, hallooing, which being heard by the People at the House, they immediately went to their Assistance, and met them and the Indians at the End of Col. Cresap Lane, about 100 Yards from his House, as mentioned before, on which the Enemy immediately fired on them, and killed Mr. Welder; the Party of White Men returned their Fire, killed one of them dead on the Spot, and wounded several more, as appeared by the Blood left in the Field, and on their Tracks. — The Colonel expects daily to be further distressed, and is in much Want of Assistance: The Indians are gone towards the Cove, below Bedford, and it is suspected they are the Party that went to the Southward some Time ago, as we have got two Rifles, and one smooth Bore, which Col. Cresap son thinks belonged to those who went there, with a great many other Implements, which they were obliged to leave behind them. The Indians were very bold and daring for some Time, and one more so in particular, who cut Mr. Welder in the Back, and divided his Ribs from the Back Bone, after he was shot down, but we prevented his being scalped. Mr. Cresap youngest Son scalped the Indian. The other Person killed was one Wade; the Person wounded Richard Morris...*

**A July newspaper article gives a gruesome account of murder on the Winchester road**
An article in the October 1763 issue of the "**Magazine of Magazines**" includes the following:

*To collect every particular case, would exceed the limits of a magazine; but a few are necessary by way of illustration. A messenger express from fort Cumberland to Winchester saw a women on the road who had been just scalped, and was then in the agonies of death; with her brains hanging over her skull, and who was afraid of staying to put an end to her misery, for fear of sharing the same fate...*

The date of this 1763 event is unknown, but it would have been sometime prior to October, in order to find its way into print overseas by October. In volume 1 of his book "**The Oregon Trail; The Conspiracy of Pontiac**", Parkman provides a transcript of a letter that the above account is obviously based on, as follows:

*I examined the Express that brought this letter from Winchester to Loudoun County, and he informed me that he was employed as an Express from Fort Cumberland to Winchester, which Place he left the 4th Instant, and that passing from the Fort to Winchester, he saw lying on the Road a Woman, who had been just scalped, and was then in the Agonies of Death, with her Brains hanging over her Skull; his Companions made a Proposal to knock her on the Head, to put and End to her Agony, but this Express apprehending the Indians were near at Hand, and not thinking it safe to lose any Time, rode off, and left the poor Woman in the Situation they found her.*

Parkman reports that this letter was printed in the "**Pennsylvania Gazette**", Issue No. 1805, and was addressed *"To Col. Francis Lee, or, in his Absence, to the next Commanding Officer in Loudoun County."* Issue No. 1805 was published July 28, 1763.

## Barrett is to march to Fort Ligonier

A July 29, 1763[1384] letter[1385] Major James Livingston wrote to Bouquet from Cumberland states:

*Having this opportunity to acquaint you, that Cap* Barrett will set out on Monday Morning, I am certain he will not get above 12 Men, he has 8 pretty good woods men; the Bearer William Linn & the Two Lads with him will be of great Service to scout, or will go to Pitt, if you require it, as they are the best woods men in those Parts, & have been on several Scouts last War. Cap* Field left this Garrison yesterday at Noon, & purposes to be here on Sunday next by Dinner, with what men he can raise, when he and Cap* Barrett will march together through the Woods to Ligonier.*

*An Express came from the South Branch from John M*Collock to let me know there were 42 Horses ready. I have sent him word, you could not spare an Escort. There have not been seen any Signs of Indians for this Week past, which makes me think, they are all called in, as they no doubt have seen you on your March.*

*I sent Gover*  Sharpe an Express on the first breaking out of the Savages, he sent some Militia to Fort Frederick to scout round that Place, but am informed he will not send any above that Fort.*

*I sent to Col*  Stephen for a Company to be stationed over the River at the Ohio Store, where they might be of great Service to this Garrison, I do not doubt, but he will order them into the Fort, untill I hear from you. I wish you Success and Safety to the End of your Journey*

*I am obliged to give the married Persons Families who are of Cap*  Barretts Comp*  of Rangers, Provisions, otherwise the Men could not have come to you.*

## The general disposition at Fort Cumberland on August 1, 1763

A synopsis of an August 1, 1763 letter[1386] from Cumberland states, *"James Livingston to Bouquet. Has mustered 14 of the best men; has promised to look after the wives and children left behind. Capt. Field expected; rations for the men. Has purchased flour for the garrison; McCulloch can take 30 horses to Bedford after delivering the flour. His garrison very weak. Has advanced money to Barret and has given lead for bullets and powder."*

In this letter, Livingston describes Barrett's scouts as the best men from his garrison. Livingston wrote that he gave each scout 30 balls for muskets or lead for rifles, and two pounds of gunpowder. One of the scouts, Richardson is described as having eight children and a wife and is identified as a good woodsmen. Another of the scouts, Elias Jarett, had six children and a wife. Livingston promised to take care of them until Bouquet reaches Fort Pitt. The flour was bought from McCollock. Livingston planned to load McCollack's horses with ball to deliver to Fort Bedford.

---

[1384] Regrettably, this date was erroneously reported as July 29, 1762 in "**Fort Cumberland: The Missing Years**".
[1385] "**The Papers of Col. Henry Bouquet**", 1942.
[1386] A transcript of the letter is included in "**The Papers of Henry Bouquet**", Volume VI, 1994.

## Peace with France is announced in Maryland

In the August 4, 1763 issue of the "**Maryland Gazette**" Governor Sharpe announced the ratification of peace with France and Spain and proclaimed a day of public thanksgiving to be held on August 23, 1763.

## Barett's men sortie from Fort Cumberland to engage in the 1763 battle of Bushy Run

The battle of Bushy Run was fought during Bouquet's march to relieve Fort Cumberland. Lemuel Barrett wrote out a list[1387] of equipment that was lost in the battle. The list, which indicates the Rangers sortied from Fort Cumberland, states:

| | | |
|---|---|---|
| *Augst ye 5ᵗʰ 1764 (sic)* | | *Lost in Battol att Bushy Run* |
| *2 shorts and one pair Draws* | | *£ 3 – 10 – 0* |
| *1Blanciᵗ* | | *1 – 0 – 0* |
| *Belonging to my men* | *1 Blanciᵗ* | *0 – 15 – 0* |
| *James parkes* | | |
| *James Spencor* | *1 ditto* | *0 – 15 – 0* |
| *Eias Jarod* | *1 ditto* | *0 – 15 – 0* |
| *Hennry Doring* | *1 ditto* | *0 – 15 – 0* |
| *John Jemeson* | *1 ditto* | *0 – 15 – 0* |
| *William Spencor* | *1 ditto* | *0 – 15 – 0* |
| *Thomas Beate* | *1 ditto* | *0 – 15 – 0* |
| *Michel Ashford* | *1 ditto* | *0 – 15 – 0* |
| *John MᶜMillyon* | *1 ditto* | *0 – 15 – 0* |
| *Nathaniel Stedmon* | *1 ditto* | *0 – 15 – 0* |
| *William Spencor* | *1 ditto* | *0 – 15 – 0* |
| *Thomas Symson* | *1 ditto* | *0 – 15 – 0* |
| *4 Shortes at 15ˢ* | *each* | *3 – 0 – 0* |
| | | *£ 16 – 10 – 0* |

*the above accounᵗ is a true lisᵗ of things Losᵗ in yᵉ Battel of Coll Buqate att Bushy Run furneseed on my one Expenes when I marcheᵈ with my man from forᵗ Cumberland tesᵗ·*

*Lemᶫ Barritt Capᵗ*

*To Henery Buquat Esqʳ Commandor of the troops in that Batel*

The above list was accompanied by a February 20, 1765 letter from Barritt to Bouquet that states:

[1387] "**The Papers of Col. Henry Bouquet**", Series 21651, Federal Works Agency, 1943.

*I humbely wold Beag Leave to Recommend to your Consideration the Los<sup>t</sup> of me and my partey of Rangers that was in y<sup>e</sup> Battel with your honer att Bushey Run on y<sup>e</sup> 5<sup>th</sup> and 6 of August 1764 (sic) Which your honor is Very Senecible of and gives me Libety to Remind your honor of your promises of your honor asistantes in my having Sum Satesfaction and as there is privision made for y<sup>e</sup> Same would humpely pray that your honor wold asis<sup>t</sup> me in this afaier as I was Obliged to furnish my men with those nescasarys Befor y<sup>e</sup> marched, and to gather with y<sup>e</sup> other losis I have Sostained on y<sup>e</sup> Same Acot Living on y<sup>e</sup> fruntears of this provine of pencelvania By which I am a greate Sufor<sup>r</sup> thare By I in Close<sup>d</sup> a true Lis<sup>t</sup> of y<sup>e</sup> things Los<sup>t</sup> and your honors asistence will much oblige your honors most humble Sv<sup>t</sup> in Dutey Bound shall Ever pray*

### Barrett suggests the winning strategy

According to the 1883 book "**Col. Henry Bouquet and His Campaigns of 1763 and 1764**", Barritt proposed the strategy that won the battle. While not documentary evidence, the book states:

*A Captain or Lieutenant Barret, commanding it is said a small Maryland detachment of provincial rangers, pointed out to Bouquet a place where a large body of the boldest of the Indians might be taken on the flank and rear by a well directed bayonet charge around the hill and up a hollow or ravine. Andrew Byerly was with Bouquet at the time, and heard Barret make the suggestion, which the Colonel quickly put into execution on a large scale by a masterly piece of strategy. Immediately Major Campbell was directed to make a rapid circuit through the woods on the right flank of the savages around the hill aforesaid, taking them in flank and rear. Captain Basset of the Royal Engineers was directed to arrange the other companies, so as to co-operate promptly with the strategic movement at the right moment. The thin line of troops that took the place of the two companies withdrawn from the front, gave away before the impetuous onset of the exultant savages and fell back upon the convoy, where they presented a line of bristling steel. The Indians fell completely into the snare and rushed with demoniac fury into the camp, certain that the fight was won.*

*But just as they supposed themselves masters of the field the Highlanders charged in with a wild battle cry upon their right flank. A volley was fired upon the amazed and huddled savages, but they stood their ground with wonderful intrepidity, not willing to loose a decisive victory and the great booty of stores and scalps which a moment before they felt was within their grasp. It is agreed on all hands that on this occasion, not only in the attack and the assault, but in meeting the unexpected charge on their flank and rear, the Indians displayed unusual courage and firmness.*

*But a well directed bayonet charge no body of Indians ever did or will stand. Here Bouquet had them at last where he wanted them, at close quarters where there could be no dodging or popping from behind the trees. The Highlanders were at home with the bayonet and only too glad to get a good chance at the painted villains who had skulked behind trees while they shot their brave comrades during the past two days. Still the savages struggled in hope of gaining the day, but the shock was irresistible and, perceiving that they had been caught in a trap, they fled in tumultuous disorder. In doing so they were obliged to pass in front of the companies brought up on the opposite side by Capt. Basset, from whom they received another volley. The four companies now vied with each other in driving the savages through the woods beyond Bushy Run without giving them time to reload their empty rifles. Many of their chief warriors were killed and the rest utterly routed. Among others, Kukyuskung, the ungrateful and blatant blackguard, and the famous war Chief called "The Wolf," were slain.*

### Ormsby credits Barrett with the winning strategy at Bushy Run

The January 1847 issue of "**The Olden Time**" includes a transcript of a narrative written by John Ormsby, that includes the following:

*About the time the Indians murdered my clerks, they also laid siege to the Fort, and as I had a house at Pittsburgh, and a few goods, in remnants, &c., I chose to stay and help to defend it against the savages. The Indians continued block up the garrison for near three months, when Colonel Bouquet was ordered to proceed to Pittsburgh with about 1500 men, part regulars. The Indians having early intelligence of his march, watched his movements very closely, till the army encamped on a dry ridge, within about thirty miles of Pittsburgh. Here the enemy had collected all their forces, and attacked Bouquet's army in a furious manner, confident that they could use him as they used Braddock eight years before. The English troops were in a wretched situation, as the Indians very artfully secured all the springs of water in the neighborhood. Thus they (the English) fought all day without water, except what they sucked out of the tracks of beasts, as happily a small rain fell. As Bouquet in the beginning ordered an encampment to be made of bags, saddles, &c, the Indians still advanced that way, where the sick and wounded lay in a deplorable condition. In this desperate situation of the English army, a certain Captain Barret, who commanded a small detachment of Maryland volunteers, informed Bouquet that he and his army would be cut off, if they followed that mode of fighting. Bouquet then agreed to his proposal, which was, that a quick march should be ordered towards the breastwork, which would take up the attention of the savages, while two small squads should run around them, and upon beating a flam,[1388] they should rush up and give them a general volley in the rear, which had the desired effect, for the Indians were sure a reinforcement attacked them. Being thus alarmed, they broke, and yelped, and ran up the hills, being pursued by the English as far as prudence would permit. The army then commenced its march, and arrived safe at Pittsburgh next day, without being molested by the copper gentry. If Captain Barret had not suggested the above mentioned movement, the savages intended to storm the camp, and would very probably have massacred the chief part of the army.*

*At the time of the arrival of Bouquet at Fort Pitt there was not a pound of good flour or meat there, so that if he had failed we would have starved or been tomahawked. Notwithstanding it was understood that our preservation was owing to Captain Barret, yet when Bouquet and his officers were regaling themselves in luxurious living not one of them offered the brave New Englander a cup of cold water; nay, would not own that the victory was any way due to him.*

### Bouquet's description of the first day of battle
The aforementioned 1883 book includes the letters Bouquet wrote from the battlefield, describing the events. The letter written on the first day of the battle of Bushy Run states:

*Camp At Edge Hill, 26 Miles From Fort Pitt, 5th Aug. 1763.*

*Sir: The second instant the troops and convoy arrived at Ligonier, where I could obtain no intelligence of the enemy. The expresses sent since the beginning of July, having been either killed or obliged to return, all the passes being occupied by the enemy. In this uncertainty, I determined to leave all the wagons, with the powder, and a quantity of stores and provisions, at Ligonier, and on the 4th proceeded with the troops and about 340 horses loaded with flour.*

*I intended to have halted to-day at Bushy Run, (a mile beyond this camp), and after having refreshed the men and horses, to have marched in the night over Turtle Creek, a very dangerous defile of several miles, commanded by high and rugged hills; but at one o'clock this afternoon, after a march of 17 miles, the savages suddenly attacked our advance guard, which was immediately supported by the two Light Infantry companies of the 42d regiment, who drove the enemy from their ambuscade and pursued them a good way. The savages returned to the attack, and the fire being obstinate on our front and extending along our flanks, we made a general charge with the whole line to dislodge the savages from the heights,*

---

[1388] Based on the 1760 book "**An Abstract of General Bland's Treatise of Military Discipline…**", I believe that a flam is a specific drum beat that was used as a signal.

*in which attempt we succeded, without by it obtaining any decisive advantage, for as soon as they were driven from one post, they appeared on another, till, by continued reinforcements, they were at last able to surround us and attacked the convoy left in our rear; this obliged us to march back to protect it. The action then became general, and though we were attacked on every side, and the savages exerted themselves with uncommon resolution, they were constantly repulsed with loss; we also suffered considerably. Capt. Lieut. Graham and Lieut. James Mcintosh, of the 42d, are killed, and Capt. Graham wounded. Of the Royal American Regt., Lieut. Dow, who acted as A. D. Q. M. G., is shot through the body. Of the 77th, Lieut. Donald Campbell and Mr. Peebles, a volunteer, are wounded. Our loss in men, including rangers and drivers, exceeds sixty killed or wounded.*

*The action has lasted from one o'clock till night, and we expect to begin at daybreak.*

*Whatever our fate may be, I thought it necessary to give your Excellency this early information, that you may at all events take such measures as you think proper with the Provinces, for their own safety, and the effectual relief of Fort Pitt, as in case of another engagement, I fear insurmountable difficulties in protecting and transporting our provisions, being already so much weakened by the losses of this day in men and horses, besides the additional necessity of carrying the wounded, whose situation is truly deplorable.*

*I cannot sufficiently acknowledge the constant assistance I have received from Major Campbell during this long action, nor express my admiration of the cool and steady behavior of the troops, who did not fire a shot without orders, and drove the enemy from their posts with fixed bayonets. The conduct of the officers is much above my praises.*

*I have the honor to be with great respect,*

*Sir, &c. Henry Bouquet*

### Bouquet's description of the second day of the battle of Bushy Run
Bouquet's letter from the second day of the battle of Bushy Run states:

*Camp At Bushy Run, 6th Aug. 1763.*

*Sir: I had the honor to inform your Excellency in my letter of yesterday of our first engagement with the savages.*

*We took the post last night on the hill where our convoy halted, when the front was attacked, (a commodious piece of ground and just spacious enough for our purpose). There we encircled the whole and covered our wounded with flour bags.*

*In the morning the savages surrounded our camp, at the distance of 500 yards, and by shouting and yelping, quite round that extensive circumference, thought to have terrified us with their numbers. They attacked us early, and under favor of an incessant fire, made several bold efforts to penetrate our camp, and though they failed in the attempt, our situation was not the less perplexing, having experienced that brisk attacks had little effect upon an enemy who always gave way when pressed, and appeared again immediately. Our troops were, besides, extremely fatigued with the long march and as long action of the preceding day, and distressed to the last degree, by a total want of water, much more intolerable than the enemy's fire.*

*Tied to our convoy, we could not lose sight of it without exposing it and our wounded to fall a prey to the savages, who pressed upon us, on every side, and to move it was impracticable, having lost many horses, and most of the drivers, stupified by fear, hid themselves in the bushes, or were incapable of hearing or obeying orders. The savages growing every moment more audacious, it was thought proper to still*

711

*increase their confidence by that means, if possible, to entice them to come close upon us, or to stand their ground when attacked. With this view two companies of Light Infantry where ordered within the circle, and the troops on their right and left opened their files and filled up the space, that it might seem they were intended to cover the retreat. The Third Light Infantry company and the Grenadiers of the 42d were ordered to support the two first companies. This manoeuvre succeeded to our wish, for the few troops who took possession of the ground lately occupied by the two Light Infantry companies being brought in nearer to the centre of the circle, the barbarians mistaking these motions for a retreat, hurried headlong on, and advancing upon us, with the most daring intrepidity, galled us excessively with their heavy fire; but at the very moment that they felt certain of success, and thought themselves masters of the camp, Major Campbell, at the head of the first companies, sallied out from a part of the hill they could not observe, and fell upon their right flank. They resolutely returned the fire, but could not stand the irresistible shock of our men, who, rushing in among them, killed many of them and put the rest to flight. The orders sent to the other two companies were delivered so timely by Captain Basset,[1389] and executed with such celerity and spirit, that the routed savages who happened that moment to run before their front, received their full fire, when uncovered by the trees. The four companies did not give them time to load a second time, nor even to look behind them, but pursued them till they were totally dispersed. The left of the savages, which had not been attacked, were kept in awe by the remains of our troops, posted on the brow of the hill for that purpose; nor durst they attempt to support or assist their right, but being witness to their defeat, followed their example and fled. Our brave men disdained so much as to touch the dead body of a vanquished enemy that scarce a scalp was taken except by the Rangers and pack-horse drivers.*

*The woods being now cleared and the pursuit over, the four companies took possession of a hill in our front, and as soon as litters could be made for the wounded, and the flour and everything destroyed, which, for want of horses, could not be carried, we marched without molestation to this camp. After the severe correction we had given the savages a few hours before, it was natural to suppose we should enjoy some rest, but we had hardly fixed our camp, when they fired upon us again. This was very provoking; however, the Light Infantry dispersed them before they could receive orders for that purpose. I hope we shall be no more disturbed, for, if we have another action, we shall hardly be able to carry our wounded.*

*The behavior of the troops on this occasion, speaks for itself so strongly, that for me to attempt their eulogium would but detract from their merit.*

*I have the honor to be, most respectfully, Sir, &c.*

*Henry Bouquet*

## James Smith's commentary on Bushy Run

Colonel James Smith's 1812 book, "**A treatise on the mode and manner of Indian war...**" makes the following statement about Lemuel Barrett's participation in the battle of Bushy Run:

*The Indians had no aid from the French or any other power when they besieged Fort Pit, in 1763, and cut off the communication between that post and Fort Loudon, for about 6 months, and would have defeated gen. Bouquets' army, who were on the way to raise the siege, had it not been for the assistsance of the Virginia volunteers. Col. Barret with his volunteers fought in the front for some time, but was overpowered by numbers and drove in; Col. Barrett then went to the general, and told him to force his men out on every direction so as to form a hollow square, and get behind trees, and if they did not do this, the army would be cut off. The general complied with this advice. Then Col. Barret also applied to the gen. for four hundred of his men; this was also granted. Col. Barrett then collected those men to the*

---

[1389] One has to wonder if this is a misreading of *"Barret"*.

*centre of the square, and ordered them to strip to their shirts & tie handkerchiefs round their heads which was the dress that the volunteers wore. As the army was not altogether surrounded, the Col. With these men and the volunteers, sallied out at a gap and came round behind the Indians. And they finding that they were between two fires immediately fled, and never attempted attacking the army again. — Had it not been for Col. Barret Fort-Pitt would then have fallen into the hands of the enemy; for they were almost out of provisions; and another army could not have been sent that year, as it was now late in the fall. — Thus the Generalship and bravery of Col. Barrett, and his Virginia volunteers; were the means of saving the army and Fort-Pitt. — When the British made their official report to England, the Virginians or Col. Barrett were not mentioned. — It was stated that the Red-Coats had done all!*

## Captain Stanton is killed on the South Branch on August 9, 1763

The 1977 book "**Genealogical Data from Colonial New York Newspapers**" states that an article in a 1763 issue of the "**New-York Mercury**" reports that Captain Stanton, a member of the Virginia Militia was killed by Indians on August 9, 1763 at a fort on the South Branch above Pearsall's. This event was described as occurring near Fort Cumberland, even though it took place above Pearsall's.

The August 25, 1763 issue of the "**Pennsylvania Gazette**" published an extract of an August 9, 1763 letter from Fort Cumberland that includes the following:

*I have just received Advice by Express, that this Day the Savages killed one Captain Staunton, and another Man, of the Virginia Militia, and wounded three others dangerously, at a Fort above Pearsall, on the South Branch, but scalped none. There were eleven Men in the Fort; the Party of Indians was between Thirty and Forty, three of whom are thought to be killed. As he has the Command of the Militia of several Counties, he has promised to assist all in his Power, by protecting Bedford and this Garrison.*

## Bouquet writes from Fort Pitt on August 11, 1763

The October 15-18, 1763 edition of the "**The London Chronicle**" contains the following letter from Colonel Bouquet:

*Fort Pitt, August 11, 1763. Account transmitted by Colonel Bouquet to Sir Jeffery Amherst.*

*Sir,*

*We arrived hear yesterday without further opposition than scattered shots along the road.*

*The Delawares, Shawnese, Wiandots, and Mingoes, had closely beset and attacked this fort From the 27th of July to the first instant, when they quitted it to march against us.*

*The boldness of those savages is hardly credible: they had taken posts under the banks of both rivers, close to the fort, where digging holes they kept an incessant fire and threw fire arrows. They are good marksmen, and though our people were under cover, they killed one, and wounded seven. Capt. Ecuyer is wounded in the leg by an arrow. I shall not do justice to that officer should I omit mentioning, that without an engineer, or any artificers than a few shipwrights, has raised a parapet of logs round the fort, above the old one (which, having not been finished, was too low and enfiladed) palisadoed the inside of the area, constructed a fire engine, and, in short, has taken all precautions, which art and judgment could suggest, for the preservation of his post, open before on the three sides, which had suffered by the floods. The inhabitants have acted with spirit against the enemy, and in the repairs of the fort. Captain Ecuyer expresses an entire satisfaction in their work.*

## The impact of the battle of Bushy Run

The 1847 book "**Early History of Western Pennsylvania**" describes the impact of the battle of Bushy Run as follows:

*This terminated the successful campaign of 1763. The signal victory gained over the Indians by Col. Bouquet, at Brush Creek, had so dismayed them, that they not only gave up all designs against Fort Pitt, but withdrew from the frontiers, retreating far beyond the Ohio, and abandoning all the country between Presque Isle and Sandusky; not thinking themselves safe till they arrived at Muskingum.*

Bouquet would eventually follow the Indians to Muskingum in 1764, and there intimidate them into returning their captives, and agreeing to peace.

## George Washington takes a sarcastic swipe at Adam Stephen

George Washington wrote a letter to Robert Stewart on August 13, 1763 that contains the following:

*Another tempest has arose upon our Frontiers, and the alarm spread wider than ever; in short the Inhabitants are so apprehensive of danger that no Families stands above the Conogocheage road and many are gone of below it — their Harvests are in a manner lost, and the distresses of the Settlement appear too evident and manifold to need description: In Augusta many People have been killed and numbers fled, and confusion and despair prevails in every Quarter — At this Instant a calm is taking place which forebodes some mischief to Coll⁰· Bouquet at least those who wish well to the Convoy are apprehensive for him since it is not unlikely that the retreat of all the Indian Parties at one and the same time from our Frontiers is a probable proof of their Assembling a force somewhere, & for some particular purpose; none more likely than to oppose his March.*

*It was expected that our Assembly woud have been called in such exegencies as these but its concluded (as I have been informed) that an Assembly without Money coud be no eligable plan — to comprehend the meaning of this expression, you must know, the Board of Trade at the Instance of the British Merchants have undertaken to rebuke us in the most ample manner for our Paper Emissions — and therefore the Governor and Council hath directed 1000 Militia to be employed for the protection of the Frontiers 500 of which to be Drafted from Hampshire &ca — and be under the Command of Coll⁰· Stephen whose Military Courage and Capacity (says the Governor) is well established — The other 500 from the Southern Frontiers Counties are to be conducted by Major Lewis so that you may readily conceive what an enormous expence must attend these Measures. Stephens immediately upon the Indians retiring, advanced to Fort Cumberland with 200 or 250 Militia in great parade and will doubtless achieve some signal advantage of which the Publick will soon be informed.*

*I think I have now communicated the only News which these parts afford — it is of a melancholy nature indeed and yet we cannot tell how, or when it is to end...*

## Captain Ourry reaches Fort Cumberland with 400 men

A letter[1390] General Amherst sent to Colonel Bouquet from New York on August 25, 1763 includes the statement:

*The Infatuated Obstinacy of the People in Power of the Province of Pensylvania Renders any further Application from me unnecessary, as they have not Paid the least regard to the Pressing Instances, I have from time to time, Urged to the Governor, for exerting themselves like Men, in the Defence of the Lives*

---

[1390] "**The papers of Col. Henry Bouquet**", 1940.

*& Properties of the Back Settlers; But I have a very Different Account from Virginia; for the L<sup>t.</sup> Governor, Immediately on the Receipt of my Letter, Desiring him to Concert the properest Methods for the Protection of that Colony, by Virtue of the Militia Law, which happily Subsists there, gave orders for Assembling One Thousand Men, in two Bodys, of 500 Each, giving the Command to Colonel Stephen and Colonel Lewis; The Former, I find by a Letter from Captain Ourry of the 17<sup>th</sup> Instant, and which came to hand with yours, has Reached Fort Cumberland, with about 400 men; And that he had on his March thither, by a Detachment Routed a Party of Indians; Killed and Scalped one; Wounded Several; & Recovered two Prisoners and three Scalps: A Spirit-like this, will soon Intimidate the Villains.*

## Colonel Stephen has militia at Fort Cumberland and Fort Bedford

An August 27, 1763 letter[1391] Sir Jeffery Amherst wrote to Sir William Johnson from New York includes the following statement:

*Some random shots were fired on the army between Bushy Run and Fort Pitt; but this seasonable check I believe will put an effectual stop to any further mischief being done on that communication; particularly as Colonel Stephen with a body of 4 or 500 men of the Virginia Militia is advanced as far as Forts Cumberland and Bedford, with a view not only of covering the frontiers, but of acting offensively against the Savages. This publick spirited Colony has also sent a body of the like number of men under the command of Colonel Lewis for the defence and protection of their South West frontiers. What a contrast this makes between the conduct of the Pennsylvanians and Virginians, highly to the honor of the latter, but places the former in the most despicable light imaginable.*

## An August 29, 1763 letter mentions the battle of Bushy Run

In an August 29, 1763 letter written from New York to Lieutenant Governor Fauquier, General Jeffery Amherst mentions the battle of Bushy Run as follows:

*I enclose you a copy of a Letter which I Writ to Colonel Stephen, on hearing of his arrival at Fort Cumberland; and since then Captain Bassett, who brought me the agreeable Accounts of Colonel Bouquets' having totally Routed the Body of Indians who had attacked his Little Army near Bushy Run (the Particulars of which you will certainly hear, before this can Reach you) Acquaints me that Col. Stephen was at Fort Bedford when he came past that Place.*

*As a severe Punishment of the Savages at this time will be the most effectual security to the Back Inhabitants for the future; I should be glad the Virginia Volunteers were employed in Destroying the Shawanese Settlements, which I imagine might be easily effected and altho' I have work enough alredy for the small number of Regulars at Fort Pitt, yet I would Try to spare some form thence to Joyn the Virginians in offensive operations against the Shawanese Towns, on the Banks of the Ohio. I shall write to Colonel Bouquet on this subject, and if Colonel Stephen can get men for that service, I should hope it might be executed with success. ...*

A transcript of this letter is published in the 1911 reprint of "**Michigan Historical Collections**", Volume 19. A footnote to the letter in that book states, *"On Amherst's call for troops, Virginia raised 1,000 volunteers and placed them under Cols. Adam, Stephen and Lewis."*

---

[1391] "**Documents relative to the colonial history of the state of New York**", 1856.

## Colonel Stephen reaches Fort Cumberland with volunteers from Virginia

An August 31, 1763 letter[1392] Sir Jeffery Amherst wrote to Bouquet from New York includes the following:

*I Have already Ordered the Agents to forward whatever Supplys Captain Ourry might Demand for the Troops under your Command, without waiting for Orders from You: And as I Learnt by a Letter from Captain Ourry that Colonel Stephen had Reached Fort Cumberland with a Large Body of Virginia Volunteers, I Immediately Wrote to the Colonel, Desiring he might upon this Occasion, Employ his men, on the Communication, for Escorting Provisions &ca to Fort Pitt, that you might be the better Enabled to Execute my Orders for Punishing the Savages...*

## A scouting party engages a party of Indians about 25 miles from Fort Cumberland

The September 1, 1763 issue of "**The Pennsylvania Gazette**" states:

*...From Fort Bedford we have Advice, that a scouting Party of Colonel Stevens Voluntiers on the Virginia Frontier, towards Winchester, lately fell in with a Party of Indians on Potowmack, about 25 Miles from Fort Cumberland, and routed them, killing and scalping One, wounding several, and recovering two Prisoners, and three Scalps, taken four Days before; they took from the Enemy four Rifles, and many Horses as were reckoned worth One Hundred Pounds, and a great Deal of other Plunder; and all without having a Man killed or wounded...*

## Fort Cumberland can have fresh meat

A September 11, 1763 letter[1393] Bouquet wrote to William Plumstead and David Franks from Fort Pitt includes the following statement, which begins with a sentence about salt:

*Forty Bushels more will Serve Ligonier and the same Quantity for Bedford, and Cumberland, but the two last Posts can have fresh Meat, and will take Care of themselves.*

*The Garrisons of those Posts are not fixed yet, and may be supposed including Passengers to amount to fifty Rations per Day during these Disturbances.*

## Investigating the issuance of provisions to refugees at Fort Cumberland in September 1763

A September 12, 1763 letter[1394] General Amherst wrote to Bouquet from New York states:

*Mr Leake having Represented to me that Mr Reade his Deputy in the Southern District, has Acquainted him, that he has Lately Received a great many Certificates, for Provisions Issued at Fort Cumberland, & the Communication in that Neighborhood, to Provincials & Inhabitants: the Certificates Signed by Fort Major Livingston; I Have Told Mr Leake to Write to his Deputy that he is to be guided by the Directions he may Receive from you, in regard to Allowing the said Certificates; The Inhabitants who were in real want, and could not have Subsisted without being Supplyed, when they Left their Settlements on the Alarm of the Indians; and Such of the Virginia Volunteers as were, or may be Employed, in Acting Offensively, in Conjunction with the King's Troops against the Savages, are the only Persons that I would Allow Provisions to for it must not be thought that every Inhabitant that runs to the Posts for Shelter is to receive*

---

[1392] "**The papers of Col. Henry Bouquet**", 1940.
[1393] "**The papers of Col. Henry Bouquet**", 1940.
[1394] "**The papers of Col. Henry Bouquet**", 1940.

*Provisions from the Crown: There would be no End to that; you will therefore be pleased to give Mʳ Reede your Orders accordingly.*

### The Royal Americans at Fort Cumberland are to go to Fort Pitt

A September 15, 1763 letter[1395] Bouquet wrote to Major Allan Campbell from Fort Pitt includes the statement, *"All the Royal Americans including those at Fort Cumberland are to Return here with your Detachment."*

### Instructions concerning the feeding of refugees in September 1763

A September 30, 1763 letter[1396] Bouquet wrote to Fort Major Livingston from Fort Pitt states:

*Having been informed when I was last at Fort Bedford, that there was a Considerable Number of Inhabitants who having taken Shelter at Fort Cumberland were then Victualed at the Kings Expence, I desired Captain Ourry to Write to you from me, to put a Stop to it, and I specified the Persons who were for the future to receive the Kings Allowance of Provisions: I hope those Orders have been Complyed with, and that the Complaints which have Occasioned the enclosed Letter from the General to me, have in View Certificates of a Prior Date, You will please to explain it to me and hereafter Conform yourself Exactly to the Present Orders from Sir Jeffery Amherst.*

This, and the September 12 letter above, show that local inhabitants were taking refuge at Fort Cumberland. A related letter,[1397] written to General Jeffery Amherst by Colonel Henry Bouquet from Fort Pitt on September 30, 1763, includes the following statement:

*I write to Mr. Read how he is to act in regard to the certification transmitted to him from Fort Cumberland. I had set orders from Carlisle to Captain Ourray to allow no Provisions (past the first moment of alarm) but to such persons as could be of service for the defense of the Post, and from Bedford I put the same stop to the Provisions at Fort Cumberland. Mr. Read will inform me from the Dates of the certificates, whether those orders have been observed, and he will receive directions accordingly.*

### The administrator of Welder's estate is summoned

On October 4, 1763, a summons was issued by the Frederick County, Virginia court that required the appearance of the administrator of Samuel Stansby Welder's estate, Robert Adams.[1398] The subject was a debt of slightly over £36 that was owed to John Carlyle and documented in an August 9, 1759 promissory note.

### The Royal Proclamation on North America, October 7, 1763

The following is an extract of the portions of the British Proclamation of 1763 that deal with settlement on Indian lands in the area of interest covered by this book:

*Whereas we have taken into our royal consideration the extensive and valuable acquisitions in America secured to our Crown by the late definitive treaty of peace concluded at Paris on the 10th day of February last; and being desirous that all our loving subjects, as well of our kingdom as of our colonies in America,*

---

[1395] "**The papers of Col. Henry Bouquet**", 1940.

[1396] "**The papers of Col. Henry Bouquet**", 1940.

[1397] "**Michigan Historical Collections**", Volume 19, 1911 reprint of 1892 book.

[1398] "**Colonial Records of the Upper Potomac**", Volume 6.

*may avail themselves, with all convenient speed, of the great benefits and advantages which must accrue therefrom to their commerce, manufactures, and navigation...*

*And whereas it is just and reasonable, and essential to our interest and the security of our colonies, that the several nations or tribes of Indians with whom we are connected, and who live under our protection, should not be molested or disturbed in the possession of such parts of our dominions and territories as, not having been ceded to or purchased by us, are reserved to them, or any of them, as their hunting-grounds; we do therefore, with the advice of our Privy Council, declare it to be our royal will and pleasure, that no Governor or commander in chief, in any of our colonies of Quebec, East Florida, or West Florida, do presume, upon any pretence whatever, to grant warrants of survey, or pass any patents for lands beyond the bounds of their respective governments, as described in their commissions; as also that no Governor or commander in chief of our other colonies or plantations in America do presume for the present, and until our further pleasure be known, to grant warrants of survey or pass patents for any lands beyond the heads or sources of any of the rivers which fall into the Atlantic Ocean from the west or northwest; or upon any lands whatever, which, not having been ceded to or purchased by us, as aforesaid, are reserved to the said Indians, or any of them. ...*

*And whereas great frauds and abuses have been committed in the purchasing lands of the Indians, to the great prejudice of our interests, and to the great dissatisfaction of the said Indians; in order, therefore, to prevent such irregularities for the future, and to the end that the Indians may be convinced of our justice and determined resolution to remove all reasonable cause of discontent, we do, with the advice of our Privy Council, strictly enjoin and require, that no private person do presume to make any purchase from the said Indians of any lands reserved to the said Indians within those parts of our colonies where we have thought proper to allow settlement; but that if at any time any of the said Indians should be inclined to dispose of the said lands, the same shall be purchased only for us, in our name, at some public meeting or assembly of the said Indians, to be held for that purpose by the Governor or commander in chief of our colony respectively within which they shall lie: and in case they shall lie within the limits of any proprietary government, they shall be purchased only for the use and in the name of such proprietaries, conformable to such directions and instructions as we or they shall think proper to give for that purpose. And we do, by the advice of our Privy Council, declare and enjoin, that the trade with the said Indians shall be free and open to all our subjects whatever, provided that every person who may incline to trade with the said Indians do take out a license for carrying on such trade, from the Governor or commander in chief of any of our colonies respectively where such person shall reside, and also give security to observe such regulations as we shall at any time think fit, by ourselves or commissaries to be appointed for this purpose, to direct and appoint for the benefit of the said trade. And we do hereby authorize, enjoin, and require the Governors and commanders in chief of all our colonies respectively, as well those under our immediate government as those under the government and direction of proprietaries, to grant such licenses without fee or reward, taking especial care to insert therein a condition that such license shall be void, and the security forfeited, in case the person to whom the same is granted shall refuse or neglect to observe such regulations as we shall think proper to prescribe as aforesaid. ...*

*Given at our Court at St. James's, the 7th day of October 1763, in the third year of our reign.*

## Feeding refugees at Fort Cumberland

A synopsis[1399] of an October 9, 1763 letter Major Livingston wrote to Bouquet from Cumberland states, *"To whom he supplied provisions in accordance with instructions, in addition to what were given to poor*

---

[1399] **"Sessional Papers of the Dominion of Canada"**, Volume 23, 1890.

*people who would otherwise have perished, but none received provisions who could subsist themselves. His garrison is now reduced to twenty-one persons."*

### Men from Fort Cumberland reach Fort Bedford in October 1763

A synopsis of an October 10, 1763 letter written from Bedford to Bouquet by Captain Ralph Phillips includes the following, *"McKinley arrived this morning with his party from Fort Cumberland."*

### All is quiet from Philadelphia to Fort Pitt on October 10, 1763

The November 8-10, 1763 edition of the "**The London Chronicle**" contains the following extract of an October 10, 1763 newspaper account:

*New-York, Oct. 10 By the Philadelphia Post we have the pleasure to learn, that all is quiet on the communication between that Place and Fort Pit.*

### A Maryland act for prohibiting trade with the Indians

The minutes from an October 24, 1763 meeting of the lower house state:

*Col.° Tilghman brings in and delivers to Mr Speaker the Bill Ent.ᵈ An Act for prohibiting all trade with the Indians for the time therein mentioned with the Amendments made thereto proposed by the Upper house which was read Agreed to and passed for Ingrossing.*

The bill *"An Act for prohibiting all Trade with the Indians, for the Time therein mentioned"* was passed on November 21, 1763.[1400]

### The Royal Americans at Fort Cumberland in October 1763

An October 24, 1763 letter[1401] written from Fort Pitt by Colonel Henry Bouquet to General Jeffery Amherst mentions companies at Fort Pitt, Ligonier, and Bedford, and then states:

*The Royal Americans at Fort Cumberland and the rest to the Settlements that Corps having been six years in the Woods, and their spirit so much cast down, I would hope that a little rest would recruit them, and make them more fit for service in the Spring. If they are kept here another winter, I foresee a great Desertion and the rest discouraged will be good for nothing.*

### A substantial quantity of small arms was removed in the circa 1763-time frame

In the "**Proceedings and Acts of the General Assembly, 1762-1763**" the October 27, 1763 minutes of the Maryland General Assembly include the following statement regarding arms in the Annapolis armory:

*Your Committee find that Since the last Report of the State of the Arms, and Amunition there have been received by the Armourer into the Magazine from Fort Frederick & Fort Cumberland three hundred Muskets one hundred Gun & Carbine & Carbine Barrels two hundred Bayonets said to be much eaten with rust when they were received into the Magazine but your Committee apprehend they may have gathered much more Rust since they were received as they are deposited in the Cellar below the Conference Chamber which is very Damp and we imagine a very unfit place for fire Arms to be kept in*

---

[1400] "**Laws of Maryland at large with proper indexes…**"
[1401] "**Michigan Historical Collections**", Volume 19, 1911 reprint of 1892 book.

*which unless soon removed and cleaned will be eat out with rust, also Received from said Forts, Two hundred and fifty Cartouch Boxes much rat eaten and fifty Bullet Molds very Rusty.*

### Colonel Stephen offers to send flour to Fort Cumberland in November of 1763

A synopsis of a November 7, 1763 letter from Winchester includes the following, "*Col. Adam Stephen to Bouquet. ... Offers the product of his farm delivered at Cumberland or Bedford on equal terms with other people.*"

### Joseph Mounts becomes constable of the Cumberland Hundred

On November 15, 1763, Joseph Mounts was appointed[1402] to serve as the constable for the Cumberland Hundred by the Frederick County, Maryland court, and James Crabtree was appointed to serve as the constable for the Old Town Hundred. It seems reasonable to interpret the formation of the Cumberland Hundred as indicative of the increasing population near Fort Cumberland.

### A reward is granted for the scalps of Indians killed at Cresaps and Georges Creek

In a session of the Maryland Assembly, the following legislation, titled, "*An ACT for giving a Bounty for taking Indian Prisoners; and other Purposes therein mentioned.*" was passed on November 21, 1763:

*Whereas the Commissioners or Trustees for Emitting Bills of Credit have still remaining in their Hands the sum of Two Thousand one hundred and twenty Pounds of the several sums of Money Appropriated to the payment for Indian Prisoners or Scalps by Virtue of an Act entituled an Act for his Majestys Service and further Security and Defence of the Province, And Whereas Daniel Cresap Michael Cresap, John Walker[1403] Nathan Friggs William Young Abraham Richardson and Ezekiel Johnson by their humble Petition have represented to this General Assembly that some time in the Month of July last a party of Indians Came to Col.º Thomas Cresaps of Frederick County in a War like Manner to Attack the said House and family where the Petitioners then were and that upon their being discovered the Petitioners met them in the Field about an hundred Yards from the House, on which an Engagement begun and the Petitioners were so fortunate as to rout the Indians, kill one on the Spot (whose Scalp they presented with the said Petition) wound several others and take some of their Arms, and prayed a reward for the same Scalp and whereas also James Davis of the Colony of Virginia by his humble Petition hath represented to this General Assembly, That in the Month of August last the Petitioner and twenty eight Others who lived on Potomack being informed that a party of Indians had made an Incursion and carried away a certain James Ciniston and his Wife who lived at Cape Capon on the South side of Potomack, Armed themselves and went in Pursuit of the said Indians who were ten in Number that on the Eleventh day of the same Month they came up with them at a place Called Georges Creek within this Province and released the said Prisoners and in an Engagement which ensued the Petitioner Shot one of the Indians through the Body and Afterwards took of the said Indians Scalp and prayed a reward for the same, All which facts contained in the said Petition do Appear to this General Assembly by proper legal Affidavits to be true,*

*Be it therefore Enacted by the Right Honourable the Lord Proprietary by and with the Advice and Consent of his Lordships Governor and the Upper and Lower Houses of Assembly and the Authority of the same*

---

[1402] "**Colonial Records of the Upper Potomac**", Volume 6.

[1403] In his 1833 book, "**History of the Valley of Virginia**", Samuel Kercheval states, "*At a battle at Oldtown, John Walker killed an Indian and wounded another. Walker cut out a part of the dead Indian's flesh from the thick part of his thigh, and threw it to his dog, who ate it. He otherwise mutilated his body, and thrust parts of it into his mouth.*"

*that the said Commissioners or Trustees for emitting Bills of Credit shall and may and are hereby Ordered and Directed to pay unto the said Daniel Cresap, Michael Cresap, John Walker Nathan Friggs, William Young Abraham Richardson and Ezekiel Johnson the sum of fifty Pounds out of the said sum of two Thousand one hundred and twenty pounds as aforesaid remaining in their Hands and to the said James Davis the sum of fifty Pounds out of the same sum of Two thousand one hundred and twenty Pounds as rewards for the said Scalps so by them Respectively taken,*

*And Whereas it will greatly tend to the Security of the Frontier Inhabitants amidst the present Indian Disturbances and Incursions to Appropriate the residue of the said sum of two thousand one hundred and twenty Pounds to the taking of Indian Prisoners and Scalps, Be it further enacted that the residue of the said sum of Money in the Hands of the said Commissioners or Trustees after the payment of the said rewards hereby given for the Scalps aforesaid shall be Applied to the payment for Indian Prisoners or Scalps in manner herein after mentioned, That is to say for every Scalp of an Indian Enemy (being the skin of the Crown of the Head) and for every live Indian Enemy, which any Inhabitant of the Province, not being in the pay of this Province as a Soldier, or Indian in Friendship and Alliance with his Majestys Subjects shall produce to any Magistrate of this Province and for every such Scalp taken from any Indian Enemy killed within this Province and every Indian Enemy taken a live within the same by any Person who shall be a resident of any other Province and shall be Produced to a Magistrate as af'd such Magistrate (after Burning or destroying such Scalp shall immediately give such Person or Indian Friend a Certificate under his Hand, which Certificate being produced to the said Commissioners or Trustees such Commissioners or Trustees shall immediately pay to the Person producing the same the sum of fifty Pounds Current Money and the receipt of such Person or Indian on such Certificate shall for such sum be a sufficient Voucher for the said Commissioners or Trustees their Payment of the said sum, And whenever any Person or ffriend Indian shall produce any such Indian Enemy to any Magistrate such Magistrate shall by such Person or Friend Indian with Assistance of such other Person or Persons as by Warrant under his Hand he shall Order and direct, and such Indian Enemy to the Sheriff of the respective County who shall receive into his Goal, and safe keep such Indian Enemy at the Public expence of this Province till legally discharged, Provided always and be it Enacted, That every Person other than an Inhabitant of this Province or Friend Indian who shall produce a Scalp or Indian Prisoner to any Magistrate shall before he receives a Certificate for the same make Oath before the said Magistrate, or give such other Evidence as shall satisfy such Magistrate, that such Indian Prisoner was taken or such Scalp taken from off an Indian Enemy killed within this Province And that every Inhabitant of this Province who shall Produce a Scalp or Indian Prisoner as aforesaid before he shall receive a Certificate as aforesaid shall make Appear as aforesaid that such Scalp was by him taken from off an Enemy Indian slayn by him or by some other Person under whom or in Company with whom he has a right to claim the reward aforesaid or that such Indian Prisoner was Captured by him or by some other Person such as aforesaid*

*And Whereas there is now remaining in the Hands of the Agents for carrying into Execution the said recited Act and another Act of Assembly entituled an act for granting a Supply of Forty thousand Pounds for his Majestys Service and Striking thirty four thousand fifteen Pounds six shillings thereof in Bills of Credit and raising a fund for sinking the same, a small Ballance unapplied; Be it enacted by the Authority advice and Consent aforesaid that the said Agents shall and may and are hereby directed to pay into the Hands of the said Commissioners or Trustees all such sum or sums of Money as they have received in Virtue of the said recited Acts and is or are now in their Hands unapplied which said Ballance is hereby Appropriated to the Payment for Indian Prisoners and Scalps in manner aforesaid.*

## Writing to Innis at Fort Cumberland about hogs for Fort Pitt

A December 3, 1763 letter Ourry wrote to Bouquet from Fort Bedford states that Ourry has instructed the Commissary at Fort Bedford to correspond with Mr. Innis of Fort Cumberland to inquire about the price Mr. Innis would charge to deliver hogs to Fort Pitt. This appears to be a reference to Enoch Innis.

## Enoch Innis witnesses a deed

On December 13, 1763, Enoch Innis witnessed the deed for John Hopkins' sale of South Branch Lot No. 64 to Marylander Thomas Cresap.[1404] Job Pearsall served in the capacity of attorney for Hopkins, who was living in North Carolina at the time of the sale. Lot No. 64 was located on the east side of the mouth of the South Branch of the Potomac River, approximately at Latitude 39.52217°, Longitude -78.58192°.

## Lemuell Barrett is called to court over the estate of Samuel Welder

Lemuell Barrett was called to appear before the Frederick County, Maryland court in December of 1763 to answer Michael Cresap in a matter relating to the estate of Samuel Stansby Welder.[1405] Michael Cresap was the administrator of the estate.

---

[1404] "**Colonial Records of the Upper Potomac**", Volume 3.
[1405] "**Colonial Records of the Upper Potomac**", Volume 6.

# 16. 1764: Bouquet prevails at Muskingum

### A traders' lawsuit

A section titled, *"Imparlances to June Court Anno Domini 1764"* in the Maryland book "**Frederick County Four Docquets For 1764**" includes a record no. 31 dated January 27 that must be fascinating. It is a case of *"Evan Shelby Sam<sup>l</sup> Postlethwait and Edm<sup>d</sup> Moran"* versus John Williams, and references *"Nich<sup>l</sup> Philips & Adam Furrie Bail"*. Samuel Postlethwaite and Edmund Moran were traders who visited Fort Cumberland, and a Samuel Postlewait appears in Deakins' list of settlers westward of Fort Cumberland.

### Vachel Hinton is involved in a lawsuit

A section titled, *"Original writs to March Court 1764"* in the Maryland book "**Frederick County Four Docquets For 1764**" contains a record no. 300 dated February 26 for the case of Tho<sup>s</sup> Beatty versus Vachel Hinton. A Vachel Hinton later appears in the 1783 Cumberland hundreds list.

### A land transaction on Patterson Creek

The 1939 book "**Early Records Hampshire County Virginia**" records the following for March 19, 1764, *"ICE, Frederick of Hampshire Co. to Robert Gregg of Hampshire Co. (lease and release) 100 a. on Patterson Creek; rec. 8-14-1765. Wit.: Wm. Dopson, John Forman, Humphrey Wastell, David Gregg."*

### Richard Morris is appointed constable of the Old Town Hundred

Richard Morris was appointed by the Frederick County, Maryland court to be the constable for the Old Town Hundred on March 20, 1764, replacing James Crabtree, who had left Maryland.[1406] This implies that Morris recovered from the wound received at Cresap's on July 14, 1763. A Richard Morris is on the 1761 Old Town Hundred list.

### Thomas Cresap is involved in two lawsuits, one related to trespass

A section titled, *"Continuance Docquet Anno 1764"* in the Maryland book "**Frederick County Four Docquets For 1764**" contains a record no. 7 dated March 22 for the case of Thomas Cresap versus John Jones, and contains a record no. 8 of the same date for the case of Thomas Cresap versus Joseph Williams relating to trespass. A John Jones later shows up in Deakins' list of settlers west of Fort Cumberland.

### People living on the Cumberland road

A March 24, 1764 letter Ourry wrote to Bouquet from Fort Bedford indicates that he was planning to warn people living on the Cumberland road about Indian depredations.

### Nathan Wells and John Nicholas are involved in court cases

A section titled, *"Original Writs to June Court 1764"* in the Maryland book "**Frederick County Four Docquets For 1764**" includes record no. 100 dated March 26 for the case of Tho<sup>s</sup> Beatty & Comp<sup>y</sup> versus

---

[1406] "**Colonial Records of the Upper Potomac**", Volume 6.

Nathan Wells. It was one of many lawsuits brought by Beatty that day. A section titled, *"Original writs to March Court 1764"* in the same book contains a record no. 379 dated February 16 for the *"James Dickson Case"* versus John Nicholas and contains a record no. 385 dated February for the *"James Dickson Case"* versus Nathan Wells. An individual named Nathan Wells witnessed an April 3, 1751 will of Hugh Parker. A section titled, *"Recognizances to August Court 1764"* includes an £10 bond of John Nicholas.

### Michael Cresap is serving as the administrator for the estate of Samuel Stansby Weldor

A section titled, *"Original Writs to June Court 1764"* in the Maryland book **"Frederick County Four Docquets For 1764"** includes several records of the lawsuits of *"Michael Cresap Adm$^r$ Sam$^l$ Weldor"* dated March 26, including record no. 111 against James Gregson, record no. 112 against James Kelly, record no. 113 against Lemuel Barrett, and record no. 114 against Casper Everly.

A section titled, *"Original writs to March Court 1764"* in the same book contains a record no. 59 dated December 24 for the case of *"Mich$^l$ Cresap Adm$^r$ of S S Weldor"* versus Lemuel Barrett, and also contains a record no. 60 of the same date for the same administrator versus Casper Everly. This section also has January 27 records for the same administrator, including record no. 173 for a suit against James Gregson, record no. 174 for a suit against James Spencer, and record no. 175 for a suit against James Kelly

### Flour sent to the troops is refused

A synopsis[1407] of an April 16, 1764 letter from Fort Cumberland states, *"Col. Stephen to Bouquet. Complains that the flour he sent for the troops had been refused."* The letter[1408] states:

> I am extreamly concerned that my endeavours to serve you by exerting my self at the risk of my fortune, & Credit in the Government of Virginia, in order to fullfil your intentions in forwarding the Kings Service, should produce no Other Effect, than the greatest & only Injury you could do me; I mean the Refusal of my floor to be deliverd at Bedford and that, on the very day after the Expiration of the term in the Agreement

> A Quantity of it has been carried for the Use of the Militia employd on Patterson Creek; the remainder about 26,000 lb lies in a hundred dollars worth of good Baggs at this place, if you can give directions about it, I will endeavor to Return the favour.

> The Flour is of good Quality, as any designed for the West India Market, A the bags of New Sacking.

> Your Sentiments on this heed will determine whether I shall be Obliged to Wait on the Gen$^l$ about the affair

> Several Parties of Indians are down in Hampshire, but I have a Number of Chosen Rifflemen on the hunt after them.

### Reserving 10,000 acres for the Lord Proprietary

Governor Sharpe issued the following instructions[1409] to the judges of the land office on April 16, 1764:[1410]

---

[1407] The synopses of correspondence in this chapter are from Volume 23 of the **"Sessional Papers…"**

[1408] **"The Papers of Henry Bouquet"**, Series 21650, Part I, 1942.

[1409] **"Kilty's Land-Holder's Assistant, and Land-Office Guide"**.

[1410] Volume 32 of the **"Archives of Maryland"** gives the date as April 10, 1764.

*GENTLEMEN,*

*The lord proprietary being desirous to have 10,000 acres of land reserved in the western part of Frederick county for a manor, I have given the surveyor of that county instructions to execute no warrants whatever on the lands lying beyond Fort Cumberland till the above quantity is surveyed and laid out for his lordship; of which you will be pleased to take notice and cause the same to be communicated to any person that may apply for warrants that may affect land in that part of the province.*

*I am, Gentlemen,*

*Your h'ble servant,*

*Horo. Sharpe.*

## Do not feed the militia coming to Fort Cumberland unless they have an order for it

An April 28, 1764 memorandum[1411] Bouquet wrote includes the statement:

*Regulate the Charges of Provisions & Contingencies at Fort Cumberland, after I receive the answers of the southern Governments; The Militia coming there not to be victualed at the king's Expence unless they have an order for it.*

## Closing the accounts from the last campaign

A May 21, 1764 letter[1412] Gage wrote to Bouquet from New York includes the following statement:

*Colonel Reid has given me a Copy of the Acc$^{ts}$ made out at Carlisle, and I hope those agreed upon to have been just and equitable Demands, by all Parties, have been acquitted. I observe one Article is left open to the first of June, and another for Acc$^{ts}$ uncollected at Forts-Pitt & Cumberland, which it's supposed can't amount to less than £1000 is left to no determined Time. I must beg the Favor of you to get all this finaly closed, for it is Time to Settle every thing with Mess$^{rs}$ Plumsted and Franks, with whom I will finish every thing at once, and leave nothing open; or allow any Article of the last Campain to come into the Expences of this. The Pay-Master General has often represented to me that the Transactions with those Gentlemen have been left in a loose Way, for too long a Time, and is very uneasy to have his Warrant for the whole Disbursement, which I can not have made out, till every thing is finaly closed.*

## A larger garrison is requested for Fort Cumberland in June of 1764

A June 5, 1764 letter[1413] Major James Livingston wrote to Bouquet from Fort Cumberland states:

*I wrote you the 23$^d$ of May acquainting you with the State of this Garrison. Coll$^o$ Stephen has been Obliged to Call his men away by Order of the Govourner therefore am at present Quite Distituts of men only 1 Corp$^l$ & 6 which I prevailed on Cap$^t$ M$^c$Donald to Leave with me till I coud get a Relief if within a Short time but Expect them now Every day to be Calld away as there has been so much mischief done on the Frontiers of Virginia within this few Days an Account of which is that on the 26th Ult. a Large Body of Indians fell on a party of white people working in a Field near Fort Dinwiddie in Augusta County Virginia*

---

[1411] **"The papers of Col. Henry Bouquet"**, 1940.
[1412] **"The Critical Period 1763-1765"**, 1915.
[1413] **"The papers of Col. Henry Bouquet"**, 1942.

*Killd 15 & wounded & took 16 more they Immediately Attackd the Fort & Fired 6 hours Successively on it but Coud not prevail*

*I have this day Received an Express from. Coll⁰ Stephen who Informes me that on the 4th Insᵗ Capt Nimrod Ashby & a man of the Viriginia Voluntiers was taken prisoners on the South Branch of Potomack the same day a Negro Fillow belonging to one Linch was taken as he was driving a Wagon the Horses was Killd & the Wagon Broke to pieces allso at the same time a man his wife & Child was taken away from Ceedir Crick within 10 mile of Winchester & it is Supposed by the Great Number of Tracts that are Discovourd that there must be Three or four Large Bodys of the Enemy now down About us, as there is So great sn Appearance of a hott Campain in this Quarter Imagine as Large a Garrison as can be well sparrd woud be Necessary as the Inhabitants are Chiefly gon or going Unless there is Some protection for them.*

The historic marker for Fort Dinwiddie is located about four miles west of Warm Springs, Virginia, which is 143 miles south-southwest of Cumberland.


## Joseph Tomlinson is involved in a court matter

A section titled, *"Original Writs to June Court 1764"* in the Maryland book **"Frederick County Four Docquets For 1764"** includes record no. 459 dated June 8 for the case of Joseph Tomlinson versus Jacob Miller.


## Inhabitants are prohibited from receiving provisions at Fort Cumberland in June of 1764

A June 11, 1764 letter[1414] Bouquet sent to Major James Livingston from Philadelphia includes the following:

*I have ordered a detachment of Twenty Men to Garrison Fort Cumberland, and when they arrive you are not to issue any more provisions to any body Else. If the Inhabitants will not, or can not Subsist themselves, it is not in my power to victual them.*

*In every other respect you will, receive them in the Fort, & give them all the assistance & Protection in Your Power.*

*The Provincials this way are getting ready as fast as it is possible and I shall advance them immediately to draw the Attention of the Enemy from our unfortunate Inhabitants. You will send me Regularly Every Month dated the 24ᵗʰ Returns of the Garrison Provisions, Stores & Issuings at your Post. You know that no Provisions are allowed to Women or Children, on any Account whatever & that an Officer is only intitled to one Ration*


## Fort Cumberland is garrisoned

A synopsis of a June 12, 1764 letter Bouquet wrote to General Gage includes the statement *"Murders by Indians. Fort Cumberland garrisoned."*

A June 17, 1764 letter[1415] Captain Schlosser wrote to Bouquet from a *"Camp near Fort Loudoun"* includes the following:

---

[1414] **"The papers of Col. Henry Bouquet"**, 1942.
[1415] **"The papers of Col. Henry Bouquet"**, 1942.

*Lieutenant M<sup>c</sup>Intosh who by his ancienity hapens to be the first for Command in this Camp, has set off this Morning with One Serjeant Five Private of ouers, and One Corporal and 14 Private of the 42<sup>d</sup> to Garrison Fort Cumberland...*

## Bouquet proposes storing supplies at Fort Cumberland for a march to Fort Pitt

A June 18, 1764 letter[1416] Bouquet wrote to William Rutherford from Philadelphia states:

*Captain Callender hath-acquainted me, that in Your opinion a Number of Voluntiers from the Province of Virginia would willingly join the Troops under my Command, & serve without pay in an Expedition against the Indian Towns beyond the Ohio; if they could only obtain the King's Provisions during that time.*

*Desirous to encourage those Good dispositions I beg You would take an Oportunity to inform them that I accept Chearfully of their Services, and would be very glad to have them with me, and I will Supply with Amunition and Provision the Voluntiers who will join the King's Troops at Fort Pitt, on the 1<sup>st</sup> day of October next, The fall being the best Season to attack the Savages in their Towns. The first part of the Campaign will necessarily be taken up in forwarding the Provisions to Fort Pitt and preparing every thing to be ready to proceed the moment they join me at the time and Place above mentioned; they shall not be a Moment detained at our Return but will have entire Liberty to retire home.*

*The Deficulty & Expence of Carrying Provisions so far being very great I would not chuse to carry more than is wanted to serve our Troops.*

*Therefore it would be necessary that I should know as soon as possible what Number of Voluntiers I could be Certain of and the only way for those who have a Mind to assist in bringing this War to issue is to enter their Names in a Book, and You would send me the list, that I may be prepared accordingly, and lodge Provisions for them at Fort Cumberland from whence they might proceed by Braddock's Road to Fort Pitt so as to reach that Post at the precise Time appointed.*

*They will of Course appoint among themselves a proper Number of Officers to Command them, for the Preservation of Order and Regularity.*

*I shall think myself much obliged to You for Your good Offices on this Occasion; I wish a Number of the Voluntiers would serve on Horse Back and join our light Horse, who I hope will be Successfully employed in the pursuit of Indians when once routed, large Dogs likewise might be of Service to discover and pursue the Enemy.*

## Thomas Cresap asks where his volunteers should meet Bouquet

A June 18, 1764 letter[1417] Colonel Thomas Cresap wrote to Bouquet states:

*As I am informed that you are to march out with a considerable Number of Men against the Indian Towns, I beg the Favour of you to acquaint me by a Letter, when & where I shall meet you, for I believe I or my Son can join you with a Party of Volunteers provided I have timely Notice; if I cannot come in Person, I will endeavour to procure as many Men as in my Power lies to come & join you at the Time and Place appointed.*

---

[1416] "**The papers of Col. Henry Bouquet**", 1942.

[1417] "**The papers of Col. Henry Bouquet**", 1942.

## No provisions for troops arriving at Fort Cumberland

A June 23, 1764 letter[1418] Major John Field wrote to Bouquet from Fort Cumberland states:

*I was greatly Surprisd when I arriv'd at this garison after 13 Days and nights hard Duty ascouring the mountains and the Waters of Cheet and Maholangany Rivers Being Severall Days without Provisions Unless what we Cold kill in the woods when we cold Ventor to shoot, and had it not have Been for Majʳ Leviston shold have gone without I allways Understood that there was a sofisent quantity Laid in this garison to answer the Purpose of Scouring the woods By the Virginia Vollintears which is the only Protection the inhabitants of marylanders have. I have Been informᵈ by Leut Mᶜintush that you are joined By a 1000 of the Pensylvanians the Legislative Body in Virginia has not made any preparations to assist you with any men. But I may Vontor to say that you will Likely have a large assistance from this quarter of Brave Vollintears Cold we know the time you will march I shold Be glad to have a line from you as soon as possable of the Particulars Relating thereto. great numbers of murders have Been Committed on our Fruntears this spring when you are Ready to march you will Let me know Wherther you think it Proper to meet you at Bedford or to make a push along Bradocks Road to Pitt*

## Ordering Butchers, Salters, and Coopers to Fort Cumberland

In June 23, 1764 orders[1419] to contractors' agents in Philadelphia, Bouquet directed the agents to determine the flour and cattle needed to feed 450 people for the entire year of 1765, including 30 men at Fort Cumberland. The order goes on to state:

*...you will Send to Each of the Said Posts, Butchers, & Salters to Slaughter, Salt & pack the meat with Coopers to repair & make the number of Barrels wanted to hold the meat. You will Send to Fort Loudoun, Two Hundred Bushells of Salt more, to be distributed during the Campaign to the Troops, when they have Fresh meat, and as this article is not to be a Charge to the Crown; The Troops are to pay for it the first Cost & Carriage.*

## June 24, 1764 letters from Fort Cumberland

A June 24, 1764 letter[1420] Major James Livingston wrote to Bouquet from Fort Cumberland states:

*I had the Honʳ of yours dated the 11ᵗʰ with your Instructions about Provisions which have been punctualy obeyed by me this year only to 17: of Capᵗ MᶜDonalds Men that was Station'd here who Was Serv'd to the 28ᵗʰ Instant and is gone to Joyn their Compʸ on the arrival of Lieuᵗ MᶜIntosh of the R: A.*

*I have Sent you as an Exact a return as possibl I could for the Ball being put into Barrells Cannot Say how maney Boxes they will fill as to provisions I am afraid I have too much.*

*I was oblidgd to hang both pork & Beeff or Els Should Lost a great deal of it if not all I Lost Some and blames nothing but the New Casks for it as to Flower I let the Country people have what they Wanted at the price the Carrige and Flower Cost in order to get the bags Empty to return them as they Came Verrey high I fill'd 7 Hogsheads which I Imagine holds 7000 besids Some bags I had in Store belonging to the Garrison. Therefor in the whole I Conclude there is the Quanntety mentiond in the return the Meat I only Can Compute as its all hanging up I have plenty of Live Stock but the Garrison being So Small Cannot presume to kill any Cattle, as you will See by the State of the Garrison*

---

[1418] **"The papers of Col. Henry Bouquet"**, 1942.

[1419] **"The papers of Col. Henry Bouquet"**, 1940.

[1420] **"The papers of Col. Henry Bouquet"**, 1942.

*I had a Letter Inclosd to me from Cap^t Postlweight & Derected to him from Cap^t Ourry by your order about flints I never took any but 3000 of which 3000 remain in Store as you Will see by the return the rest was given to a Merch^t at this post to Sell by his order therefor have given him a receipt for the above quanntety which was never required of me befor*

*Maj^r Field left this yesterday when I Issued 200 weight of Flower & Bacon on the Same footing the Country people gets it untill I hear from you*

*Col Militia in augusta Virginia have kill'd 5 Savages the 13^th Ins^t on the fronteres of that County. We are verrey quit on this Qu^r which I hope will Continue...*

A June 24, 1764 letter[1421] Lieutenant George McIntosh wrote to Bouquet from Fort Cumberland states:

*By An Order from Captain Murray I left Fort Loudoun Camp, on the 17^th & on the 21^st Instant, arrived here With A Command of one Serjeant, one Corporal & 19 private men of the 42^d & 60^th Regiment^s and am Ordered to command here till further Orders, and not to permitt any provisions to be issued but to the Kings troopes and as Major Livingston tells me, that he with one Servant, & the Contractors Clark, draws provis^ns out of the Kings Store, Therefore you Will be pleased to let me know, if such Will be Allowed as I imagine its by my Voucher's that the King Will be Charged for the time that I may Comm^d here.*

*And as major Livingston tells me that you desired the Returns, & State of the Garisson from him, Shall refair to it as he Sends by this Occasion, He having Charge of all the Stor's.*

### William Teagard is involved in a Maryland court case
A section titled, *"Continuance Docquet Anno 1764"* in the Maryland book "**Frederick County Four Docquets For 1764**" contains a record no. 54 dated June 28 for the case of Fran^s Sanderson versus Will^m Tegard. A William Teagard occupied Lot No. 7 at the time of the Genn's November 1748 survey along Patterson Creek.

### A plan to store supplies at Fort Cumberland for an expedition against the Ohio Indians
The following letter,[1422] written from Philadelphia to Colonel Stephen by Colonel Bouquet on July 5, 1764, describes a plan to store supplies at Fort Cumberland for an expedition against Indian towns:

*Governor Fauquier having been pleased to acquaint me that you would assist me in the Expedition intended against the Indian Towns upon the Ohio, as far as your orders and the Law would permit. I beg leave to request that you would give Encouragement to good woodsmen on your Frontiers to Join as Volunteers the Troops under my command; it is not in my Power to give them any pay, and I can only supply them with Provisions and Ammunition during the campaign. It would be necessary that I could be informed as early as possible of the number I could depend upon in order to lodge Provisions and Ammunition at Fort Cumberland for them, that they may Join us at Fort Pitt by Braddock's Road, which will be the shortest way, and as I would not occasion them any unnecessary fatigue, they might Join me at Fort Pitt, about the 25^th September next, when I shall be ready to cross the River and march to the Enemy. We have the same Regular Troops we had last year, and one thousand men from this province. They grant besides a considerable Reward for Scalps, which do doubt will be a strong inducement to several woodsmen and hunters, to come with us. But I have so great an opinion of the courage and*

---

[1421] "**The papers of Col. Henry Bouquet**", 1942.
[1422] "**Michigan Historical Collections**", Volume 19, 1911 reprint of 1892 book.

*Experience of your Frontiers, that I would think myself certain of success could I be Joined by three or four hundred of them under proper officers of their own choice.*

*The fate of this war must depend in a great measure upon the success of this Campaign, as from the difficulty of obtaining hereafter Provincial Troops and the heavy Expense accruing to the Crown, it is easy to foresee that this will be the last Expedition this way. Therefore it is an opportunity not to be neglected by our Frontier People who are so much exposed to the Depredations of the Savages.*

*I shall be particularly obliged to you for your good offices and interest on this important occasion. Sent a duplicate of the above letter to Colonel Lewis.*

### A birth near Fort Cumberland in July of 1764

The military pension file of Thomas Mounts (S.17594) indicates that he was born on July 8, 1764 near Fort Cumberland, served under both his father Providence Mounts and his brother Caleb Mounts during the Revolutionary War, lived 27 years in Pennsylvania, 15 years in Kentucky, and then moved to Indiana. The June 12, 1932 issue of the "**Indianapolis Star**" mentions the July 8, 1764 birth of Thomas Mounts near Fort Cumberland, and various Revolutionary War services, beginning with enlistment at age 15. As described below, in 1779, Providence Mounts helped to build a military supply road that ran from Fort Cumberland to the environs of Hunker, Pennsylvania, where it merged with Braddock's road.

### Fred Dunfield is involved in a court case

A section titled, *"Continuance Docquet Anno 1764"* in the Maryland book "**Frederick County Four Docquets For 1764**" contains a record no. 68 dated July 22 for the case of Jos Volgamot versus Fred Dunfield.

### Tracks seen in the woods near Muddy Creek in July of 1764

A July 24, 1764 letter[1423] Major Mames Livingston wrote to Bouquet from Fort Cumberland states:

*I have here inclosed you the Return for this Month there is no News here more then that a few days ago a Small party of Scouts being Out from Virginia at a place Call'd Muddy Creek about 30 miles Above this place Discover'd a Number of Maukison Tracts & heard Several gunns fired in the woods About them they Immediately Returned & a Capt'n & 40 men went Off in Quest of the Enemy but have not yet Returned. We allso had Accot's this day that a party of Indians were a day or two ago Seen at Fort George[1424] on the South Branch but were drove off by the Scouters who are Still in persuit of them.*

### The fort and barracks are untenable in July of 1764

A July 25, 1764 letter[1425] Lieutenant George McIntosh wrote to Bouquet from Fort Cumberland states:

*I had the Honour of Writing to you the 25th Ultimo Wherin I acquainted you of my Arrival here, With A Detach' of the 42d & 60th Reg'ts from Fort Loudoun And in my leter Acquainted you that Major Livingston drew provision for himself Servant, and Contractors Clerk out of the Kings Store I made Some Scruple of granting A Vouchor for the Contract's Clerk the 24th Instant til M' Livingston told me it Was Always*

---

[1423] "**The papers of Col. Henry Bouquet**", Kent, 1942.

[1424] The September 7, 1769 issue of the "**Virginia Gazette**" includes a July 31, 1769 letter that provides an additional clue regarding the location of Fort George, via this statement, *"There have been three Indians killed on the south branch of Potowmack...about 70 or 80 miles up the branch, at a place called Fort George..."*

[1425] "**The papers of Col. Henry Bouquet**", Kent, 1942.

*Allowed. and now we draw provision for 26 person's as you may See by this return as my Servant joynd the 13ᵗʰ Instant, being Obligeᵈ to leave him Sick at Fort Loudoun when I Was ordered here.*

*I See by your leter to Major Livingston that you desire a Return of the Artilery Stores & provision from him So Shall Refare to it. as he Sends by this Oppertunity to Bedford He likewise Acquaints me that you know that the fort & Barracks, are but of repair*

*I Shall only add that Neither are tenable Should a Detachᵗ Stay here till the Season Advance, they can not be lodged Without the Barracks Are Repaired.*

### August 1764 orders to relieve Lieutenant McIntosh at Fort Cumberland

An August 14, 1764 letter[1426] Bouquet wrote to Captain Schlosser from Fort Loudon includes the following statement, which references Lieutenant Carre, *"The Lieutᵗ and Party of the Pennsilvania Regt who marches with you, is to proceed to Fort Cumberland to relieve Lieutᵗ McIntosh who is to join you at Bedford, and remain there till further orders."*

Bouquet's August 14, 1764 order[1427] to Captain Schlosser, written from Fort Loudoun, includes the statement:

*The Lieutᵗ and Party of the Pennsylvania Troops are to proceed from Bedford to Fort Cumberland to relieve Lieutᵗ McIntosh who is to come to Bedford, and garrison that Fort with the twenty one Men and of the Royal Americans & Ten Provincials which Colˡ Reid will leave there Lieutenant Carre will deliver to Lieutᵗ McIntosh his Instructions, and the Kings stores, The Company of the 42ᵈ Regiment will join Colˡ Reid and Lieut. Carre Capt Schlosser's Detachment.*

### Macintosh is relieved at Fort Cumberland on August 20, 1764

A January 14, 1765 letter[1428] that Captain John Schlosser wrote to Colonel Henry Bouquet from Lancaster includes the statement, *"Lieutᵗ McIntosh was relieved on the 20ˢᵗ of August by Lieutᵗ Christian Seal at Fort Cumberland on the 21ˢᵗ of August he relieved Again Lieutᵗ Carre at Bedford, the 8ᵗʰ of September he was relieved again aby Lieutᵗ Hunter of the Pensylvanians"*

### Men are moved From Fort Cumberland to Fort Bedford in August of 1764

An August 21, 1764[1429] letter Lieutenant George McIntosh wrote to Bouquet from Bedford states:

*As I imagine Lieutᵗ Colᵒ Reid wrote you fully concerning the State of the Garrison here I Shall have No Occasion to trouble you with any a repitition; I most likewise beg leave to acquaint you that I imagine that I had Acted up to the Order express't in your leter of the 14ᵗʰ Instant, by marching the Royal American's Only from Fort Cumberland to this place. But as Colᵒ Reid think's, from a part of your instruction's to him, that you intended I Should have marched my whole party, I have therefore by his Advice Sent for the men of the 42ᵈ Regiment left there, & have taken the liberty to Send you a Copy of your orders to me; Likewise that part of Lieut. Seeals Instimetions that regards it, Which is as follows.*

1426 **"The papers of Col. Henry Bouquet"**, 1940.

1427 **"The papers of Col. Henry Bouquet"**, 1940.

1428 **"The Papers of Col. Henry Bouquet"**, Series 21651, Federal Works Agency, 1943.

1429 **"The papers of Col. Henry Bouquet"**, Kent, 1942.

*You Will deliver Copy of your instructions to the Officer who reliev's you L$^t$ Christ Sealy and march all your Garrison of the Royal Americans, to Bedford where you Are to joyn Without delay Captain Schlosser.*

*L$^t$ Sealys Instruction's. you Are to proceed By the Way of Bedford to Fort Cumberland Where you Are to Releive L$^t$ M$^c$Intosh of the Royal Americans and the men of that Corps.*

*I Received the inclosed leter broke at the end, from Rob$^t$ Shaw of Cap$^t$ Carn's Company of Light infantry, and He Says, that he received it in that condition from His Captain.*

Colonel John Reid's August 21, 1764 letter[1430] to Bouquet, also written from Bedford, includes the statement:

*...had Lieutenant Macintosh who is arrived brought his whole Party with him from Fort Cumberland ... but he has only brought a few Royal Americans who were of that party, owing to his misapprehending your order to him, which he will acquaint You of; but as it appear'd plain from a part of Your instructions to me, that you intended his whole Party to march from Fort Cumberland, I have therefore advised him to send for them. Cap$^t$ Slocer has exchanged two or three Men w$^h$ L$^t$ Macintosh who were not fit to march, so that L$^t$ Macintosh will have his full Complement of Men when the rest of his Party arrives.*

An August 24, 1764[1431] letter McIntosh wrote to Bouquet from Bedford includes the statement, *"The Detach$^t$ of the 42d Regiment from Fort Cumberland joined me here Wednesday night."*

### Enoch Innes is involved in a court matter

A section titled, *"Imparlance Docquet 1764"* in the Maryland book "**Frederick County Four Docquets For 1764**" contains a record no. 29 dated August 25 for the case of Henry Hinezman versus Enoch Innis that references *"Tho$^s$ Johnson Bail"*.

### A woman was killed near Fort Cumberland on August 25, 1764

A September 5, 1764 letter that Colonel Henry Bouquet wrote to Bradstreet from Fort Bedford indicates that six persons were killed in Virginia and four were taken prisoner on August 22, Isaac Stimble was killed and scalped near Fort Bedford on the same day, and a woman was killed near Fort Cumberland on August 25. The party of Indians who killed her were overtaken by Virginia Militia, two of Indians were killed and scalped, and a white woman was rescued.

### A report of the provisions at Fort Cumberland is forwarded in August of 1764

A synopsis of an August 26, 1764 letter written to Bouquet from Bedford by John Reed states, *"John Read, commissary, to the same. Sends return of provisions at fort Cumberland. Has brought new bags, &c."*

### Cresap sues Thomas Walker

According to Volume 1 of the 1912 book "**Chronicles of the Scotch-Irish Settlement in Virginia**", the August 1764 records of the Augusta County Virginia court include the case of:

*Col. Thomas Cresap vs. Dr. Thomas Walker. — Van Swearingen's deposition taken in Frederick County, Maryland, 1764. He pastured horses in 1755 for Dr. Walker, who, he understood, was the King's*

---

[1430] "**The papers of Col. Henry Bouquet**", Kent, 1942.
[1431] "**The papers of Col. Henry Bouquet**", Kent, 1942.

*Commissary. Cresap was from "Old Town." This suit was to recover costs and expenses in Braddock's expedition. Advertisement by Robert Leahe, Commissary, 13th February, 1756, that the Commissioners to settle accounts (Edward Shippen, Samuel Morris, Alexander Stedman and Samuel McCall) would attend at Lancaster, Pennsylvania, to settle accounts. Letter from Cresap to Walker and from Walker to Cresap. Walker's letter dated Castle Hill.*

For the same month and year, the 1912 book also reports:

*Cresap vs. Walker. — Debtor Dr. Thomas Walker: 1755 — March 17, To 54 ells of oznabrigs for bags; paid for making 20 bags, 10/; thread, 1/6. March 19, paid William Ives for carriage of 10 horseloads of flour to Fort Cumberland; paid Notley Pigman for water carriage of 87 ½ bushels of wheat, weight 5,250 pounds, at 3/. March 21, paid Edmond Martin for carriage of 24½ bushels of wheat, weight 1,400 pounds, at 3/; paid James Hayton for carriage of 40 bushels of wheat, weight 2,400 pounds, at 3/. March 28, paid Daniel Lynn for carriage of 12 casks of flour; paid Daniel Lynn for carriage of 33 pounds wheat; to 21 yards oznabrigs for bags; paid for making of six bags, 3/, thread, 6d.; paid William Ives for carriage of 16 horseloads of flour to Fort Cumberland; paid Nathan Triggs for water carriage of 38 bushels wheat; paid Nathan Triggs for water carriage of 200 pounds of flour; paid William Triggs for water carriage of 35 ½ bushels wheat; paid William Reynolds for water carriage of 39 ¾ bushels of wheat. April 7, paid William Wiggins for water carriage of 38 bushels of wheat. April 8, paid Samuel Hayton for water carriage of 30 bushels of wheat; paid Samuel Hayton for water carriage of 2 casks of flour. April 17, paid Zebulon Robinet for water carriage of 6 casks of flour and 19 ¼ bushels of wheat; paid John Crisp for materials for the flat. April 26, paid Isaac Crumwell per your order. May 7, paid William Williams for water carriage of 58 bushels of wheat; paid Joseph Flint's order on you. May 26, paid Vann Swearingen for wintering 20 wagon horses purchased by Governor Sharp for his Majesty's service; paid William Reynolds for water carriage of 2,388 pounds of flour, at 3/. Maryland, Frederick County, to wit: June 30, 1762. Sworn to by Thomas Cresap, gent, before Thomas Norris. Certificate with seal by John Darnall, clerk, that Thomas Norris "is one of his Lordships the Right Honorable the Lord Proprietory his Justices of the Peace" for Frederick County. Castle Hill, September 30, 1760. Sir: Your favor of ye 30th of August came to hand the other day. The contents thereof surprises me, I suppose, as much as Mrs. Hoops's answer did you. I shall not at present enter into the justness, or reasonableness, of the account, as I presume that is out of the question. You, I make no doubt, are sensible the money ought to have been paid by the Crown, and I should have thought your experience from the year 1755 would have convinced you that it was necessary to apply either before or at the time the Commissioners settled the accounts for the campaign of 1758, as no regard has been paid to any accounts that were not brought in before such settlements of any campaign were finished. As to your seeking justice in Virginia, I presume no Court, or jury, can be of opinion that I am to pay the debts due from the Crown which remain unpaid from the neglect of the creditors. Could I assist you I should with the greatest pleasure, but as I cannot, must leave you to take any method you may think just and most likely to recover your due. I am, your most humble servant, (Signed) Thomas Walker. Col. Thomas Cresap, the Old Town, Maryland. James Heaton's receipt to Thomas Cresap, 21st March, 1755, £3.12.0. Edmond Martin's (mark) receipt to Thomas Cresap, 21st March, 1755, £2.2.0. William Frigg's receipt to Thomas Cresap, 28th March, 1755, £2.12.0. John Crisp's order on Mr. Thomas Walker, Commissary, 13th April, 1755. William Williams's receipt. (Test, Jarvis Hougham.) Isaac Cromwell's order. Notley Pigman's receipt. William Reynold's receipt. William Wigins's receipt. William Ives's receipt. William Reynold's receipt. Zebulon Robinet's receipt. Daniel Linns's receipt. Nathan Trigg's receipt. Joseph Flint's receipt. Samuel Haton's receipt. I do certify that sixty head of beef cattle and fifty head of sheep, bought by the contractors for the use of the forces under the command of Col. George Washington, were grazed upon the plantation of Col. Thomas Cresap, at Old Town, from the 15th of July to the 15th of September, inclusive. (Signed) Joseph Galbreath, assistant to the contractors. Fort Cumberland, September 21, 1758. Attachment against Thomas Walker, addressed to sheriff of Augusta, to answer Thomas Cresap, dated 17th February, in second year of our reign. Daniel Linn's receipt. William Ives's receipt. March 1, 1764. — Van Swearinger. Sr., deposes before Joseph Smith, James Smith, Justices for Frederick County, Maryland, aged seventy years, or thereabouts: That on 25th May, 1755, the deponent attended Dr. Thomas Walker, who, he understood, was the King's commissary, with an account for wintering 20 wagon horses, which horses were sent him by Col. Thomas Cresap, who informed him that the said horses were the King's and were purchased by the Governor of Maryland of Mr. Robert Callender, and ordered by the Governor to him, the said Cresap, to have them wintered. Some time in the spring the said horses, with the wagons, which were ordered away from his house by Dr. Thomas Walker, without acquainting him at the time to whom he was to apply for the payment of his account, on which he applied to Colonel Cresap, as he had sent the horses to him, who went with the deponent to Fort Cumberland on the day and date above mentioned, where was Dr. Thomas Walker, to whom the deponent presented his account, which the said commissary perused and made no objection to any part thereof, but told him they had not cash at that time to discharge it, but that as soon as Colonel Washington came up from Virginia, by whom he expected a sum of money, he would pay the account. The deponent informed them that as he lived at a great distance, and it would put him to considerable trouble to be coming after his money, he should for the future expect his money from Colonel Cresap, who he looked upon to be liable to him for it, upon which Dr. Walker desired Colonel Cresap to pay me the money, the amount of which was £30.17.0, which sum the Colonel payed me the next day. Agreeable to his request for which I gave a receipt and never received anything for the same but from Colonel Cresap. (Signed) Van Swearingen, Sr.*

*ADVERTISEMENT.*

*Philadelphia, January 31, 1756. Whereas, Application hath been made to his Excellency, General Shirley, on behalf of the owners of the wagons, teams, carriages, horses, and other things contracted for and employed in his service under the late General Braddock ; and his said Excellency, General Shirley, having given orders for the settling and discharging all such accounts as yet remain unsatisfied for the said wagons, teams, horses, etc.; and Edward Shippen, Samuel Morris, Alexander Stedman, and Samuel McCall, Jr., Esqs., being, by the directions of the said General Shirley, commissionated and appointed to audit, adjust, and settle the said accounts in conjunction with Robert Leake, Esq., commissary to his Majesty's forces in North America; notice is hereby given that the said Robert Leake, with the said commissioners, will attend at Lancaster, from the third until the thirteenth day of February next, both inclusive, for the settling, adjusting, and discharging all accounts and demands relative to the said wagoners, horses, and other things. When and where all persons concerned are hereby required to appear with their several accounts and contracts (and their proofs and vouchers) relating to the premises, in order to have the same settled and paid by Robert Leake, commissary. Lancaster, 13th February, 1756. The said commissioners and commissary will attend at Philadelphia, where all persons are desired to come immediately who have any demands as above. (Signed) R. Leake, commissary.*


### Lieutenant McDonald goes out to meet approaching Indians in September of 1764

A synopsis of a September 3, 1764 letter states, "*Intelligence from Fort Cumberland of the advance of Indians, whom Lieut. McDonald has gone out to meet. Lieut. Sealy writes to Major Livingston, sending a copy of McDonald's letter.*"

### The Virginia volunteers to be at Fort Cumberland, according to a September 1764 letter

A September 5, 1764 letter [1432] that Colonel Henry Bouquet wrote to General Thomas Gage from Fort Bedford includes the following statements that are relevant to Fort Cumberland:

*...as I cannot suppose that Co. Bradstreet had received your last orders when he granted Peace to the Delaware & Shawanese, I have sent him by Two Traders well acquainted with the country, the Paragraph you have been pleased to include to me, and desired he would if possible postpone the final conclusion of the Treaty till I could transmit him your Intentions.*

*In the mean time some Parties of Savages continue to shew themselves on the Frontiers and on the 27th Ulto Two were killed and scalped beyond Fort Cumberland by the Militia of Virginia, and a woman they had made Prisoner released; and I am this moment informed that three Indians with Bows & Arrows have attempted to take one of our Drivers at the Grass Guard.*

*I have been here since the first Instant...*

*The Desertion continues amongst the Provincials, with the additional loss of Horses and Arms, which they carry off; I shall never more depend upon new raised Troops.*

*By Col. Lewis Letter a good Reinforcement of Volunteers from Virginia, will be at Fort Cumberland by the 10th Inst, but he could not fix the number.*

### Cresap sues in his capacity of Hugh Parker's executor

William Chapline's executors (Joseph Chapline and James & Ann Forman) were summoned by the Frederick County, Virginia Court on September 7, 1764 to answer Hugh Parker's executors (Jeremiah Warder and Thomas Cresap) regarding an unpaid debt of William Chapline.[1433] Ann was William Chapline's widow.

### A 1764 military pass for the trader Edmund Moran is signed at Fort Cumberland

The Library of Congress has the military pass of Edmund Moran that was written at Fort Loudoun on September 13, 1764, and subsequently signed at Fort Cumberland by *"J. H. C. Sealy Comanding"* on September 19, 1764. The addition to the pass that was written at Fort Cumberland states, *"as Mr. Moran has come to Fort Cumberland with a party of Maryland Volunteers on their way to Fort Pitt & not finding any Liquors with him & Goods only fitt for the Campain have thought Propper to Let him pass this post"*.

### Fort Cumberland is reported as being repaired

A September 24, 1764 letter[1434] that Lieutenant J. H. C. Sealy wrote to Bouquet from Fort Cumberland states:

*Inclosed is a Return for the Last Month which hope will Come safe to hand. We have not had a Sillable of News Since Collo McNeals departure from hear & any Before he will Acquaint You with.*

*The Fort is Repaird in the Best manner it will admit of I believe it will Answer for the Ensuing Season, being Station'd at this Out Post hope you will not forget me the First Vacancy...*

---

[1432] **"Michigan Historical Collections"**, Volume 19, 1911 reprint of 1892 book.
[1433] **"Colonial Records of the Upper Potomac"**, Volume 6.
[1434] **"The papers of Col. Henry Bouquet"**, Kent, 1942.

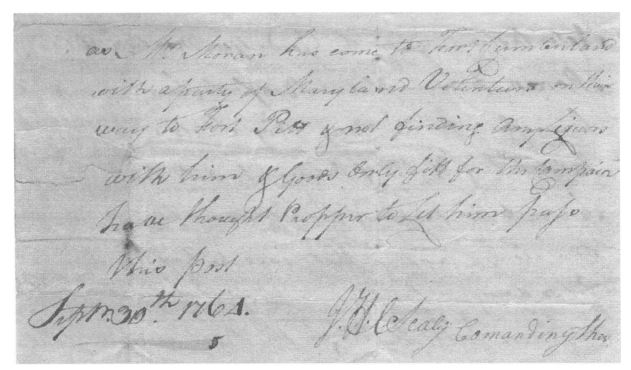

This is the 1764 pass of the trader Edmund Moran that was signed at Fort Cumberland.

## A store, tavern, and families at Fort Cumberland

A September 30, 1764 letter that Lieutenant J. H. C. Sealy, of the Pennsylvania Regiment, wrote to Bouquet from Fort Cumberland is translated as follows in the 1942 book "**The papers of Col. Henry Bouquet**":

*Most humbly we report that Captain Volgomot arrived here the 25th of September with 18 volunteers from Maryland, and paid his respects to Captain McClean, who reached here the 28th instant. Both companies set out from here the 30th and by Your Honor's stipulated order, I have provided them with ammunition and provisions for 7 days of their march to Fort Pitt. Fort Major Livingston started for Winchester the 25th of this month. As soon as the honorable Major Livingston returns, will Your Honor investigate the following complaint, that Major Livingston his associate, Justice Innes, whose [store?] and tavern are at the fort, took it upon themselves and sold lead, and the like. For my part, I am obliged to believe some of it because I have found the [back?] door of the store open. So I had my sergeant close it and give the key into my hand until further orders from Your Honor, whether I should turn it over to Major Livingston or not. Major Livingston said Colonel Bouquet gave him these orders and I must do as he commands. There are 8 families here and they cannot support themselves, but at least they are getting along as well as they did [before?]; so they are all jealous of me. If Your Honor can grant me an interview, please let me know, at any time, at what place I may see you, for the honor of King and Country, and lastly my own honor. Having received Your Honor's [orders?] and awaiting further notice, I am,*

> *Your Right Honorable Worship's obedient servant,*
>
> *J. H. C. Sealy, Lieutenant*
>
> *In the Pennsylvania Regiment,*
>
> *Commanding at Fort Cumberland by your order.*

*N. B. The barracks are being put in good order again, the post repaired with facines, ½ dozen ramrods and [sponges?] made for the cannon here.*

This is an important letter in several respects. First, it's the earliest known reference to a tavern and a civilian store at Fort Cumberland. This provides support for the many traditions of settlers coming to Fort Cumberland for supplies. Having intensely studied the issue of an early store in the vicinity of Fort Cumberland, I believe that the referenced store is that of Enoch Innis. Innis shows up in other letters herein as a storekeeper. Second, the letter references repairing the Fort Cumberland with fascines. This is the last known phase of fort modifications. Fascines are bundles of light wood, like saplings. They are used to shore up earthen ramparts. The use of fascines was a military engineering art. An 1855 military dictionary has over a page of definitions for fascine-related words. At Fort Cumberland, the fascines were somehow used in place of logs, to hold the earthworks in position. Thirdly, the letter references eight families living at the fort.

## Enoch Innis was living in Maryland in 1764

On June 19, 1766, Enoch Innis swore out a deposition[1435] that includes the following:

*The Deposition of Enoch Innis aged Twenty seven years, or thereabouts being first Sworn on the Holy Evangels of Almighty God Deposeth and Sayeth that one James Spencer an Inhabitant of Maryland in the year 1764 Came before him (he being a Justice of the Peace for the said County in the Province of Maryland) and made Oath to the following Purport. That he the said Spencer in the Month of August in the year 1763 being present in an Engagemen between his Majesty's Troops and the Indians at a Place called Bushy run…*

This proves as well as any document can that Enoch Innis was a resident of Maryland in 1764. Since tavern keepers typically resided in their taverns, this suggests that the tavern mentioned in Lieutenant Sealy's September 30, 1764 letter was located on the Maryland side of the Potomac River. Added to this, it seems like 1764 would have been a dangerous time to have a store and tavern on the opposite side of the river from the fort.

## Bouquet's 1764 expedition results in a peace conference with the Indians

Regarding Pontiac's insurrection, the 1847 book "**Early History of Western Pennsylvania**" states:

*It was therefore resolved that a decisive blow should be struck, and the merciless depredators be awed into silence and subjection. It was proposed to attack them at two different points, and "carry the war in the heart of their own country."*

*With this view, Co. Bradstreet was sent, with a body of troops, to act against the Wyandotts, Ottawas, Chippewas, and other nations living in the vicinity of the Lakes; while Colonel Bouquet should pass an army through Pennsylvania into Ohio, and attack the Delewares, Shawanese, Mingoes, Mohicans, and other nations between the Ohio and the Lakes.*

*These two divisions of the army were to act in concert. Colonel Bradstreet was to proceed to Detroit, and Michilimackinac, in the first place, and on his return he was ordered to encamp and remain at Sandusky, to awe and hold in check the numerous north-western tribes, so as to prevent them from sending any assistance to the Ohio Indians, while Colonel Bouquet should march from Fort Pitt, and attack them in their settlements upon the Muskingum.*

---

[1435] "**Archives of Maryland, Proceedings of the Council of Maryland, April 15, 1761 – September 24, 1770**", 1912.

Colonel Bouquet left Fort Pitt for Muskingum with a large force on October 3, 1764. A conference was held with the Indians at Muskingum on October 20, 1764, where Bouquet demanded the return of all captives, stating:

*I have brought with me, the relations of the people you have massacred, or taken prisoners. They are impatient for revenge; and it is with difficulty that I can protect you against their just resentment, which is only restrained by the assurances given them, that no peace shall ever be concluded till you have given full satisfaction.*

*Your former allies, the Ottawas, Chippewas, Wyandotts, and others, have made peace with us. The Six Nations have joined us against you. We now surround you, having possession of all the waters of the Ohio, the Mississippi, and the Lakes. All the French living in those parts are now subjects of Great Britain, and dare no longer assist you. It is therefore in our power totally to extirpate you from being a people. But the English are a merciful and generous nation, averse to shed the blood even of their most cruel enemies; and if it were possible that you could convince us that you sincerely repent of your past perfidy, and that we could depend on your good behavior for the future, you might yet hope for mercy and peace. If I find you faithfully execute the following preliminary conditions, I will not treat you with the severity you deserve. I give you twelve days to deliver into my hands all the prisoners in your possession, without any exception; Englishmen, Frenchmen, women and children, whether adopted in your tribes, married, or living amongst you under any denomination and pretence, whatsoever, together with all the negroes. And you are to furnish the said prisoners with clothing, provisions, and horses, to carry them to Fort Pitt. When you have fully complied with these conditions, you shall then know on what terms you may obtain the peace you ask for.*

The Indians delivered 206 captives to Bouquet on November 9, 1764. On November 12, the Shawanese delivered more prisoners to Bouquet, and promised to deliver the rest at Fort Pitt the following spring.

### The militia retakes a prisoner from an Indian raiding party
General Thomas Gage wrote a letter[1436] from Fort Loudoun on October 20, 1764 that states:

*Yesterday an Express arrived here, which was Sent to me from Fort Cumberland aquainting me that on the 6th Instant three miles from Staunton in Augusta County, there were two persons Killed and one taken by the Indians, but by the Vigilance of Colonel Lewis' Militia, the Prisoner was Retaken with the loss of all the Savages Baggage; the Commanding officer says in his Letter this is Confirmed to me by Colonel Stephens. But does not say what Nation they are, but by a Man that came here about an hour ago from Virginia am told they are Wyondots.*

### A court summons for Thomas Spencer.
An October 27, 1764 Frederick County, Virginia court summons to Thomas Spencer requires him to answer in court for an £2/13/6 debt alleged by Daniel Cresap.

### Colonel Bouquet writes from Muskingum
Colonel Henry Bouquet wrote a letter[1437] to Captain David Hay from the *"Camp upon the Muskinghum 128 Miles from Fort Pitt Nov[r] 9th 1764"* that includes the following statement:

---

[1436] This letter was provided by Tim Fisher.
[1437] **"The Papers of Col. Henry Bouquet"**, Series 21651, Federal Works Agency, 1943.

*I send you by ~~Col~~ Cap^t Blueford of the Virginia Voluntiers Prisoners, who are to remain at Fort Pitt, till further Orders; the Men are to be lodged Separately from the Women and Children, and as most of them, particularly these who have been a long time among the Indians will take the first Opportunity to run away, they are to be closely watched and well Secured: Some of them may have full Liberty to walk about the Fort, and are to assist in taking Care of the Rest: Their Escort consists of an Officer a Serjeant, and Twenty Men of the Penn^y Regt who are to join your Garrison, and thirty Virginia Voluntiers, who are to be sent home with Provisions to Fort Cumberland, except such part of them as Cap^t Blueford will chuse to keep with him till we return, and these must be very few. An Officer of the Penn^y Reg^t under the Sentence of a Court Martial is likewise sent in Arrest to Fort Pitt, where he is to remain in confinment, with the Liberty of Walking in the Fort only in the day Time, till the General's Pleasure ~~is known~~ can be known.*

*The Pack Horses must be discharged & sent down without delay. Those from Virginia may go if they chuse it by Cumberland road. Capt Ourry writes you on that head.*

## The Virginia volunteers are to march to Fort Cumberland

Major John Small wrote a letter[1438] to Captain Thomas Buford from the *"Head quarters Camp Near the Forks of Muskingum, November 9^th 1764"* that includes the following statement:

*The Collonel reposing a particular Confidence, in you, being assur'd of your Zeal & diligence in the Publick Service, has made Choice of you to perform this Essential duty of Conducting these <u>Captives</u> to Pittsburgh where you will deliver them over to Cap^t David Hay of the Royal Regiment of Artillery Commanding his Majesties troops at that Fortress. The officer & Detachment of the Pensilvania Troops that proceed with you are to Join that Garrison & remmain under Captain Hays Command. You will also remmain yourself at Pittsburgh till the Army returns thither; or till you receive orders from Collonel Bouquet to the Contrary.*

*You will Detain Such of the Virginia Voluntiers (<u>who are to remmain with you at Fort Pitt</u>) as you Shall think propper to pitch upon for that purpose; The ~~Remaining~~ other Voluntiers that now proceed with you; are to Receive provisions at Pittsburgh, to carry them To Fort Cumberland, to which place you will give them orders to March as soon as possible.*

## No payment for horses that gave out on the way to Virginia via Cumberland

Captain Thomas Barnsley wrote a letter[1439] to Colonel Henry Bouquet from *"Fort Loudoun the 11^th November 1764"* that includes the following statement:

*Yesterday two of the Horse Masters Viz Barclay & Blane Arrived here with their drivers and Some Horses. The other two went to Virginia by way of Cumberland, they inform me a good many of their horses Tyred and gave out, so that they was obligd to leave them on the road. I advised them to acquaint their owner with it; as they might be Assured no Horses would be paid for but Such as were killed or taken by the Enemy &c^a.*

---

[1438] **"The Papers of Col. Henry Bouquet"**, Series 21651, Federal Works Agency, 1943.
[1439] **"The Papers of Col. Henry Bouquet"**, Series 21651, Federal Works Agency, 1943.

## Hoping to obtain horses at Fort Cumberland

Colonel Henry Bouquet wrote a letter[1440] to Colonel John McNeill from the *"Camp at the Forks of Muskingham 15th Nover 1764"* that includes the following statement:

*Captn Lewis will take your Orders at Fort Pitt, as we have no more Horses from Virginia. I wish he could discharge at Fort Cumberland, those belonging to Pensylvania, & hire or Impress the Horses he will want for the Detachment & Prisoners, for which I am willing to pay upon his or your Certificate directed to Captn Barnsley A. D. Q M. G. at Fort Loudon.*

## The Virginia prisoners are to be delivered home via Fort Cumberland

Colonel Henry Bouquet wrote a letter[1441] to Captain David Hay from the *"Camp at the Forks Muskinghum Novbr 15h 1764"* that includes the following statement:

*After you have received the Prisoners from Captn Lewis, you will please to deliver to him or to Coll McNeil if he chuses it, all the Prisoners belonging to their district in Virginia, making two descriptive Lists of them, both signd by You & the Officer who receives them, One of which you will deliver to Me, with the Receipt at the Bottom, & give the other with the Captives.*

*You will provide them with the Horses absolutely necessary for their March to Fort Cumberland, from whence I would if possible have them to hire or impress from Stage to Stage country Horses as Augusta County is too far for our starved Creatures to reach it & return to their Owners.*

*They will draw Provisions at the Fort to carry them to Fort Cumberland where they will draw again.*

## Orders concerning Indian traders are issued to the forts in November 1764

Colonel Henry Bouquet issued an order[1442] related to the Indian trade on November 29, 1764 that includes Fort Cumberland:

*By Henry Bouquet Esquire Colonel of Foot Commanding His Majesty's Forces in the Southern District of North America.*

*Whereas a suspension of Arms has been granted to the Indian Tribes of the Mingoes, Wiandots, Delawares & Shawanese any of their people coming to our Posts are to be Treated as our friends, but as no Trade can be carried on with the said Indians till a Definite Treaty of Peace be concluded with them, and the manner of carrying on the said Trade be regulated by Authority. The officers commanding at Fort Bedford, Cumberland, Ligonier, Fort Pitt & all other Posts on the communication to the Ohio, are not to permit Liquors Dry Goods or Merchandise either going to Fort Pitt or further to pass at their respective Posts, and in case any Traders, Settlers or others should contrary to this order, attempt to carry Liquors Dry Goods or Merchandize in a clandestine manner: the Cargoes of such Delinquents are to be seized and lodged in the Kings Stores till orders can be had thereupon from the General & it is particularly forbid to any Persons at Fort Pitt to have any Dealings whatever with the Indians & to sell or give them any Ammunition Liquors or Dry Goods without orders from the commanding officer at that Post, who will give such orders in cases only where His Majestys Service shall absolutely require it.*

*All kinds of eatables & the Stores necessary for the use of the officers & soldiers of his Majestys Troops in Garrison at those Posts are permitted to pass provided the Carriers produce to the officers*

---

[1440] "**The Papers of Col. Henry Bouquet**", Series 21651, Federal Works Agency, 1943.
[1441] "**The Papers of Col. Henry Bouquet**", Series 21651, Federal Works Agency, 1943.
[1442] "**Michigan Historical Collections**", Volume 19, 1911 reprint of 1892 book.

*commanding at such Post Permits signed by the Genl. The officers commanding in this Department or the officers commanding at Fort Pitt. This order to be made Publick at each Post for the Information of all Persons whom it may concern.*

*Given under my hand at Head Quarters in Fort Pitt this 29th day of November 1764.*

*Henry Bouquet.*

### Members of the 42nd were in garrison at Fort Cumberland in November 1764

A letter,[1443] written from Fort Pitt by Colonel Bouquet on November 30, 1764 to General Thomas Gage, includes the statement:

*Fort Pitt is garrisoned by Five Companies of the 42nd Reg. under the command of Capt. William Murray. Fort Ligonier, has a company of the same corps, under the Command of Captain Steward, Fort Bedford another Company commanded by Capt. William Grant. Fort Cumberland, half a company commanded by Lieut James Eddington.*

### William Ross's son Taverner is among the returned captives

A list of items given to captives from the northern district of Virginia accompanied a November 30, 1764 letter from Bouquet to Gage.[1444] The list identifies Taverner Ross as one of the captives, and shows that he was provided with a shirt, shoe packs, and a blanket. Eve, William, Lewis, John, Thomas, Elizabeth, and Catherine Ice are also included in the list.

The January 17, 1765 issue of the "**Pennsylvania Gazette**" includes a *"List of captives taken by the Indians, and delivered to Colonel Bouquet, by the Mingos, Delawares, Shawanese, Wyondots and Mohickons, at Tuscarawas and Muskingam, in November, 1764."* Among the females and children of the northern district of Virginia, are, *"Eve Ice; William; Lewis, John, Thomas, Elisabeth and Catherine Ice"*. These are believed to be the family of Frederick Ice.

### Charges against Colonel Adam Stephen are considered

The 1907 book "**Journals of the House of Burgesses of Virginia 1761-1765**" contains the following entry from December 5, 1764:

*Mr Attorney, from the Committee of Propositions and Grievances, reported that the said Committee had had under their Consideration that Part of the Report of the Commissioners appointed by an Act of Assembly entitled An Act for appointing Commissioners to examine and state the Accounts of the Militia lately ordered out into actual Service, and for other Purposes therein mentioned, as relates to the Conduct and Services of Col. Adam Stephen therein named; also the Charge exhibited in Writing against the said Col. Stephen, and reflecting upon his Conduct, by Mr Thomas Rutherford, a Member of this House, to them referred; and having heard as well the said Mr Rutherford as Col. Stephen, and the Depositions of sundry Witnesses taken by Order of the House upon the Subject Matter of the said Charge, had agreed upon a Report, and come to several Resolutions thereon; which he read in his Place, and then delivered in at the Table, where they were again twice read, and agreed to by the House, with some Amendments, as follow:*

---

[1443] "**Michigan Historical Collections**", Volume 19, 1911 reprint of 1892 book.
[1444] "**The Western Pennsylvania Historical Magazine**", Volume 39, Number 3, Fall 1956.

*Your Committee beg Leave to inform the House that the Charge exhibited by Mr Rutherford against Col. Stephen consists of the following Aritcles, viz.*

*1st. That he had, by Persuasions, Orders, Threats, and Influences, prevented many Persons from joining as Volunteers in the Expedition commanded by Col. Bouquet against the Indian Towns the Ohio, &c.*

*2d. That he had at several Times ordered the Militia in the actual Service of the Country out of this Colony, to the Forts Cumberland in Maryland, and Bedford in Pennsylvania, to escort Waggons and Pack-Horses, with Flower and Beeves, his own Property, in Compliance with his own private Engagements, &c. and that the drawing off the Militia at such particular Times rendered the several Garrisons from whence they were taken so weak that they were insufficient to protect the Frontiers from the Incursions of the Indians, who at that Season were daily expected, and did actually come down within the Settlements, and kill and carry away many of the Inhabitants. And*

*3d. That he sent Waggons from the South Branch to Hite's Mill, near his own Plantation, for his own Flower, to supply the several Garrisons on the Frontiers, when the same might have been had much nearer, as cheap and as good.*

*As to the first Article of the said Charge, your Committee beg Leave to inform the House that it appears to them that Mr Rutherford having intimated to Col. Bouquet that in his Opinion a Number of Volunteers might be raised in this Colony, to join him in his intended Expedition against the Indians, Col. Bouquet, by Letter of the 18th of June 1764 to Mr Rutherford, expressed his Cheerful Acceptance of their Services, and promised to supply such Volunteers as would join him; therein with Ammunition and Provisions, desiring his good Offices in promoting that Service, and advising that some of them would serve on Horseback, to join his Light Horse, and giving it as his Opinion that large Dogs might also be of Service to discover and pursue the Enemy: That Mr Rutherford, in Answer to this Letter, informed Col. Bouquet that he would write to the Governour to desire his Permission for a Number of the Militia then in Service on the Frontiers to enter themselves as Volunteers in the said Expedition; and that if the Governour should be averse to his Proposal, he would then exert all his Interest to procure a Number of Volunteers to go upon his Terms: That Col. Lewis commanded the Militia in Augusta; that he was a Gentleman of great Interest in that County, and had the Common Cause much at Heart; that a few Lines to him upon the Subject might not be amiss; and that Col. Stephen, who commanded the Militia in Frederick and Hampshire, might possibly look for the like Compliment; That soon after Mr Rutherford, in Company with Mr James Keith and others, laid Col. Bouquet's Letter to him before Col. Stephen, who expressed his Disapprobation of the intended Expedition; that he thought Col. Bouquet the most improper Person for that Command, and that he was convinced he would proceed no further than Pittsburg; that all he wanted was to make a Noise and Parade, and so the Matter would end; that the Colony was very capable of undertaking the Expedition themselves, and that it was a Shame to give that Credit and Honour to Col. Bouquet, which we might reap ourselves; That Col. Stephen at other Times expressed his Dislike of the said intended Expedition in much the same Terms, and threatened some of the Officers and Soldiers under his Command that if they went out as Volunteers in the said Expedition they should be deprived of their Commissions, and should not receive any Pay for the Services they had done. On the other Hand, your Committee beg Leave to observe that many other Persons were examined (who were present at the Time it was said Col. Stephen attempted to dissuade People from entering as Volunteers in the said Expedition, particularly at the House of one Robert Cunninghame, where one James Chew, who was a Lieutenant in Capt. Morgan's Company of Militia, and others, deposed that they heard him make Use of such Dissuasions and Threatenings) who declared that they did not hear Col. Stephen at that, or any other Time, attempt to discourage the Volunteer Scheme, or endeavour to dissuade any Person whatsoever, either by Threats or any other indirect Practices, from joining Col. Bouquet on his Expedition: And it further appears to your Committee that Col. Stephen, having received a Letter from his Honour the*

*Governour of the 18th and 20th of August last, granting his Permission to all Persons that should think proper to join Col. Bouquet as Volunteers, on the Encouragement and Terms he should offer them, and directing him to second his Intentions as far as the Laws of the Colony would permit, Col. Stephen thereupon immediately sent circular Orders to the Officers of the Militia under his Command, at their different Posts, to encourage and promote the enlisting Volunteers for the said Expedition, and did use his best Endeavours in that Service: And therefore,*

*Resolved, That the said Col. Stephen has not fully acquitted himself of the first Article of the said Charge.*

*Your Committee then proceeded to examine the Evidence offered on both Sides, on the second Article of the said Charge, and beg Leave to inform the House that it appears to them that in the Year 1763 Col. Stephen having engaged with the Contractors for supplying the King's Forces with Provisions, to furnish them with a Quantity of Flower to be delivered at Forts Cumberland and Bedford, and a Number of Beeves to be delivered at Fort Bedford, employed Parties of the Militia under his Command to escort them thither respectively, which was accordingly executed, and were a very seasonable supply to the Garrison at Fort Bedford, who were short of Provisions at the Time of their being sent there, and had pressed Col. Stephen very much to assist them; and that Col. Stephen paid the Expense of the Pasturage of the Cattle on their Way up himself.*

*It further appears to your Committee that in the Spring of the following Year Col. Stephen received a Letter from Capt. Ourry, Commandant at Fort Bedford, enclosing another from the above mentioned Contractors, in which they informed him that as he had not complied with his Contract, in delivering the Flower he had engaged at the Times agreed on, he could not take it hard if they did not receive it according to the Terms of the first Contract; but that they had, upon the Request of Col. Bouquet, come to a Determination to receive what he could deliver by the 4th of June at Bedford, or the 4th of September at Pittsburg, and allow him the Market Price: That Col. Stephen thereupon impressed a Number of Waggons, and ordered out Parties of the Militia, stationed at several of the Forts and Posts in his Department, to escort them to Fort Cumberland, and gave out that they were to go no further: That they were there loaded with Flower belonging to Col. Stephen, which he had in Store at that Fort, and from thence proceeded to Fort Bedford under the same Escort, many of whom declared that they did not think themselves obliged to that Service, being out of the Colony, and threatened to return home, but were at length prevailed on by Col. Stephen to proceed; That Col. Stephen himself paid for the Waggonage of the Flower, and that they were about three Days engaged in that Service, and that Col. Stephen gave orders to escort any Persons carrying their Commodities to Fort Bedford.*

*It appears that during the Absence of these Parties from their Posts two Men were killed in the Neighbourhood of Foreman's Fort by the Indians, and some near Winchester; but that those Forts were not more weakened by those Draughts than they usually were upon sending out scouting Parties.*

*It further appears to your Committee that as well the Militia who were in actual Service at and about Fort Cumberland, as the Inhabitants who were driven from their Plantations by the Indians, and took Refuge there, were supplied with Provisions out of the King's Stores at that Fort.*

*Resolved, That Mr Rutherford had proved the second Article of the said Charge against Col. Stephen, and that he was guilty of a Breach of his Duty in sending out Escorts of the Militia under his Command in such Services.*

*Your Committee then proceeded to an Inquiry and Examination of the third and last Article of the said Charge, and beg Leave to inform the House that it appears to them that it being impracticable to procure Flower for the Use of the Militia stationed on and about the South Branch and Patterson's Creek, in that Neighbourhood, Col. Stephen impressed a Number of Waggons, and sent them to Jacob Hite's Mill, near his own Plantation, and one also to John Hite's Mill, where they took in as well as his own Flower as some he had purchased of other People, which was transported to those Posts for the Use of the Militia: It appears that Jacob Hite's Mill was about 19 Miles, and John Hite's 4 Miles, distant from Winchester; and that Flower might have been procured at a less Distance, but it does not appear that Col. Stephen knew it; And it appears to your Committee to have been the constant Tenour of Col. Stephen's Orders, to the Officers of the Militia under his Command, to procure Flower and other Provisions for their Men as near them, and with as little Expense to the Country, as they possibly could.*

*Resolved, That Col. Stephen hath acquitted himself of the third Article of the said Charge.*

*Resolved, That the said Col. Stephen ought to be allowed the Pay of a County Lieutenant only during the Time he was employed in the Service of the Country.*

*Resolved, That Col. Adam Stephen hath discharged his Duty (saving in the two Instances before mentioned) as a brave, active, and skilful Officer.*

### Reporting on the number of refugees fed at Fort Cumberland

Major James Livingston wrote a letter[1445] to Colonel Henry Bouquet from Fort Cumberland on December 8, 1764 that states:

*I expected to have had the Pleasure of waiting on you at Bedford on your way Down but am Prevented by the Gout which I have had for a Considerable time past Extreemly Bad, I must therefore by way of Letter Sincearly Congratulate you on your Happy Success & Safe Return, the good Consequences of which every Person in this Country are Truly Sensable therefore hope they may Continue. I have herewith sent you an Exact Coppy of an Abstract of Provisions Issued Since March 1763 & agreeable to your Directions have got as many of the Principle Inhabitants of this Place as are Convinient to Certify that, to the Best of their Knoledge & Belief, there was the Number of Refugees at the Different Times in this Garrison & that they Drew Provisions out of the Kings Stores. I therefore hope their Certificate will be fully Sattisfactory in that Matter.*

### Reporting on horse thieves and the return of captives

Major John Field wrote a letter[1446] to Colonel Henry Bouquet from Fort Pleasant on December 13, 1764 that includes the following:

*We arrivd at this garason Yesterday, And as I Before amajined William Spensor Jo^s^ Tumoleston and ~~Joseph~~ W^m^ Ice ware the only offenders from our Colony who had stolen horses which persons it was altogether out of my power to apprehend them for their Villany as they kept out of the Way and as it was out of my power to wait, But as two of them Live mariland and Ice in Virginia which is near Cumberland therefore you will deal with them as you think proper.*

*We have delivered up all the Captives in our possession to their Relations Except three…*

A William Ice is listed as one of the Indian captives who was returned in November of 1764.

---

[1445] "**The Papers of Col. Henry Bouquet**", Series 21651, Federal Works Agency, 1943.
[1446] "**The Papers of Col. Henry Bouquet**", Series 21651, Federal Works Agency, 1943.

## Ennis is minding the store at Fort Cumberland

A December 16, 1764 letter[1447] that Captain Thomas Buford wrote to Colonel Henry Bouquet states:

*According to your derection I have Delivered all the Captives that was under my deraction to their respective friends only five whitch I left with Col[o.] Abraham Hight in Hamsher County who is to send to their friends to fetch them to their respective homes.*

*There are three horses whitch was stolen by our Vollentears in the posestion of Joseph Tumblestone, W[m.] Spencer, and W[m.] Ice but they was apprehensive that I should confine them, and so kept out of my way, thot hay all live Near fort Cumberland and major Field has wrote to M[r.] Ennis storekeeper at Fort Comberland to uppere hand them so I hope the poor Indions will git their horses*

This isn't the only 1764 letter stating that Innis had a store at Fort Cumberland.

## The estimated date of construction for Michael Cresap's stone house

According the historical marker at the site, the estimated date of construction of Michael Cresap's stone house at Oldtown is 1764. The house is located at Latitude 39.541859°, Longitude -78.611512°, and is property AL-II-B-002 on the Maryland Historical Trust's Inventory of Historic Properties.

---

[1447] Francis Bridges found a synopsis of this letter, and that led to the discovery of a transcript of the entire letter.

# 17. 1765: Resistance to the Stamp act

### John Morris obtains property on the east side of Martins Mountain

*"Jno. Morris"* is one of the individuals named on the 1761 Old Town Hundreds list. The 50-acre *"Johnsons Folley"* tract (Frederick County Patent Certificate 2214, MSA S1197 2280) was surveyed for John Morris on February 18, 1765 and patented to him the same day. The survey reads, *"... I have Carefully Surveyd and Laid out for and in the name of him the said John Morris all that Tract of Land Called Johnsons Folley Lying in the County afsd Beginning at Two Bounded white oaks Standing on the East side of Martins Mountain near the head of a Draught of Flint Stone Creek ..."*

### Western immigration was already well in progress in 1765

An April 30, 1765 letter[1448] from Winchester, Virginia[1449] states, *"The frontier inhabitants of this colony and Maryland are removing fast over the Allegheny mountains, in order to settle and live there."*

### The British approach the Indians about a new boundary line for British lands

Volume 5 of "**The Complete Works of Benjamin Franklin**" includes the following:

*...orders were transmitted to Sir William Johnson, in the year 1764, to call together the Six Nations, lay this proposition of the boundary before them, and take their opinion upon it. This, we apprehend, will appear evident from the following speech, made by Sir William to the Six Nations, at a conference which he held with them at Johnson Hall, May the 2d, 1765.*

*Brethren:*

*The last, but the most important affair I have at this time to mention is, with regard to the settling a boundary between you and the English. I sent a message to some of your nation some time ago, to acquaint you that I should confer with you at this meeting upon it. The king, whose generosity and forgiveness you have already experienced, being very desirous to put a final end to disputes between his people and you concerning lands, and to do you strict justice, has fallen upon the plan of a boundary between our provinces and the Indians, which no white man shall dare to invade, as the best and surest method of ending such like disputes, and securing your property to you beyond a possibility of disturbance. This will, 1 hope, appear to you so reasonable, so just on the part of the king, and so advantageous to you and your posterity, that I can have no doubt of your cheerfully joining with me in settling such a division line, as will be best for the advantage of both white men and Indians, and as shall best agree with the extent and increase of each province, and the governors, whom 1 shall consult upon that occasion, so soon as I am fully empowered; but in the meantime I am desirous to know in what manner you would choose to extend it, and what you will agree heartily to, and abide by, in general terms. At the same time I am to acquaint you that whenever the whole is settled, and that it shall appear you have so far consulted the increasing state of our people as to make any convenient cessions of ground where it is most wanted, then you will receive a considerable present in return for your friendship.*

---

[1448] "**The Monongahela of Old**", James Veech.

[1449] The material from the letter is quoted from page 58 of the 1884 book "**History of Bedford, Somerset and Fulton Counties...**"

*To this speech the sachems and warriors of the Six Nations, after conferring some time among themselves, gave an answer to Sir William Johnson, and agreed to the proposition of the boundary line; which answer, and the other transactions of this conference, Sir William transmitted to the office of the Lords Commissioners for Trade and Plantations.*

## Peace with the Indians is ratified on May 9, 1765, opening the way for western settlement

The 1847 book "**Early History of Western Pennsylvania**" concludes its coverage of Pontiac's war by stating:

*In the ensuing spring, when the ninth of May, the time designated for holding the council for ratifying the treaty of peace, arrived, ten chiefs and about fifty warriors, accompanied by a large body of the Delaware, Seneca, Sandusky, and Muncy tribes, made their appearance at Fort Pitt, for the faithful fulfillment of their promises. They brought with them all the prisoners except a few, who they said were absent with their hunting parties—such as probably preferred a savage life.*

*The Shawanese now, as well as the other nations, expressed their entire satisfaction at the treaty of peace. Their tone was completely changed, and they seemed indeed rejoiced in perfectly brightening "the chain of friendship." Peace was ratified, and the Indians returned to their homes in the wilderness; and the deserted hearth stones of the white inhabitants, upon the frontiers, were again revisited, and the wave of population began to move on westward.*

*Thus closed the memorable Kivashuts and Pontiac war — one of short duration, but nevertheless, productive of more distracting disquietude and serious injury to the frontier settlements, than had been experienced during the years of previous hostility. The peace that now ensued lasted until a short time prior to the revolution, and gave confidence and security to the pioneers of the west. It was during this period of quietude that emigration to the valley west of the Alleghenies, was permanently commenced, — when the foundations were laid of great and powerful States, now holding a controlling influence in the American Union.*

## Abram's cabin at Turkeyfoot was built in 1765

According to page 35 of the 1906 book "**History of Bedford and Somerset Counties…**" Volume II, a circa 1798 document by surveyor Alexander McLean references *"the first cabin built by Henry Abrams, in 1765."*, and also references *"The second cabin built in 1769"* and *"His latest dwelling house."* As shown by the 1790 Abrams survey (Book C2 Page 89), Abrams' property was located at the junction of the Youghiogheny and Casselman rivers. The survey refers to the Casselman River as the *"Little Crossings"*.

## Fort Cumberland was scheduled to be abandoned by the military in 1765

The abandonment of Fort Cumberland is presaged by a May 12, 1765 letter[1450] from General Gage to Governor Sharpe that includes the statement:

*As I shall soon find it necessary to withdraw the Troops which are now in Garrison in Fort Cumberland in your Province, I think it proper to acquaint you of it, that you may give such Directions concerning the Fort, or any stores which there may be belonging to your Province, as you shall Judge necessary.*

---

[1450] "**Archives of Maryland**", Volume 14.

## Gage orders the abandonment of Fort Cumberland

A June 1, 1765 letter[1451] General Gage sent to the Earl of Halifax from New York includes the statement, *"I am to acquaint your Lordship, that finding Fort Cumberland on the frontiers of Virginia and Maryland of no use at present, and that those provinces have declined being at any further Expence in the preservation of it, I have ordered it to be abandoned."*

## Sugar Bottom was already cleared in 1763 and patented in June 1765

The Sugar Bottom tract, located within the horseshoe bend of the Potomac River, near Pinto, Maryland, has been mentioned several times in previous chapters. Although it is beyond the scope of this or any book to follow the history of every tract of land near Fort Cumberland, the Sugar Bottom tract is one that is revisited several times herein as an example. Following his previously described property dispute with Thomas Bladen, David Ross was awarded Frederick County Patented Certificate 4646[1452] for a May 25, 1763 survey of Sugar Bottom on June 24, 1765. Ross's patent certificate indicates that Edw. Lloyd acknowledged receipt of four pounds[1453] for improvements on the property, which consisted of *"Three Sorry Log Cabbins 1 of Which is 16 foot by 14 one other 14 foot by 12 The other 10 foot by 8 each covered with puncheons 6146 fence Rails and 30 Acres of Cleared Land".*[1454] The large amount of cleared land indicates that the Sugar Bottom property had already been occupied for a number of years prior to 1763.

Edward Lloyd was a very wealthy individual who served as an Agent and Receiver General for Lord Baltimore. Lloyd's signature is present on the Sugar Bottom survey in this official capacity and can be found on other early surveys acknowledging receipt of similar payments to Lord Baltimore.

Given his wealth and high status, and his official reason for signing the survey, Edward Lloyd is clearly not the individual who made the improvements on the Sugar Bottom property. The unanswerable question is who did make those improvements? It would have been a huge undertaking to cut 6146 fence rails[1455], and the decade preceding the May 25, 1763 survey was an exceedingly dangerous time to be living west of Fort Cumberland. The hazardous living conditions would seem to make it unlikely that a private individual or individuals made the improvements — but certainly not impossible. James Livingston's previously quoted July 16, 1763 letter indicates that Joseph Mounts was already living along the Potomac River, above Fort Cumberland on the date of the letter — so perhaps the Mounts family was already living on and improving the Sugar Bottom property long before purchasing it from Ross in 1768.

## John Johnson, Isaac Cox, and Daniel Pursley witness a Virginia property transaction

The 1939 book "**Early Records Hampshire County Virginia**" records the following for August 9, 1765, *"FRIEND, John (w. Carenhapech) of Hampshire Co. to Dennis Pursley of Frederick Co. (lease and release) 194 a. on Potomac River; rec. 10-8-1765. Wit.: John Johnson, Isaac Cox, Daniel Pursley."*

---

[1451] Lois Mulkearn's 1954 book mistakenly gives the date of the letter as June 8, 1765. Timothy Fisher tracked down Gage's copy of the letter and provided photographs.

[1452] MSA S1197-5069.

[1453] Lloyd's affidavit states, *"I have received four pounds for the within Improvements and One pound four Shillings and four pence for Two years Rent on the Within Lands __Mid___ 1765 Patant may therefore issue with is Excellencys Approbation 21 Decem$^r$ 1764 Edw. Lloyd. Approved H. Sharpe"*

[1454] Julia Jackson found the description of the improvements on Sugar Bottom and determined that the individual who acknowledged receipt for the improvements and rent was Edward Lloyd, rather than Edward Boyd.

[1455] I estimate that 6146 fence rails is enough to fence in about 41-1/2 acres.

### A 1765 reference to a local sawmill

Michael Cresap's October 4, 1765 survey of the 80-acre Alder Thickett tract (Frederick County, Maryland Patent No. 263) includes the statement, *"Beginning at a bounded White Oak standing on the point of a ridge opposite the sawmill..."*[1456]

This is likely to be a reference to Colonel Thomas Cresap's sawmill, which is mentioned in the previously quoted October 17, 1760 resolution of the committee of the Ohio Company. The beginning point of Alder Thickett is in the general vicinity of Latitude 39.526375°, Longitude -78.545409°, on a ridge in a bend of Town Creek. The phrase *"opposite the sawmill"* probably means on the opposite side of Town Creek. There is a potential mill stream illustrated opposite the ridge on topographical maps, emptying into Town Creek approximately at Latitude 39.528801 °, Longitude -78.542100°. This seems to be about where Craig's mill is located on the 1795 Griffith map. It may be that Craig's mill reused Cresap's mill race.

### Frederick Ice is involved in a land transaction on Patterson Creek

The 1939 book "**Early Records Hampshire County Virginia**" documents the following for October 25, 1765, *"ICE, Frederick of Frederick Co., Md. (w. Eleanor) to John Greenfield of Frederick Co., Va. (lease and release) 187 a. on Patterson Creek; rec. 4-14-1767. Wit.: Bryan Bruen, Robt. Gregg, John Lyne, Jno. Moffet, Henry Heth. Thos. Wood."*

### The Frederick County court repudiates the stamp act in November 1765

According to J. Thomas Scharf's 1882 book "**History of Western Maryland**", the stamp act became law on March 22, 1765, the stamp distributor for Maryland was burned in effigy at Frederick Town on August 29, 1765, and the Frederick County Court decided to proceed without stamped paper in November 1765. The stamp act, and other parliamentary acts, produced American resistance to the Crown that ultimately led to the War for Independence. An excellent account of events leading to the war, and reactions in Maryland, is provided in the "**History of Western Maryland**". The still-celebrated order of the Frederick County Court states:

> *It is the unanimous resolution and opinion of this court that all the business thereof shall and ought to be transacted in the usual and accustomed manner without any inconvenience or delay to be occasioned from the want of stamped paper, parchment, or vellum, and that all proceedings shall be valid and effectual without the use of stamps, and they enjoin and order all sheriffs, clerks, counsellors, attorneys, and all officers of the court to proceed in their several avocations as usual, which resolution and opinion are grounded on the following and other reasons: —*

> *First. It is conceived there hath not been a legal publication yet made of any act of Parliament imposing a stamp duty on the Colonies. Therefore this court are of the opinion that until the existence of such an act is properly notified it would be culpable in them to permit or suffer a total stagnation of business which must inevitably be productive of innumerable injuries and have a tendency to subvert all principles of civil government.*

> *Second. As no stamps are yet arrived in this Province, and the inhabitants have no means of procuring any, this court are of opinion that it would be an instance of the most wanton oppression to deprive any person of a legal remedy for the recovery of his property for omitting that which it is impossible to perform.*

---

[1456] This patent description was found as a result of Steve Colby's research.

## A Maryland 'funeral' for the stamp act

The December 16, 1765 issue[1457] of the "**Maryland Gazette**" includes the following:

*The Stamp Act having received a mortal stab at the hands of justice on Saturday last, gave up the ghost to the great joy of the inhabitants of Frederick County. The lifeless body lay exposed to public ignominy till yesterday when it was thought proper, to prevent infection from its stench, to bury it in the following manner: The Sons of Liberty assembled at the house of Mr. Samuel Swearingen in the afternoon and the coffin was taken up exactly at 3 o'clock.*

*FORM OF THE FUNERAL.*

*1 — The colors of the town company.*

*2 — Drums.*

*3 — The banner displayed with this inscription in large characters, 'Constitutional Liberty Asserted by the Magistrates of Frederick County, 22, November, 1765.'*

*4 — The Cap of Liberty mounted on a staff with the several following inscriptions: 'Magna Charter,' 'Charter of Maryland,' 'Trial by Jury Restored,' 'Oppression Removed,' 'Liberty and Loyalty.'*

*5 — Conductors.*

*6 — The coffin with this inscription on the lid: 'The Stamp Act expired of a mortal stab received from the genius of liberty in Frederick County court, 22 November, 1765, aged 22 days.' On the ends, sides and ledges of the coffin appeared several inscriptions which were all together deposited in the ground as appendages to the Stamp Act, viz.: 'Tyrrany,' 'Villenage,' 'Military Execution,' 'Soldiers quartered in private houses,' 'Court of Vice Admiralty,' 'Guarda de Costas to prevent corruption in North Americans, from a redundancy of Spanish dollars,' 'Britons employed in fastening chains on the necks of British subjects,' 'Fines,' 'Imprisonment,' 'Ruin,' 'Desolation,' 'Slavery, taking possession of America in order to extend her dominion over Great Britain.'*

*7 — Z. H. Esq. (Zachariah Hood, the stamp agent) as sole mourner carried in an open chariot. His countenance pale and dejected, his dress disorderly, unsuitable to his rank and betraying great inward distraction of mind, and his tottering situation, being scarce able to keep his seat, demonstrated the weakness to which he was reduced and plainly indicated the melancholy catastrophe which shortly ensued.*

*8 — Sons of Liberty, two by two.*

*During the whole procession, which marched through the principal streets until it arrived at the gallows erected on the Court House green, the bells continued ringing; and on every huzza by the crowd or loud laugh of female spectators, Z. H. Esq. was observed to nod or drop his head into his bosom in token of the utmost sorrow and confusion.*

*On their arrival at the gallows Z. H. Esq., unable to say anything, was seen to give a faint nod of approbation when he was asked if the paper taken from his pocket contained the substance of what he had to say. In this paper he spoke of his devotion to the Stamp Act and asked to be buried in the same grave with it. As soon as the person appointed had finished reading, he was seen to sink suddenly down and tumble out of the chariot, his body becoming instantaneously cold and stiff, so violent an assault had grief made on all his vital faculties. A loud noise and roll of drums followed and according to his own request his corpse was deposited in the earth, together with that of his beloved.*

[1457] "**Luther League Review**", Volume 32, 1919.

*The grave being filled up, and acclamations repeated, the company marched in their former order with colors, banners, etc., to the house of Mr. Samuel Swearingen, where an elegant supper was prepared and a ball given to the ladies, who made a brilliant appearance on the occasion.*

Although not documentary evidence, Volume 10 of the "**Ohio Archæological and Historical Quarterly**" (1901) states that the Sons of Liberty was organized by Colonel Thomas Cresap; Samuel Swearingen's sisters Ruth and Drusilla married Colonel Cresap's sons Daniel and Thomas; and Samuel Swearingen's daughter married Colonel Cresap's grandson Daniel Cresap, Jr.

### Gordon proposes supplying the forts on the Mississippi via Fort Cumberland

Harry Gordon's December 17, 1765 *"A Memorial concerning the back Forts in N America"* includes the following:

*If the Forts on the Mississipi are to be garrisoned I cannot help reflecting on the unnatural Choice of the Way of communicating with, and sending Troops to them — They enter by PENSACOLA or MOBILE, unhealthy Places at that Season, at which they take Provisions sent from here — Then they strugle against the Stream of the Mississippi for 12 or 1300 Miles, and as it is only to be ascended when there is a Flood in the River, that by spreading over its Banks diminishes the Strength of the Current, which is prodigious when confin'd within them; therefore the Passage up this River is long, fatiguing, incertain, expensive, and thence becomes dangerous — Whereas were the Troops to be landed from England in any of the Northern Colonies or Provinces, Provisions bought near and sent up the Potowmack along with them to Fort Cumberland, from thence transported, & the Troops marched, along the Passage opened by order of General Braddock across the Alegheny Mountains, to the Monongehela — They then would pass thro' a healthy Country, be plentifully supplied with all Kinds of Necessaries, and goe down Stream to within 100 Miles of their Quarters, by the finest River, that runs thro' the finest of Countries, in large Craft, without any Risque, (provided any Measures are kept or any Attention pay'd to the only two Nations of the Delawares & Shawnese) and be able to perform their Route in two Months from their Landing, whereas the other cannot be well done in less than Six, & perhaps take two Floods, which seldom happen above once a Year —*

# 18. 1766: A friendly Indian is murdered

**An Indian is murdered between Fort Cumberland and Fort Bedford on January 11, 1766**
Volume 9 of the 1852 book "**Minutes of the Provincial Council of Pennsylvania**" includes three items relating to an Indian who was murdered 12 miles from Fort Cumberland. The following statement is from the March 6, 1766 council proceedings:

*The Governor acquainted the Council that a few days since he had received Information from Captain Lemuel Barrit, of Cumberland Valley, that on the 11th day of January last, a Mohawk Indian, on his return from the Country of the Cherokees, was murdered & Scalp'd about 12 miles from Fort Cumberland, on the road leading from thence to Fort Bedford, and proposed to issue a Proclamation offering a reward for the discovery, and apprehending the murderer that he might be brought to Condign Punishment; But Captain Barrit attending the Board, at the Governor's request, he was farther examined, and his deposition taken in writing, when there appeared from sundry Circumstances, great reason to suspect the Murder had been committed by a certain Sam[l.] Jacobs, who had absconded, and was supposed to have gone to the Frontiers of Virginia and Maryland; The Council, therefore, advised the Governor to delay issuing a Proclamation, till means were tried for apprehending the person suspected; and for that purpose to write to the Governors of Maryland and Virginia, enclosing them Copies of Capt[n.] Barrit's Deposition, & desiring they would be pleas'd to order a strict Search to be made for the said Samuel Jacobs, through their respective provinces, & also to write to Sir William Johnson, acquainting him with the matter.*

*John Penn sends letters regarding the murder*
The following letter was sent from Philadelphia by Governor John Penn of Pennsylvania to Governor Sharpe of Maryland and Governor Fauquiere of Virginia on March 11, 1766:

*I lately received information that one of the six Nations Indians, returning from the Cherokee Country, was Murdered on the 11th of January last, on the road between Fort Cumberland and Fort Bedford, within this Province. I intended to have issued a proclamation offering a reward for discovering & apprehending the Murderer, but finding by the examination of Captain Lemuel Barrit, who lives near the place where the Indian was found, that there is great reason to believe the Murder was committed by one Samuel Jacobs,[1458] who is said to have fled into the back parts of Virginia or Maryland, I think it most*

---

[1458] According to Veech's book "**The Monongahela of Old…**", a man named Samuel Jacobs killed an Indian known as Indian Stephen *"at or near Stewart's Crosings"*, and was *"aided and abetted by one John Ingman, an 'indentured servant' of Capt. Wm. Crawford…"* I don't know if this is the same Samuel Jacobs referred to in John Penn's March 11, 1766 letters, but it seems likely. Veech also states, *"The case acquired importance from the fact that the Governor of Virginia, contrary to the claim of that province to the territory embracing the locality of the killing, had sent one of the offenders back from Virginia to Pennsylvania to be tried for the offense."* According to the "**Pennsylvania Archives**", Botetourt, the Governor of Virginia, wrote a letter to John Penn, the Governor of Pennsylvania, on March 20, 1770 that states, *"I have the honor to inclose two Depositions, together with an answer to a letter wrote by Mr. Attorney General at my desire, and have sent to your Excellency, by Lieutenant Inglis, the Body of John Ingman, he having confessed himself concerned in the murder of Indian Stephen, which, from the best information I can obtain, was committed on a spot of Ground claimed by your Government. You will find, by the Paper I have inclosed, that there never was an Act of Villainy more unprovoked or more deliberately undertaken, it is therefore extremely my wish that the Laws may enable you to do justice and appease, by rigid punishment, a Nation of offended Indians. Mr. William Crawford, who is Master of John Ingman, has promised to attend you the beginning of April, and has engaged to do his utmost to procore any Evidence which you may think material to be examined."* The 1833 book, "**History of the Valley of Virginia**" provides a detailed account of an un-named Irish servant of William Crawford who was arrested and jailed at Winchester for participating in the killing of two Indians in 1768. The story ends with the servant and his companion William White

*advisable to defer my proclamation till I have first tried every other means in my power to secure the Offender. I take the liberty of inclosing you Capt[n.] Barrit's deposition & description of Jacobs' person, at the same time requesting you will cause strict search to be made for him throughout your Province, as you must be sensible of the ill Consequences that will ensue if all necessary steps are not pursued in order to bring to Justice this lawless Villain, as well to convince the Indians of our good Intentions towards them as to deter others from the same Conduct, which, if we cannot fall upon some means of putting a stop to, we may reasonably expect to be again involved in the Miseries of an other Indian War. I shall make Sir William Johnson acquainted with this unhappy affair, and the measures taken to give our Friends, the Six Nations, all the satisfaction in our power, that he may represent the matter in a proper light to them, so as to prevent any ill Consequences that might otherwise happen from their resentment.*

The following letter was written from Philadelphia by Governor John Penn to Sir William Johnson on March 11, 1766:

*It was with a very great Concern that a few days ago I received certain Information by Capt[n.] Samuel Barrit, that on the 11th of January last, a Mohawk Indian, in his return from the Cherokee Country, was Murdered on the Road between Fort Cumberland & Fort Bedford, in this Province.*

*This unhappy affair will no doubt give great Offence to the Indians of the Six Nations, and may be attended with very bad consequences. But I shall think it my indispensable duty, from motives of Justice as well as good Policy, to give them all the Satisfaction in my power for this Injury, and I beg you will be pleased to take the first Opportunity to acquaint them that I heartily condole with them on this occasion, and that all means shall be used for apprehending the Murderer and bringing him to Condign Punishment. I intended to have issued a Proclamation, offering a Reward for that purpose; but as there appears by Capt[n.] Barrit's deposition, a Copy of which you have enclosed, very great reason to think the Murder was committed by one Samuel Jacobs, who is supposed to have fled to the back parts of Maryland and Virginia, I shall suspend the Proclamation till better means have been tried to apprehend him, for which purpose I have written to the Governors of Maryland and Virginia, to request they would cause a strict search to be made for him throughout their perspective Provinces. If we should be so fortunate as to secure this Lawless Villain, I will immediately acquaint you therewith, that you may have it in your power to satisfy the Indians of our good disposition towards them, and our desire and readiness to do them the strictest Justice upon all Occasions.*

### *Barrett's deposition regarding the murder of the friendly Indian*
The book "**Proceedings of the Council of Maryland, 1761-1769**" quotes the March 6, 1766 deposition of Lemuel Barrett, as follows:

*Copy Lemuel Barrett of Cumberland Valley in Cumberland County in the Province of Pensylvania, being Sworn on the holy Evangelists of Almighty God Deposeth and Saith That on the Twenty fourth day of January last past this Deponent being informed that the body of an Indian had been found by one Edward Askin, near the high Road leading from Fort Cumberland to Fort Bedford, he this Deponent Collected together upwards of twenty of his Neighbours, among whom was a certain Samuel Jacobs, and went with them to View and bury the Body of the said Indian. That upon inspecting the said Body, he found that the said Indian had been Shot with a Bullet thro' his Body the Ball appearing to have entered in at his Breast a little above the Pit of his Stomach, and to have come out between his Shoulders, That the head was Scalp'd and his Belly and Breast ripped open. That he this Deponent was informed (after he first heard of the said Indian's being Murdered) by his Servant Man Samuel Lyon that on the eleventh day of the same Month of January he saw the said Indian pass along the high Road and Conversed with him about half a Mile from the place where his Body was found, and that the aforesaid Samuel Jacobs had Cross'd the said Road with a Gun in his hand a few Minutes after the Indian had left the said Samuel Lyon, and*

---

being sprung from jail by a large force of civilians led by Abraham Fry. Since Ingman is an Irish name, the un-named Irish servant in the story was probably John Ingman.

*further that within a Quarter of an hour afterwards he the said Samuel Lyon had heard the Report of a Gun about the place where the said Indian was killed, from whence this Deponent suspected that the said Samuel Jacobs had been concerned in the said Indian's Murder. This Deponent further saith that he informed his Neighbours as they stood round the said Indians Body that he had heard it asserted, that if a Murderer touch'd the Dead Body of the Person he had Slain, the Carcass tho' Lifeless would bleed, and therefore he proposed to them to try the Experiment and by that Method they would either acquit themselves of all Suspicion of having killed the said Indian or if any Person then present had really killed him he would be discovered and his Guilt be made Evident or to that purpose. That this proposal being generally agreed to, he this Deponent and all the Rest of the Company (except the aforesaid Samuel Jacobs) very ready touch'd alternately the said Indian's Body, but the said Samuel made some hesitation when it came to his turn, and his Countenance changed and he appeared Confused, but at last on the Importunity of the Company, touch'd the said Body, That this Behaviour of the said Samuel induced the Company to Suspect and charge the said Jacobs with the killing the said Indian, but he absolutely denied it. That after they had buried the said Indian, this Deponent was informed by one of the Company whose name is Thomas Elby, that in some Conversation with the said Jacobs, the said Elby persuading him to discover where the said Indian's Gun was, the said Jacobs had denied that he knew any thing about the said Gun, but told the said Elby that the night before he had dreamt that it was hid under a logg about two hundred yards from the Main Road near a Run of Water which crossed the said Road. That on this information this Deponent took one Thomas Jones with him and left the Company with an intent to search for the Gun, at the Place described which he was well acquainted with, and after they had taken a Circuit a different way in the Woods to conceal from the said Jacobs and the rest of the Company what their real design was, he this Deponent and the said Thomas Jones went down to the before mentioned Run, and found the said Indian's Gun his Powder horn and Shot Bagg lying under a log about two hundred yards from the Road aforesaid, That they thereupon were Confirmed in their former Suspicions that the said Jacobs was the Murderer of the said Indian and immediately returned to the said Company with an Intent to apprehend and carry him before a Justice of Peace to be dealt with according to Law, but to their great surprize were informed by the Company that the said Jacobs had followed him the said Jones and this Deponent into the Woods and that they had not seen him since. This Deponent further saith that it was then Evening and too late to pursue him, and that the said Jacobs hath absconded and never made his appearance in that part of the Country since, but that he has been informed he was seen soon afterwards in the back parts of the Colony of Virginia, and further this Deponent saith not,*

*Taken and Sworn March 6th 1766. Lemuel Barritt*

*Before me Will^m Allen Chief Justice.*

The deposition indicates that Barrrtt had about 20 neighbors he was able to call on for help in 1766.

The same book also includes the following:

*A Description of Samuel Jacobs, the Person suspected to have Murdered the Mohock Indian on the 11th of January 1766.*

*A thick well set Man with a bold look about 5 feet 8 Inches high 27 years of Age wears his own hair which is Short, and frizled, of a light brown Colour, pock marked and has a Scar on the Right side of his Belly near the bottom, he was born in America and Speaks English very distinctly but rather slow. It is the humble Advice of this Board that his Excellency should write to M^r Darnall recommending to him to issue his Warrant, and use his utmost endeavours to get the above described Samuel Jacobs Apprehended.*

*Copy of the Deposition and Description of Jacobs being made out for M^r Darnall was transmitted accordingly.*

### A 1766 survey mentions John Friend's residence

Michael Cresap's May 9, 1766 survey of the 70-acre Bettys Blessing tract (Frederick County, Maryland Patent No. 513) includes the statement, *"Beginning at a bounded Hickory and Popular standing near Potomack River & nearby opposite John Friends on the Virginia side of the River".*[1459]

### Sharpe writes to Lord Baltimore about the effect and repeal of the stamp act

On May 15, 1766, Governor Sharpe wrote a letter[1460] to Lord Baltimore that includes the following:

*In the Letters I address't to your Ldp & M$^r$ Calvert last Winter I inform'd you that an entire Stop had been then put to all Business & that the Courts of Law except in two or three of the most distant Counties were shut up; in this situation Things remained till the Provincial Court met here the 1$^{st}$ Day of April agreeable to their Adjournment when a Number of People who were assembled here from different parts of the Province impatient at the Provincial Office being so Long shut up went in a Body to the Judges & insisted on its being opened so that Writs may issue as usual without Stampt paper & in order to prevent farther Clamour or Disturbance the Judges so far complied with their Demand as to make an Order to that Effect & then Adjourn'd the Court to the 21$^{st}$ of next July at which time as we have now received an Account of the Stamp Acts being certainly repealed the Court will sit & proceed to Business in the usual manner. I find by several Letters in which Mr Hamersley has been so kind as to communicate to me what passed in the two Houses of Parliament relative to the Repeal of the Stamp Act that it has not been carried without great Opposition & Difficulty & that it is at length repealed not on the principle contended for by the Colonies but purely out of regard to the Commercial Interests of Great Britain: Whatever was the Motive for the Repeal the Measure will I flatter myself be immediately productive of the best Consequences, the Restoration of Tranquillity to the Colonies & of mutual Intercourse & Affection between His Majesty's British & American Subjects.*

On May 28, 1766, Sharpe wrote a letter[1461] to Hamersley that includes the following statement:

*Thanks for the several Letters you were so kind as to favour me with the 20$^{th}$ & 26$^{th}$ of Decem$^r$ last, the 20$^{th}$ & 25$^{th}$ of February & 1$^{st}$ of March by which I perceive there was a very great Opposition in the House of Lords especially to the Motion for Repealing the Stamp Act & that the Commercial Interest of Great Britain & not the Claim or Clamour of the Colonies has been urged as the sole or at least the most proper Reason to be given for the Repeal. You'll see by the inclosed Gazette that a Copy of the Act has already reached us whereupon all the Offices are opened & I hope there is now an End to the Disturbances & Discontent the Stamp Act had occasioned for tho I perceive by the Northern Papers that there are Men both in New England & New York who deny the Right of the British Legislature to bind the Colonies by any Laws whatever I do not think such Doctrine is agreeable to the Sense of these Southern Colonies.*

Sharpe was off by more than a little bit in his last remarks. The resentment continued to grow, leading to war with the mother country within a decade.

### A road between Cumberland and Bedford on the east side of Wills Mountain

The journal from Mason and Dixon's survey has a May 29, 1766 journal entry that identifies a road from Fort Cumberland to Fort Bedford that was located on the east side of Wills Mountain, stating, *"At 157 miles 75 chains, crossed the Road Leading from Fort Cumberland to Bedford."* The road is illustrated on Mason and Dixon's map of the survey. This may be the road Washington cut to Rays Town in 1758, during the

---

[1459] This patent description was found as a result of Steve Colby's research.
[1460] "**Archives of Maryland**", Volume 14.
[1461] "**Archives of Maryland**", Volume 14.

French and Indian war. I have converted the surveyors' measurements to GPS coordinates using the landmarks they reference and find the stated location of the 1766 road to Bedford[1462] to be very near where the modern road crosses the Mason-Dixon line.

### People were living near the state line in 1766

The May 31, 1766 entry in Mason and Dixon's survey journal states:

*Continued the line. At 159 m, 71 ch, the summit of Wills creek Mountain. Here by the estimation of some who live near this place, Fort Cumberland bears south, distant between 5 and 6 miles. At 161 m, 25 ch, cross'd Wills creek.*

### Enoch Innis has family ties with Thomas and Michael Cresap

The June 19, 1766 deposition[1463] of Enoch Innis establishes his age with the statement, *"The Deposition of Enoch Innis aged Twenty seven years, or thereabouts..."* The December 9, 1766 deposition[1464] of Thomas Bowles establishes family ties between Enoch Innis and Thomas Cresap with the statement, *"...except from Col° Cresap or his Son in Law Enoch Innis..."* In his book, "**A biographical sketch of the life of the late Captain Michael Cresap**", John Jacob states, *"Sarah, daughter of Colonel Thomas Cresap, was twice married; first to Colonel Enoch Innis, and afterward to a Mr. John Foster. They are all dead, and she had no children."*

Thomas Cresap had storekeeping experience and was a member of the Ohio Company. Thomas's son Michael also had storekeeping experience. The family ties Enoch Innis had with Thomas and Michael Cresap may help to explain why a Mr. Ennis was described as being the storekeeper at Fort Cumberland in a December 16, 1764 letter, how Enoch Innis and Michael Cresap came to sell a large amount of supplies to Mason and Dixon in 1767, how a Mr. Innis was documented at the New Store opposite Fort Cumberland on November 27, 1770, and why someone was able to stay a day with Major Ennis at Fort Cumberland in 1772. It appears that Enoch Innis was minding store at Wills Creek, which, if true, helps to explain the various traditions relating to western settlers obtaining supplies at Fort Cumberland before the formation of the town.

### An eyewitness says the fort was dilapidated in 1766, but still had ten cannons

On Sunday, June 22, 1766, after Fort Cumberland had been abandoned, Charles Mason (of Mason and Dixon fame) wrote the following in his journal:

*Went to see Fort Cumberland: It is beautifully situated on a rising ground, close in the Northwest fork made by the falling in of Wills Creek into Potowmack; The Fort is in bad repair; has in it at present only 10 Six Pounders. Going to the Fort I fell into General Braddock's Road, which he cut through the Mountains to lead the Army under his command to the Westward in the year 1755, but fate; how hard: made through the desert a path, himself to pass; and never; never to return.*

---

[1462] In his 1803 journal, Thaddeus Harris describes Bedford as follows, *"It is regularly laid out, and there are several houses on the main street built with bricks; even the others, which are of hewn logs, have a distinguishing neatness in their appearance. The Court House, Market House, and Record Office, are brick; the Gaol is built of stone. The inhabitants are supplied with water brought in pipes to a large reservoir in the middle of the town. On the northerly skirt of the town flows Rayston creek, a considerable branch of the Juniata."*

[1463] "**Archives of Maryland**", Volume 32.

[1464] "**Archives of Maryland**", Volume 32.

As described in other chapters herein, Maryland and Virginia sought to acquire the referenced cannon for use in the Revolutionary War.

### A 1766 building at the site of Corriganville

Mason and Dixon's map of their 1766 boundary line survey illustrates a building at the mouth of Jennings Run, and another to the northward, on the west side of Wills Creek. These buildings substantiate the existence of a path or road along the west side of Wills Creek in 1766, and settlers.

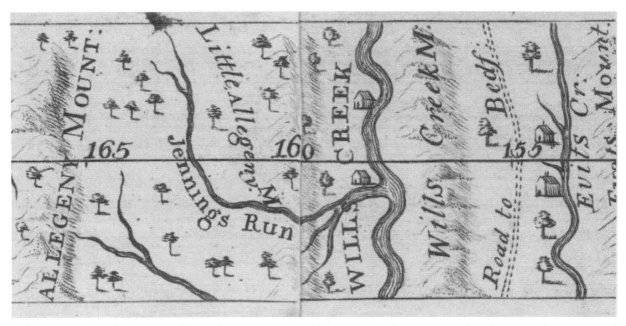

This is a portion of Mason and Dixon's map of their state boundary line survey, showing a portion surveyed in 1766, east of Maryland Route 47. The map shows a building at the mouth of Jennings Run, and a building north of Jennings Run, and two buildings on the road to Bedford. (Courtesy of T. M. Babcock, PLS.)

### Part of a Mill Race

The July 10, 1766 Joseph Shirt survey (Frederick County unpatented certificate 330) that began *"at the end of Sixteenth line of a Tract of Land called Wills Town"* mentions the following improvements, *"2 acres of Cleared Land where on is part of an old Cabbin & Part of a Mill Race".*[1465] Joseph Shirt appears on Veatch's map of Deakins' survey and is in the general vicinity of Corriganville.

### Michael Cresap patents an improved property

Michael Cresap's July 15, 1766 survey of the 28-1/2-acre Ash Bottom tract (Frederick County, Maryland Patent No. 352) includes the statement, *"3 acres of cleared land where on is 500 rails & a cabbin 12 feet by 14 feet".*[1466] The 500 fence rails were enough to fence in all of the cleared ground, by my calculations.

---

[1465] This improvement was identified by Francis Bridges.

[1466] This patent description was found as a result of Steve Colby's research.

## Land gobbers

Matthew Clarkson, an employee of the firm of Baynton, Wharton, & Morgan, was taking a business trip for the firm in the summer of 1766. His August 15, 1766 journal entry, partially quoted here, tells of buying a large amount of land in the general area:

*This day, halted at Bedford to rest myself and horses. Entered into an agreement with George Woods about five tracts of land, three of them in Cumberland valley, about seventeen miles from Bedford on the road to Fort Cumberland — one on the waters of Dunning's Creek, about three miles to the north-east of Bedford, and one other in Woodcock valley, about forty miles north of Bedford, and two miles west of Standing Stone — amounting together to 1800 acres, one half of which I am to have on paying him £90 three months after they are warranted and accepted at the Surveyor's office, provided Edward Duffield, of Philadelphia, agrees hereto in that time. Was obliged to borrow of George Wood, £3 10s., to assist the bateaux-men on to the fort, as they had spent all their money. Drew an order on B., W., and M., in favor of Wood, for it.*

## Richard Morris obtains a land patent

Richard Morris is one of the individuals named on the 1761 Old Town Hundreds list. The 80-acre Morris's Luck tract was surveyed for Richard Morris on September 23, 1766 and patented to him the same day (Frederick County Patent Certificate 2673, MSA S1197-2976). The survey reads, *"... I have Carefully Surveyd and laid out for and in the name of him the said Richard Morris all that Tract of Land Called Morris's Luck Lying in the County afsd Beginning at the end of Thirty Eight Pole a long the first line of a Tract of Land Called "Morris's Choice..."* This seems to be a reference to the 100-acre Morris's Chase tract that was surveyed for Joseph Flint on June 16, 1751 and patented to Joseph Flint on August 10, 1753. The survey reads, *"... I have Carefully laid out for and in the name of him the said Flint all that tract of Land called Morris's Chase beg at two bounded White Oaks standing on the Town Creek about Six Miles from the Mouth thereof in the North West corner of this Province ..."*

## Imported stones are to be set up on the new boundary in the presence of commissioners

A letter Governor Sharpe wrote to Hamersley from Annapolis on October 22, 1766 includes the following:

*The two Surveyors who came from England to run the Boundary Lines under the Direction of the Commissioners having at last described them all it is agreed that the Stones which were imported last Summer shall be immediately set up in the Presence of a Comm^n on each Side & that there shall be then a general Meeting in order to draw up a State of our Proceedings & return the same to the High Court of Chancery according to the Tenor of the Articles of Agreement & our Commission, but as the setting up the Stones & the Drawing such State afterwards might take up so much time as to make it impossible for us to transmit the same before the last of Decem^r next when our last Comm^n will expire I submit it to you whether it will not be necessary that a new Commission be sent us, which indeed must be the Case if His Ldp & the Proprietors of Penns' have agreed that the East & West Line shall be next Summer extended to the Westernmost Limits of Penns^a for it now stops at Savage Mountain a Ridge of the Allegany not more than five or six Miles Westward of Fort Cumberland.*

## Money appropriated for road improvements west of Fort Cumberland in 1766

The 1910 book **"History of Harrison County, West Virginia"** states that in November 1766, the Virginia Assembly appointed commissioners *"To view, lay out and direct a road to be cleared from the North branch of the Potomac to Fort Pitt on the Ohio, by or near the road called Braddock's road, in the most direct and cheapest manner the said commissioners think fit, and two hundred pounds were appropriated for that* *purpose.*" The November 7, 1766 act is recorded in "**Hening's Statutes at Large**", and begins with the statement, "*Whereas it is represented to this present general assembly, that by opening a road from the frontiers of this colony to Fort Pitt on the Ohio, a very advantageous trade might be carried on with the Indians, in alliance with the British crown on the western frontiers of this dominion, and the king's garrisons be better supplied with provisions...*"

### John Penn follows up on the murder of the friendly Mohawk Indian

The book "**The Statutes at Large of Pennsylvania from 1682-1801**", Volume 7, includes a November 15, 1766 letter from Governor John Penn of Pennsylvania, to the Governor of Virginia, written from Philadelphia, that includes the following:

*I did myself the honor to write you on the 11th March, concerning the murder of a friendly Indian near Fort Cumberland in January last, suspected, with great reason, from the deposition of Captain Lemuel Barrit, to have been perpetrated by one Samuel Jacobs, who afterwards, as was believed, fled into the back parts of Virginia, and having requested you would cause strict search to be made for him throughout your colony, I beg you will now be kind enough to acquaint me what has been done in consequence of your orders therein, and whether any intelligence has been obtained about that villain, as I am very anxious that offenders of this kind should be discovered and brought to punishment, as well to convince the Indians of our disposition to do them every act of justice in our power, as to prevent the terrible calamities of another war.*

### Sharpe hopes Johnson will obtain consent for Mason and Dixon to continue their line

A December 15, 1766 letter Governor Horatio Sharpe wrote to Sir William Johnson from Annapolis states:

*Lord Baltimore the Proprietary of Maryland & Messrs. Penns the Proprietors of Pennsylvania having some Years ago entered into an Agreement for Running Divisional Lines between their respective Provinces appointed certain Commissioners to carry the Said Agreement into Execution who have at length caused all the Lines to be actually run & described by Vistoes except One which is also extended a few Miles farther Westward than Fort Cumberland. According to the Articles of Agreement this Line is to be continued to the extreme Western Limit of Pennsylvania but the Conmmissioners being apprehensive that the Indians may take Umbrage at it's being done without their Consent I am desired as You will see by the inclosed Copy of the Commissioners Minutes to represent as much to You & to desire that You will on behalf of the Proprietors apply to the Indians concerned for such Consent so that the Surveyors may proceed with the Line the End of March or Beginning of April next. As I presume Governor Penn has already wrote to You on the Subject I shall only add that I hope You will endeavour to prevail on the Indians to give their Consent that the Line may be now run so that there may not hereafter be any Dispute between the Inhabitants of Pennsulvania & this Province about the Boundaries which has been too much the Case for many Years past.*

### The difficulty of preventing settlement west of the limits of the Royal Proclamation

A December 23, 1766 letter[1467] written from Annapolis to the Earl of Shelborne by Deputy Governor Sharpe states:

*Since I had the honour to receive Your Lordships Letter dated the 13th of Septr last I have made Enquiry but cannot find that any Violence hath been committed within this Province on any Indian since the Conclusion of the late War, nor have any Lands been granted in Maryland beyond the Limits described in His Majestys Proclamation of 1763 or even to the Westward of Fort Cumberland, if therefore any*

---

[1467] "**Correspondence of Governor Sharpe, 1761-1771**".

*Settlement has been made on Lands to which the Indians have any Pretensions it has not been by Persons claiming Protection under this Government & your Ldp may be assured that I shall never Countenance the making any Settlement that can possibly give the Indians the least Cause of Offence & If any of the Inhabitants of this Province shall injure them in any respect I will endeavour to have the Offender punished; but as there are on the Frontiers of these Provinces Persons that support themselves by Hunting & among them Men of no Character or principle It will I am afraid be impossible to prevent such from going & building Houses or Cabbins beyond the Limits prescribed by the Royal Proclamation unless the Military to the Westward of these provinces are directed to destroy such Houses & otherwise to punish such Offenders. Should I hear of any Transaction within or in the neighbourhood of this province likely to give the Indians Uneasiness I shall immediately advise both General Gage & Sr William Johnson thereof & will use all means in my power to prevent the ill Consequences of such Uneasiness & to preserve Peace & Harmony between the Neighbouring Indians & His Majestys Subjects in this province.*

## A reference to Nemacolin in 1766

Lieutenant Thomas Hutchins' circa 1766[1468] *"A Description of part of the Country Westward of the River Ohio, with the Distances Computed from Fort Pitt to the several Indian Towns by Land & Water"* describes a place 20 miles from the Hocking River, as follows, *"15 Miles from the Canoe place is A Shelving Rock, under which Neal McCollen, a Delaware Indian, Built a Cabbin."*

## A tradition of a family living at Fort Cumberland in the 1766 to 1769 timeframe

Although not documentary evidence, the 1883 book "**History of Monongalia County, West Virginia**" includes the following statement:

*Col. John Evans was born in Loudon County, Virginia, whither his father emigrated from Wales when a young man, and settled in and married there. While he was still a small boy and only child, his father died from the bite of a rattlesnake. The widowed mother bestowed upon her son a liberal education for those times. After leaving school at Alexandria, he returned to his mother in Loudon County, where he subsequently married Ann Martin.*

*Between 1762 or 1764, braving the dangers incident to such an expedition, he crossed the mountains and secured a tomahawk right[1469] by hacking the outlines of a fertile tract of land on the eastern side of the Monongahela River, about a mile north of the mouth of Decker's Creek. David Moran's farm, on which, in 1783, the county-seat of Monongalia was located, lay immediately north of said creek, and was afterwards called Morgantown. In the year following (1765), he again visited his land on the Monongahela, and built a cabin and made an improvement on it. In the following year (1766), he started from his home in Loudoun County with his family, consisting of his mother, his Wife, two children, and a family of negroes, intending to take them to the new home he had prepared for them west of the Alleghanies. Learning that the Indians still made occasional invasions into northwest Virginia, he left his family at Fort Cumberland (now Cumberland, Md.), where they remained until 1769, and where his son John was born. Col. Evans, in the meantime, occasionally visited his new home. In 1769, he obtained a patent on his tomahawk settlement for 400 acres of land, including his improvement thereon, to which,*

---

[1468] Although the referenced Hutchins papers are undated, 1766 is the year Thomas Hutchins, Henry Gordon, and George Croghan began their surveying expedition down the Ohio River. Hutchins' papers are collection 308 of the Historical Society of Pennsylvania.

[1469] Volume 2, page 90 of the 1906 book "**History of Bedford and Somerset Counties...**" states, *"The improvement right or claim was considered legal, and was looked on as being just and respectable. A tomahawk claim, unless followed by speedy settlement, was usually looked on and treated with contempt."* Page 103 of the same book states, *"...many of the settlers were poor and could not at the time pay the necessary fees and expenses to have their lands surveyed. They simply held them under improvement rights, their being on them and in possession being usually looked on as a sufficient title to keep others off."*

*in that year, he removed his family, and upon which he settled and lived until his death, find which he named "Walnut Hill," by which name it is still known.*

# 19. 1767: Mason and Dixon return

### Mount Pleasant has an old improvement

Normand Bruce's April 1, 1767 *"Mount Pleasant"* survey (Frederick County Patented Certificate 2727) describes the following Improvements: *"2 Acres of cleared Land Thereon is 1. Old Cabbin 16 by 12 feet 300, old fence Rails"*.[1470] This 440-acre tract includes some of the land where Mount Savage is now located.

### Walnut Valley is surveyed for John Nicholls, Jr.

*"John Nickols Junr"* appears on the 1761 Old Town Hundreds list. On May 1, 1767 John Murdock surveyed the 62-acre tract *"Walnut Valey"* for John Nicholls, Jr.[1471] The tract was patented to John Nicholls, Jr. on July 26, 1768 (Frederick County Patent Certificate 4991). The survey began *"at two bounded Walnuts Standing at the head of a Drane that Emptys itself into Evits Creek near the mouth..."*

### Surveying instruments arrive at Fort Cumberland on July 7, 1767

Mason and Dixon's journal entry for July 7, 1767 states, *"The Waggons arrived at Fort Cumberland with the Instruments, Tents, &c."* On January 29, 1768, Mason and Dixon wrote a letter to Hugh Hamersley, Principal Secretary of Maryland, that includes the statement, *"On July the 7th the Waggons arrived at Fort Cumberland with the Instruments Tents etc. Having collected Hands we proceeded to the Place in the Allegany Mounts Where we left off at Last Year..."* This letter suggests that they hired workmen from the Fort Cumberland locale.

### Enoch Innis sells supplies to Mason and Dixon

The account records of Mason and Dixon show that Enoch Innis was paid 309 pounds for supplying Mason and Dixon between July 11, 1767 and November 6, 1767, that Enoch Innis gave a refund of 3 pounds to Mason and Dixon on November 8, 1767 for a cow that he did not deliver to them, and that Mason and Dixon received 9 pounds 10 shillings for hides from Enoch Innis on January 29, 1768. It also shows that Enoch Innis bought a tea canister from Mason and Dixon at an auction. During the same period, Michael Cresap had even larger transactions with Mason and Dixon. These large transactions suggested to one historian that both men were merchants or large farmers.[1472] We know that Michael Cresap indeed was a merchant, and the large purchases from Enoch Innis suggest that he was too. The purchase of hides is also suggestive of trading post-type activity.

The records indicate that Joseph Mounts, Samuel Plum, and William Tissue also sold supplies to Mason and Dixon. Phinehas and Mary Killam are also listed as selling supplies to Mason and Dixon; this may be the names of the Killam's who are mentioned in George Washington's journal.

---

[1470] This survey was identified by Francis Bridges.

[1471] This survey was identified by Francis Bridges.

[1472] This paragraph is a summary of material, including original records, published in A. J. W. Headlee's 41-page booklet **"We Axed America"**.

### John Greenfield is involved in a property transaction on Little Cacapon

The 1939 book "**Early Records Hampshire County Virginia**" records the following for August 4, 1767, "*GREENFIELD, John of Frederick Co., Va. LIVINGSTON, John of Frederick Co., Md. to Isaac Cox of Hampshire Co. (lease and release) 143 a. on Little Capon; rec. 8-12-1767. Wit.: Alexr. White, Thos. Edmondson, Peter Stalker, Angus McDonald, Luke Collins, John Lyne, John Hardin.*

### John Greenfield is involved in a property transaction on Patterson's Creek

The 1939 book "**Early Records Hampshire County Virginia**" records the following for September 2, 1767, "*GREENFIELD, John of Frederick Co., Va. to Alexr. Gibbony of Hampshire Co. (lease and release) 200 a. on Patterson Creek; rec. 10-13-1797. Wit.: Henry Heth, Bryan Bruen, Edward McGuire, Alexr Wodrow, John Lyne, Ja. Keight, Alexr. White.*"

### James Livingston gives power of attorney to Enoch Innis for selling property

The 1939 book "**Early Records Hampshire County Virginia**" records the following for September 7, 1767, "*LIVINGSTON, James of Frederick Co., Md. to Enoch Innis of Hampshire Co. (power of atty.) Power to sell land in Virginia and Pennsylvania. Rec. 3-9-1768. Wit.: David Cox, John Nicholas, Jonathan Hammar, Thos. Spencer, Joseph Tombinson, Jr., John Pierpoint.*"

### Indians request a conference at Fort Cumberland or Colonel Cresap's place

Volume 2 of the 1908 "**Annual Report**" provides the following synopsis of a September 10, 1767 speech at Old Town, "*Speech by Indians representing Dillaways, Shawnes and Waindots (copy) to the Governor of Virginia, asking for a mid-September conference at Fort Cumberland; interpreted by John Wolker.*"

A transcript of the speech is included in Volume V of the 1927 book "**The Papers of Sir William Johnson**". The transcript is missing a great deal of text due to damage sustained by the contemporaneous copy it is based on. One of the more interesting fragments of text is the statement, "*having heard many bad Stories of you, and we make no doubt but that you have heard the same of us. There is _____ bad white people among you; so there are of our people and us. we have sundry Grievances to Complain off when you give us an Opportunity.*"

The heart of the speech is as follows:

> *In as much as your Excellency the Governor of Virginia has not as yet shook hands with us and brighten'd the Chain of Friendship as the other Governors have done. We are in some concern to know if it is not your Honour that threatens our Distruction; if it Should not we should be very glad your Honour will give us the Opportunity to shake hands with you. at which time we shall communicate to your Honour every thing that is material, in regard to removing all doubt_____ appoint John Wolker, who_____ to be our Interpreter. There is also _____ Nations of Indians who are desirous ____ with your honor if you should think ____ us. The time that best suits us to _____ first or middle or September when our ___ting is over, and we should also be glad _____ suit your Honor to meet at Fort Cumberland or Col°. Cressap's, as our going further down the Country wou'd be attended with a great Expence, and perhaps our people by getting drunk might be very troublesome. We send you this by Order of our King called the New Comer, with our Names under written.*

After the names of the Indians, the following is written, "*The above is the true Speeches made by the above subscribers & was delivered to me verbally by John Wolker, Interpreter.*"

## Mason and Dixon send to Fort Cumberland for more helpers on October 2, 1767

Mason and Dixon's journal entry for October 2, 1767 states, *"Continued the line. Sent to Fort Cumberland for more Hands."* For them to send to Fort Cumberland for workers indicates they were aware that potential employees were then living in the Fort Cumberland locale. Mason and Dixon needed a lot of extra help at the time; their September 29, 1767 journal entry states, *"Twenty-six of our Men left us. They would not pass the River for fear of the Shawanes and Delaware Indians. But we prevailed upon 15 Ax Men to proceed with us; and with them we continued the Line Westward."*

## Mason and Dixon wrote a letter to a state governor

On October 28, 1767,[1473] Mason and Dixon finished a letter[1474] to one of the state governors from *"near the 230th Mile Post"* that includes the following:

> *In our last of the 2d Inst. we informed you of the Desertion amongst our Men at the Monanegehela: Their Places we soon supply'd by Hands from Fort Cumberland and Raystown and should have finished the Line before the End of this Month. But on the 9th Ins. we cross'd a Warrior Path (used by the Six Nations to go against their enemies the Cheroquees) there we were informed by the Chief of our Indians that he was "come to the Extent of his Commission from the Six Nations to go with us on the Line; and that he would not proceed one Step further.*

This letter demonstrates that Mason and Dixon were able to replace some of their workers from the Fort Cumberland locale.

## Enoch Innis was a resident of Virginia in 1767

The *"April, July, 1921"* issue of the **"Bulletin of the Virginia State Library"** also bears the title, **"Justices of the Peace of Colonial Virginia 1757-1775"**. This issue contains a transcript of an original Hampshire County list dated October 29, 1767 that includes Enoch Innis as a Justice of the Peace. This demonstrates that he was then a resident of Virginia.

## Kellams was living at the gap in Savage Mountain on November 20, 1767

Mason and Dixon's journal entry for November 19, 1767 indicates that they were at Laurel Run, on the west side of Savage Mountain. The November 20, 1767 journal entry states, *"The weather being so bad our Hands would not proceed on their work. We then proceeded to Mr. Kellams (in the road from Fort Pit to Fort Cumberland) at the Gap in Savage Mountain."* This entry documents a private residence along Braddock's road, near Fort Cumberland, in 1767.

## Tomlinson was living in the valley of Wills Creek on November 22, 1767

Mason and Dixon's journal entry for November 21, 1767 states, *"Seven of our hands left us."* The entry for November 22, 1767 states, *"Proceeded to Mr. Tumblestone's in Wills Creek Valley. Employed more hands."* Tumblestone is a spelling variation of Tomlinson. The November 22 journal entry indicates that people were living near, or congregating at, Tomlinson's place.

---

[1473] Different sources give various dates for this letter. At least one manuscript version bears both October 22 and October 28 dates.

[1474] The existence of this letter was brought to my attention by Francis Bridges.

### Fauquier accuses Cresap of meddling in Indian affairs

A November 23, 1767 letter Governor Francis Fauquier wrote to Sir William Johnson from Williamsburgh states:

*I enclose to you under Cover with this, the Copy of a Talk from Some northern Indians in your District, sent me down by Colonel Cressap near Fort Cumberland in the Colony of Maryland. That Gentleman, has on other Occasions as well as the present very improperly as well as officiously interfered in matters that dont at all concern him: as his Majesty has very judiciously committed the management of the Indians Affairs into your hands, I have wrote my Sentiments fully to Colonel Cressap on this head. If you should think it necessary or useful that the Indians should see me, I shall with the greatest readyness comply with every thing You shall desire to cultivate and confirm the Friendship subsisting between his Majestys white Subjects and themselves. Of this I beg the favor of you to assure them, and that We have not the least Inclination or wish to let go the Chain: And if you think it necessary I should tell them this in a Talk under my hand, on your acquainting me of the expediency of such a measure, I will immediately send one as you shall desire. It appears also to me that it would be proper to inform the Indians that any application to Colonel Cressap or any other person but your self, will not have the Regard paid to it as if it came from you But in this you will act according to your own Discretion, being a much better Judge of these matters than I can be.*

# 20. 1768: Steel reports from Fort Cumberland

**Pennsylvania decides to get tough on trespassing settlers**

The "**Pennsylvania Archives**" records the following act, titled, *"An act to remove the persons now settled, &c, and to prevent others from settling on any lands in this province not purchased of the Indians, 1768"*, which was signed into law on February 3, 1768:

*WHEREAS, many disorderly People, in Violation of His Majesty's Proclamation, have presumed to settle upon Lands not yet purchased from the Indians, to their Damage and great dissatisfaction, which may be attended with dangerous and fatal Consequences to the Peace and Safety of this Province. Be it therefore enacted by the Honourable John Penn, Esquire, Lieutenant Governor under the Honourable Thomas Penn & Richard Penn, true and absolute Proprietaries of the Province of Pennsylvania and Counties of New Castle, Kent and Sussex upon Delaware, by and with the advice and Consent of the Representatives of the Freemen of the said Province in General Assembly met, and by the authority of the same. That if any person or persons settled upon any Lands within the Boundaries of this Province not purchased of the Indians by the Proprietaries thereof, shall neglect or Refuse to remove themselves & Families off and from the same Lands within the Space of Thirty days, after he or they shall be required so to do, either by such persons as the Governor of this Province shall appoint for that purpose, or by his Proclamations to be set up in the most Public places of the Settlements on such unpurchased Lands, or if any person or persons being so removed shall afterwards return to his or their Settlement, or the Settlement of any other person with his or their Family, or without any Family, to remain and Settle on such Lands, or if any person shall after the said Notice to be given as aforesaid, reside and settle on such Lands, every such person and persons so neglecting or refusing to remove with his or their Family, or returning to settle as aforesaid, or that shall settle on any such Lands after the Requisition or Notice aforesaid, being thereof legally convicted by their own Confession or the Verdict of a Jury, shall suffer Death without the Benefit of Clergy. Provided always nevertheless, That nothing herein contained shall be deemed or construed to extend to any person or persons who now are, or hereafter may be settled on the main Roads or Communications leading through this Province to Fort Pitt, under the approbation and permission of the Commander-in-Chief of His Majesty's Forces in North America, or of the Chief Officer commanding in the Western District to the Ohio for the Time being for the more convenient accommodation of the Soldiery and others, or to such person or persons as are or shall be settled in the Neighbourhood of Fort Pitt, under the approbation and permission aforesaid, or to a Settlement made by George Croghan, Esq'., Deputy Superintendant of Indian Affairs under Sir William Johnson on the Ohio, above the said Fort, any thing herein contained to the contrary in any wise notwithstanding. And be it further enacted by the authority aforesaid, That Joseph Galloway, Benjamin Chew and Joseph Fox, Esquires, or the majority of them, with the Consent and approbation of the Governor or Commander-in-Chief of this Province for the Time being, and not otherwise, shall have, receive, and take out of the remaining part of the Sum appropriated by the Act entitled "An Act for granting to His Majesty the sum of Twenty-three thousand five hundred Pounds," &c., for defraying the Expence of the late Indian Treaties held at Easton and Lancaster, any sum or sums of money not exceeding the sum of Three hundred Pounds, and apply, order and dispose of the same for & towards defraying the necessary Expences of giving Notice to all persons settled upon any of the Lands not purchased of the Indians as aforesaid, within the Boundaries of this Province, to remove from their s^d settlements. And be it further enacted by the authority aforesaid, That the said Joseph Galloway, Benjamin Chew & Joseph Fox, or a majority of them, shall and they are hereby* *enjoined and required to draw Orders on the late Trustees of the General Loan Office of this Province for the purposes aforesaid, the same purposes being severally first approved of and agreed to by the Governor or Commander-in-Chief of this Province for the Time being; which Orders so drawn, the said late Trustees shall pay and discharge out of, and with the monies aforesaid, and when paid shall be produced to the Committee of Assembly for the Time being, and by them be allowed in discharge of so much of the monies remaining in their hands for the Uses aforesaid. And be it further enacted by the authority aforesaid, That if any person or persons after the publication of this Act, either singly or in companies, shall presume to enter upon any Lands, the same not being purchased as aforesaid, and make surveys thereof, mark, or cut down Trees thereon, such person or persons so offending, and being legally convicted in any Court of Quarter Sessions of the county where such offender shall be apprehended, (in which said Court the same offence is hereby made cognizable) by the oath or affirmation of one or more witnesses, or by the Confession of the Party, every person so offending shall forfeit and pay for every such Offence the sum of Fifty Pounds, and suffer three months' Imprisonment without Bail or mainprize. One moiety of which Fine shall be paid to the Prosecutor, and the other moiety to the Overseers of the Poor of the Township where such Offender shall reside, for the Use of the Poor of the said Township, if Resident within this Province, if otherwise, for the Use of the Poor where such Offender shall be apprehended. And be it further enacted by the authority af$^{sd}$, That all Offences by this Act declared capital or Felonies of Death shall be enquired of, heard, adjudged and determined before the Justices of the Supream Court or the Justices of the Courts of Oyer and Terminer and General Goal Delivery, to be held in the County of Philadelphia, by Inquest Indictments and Verdicts to be taken of good and lawful men, Inhabitants of the same County, in like manner and form as if such Capital Offence or Offences had been committed, perpetrated and done within the said County, any Law, Custom or Usage to the contrary thereof in any wise notwithstanding. And be it further enacted by the authority aforesaid, That this Act shall continue in force during the Term of One year, and from thence to the end of the next Sitting of Assembly and no longer.*

This act is relevant to the settlement of a portion of the environs of Fort Cumberland that was in nearby Pennsylvania. It is clear that this act did not cover present-day Southampton Township, Somerset County, Pennsylvania, because there were a number of 1767 surveys there that were performed on 1767 orders.

Benjamin Chew, who is mentioned in the act, would later take advantage of the opening of the sale of western Pennsylvania lands, buying up many tracts. According to Volume II of the 1906 book "**The History of Bedford and Somerset Counties…**", *"For, even in those early days, the land hunter (as he must be designated to distinguish him from the home seeker, for he was not seeking a home for himself, but keeping well up with the advancing tide of settlers) was ever on the lookout for choice tracts of land, on which he obtained patents in the hope of gaining a profit therefrom from the increased value given by them by the settlement of adjacent lands. Among these speculators who thus acquired lands in Somerset county were two citizens of Philadelphia – Benjamin Chew, and Alexander Wilcocks. These two men alone had, as shown in the record in the Survey book, not less than forty-nine tracts of land in Somerset county, aggregating some ten thousand acres, surveyed to them."*

## McCracken property transactions on Patterson Creek

The 1939 book "**Early Records Hampshire County Virginia**" records the following for sometime in 1768, *"McCRACKEN, Margaret, RUTHERFORD; Benjamin (w. Elizabeth); WORTHINGTON, Robert (w. Ann) of Frederick Co., Va. To John Hardin of Hampshire Co. (lease and release) 201 a., 306 a., Pattersons Creek; rec. 3-18-1768. Wit., Ja. Keith, Enoch Innis, Rich'd Hougland, Job Pearsall."* (Semicolons added where needed for separation of names.)

## Sugar Bottom is sold to Joseph Mounts

David Ross sold the Sugar Bottom tract to Joseph Mounts on March 21, 1768.[1475] By 1783, Mounts would have a mill and some kind of commercial horse operation on the property.

## Lord Baltimore, Proprietor of Maryland, is put on trial for the rape of Sarah Woodcock

The jury trial of Frederick Calvert (Lord Baltimore, Proprietor of Maryland) for the rape of Sarah Woodcock began on March 26, 1768. A complete transcript of the trial is provided in the 1768 book titled **"The Trial of Frederick Calvert, Esq; Baron of Baltimore in the Kingdom of Ireland, for a Rape on the Body of Sarah Woodcock; and of Eliz. Griffinburg, and Ann Harvey, otherwise Darby, as accessories before the Fact, For procuring, aiding, and abetting him in committing the said Rape…"**

The trial was held before Baron Sydney Stafford Smythe, and the book reports that he instructed the jury as follows:

*Gentlemen of the jury, The prisoner at the bar, lord Baltimore, stands indicted for feloniously ravishing and carnally knowing Sarah Woodcock, spinster, against her will, on the 22d of December last, at Epsom, against the statute which makes this offence felony; and the other two prisoners are indicted as accessàries before the fact, by feloniously and maliciously procuring, aiding, and abetting lord Baltimore to commit the said rape, at the said time and place. To this they have pleaded Not Guilty; and you are to try if they are guilty. Before I state to you the evidence, I will mention to you two or three things: In the first place, my lord complains of libels, and printed accounts of this transaction, which have been circulated. It is a most unjustifiable practice, and tends to the perversion of publick justice; and therefore if you have seen any thing printed on the sides of the prosecutrix or the prisoners, I must desire you to divest yourselves of any prejudice that such publication may have occasioned, and give your verdict only on the evidence now laid before you. Another thing I desire is, that whichever way the verdict is given, none of the friends of any of the parties will make use of any expressions of approbation or applause, which are extremely improper and indecent in a court of justice, and I shall certainly commit any person whom I shall know to be guilty of it. The last thing I shall mention to you is, to desire that no resentment you may feel at the manner in which she was carried to lord Baltimore's house, may have any influence on your verdict; for however unwarrantable the manner was, in which she came into his power, if at the time he lay with her it was by her consent, he is not guilty of the offence of which he is indicted; though it was proper to be given in evidence in this trial, to account for her being with him, and his having an opportunity of committing the crime; and to shew, from the indirect manner of getting her to his house, the greater probability that her account is true.*

*Having said this, I will now state to you the whole evidence as particularly as I can.*

*Mr. Baron Smythe then stated the whole of the evidence to the jury, as before given, which took up three hours, and on account of the length of it is not repeated here, and then concluded:*

*In point of law the fact is fully proved on my lord and the two other prisoners, if you believe the evidence of Sarah Woodcock. It is a crime which in its nature can only be proved by the woman on whom it is committed; for she only can tell whether she consented or no; it is, as my lord observes, very easy to be*

---

[1475] Reported by Francis Bridges, who also notes that a Joseph Mounts is included in the 1761 Old Town hundreds list. Some secondary sources assert that Joseph was the brother of Providence Mounts, who would later cut the northern part of the Turkey Foot Road, in 1779, to rush supplies from Fort Cumberland to Fort Pitt. This assertion may be true, since Joseph Mounts' will indicates that he had a son who was also named Providence Mounts (Joseph Mounts' will was located by Scott Williams.)

*made, and hard to be disproved; and the defence can only be collected from circumstances; from these you must judge whether her evidence is or is not to be believed. Lord Hale, in his History of the Pleas of the Crown, lays down two rules: 1. If complaint is not made soon after the injury is supposed to be received; 2. If it is not followed by a recent prosecution, a strong presumption arises that the complaint is malicious. She has owned the injury was received December 21st, and the complaint was not made till December 29th; but she has accounted for it in the manner you have heard. The strong part of the case, on behalf of the prisoners, is, her not complaining when she was at lord Mansfield's, the supreme magistrate in the kingdom in criminal matters; you have heard how she has explained and accounted for her conduct in that particular, which you will judge of. Upon the whole, if you believe that she made the discovery as soon as she knew she had an opportunity of doing it, and that her account is true, you will find all the prisoners guilty; if you believe that she did not make the discovery as soon as she had an opportunity, and from thence, or other circumstances, are not satisfied her account is true, you will find them all not guilty; for if he is not guilty, they cannot be so; for they cannot be accessary to a crime which was never committed.*

After about an hour and twenty minutes of deliberation, the jury acquitted Lord Baltimore, apparently believing Sarah didn't try hard enough to escape her abductors. The scandal arising from the trial destroyed Lord Baltimore's reputation, and shortly after the trial, he left the country, continuing to live a life of debauchery. During the same year as the trial, one of his former mistresses wrote a book titled "**Memoirs of the Seraglio of the Bashaw of Merryland, by a Discarded Sultana**" that further destroyed Lord Baltimore's reputation. The 1825 book "**The Newgate Calendar: Comprising Interesting Memoirs of the Most Notorious Characters...**" has an article describing the infamous abduction and rape of Sarah Woodcock.

## Sharpe writes to Hamersley about laying out a manor west of Fort Cumberland

On April 1, 1768, Sharpe wrote a letter[1476] to Hamersley from Annapolis, via Captain McLachlan, that includes the following:

*From Mr Jordan His Ldp will likewise receive an Account of the Proceedings of the Commissioners whom His Ldp was pleased to appoint to examine & settle His Agents Accounts, & also a Report of what has been done by us under the Commission impowering us to sell his several Mannours; but lest any Accident should happen to the Ship in which Mr Jordan takes his Passage Mr Dulany & I have thought proper by this Opportunity to transmit such a State of the Sales of the Mannours as will shew His Ldp at one View how much Land has been already sold, at what price, the Amount of Deposits or Payments already made by the Purchasers, Amount of Disbursements for surveying &c. the Amount of Bills of Exchange remitted to this time & the Sums to be received & remitted hereafter. I shall likewise inclose you in order that you may lay it before His Ldp a Plan or Draft of a large Tract of Land which as His Ldp seemed desirous to have other Mannours laid out I have caused to be surveyed & reserved for that purpose. It lies as you will observe just beyond Fort Cumberland extending Northwards from the Bottom or Low Land lying on Potowmack to the Line that divides Pennsylvania from this Province & Westward so far as to include the Eastern Ridges of the Allegany Mountain. Some of the Land included as I am informed very good, other Parcells indifferent & a good deal hilly & broken, the Reason I ordered so large a Quantity to be included was that it might be at His Ldp's Choice to have either One or more Mannours laid out & because the good Land does not lye contiguous but in parcels, a quantity of good Land so large as four or fjve thousand Acres together not being at this time to be found vacant on this*

---

*side the Allegany Mountain. If the Indians remain quiet I doubt not but His Ldp might if he pleases sell the whole within these few years at a better price than he now grants uncultivated vacant Land or if he chooses to have the level & best Parts of the Survey laid out immediately in Tenements they may I am told be leased for a Term of years at Ten Shillings pr Annum the hundred Acres with a Condition in the Leases that the Tenants shall make thereon certain Improvements. As some Tracts of patented Land lye within the Bounds of this large Survey I have caused another of 2524 Acres to be made beyond it on a Branch of The Yoghiogany near a Place called the little Meadows, imagining that His Ldp may hereafter if he pleases therewith purchase (by way of Exchange) such patented Tracts lying within the large Survey in case he should choose to erect the whole into one Mannour. In His Majestys proclamation of the 7th of Oct' 1763 of which I send you an Extract there is a prohibition as to the Granting Lands lying Westward of the Heads of the Rivers that run into the Atlantic Ocean, wherefore the Surveyor of Frederick County does not execute any Warrant at this time beyond the Alegany Mountain nor will he do so till His Ldp shall be pleased to send Orders for that purpose. I intimated to you in my Letter dated the 11th of Feb^ry that in Consequence of a Complaint from the Indians a Parcel of People who had made a Settlement in the Western part of Pennsylvania at a Place called Red Stone Creek would be this Spring compelled to retire, in a late Pennsylvania Gazette is published an Act of Assembly that has been made there for that purpose & I understand the Virginians also talk of obliging the People who have settled in that Dominion beyond the Allegany to break up their Settlements, lest otherwise they should be the means of another Indian War.*

## A 1768 report to John Penn, written from Fort Cumberland

Volume 9 of the 1852 book "**Minutes of the Provincial Council of Pennsylvania**" includes the following letter that was written to John Penn, Governor of Pennsylvania, from Fort Cumberland by Reverend John Steel, John Allison and Christopher Lemes, Esquires, and Captain James Potter on April 2, 1768:

*Having in our Return reached Fort Cumberland, and being here to part, We concluded it necessary to prepare an Extract from our Journal of what appeared to us most important, which We Ordered to be transmitted to your Honour by Mr. Steel.*

*We arrived at the Settlement on Red Stone, on the twenty third Day of March. The People having heard of our coming had appointed a Meeting among themselves on the twenty-fourth, to consult what Measures they should take. We took the advantage of this Meeting, Read the Act of Assembly, and Proclamation, explaining the Law, and giving the Reasons of it as well as we could, and used our Endeavors to persuade them to comply, alleging to them that it was the most probably Method to entitle them to favour with the Honourable Proprietaries when the Land was purchased. After Lamenting their distressed Condition, they told us the People were not fully collected, but as they expected all would attend on Sabbath following, and then they would give us an Answer. They, however, affirmed that the Indians were very Peaceable, and seemed sorry that they were to be removed, And said they apprehended the English intended to make War upon the Indians, as they were moving off their People from their Neighborhood.*

*We labored to persuade them that they were imposed on by a few straggling Indians, that Sir William Johnson, who had informed our Government must be better acquainted with the mind of the Six Nations, and that they were displeased with the White People's settling on their unpurchased lands. On Sabbath, the twenty-seventh day of March, a considerable Number attended, (their Names are Subjoined) and most of them told us they were resolved to move off, and would Petition your Honour for a Preference in obtaining their Improvements when a Purchase was made. While We were conversing we were informed that a number of Indians were come to Indian Peters; We judging it might be subservient to our main design, that the Indians should be present, while We were advising the People to obey the Law, sent for them; They came; and after Sermon delivered a Speech, with a String of Wampum to be transmitted to Your Honour. Their Speech was, "Ye are come, sent by your Great men, to tell these People to go away from the Land, which Ye say is ours, And We are sent by our Great Men, and are glad We have met there this day. We tell you the White People must Stop, and We stop them 'till the Treaty, and when George Croghan, and our great Men will talk together, we will tell them what to do." The Names of the Indians are subjoined. The Indians were from the Mingo-Town, about Eighty Miles from Red Stone. After this the People were more confirmed that there was no danger of War. They drop't the design of Petitioning, and said they would wait till the issue of the Treaty; Some, however, declared they would move off. We had sent a Messenger to Cheat River, and to Stewart's Crossings, of Yougheogenny, with Several Proclamations, requesting them to meet us at Guesse's place, as most Central for both Settlements. On the thirtieth of March about thirty or fourty Men met us there; We proceeded as at Red Stone, reading the Act of Assembly, and a Proclamation, and endeavored to convince them of the Necessity and Reasonableness of quitting the unpurchased Land, but to no Purpose; They had heard what the Indians had said at Red Stone, and reasoned in the same manner, declaring they had no Apprehensions of a War; that they would attend the Treaty, and take their Measures accordingly. Many severe Things were said of Mr. Croghan, and one Lawrence Harrison treated the Law, and our Government, with, too much disrespect. On the thirty-first of March, We came to the great Crossings of Yougheogenny, and being informed by one Speer, that eight or ten Families lived in a Place called Turkey-Foot, We sent some Proclamations thither by said Speer, as We did to a few Families nigh the Crossings of little Yough, Judging it unnecessary to go amongst them. It is our Opinion that some will move off in Obedience to the Law, that the greatest Part will wait the Treaty, and if they find that the Indians are indeed dissatisfied, We think the whole will be persuaded to Remove. The Indians coming to Red Stone, and delivering their Speech, greatly obstructed our design.*

The names of the individuals residing at Turkeyfoot were Henry Abrahams, Eze. Dewit, Jam[s] Spencer, Benj. Jennings, Jn[o.] Cooper, Eze. Hickman, Jn[o.] Euslow, Henry Euslow, and Benj. Pursley.

## Braddock's road west of Fort Cumberland was heavily settled by 1768

On May 17, 1768, George Washington wrote a letter to John Blair, acting Governor of Virginia, that stated:

*At present the road from Fort Cumberland to Pittsburg is very thickly Inhabited; so much so at least, as to render the communication easy and convenient for Travellers, and for the transportation of Provisions &ca. from the Frontiers of this Colony to the last mentioned Garrison, and to the Settlers that now are, or may hereafter be fixed on the Ohio…*

## Paying for the survey of Lord Baltimore's manor west of Fort Cumberland

The book "**Proceedings of the Council of Maryland, 1761-1769**" includes the following minutes from a September 1, 1768 meeting of the Board of Revenue:

*His Excellency is pleased to lay before the Board an Account from the Surveyor employed in laying off a Manor for His Lordship's use, to the Westward of Fort Cumberland, desiring their Advice in regard to the sum to be allowed him (exclusive of other necessary Charges) during his being employed on that Service. The Board are unanimously of opinion that 15/ Cur[t] Money p diem be paid him as a Compensation for the same.*

*The Instructions to the several Officers concerned in the management & Receipt of His Lordship's Revenue were again read, It is the opinion of the Board & therefore ordered That the Rent Roll Keepers do give Bond for the faithful discharge of their Duty agreeable to Instructions to be to them delivered and that an additional Clause be added to the said Instructions, requiring a due return of all Books and Papers, relative to His Lordship's affairs, into the Revenue Office when they, or either of them shall be called upon for the same by the Board of Officers.*

*The Farmers and Receivers to have a Clause added in their Instructions to the same Purport.*

### A land transaction between James Livingston and Daniel Cresap

The 1939 book "**Early Records Hampshire County Virginia**" records the following for September 13, 1768, *"LIVINGSTON, James of Frederick Co., Md. to Daniel Cresap Frederick Co., Md. (lease & release) 159 a. on North Branch of Potomac; rec. 9-13-1768. Wit.: Bryan Bruen, W. Hancher, John Lyne, John Keating."*

### The Fort Stanwix treaty was signed on November 5, 1768

During the Fort Stanwix treaty, also known as the *"purchase of 1768"*, the Six Nations granted a vast amount of land to the Crown. The land office of Pennsylvania opened this area up for settlement in April of the following year.[1477] The text of the *"purchase of 1768"* is as follows:

*GRANT FROM THE SIX UNITED NATIONS TO THE KING OF ENGLAND.*

*To all to whom these presents shall come, or may concern: — We, the sachems and chiefs of the Six Confederate Nations, and of the Shawnesse, Delawares, Mingoes of Ohio, and other dependent tribes, on behalf of ourselves, and of the rest of our several nations, the chiefs and warriors of whom are now here convened by Sir William Johnson, baronet, his majesty's superintendent of our affairs, send greeting:*

*Whereas his majesty was graciously pleased to propose to us, in the year one thousand seven hundred and sixty-five, that a boundary line should be fixed between the English and us, to ascertain and establish our limits, and prevent those intrusions and encroachments, of which we had so long and loudly complained; and to put a stop to the many fraudulent advantages which had been so often taken of us; which boundary appearing to us as a wise and good measure, we did then agree to a part of a line, and promised to settle the whole finally, whensoever Sir William Johnson should be fully empowered to treat with us for that purpose:*

*And whereas his said majesty has at length given Sir William Johnson orders to complete the said boundary line between the provinces and Indians; in conformity to which orders, Sir William Johnson has convened the chiefs and warriors of our respective nations, who are the true and absolute proprietors of the lands in question, and who are here now to a very considerable number: And whereas many uneasinesses and doubts have arisen amongst us, which have given rise to an apprehension that the line may not be strictly observed on the part of the English, in which case matters may be worse than before; which apprehension, together with the dependent state of some of our tribes, and other circumstances; retarded the settlement, and became the subject of some debate; Sir William Johnson has at length so far satisfied us upon it, as to induce us to come to an agreement concerning the line, which is now brought to a conclusion, the whole being fully explained to us in a large assembly of our people, before Sir William Johnson, and in the presence of his excellency the Governor of New Jersey, the Commissioners from the provinces of Virginia and Pennsylvania, and sundry other gentlemen; by which line so agreed upon, a*

---

[1477] Volume II, Chapter 4 of the 1906 book "**The History of Bedford and Somerset Counties…**"

*considerable tract of country, along several provinces, is by us ceded to his said majesty, which we are induced to, and do hereby ratify and confirm to his said majesty, from the expectation and confidence we place in his royal goodness, that he will graciously comply with our humble requests, as the same are expressed in the speech of the several nations, addressed to his majesty, through Sir William Johnson, on Tuesday, the first day of the present month of November; wherein we have declared our expectations of the continuance of his majesty's favor, and our desire that our ancient engagements be observed, and our affairs attended to by the officer who has the management thereof, enabling him to discharge all the matters properly for our interest: That the lands occupied by the Mohocks, around their villages, as well as by any other nation affected by this our cession, may effectually remain to them, and to their posterity; and that any engagements regarding property, which they may now be under, may be prosecuted, and our present grants deemed valid on our parts, with the several other humble requests contained in our said speech:*

*And whereas, at the settling of the said line, it appeared that the line described by his majesty's order, was not extended to the northward of Owegy, or to the southward of Great Kanhawa river; we have agreed to and continued the line to the northward, on a supposition that it was omitted, by reason of our not having come to any determination concerning its course, at the congress held in one thousand seven hundred and sixty-five: And inasmuch as the line to the northward became the most necessary of any, for preventing encroachments on our very towns and residences; and we have given this line more favorably to Pennsylvania, for the reasons and considerations mentioned in the treaty: we have likewise continued it south to the Cherokee river, because the same is, and we do declare it to be our true bounds with the southern Indians, and that we have an undoubted right to the country as far south as that river, which makes our cession to his majesty much more advantageous than that proposed:*

*Now, therefore, know ye, that we, the sachems and chiefs aforementioned, native Indians and proprietors of the lands hereafter described, for and in behalf of ourselves and the whole of our confederacy, for the considerations herein before mentioned, and also for and in consideration of a valuable present of the several articles in use amongst Indians, which, together with a large sum of money, amount, in the whole, to the sum of ten thousand four hundred and sixty pounds seven shillings and three pence sterling, to us now delivered and paid by Sir William Johnson, baronet, his majesty's sole agent and superintendant of Indian affairs for the northern department of America, in the name and behalf of our sovereign lord George the Third, by the grace of God, of Great Britain, France and Ireland, King, Defender of the Faith; the receipt whereof we do hereby acknowledge; we, the said Indians, have, for us, our heirs and successors, granted, bargained, sold, released and confirmed, and by these presents, do grant, bargain, sell, release and confirm, unto our said sovereign lord King George the Third, all that tract of land situate in North America, at the back of the British settlements, bounded by a line which we have now agreed upon, and do hereby establish as the Boundary between us and the British colonies in America; beginning at the mouth of the Cherokee or Hogohege river, where it empties into the river Ohio; and running from thence upwards along the south side of the said river to Kitanning, which is above Fort Pitt; from thence by a direct line to the nearest fork of the west branch of Susquehannah; thence through the Allegany mountains, along the south side of the said west branch, till it comes opposite to the mouth of a creek called Tiadaghion; thence across the west branch, and along the south side of that creek, and along the north side of Burnet's hills, to a creek called Awandae; thence down the same to the east branch of Susquehannah, and across the same, and up the east side of that river to Owegy; from thence east to Delaware river, and up that river to opposite to where Tianaderha falls into Susquehannah; thence to Tianaderha, and up the west side thereof, and the west tide of its west branch to the head thereof; and thence by a direct line to Canada creek, where it empties into Wood creek, at the west end of the carrying place beyond Fort Stanwix, and extending eastward from every part of the said line, as far as the lands formerly purchased, so as to comprehend the whole of the lands between the said line and the purchased lands or settlements, except what is within the province of Pennsylvania; together with all the hereditaments and appurtenances to the same, belonging or appertaining, in the fullest and most ample manner; and all the estate, right, title, interest, property, possession, benefit, claim and demand, either in law or equity, of each and every of us, of, in, or to the same, or any part thereof; To have and to hold the whole lands and premises hereby granted, bargained, sold, released, and confirmed, as aforesaid, with the hereditaments and appurtenances thereunto belonging; under the reservations made in the treaty, unto our said sovereign lord King George the Third, his heirs and successors, to and for his and their own proper use and behoof, for ever.*

*In witness whereof, we, the chiefs of the confederacy, have hereunto set our marks and seals, at Fort Stanwix, the fifth day of November, one thousand seven hundred and sixty-eight, in the ninth year of his majesty's reign.*

The document was signed by Abraham, Chief of the Mohawks, Hendrick, Chief of the Tuscaroras, Conahquieso, Chief of the Oneidas, Bunt, Chief of the Onondagas, Tagaaia, Chief of the Cayugas, and Gaustarax, Chief of the Senecas.


### Baptisms and church services near Fort Cumberland in November of 1768

Volume 2 of the 1872 book "**The Fathers of the German Reformed Church in Europe and America**" references John Conrad Bucher's records, and indicates that he preached *"near Fort Cumberland"* and *"at Big Crossings of Yogheheny"* in 1768. This indicates settlements of some kind in the environs of Fort Cumberland in 1768.

The book "**History of Dauphin County, Pennsylvania**" contains a record of baptisms performed by John Conrad Bucher. At the *"Bick Crossing of Jaghegheny"* Bucher baptized Jacob, the son of Peter and Maria Risner, who was born August 12, 1768, and baptized *"Cath ina"*, daughter of Nicholas and Sarah Christ, who was born September 24, 1767. These baptisms were performed on November 10, 1768. The witnesses for both baptisms were Paulus Frohman and Mater Puellae. On November 21, 1768, Bucher baptized Joseph Tomlinson, son of John and Mary Tomlinson *"near Fort Cumberland"*. The witnesses were Henry Leane and Rebecca Tomlinson. The baptism record indicates that Joseph was born on September 3, 1767.

Paul Froman shows up in the 1772 Brothersvalley tax list, which is included in another chapter herein.


### Enoch Innis was living in Virginia in December 1768

The December 20, 1768 deposition of Enoch Innis indicates at the time of the deposition, he was *"an Inhabitant of the Colony of Virginia"*. This is harmonious with the theory that Enoch Innis was the *"Mr. Innis"* that George Washington ate breakfast with on November 27, 1770 at the new store in Virginia.

# 21. 1769: Western settlement approved

**Land patents may be issued on surveys west of Fort Cumberland**

The book "**Proceedings of the Council of Maryland, 1761-1769**" includes minutes of the January 2, 1769 meeting of the Board of Revenue, which include the following:

*His Excellency the Governor lays before the Board Plats and certificates of Lands reserved for His Lordship's use in the western Frontier of this Province and desires the opinion of the Board: Whether it would not be necessary to give notice to all Persons who may have Purchased Warrants and made Surveys & who have hitherto been restrained from obtaining Patents thereon by reason of a prohibitory order to the Judges of the Land Office, that on their laying a true State of their Pretensions before the Board, such orders might issue thereon as should be thought just & Reasonable.*

*The Board being of opinion that such a Step would be necessary, Ordered.*

*That the Clerk do cause the following Advertisement to be Printed both in English and Dutch for the better Information of all Concerned.*

*Annapolis Janry 2d 1769*

*Whereas sundry Persons have heretofore purchased Warrants and made Surveys with a view of securing Land in the Western part of the Province beyond Fort Cumberland, but have been restrained from obtaining Patents on the same by reason of a prohibitory Order signified to the Judges of the Land Office, and as the Reasons for continuing such prohibitory order no longer subsist; It is hereby notified to all Persons who have purchased Warrants or made Surveys for the Purpose above mentioned, that they lay before His Lordship's Board of Revenue on the Twentieth Day of February next a true State of their Pretensions, that such orders may issue for granting them the Benefit of their respective Warrants, or Surveys, according to the priority thereof as may be thought just and reasonable.*

*Signed p order*

The book "**Proceedings of the Council of Maryland, 1761-1769**" includes minutes from the February 22, 1769 meeting of the Board of Revenue, which include the following:

*In pursuance of the determination of the Board at their last meeting, The Persons attending, deliver in to the Clerk of the Board their several pretensions in Writing, but it appearing to the Board that many others, who have obtained Warrants and made surveys to the Westward of Fort Cumberland, are Absent, either from Sickness or want of Information; and as 'tis probable different Warrants may have been Located on one & the Same Tracts or Parcels of Land. The Board determine to wait until all the Parties shall have stated their Pretensions in Writing, after which the Board will consider them respectively & represent their Opinion to His Lordship, by whose Instructions the Board determine finally to be Governed.*

**A land sale on Patterson Creek**

The 1939 book "**Early Records Hampshire County Virginia**" records the following for February 2, 1769, "*McCRACKEN, Jane; McCRAKEN, Margaret; RUTHERFORD, Benjamin (w. Elizabeth);*

*WORTHINGTON, Robert (w. Ann) of Frederick Co., Va. to John Harden of Hampshire Co. 306 a. Patterson's Creek; rec 3-14-1769. Wit.: Ja. Keith, Edward McGuire, Alex White, Pet. Hog."*

### Pennsylvania announces that it will sell land within the new purchase

The land office of Pennsylvania made the following announcement[1478] on February 23, 1769, opening lands west of the Allegheny Mountain for sale commencing April 3, 1769:

*The Land Office will be opened on the 3d day of April next, at 10 o'clock in the morning, to receive applications from all persons inclinable to take up lands in the New Purchase, upon terms of five pounds Sterling per hundred acres, and one penny per acre per annum quit-rent. No person will be allowed to take up more than three hundred acres, without a special license from the Proprietaries or Governor. The surveys upon all applications are to be made and returned within six months, and the whole purchase money paid at one payment, and patent taken out within twelve months from the date of the application, with interest and quit-rent from six months after the application. If there be a failure on the side of the party applying, in either proving his survey and return to be made, or in paying the purchase money and obtaining the patent, the application and survey will be utterly void, and the Proprietaries will be at liberty to dispose of the land to any other person whatever. And as these terms will be strictly adhered to by the Proprietaries, all persons are hereby warned and cautioned not to apply for more land than they will be able to pay for in the time hereby given for that purpose.*

*By order of the Governor.*

*James Tilghman,*

*Secretary of the Land Office.*

*Philadelphia Land Office. February 23, 1769.*

### A land transaction between Phillip Ross and Michael Cresap

The 1939 book "**Early Records Hampshire County Virginia**" records the following for March 14, 1769, *"ROSS, Phillip (w. Elizabeth) of Hampshire Co. to Michael Cresap of Frederick Co., Md. (lease and release) 408 a. on North Branch of Potomac; rec. 8-15-1796.[1479] Wit.: None."*

### Non-importation of British goods is discussed at high levels in 1769

Doctor David Ross[1480] corresponded with George Washington and George Mason about non-importation of British goods in 1769. An April 5, 1769 letter George Washington wrote to George Mason from Mount Vernon includes the following:

---

[1478] "**History of Lycoming County, Pennsylvania**".

[1479] This seems to be a typographical error, and most likely should read 1769.

[1480] Dr. Ross owned various property in the vicinity of Fort Cumberland. For example, a deed recorded July 25, 1805 documents the fact that Archibald Arnold bought *"White Oak Point"* from the estate of Doctor David Ross. A May 4, 1801 Chancery Court record relates to the case of Archibald Arnold versus David Ross, Horatio Ridout, Samuel Ridout, and William Stewart, which is about a contract to purchase the Level Ridge tract, which is located along a surviving segment of the Turkey Foot Road in Arnold's settlement. The 150-acre 1762 *"Level Ridge"* tract was patented to David Ross, according to Patent Record BC and GS 15, page 440. This is probably the same Doctor David Ross who was elected as one of the managers of the Potomac Company in May 1762; see page 518 of Scharf's 1879 book "**History of Maryland: 1765-1812**", Volume II.

*Herewith you will receive a letter and Sundry papers which were forwarded to me a day or two ago by Doctor Ross of Bladensburg. I transmit them with the greater pleasure, as my own desire of knowing your sentiments upon a matter of this importance exactly coincides with the Doctors inclinations.*

*At a time when our lordly Masters in Great Britain will be satisfied with nothing less than the deprication of American freedom, it seems highly necessary that some thing shou'd be done to avert the stroke and maintain the liberty which we have derived from our Ancestors; but the manner of doing it to answer the purpose effectually is the point in question.*

*That no man shou'd scruple, or hesitate a moment to use arms in defence of so valuable a blessing, on which all the good and evil of life depends; is clearly my opinion; yet Arms I wou'd beg leave to add, should be the last resource; the denier resort. Addresses to the Throne, and remonstrances to parliament, we have already, it is said, proved the inefficacy of; how far then their attention to our rights and priviledges is to be awakened or alarmed by starving their Trade and manufactures, remains to be tryed.*

*The northern Colonies, it appears, are endeavouring to adopt this scheme. In my opinion it is a good one, and must be attended with salutary effects, provided it can be carried pretty generally into execution; but how far it is practicable to do so, I will not take upon me to determine. That there will be difficulties attending the execution of it every where, from clashing interests, and selfish designing men (ever attentive to their own gain, and watchful of every turn that can assist their lucrative views, in preference to any other consideration) cannot be denied; but in the Tobacco Colonies where the Trade is so diffused, and in a manner wholly conducted by Factors for their principals at home, these difficulties are certainly enhanced, but I think not insurmountably increased, if the Gentlemen in their several Counties wou'd be at some pains to explain matters to the people, and stimulate them to a cordial agreement to purchase none but certain innumerated Articles out of any of the Stores after such a period, not import nor purchase any themselves. This, if it did not effectually withdraw the Factors from their Importations, wou'd at least make them extremely cautious in doing it, as the prohibited Goods could be vended to none but the non-associator, or those who wou'd pay no regard to their association; both of whom ought to be stigmatized, and made the objects of publick reproach.*

*The more I consider a Scheme of this sort, the more ardently I wish success to it, because I think there are private, as well as public advantages to result from it; the former certain, however precarious the other may prove; for in respect to the latter I have always thought that by virtue of the same power (for here alone the authority derives) which assume's the right of Taxation, they may attempt at least to restrain our manufactories; especially those of a public nature; the same equity and justice prevailing in the one case as the other, it being no greater hardship to forbid my manufacturing, than it is to order me to buy Goods of them loaded with Duties, for the express purpose of raising a revenue. But as a measure of this sort will be an additional exertion of arbitrary power, we cannot be worsted I think in putting it to the Test. ...*

*Upon the whole therefore, I think the Scheme a good one, and that it ought to be tryed here, with such alterations as the exigency of our circumstances render absolutely necessary; but how, and in what manner to begin the work, is a matter worthy of consideration, and whether it can be attempted with propriety, or efficacy (further than a communication of sentiments to one another) before May, when the Court and Assembly will meet together in Williamsburg, and a uniform plan can be concerted, and sent into the different counties to operate at the same time, and in the same manner every where, is a thing I am somewhat in doubt upon, and shou'd be glad to know your opinion of.*

Although not documentary evidence, Volume 5 of the "**Casket**" (1830) states:

*In the session of the house of burgesses of 1769, Mr. Lee brought forward his resolutions against the assumed right of the British parliament to bind the colonies. He also, as chairman of a committee on internal regulations, brought in a report recommending the improvement of the navigation of the Potomac as high as fort Cumberland. The house of burgesses was dissolved. The members met in a private chamber, and recommended their fellow-citizens to abstain from such of the luxuries, and even of what might be called the necessaries of life, as were not the product of their native land. — Non-importation societies were formed, and rapidly increased throughout the colony.*

## A July 1769 receipt for the land the Penns purchased from the Six Nations

On July 28, 1769, the Six Nations gave a receipt[1481] to the Penns, proprietaries of Pennsylvania, acknowledging payment for the land they sold at the treaty of Fort Stanwix in 1768. The receipt was signed by 13 chiefs using pictorial symbols.

## A Uniontown tradition of procuring salt and iron from Cumberland circa 1769

While not documentary evidence, the 1843 book "**Historical Collections of the State of Pennsylvania**" states:

*Uniontown[1482] was laid out by Henry Beeson about the year 1767 or '69. Mr. Beeson was a Quaker from Berkeley co., Virginia. His cabin stood upon the place now occupied by the residence of Mr. Veech, at the west end of the town. At that time all the iron and salt for this region was transported on pack-horses from Cumberland; and while Mr. Beeson was absent on one of these expeditions, his wife was greatly alarmed at seeing several groups of Indians skulking about the house, apparently with hostile intentions, and occasionally engaged in earnest conversation. She could understand a little of the French and Indian of one old man who was evidently communicating to his comrades the fact that Mr. Beeson was one of the "broad brims," or Wm. Penn's men, and that his family ought therefore to pass unmolested. The Indians soon after this dispersed without doing any injury: — a beautiful commentary on the peaceful policy of Wm. Penn. Jacob Beeson came several years after Henry, and purchased the Veech place from his brother, who removed to the south part of the town. Jacob Beeson was the former owner of the site of Mr. Stockton's elegant mansion at the west end. Windle Brown and his two sons, and Frederick Waltzer, lived about four miles west of Uniontown before Braddock's defeat. Mr. Freeman Lewis[1483] came here in 1796; and about that time the courthouse and market-house were erected. Since then the town has gradually increased with the opening of the country.*

---

[1481] The Gilder Lehrman Institute of American History.

[1482] John Ewing's June 28, 1784 journal entry describes Uniontown as follows, *"At Beeson's Town we crossed Redstone Creek where ye water is brought through ye town to turn a saw mill. There are near 30 houses in this place which is made the County town of Fiatt."* Samuel Vaughn's 1787 journal describes Uniontown as follows, *"To Union town, lately called Beaston. Borough town to Fayette county. Has a Court house Goal a Prisbetarian & Methodist Church & 120 houses mostly Log & built within 2 years, the land easy hills with some stone, soil good, having Red Stone Creek running through the town on which are grist mills."* Thaddeus Harris's 1803 journal describes Uniontown as follows, *"Uniontown is the shire town of the County. It is a very pleasant and thriving place, situated near Redstone Creek, and principally built upon one straight street, the side walks of which are neatly paved with large flat stones. It contains about one hundred and twenty houses, many of them well built, and some quite handsome. The public buildings are a meeting-house, and a stone Gaol. There is a printing office in the town which issues a weekly news-paper. Several manufacturers are carried on in the place, and much business is done in the mercantile line to very great advantage. Though the town has been settled but fifteen years, it is, next to Pittsburg and Wheeling, the most flourishing town through which we passed on the western side of the mountain."*

[1483] Uniontown surveyor Freeman Lewis attempted to create a history of Fayette County. It may be that the Beeson tradition came from him.

## A Cresap-related land transaction

The 1939 book "**Early Records Hampshire County Virginia**" records the following for October 2, 1769, *"NICHOLAS, John of Frederick Co., Va. to Joseph McHenry (w. Hannah) Parcel of land on Patterson's Creek; rec. 11-14-1769. Wit.: John Hartly, Richard Harrison, Enoch Innis."*

## John Jones is involved in a land transaction on Patterson Creek

The 1939 book "**Early Records Hampshire County Virginia**" records the following for November 14, 1769, *"TEPOLT, Michael of Hampshire Co. to John Jones of Hampshire Co. (lease and release) 170 a. on drain of Patterson Creek; rec. 11-15-1769. Wit.: John Rouesaw, John Reno."* A John Jones later shows up in Deakins' list of settlers west of Fort Cumberland.

## Clearing the Potomac, to make it more navigable to Fort Cumberland, is discussed in 1769

The journal of the Virginia House of Burgesses contains the following entry[1484] for December 5, 1769:

> *Ordered, That leave be given to bring in a bill for clearing and making navigable the river Potomack, from the Great Falls of the said river up to Fort Cumberland; and that M$^r$. Richard Henry Lee and M$^r$. Washington do prepare and bring in the same.*

## George French's father claimed land west of Fort Cumberland in 1769

Volume 192 of the "**Laws of Maryland...**" includes the following record from the November 1789 session of the General Assembly of Maryland:

> *WHEREAS it appears to this general assembly, that on the 21st of April, 1775, a patent was granted to George French, for a tract of land called George's Adventure, containing 456 acres, and that on the 27th of April and 24th of October, 1776, patents were granted to the said George French, for another tract called the Vale, containing 1627 acres, lying to the westward of Fort Cumberland, and that the same has been held by the father of the petitioner, and those claiming under him, since the year 1769, and have been considerably improved, RESOLVED, That the right of the state to the said lands be relinquished, any former claim to the said lands on behalf of the state notwithstanding.*

---

[1484] "**Proceedings and Addresses: Celebration of the Beginning of the Second Century of the American Patent System**", 1891.

# 22. 1770: Mr. Innis at the new store

**Killam's on a branch of Georges Creek, and Turner's mill near Short Gap, in 1770**

On the morning of October 11, 1770, Washington *"set off"* from a location he described the previous day as *"Wise's (now Turner's) mill"*, which was at or near the present-day site of the village of Short Gap, West Virginia. His journal entries[1485] from the 11th and 12th state:

*11th. – The morning being wet and heavy we did not set off till eleven o'clock, and arrived that night at one Killam's, on a branch of George's Creek, distant ten and a half measured miles from the north branch of the Potomac, where we crossed at the lower end of my deceased brother Augustine's land, known by the name of Pendergrass's. This crossing is two miles from the aforesaid mill and the road bad, as it likewise is to Killam's, the country being very hilly and stony. From Killam's to Fort Cumberland is the same distance, that it is to the crossing above mentioned, and the road from thence to Jolliff's by the Old Town much better.*

*12th. – We left Killem's early in the morning; breakfasted at the Little Meadows, ten miles off, and lodged at the Great Crossing twenty miles further; which we found a tolerably good day's work. The country we travelled over to-day was very mountainous and stony, with but very little good land, and that lying in spots.*

As previously quoted in more detail, Mason and Dixon's November 20, 1767 journal entry references *"Mr. Kellams (in the Road from Fort Pit to Fort Cumberland) at the Gap in Savage Mountain."* Washington's journal shows that Kellam was still living there in 1770.

### *The significance of Turner's 1770 mill*

As described in a previous chapter, the Pendergrass property was in Virginia (now West Virginia) at the present-day site of the Allegany Ballistics Laboratory. As described in a subsequent chapter, this puts Turner's mill along Turners Run (formerly Turner's Mill Run) somewhere near the town of Short Gap. The early presence of Turner's mill suggests the presence of a substantial farming community to support it. On present-day roads, both Pinto and Short Gap are 8.6 miles from Cumberland.

Another thing Washington's journal tells us is that in 1770, a road forked from Braddock's Road and passed through the vicinities of Pinto, Maryland and Short Gap, West Virginia.

**Washington returns to Killam's on November 26, 1770**

George Washington's November 26, 1770 journal entry states:

*Reached Killam's, on Georges Creek, where we met several families going over the mountains to live; some without having any places provided. The snow upon the Allegany Mountains was near knee deep.*

One has to marvel at intrepidity of families migrating west in deep November snow, planning to seek out new ground to live on, and wonder what they planned to subsist on until they could clear fields, and then plant and harvest crops.

---

[1485] **"The Writings of George Washington"**, Volume II, by Jared Sparks.

## Innes had a residence in the environs of Fort Cumberland in the 1770 timeframe

George Washington's November 27, 1770 journal entry states:

> We got to Colonel Cresap's at the Old Town, after calling at Fort Cumberland and breakfasting with one Mr. Innis at the new store opposite."

It seems reasonable to interpret this diary entry as meaning that George Washington visited with one or more people on the Fort Cumberland side of the Potomac River, and then ate breakfast with Mr. Innes at the replacement new storehouse, on the opposite side of the river. One can reasonably wonder if Mr. Innes was operating the new store as an actual public store in the 1770 timeframe. If he did, it would help to explain the traditions that western settlers came to Fort Cumberland for necessities, such as salt and iron.

### *The location of the replacement New Store*

The location of the replacement *"new store"* was much different than the location of the famous original new store that is shown on several French and Indian War maps that highlight the configuration of the Fort Cumberland structure. The location of the replacement new store is described in Alfred Procter James' book **"The Ohio Company: Its Inner History"**, as follows:

> The resurvey of the Lots 14, 15, and 16 of the New Store Tract in Virginia, opposite the mouth of Wills Creek, authorized by the warrant of March 1, 1768, was made by John Moffett on the 3rd, 4th, and 5th of May 1768. The resurvey included the intermediate waste land and totaled 1,083 acres. The resurvey, properly endorsed, is accompanied by a rough draft of the acreage and the surrounding territories, showing the hairpin curve of the Potomac River, Fort Cumberland, and the mouth of Wills Creek with the new store immediately opposite, on the extreme point of Virginia of that day, but now of Mineral County, West Virginia.

## St. Catherine's, near Killam's

The December 13, 1770 issue of the **"Maryland Gazette"** carries the following advertisement:[1486]

### FIVE POUNDS REWARD

*RAN away on the 11th Instant from the Subscriber, living at St. Catherine's, near Killam's, by George's Creek, Allegany Mountain, an Irish Convict Servant Man, named THOMAS BURN, alias Bryan, about 26 Years of Age, 5 Feet 6 Inches high, blind of the left Eye, wears his own Hair, and is by Trade a Mason: Had on and took with him a Blanket Coat, Two Osnabrig Shrits, Two Pair of Trousers, a Surtout Coat, and Felt Hat. Whoever secures the said Serevant, so that his Master gets him again, shall receive the above Reward, and reasonable Charges if brought home, paid by*

*(4w)*                *THOMAS FRENCH.*

*N.b. He is remarkably cut on the Buttocks by a Flogging he received from a former Master, and it is probable he may change his Name.*

This record tells us approximately where Thomas French was living in the year 1770.

---

[1486] This advertisement was identified by Scott Williams.

## Benjamin Tomlinson was living on the Ohio in the early 1770s

On April 17, 1797 Cumberland area resident Benjamin Tomlinson gave written answers to questions on an affidavit that was signed in Cumberland. His answer to the tenth question indicates he was living on the Ohio River in 1770:

*Ques. 10th. Were not some white men killed by the Indians in the year 1773?*

*Ans. Yes; John Martin and two of his men were killed on Hockhocking, about one year before Dunmore's army went out, and his canoe was plundered of above £200 worth of goods.*

*I lived on the river Ohio, and near the mouth of Yellow Creek, from the year 1770 until the Indians were killed at Yellow Creek, and several years after; I was present when the Indians were killed, and also present at the treaty in September or October 1774, near Chillicothe, on the Scioto...*

## Hauling commodities from Fort Cumberland, circa 1770

Although not documentary evidence, Volume 2 of the 1912 book "**Genealogical and Personal History of Fayette County Pennsylvania**" states:

*William, son of Dr. John McCormick, was born about 1736, he being the next son to Francis, born 1734. He was probably born in Virginia, as the record of the deed mentioned was 1740. He came to southwestern Pennsylvania about the year 1770, and was the first settler within the limits of the later borough of Connellsville, preceding by a few years Zachariah Connell, in whose honor the town was named. William McCormick came to Connellsville from Winchester, Virginia, bringing with him a number of pack-horses, which he employed in the transportation of salt and iron and other commodities from Cumberland, Maryland, to the Youghiogheny and Monongahela river settlements. There were no railroads, and Cumberland was the nearest point on the old National Pike. He settled on the Connellsville side of the river, building his first home of logs on the river bank directly opposite the home of Colonel William Crawford, on the west side of the Youghiogheny river, in 1767, at Stewart's Crossing,[1487] later the borough of New Haven, now a part of the city of Connellsville.[1488] He died in 1816, aged about eighty years. He married Effie, daughter of Colonel William Crawford, the revolutionary officer and famous Indian fighter, whose life and tragic death[1489] at the hands of his savage foes has inspired the pen of so*

---

[1487] Chapter CMLXXVII of the "**Pennsylvania Statutes at Large**" gave William Crawford the right to establish a ferry at Stewart's Crossing. The act, which was passed April 13, 1782, was titled *"An act for establishing ferries on the rivers Monongahela and Youghiogheny"*. William Crawford's 1793 survey (Book W, Page 238) for property along the Youghiogheny River just north of Mounts Creek states that it is *"Situate on the North side of Stewart's Crossing of Youghio Geni River"*. This survey is connected to Crawford's April 3, 1769 *"New Purchase"* application number 374. The "**New Purchase Register**" describes this property as being *"On the North side of Youghogany River on the mouth of a Creek that empties into said River where Braddocks Road crosses said River including his improvement made by permission of the Commanding officer at Fort Pitt."* These Crawford documents prove that Braddock's road crossed the Youghiogheny River at Stewart's Crossing. Additionally, Gist's journal from Braddock's campaign mentions the *"Camp by Stewards"*. The W.P.A. Warrant map of Dunbar Township labels the road coming into Stewart's Crossing as Braddock's road, but the underlying surveys do not name the road. Edward Cook's 1769 survey of John Crawford's property at Stewart's Crossing (Book C-25, Page 290) shows roads going to Broad Ford and Stewart's Crossing, but does not name them. The adjacent 1769 survey of Lawrence Harrison, Senior (Book E, Page 217) also shows the road to Stewart's Crossing, but does not name it. The 1873 Robinson survey, 1846 Harrison survey, 1873 Banning survey, and 1786 Ross survey that are shown on the W.P.A. map do not show the road.

[1488] Thaddeus Harris' 1803 journal describes Connellsville as follows, *"This town has been settled eight years. It is pleasantly situated on the Yohiogany; and contains about eighty houses, and four hundred inhabitants."*

[1489] An eyewitness, fellow prisoner Dr. Knight, described William Crawford's 1782 murder as follows, *"When we went to the fire, the colonel was stripped naked, ordered to sit down by the fire, and beat. Afterward I was treated in the same way. They then tied a rope to a post about fifteen feet high, bound the colonel's hands behind his back anil fastened the rope to the ligature between his wrists. The rope was long enough for him to sit down or walk around the post once*

*many writers. Colonel Crawford's coming to Western Pennsylvania antedated William McCormick's by several years…*

The reference to the National Pike is incorrect, as it was not built yet in the 1770s. Nevertheless, such biographies are based on stories handed down in families, and at least part of this biography rings true. The earliest version of the McCormick story that I can find is from Volume 1 the 1900 book "**Nelson's Biographical Dictionary and Historical Reference Book of Fayette County Pennsylvania**", which states:

*The first settler within the limits of Connellsville, as it is now constituted, was William McCormick, who came from Winchester, in the historic and beautiful valley of Virginia, in 1770. He was transporting salt, iron and other commodities from Cumberland, Maryland, to the Youghiogheny and Allegheny rivers. His name points to a Scotch-Irish origin, and he was probably identified with that sturdy and vigorous race which has impressed itself so deeply and in so many spheres of thought and action upon the history and development of the American nation. His wife was Effie Crawford, daughter of Col. William Crawford, who had established himself on the left bank of the Youghiogheny, near the northern boundary of the present borough of New Haven. His first home was a log house on the river bank, in accordance with the primitive fashion of the times. He lived to a ripe old age, dying in 1816, having passed his three score and ten, and leaving a large family—eleven children. Some of these found homes in the great west, others remained in Connellsville. They seem to have been characterized by energy and industry, and one, at least, of his descendants, Provance McCormick, had a versatile talent, pursued a variety of occupations and attained to the office of a justice of the peace. Zachariah Connell, founder of the town, came in a few years later than William McCormick, and married Ann Crawford, sister of the wife of William McCormick.*

---

*or twice, and back the same way. The colonel called to Girty to know if they intended to burn him, and Girty answerd, 'Yes,' when the colonel said he would take it all patiently. Captain Pipe made a speech to the Indians — thirty or forty men, sixty or seventy squaws and boys.*

*When the speech was ended they all veiled a hideous and hearty amen to what he had said. The Indian men took up their guns and shot powder into the colonel from his feet to his neck — I think not less than seventy loads. They then crowded around him, and, to the best of my observation, cut off his ears; when they dispersed a little I saw the blood running from both sides of his head. The fire was about six or seven yards from the post to which he was tied, and was made of small hickory poles, burnt quite through in the middle, each end of the pole remaining about six feet in length. Three or four Indians by turn would take up a burning piece of wood and apply it to his body, already burnt black with powder. These tormentors presented themselves on every side of him with burning fagots and poles. Some of the squaws took broad boards on which they could carry a quantity of burning coals and hot embers and threw on him, so that soon he had nothing but hot coals and ashes to walk on. In the midst of these extreme tortures he called to Girty and begged him to shoot him; Girty making no answer he called again, when Girty deridingly answered he had no gun, and laughed heartily.*

*Colonel Crawford now besought the Almighty to have mercy on his soul, spoke very low, and bore his torment with manly fortitude. He continued in this extremity of pain a couple of hours, when, exhausted, he lay down on his belly. They then scalped him, and repeatedly threw the scalp in my face, telling me that it was my 'great captain.' An old squaw (whose appearance every way answered the idea people entertain of the devil) got a board, took a parcel of coals and ashes and laid them on his head and back after he had been scalped. He raised himself on his feet again, and began to walk around the post. They put a burning stick to him again, but he seemed more insensible of pain.*

*The Indian fellow who had me in charge now took me away to Captain Pipe's house, and thus I was prevented from seeing the last of the horrid spectacle." ("**Sketches of Western Adventure…**", McClung, 1847.)*

# 23. 1771: Tomlinson millwrights

### Philp Martin leases various lots on Patterson Creek

Philip Martin had lot no. 22 on Patterson's Creek in 1749, which is at the mouth of the creek. The 1939 book "**Early Records Hampshire County Virginia**" records several property transactions for Phillip Martin that were recorded on May 15, 1771, and all of them were leases to persons living in Hampshire County. Each lease indicates that Philip Martin is a Captain stationed at Newfoundland, and one of them indicates he is a Captain of the Artillery. Each lease is witnessed by Peter Hog, John Magill, George Brent, and Phil Pendleton. A May 14, 1771 lease for *"625 a. — Lot No. 3, on Patterson Creek"* was to Richard Boyce. A May 14, 1771 lease for *"335 a. — Lot No. 7, on Patterson Creek"* was to Andrew Corn. A May 14, 1771 lease for *"421 a. — Lot No. 6, on Patterson Creek"* was to John Gilmore. A May 14, 1771 lease for *"280 a. — Lot No. 8, on Patterson Creek"* was to George Miller. A May 14, 1771 lease for *"295 a. — Lot No. 10, on Patterson Creek"* was to John Parker. A May 14, 1771 lease for *"278 a. — Lot No. 9, on Patterson Creek"* was to John Ramsey. A May 15, 1771 lease for *"299 a. — Lot No. 2, on Patterson Creek"* was to William Vause.

### John Tomlinson, millwright

John Tomlinson was already a millwright in 1771. Pages 103 to 104 of Frederick County Maryland Deed Book O (MSA CE 108-11) include the following:

*At the request of John Tomlinson the following Deed was Recorded March the 26, 1771, To Wit .... This Indenture made this Sixteenth Day of March in the year of our Lord One thousand Seven hundred Seventy One Between Joseph Tomlinson of Frederick County and Province of Maryland of the one part and John Tomlinson of Frederick County and Province aforesaid mill wright of the Other part witnesseth that the said Joseph Tomlinson in Consideration of the sum of ninety four pds in Dollars at Seven Shillings and Six pence Each Dollar to him in hand paid ... doeth give grand bargain Sell ... unto him he said John Tomlinson ... the following tract or parcel of Land Called the Second part of Wills Town ... Beginning at a Stone Set up in the given line of the Original Tract Called Wills Town ... together with all wrights Benefits and Profits whatsoever being o_ on the said tract or parcel of Land with all wrights Claims and Demands whatsoever of or from him the sd Joseph Tomlinson To have and to hold the said tract or parcel of Land aforesaid with all Rights and Profits whatsoever thereunto belonging unto him the Said John Tomlinson ...*

### Sharpe reminds Lord Baltimore about the reserve west of Fort Cumberland

A letter[1490] that Sharpe wrote to Lord Baltimore on June 5, 1771 via Hanbury includes the statement:

*In answer to that part of your Ldps Letter where you say that you understand there was some Land which I was desirous of but that you had not been informed where it lay I must beg leave to put your Ldp in mind that in Consequence of your Ldps Inclinations to reserve more Lands in the Province by Way of Manours a Reserve was a few years ago laid on a large Tract 96610 Acres lying just beyond Fort Cumberland & extending from Potowmack to the Dividing Line Northward & Westward so far as to include the Eastern Ridges of the Alegany Mountains, the Reason given for laying a Reserve on so large*

---

[1490] "**Archives of Maryland**", Volume 14.

*a Tract was that the good Land did not lye contiguous but in parcels interspersed with a good deal of hilly broken & barren Land & that it might be at your Ldps Choice to have one or more Manors laid out within such large reserved Tract. There was also at the same time a Tract of 2524 Acres surveyed & reserved for your Ldp farther to the Westward on the Branches of Yoghiogany River. In the Spring of 1768 Three other Tracts lying among the Branches of the Yoghyogany were surveyed as Manours for your Ldp & Plats thereof returned to the Land or Revenue Office viz One Tract containing 17750 Acres, Another 6030 Acres & the Third 4740 Acres. When I was given to understand by M<sup>r</sup> Hamersley's Letter dated in July 1768 that your Ldp did not desire to hold so much Land in the Nature of Manors but were rather inclined to patent most of it reserving a Quit Rent I in a Letter to your Ldp bearing Date the 28th Nov<sup>r</sup> 1768 wrote as follows. "If that is the Case (viz that your Ldp chooses to part with those Lands) I will if your Ldp pleases deposit the usual Caution Money for Either of the small Tracts & very probably other Persons may be found to take up the Rest if your Ldp is willing to part with it on the same Terms." This Letter of mine might not perhaps have reached your Ldp before you left England but in that Case I presume Mr Hamersley forwarded it to you; What I mean't & ask't by the part of it which I have quoted was that if your Ldp should choose to sell those Tracts of uncultivated Land on the usual Terms of Vacant unimproved Land viz £5 pr 100 Acres Caution Money & four shillings p<sup>r</sup> 100 Acres Quit Rent I would be glad to have the preemption of One or two of the small Tracts, to be granted to Me by one Patent, & if your Ldp pleases to accept my Offer & to give a special Order or Instruction for the Patents being issued I am still willing to purchase on those Terms for I believe none of those Lands are as yet disposed of.*

## Nathaniel Tomlinson, millwright

Nathaniel Tomlinson was already a millwright in 1771. Pages 594 to 595 of Frederick County Maryland Deed Book O (MSA CE 108-11) include the following:

*At the request of Nathaniel Tomlinson the following Deed was recorded Oct 28, 1771 — This Indenture made the nineteenth day of Sept in the year of our Lord One Thousand Seven Hundred Seventy one Between Joseph Tomlinson of Frederick County and province of Maryland of the one part & Nathaniel Tomlinson of Frederick County and province aforesaid cy Mill Wright of the other part Withnesseth that the said Joseph Tomlinson for and in consideration of the sum of One Hundred & forty four pounds in Dollars at Seven Shilling Six pence each Dollar to him in hand paid by the said Nathaniel Tomlinson ... doth give grant Bargain sell, alienate, Release, & Confirm unto him the said Nathaniel Tomlinson ... the following tract of Land lying & being in Fred<sup>k</sup> County & province aforesaid calld the first part of Wills Town ...*

John and Nathaniel Tomlinson are believed to be children of Joseph Tomlinson. Joseph Tomlinson, Junior, acting as an attorney for Nathaniel Tomlinson, deeded the first lot of the Wills Town tract to Benjamin Tomlinson on March 3, 1788. The 263-acre tract was located on Wills Creek, *"Beginning On The West Branch On Jennings Run"*. The deed states that John Tomlinson's property adjoined the north side of this property. The September 12, 1806 *"General Journal"* compiled by the commissioners for the National Road mentions Benjamin Tomlinson's mill as follows, *"Set out from Musselmans to Jenings run with a view to a critical examination of the capacity of the ground in that valley, and found from the meanders of the run frequently running close up to bold & rocky banks three crossings of the run will be unavoidable and that the best route will be to cross the run at Ben Tomlinsons old Mill near the present road & pass up on a plat of land above the level of the valley to recross the run at the lower end of a steep rocky bluff, then in direct course thro a little orchard."* This reference puts Benjamin Tomlinson's mill along Jennings Run and the Turkey Foot Road. The location of *"Musselmans"* was at the present-day site of Frostburg.

## Frederick Calvert, Lord Proprietor, dies in September 1771

The 1979 book "**A Biographical Dictionary of the Maryland Legislature 1635-1789**", by Edward C. Papenfuse, et. al. indicates that Frederick Calvert, Sixth Lord Baltimore, died in 1771, and willed his proprietorship to his Harford children, who were illegitimate. The will was contested, and litigation continued until 1781. Henry Harford inherited the rights of the proprietor to property in Maryland, but the Revolutionary War and the lawsuit meant that these rights no longer had much value. Henry estimated that these rights gave him 125,000 undeveloped acres west of Fort Cumberland, and other land amounting to 71,000 acres.

The 1826 U.S. Supreme Court case[1491] Cassell v. Carroll 24 U.S. 134 explains what became of the proprietary rights, as follows:

*The said Frederick Lord Baltimore died without lawful issue on 4 September, 1771. ...*

*On 4 March, 1771, Frederick Lord Baltimore made his will, and devised the Province of Maryland, and all its appurtenances, to Henry Harford. That upon the death of the said last mentioned Frederick, Baron of Baltimore, Henry Harford, the devisee named in his will, was a minor, and a ward under the guardianship of the Court of Chancery in England, and so continued until 1779. That the said Henry Harford, as devisee as aforesaid, was recognized and acknowledged by the provincial government of Maryland as the lawful proprietor under the charter, and by his guardians, with the knowledge and consent of the British government, entered into the possession of the government of the Province of Maryland and received the rents and revenues thereof as proprietor until the beginning of the disturbances which separated the United States of America from the British government. That those disturbances began in 1774, at which time the people of the Province of Maryland took the government of the said province into their own hands and ousted the officers of the proprietor, and the government of the said province so continued in the hands of the people until the Declaration of Independence, 4 July, 1776. That no quit rents nor any revenues which fell due in the said province after the year 1773, were paid to the proprietor or his officers; that after the Revolutionary War, the British government paid to the said Henry Harford 60,000, as a compensation for his losses in Maryland by the Revolution, and paid to the above-mentioned John Browning and to Robert Eden, who married the above-mentioned Caroline, 10,000 each as a compensation for their losses in the said province by the said Revolution. That suits in the Chancery Court of England were instituted in 1772 by the said Browning and wife and the said Eden and wife against the said Harford to recover the province and revenues of the said Province of Maryland, which suits continued until 1782, when the said bills were dismissed by the complainants.*

*In 1780, the Legislature of Maryland passed an act which declares that "The citizens of Maryland, from the declaration of independence, and forever, be and they are hereby declared to be exonerated and discharged from the payment of the aforesaid quit rents, and that the same shall be forever abolished and discontinued."*

## The estate of John Greenfield sells the 149-acre tract on the Little Cacapon River

The 1939 book "**Early Records Hampshire County Virginia**" records the following for November 8, 1771, "*GREENFIELD, John, dec'd, by McDONALD, Angus, WHITE, Alexander, Executors, and LIVINGSTON, Mayor James to Peter Hog, Attorney, of Augusta Co. for 149 a. on Little Cacapeon; rec 9-13-1772. Wit.: John Magill, Abraham Hite, Phil Pendleton.*"

---

[1491] This court case was located by Alan Williams of Cumberland, Maryland.

### Dickerson Simpkins lived in the vicinity of Fort Cumberland circa 1771

The court case of *"Beal vs. Lynn"* is included in the 1883 book "**Reports of Cases Argued and Adjudged in the Court of Appeals ...**", and includes the following statement:

*The plaintiff further offered in evidence, by Dickinson Simkings, a competent witness, that he has known the land called The Brothers for about fifty years. Witness went to live in the neighborhood of the land about 1771, and has lived in that neighborhood ever since. About twenty-six or twenty-seven years ago, Beall laid off an addition to Cumberland on the tract called The Brothers, on the east side of Wills Creek, and sold out the lots to different persons, Beall at the same time claiming title to the whole tract as purchased from Abraham Faw, except where he had sold out parts of it.*

### Cresap finds the source of the South Branch

The United States Supreme Court case of *"The State of Maryland vs. The Commonwealth of Virginia"* contains the following:[1492]

*That, after these difficulties had subsided the Governor of Maryland, some time in the year 1771 appointed commissioners, with authority to proceed to the head of the South branch of the Potomac, in search of its most western fountain, to get a meridian, and to ascertain the relative extent and bearings to the West of the first fountain of the North and South branches aforesaid; that the said commissioners undertook the trust, and after having made, in part, an actual survey and plot thereof, they reported to the Governor in the form of a letter signed by Thomas Cresap, one of the said commissioners, among other things, that agreeably to his Excellencys commission he (Thomas Cresap) proceeded to the head of the South Branch in company with the other two commissioners, and two surveyors with a number of pack horses and choppers, and two chain carriers; that after a diligent search they found the most westerly fountain to be a fountain of the North fork of the South branch of the Potomac; that the spring from which they proceeded with their North line, was small but about a hundred rods from it a little more easterly, broke out twelve springs, which made a large branch at once, that at a small distance from it over a small ridge was one of the fountains of James River, south of the other and to the West, was a fountain of green briar as they were informed; that they made a small wall of stone around the spring, from which they proceeded, and covered it with a large broad stone, on which they cut these letters C. Ld B. the initials of the name and title of Lord Baltimore, from which they continued their line for upwards of nine miles, to a smart creek, about two or three roods wide running to the west as well as all the waters they crossed in the above distance and for some miles further the water continued running to the west; that the next water they came to was two branches of cheat and soon afterwards they left off running; that the reason of their breaking up and coming home before finishing was for want of provisions and money to pay off pack-horse-men and choppers; that the hire of pack horses was very high for they had killed three, and several of the others were not able to travel home; that since their return home they had received his Excellencys letter informing them that a surveyor was coming to assist with some particulars such as staff and plum, those they made use of in the same manner Mr. Dixon and Mason did in running the province line; that they were threatened very hard by some of the Virginia people before they set out, that fifty men were appointed to meet them, and take them prisoners; but they were not molested by any person: That on this survey of the two branches a plot was made by them on which the South and North branches were delineated with a meridian ruuning through the head of each, and the meridian through the head of the South branch was upwards of twenty miles more west than the meridian through the head of the North branch, which said report and plot on the survey af'd were deposited and now remain in the*

---

[1492] "**Transcript of Record. Supreme Court of the United States October Term, 1908**", Volume II.

790

*archives and among the records of the province as by reference thereto will more fully appear and which are ready to be produced when required.*

# 24. 1772: Settlers north of the state line

**Luther Martin lodged with Innes at Fort Cumberland in 1772**

In the 1802 book "**Modern Gratitude, in Five Numbers**", Luther Martin describes staying at Fort Cumberland in 1772:

> *At Fort-Pitt, and the settlement in the neighborhood of Red-Stone, I remained, I believe, upwards of three weeks. — On my return, I staid a day with Major Ennis at Fort-Cumberland—I then arrived at Old-Town, where I spent a few days with the two Mr. Cresaps, — the father and the son. — The kind attentions, — the friendly civilities, I on this journey received from that truly hospitable family, gave rise to that connexion, which eleven years after took place between them and myself, — and by which I became the happy husband of the amiable daughter of the one, and grand daughter of the other.*

A footnote to this paragraph states:

> *As Miss Cresap was returning home from Philadelphia, where she had been educated under Mrs. Brodeau, she made a short stay in Baltimore; accidentally hearing that a young lady of that name was in town, I originally waited upon her solely from the motive of in some measure repaying, by my attentions to a daughter of the family, the kindness and hospitality I had received from her parents and relations. — But for that circumstance, it is more than probable I should never have seen her.*

This *"Major Ennis"* appears to be the *"Mr. Innis"* that George Washington ate breakfast with on November 27, 1770 at the new store. According to an extensive biography in the preface to Volume 5 of the "**Colonial Records of North Carolina**", the Colonel Innes who built Fort Cumberland died on September 5, 1759, at Wilmington. If true, this 1772 *"Major Ennis"* cannot be the Colonel Innes that originally built Fort Cumberland. I believe it is a reference to Enoch Innis.

Below, you will see that a Colonel Innes conditionally rented his plantation at Fort Cumberland to David Meriwether in 1782. This suggests that Innes may have been a resident at a community known as Fort Cumberland, rather than being present in some military capacity.

**A 1772 Virginia legislative act for improving navigation on the Potomac River**

Volume 3 of the book "**Legislative Journals of the Council of Colonial Virginia...**" records the following for April 9, 1772:

> *Philip Ludwell Lee, Esquire, reported that the Gentlemen to whom, the bill, intitueled, "An act for opening and extending the Navigation of the River Potowmack from Fort Cumberland to Tide-Water, was committed, had according to Order had the same under Consideration, and made an Amendment thereto*

> *Which Amendment being read and agreed to it was ordered that the Bill, with the Amendment be read a Third time immediately.*

> *The said Bill with the Amendment, accordingly read a third Time.*

> *Resolved, that the Bill, as amended, be agreed to.*

On May 4, 1772, George Washington wrote a letter to the Reverend Dr. Jonathan Boucher from Mount Vernon that includes the statement:

*An Act has passed this session empowering Trustees (to be chosen by yᵉ Subscribers to the Scheme) to raise money by way of Subscription, & Lottery, for the purpose of opening, and extending the Navigation of Potomack from the Tide Water, to Fort Cumberland; & for perpetuating the Toll arising from vessels to the Adventurers in the scheme — but ye Execution of it must necessarily be suspended till something similar passes into a Law in your provence.*

Washington was unable to obtain the cooperatin of Maryland until 1785.

### A land transaction on the Potomac River

The 1939 book "**Early Records Hampshire County Virginia**" records the following for September 10, 1772, *"GREATHOUSE, Harman (w. Mary) of Hampshire Co. to Michael Cresap of Frederick Co. (lease and release) 275 a., 249 a., on Potomac River; rec. 9-11-1772. Wit.: None."*

### Enoch Innis receives a commission

On October 15, 1772, John Murray, the fourth Earl of Dunmore, issued a Commission of Oyer and Terminer to Hampshire County Justice of the Peace Enoch Innis, and other justices from the same county.[1493] The commission meant that they had the authority to preside over trials regarding slaves who were charged with insurrection and conspiracies.

### Gage asks if goods are being transported via Fort Cumberland

On October 20, 1772, General Thomas Gage sent a letter[1494] from New York to Captain Edmonstone of the 18ᵗʰ Regiment at Fort Pitt, concerning plans for abandoning Fort Pitt. The letter contains the following reference to Fort Cumberland:

*If you could get Information whether any Goods are sent up the Potowmack from Alexandria to Fort Cumberland, by Water, and from thence in Waggons to Redstone Creek, and the Price paid per hundred Weight for the different Transportations by Land and Water, it would be very useful to have a particular Account of it. I imagine that Communication is not kept up, or that it is very costly, for by all I can learn, the Company of Baynton Wharton and Morgan, never send their Goods by that way, but send them always by Land Directly from Philadelphia.*

The letter has a postscript that states:

*I imagine the Traders if you examine them all, will be able to give good Intelligence in the Matters required. And I would be glad to know the shortest Distance between Fort Cumberland, and the Navigable part of Redstone Creek. There are two Roads, one something shorter than the other, but its said the shortest is so bad, that the other is generally used. The Distance is commonly computed at Seventy Miles.*

---

[1493] "**The Library of Virginia Quarterly Report of Archival Accessions**", July 1 through September 30, 2010.
[1494] This letter was found by Tim Fisher.

### Cresap is paid for running the meridian line from the first fountain of the Potomac

The November 3, 1772 minutes[1495] of the Maryland Board of Revenue include the following:

*The Board proceed to take under consideration the Accounts of Colᵒ Thomas Cresap for necessaries paid for by him as a Commissioner appointed to run a true Meridian Line from the first Fountain of the River Potowmack, including an Allowance to himself, John Revely and Docʳ Charles Wheeler, Commissioners and for two Surveyors amounting in the whole to the Sum of £1056..19..7½ Current Money, which, after due examination of the Vouchers, is passed and the same is, by Order of his Lordship's Commissioners, paid out of the Moneys arising from the Sale of his Manors and Reserv'd Lands.*

### A Virginia land transaction between John Smith and Michael Cresap

The 1939 book "**Early Records Hampshire County Virginia**" records the following for November 9, 1772, "*SMITH, John of Hampshire Co. to Michael Cresap of Frederick, Md. (lease and release) 40 a. on North Branch of Potomac; rec 11-12-1772. Wit.: Michael Cresap, Jr., Joseph Stibbs, Thomas Humphres, B. Ashby.*"

### John Jacob begins minding Michael Cresap's store at Oldtown

Page 18 of John J. Jacob's 1826 book "**A biographical sketch of the life of the late Captain Michael Cresap**" indicates that he became acquainted with Captain Cresap in 1772. The introduction to the book states,

*...I became an inmate of the family of Captain Cresap in my fifteenth year, and soon after, although very young, had the principal charge of his store; and such was his confidence in me, that about one year after he branched out his goods and sent me to a stand he had selected in the Allegheny Mountains, with a small assortment. The next year, to-wit: 1774, he sent me still further west, to-wit: to the place now called Brownsville,[1496] with a pretty large cargo. This whole cargo, in consequence of his instructions, I sold to the officers and soldiers in the Virginia service, in Dunmore's war. The store being dissolved, I returned to his family, at his residence in Oldtown, now Allegheny county, Maryland. Early in the year 1775 Captain Cresap marched to Boston with a company of riflemen, and committed all his intricate and multifarious business to my care.*

### Nearby Brothersvalley Township, Bedford County, had many taxables by 1772

When Bedford County, Pennsylvania was formed in 1771,[1497] all the region west of the Allegheny Mountain was part of Brothersvalley Township. All the families living therein required supplies, such as salt, from more settled areas to the east. One source of supplies would have been Michael Cresap's store at Old Town. Another may have been the *"new store"* at Wills Creek, where George Washington had breakfast with *"Mr. Innis"* on November 27, 1770. The following list of the 1772 taxables of Brothersvalley Township is from the 1906 book "**The History of Bedford and Somerset Counties...**" and identifies improved acreage. The names of the settlers listed at Turkeyfoot in Steel's April 2, 1768 report are bolded:

---

[1495] "**Minutes of the Board of Revenue, 1768-1775.**"

[1496] Although not documentary evidence, the 1937 booklet "**Monongahela the river and the region**" indicates that Michael Cresap was operating a ferry at the site of Brownsville in the 1770s.

[1497] Bedford County was formed as a result of the passage of Chapter DCXXXIX of the Pennsylvania Statutes at Large on March 9, 1771. It was *"Referred for consideration by the King in Council October 9, 1771. And allowed to become a law by lapse of time in accordance with the proprietary charter."* The title of the act was *"An act for erecting a part of the county of Cumberland into a separate county"*.

***Henry Abrahams, acres 100; imp. 12; horses 2; cows 3***; *Frederick Ambrose, acres 200; imp. 8; horses 2; cows 2; Samuel Adams, acres 200; imp. 5; horses 2; Solomon Adams, acres 200; imp. 3; horses 1; cows 1; Richard Brown, acres 300; imp. 6; horses 1; cows 4; negro slave 1; John Bridges, acres 200; imp. 3; horses 2; cows 1; John Baxter, acres 200; imp. 8; horses 2; cows 1; Ludwick Boude, acres 100 imp. 2; horses 1; cows 1; Christopher Benuch, acres 200; imp. 3; horses 1; cows 1; Benjamin Riggs, acres 300; imp. 2; horses 2; cows 1; William Cracart, acres 200; imp. 4; James Claypole, acres 200; horses 1; Frederick Cefar, acres 100; imp. 3; horses 1; cows 1; James Campbell, acres 200; imp. 12; horses 1; cows 1; Abraham Cable or Keble, Esq., acres 200; imp. 10; horses 2; cows 4; John Catta, acres 200; imp. 4; horses 2; cows 1; Michael Cefar, acres 100; imp. 6; horses 1; cows 1; Joseph Death, acres 600; imp. 5; horses 1; cows 10; Oliver Drake, acres 100; imp. 2; horses 1; cows 2; James Dougherty, acres 200; imp. 10; horses 5; cows 2; William Dwyer, acres 150; imp. 10; horses 1; cows 4; John Dilliner, acres 100; imp. 2; cows 1;* **Henry Enslow**, *acres 100; imp. 8; horses 3; cows 4;* **John Enslow**, *acres 100; imp. 6; horses 1; cows 2; Robert Estep, acres 100; imp. 3; horses 1; Adam Flick, acres 100; imp. 1; horses 1; cows 1; Jacob Fisher, acres 200; imp. 12; horses 2; cows 3; John Ferguson, acres 300; imp. 4; horses; cows 1; Andrew Friend, acres 50; imp. 10; horses 3 cows 2;[1498] Augustine Friend, acres 100; imp. 2; horses 2; cows 3; Paul Froman, acres 700; imp. 18; horses 2; cows 5; negro slaves 2; Michael Flick, acres 200; imp. 4; horses 1; Charles Friend, acres 200; imp. 10; horses 2; John Friggs, acres 200; imp. 1; horses 2; cows 1; John Fry, acres 100; imp. 1; cows 1; John Glassner, acres 200; imp. 8; horses 2; cows 3; Joseph Greenwalt, acres 100; imp. 7; horses 2; cows 2; William Greathouse, acres 200; imp. 10; horses 2; cows 3; Thomas Green, acres 100; imp. 6; horses 2; cows 8; Walter Hite, acres 200; imp. 8; horses 2; cows 2; Michael Huff, acres 300; imp. 6; horses 3; cows 3; servants 1; Richard Hoagland, acres 350; imp. 71;[1499] horses 2; cows 3; Andrew Hendrix, acres 200; imp. 10; horses 4; cows 6;* **Benjamin Jennings**, *acres 200; imp. 36; horses 4; cows 6;[1500] William Johnston, acres 200; imp. 3; horses 1; cows 1; Solomon Kessinger, acres 100; imp. 4; horses 2; cows 1; Philip Kemble, acres 300; imp. 8; horses 2; cows 4; George Kimball, acres 100; imp. 5; horses 2; cows 2; Valentine Lout, acres 100; imp. 2; horses 1; cows 1; Daniel Lout, acres 100; imp. 3; horses 1; cows 1; John Markley, acres 200; imp. 10; horses 4; cows 5; James McMullen, acres 45; imp. 9; horses 1; cows 1; William McClee, acres 300; imp. 7; horses 2; cows 1; John Miller, acres 300; imp. 10; horses 1; cows 2; Joseph Ogle, acres 200; imp. 10; horses 2; cows 2; Adam Polen, acres 100; imp. 5; horses 1; cows 1; Francis Polen, acres 200; imp. 3; horses 2; cows 1;* **Benjamin Pursley**, *acres 100; imp. 12; horses 3; cows 2;[1501] John Pursley, acres 60; imp. 7; horses 1; cows 1; Danes Pursley, acres 100; imp. 3; horses 2; cows 3; John Peters, acres 300; imp. 12; horses 2; cows 3; Henry Rhodes, Sr., acres 200; imp. 21; horses 3; cows 4; Jacob Rhodes, acres 100; imp. 5; horses 2; cows 3; Gabriel Rhodes, acres 200; imp. 10; horses 2; cows 2; Henry Rhodes, Jr., acres 400; imp. 10; horses 1; cows 2; John Rhodes, acres 100; imp. 1; horses 1; cows 1; John Reed, acres 100; imp. 7 horses 2; cows 2; John Rice, acres 400; imp. 35; negro slaves 1; horses 7; cows 1; Cutlip Rose, acres 100; imp. 8; horses 1; cows 1; Hugh Robinson, acres 100; imp. 8;*

---

[1498] For more information on Andrew Friend, see the 1906 book "**The History of Bedford and Somerset Counties…**" and the article *Captain Andrew Friend of Turkeyfoot"* in the May 3, 1963 issue of the "**Laurel Messenger**".

[1499] Richard Hoagland's 71 acres of improved land indicates that his property had been settled for a long time.

[1500] Apparently, there were two men named Benjamin Jennings in the area. Volume 2, page 239 of the 1906 book "**History of Bedford and Somerset Counties…**" states, *"Benjamin Jennings, also from the Turkeyfoot region, and who was a son of the Benjamin Jennings named in Capt. Steele's list of the Turkeyfoot trespassing settlers of 1768, served in Capt. Kilgore's company of the 8th Regiment of the line. He is said to have been a man of great physical strength, and at the time of his death, which took place about 1845, had reached the age of 90 years; he was buried in the old graveyard at Ursina."*

[1501] Ursina is on Benjamin Pursel's *"Longbottom"* survey. Andrew Ream owned the Benjamin Pursel property by 1796. The 1939 W.P.A. map of early surveys shows *"Otho Ream in Rt of Benjamin Pursel"* at the eventual site of Ursina. The 1786 survey of Benjamin Pursel (Book C-172, Page 74) states that the property is *"Situated on the north fork of Turkey-Foot (a branch of Youghiogeni River so Called) and on the Turkey-foot Road…"* According to the February 1963 issue of the "**Laurel Messenger**", Puzzley Run was named for the early settler Benjamin Pursley.

*horses 1; cows 2; Frederick Sheaf, acres 200; imp. 4; horses 2; cows 2; John Swiser, acres 100; imp. 5; horses 2; cows 3; John Sappinton, acres 200; imp. 6; horses 2; cows 2; Adam Small, acres 300; imp. 8; Bastion Shells, acres 100; imp. 1;[1502] horses 1; cows 1;* **James Spencer**, *acres 240; imp. 21; horses 2 cows 6; Nathaniel Skinner, acres 100; imp. 5;[1503] horses 1; William St. Clair, acres 100; imp. 6; Henry Smith, acres 200; imp. 3; horses 1; cows 1; Solomon Shute, acres 100; imp. 2; horses 1; cows 1; William Tyshoe, acres 300 imp. 12; horses 1;[1504] cows 1; Abraham Vaughan, acres 100; imp. 4; horses 2; cows 2; Thomas Urie, acres 100; imp. 12; Philip Wagaly, acres 200; imp. 10; horses 2; cows 1; Frederick Weimer, acres 200; imp. 4; horses 2; cows 2; John Weimer, acres 100; imp. 2; horses 1; cows 1; Richard Wells, acres 300; imp. 10; horses 3; cows 2; George Wells, acres 50; imp. 4; horses 2; cows 1; Acquilla White, acres 200; imp. 3; horses 1;[1505] cows 2; John Winsel, acres 100; imp. 1; horses 2; cows 1; Peter Winard, acres 100; imp. 5; horses 2; cows 3; Thomas John Wailer, acres 100; imp. 1; horses 2; cows 1; Samuel Wallis, acres 300. Matthias Ditch, Thomas Stinton, John Penrod, Felix Morgan, Frederick Aker, James Winler, James Pursley, Nicholas Friend, Robert Pulclut, Ephraim Tassey, Martin Cefar, James Moore, Frederick Vandoux, Edward Grimes, Samuel Worrell, James Wells, Peter Booker, Lodowick Greenwalt, Gabriel Abrahams, James Black, Henry Bruner, George Briner, John Bowman, Casper Stoy, Joseph Jennings, Francis Hay, James Hogland, Edward Henderson, William Haskin, Edward Higgins, Matthew Judy, John St. Clair, George Shider, Henry Shidlet, Jacob Wingart, Atwell Worrell, Richard Wells, Thomas Ogle, Daniel Pursley, John Hinkbaugh.*

Some of the names in this list are recognizable to students of Somerset County history as residents of the southern part of what is now Somerset County, including Henry Abrahams, Oliver Drake, John Enslow, Andrew Friend, Thomas Green, Richard Hoagland, Benjamin Jennings, John Markley, Benjamin Pursley, John Reed, James Spencer, Nathaniel Skinner, William Tyshoe, John Weimer, and Acquilla White. Other parts of Bedford County, such as the Cumberland Valley, were also settled at the time, and represent potential customers for Maryland storekeepers. I didn't include the taxables of those areas because I am not very familiar with the names of the early settlers who lived there.

### Richard Hoagland had a great deal of ground cleared in 1772

While not documentary evidence, the 1906 book "**The History of Bedford and Somerset Counties…**" references Richard Hoagland as follows:

*Richard Hoagland must have been a very early settler, his land being on the east side of the Youghiogheny river. He also had a large tract that lay on both sides of the Braddock road. The assessment of 1772 returns him as having seventy-one acres of cleared or improved land. This is nearly four times as much cleared land as any one else had who was then living in what is now Somerset county, and it certainly indicates a number of years of previous settlement. It is not unlikely that he was one of those who were permitted to locate along the Braddock road under sanction of the military authorities, who did this sometimes because it was of some advantage to have at least some persons settled along the road. And he may have found it to his profit to clear and cultivate so much more land than others did by reason of*

---

[1502] Sebastian Shallis is one of my ancestors.

[1503] Nathaniel Skinner is buried at the Jersey Church, near Confluence, Pennsylvania. His tombstone reads *"THE BODY of NATHANIEL SKINNER Sen who was born in Woodbridge in New Jersey, lieth here He Departed this life October 1, 1801 aged 95 years"*.

[1504] For information on Tissue, see "**In Search of the Turkey Foot Road**", fourth edition.

[1505] According to Volume II, page 239 of the 1906 book "**History of Bedford and Somerset Counties…**", Aquilla White served as a corporal in the Revolutionary War. The 1775 survey of Aquila White (Book D-8, Page 216) was certified in 1801, and references an *"old path leading to Turkeyfoot"*. This survey proves there was a path in what became Milford Township that was known as the *"old path leading to Turkeyfoot"*, however, this seems to be an 1801 description, because the paragraph mentions Somerset County, which did not exist in 1775. This path is unrelated to the military road out of Fort Cumberland that was cut in 1779.

*having a ready sale for its product to those who were at all times passing over the road. He must also have been a man of some reputation, for we find that in 1773 he was commissioned a justice of the peace, the second to be commissioned in what is now Somerset county. He would, however, seem not to have been a very good manager, for he must have been insolvent at the time of his death, his lands in 1786 having been sold to Henry Smyth by the then sheriff of Bedford county, at the suit of Michael Cresap's heirs.*

### The Salisbury, Pennsylvania area settlement already existed in 1772

The Salisbury, Pennsylvania area was settled before the Revolutionary War. For example, John Hendrix, John Markley,[1506] and William Tyshoe (Tissue) appear in the 1772 Brothersvalley assessment list for 1773 taxes. Tyshoe already had 12 acres cleared, and Markley had 10 acres cleared. So much cleared land means they had already been in the area at least a few years. For another example, the early settler John Christner's property was warranted in 1775, and he and Christian Hochstetler[1507] were recorded doing business with Peter Livengood[1508] in 1776. For another example, Morgan brought his road through the area in 1779, as described in another chapter herein, because the existing settlement was a good source of forage for the packhorses.

---

[1506] I descend from John Markley through his daughter Margaret, who married John Hendricks(on). Their daughter Mary *"Polly"* Hendricks was born on March 10, 1776 in Elk Lick Township, and married Jacob Beeghley/ Beeghly/Beachly. Although the will abstract of John Hendricks in the 1900 book "**Historical Collections of Harrison County, in the State of Ohio**" lists John's daughter as Mary Picaly, I believe *"Picaly"* is an inadvertent corruption of *"Beachly"*. For more information on the Markley family, see Ruth Markley's 1980 book "**John Markley Descendants**". According to Volume 2, page 68 of the 1906 book "**History of Bedford and Somerset Counties...**", *"John Markley is considered by all the best authorities as having been the first settler here. He had taken up several tracts of land, but his home place was a large tract of several hundred acres, known under the name of 'John's Fancy,' All the older part of the town of Salisbury was platted on this tract."* In the 1772 assessment for 1773 Brothersvalley Township taxes, John Markley is listed with 200 acres total, and ten acres cleared. This means Markley was in the area long before George Morgan had the 1779 road cut to supply Fort Pitt. According to the article *"The Markley House"* in Volume LI, Number 2 of the "**Casselman Chronicle**" (2011), John Markley's log house was donated to the Highland Association.

[1507] Page 57 of the 1912 book "**Descendants of Jacob Hochstetler**" indicates that Christian, the son of Jacob Hochstetler, sold his Lancaster area farm in 1775 and was taxed on property in Somerset County in 1776. This is confirmed by the 1898 book "**Returns of taxable for the counties of Bedford (1773 to 1784...**", which lists a tax of *"7.6"* for *"Christian Hostelder"* on uncultivated land. Christian Hofstotler appears in the list of 1779 Brothersvalley Township property holders and is listed with 150 acres. I am a descendant of Christian's father Jacob, who, like Christian, survived a French and Indian War massacre in Berks County, and subsequent Indian captivity. Volume 3, page 460 of the 1906 book "**History of Bedford and Somerset Counties...**" mistakenly implies that the massacre occurred near present-day Meyersdale. The October 6, 1757 issue of the "**Pennsylvania Journal**" states, *"From Reading we have advice that last Wednesday the enemy burnt the house of one Hochsteller and killed Hochstelle's wife and a young man, and himself and three children are missing."* The October 15, 1757 issue of Philadelphia's "**Journal**" states, *"In the same week the Indians came to Hoffstettler's place; the man called on his neighbors for help; meanwhile the Indians killed his wife and carried away his children, and burned the house and barn. One son escaped."* Captain Jacob Orndt's report states, *"Highstealer's wife and one child killed and scalped; and three of his children taken captives in September, 1757, in Bern Township."* The August 13, 1762 petition to the Lieutenant Governor of Pennsylvania for the return of his captured children, by Christian's father Jacob Hochstetler, is recorded in the 1853 edition of the "**Pennsylvania Archives**", Volume IV, page 99, and includes the following, *"That about ffive Years ago yoʳ Petʳ with 2 Children were taken Prisoners, & his Wife & 2 other Children were kill'd by the Indians, that one of the said Children who is still Prisoner is named Joseph, is about 18 Years old, and Christian is abot 16 years & a half old, That his House & Improvenᵗˢ were totally ruined & destroyed. ..."*

[1508] Peter Livengood is one of my ancestors. According to the Somerset County assessment lists in John Cassaday's 1932 book "**The Somerset County Outline**", Peter *"Levergood"* first appeared as a taxable in Brothersvalley Township in 1776. A study of his business journal suggests that he came in 1775. The records suggest that he stopped weaving in April 1775 in order to move, was in the present-day Salisbury area by July 1775, and clearly already had his weaving equipment across the Allegheny Mountain by April 1777.

Regarding the Salisbury area settlement, the book "**The History of Bedford and Somerset Counties...**" states:

*Other settlers whose names are found on the first assessment list, supposed to have been made in 1772, were Bengamin Biggs, William Tissue, William Dwire, Andrew Hendricks, Hugh Robinson, William St. Clair, John St. Clair and James Claypool. Abraham Cable's name is identified with the Cox farm, and he may have lived on it, but this is by no means certain. How long they had been here at the time that this first written record was made, is not known. But some of them may have been of the trespassing settlers who were in the country prior to the time that it was legally open for settlement. Without mentioning any names, as he did when speaking of the Turkeyfoot region, Steele in his report of April, 1768, does make reference to a few settlers as "living nigh the crossing of the Little Yough," to whom some proclamations were sent. ...*

### A tradition of Indian fields in the vicinity of Salisbury at the time of white settlement

Page 548 of the 1884 book "**History of Bedford, Somerset and Fulton Counties...**" describes Indian clearings in the vicinity of Salisbury as follows:

*Peter Livengood, a native of Switzerland, came to America, married in Berks county, Pennsylvania, and removed to Elk Lick township, settling on the farm now known as the Arnold property. ... It is said that there was a small clearing on the farm which had been made by the Indians.*

Volume II, page 3 of the 1906 book "**History of Bedford and Somerset Counties...**" describes a source of the Indian field tradition:

*Grandsons of Peter Livengood, one the first settlers in this region, who were born about 1804, and who remembered their grandfather quite well, informed the writer that when he settled there he found an Indian clearing on his farm.*

This Indian clearing is evidence of fairly recent Indian occupation. When Harry Ringler, Senior was a boy, he found a rich supply of Indian artifacts on the portion of Peter Livengood's property that is located on the east side of the Casselman River.

# 25. 1773: The year of the Boston Tea Party

### Andrew Due obtains land on a draught of Old Town Creek

Andrew Due appears on Andrew Bruce's 1778 Oath of Fidelity list. The tract named *"Dues Chance"* was surveyed for Andrew Due on February 27, 1773 and patented to him on December 20, 1784 (Frederick County Patent Certificate 1211). The survey states that the survey begins *"at a Bounded White Oak Standing on the north sde of Murleys run, being a Draught of old Town Creek ..."*

### A property transaction on the North Branch of the Potomac River

The 1939 book "**Early Records Hampshire County Virginia**" records the following for March 9, 1773, *"COLLINS, Thomas (w. Elizabeth) of Hampshire Co. to Charles Prather of Hampshire Co. (lease and release) 70 a. on North Branch of Potomac; rec. 3-11-1773. Wit.: William Dopson, John Forman, Humphrey Westell, Benjamin Bowman."*

### 8,000 dollars provided for road improvement west from Fort Cumberland in 1773

A 1773 Maryland act[1509] states:

*And be it enacted that of the said Eighty Thousand Dollars to be emitted in Virtue of this Act such Number as shall be necessary not exceeding Eight thousand Dollars be and are hereby appropriated to be laid out and expended in the cutting clearing amending and putting in good Order a Waggon Road from Fort Cumberland to the nearest Battoc [batteau] navigable Water on the Western side of the Allegany Mountain and the said Eight Thousand Dollars or such part thereof as may be necessary shall and may be laid out and expended in the Work aforesaid by M.ʳ Thomas Johnson Jun.ʳ M.ʳ Henry Griffith M.ʳ Charles Beatty M.ʳ Thomas Sprigg Wootton M.ʳ Joseph Sprigg M.ʳ Thomas Price and M.ʳ Jonathan Hagar or the Major Part of them who are hereby appointed Supervisors of the said Road and the said Commissioners shall from time to time pay to the Order or Orders of the said Supervisors or the major Part of them any Part or Parts of the said Eight thousand Dollars for the purpose aforesaid of the Expenditure whereof the said Supervisors shall from time to time render to the General Assembly of this Province a full and perfect Account*

A Thomas Johnson is included in the 1783 Cumberland hundred list, and a Joseph Sprigg is included in the 1783 Skipton hundreds list. The presence of their names in the 1773 act suggests they were already living in the environs of Fort Cumberland in 1773.

### A property transaction on Patterson Creek

The 1939 book "**Early Records Hampshire County Virginia**" records the following for October 29, 1773, *"ROBINSON, Joseph of Frederick Co. to William Campbell of Frederick Co. (lease and release) 332 a. on Patterson Creek; rec. 11-9-1773. Wit.: George Rootes, Samuel Beall, Alex White, Bryan Bruin."* A Joseph Robinson had lot no. 21 on Patterson's Creek in 1749.

---

[1509] This is from the *"Assembly Proceedings, November 16-December 23, 1773"* section of "**Proceedings and Acts of the General Assembly, October 1773 to April 1774**", Volume 64.

## A property transaction on the North Branch of Potomac River

The 1939 book "**Early Records Hampshire County Virginia**" records the following for November 5, 1773, "*WORTHINGTON, Samuel, Jr. of Barkley Co. to John Vanbuskirk of Hampshire Co. (lease and release) 160 a. on North Branch of Potomac; rec. 5-10-1774. Wit.: None.*"

## The December 16, 1773 Boston Tea Party

Volume VI of the book "**Charles Knight's Popular History of England**" describes the well-known Boston Tea Party as follows:

*It was Sunday, the 28th of November, 1773, when there sailed into Boston harbour the English merchant ship Dartmouth, laden with chests of tea belonging to the East India Company. The Act of Parliament which allowed the Treasury to license vessels to export the teas of the Company to the American colonies, free of duty, was the signal for popular gatherings in Boston. ... Town meetings were held at Boston, when strong resolutions were adopted. In this state of things, on that Sunday, the 28th of November, the first tea-ship arrived. The New England colonists preserved that strict observance of the Sabbath which their puritan fathers felt the highest of duties. But it was a work of necessity to impede the landing of the tea; and a Committee met twice on that Sunday to concert measures. They obtained a promise from Rotch, the commander of the ship Dartmouth, that his vessel should not be entered till the following Tuesday. On Monday, the Committees of all the neighbouring towns assembled at Boston; and five thousand persons agreed that the tea should be sent back to the place whence it came. "Throw it overboard," cried one. The consignees, alarmed at this demonstration, declared that they would not send back the teas, but that they would store them. This proposal was received with scorn; and then the consignees agreed that the teas should not be landed. But there was a legal difficulty. If the rest of the cargo were landed, and the tea not landed, the vessel could not be cleared in Boston, and after twenty days was liable to seizure. Two more ships arrived, and anchored by the side of the Dartmouth. The people kept watch night and day to prevent any attempt at landing the teas. Thirteen days after the arrival of the Dartmouth, the owner was summoned before the Boston Committee, and told that his vessel and his tea must be taken back to London. It was out of his power to do so, he said. He certainly had not the power; for the passages out of the harbour were guarded by two king's ships, to prevent any vessel going to sea without a licence. On the 16th, the revenue officers would have a legal authority to take possession of the Dartmouth. ...*

*On the 16th of December, there was a meeting in Boston of seven thousand persons, who resolved that the tea should not be landed. The master of the Dartmouth was ordered to apply to the governor for a pass, for his vessel to proceed on her return voyage to London. The governor was at his country house. Many of the leaders had adjourned to a church, to wait his answer. The night had come on when Rotch returned, and announced that the governor had refused him a pass, because his ship had not cleared. There was no more hesitation. Forty or fifty men, disguised as Mohawks, raised the war-whoop at the porch of the church; went on to the wharf where the three ships lay alongside; took possession of them; and deliberately emptied three hundred and forty chests of tea into the waters of the bay. It was the work of three hours. Not a sound was heard, but that of breaking open the chests. The people of Boston went to their rest, as if no extraordinary event had occurred.*

This action, and the reverberations from it, helped to precipitate the Revolutionary War. The day after the event, John Adams wrote the following in his diary:[1510]

*December 17. Last night, three cargoes of Bohea tea were emptied into the sea. This morning a man-of-war sails. This is the most magnificent movement of all. There is a dignity, a majesty, a sublimity, in this last effort of the patriots, that I greatly admire. The people should never rise without doing something to be remembered, something notable and striking. This destruction of the tea is so bold, so daring, so firm,*

---

[1510] "**The Works of John Adams, Second President of the United States ...**", Volume 2, 1850.

*intrepid and inflexible, and it must have so important consequences, and so lasting, that I cannot but consider it as an epoch in history. ...*

*What measures will the Ministry take in consequence of this? Will they resent it? Will they dare to resent it? Will they punish us? How? By quartering troops upon us? by annulling our charter? by laying on more duties? by restraining our trade? by sacrifice of individuals? or how?*

*The question is, Whether the destruction of this tea was necessary? I apprehend it was absolutely and indispensably so. ... To let it be landed, would be giving up the principle of taxation by parliamentary authority, against which the continent has struggled for ten years. It was losing all our labor for ten years, and subjecting ourselves and our posterity forever to Egyptian task-masters; to burthens, indignities; to ignominy, reproach and contempt; to desolation and oppression; to poverty and servitude.*

## Joseph Doddridge's story of his pioneer experiences references Cumberland

The 1833 book "**A History of the Valley of Virginia**" includes a large section written by the Rev. Dr. Joseph Doddridge titled *"Notes on the settlement and Indian wars of the western parts of Virginia and Pennsylvania, from the year 1763 until the year 1783 inclusive. Together with a view of the state of society and manners of the first settlers of that country."* The section is taken from an 1824 book of the same title, written by Doddridge.

Doddridge states *"My father, with a small number of neighbors, made their settlements in the spring of 1773."* The settlement must have been in what is now Fayette County, Pennsylvania (then claimed by Virginia), because the book states that as a result of Dunmore's war in the spring of 1774, *"Our little settlement then broke up. The women and children were removed to Morris's fort, in Sandy Creek glade, some distance to the east of Uniontown."* This background as someone who lived the western settler's experience provides a significant degree of authority for the following extracts from the book.

### Doddridge reports that the majority of western settlers used Braddock's Road

One excerpt from the book informs us that the majority of western settlers used Braddock's road, which would have brought many of them through the Fort Cumberland region:

*I will go back to the year 1772, and trace the various steps by which our settlements advanced to their present vigorous state of existence.*

*The settlements on this side of the mountains commenced along the Monongahela, and between that river and the Laurel ridge, in the year 1772. In the succeeding year they reached the Ohio river. The greater number of the first settlers came from the upper parts of the then colonies of Maryland and Virginia. Braddock's trail, as it was called, was the route by which the greater number of them crossed the mountains. A less number of them came by the way of Bedford and Fort Ligonier, the military road from Eastern Pennsylvania to Pittsburg. They effected their removals on horses furnished with pack-saddles. This was the more easily done, as but few of these early adventurers into the wilderness were encumbered with much baggage.*

*Land was the object which invited the greater number of these people to cross the mountain; for as the saying then was, "it was to be had here for taking up." That is, building a cabin and raising a crop of grain, however small, of any kind, entitled the occupant to four hundred acres of land, and a preemption right to one thousand acres more adjoining, to be secured by a land office warrant. This right was to take effect if there happened to be so much vacant land, or any part thereof, adjoining the tract secured by the settlement right. At an early period the government of Virginia appointed three commissioners to give certificates of settlement rights. These certificates, together with the surveyor's plat, were sent to the land office of the state, where they laid six months, to await any caveat which might he offered. If none was offered the patent then issued.*

**Doddridge reports that western settlers bartered for salt and iron at Cumberland**

The following excerpt indicates that the western settlers bartered for salt and iron at Fort Cumberland:

*The acquisition of the indispensable articles of salt, iron, steel and castings, presented great difficulties to the first settlers of the western country. They had no stores of any kind, no salt, iron, nor iron works; nor had they money to make purchases where those articles were to be obtained. Peltry and furs were their only resources, before they had time to raise cattle and horses for sale in the Atlantic states.*

*Every family collected what peltry and fur they could obtain throughout the year for the purpose of sending them over the mountains for barter.*

*In the fall of the year, after seeding time, every family formed an association with some of their neighbors for starting the little caravan. A master driver was selected from among them, who was to be assisted by one or more young men, and sometimes a boy or two. The horses were fitted out with pack-saddles, to the binder part of which was fastened a pair of hobbles made of hickory withs: a bell and collar ornamented his neck. The bags provided for the conveyance of the salt were filled with feed for the horses: on the journey a part of this feed was left at convenient stages on the way down, to support the return of the caravan. Large wallets, well filled with bread, jerk, boiled ham and cheese, furnished provision for the drivers. At night, after feeding, the horses, whether put in pasture or turned out into the woods, were hobbled, and the bells were opened.*

*The barter for salt and iron was made first at Baltimore, Frederick, Hagerstown, Oldtown and Cumberland, in succession, became the place of exchange. Each horse carried two bushels of alum salt, weighing eighty-four pounds the bushel. This, to-be sure, was not a heavy load for the horses, but it was enough considering the scanty subsistence allowed them on the journey.*

*The common price of a bushel of alum salt at an early period was a good cow and calf; and until weights Were introduced, the salt was measured into the half bushel by hand as lightly as possible. No one was permitted to walk heavily over the floor while the operation was going on.*

Unfortunately, Doddridge does not indicate when Cumberland became the place of exchange. From the title of Doddridge's section of the book, which includes the statement *"from the year 1763 until the year 1783 inclusive"* it appears that he is describing a time before the town of Cumberland was founded.

# 26. 1774: Local resistance to importation

### Consideration of the petition of Thomas French is postponed

The book "**Proceedings of the Council of Maryland, 1761-1769**" provides a transcript of the minutes from the February 23, 1774 meeting of the Board of Revenue, which include the following statement:

*The Board proceed to take under Consideration the Petition of Thomas French relative to taking of the Reserve to the Westward of Fort Cumberland, except Lands actually Surveyed and Certificates thereof returned for the use of the Lord Proprietary. It appearing to the Board that the late Lord Proprietary was desirous of having 10000 Acres of Land laid off in that part of the Province for a Manor, in order to secure the same Col° Sharpe, then Governor, had thought proper to lay a general Reserve until such manor should be ascertained which had not yet been done, but that in lieu thereof Five different Tracts had been actually Surveyed and Certificates thereof returned containing in the whole the quantity of 127680 Acres of Land. The Board are of opinion, that the further consideration of the Petition should be postponed and a previous enquiry made into the Reasons for enlarging the quantity after which they will again meet, and determine the said Petition.*

### A property transaction on Patterson Creek

The 1939 book "**Early Records Hampshire County Virginia**" records the following for March 3, 1774, *"HARDIN, John to William Blackburn (lease and release) 100 a. on Patterson Creek; rec. 3-8-1774. Wit.: Alex White, Wm. Campbell, George Rootes, Peter Hog, Abraham Hite."*

### A property transaction on the North Branch of Potomac River

The 1939 book "**Early Records Hampshire County Virginia**" records the following for March 12, 1774, *"PEARCEALL, John (w. Hannah) of Hampshire Co. to Leonard Tipsord of Hampshire Co. (lease and release) 174 a. on North Branch of Potomac; rec. 3-14-1775. Wit.: Elias Posten, Okey Johnson, Nath. Kuykendall, Simon Doyle."*

### The board wants to remove the reserve on lands west of Fort Cumberland

The book "**Proceedings of the Council of Maryland, 1761-1769**" provides a transcript of the minutes from the March 26, 1774 meeting of the Board of Revenue, which includes the following:

*The Business having been previously intimated to His Excellency the Governor, who by reason of his Indisposition could not attend Personally. The Board resume the Consideration of the Propriety or Impropriety of taking off the Reserve on all Lands lying within this Province to the west-ward of Fort Cumberland, except such Lands as have been actually surveyed and Certificates thereof returned to this Office for the use of the Lord Proprietary, and after mature deliberation thereon unanimously came to the following Determination Viz.*

*Whereas it appears to this Board, that People have been restrained from making Surveys and obtaining Grants of Lands to the Westward of Fort Cumberland, in this Province, in consequence of an Instruction issued by the late Governor, Col° Sharpe, to the Judges of the Land Office, bearing Date the 10th Day of April 1764 in the following Words:*

*The Lord Proprietary being desirous to have 10000 acres of Land reserved in the western part of Frederick County for a Manor, I have given the Surveyor of that County Instructions to execute no warrants whatever on the Lands lying beyond Fort Cumberland til the above quantity is surveyed and laid out for his Lordship, of which you will be pleased to take notice and cause the same to be communicated to any Person that may apply for Warrants that may affect Land in that part of the Province. I am*

> *Gen^n*
>
> *Your hble Servant*
>
> *Hor° Sharpe*

*And as it appears by Platts thereof, that, since the said Instruction, several Surveys have been made and Lands reserved for the use of the Lord Proprietary to the westward of Fort Cumberland to wit 2550 Acres p Certificate dated the 30^th October 1767, 96610 acres p Certificate dated the 1^st of December 1767, 17750 acres p Certificate dated the 8^th May, 4740 Acres p Certificate dated the 16^th May, and 6030 Acres p Certificate dated the 20^th May in the year 1768 whereby the Intent and Design of the said Instruction to the Surveyor of Frederick County has been fully answered; and in as much as the Revenue of the Lord Proprietary would be augmented, and the Settlement of the Country be encouraged by giving liberty to all Persons to have surveyed to their use, upon Warrants already issued and that shall hereafter issue the Lands in this Province, to the Westward of Fort Cumberland, so that such Surveys in virtue of such Warrants do not run into, interefere with, or in any manner affect the above, or any of the above Surveys made for the Lord Proprietary: Therefore it is the opinion of this Board that the Deputy Surveyor of Frederick County be instructed to lay out, and Survey for such Person and Persons as for that purpose shall apply to him to execute any Warrant or Warrants on any Lands to the Westward of Fort Cumberland, in this Province, in the same manner and by the same rules as he would do in case the first mentioned Instruction had never been given or issued. Provided that in making Surveys the said Deputy Surveyor do take especial Care that he do not run into, interfere with, or in any manner affect any of the Lands laid out and surveyed for the Lord Proprietary as aforesaid. And it is also the Opinion of this Board, that Copies of the Lines, Courses and Boundaries of the aforesaid Surveys made for the Lord Proprietary, shewing the situation of the Lands surveyed and Reserved as aforesaid for his Lordship's use, he sent to the said Deputy Surveyor in order that he may be the better enabled to perform his Duty in not running into, interfering with, or in any manner affecting the Lands, or any part of them laid out and reserved for the Lord Proprietary as aforesaid.*

*Ordered, That the Clerk of this Board do immediately wait on his Excellency the Governor and lay before him the foregoing State of this Day's Proceedings, and in case his Excellency shall concur in the expediency of the Measure, that then the Certificates before recited be by the Clerk delivered into the Land Office that all Persons may have access to them; and also that Copies of the Courses be forwarded to the Deputy Surveyor of Frederick County, that he may be enabled to regulate his Conduct in all Surveys to be made in pursuance thereof, of all which Proceedings of the Board, His Excellency was pleased, after perusal thereof, to signify his entire Approbation.*

*The Board adjourn to Tuesday the 17^th Day of May next.*

## The May 17, 1774 meeting of the Board of Revenue

The book "**Proceedings of the Council of Maryland, 1761-1769**" includes minutes from a May 17, 1774 meeting of the Board of Revenue, which include the following:

*The Agent having withdrawn, Two Letters from him addressed to the Judges of the Land Office, together with the Copy of an answer from the Hon^{ble} George Steuart, Esq^r were laid before the Board and Ordered to be read, being relative to the Powers of this Board and the propriety of their having taken off the Reserve to the westward of Fort Cumberland are referred for Consideration, at the next Meeting.*

*It having been intimated to his Excellency the Governor that sundry Persons who have obtained Warrants & located them to the westward of Fort Cumberland had run their Lines within some of the Reserves surveyed for the Lord Proprietary, notwithstanding the strict orders given to the Deputy Surveyor of Frederick County not to suffer them in any manner to interfere therewith. The Attorney General is requested to frame a Clause to be inserted in all Grants that may take place in that part of the Province, which will effectually prevent any Surveys affecting any of the Reserves to the prejudice of the Proprietor.*

*M^r Jenings having promised to furnish the same, the Board adjourn to Thursday next.*

### Daniel Jenifer confronts the Board of Trade on behalf of existing settlers

The book "**Proceedings of the Council of Maryland, 1761-1769**" includes the minutes of the May 19, 1774 meeting of the Board of Revenue, considering the protest of Daniel Jenifer. The correspondence contained in the minutes indicates that settlers were living west of Fort Cumberland in 1774 and had already been living there during the time of the French and Indian War and Pontiac's war.

*The Board proceed to take under Consideration Letters from the Agent to the Judges of the Land Office with the Answers thereto, and unanimously agree to transmit Copies of the same to the Guardians of the Lord Proprietary together with their Reasons in justification of the Measure adopted with respect to granting Lands (the Lord Proprietary's Reserves excepted) to the westward of Fort Cumberland.*

*The following are copies of the Agents' Letters & the Answers thereto, mentioned in the proceeding of the 17^{th} Instant, as also the Reasons which induced this Board to take off the Reserve*

*April 29^{th} 1774.*

*Gen^n*

*I have this Day received a Letter from M^r John Hanson Deputy Surveyor of Frederick County, by which I am informed that he has Surveyed for John Swan, Walter Hanson Jenifer & Andrew Scott, nine Tracts of Land to the westward of Fort Cumberland, containing in the whole Three Thousand Acres. As the Land Office has been shut for several years and every Person in the Province, precluded the making Surveys in that part of the Country; I must beg and insist, on behalf of the Lord Proprietor that you do not make out Patents for any of the above mentioned Lands, nor Patents for any Lands Surveyed or to be Surveyed to any other Person to the westward of Fort Cumberland, until his LordShip's Pleasure be fully known, I have also received Information that James Brooks, Robert Smith Jonathan Boucher, Thomas Johnson Jun^r Anthony Stewart, James Tilghman, David Stewart & others, have made or are actually now making Surveys not only to the westward of Fort Cumberland, but have located Warrants to the westward of a Meridian Line drawn from the head of the North Branch of Potowmack River to its intersection of the west Line, run between Maryland & Pennsylvania & even have proceeded in their Locations to the Westward of the Allegany Mountains, against his Majesty's express command by his Proclamation issued the 7^{th} October 1763. You must be very sensible that the Proprietor's noble Predecessors have cautiously avoided giving any Offence, by granting Lands to the westward of the Line settled between the Crown and Lord Fairfax, for altho' there cannot be a doubt, but the Fountain Head of the South Branch, was the Spot intended where the Meridian Line was to be set off as the western Boundary of Maryland; yet, I presume, they waited for a favourable Opportunity of bringing this matter before the King in Council, when there would not be the least doubt of his Majesty's Equity & Justice: That time appears now not to be far off; for as the Pennsylvanians have imprisoned an Officer acting under Commission from Lord Dunmore, and his Lordship in return hath caused three Magistrates acting under Commission from Governor Penn to be arrested and carried to Williamsburgh; it is very likely that these Steps may very soon bring the extention of those Governments before his Majesty in Council, where only they can be settled. Should this be the Case, it would be a favourable time for the Proprietor to put in his Claim to all the Land lying to the Eastward of a Meridian drawn from the head Spring of the South Branch 'til it intersected the west Line run between Maryland and Pennsylvania. From these appearances I think it highly improper for the Proprietor or his Officers, to throw the first Stone by granting Lands over the Allegany Mountains; nor is it in my opinion just, or equitable, that the Office should have been opened for granting Land to the Westward of Fort Cumberland, before the back Inhabitants, who stood the Brunt of two Indian Wars (and some of whom I have heard obtained warrants with a view of Locating them on these Lands before the Reserve was laid) had notice, and thereby an equal Chance with others of taking up these Lands.*

*By a Rule of the Land Office, all Certificates are to lye in that Office three months before Patents can be made out, this Rule I conceive to be a very just one, and not to be dispensed with, if it should, a younger Certificate might be prefered to an elder. As I am very sensible of your Justice and Equity, as well as your inclination to promote the Interest of the Proprietor, so I am certain there will be, but one unalterable Rule of Right, by which your decissions will be guided; and as a Month or two longer than the three Months, will afford the Guardians of the Proprietor time to signify their Pleasure in this Business, I submit, to your better Judgment which will direct you, either to grant or refuse my Request. I hope you will excuse the Freedom, which my Duty has impelled me to take & believe me to be, with due Regard,*

*Gen<sup>n</sup> Your most Obed<sup>t</sup> hble Serv<sup>t</sup>*

*Danl of S<sup>t</sup> Tho<sup>s</sup> Jenifer*

*Hon<sup>ble</sup> Geo. Steuart &*

*B. Calvert, Esq<sup>re</sup>*

*Sir,*

*Yours dated the 29<sup>th</sup> Ult° directed to M<sup>r</sup> Calvert and myself I duly received. M<sup>r</sup> Calvert's distress, occasioned by the Death of his Son, prevents his coming to Town, this and the hopes of your retracting the Letter, to which this is an answer, prevented my writing to you sooner, I told you it contained an improper request and that I thought you in the wrong, in this perhaps I may be mistaken, however I meant well & friendly. It was from M<sup>r</sup> Calvert I first heard that the Governor intended to order warrants to be issued to the westward of Fort Cumberland, both of us waited on you that Instant & informed you of it, and at the same time told you that we could not consistent with our Instructions issue any Warrants until you had certified that the Caution money was paid, when you had done that it became our Duty to issue Warrants, and when the Surveyor returns Certificates of the execution of them, it is no less our Duty to make out Patents upon them, the parties complying with all the Requisites required by the Conditions of Plantations; It is inconsistent with the Honour & Justice of the Proprietor to refuse Grants to confirm the Titles of those who purchased Lands lately, any more than to those who were Purchasers formerly, under the same Conditions it becomes neither you nor me to confine the Proprietor's limits of the Province, the Charter gives him to the Fortieth Degree of North Latitude, then West until it intersects a*

*Meridian from the first Fountain of Patowmack, and for his Officers to confine him within narrower bounds is unreasonable, especially as the late Proprietor has been lately at the Expence of running a Line to the head of the South Branch of that River & when the Virginians hear that the Proprietor's Officers in Maryland doubt of the extention of his Limits, it will be an encouragement to them to begin to throw Stones, which I never heard that they had yet done, nor can I conceive that his Majesty, who is all Justice, could think of making a Reserve by Proclamation of Lands granted by his Royal Ancestors to any of his Subjects much less to Sir George Calvert who was the Grantor's Favourite and faithful Minister. Therefore upon the whole, I must in Justice to the People who purchased Warrants lately, issue Patents to them, as to others under the same Circumstances. I shall lay your Letter before the Governor and the Board of Revenue and if they think me wrong I shall submit to their better Judgment, we all mean to promote the Proprietor's Interest, we only have different sentiments as to the means to be pursued for that purpose, I know your Zeal for the common Cause, my endeavours shall not be wanting to lend a helping Hand & am*

*Sir Yrs &*

*G. Steuart*

*To the Hon: Dan^l of S^t Tho^s Jenifer Esq^r*

*May 9^th, 1774*

*Sir*

*I am sorry that the request I made, in my Letter of the 29^th Ult° should be thought improper, or wrong. It is true, that you & M^r Calvert gave me a private intimation of the Governor's Intention, and both pronounced the measure to be wrong, and at the same time you must Remember that you & M^r Calvert agreed, the Agent could not refuse Warrant to any Person that applied for it, I thought so too, and believe if I had done it, it would have been the first Instance, Locations not being made in my Office. How far it became your Duty, to issue Warrants directing the Surveyor to survey Lands to the westward of Fort Cumberland, I cannot pretend to dispute with you, as you certainly know it much better than I do, but I hope you will excuse my reminding you that I applied to you & M^r Calvert & to M^r D. Dulany before any warrant issued out of your Office, to go with me to the Governor to prevail upon his Excellency to recall the Order. And had my request been complied with I think he would readily have postponed the Measure, til the Proprietor's pleasure was known, for I must do him the Justice to say, that I have ever found him ready to take the Advice of those in whom he placed a Confidence.*

*I am far from imputing an Inclination in the Proprietor or his Guardians to do any thing inconsistent with honour & justice, but when a new Measure is about to be taken by which his Property is meant to be transferred, it would seem but reasonable that he & his Guardians should have an Opportunity of considering the propriety & Fitness of carrying that measure into Execution, before they were precluded exercising a Judgment in the Case, by Patents being given under the great Seal. This was all I requested I would not presume to do anything, which might tend to limit the Extention of the Grant to the Proprietor's noble Predecessor, nor can I conceive how such a Construction could be made upon my Letter; but as the Lands to the Westward of a Meridian drawn from the head of the North Branch, to its intersection with the West Line of the Province, have never yet been granted by the Proprietors of Maryland, however clear the Right may be, I stil think a delay of exercising that Right for a short time, cannot weaken it, or encourage the Virginians to consider it as a dereliction; and that it would be more agreeable to the Proprietor to delay granting those Lands until the Dispute was fairly Settled, than to bring on an abrupt Contest, by exercising his Right at this particular time.*

*My Conduct in this Affair has flowed from the Duty I owe to the Proprietor & the attention I shall ever pay to his Concerns here, whilst I have the Honour of being employed by him, in which tho I have not the Pleasure of your Concurrence in this Instance, yet I cannot in conformity to your wishes retract my Letter, no Reason having been as yet offered to convince me, that the Request contained therein is unreasonable, or that the Compliance with it, can possibly be attended with any ill Consequence. Your own Judgment & Discretion assisted by the advice of the Board, you mention, I doubt not will govern your Conduct in granting or delaying to grant Patents; I have only interfered so far as I thought it my Duty to do.*

*As I am informed that Surveys are now actually making within the Lands reserved for the Proprietor, it would seem fit & prudent to make such restriction in the Patents (as you seem resolute to grant them) as will prevent their having Effect so far as the location is made within such Reserves, and this Step appears to be the more necessary, as the Surveyor has signified to me, that altho' he shall do everything in his Power to prevent an Interference, yet he is fearful as the Lands lie at such a Distance, it will not be in his Power to prevent Encroachments.*

*I am well convinced of your Zeal for the Proprietor's Interest, your Actions having ever evinced it to*

*Sir, Your most Obed<sup>t</sup> hble Serv<sup>t</sup>*

*Hon. Geo. Steuart, Esq<sup>r</sup>          Dan<sup>l</sup> of St. Tho<sup>s</sup> Jenifer.*

*Sir,*

*I received yours dated yesterday nobody breathing would more chearfully co-operate with you than I would but as I am directed to advise with the Governor & Chancellor, I must in all difficult cases apply to them for assistance; the resurvation of the Proprietor's just Rights is a duty incumbent upon all his Officers, and I assure you, that it affords me great Pleasure when I have it in my power to defend his Property from every attack made against it.*

*You say that the Surveyor informs you that it is scarcely possible to prevent those who have the execution of the Warrants, lately issued, from intruding upon his Lordship's Reserves, pray get information from him who are the Intruders, that Caveats may be entered against their having Patents and this will answer the end you desire, it is my duty to do Justice to the Proprietor as well as to his Tenants and I shall exert my utmost Power to prevent any Injury to him or them. As we all aim at the same thing I hope we shall at last succeed & am*

*Sir, Your most Obed<sup>t</sup> Hble Serv<sup>t</sup>*

*Geo: Steuart*

*Annapolis May 10<sup>th</sup> 1774.*

*M<sup>r</sup> Jenifer's Interposition in his Capacity of Agent appears somewhat extraordinary in respect both of the Matter and Manner of it, From his Letter to the Judges of the Land Office we might be led to infer, that his Information concerning the Warrants for Lands to the westward of Fort Cumberland, was first communicated from the Surveyor of Frederick County were we not assured that he was fully informed thereof, before they had any notice or Intimation that the constructive Restriction on Governor Sharpe's Order had been taken off; that he had actually received the Caution money for such Warrants, and had given the usual Titlings to the Land Office, not only before warrants reached the hands of the Surveyor, but antecedent to their issuing out of the Land Office.*

*Upon the Subject, whether it was proper or not to open the Office, in respect of Lands to the westward of Fort Cumberland, we gave our opinion on the 26<sup>th</sup> March last to which we refer, and in a day or two* *afterwards, the Agent demanded an Inspection of our Proceedings, and his Requisition was submitted to by our Clerk.*

*The Course is, when Vacant Lands are to be taken up, under the Conditions of Plantation, to pay the Consideration or Caution money to the Agent, who thereupon gives an order, or Titling to the Land Office specifying the sum received by him and the number of Acres the party is to have surveyed upon this order the warrant for making the Survey issues from the Land office, directed to the Surveyor of the County where the vacant Lands are & these orders being preserved in the Land Office, are a check on the Agent in settling his accounts of the Caution Money received: When the Surveyor returns his Certificate to the Land Office, it remains there for three months before a Patent issues, after which the party is entitled to a Grant by the established Rules of the Office; wherefore we apprehend, that this Rule, after the Caution money is paid, constitutes the contract to be performed with the Party, and consequently that the Faith of Government is engaged that it shall be in this manner complied with, but if this Rule be altered (which the Agent in his Letter seems to consider as an unalterable Rule of Right) and the Alteration is to be made with a view of obtaining an order to prevent the issuing of Grants; and if the Attempt to induce such an order should be successful, the Parties will have reason to be allarmed, to complain of a breach of Contract & of the precarious dependance on Acts of Government. If there be no intention to obtain an order to prevent the issuing of Grants, we shall not undertake to conjecture, why the Agent thought it expedient to express his Zeal on this Occasion for the Interests of the Proprietor, and to insist on his behalf, that there should be a new retrospective Regulation of the Land Office; should there be in consequence of his unexpected Representation an order not to issue Patents to those who have paid the caution Money executed their Warrants in pursuance of his Titlings, return'd Certificates and entitled themselves to Grants according to the common course and invariable Rules of the Land Office, it may be with Propriety asked, how are the Parties to be indemnified? a return of the Caution Money received and repayment of the several Fees, with Interest will be insufficient for this Purpose. The Trouble & Expence in gaining information of Vacant Land are considerable and the disappointment of many who may have regulated their Affairs in expectation of Grants according to the usual Course, will be severely felt. The Rights of those who have paid for and obtained warrants and made advantageous Locations, may be transferred, and the Purchasers proceeding agreeable to the common Usage in Transactions of this nature would have greater Reason than we wish them to have to complain of Injustice, should their Grants be withheld.*

*If the Measure of opening the Office respecting Lands to the Westward of Fort Cumberland, according to our opinion above referred to, appeared improper, as the Agent was fully apprised of the meeting of this Board, the occasion of such meeting, and of both the Substance and Letter of our opinion, if he thought it his indispensable duty to oppose it, his objections & Reasons in support of them would have been then more seasonable than they were on the 29th of April last, at which time he had received Caution Money to the Amount of £3459.. — ..6 and since that time to the am° of £2200.. — .. — and actually given his Tidings for warrants, Our Authority, it seems, has been called in Question. If we imagined it no longer existed, we should not upon any possible Motive of self Interest, concern ourselves with the Proprietor's Revenue, but we apprehend as this Board was established in consequence of the late Proprietor's Instructions which have been revived and continued by the general Instruction upon the accession of the present Proprietor, so we presume to think that the Authority of the Board is in Force as well as the Conditions of Plantations, and other Matters dependant on Instruction. If our Authority has however ceased, we should be at a loss to investigate the Power of Controul which seems to be Claimed by the present Agent; his Commission does not shew it, and we believe no former Agent ever exercised, or claimed it.*

*Before the establishment of this Board, the Governor and other Officers, were vested with the power of superintending the Affairs of Revenue; & we conceive it was upon the supposition of our continued Authority, that the opinion above referred to was required by & submitted to the Governor.*

*The Reasons assigned by the Agent in his Letter to the Judges of the Land Office, why he thought proper to controul their Proceeding in issuing Patents according to the established Conditions of Plantation may be reducible to the following Heads:*

*First, That the making Surveys beyond the Allegany Mountains, would be against his Majesty's express Command by Proclamation in the year 1763.*

*Second, That the former Proprietors of this Province cautiously avoided giving offence by granting Lands to the westward of the Line settled between the Crown & Lord Fairfax (tho' the Agent alledges there cannot be a doubt but that the Fountain Head of the South Branch of Patowmack is the place referred to in the Charter of this Province) and he presumes this Caution was intended to be observed until there should be a favourable opportunity of bringing the Matter before the King in Council, and that the present Contest between Virginia and Pennsylvania will probably afford this Opportunity; he therefore thinks it highly improper for the Proprietor, or his Officers to throw the first Stone by granting Lands over the Allegany Mountains.*

*Third, That the back Inhabitants who have stood the brunt of two Indian wars ought to be preferred; and that he has heard some of them had obtained Warrants with a view of surveying Lands to the westward of Fort Cumberland, before the Reserve was laid.*

*As to the First, It must be confessed that we did not foresee the Objection, nor do we now perceive that there was any foundation for it. When the Royal Order was made in 1763, there were in the then Situation of American Affairs, particular State Reasons for such prohibition, but the purposes of this Order have been fully answered, and in consequence of the King's subsequent Proclamation very extensive Grants have issued for Land beyond the Mountains, to Officers & Soldiers who served in America & were reduced on the Peace, and we are assured that more than Two Thousand Families have since settled in Pennsylvania beyond the Allegany, under Titles from the Proprietaries, & above double that number in other parts of America over the same Range. When for Reasons of publick Utility the order of 1763 was notified, a compliance with it was decent & proper, tho' we do not imagine that it could, or was meant to abridge the Right of the Proprietor under the Charter of Maryland; and it seems to be a groundless Fear that an immediate exercise of this Right may give Offence to the Crown, after the Order of 1763 has been in the most explicit Terms superseded by the subsequent Proclamation, and so many Thousand Families have been permitted to settle beyond the mountains, in the neighbouring Colonies of Virginia and Pennsylvania. These Settlements we apprehend have been greatly disadvantageous to the Proprietary Interest, and the temptation given to many People to emigrate from hence in search of Lands on easy Terms will, if not speedily removed, prove very detrimental to the future Improvement of the Province.*

*As to the Second, We presume that the former Proprietors were not inclined to enter into Contests with the Crown; but this Intimation seems to imply that some measures or Instructions indicative of a peculiar Caution, have been pursued or given with which we are totally unacquainted, nor do we perceive how the late Dispute between the Colonies of Virginia & Pennsylvania, which has no relation to the limits of this Province, will afford an opportunity of representing the Proprietor's Claims with which no acts or Grants of the Government of Virginia, to our knowledge interfere. If the making of Surveys and issuing Patents with a view of effecting gradual & peaceable Settlements under the Charter should now be stopped upon the Principle of this objection, it may draw on, and encourage the Interposition of Virginia, and Arguments may be deduced against the Proprietor's Right from his reluctance to claim & exercise it. When the Bounds of the neighbouring Provinces are liable to controversy, settlements and*

*Improvements have been always deemed advantageous to that Colony under whose Title & Government they were made. It cannot be disputed but that all the Land to the westward of Fort Cumberland in this Province, was subject to be taken up under the common Conditions of Plantations, and that the Restriction proceeded from the Order of Governor Sharpe, pursuant to an order from the Proprietary to reserve for him 10000 Acres. As the Restriction communicated by the late Governor's order to the Surveyor of Frederick County was not general, but for the particular purpose of securing a Reserve to the Proprietor, which has been fully answered; we therefore apprehend it was expedient to inform the Surveyor that he was no longer bound by it. If the Intention had been to reserve all Land to the westward of Fort Cumberland the Reservation of parcels was unnecessary, and the Order respecting Surveys would have been absolute & general instead of qualified & special.*

*In consequence of the late Proprietor's Instruction a Line from the first Fountain Head of Patowmack was run at a considerable Expence to his Lordship, but for what Purpose was the Boundary ascertained, if no beneficial Consequence was to result from its Establishment?*

*Further it appears to us that the small number of Surveys made to the Westward of Fort Cumberland, prior to the order of Governor Sharpe, was owing to the quantity of vacant Lands more valuable & conveniently situated, which were subject to the Conditions of Plantation. Antecedent to the above Prohibitory Order, we do not find that there was any kind of Restriction to prevent surveys to the westward, and this Order having issued for particular purposes, which have been since effectually answered, we conceive the Lands in question are subject to the same Regulation & Rules of Office as those heretofore Granted.*

*As to the Third, We are not informed of those Persons who it is said, have stood the brunt of the Indian Wars, nor can we forbear remarking that if the Agent knew of any such whose particular circumstances entitled them to Regard, he would have more effectually promoted their Interests by a communication of his. knowledge to the Governor, before the 26th March last, than by his oblique Censure of our Proceedings in his Letter to the Judges of the Land Office, so late as the 29th of April. From principles of benevolence the Governor has directed the Surveyor of Frederick County to inform those who have settled to the Westward of Fort Cumberland that upon application & payment of the Proprietor's Caution Money, they shall be preferred before others; and if any Persons are possessed of, or entitled to Warrants, which they purchased with a view of surveying Land in that part of the Province, as the office is open, they have an opportunity of completing their Titles; but if these Warrants have been executed elsewhere, they can have no pretence of Claim. The Restriction with Respect to the Lands reserved for the use of the Proprietor is fully and most expressly continued, for which we refer to the proceedings of the 26th March last; and we are of opinion that every precaution should be used to prevent other Surveys from interfering with these Reserves: Should there be any suspicion of designs to evade the Restrictions respecting the Reserved Lands, we recommend that Caveats be entered until there can be a full examination into the Matter; and the more effectually to counteract every Intention of this nature we think it necessary that a special Proviso should be inserted in the Patents.*

*We apprehend that the expected Emolument from the Proprietor's reservation will be entirely lost if the adjacent Lands remain uncultivated; the Mountainous situation of the Country and its distance from Navigable Water preclude the hopes of an extensive Commerce, and unless opportunities be afforded to the Tenants of interchanging their Commodities with the neighbouring Inhabitants, we conceive but few Persons & those of the lowest Estimation would incline to settle in this solitary part of the Province, shut out from the intercourse of Mankind.*

*It being intimated, that the Hon^ble Daniel of S^t Thomas Jenifer, Esq^r is desirous of inspecting the proceedings of this Board relative to the Letters addressed by him to the Judges of the Land Office.*

*Ordered that the Clerk do inform him, that the Board have not any objection to his perusing the same and that on application he may be furnished with Copies thereof,*

*M͏ͬ Dulany being much indisposed his attendance is dispens'd with.*

*The Board take under consideration the propriety of adopting a measure for the encouragement of such of the back Inhabitants as may have settled & made small Improvements, and are unanimously of Opinion; That his Excellency the Governor hath a Power, agreeable to Instructions from the late Proprietor to the Judges of the Land Office (a Copy of which they are to furnish) to order Warrants to issue for small Parcels of Land, not exceeding one hundred Acres each, to be surveyed for those as shall apply therefor, with the Indulgence of making Payment of the Composition money & Other Charges at any time within Two years from the Date of such Warrants.*

*It is the opinion of this Board that a proviso be inserted in all Grants that may issue for Lands to the Westward of Fort Cumberland effectually to make void such part or parts thereof as shall be found situated lying and being within any of the Lord Proprietor's reserved Lands in that part of the Province.*

*On further examination of the Agent's Accounts with the Executors of the late Lord Proprietor, the Board unanimously pass the same.*

## Richard Lee requests a list of settlements made west of Fort Cumberland

A letter[1511] written from Annapolis on October 6, 1774 by Richard Lee states:

*By virtue of an instruction from Hugh Hamersly, Esquire, one of the guardians of the right honourable Henry Harford, Esq. proprietor of Maryland, dated at Spring Gardens, Westminster, the 30th of July 1774, I am directed to signify unto you, that it is the pleasure of the lord proprietary's guardians, that all further proceedings upon the governor's order to you, of the 22d of March last be suspended, and that all locations, settlements, and grants of land to the westward of Fort Cumberland be stopped until their further pleasure shall be signified to the contrary; of which you will be pleased to take notice and govern yourselves accordingly. I am likewise directed to transmit to the lord proprietary's guardians, by the earliest opportunity, an account of every step taken in consequence of the above mentioned order, and also of all such settlements and locations of land (if any) as have been at any time made beyond the limits mentioned in it, since the year 1763, and more particularly since the death of the late lord proprietary; you will therefore be pleased to furnish me with a list of all the warrants that have been issued out of your office from the year 1763, to the present time, to affect any lands to the westward of Fort Cumberland, with their respective dates and locations, and also, with a list of all the certificates of surveys made and returned by the surveyor in pursuance of such warrants; that I may agreeable to the instructions which I have received, transmit the same to the lord proprietary's guardians*

## Kilty explains Jenifer's conflict with the Board of Trade

The 1808 book "**Kilty's Land-Holder's Assistant, and Land-Office Guide**" includes the following explanation of the conflict between Jenifer and the Board of Trade:

*On the 23d of February, 1774, Mr. Harford being then proprietary of the province, and Robert Eden, Esq. governor, a petition from Thomas French relative to the "taking off the reserve to the westward of Fort Cumberland, except lands actually surveyed and certificates thereof returned for the use of the lord proprietary," was taken up by the revenue board: On this occasion, an entry was made, reciting that the*

---

[1511] "**Kilty's Land-Holder's Assistant, and Land-Office Guide**".

*late lord proprietary had been desirous of having 10,000 acres of land laid off in that part of the province for a manor, and that, in order to secure the same, governor Sharpe had thought proper to lay a general reserve until such manor should be ascertained, which had not been done, but that in lieu thereof five different tracts had been actually surveyed, and certificates thereof returned, containing in the whole the quantity of 127,680 acres. After stating those general facts in relation to the object of Mr. French's petition, they postponed the further consideration of it for the purpose of a previous enquiry into the reasons which had occasioned the quantity of ten thousand acres to be thus exceeded.*

*On the 26th of March following, the board took this business again into consideration, and after reciting the several surveys that had been made as aforesaid, whereby, they observed, the intent and design of the reserve had been fully answered, and after suggesting as motives for the measure the augmentation of the proprietary's revenues, and the settlement of the back country, they resolved that the deputy surveyor of Frederick county should be instructed to execute such warrants as should be put in his hands on lands westward of Fort Cumberland, provided that he did not run into or interfere with any of the surveys made for the lord proprietary, for the purpose of avoiding which he was to be furnished with copies of the lines, courses and boundaries of the said surveys: — The governor was not present at these proceedings, but approved of them when presented to him;*

*The land office being thus opened in respect to the lands westward of Fort Cumberland, large warrants were immediately taken out, chiefly by persons of note, who from their situations were probably apprised before hand of the measure intended, and enabled to make preparation for benefiting by it. The proprietary's agent, Mr. Jenifer, on this occasion ventured to disapprove of what had been done, and addressed a letter to the judges of the land office, in which, after mentioning several surveys already made, and others then making, of these western lands, he desired and insisted, on the part of the proprietary, that no patents should be issued for them until his lordship's pleasure should be known: — He represented that some of these surveys were located beyond the Allegany mountains, in contravention of the king's proclamation of the 7th October, 1763. In addition to the impolicy which he attributed to the whole proceeding, he censured it as unjust in reference to the back inhabitants, who had "stood the brunt of two Indian wars," and some of whom had obtained warrants, with a view of locating them on those lands, before the reserve was laid, and now, for want of notice, had not an equal chance with others for making advantageous locations. One of the judges, in answer to this letter, stated that the agent had received notice of the governor's intention to take off the reserve, and had been informed that the issuing of warrants must depend on him, as they could not be granted until he the agent had certified that the caution money was paid: that when this was done, the rest followed in course: the person bringing a tiding must have a warrant, and he who returned a certificate must have a patent, supposing all requisites to be complied with. The agent rejoined by throwing the responsibility in regard to location on the judges of the land office, as he could not refuse warrant to any person that applied for it, but gave no direction that the surveys should be made westward of Fort Cumberland. The rest of the dispute turned upon the policy of the proprietary's enforcing his claim at that juncture to what they both agreed were his just limits, to wit, a meridian line drawn from the head of the south instead of the north branch of the Potomack. The board of revenue finally took up the contest, by a kind of manifesto, entered on their journal, in which, after reciting the correspondence just mentioned, they justified their proceedings by a variety of reasons, very warmly urged, and found great fault with the agent's interference. — This defence appears to have been transmitted to the new proprietary, or rather to his guardians, to whom Mr. Jenifer is also supposed to have made an appeal. The result of the contest was that, on the 6th of October, 1774, the judges of the land office received instructions to suspend all further proceedings upon the governor's order to them of the (a) 22d March preceding, and to prepare, for the use of proprietary's guardians, accurate lists and statements of all warrants issued, and measures taken, in consequence of that order, and also of all settlements and locations made within the limits therein mentioned since the year 1763.*

*In short, the proceeding in question was disapproved, and the agent came off with advantage: but, the board of revenue, and the proprietary government, with all its establishments, were now drawing to a close: the last sitting of the board was on the 11ᵗʰ of January, 1775, at which time they passed a vote affirming the power of the governor, under instructions from the late proprietary to the judges of the land office, to grant warrants, not exceeding 100 acres each, on a credit of two years, for the purpose of encouraging settlements in the back part of the province. This vote seemed to be intended for the benefit of people who had already settled and made small improvements in the back country, and, was probably occasioned by the animadversion of the agent on the conduct of the board in authorizing surveys west of Fort Cumberland without such notice as might have given those distant inhabitants an equal chance for good locations: but it is not perceived that warrants were issued on the terms which have been mentioned.*

*(a) There is some disagreement concerning the date of this order; the proceeding of the board of revenue being on the 26th, but this is the date assumed by the state government in the measures which it took respecting the unfinished business arising out of this transaction.*

Even if Kilty is correct that *"it is not perceived that warrants were issued on the terms which have been mentioned"*, the fact that Jennifer stood up for settlers west of Fort Cumberland who had *"stood the Brunt of two Indian Wars"* indicates that such settlers indeed existed. The referenced lack of warrents issuing seems like no surprise, considering that the existence of the proprietary government, including the Board of Revenue, was coming to an end.


### The British proprietary government is ousted from Maryland

As quoted previously in more detail, the 1826 U.S. Supreme Court case Cassell v. Carroll 24 U.S. 134 states:

*Henry Harford ... entered into the possession of the government of the Province of Maryland and received the rents and revenues thereof as proprietor until the beginning of the disturbances which separated the United States of America from the British government. That those disturbances began in 1774, at which time the people of the Province of Maryland took the government of the said province into their own hands and ousted the officers of the proprietor...*


### Local resistance to importation from Britain in 1774

Charles Clinton[1512] was already living somewhere in Cumberland area by 1774, where he was working on non-importation, etc., eventually receiving military rank and command of some western Maryland forces. Later, in 1779, he helped to cut a new supply road from Fort Cumberland to resupply Fort Pitt.

Scharf's 1882 book "**History of Western Maryland**" states, "*On the 22d of June, 1774, deputies from all the counties assembled in general convention at Annapolis and adopted non-importation resolutions of the strongest character. ... On the 5th of September, 1774, the Continental Congress, which was first proposed by Maryland ... adopted a plan 'for carrying into effect the non-importation, non-consumption, and non-exportation' association.*" At a November 18, 1774 meeting at the Frederick County courthouse, Charles

---

[1512] Guy Clinton's 1936 manuscript "**The Clintons Appearing in Early American Records**", which is available at the Library of Congress, includes the statement, "In Book O, page 56 of the Frederick, Md. County Registry of Deeds we find this entry: Feb. 7, 1771 Joseph Reynolds gave a bill of sale to Charles Clinton for one bay mare and one copper still for 28 pounds and 18 shillings Pennsylvania money. Reynolds was a resident of Antitam District, now of Washington County." At the time, Frederick County comprised what became Allegany County. (Reference found by Francis Bridges.)

Clinton was one of a number of men appointed to *"be a committee to represent this county to carry into execution the association agreed on by the American Continental Congress…"*

### Military companies are formed 'to act in any emergency'
Scharf's book goes on to state:

> *This convention, after an adjournment from the 21st of November to the 8th of December, adopted resolutions encouraging the colonies to rely upon the products of their own fields and their own industry, and recommending "such of the inhabitants of this province as are from sixteen to fifty years of age to form themselves into companies of sixty-eight men; to choose a captain, two lieutenants, an ensign, four sergeants, four corporals, and one drummer for each company, and to use their utmost endeavors to make themselves masters of the military exercise. That each man be provided with a good firelock and bayonet fixed thereon, half a pound of powder, two pounds of lead, and a cartouch-box or powder horn, and a bag for ball, and be in readiness to act in any emergency." It was further recommended that £1333 should be raised in Frederick by subscription to be expended by the committee of the county in the purchase of arms and ammunition.*

> *At a meeting of the inhabitants of Frederick County,[1513] held at the court-house, on Tuesday, the 24th of January, 1775…the association and resolves of the American Congress and the proceedings of the last Provincial Convention were read and unanimously approved.*

At the same meeting, Charles Clinton was one of a number of men appointed to *"be a committee of observation, with full powers to prevent any infraction of the said institution, and to carry the resolves of the American Congress and of the Provincial Convention into execution…"*

At the same meeting, it was *"Resolved, As the most convenient and effectual method of raising the sum of $1333, being this County's proportion of the $10,000 which the provincial convention has appointed to be raised for the purchase of arms and ammunition, that a subscription be immediately opened in every part of the County, and the following gentlemen be appointed to promote such subscriptions in their several Hundreds:"* In the list of appointments that followed, Clinton is listed as *"For Cumberland Hundred, Charles Clinton."* This places him in the Cumberland area.

### Passing through Fort Cumberland on the way to the battle of Point Pleasant in 1774
The 1909 book "**History of the battle of Point Pleasant, fought between white men and Indians at the mouth of the Great Kanawha River (now Point Pleasant, West Virginia) Monday, October 10th, 1774. The chief event of Lord Dunmore's war.**" was written by Vigil A. Lewis, West Virginia State Historian and Archivist. Although not documentary evidence, Lewis states:

> *Two regiments were formed, a first, the "Frederick county Regiment" Colonel William Crawford, commanding; and a second, the "Berkeley county Regiment;" at the head of which was Colonel Adam Stephen; Lord Dunmore was Commander-in-Chief, and the march to the West began. The Berkeley county Regiment left the site of the present city of Winchester August 27th. Dunmore with the Frederick county Regiment followed Braddock's Road, opened seventeen years before, from Winchester, and arrived at the mouth of the South Branch of the Potomac on the 30th of August. Thence onward by way of old Fort Cumberland — now Cumberland City, Maryland — thence over the road constructed for this purpose, by Abraham Hite, Thomas Rutherford and James Wood through the mountains from the Virginia Frontier, to the mouth of Redstone creek on the Monongahela, where the regiments were separated, the*

---

[1513] At the time, Frederick County included what eventually became Allegany County.

*Frederick county men going by way of Fort Dunmore; while the Berkeley men with the beef cattle, crossed the country to Wheeling.*

Lewis states, *"... the only material used has been drawn from original sources, documents, and writings which were contemporaneous with the occurrence of the events described"*. His evidence for Dunmore's route via Fort Cumberland has not been found.


## The battle of Point Pleasant

A letter[1514] written from Point Pleasant on October 17, 1774 describes the October 10, 1774 battle of Point Pleasant:

*For the satisfaction of the public, in this letter they have the true state of the battle fought at this place, on the 10th instant.*

*On Monday morning, about half an hour before sunrise, two of Captain Russell's company discovered a large party of Indians about a mile from the camp, one of which men was shot down by the Indians, the other made his escape and brought the intelligence. In two or three minutes after, two of Captain Shelbey's came in and confirmed the account. Colonel Andrew Lewis being informed thereof, immediately ordered out Colonel Charles Lewis to take the command of one hundred and fifty of the Augusta troops, and with him went Captain Dickinson, Captain Harrison, Captain Wilson, Captain John Lewis, of Augusta, and Captain Lockridge, which made the first division. Captain Fleming was also ordered to take the command of one hundred and fifty more of the Botetourt, Bedford, and Fincastle troops, viz: Captain Thomas Buford, from Bedford, Captain Love, of Botetourt, Captain Shelbey, and Captain Russell, of Fincastle, which made the second division. Colonel Charles Lewis' division marched to the right, some distance from the Ohio; and Colonel Fleming, with his division, on the bank of the Ohio, to the left. — Colonel Charles Lewis' division had not marched quite a half mile from camp, when, about sunrise, an attack was made on the front of his division, in a most vigorous manner, by united tribes of Indians, Shawanese, Delawares, Mingoes, Tawas, and several other nations, in number not less than eight hundred, and by many thought to be a thousand. In this heavy attack, Colonel Charles Lewis received a wound, which in a few hours caused his death, and several of his men fell on the spot. In fact, the Augusta division was forced to give way to the heavy fire of the enemy. In about a second of a minute after the attack on Colonel Lewis' division, the enemy engaged the front of Colonel Fleming's division, on the Ohio, and in a short time the Colonel received two balls through his left arm, and one through his breast; and, after animating the officers and soldiers in a most calm manner, to the pursuit of victory, retired to the camp. The loss from the field was sensibly felt by the officers in particular; but the Augusta troops being shortly re-inforced from the camp, by Colonel Field, with his company, together with Captain McDowell, Captain Matthews, and Captain Stewart, form Augusta, Captain John Lewis, Captain Paulin, Captain Arbuckle, and Captain McClenachan, from Botetourt, the enemy, no longer able to maintain their ground, was forced to give way till they were in a line with the troops, Colonel Fleming being left in action on the bank of Ohio. In this precipitate retreat, Colonel Field was killed. During this time, which was till after twelve o'clock, the action continued extremely hot. The close underwood, many steep banks and logs, greatly favored their retreat; and the bravest of their men made the best use of them, whilst others were throwing their dead into the Ohio, and carrying off their wounded. After twelve, the action in a small degree abated, but continued, except at short intervals, sharp enough till after one o'clock. — Their long retreat gave them a most advantageous spot of ground, from whence it appeared to the officers difficult to dislodge them, that it was thought most advisable to stand, as the line was then*

---

[1514] **"Early History of Western Pennsylvania"**, 1847.

*formed, which was about a mile and a quarter in length, and had sustained till then, a constant and equal weight of the action, from wing to wing. It was till about half an hour of sunset they continued firing on us scattering shots, which we returned to their disadvantage. At length night coming on, they found a safe retreat.*

*They had not the satisfaction of carrying off any of our men's scalps, save one or two stragglers, whom they killed before the engagement. Many of their dead they scalped, rather than we should have them; but our troops scalped upwards of twenty of their men that were first killed. It is beyond doubt their loss in number far exceeds ours, which is considerable.*

*The Indians at the approach of night, skipped off and left us in the field; but carried away all their wounded and many slain. However we got twenty-one of their dead on the ground; and afterwards heard they had 223 killed and wounded; but I cannot say that is true. We had 40 men killed that night, and ninety-six wounded, twenty odd of whom are since dead.*

In his book "**A Biographical Sketch of the Life of the Late Captain Michael Cresap…**", Cresap's biographer and former employee John J. Jacob presents a strong case that Dunmore instigated the Indian war to strengthen the British position by dividing and thereby weakening American forces.

A massive Virginia list[1515] of claims for payment in support of Lord Dunmore's War shows that it was something of a community-supported military campaign. Here are some local names that I could identify. Captain John Ashby had a claim for repairing guns as an assignee of Adam Haymaker. Captain Lemuel Barrett had a claim for a horse that was lost, with some connection to Peter Tittle. Charles Clinton had a claim for ammunition and provisions that was somehow connected with Enoch Innis. Colonel Henry Van meter had a claim for provisions, and a gun, and as an assignee of Peter Haut, for pack horses. Colonel Adam Stephen had a claim for his pay and a claim for provisions. Frederick Ice had a claim for a horse for hire. Henry Hazles had a claim for wagonage and forage. John Peirceall (Pearsal) had a claim for wagonage and forage. John Frazer had a claim for a horse that was lost. Joseph Gest had claims for a gun and wagonage. Enoch Innis had a claim for provisions. Marquis Calmees had a claim for a horse that was lost. Colonel Thomas Cresap had a claim for provisions and services. One of Thomas Cresap's claims was connected with John Jacobs, proving they were acquainted. Michael Cresap had claims for advances to Captain Daniel Morgan, Captain Hugh Stephenson, Captain Joseph Mitchell, Captain Sam Beeler, Captain Lemuel Barrett, Go. Wale's Company, James Morrison's Company and Peter Helvinston's Company, and for sundries advanced to Captain William Hancher's Company, and for supplying provisions, and some of these claims had some relation to John Jacobs. Michael Cresap, Jr. had a claim for a hired horse. Peter Buzzard had a claim for packing. Peter Tottle (Tittle) had claims for provisions, forage smith's work, rent, and etc. Phinias Killam had a claim for bacon and powder. Robert Parker had a claim for provisions and wagonage. John Ramsey had a claim for meal. Although not from the area of interest, General George Washington even had a claim for bags and salt.

### An 1844 magazine estimates that Arnold's Settlement was established circa 1774

Page 675 of the January 1844 issue of "**The United States Catholic Magazine and Monthly Review**" has an article that estimates that Arnold's settlement (above the present-day village of Mount Savage) was established circa 1774:

*Arnold's Settlement. — This settlement, eight miles west of Cumberland was made about seventy years ago. Situated on the east side of Savage mountain, it enjoys all the advantages of a rural and mountainous*

---

[1515] Library of Virginia.

*district. Though one thousand feet higher than Cumberland, the climate is pleasant. The soil is strong, producing all the variety of crops common to the same latitude.*

## A Crist property transaction on Patterson Creek

The 1939 book "**Early Records Hampshire County Virginia**" records the following for November 5, 1774: *"CRIST, Jacob (w. Hannah) of Hampshire Co. to Okey Johnson of Hampshire Co. (lease and release) 167 a. on Patterson Creek; rec. 5-9-1775. Wit.: Abraham Johnson, Nicholas Carpenter, Mary Johnson."* It isn't known if this relates to the property of Nicholas Crist, who was an early resident along Patterson Creek.

# 27. 1775: A British scheme to garrison the fort

**Thomas Cresap was renting out property near Pinto, Maryland in 1775**

George Washington wrote a letter to Thomas Cresap from Mount Vernon on February 7, 1775 that states:

*The acting Executors of my Brother Augustine, have been lately informed that you have taken possession of the Land, belonging to his younger Son,[1516] above Fort Cumberland — that you have filled it with Tenants — receive rents — and, that the Land is in a fair way of being injured, to the great prejudice of the orphan. As they cannot conceive under what pretext this is done, they would fain hope that the information is groundless; but that they may know from yourself the certainty of this report, & if true, under what pretence it is done, I have at their request (for I have never qualified as an Executor myself) given you the trouble of this Letter; sincerely hoping, that you do not mean to involve them in a disagreeable Law contest in support of a Right, which was never before questioned, and which you yourself, within these five years, so far acknowledged to me, as to express a desire of buying the Land. I shall be glad to hear from you on this head, and am Sir Your most humble Servant*

*G: Washington*

Cresap replied from Skipton on March 21, 1775, stating,

*I have just now Received Yours of Feby 7 last, wherein You tell me that the Executors of Your Brother have been lately informed of my having taken Possession of some Lands belonging to him, which Information is not true; for I only claim my Own which I have been always in Possession of, And the very Person who made that Complaint has Rented it of me these two Years past and being called on for Rent thinks to come off from paying by this Method and carrying a Falshood. I have been in peaceable Possession upwards of Twenty Years, and what Buildings there are on the Land which I claim, was Built by me. Your Brother has a Lott adjoining to mine, which was mine, I having bought it of one Pindergras in the presence of several Gentlemen & paid him the Money down of the spot; after which (he Sold it) to your Bror When Your Bror came to understand the Matter, he informed me of it, and there being a good Understandg between him & me (& to prevent a Law-suit), I told him I wod give him my Right to it, As Pindergras had run away and cod not be come at, therefore must have lost his Money. This Complainant has Lived sevl Years on Your Brother's Land and Claims it as his Own.*

*I have no Objection to by or Sell, if You shd have any inclination. I am Sr Yr most Obedt Servt*

*Ths Cresap*

On October 26, 1778, George Washington, who was rather busy fighting a war, took the time to write a letter to his brother John Augustine Washington from Fredericksburg, New York that includes the following statement:

*In overhauling some old Papers the other day, I came across the Inclosed Letter from Colo. Cresap to me — written, as he says, in answer to one of mine on the information of his having set up a claim to*

---

[1516] Lawrence Washington's June 20, 1752 will includes the statement, *"First I give and Bequeath unto my Loveing Brother Augustine Washington and his heirs for ever … two Tracts of Land lying and being in Frederick County which I Purchased of Col$^o$ Cresap [and] Jerrard Pendergrass…"* (**"Letters to Washington and Accompanying Papers: 1758-1770"**, Volume III, 1901.)

*some part of the Land formerly owned by our deceased Brother Lawrence, & given by him to my Brother Austin. It is essential, as I have upon other occasions mentioned to you, that this matter should be enquired into; or, a hundred to one but Cresap Chouses the Hier at Law out of part of these Lands, under various pleas, strengthen'd by possession. At first he began to Rent them in behalf of my Brother's Estate (pocketing I dare say the Money) — Now (by the Inclos'd Letter I find) he lays claim to one Lott, when, if my Memory does not fail me exceedingly, my Brother had Patents for both, and never was their the Shadow of a claim set up towards either till lately. As it is a Tract however that I never had any personal knowledge of, I may be mistaken in my conception of the matter, but as before think there were two Lotts; one of which my Brother purchased of Pendergrass, & the other of Cresap. The fact may, I presume, be ascertained by having recourse to the Deeds, & other Land Papers belonging to that Estate, or to the records in the Proprietors Office; & in my judgment no time should be lost in the Search, as Cresap is extremely artful, & his claim will obtain strength by length of Possession.*

### *Locating Turner's mill*

George Washington's October 11, 1770 journal entry indicates that he crossed the Potomac River at the lower end of the Pendergrass property,[1517] and two miles from the mill he described on October 10, 1770 as *"Wise's (now Turner's) mill"*. Volume 3 of the book **"Virginia Northern Neck Land Grants, 1775-1800"** indicates that on July 26, 1783, Francis and William Deakins bought property on Knobley Mountain adjoining Turner's Mill Run. The stream helps to roughly locate Turner's Mill. What is now known simply as Turners Run begins at the joining of its two fountainheads, about one mile south-southwest of Pinto, Maryland, and empties into Patterson Creek at Latitude 39.517631°, Longitude -78.757983°. The same book indicates that William Turner had Hampshire County property surveyed on February 15, 1781 that adjoined the Waggon Road, his own land, Knobley Mountain, Plum Run, and Turner's Mill Run. The source of Plum Run is at the town of Short Gap, West Virginia, and Turner's Run goes through the town. Based on this, there seems to be a pretty good chance that Turner's mill was at or near the town.

A secondary source[1518] indicates that Turner's mill was at the site of *"Cremers Mill"* that is shown on the 1755 Fry and Jefferson map, and was located near the town of Short Gap.[1519] David Vance surveyed the 203-acre tract where Oliver Creamer was living on April 26, 1753.[1520] This tract was granted to Mary Creamer on February 24, 1761, and she sold the tract to Abraham Wise on September 9, 1761 for £50.[1521] Abraham Wise sold the tract to William Turner on August 15, 1770.[1522]

Gottschalk, a Moravian minister, kept a diary[1523] in 1748[1524] that references Oliver Creamer, stating:

*On March 19-30, I preached, at "Bateson's Creek," [Patterson Creek] German in the forenoon and English in the afternoon. Immediately after the sermon I started out to go to Matthaes Jochem's. But a man, named Oliver Craemer, followed me. He asked me not to start on my journey alone on foot at night, but go with him to his house, and he would accompany me to Matthaes Jochem's. As I recognized plainly*

---

[1517] According to Francis Bridges, Garret Pendergrass's property extended along the Potomac River from approximately Latitude 39.563088°, Longitude -78.841839° to approximately Latitude 39.565404°, Longitude -78.833342°.

[1518] The secondary source, the *"National Register of Historic Places Registration Form"* for *"Stewart's Tavern"*, was identified by Julia Jackson.

[1519] A post-1779 map identified by Robert L. Bantz still identifies the mill as *"Cramer's"*. This then-obsolete mill identification may have been copied from the 1755 Fry and Jefferson map.

[1520] **"Colonial Records of the Upper Potomac"**, Volume 4.

[1521] **"Colonial Records of the Upper Potomac"**, Volume 4.

[1522] **"Colonial Records of the Upper Potomac"**, Volume 4.

[1523] *"Extracts From The Diary Of Bro. Gottschalk's Journey Through Maryland And Virginia, March 5 - April 20, 1748"* in the **"Virginia Magazine of History and Biography"**, Vol. XII, No. 4, July 1904.

[1524] This appears to be based on the Gregorian calendar, which we presently use.

*that the Lord had sent this man, because it would have been difficult for me to pass through so much water in a dark night over an unfamiliar road of 45 miles, traveling until the next morning at ten o'clock, I accepted his offer with many thanks, and accompanied by this man I arrived at Jochem's on Sunday, March 20-31, about ten o'clock.*

Oliver Creamer's name also appears on an August 8, 1749 petition *"for a road from the lower part of Patterson's Creek by Power Hazels into the wagon road which leads from the Courthouse to the South Branch..."* The 1833 book "**A History of the Valley of Virginia**" states, *"The Indians killed Oliver Kremer in Short Gap, and took his wife prisoner."*[1525] An 1897 topographical map indicates that *"Short Gap"* was the name of a mountain pass between Pinto, Maryland and the current town of Short Gap that is located at Latitude 39.555790°, Longitude -78.822529°. The map shows a road passing through the gap and continuing to Pinto.

### *Locating Cresap's property*
Turners Run also helps to identify the property Thomas Cresap had built on, and was renting in 1775, as being his previously described property at the present-day site of the Allegany Ballistics Laboratory.

Daniel Cresap's May 4, 1752 *"Little Meadow"* survey is located immediately north of Sugar Bottom and is shown on Deakin's map. The beginning point of the property is described as, *"By the side of a small ridge near some Sink holes about a quarter of a Mile from potowmack river near the upper old Indian Town."* This tract was surveyed for Thomas Cresap by Isaac Brooke on November 30, 1751.

### Michael Cresap, Sr. is involved in two Virginia land transactions the same day
The 1939 book "**Early Records Hampshire County Virginia**" records the following for March 13, 1775, *"CRESAP, Michael, Sr. (w. Mary) of Frederick Co. to William Lockwood of Frederick Co. (lease and release) 40 a. on North Branch Potomac; rec. 3-14-1775. Wit.: None."* and for the same day also records, *"CRESAP, Michael, Sr. (w. Mary) of Frederick Co., Md. To David Mitchell Frederick Co., Md. (lease and release) 275a. on South Branch; rec. 3-14-1775. Wit.: None."*

### Nicholas Cresswell's April 1775 journal entries
Nicholas Cresswell's April 7, 1775 journal entry states:

*Slept very little last night. Mr. Rice tells me it is because I did not take off my clothes. Water froze in Kettle about 10 foot from the fire. Crossed Little Cape Capon Creek and the south mountain, which is one entire rock. Dined at Runnel's Tavern. Travelled over barren hills to Ashby's Fort on Patterson's Creek. Camped about 2 miles to the West of it. About 30 miles to-day.*

Cresswell's April 8, 1775 journal entry apparently describes crossing Knobley Mountain at the Short Gap mountain pass, and then following Braddock's road westward, stating:

*Slept very well last night, considering the hardness of our bed. Crossed the Knobby Mountain. Called at Creig's Tavern for a supply of Rum, then over the Devil's Hunting Ground to Tittle's Tavern. This is the worst road I ever saw, large rocks and bogs. Crossed the Savage Mountain and through the Shades of*

---

[1525] The *"Stewart's Tavern"* form indicates that the mill property on Turner's was about 208 acres and was sold to Wise in 1761 for £50. An abstract in Volume II of the book "**Virginia Northern Neck Land Grants, 1742-1775**" indicates that Oliver Creamer, deceased, had also been the owner Lot No. 35 (385 acres) in Hampshire County on the waters of the South Branch of the Potomac River by virtue of an August 11, 1749 deed. The abstract is difficult to understand but seems to indicate that ownership the property went to Oliver's widow Mary on March 1, 1764. Turners Run is not part of the South Branch watershed, which suggests the deed is for some other Creamer property, unrelated to the millsite. The South Branch-related abstracts are referenced because they indicate that Oliver Creamer was deceased by 1764.

*Death. This is one of the most dismal places I ever saw. The lofty Pines obscure the Sun, and the thick Laurels are like a Hedge on each side, the Road is very narrow and full of large stones and bogs. I measured a Pine that was blown down, 130 ft. long. Camped about 2 miles west of the Shades. 28m.*

Cresswell's April 9, 1775 journal entry states:

*Crossed the Little Meadow Mountain, supposed to be the highest part of the Appalachian or Allegany Mountain. The waters begin to fall to the westward. Crossed the Negro Mountain and the winding ridge. Crossed the line between Maryland and Pennsylvania. It is cut through the woods in a west course 63 from some part of Delaware Bay about 20 yards wide. It is on the top of the winding ridge. Crossed the Yaughaganey River at the Begg crossings. Camped 2 miles west of it. Shot some Pheasants, which have made a good supper.*

## A 1775 traveler writes home from the road, five miles west of Fort Cumberland

A Volume XIX (1925) of "**The Journal of American History**" includes the following April 16, 1775 letter written by James Nourse on a journey from Virginia to Kentucky:

*Easter Day, 5 Mile[1526] Beyond Fort Cumberland, 1775*

*My dear Love — Having met a gentleman bound for Winchester, I catch the opportunity of letting you know I am well ... dined yesterday at Old Town ... Mr. Taylor is a very obliging, kind fellow-traveler. My dear love, trust with confidence that I shall see you about harvest. My heart rises and my eyes run over, when I think of the joy of meeting my love again. Adieu, the support of the Almighty be with you all.*

*From your most affectionate husband,*

*James Nourse*

## Lexington and Concord

The first military engagements of the Revolutionary War took place at Lexington and Concord Massachusetts on April 19, 1775. The general flavor of this running fight is provided by the following extract[1527] from an intercepted British letter, written from Boston on April 28, 1775:

*The grenadiers and light infantry marched for Concord, where were powder and ball, arms, and cannon mounted on carriages; but before we could destroy them all, we were fired on by the country people, who are not brought up in the military way as ourselves: we were surrounded always in the woods; the firing was very hot on both sides; about two in the afternoon the second brigade came up, which were four regiments and part of the artillery; which were of no use to us, as the enemy were in the woods; and when we found they fired from houses, we set them on fire, and they ran to the woods. We were obliged to retreat to Boston again, over Charles river, our ammunition being all fired away. We had one hundred and fifty wounded and killed, and some taken prisoners. We were forced to leave some behind, who were wounded. We got back to Boston about two o'clock next morning; and they that were able to walk were forced to mount guard and lie in the field. I never broke my fast for forty-eight hours, for we carried no provisions, and thought to be back next morning.*

---

[1526] Based on the five-mile statement, James Nourse was probably writing from Gwinn's tavern.
[1527] "**Journals of Each Provincial Congress of Massachusetts**", 1838.

*I had my hat shot off my head three times, two balls through my coat, and my bayonet carried away by my side, and near being killed. The people of Boston are in great trouble, for General Gage will not let the town's people go out Direct for me to Chatham's division of marines.*

This battle was quickly followed by the May 10, 1775 Battle of Fort Ticonderoga and the June 17, 1775 Battle of Bunker Hill.

## Before the Revolution, people from Fayette County went to Fort Cumberland for flour

Although not documentary evidence, the Georges Township chapter of Franklin Ellis's 1882 book "**History of Fayette County, Pennsylvania**" states:

*One of the earliest industries of the township was the erection of mills. One of the first mills west of the mountains was that at Georgetown, now Haydentown. Before the erection of this mill, and Beeson's, at Uniontown, the people went to Fort Cumberland for their flour. This mill was built, it is said, by Robert Peoples and Jonathan Reese, two of the most energetic business men of the frontier country. It was in existence at the opening of the Revolutionary war...*

## The birthday of the United States Army

The "**Journals of the Continental Congress**" for June 14, 1775 includes the following:

*The Congress met and agreeable to the order of the day, resolved itself into a committee of the whole, to take into consideration &c. After some time spent thereon, the president resumed the chair, and Mr [Samuel] Ward reported, that not having yet come to a conclusion they desired him to move for leave to sit again. At the same time they desired him to report some resolutions which they had come into.*

*The resolutions being read, were adopted as follows:*

*Resolved, That six companies of expert rifflemen, be immediately raised in Pensylvania, two in Maryland, and two in Virginia; that each company consist of a captain, three lieutenants, four serjeants, four corporals, a drummer or trumpeter, and sixty-eight privates.*

*That each company, as soon as compleated, shall march and join the army near Boston, to be there employed as light infantry, under the command of the chief Officer in that army.*

*That the pay of the Officers and privates be as follows, viz. a captain @ 20 dollars per month; a lieutenant @ 13 1/3 dollars; a serjeant @ 8 dollars; a corporal @ 7 1/3 dollars; drummer or [trumpeter] @ 7 1/3 doll.; privates @ 6 2/3 dollars; to find their own arms and cloaths.*

*That the form of the enlistment be in the following words:*

*I _____ have, this day, voluntarily enlisted myself, as a soldier, in the American continental army, for one year, unless sooner discharged: And I do bind myself to conform, in all instances, to such rules and regulations, as are, or shall be, established for the government of the sa$^d$. Army.*

*Upon motion, Resolved, That Mr. [George] Washington, Mr. [Philip] Schuyler, Mr. [Silas] Deane, Mr. [Thomas] Cushing, and Mr. [Joseph] Hewes be a committee to bring in a dra$^{ft}$ of Rules and regulations for the government of the army.*

One of the *"companies of expert rifflemen"* that was formed was Michael Cresap's First Company, Maryland Rifles.

## Michael Cresap's First Company, Maryland Rifles

In regard to Michael Cresap's First Company, Maryland Rifles, an August 1, 1775 letter[1528] from Frederick Town states:

*Notwithstanding the urgency of my business, I have been detained three days in this place by an occurrence truly agreeable. I have had the happiness of seeing Captain Michael Cresap marching at the head of a formidable company of upwards of one hundred and thirty men from the mountains and backwoods, painted like Indians, armed with tomahawks and rifles, dressed in hunting shirts and moccasins, and though some of them had travelled near eight hundred miles from the banks of the Ohio, they seemed to walk light and easy, and not with less spirit than at the first hour of their march. Health and vigor, after what they had undergone, declared them to be intimate with hardship and familiar with danger. Joy and satisfaction were visible in the crowd that met them. Had Lord North been present, and been assured that the brave leader could raise thousands of such like to defend his country, what think you, would not the hatchet and the block have intruded on his mind? I had an opportunity of attending the Captain during his stay in town, and watched the behaviour of his men, and the manner in which he treated them; for it seems that all who go out to war under him do not only pay the most willing obedience to him as their commander, but, in every instance of distress look up to him as their friend and father. A great part of his time was spent in listening to and relieving their wants, without any apparent sense of fatigue and trouble. When complaints were before him, he determined with kindness and spirit, and on every occasion condescended to please without losing his dignity.*

*Yesterday the company were supplied with a small quantity of powder from the magazine, which wanted airing, and was not in good order for rifles; in the evening, however, they were drawn out to show the gentlemen of the town their dexterity at shooting. A clapboard with a mark the size of a dollar, was put up; they began to fire off-hand, and the bystanders were surprised, few shots being made that were not close to or in the paper. When they had shot for a time in this way, some lay on their backs, some on their breast or side, others ran twenty or thirty steps, and firing, appeared to be equally certain of the mark. With this performance the company were more than satisfied, when a young man took up the board in his hand, not by the end but by the side, and holding it up, his brother walked to the distance and very coolly shot into the white; laying down his rifle, he took the board and holding it as it was held before, the second brother shot as the first had done. By this exercise I was more astonished than pleased. But will you believe me when I tell you that one of the men took the board, and placing it between his legs, stood with his back to a tree while another drove the centre!*

*What would a regular army of considerable strength in the forests of America do with one thousand of these men, who want nothing to preserve their health and courage but water from the spring, with a little parched corn, with what they may easily procure in hunting; and who, wrapped in their blankets, in the damp of night, would choose the shade of a tree for their covering and the earth for their bed.*

## A Virginia property transaction on the North Branch of the Potomac River

The 1939 book "**Early Records Hampshire County Virginia**" records the following for August 12, 1775, *"WALKER, John, Sr. of Hampshire Co to Thomas Walker of Hampshire Co. (lease and release) 35 a. on North Branch of Potomac; rec. 8-13-1776. Wit.: None."*

---

[1528] "**Annual Report Of The President Of The Maryland Historical Society…**", 1850. I believe the original source is the August 16, 1775 issue of the "**Pennsylvania Gazette**".

## The Jersey Baptist Church was formed in August of 1775

The 1884 book "**History of Bedford, Somerset and Fulton Counties...**" describes the Jersey Baptist Church as follows:

*Turkey-Foot Baptist Church — This organization, which is more commonly known as the Jersey Baptist church, is the oldest Baptist church west of the Allegheny mountains. It is the oldest church of any kind in Somerset county, and perhaps the oldest in Southwestern Pennsylvania. ... The Turkey-Foot church is the parent of all the Baptist churches included in a region hundreds of miles in extent. The following is an exact copy of page seven of the minute[1529] of the Turkey-Foot Baptist Church:*

*"The minutes of the proceedings of the church belonging to Turkey-Foot and Sandy Creek Glades. On Wednesday, the fourteenth day [of August], Anno Domini 1775, the Rev. Mr. Isaac Sutton and John Corbley met this church at the house of Moses Halls in Turkey-Foot, and after a sermon on the occasion they solemnly constituted a church in these places..."*

## Funding for Cresap's rifle company

The Saturday, September 23, 1775 minutes of the Continental Congress include the following:

*The Committee of acco[ts] produced two rec[s] for money rec[d] of James Whitehead, one from Richard Brown, || a captain of one of the rifle companies from Maryland, || for fifty pounds || Pennsylvania currency, 133 1/3 dollars. || The other signed by Michael Cressop, [Cresap] || a captain of the other rifle company from Maryland, || for one hundred pounds || Pennsylvania currency, 266 2/3 dollars, || rec[d] for the use of their respective companies, marching to Boston in the continental service.*

*Ordered, That they be paid by the Committee.*

## Locating the residence of Enoch Innes in 1775

On October 9, 1775 Nathaniel Smith had a 141-acre tract surveyed in Hampshire County, Virginia. The tract was located on Knobley Mountain within the drainage of Plum Run and somewhere close to Enoch Innes. This tells us that Enoch Innes was then living somewhere near the site of the present-day village of Short Gap, West Virginia. Smith received a grant for the property on September 14, 1789; see grant book U, page 247.[1530]

## Taverns along Braddock's road, west of Fort Cumberland, in 1775

Nicholas Cresswell's October 11, 1775 journal entry[1531] states:

*Crossed the Falling Timbers, Yaough-a-ga-ny River, at the Great Crossing Laurel mountain. Breakfasted at Rice's Tavern. Then over the winding ridge. Crossed the Maryland line, and Negro Mountain. Lodged at Tumblestones Tavern on top of the Allegany Mountain.*

## An eyewitness reports that Fort Cumberland was deserted and demolished in 1775

Cresswell's October 12, 1775 journal entry states:

---

[1529] Some of the early minutes of the church are included in the August 1981 issue of the "**Laurel Messenger**".
[1530] "**Virginia Northern Neck Land Grants, 1775-1800**", Volume 3, 1993.
[1531] "**The Journal of Nicholas Cresswell**", 1924.

*Crossed the little meadow mountain, Shades of Death, and the Savage Mountain. Crossed the little meadow mountain, Shades of Death, and the Savage Mountain. Breakfasted at Tittle's Tavern. Then to Greg's Tavern, Fort Cumberland now deserted and demolished on Wills Creek and Potowmeck River. Got to Old Town in Maryland, 14 miles from Fort Cumberland. Lodged at one Rollin's Tavern.*

Although Cresswell describes the fort as *"deserted and demolished"*, a December 9, 1775 letter states that there were still six cannons there, in good working order. Tittle's tavern was somewhere in the vicinity of Frostburg.[1532]

By 1782, Thomas Jefferson refers to Fort Cumberland in the past tense stating, *"Wills Creek, at the mouth of which was Fort Cumberland..."* By 1787, Samuel Vaughn mentions the *"remains of the Earth fort"*, which suggests that there was nothing left by 1787 to inform him that the fort ever had a wooden stockade.

At some point in the ongoing process of the disintegration of the wooden components of the fort, some of the references to it must relate to an earthen landmark or a populated place.

The squared logs that held the 12-foot-tall, 20-foot-thick earthen fill of the ramparts would have been subject to accelerated rot from continual contact the moist earthen fill. Likewise, the underground portion of the original stockade logs would have been subject to accelerated rot. Techniques were known for protecting the underground portion of posts from rot, such as charring, but it is not known whether such techniques were employed in the haste of erecting the stockade fort in less than a month.

## Michael Cresap died at New York on October 18, 1775

The November 1, 1775 issue of the "**Maryland Journal**" includes an October 26, 1775 letter[1533] from New York that describes Michael Cresap's death and burial:

*On the 12th instant arrived here on his return from the Provincial Camp, at Cambridge, and, on the 18th, departed this life, of a fever, in the 28th year of his age[1534] Michael Cressop, Esqre, eldest son of Col. Thomas Cressop, of Potomack in Virginia. He was Captain of a Rifle company now in the Continental army before Boston. He served as a Captain, under the command of Lord Dunmore in the late expedition against the Indians, in which he eminently distinguished himself by his prudence, firmness and intrepidity as a brave officer; and, in the present contest between the parent state and the colonies, gave proofs of his attachment to the rights and liberties of his country. He has left a widow and four children to deplore the loss of a husband and father; and by his death his country is deprived of a worthy and esteemed citizen. His remains were interred the day following, in Trinity Church-yard, with military honors, attended by a vast concourse of people.*

The October 23, 1775 issue of the "**New York Gazette**" includes the following:

*... led by a Serjeant Major walked the Grenadiers of the First Battalion with their Flintlocks reversed. Behind two Lieutenants marched a fife & drum corps. Next came a Captain of Grenadiers flanked by two Serjeants aides. Two Adjutants appointed to conduct the funeral came next and were followed by a*

---

[1532] The 1822 Lucas map and the 1836 Tanner map still show the town as *"Mount Pleasant"*. The 1826 Melish map of Pennsylvania and the 1843 "**Map of the county west of Cumberland towards the Ohio river, showing the various lines surveyed or reconnoitered for the present extension of the Baltimore & Ohio Rail Road to its western terminus**" show the town name as Frostburg. The tombstone of Meshach Frost is in Frostburg at Latitude 39.656983°, Longitude -78.927417°, and a nearby historical marker includes photographs of him and his wife.

[1533] "**Tah-gah-jute: Or, Logan and Cresap, an Historical Essay**", 1867. The tombstone is presently preserved in a Philadelphia museum, and to the best I can read it, the carving states, *"In Memory of Michael Cresap First Capt Of the Rifle Batalions And Son to Col Thomas Cresap Who Departed this Life October the 18, 1775"*.

[1534] Michael Cresap's age at the time of his death is reported by some as age 33.

*military band. Immediately proceeding the Casket walked the Clergyman and alongside the Caisson bearing the body of Captain Cresap walked eight pallbearers all Captains. The Captain's Coffin was followed by the mourners, probably Army friends of the deceased. The rear of the Funeral Cartage was composed of no less than three Infantry Battalions, an entire Battalion made up of Officers and a large assemblage of Civilians.*

## Two colonies hoped to retrieve cannon from Fort Cumberland in 1775

The December 9, 1775 instructions that the Committee of Correspondence for the county of Fairfax, Virginia gave to their representatives of the general convention include the following statement:

*When ministerial Tools are employing every wicked Machination to accomplish their unjust Purposes, 'tis high time every virtuous Citizen should be on the Watch guarding those Liberties, which the Tyrants have mark'd out for Destruction; Actuated by these Motives and wishing to contribute to the Protection of this Colony & the common Cause; We the Committee of Correspondence for the County of Fairfax beg leave to present you our Representatives in Genel Convention w'th a few such Observations, as We think may be usefull at this Period of imminent Danger. ...*

*Be pleas'd to acquaint the Convention, that there are at Winchester fourteen Cannon at Cressaps two, at Fort Cumberland six in good order and belonging to the Colony, these might be useful on Navigation, at their present Situations not wanted, the Committee of Safety have been wrote to on this Subject, but no answer given to the Letter.*

A December 13, 1775 record from the "**Proceedings of the Conventions of the providence of Maryland**" states:

*The covention (sic) being informed that there are a number of cannon and shot at Fort Cumberland, Old Town, and Fort Frederick, and also a number of small arms at Isaac Baker's in Frederick county belonging to the public,*

*Resolved, That the committee for inquiring into the state of arms and ammunition, agree with some person or persons for the carriage of such of the said cannon as are fit for use, and shot, to Baltimore Town...*

## Introducing George Morgan

George Morgan played a significant role in the history of Fort Cumberland in 1779. In keeping with the general theme of this book, events in his life, beyond this introduction, are presented in chronological order when practicable.

George Morgan was born in Philadelphia in 1743. His mother died giving birth to him, and his father died when he was five.[1535] As a young teenager, he began working as an apprentice at the firm of Baynton and Wharton.[1536] That company was engaged in many different trading activities, including trade with the Indians. After about four years, he became a bookkeeper for the firm; and by 1762, he was testing the waters of private business venture.

---

[1535] The introductory information about George Morgan that does not reference supporting documentary evidence is based on Max Savelle's 1932 book "*George Morgan Colony Builder*".

[1536] According to the 1904 "**History of Beaver County...**", George Morgan married John Baynton's daughter Mary on October 24, 1764.

Baynton and Wharton had financial difficulties in 1763, including the loss of Indian trade consignments due to Pontiac's War.[1537] George Morgan used inherited money to join and recapitalize the firm, which then became the partnership of Baynton, Wharton and Morgan.

*Morgan gains experience dealing with large-scale logistical problems*

Due to his young age and freedom from other commitments, Morgan was available to take on, though reluctantly, the responsibility of overseeing the transportation of a large shipment of Indian trade goods to the Illinois country. First, he had to organize transportation to Fort Pitt, using wagons and hundreds of packhorses. At Fort Pitt, he had to arrange for temporary storage. Next, he had to arrange for shipments down the Ohio River, and up the Mississippi. This involved large-scale boat building and hiring over 300 crewmembers. In the fall of 1766, 65 boatloads of goods were sent to the Illinois country under his supervision.

In addition to the Indian trade, the firm eventually became engaged in provisioning soldiers in the Illinois country, providing government agents with gifts for Indian tribes, and supplying settlers. In the long run, they were unable to successfully compete with French and Spanish traders, and their business in the Illinois country declined. They abandoned the effort in 1772 and had to sell their assets to pay creditors. The company effectively ceased to exist by 1776, but Morgan had gained a tremendous amount of experience in dealing with large-scale logistical problems.

## The British army had a scheme to garrison Fort Cumberland in 1775

Volume 1 of the 1785 British book "**History of the War with America, France, Spain and Holland commencing in 1775 ...**" tells of a 1775 British plan to garrison Fort Cumberland and fortify Alexandria:

*While Lord Dunmore was thus exerting himself on the coasts of Virginia, a plan was forming to invade it, together with the other southern colonies, on their back and inland parts. The people in those settlements were considered as strongly attached to the English government, and it was expected that large numbers of them would be disposed to take up arms in its support. It was also supposed that some of the Indian tribes in the neighborhood of those parts might be brought to join them. All this would form a force sufficient to make an effectual impression on the enemy, and to open a passage in the very heart of the Colonies, through which they might make an irruption into any Province they chose particularly to attack.*

*Virginia was the Colony chiefly aimed at by this scheme. The projector of it was Mr. Conelly, a Pennsylvanian, a man completely qualified for its execution. He was one of those restless and daring individuals that seemed born for the tempestuous period they lived in, and with whom America abounded at this time.*

---

[1537] In 1765, after Morgan became a partner, the firm tried to send a shipment of Indian trade goods westward before legal trade was reopened by the government. The pack train was attacked by the *"Black Boys"*, and most of the goods were destroyed. See the story beginning on page 49 of the 1884 "**History of Bedford, Somerset, and Fulton Counties**", and Savelle's book. The August 17, 1769 issue of the "**Pennsylvania Gazette**" describes a 1769 event similar to this, stating, *"We learn from good Authority, that on the 10th Instant, at 9 o'Clock in the Morning, about 2 Miles beyond Juniata, 25 Horse loads of Indian Goods, going to Fort Pitt, belonging to Mr. Robert Callender, were stopped by about 30 Men armed, and their Faces painted black, swearing at the Drivers, that unless they quitted the Horses, they would fire upon them; that it was War with the Indians, and they would destroy the Goods. The Drivers begged they would not destroy the Goods, as they would return with them, or store them; but the People would not consent, and began to unload the Horses, burn and destroy the Goods, when Justice Limes fortunately came up, and thereby prevented their destroying them all. Those they have destroyed, or carried off, are 3 Keggs of Powder, 8 Pieces of Strouds, 8 Rifles, a large Number of Shirts, 14 Match Coats, and 4 Pieces of Halfthicks. The Goods that were saved, are stored about 8 Miles on this Side Fort Bedford."*

*He communicated his project to Lord Dunmore, with the activity and resoluteness of whose temper it perfectly corresponded. It met accordingly with his entire approbation; and Mr. Conelly set out immediately to carry it forwards with all possible expedition. Through a multiplicity of obstacles he reached the back settlements, and there found means to negotiate with great secrecy, a treaty with the Indians situated on the Ohio, and to bring over to his design the people in those remote districts. On his returning to Lord Dunmore with the intelligence of his success, he was dispatched to Boston with proper recommendations. Here he was commissioned by General Gage to act in this business as Colonel and Commander, with promises of being thoroughly supported.*

*By this plan it was agreed, that the British forces at Detroit, and the forts in its vicinity, with those that were stationed in others of those distance settlements, would each furnish as many men as could possibly be spared. With these, which would altogether form a considerable body, the Colonel was to proceed as early the next spring as practicable, to Pittsburgh, where he was to establish his head quarters, till the disaffected party there was entirely suppressed, and the friends of government collected to a sufficient number to form them into regiments. From Pittsburgh he was to cross the Allegany Mountains, and penetrate into Virginia. Here, after leaving fort Cumberland strongly garrisoned, he was to fall down the river Potomack, and seize upon Alexandria, where it was concerted that Lord Dunmore should meet him with a fleet under his command, and all the force he could gather. Alexandria was then to be strongly fortified, and made a place of arms, and the centre of their operations. By these means the friends of government would be able to declare themselves without restraint, and to form a general junction with facility; and what was of more importance than all the rest, the communication between the northern and southern Colonies would be effectually cut off.*

*Such was the vast and comprehensive plan projected by Mr. Conelly. He had made a considerable progress on his journey towards Detroit; and was now on the back frontiers of Maryland, and had seemingly escaped the principal dangers, when he was unluckily discovered by one of those unexpected accidents that so often baffle the best concerted designs.*

*A tradesman with whom he was acquainted and had dealt, met him on the road, and directly gave information to the nearest committee; he was immediately seized upon suspicion, and his papers discovered the whole design. They were communicated to Congress, and the Colonel was thrown into prison.*

For more information on Conelly, and his relationship with Dunmore, see the 1833 book "**A History of the Valley of Virginia**".

A man named J. F. D. Smyth was also part of the scheme. He left a written account of the plan, his capture by rebels, and his escapes in Volume 2 of a 1784 book titled "**A Tour in the United States of America…**" Some of his statements concerning 1775 include:

*AFTER these groundless and most ridiculous suspicions were happily cleared up, the.whole intention and substance of a secret expedition to the back country, under the command of Lieutenant-Colonel Connolly, then appointed Commandant of the Queen's royal regiment of Rangers, was disclosed to me, and I was earnestly solicited by the Colonel to accompany him, along with another gentleman named Cameron; to this I most chearfully consented, and in the above regiment we all received our commissions.*

*On the day following I received an order to take any vessel in the harbour, and also such of the pilots on board his Majesty's sloop the Otter as I judged proper, for the use of this expedition.*

*This circumstance was no small satisfaction to me, as I thereby convinced Captain Squire of my being no spy, as he had alledged; and on going on board his ship made choice of two of his best pilots.*

*When we departed from Norfolk on this expedition, I was obliged to leave behind me my servant and all the property I had been able to bring down there. My servant and horses, which were valuable, were to be sent to the plantation of Mr. Atchison, at lord Dunmore's request; and the rest of my property I left in the house of a Mr. Pierce at Portsmouth, but I have never since that time heard the least account of any thing belonging to me.*

*We embarked on board a flat-bottomed decked schooner, which I had engaged for that purpose, with our horses, and only one servant who belonged to the Colonel.*

*Our small party consisted of Lieutenant-Colonel Connolly, Mr. Cameron, myself, and the servant; and we intended to proceed in this vessel up the Chesapeak, into Potomack River, and land if possible near to my house or Port Tobacco Creek, and afterwards to pass through the country on horseback until we arrived at Detroit in Canada.*

*It was proposed that I should pass through Pittsburg, with dispatches to Mr. M'Kie the Indian superintendant, and to some other friends of, government, then proceed down the river Ohio to the mouth of the Siotto, and from thence up that river, through the Shawnese, Detawares, and Wiandotts, and down Sanduski River to Sanduski Old Fort, from thence I was to cross lake Erie, by the Rattle Snake Islands, to Detroit. While the other two gentlemen were to cross the Allegany River at the Kittanning, and proceed by the nearest and most direct rout to Detroit. Here a very considerable force was to be collected from all the nearest posts in Canada, and transported, early in the spring, across the lake Erie to Presquisle, where I was to be employed during the winter with a detachment of two hundred men in covering and conducting the building batteaux, and collecting provisions, in order to proceed by the way of French Creek, Venango, and the Allegany River, to Pittsburgh which we were to seize on and establish as head-quarters, until the disaffected interest was entirely crushed, and the whole strength of the country collected and formed into regular disciplined regiments.*

*After leaving a sufficient garrison at Pittsburg, we were to advance across the Allegany Mountains with our whole force upon the back of Virginia; and after establishing a strong post at Fort Cumberland, it was proposed to fall down the river Potomack, and seize on Alexandria, where the Earl of Dunmore was to meet us with the fleet, and all the force of the lower part of the province. Alexandria was to be strongly fortified, as a place of arms, and the communication between the southern and northern parts of the continent thereby cut off.*

*If a misfortune, of such magnitude, should have happened, as to oblige us to give up this enterprize at any particular stage thereof, our retreat was then secured by these posts which we occupied in our rear; and if it would have failed in the first part of the expedition, by our finding it impracticable to seize upon Pittsburg, we were to fall down the Ohio in our batteaux to the Mississippi; where we were to be joined by the garrison, artillery, and stores from Fort Gage of Kiskuskias at the Illonois; and then to proceed down to the mouth of the river Mississippi in West Florida; where we were to embark in transports, and come round to Norfolk in Virginia, there to join the Earl of Dunmore.*

*For the execution of this well formed, judicious, and vast undertaking, Lieutenant-Colonel Connolly was furnished with the proper and necessary powers, both from General Gage the Commander in Chief, and from the Earl of Dunmore, and with ample instructions for his future conduct, as well as commissions for the formation of a complete regiment at Detroit, or Pittsburg; all of which, containing no less than eighteen sheets of paper, we carried along with us in a secret manner invented by and executed under the inspection of his lordship.*

*All these papers were concealed in the mail pillion-sticks on which the servant carried his portmanteau, they being made hollow, for that purposes and covered with tin plates, and then canvass glued therein as usual; this was so dextrously and completely executed that it could not be discovered on the strictest examination.*

*We sailed up the Potomack, almost as far as Lower Cedar Point, when a most violent gale came on from the north-west, which obliged us to stand down the river again, and run up into St. Mary's River in Maryland, where we landed on the twelfth of November, without occasioning the least suspicion, having sent off the vessel again immediately after we had taken out our horses.*

*Here I undertook to be the conductor through the country for above two hundred miles; and it was not without the utmost address, precaution, difficulty and danger that I carried them, and passed myself quite safe and unsuspected, through all that extent of thick settled country, wherein my person and principles were so well known, and without being once discovered myself.*

*However we were frequently very much alarmed, particularly at Frederick Town, where we arrived on the evening of a general muster, or field-day of the armed associators. At the inn where we put up, each of us calling for something different from the others, caused an enquiry, and of course a suspicion concerning us, and it was proposed to bring us before the committee in the morning for examination. This plan we accidentally disconcerted by setting out from Frederick Town in the morning at daybreak; and as the committee had all got intoxicated over night, it was too late next day, before they arose, and recollected any circumstances concerning us, to send in pursuit after us.*

*We pasted through a village named Middle Town, about eight miles beyond Frederick; and in the South Mountain, four miles farther, we took the wrong road, which led us to another village named Funk's Town, after Jacob Funk a German, the proprietor.*

*We dined in this place, and passed on through a considerable town called Hagar's Town, named so also after the proprietor, a German; a few miles beyond which we unfortunately met a little man, a hatter, who knew Colonel Connolly at Pittsburg, where he had lived, and now recollected him again, and spoke to him.*

*This accident giving me great uneasiness, I mentioned to the Colonel my apprehensions of our being discovered thereby, and proposed for us to change our route. But he being of a different opinion, and thinking there was no danger, it gave me inexpressible concern, and had it not been for two reasons which prevented me, I would then have left him and provided for my own safety.*

*The first was, that being under his command I could not disobey; but of that I was sensible he had too much generosity to take advantage, therefore it was not this that deterred me.*

*The second reason was, the former ridiculous suspicions against me at Norfolk; and it was on that account I determined to stand or fall with him, and to wait the event with patience, should captivity, or even death be the consequence.*

*We lodged at one Doctor Snayvelley's, a German, about five or six miles beyond Hagars Town, upon the banks of the river Connegocheague and accordingly as I had dreaded, about midnight we were all seized on in our beds and made prisoners by a company of riflemen from Hagar's Town, who were ordered out for that purpose in consequence of the little hatter's information.*

*This company consisted of thirty-six men exclusive of officers, who rushing suddenly into our room, with their rifles cocked and presented close to our heads while in bed, obliged us to surrender. This happened in the night of the nineteenth of November, one thousand seven hundred and seventy-five.*

*This party consisting solely of rude unfeeling German ruffians, fit for assassinations, murder, and death, treated us with great great ignominy and insult; and without the least provocation abused us perpetually with every opprobrious epithet language can afford.*

*We were then carried to Hagar's Town, and examined separately before the committee there, after being searched for papers; our saddles and baggage also underwent a strict scrutiny and inspection, but nothing was discovered against us. This committee was ignorant, rude, abusive, and illiberal, and ordered us to be carried to Frederick Town, under a strong guard, for further examination. The same ruffians continued to guard us, and were perpetually threatening to take our lives. As we rode along (for as yet they had not deprived us of our own horses) some of them in the rear every now and then fired off a rifle directed very near us, as I could hear the ball whistle past within a few feet of us, every time they fired.*

*At Frederick town I was told that I need not expect to get clear, for I was a noted noted friend to Britain, and they had long endeavoured to get me in their power.*

*Here we were stripped and searched again, and examined separately before the committee, where one of the most illiberal, inveterate and violent rebels named Samuel Chase, (son to a respectable and very worthy clergyman of this province) a lawyer, and a member of the Congress presided.*

*At this place we were not a little alarmed lest they should discover our instructions, papers, &c. as they examined every thing so strictly as to take our saddles to pieces, and take out the stuffing, and even rip open the soals of our boots, in vain, for the object of their search was not found, although they so frequently handled what contained it.*

*However, by some neglect of Colonel Connolly's servant, an old torn piece of paper was found in his portmanteau, which discovered part of our design; and then Colonel Connolly, to prevent our falling immediate sacrifices to a frantic mob, acknowledged our commissions.*

*Upon this we were actually robbed of our money, by Samuel Chase and the committee, the chairman of which was named John Hanson, and he has since then become a President of the American Congress, who left us only one guinea each; and we were put under a strong guard in the house of one Charles Beatty, in a close room three stories high, with the windows screwed fast down, restricted from pen, ink, and paper, and no person allowed to speak to us.*

*Thus were we confined, for seven weeks, all in one room, under a strong guard, suffering every species of insult daily, and in danger and dread of being murdered every night.*

*The servant however, who was faithful to his trust, being allowed to go at large from the first of our confinement, took care to destroy the mail pillion-sticks, containing the papers, commissions, and instructions, which we dreaded so much being discovered, as soon as he could effect it with safety, which put an end to our anxiety and alarms on that account.*

*Fredrick Town is a fine large town, built of brick and stone, there being very few timber houses in it, it is an inland town, being at least fifty miles from George Town, which is the nearest navigation or port, and is not situated upon any river or water course; the nearest to it being Monoccacy Creek, which is four miles distant, and Potomack River, which is about eight miles from it.*

*The land around Fredrick Town is heavy, strong, and rich, well calculated for wheat, with which it abounds; this being as plentiful a country as any in the world.*

*The face of the country here swells into beautiful hills and dales, and twelve miles beyond the town it arises into mountains, named the South Mountain. The soil is generally of a deep rusty brown colour, and strongly impregnated with iron.*

*Fredrick Town is not so large as Alexandria, but more considerable than Williamsburg, or Annapolis, and contains upwards of two thousand inhabitants, who abound in provisions, and all the necessaries of life.*

*Beyond the mountain Elizabeth Town, or Hagar's Town as it is generally called, astonishes you by its magnitude, beauty, and good buildings, chiefly composed of stone and lime.*

*It is situated on a plain, in the great valley between the two mighty ridges named the South Mountain, or Blue Ridge, and the North Mountain, or Great Ridge.*

*This valley is about thirty miles wide, extending many hundred miles in length, and contains a body of the richest land in the world. It abounds with the most clear and pellucid water-courses, and all the stones and rocks are lime-stone.*

*Both Frederick Town and Hagar's Town, as well as the greatest part of the back country of Maryland and Pennsylvania, are inhabited chiefly by Germans and Irish, but the first are the most numerous; and carry on almost every kind of manufacture, as well as a considerable share of trade. Neither of them stand upon any large water-course; but there is abundance of mills, forges, furnaces, and iron works, all around them, throughout the adjacent country.*

*Many of the Irish here can scarcely speak in English; and thousands of the Germans understand no language but High Dutch; however they are all very laborious, and extremely industrious, having improved this part of the country beyond conception; but they have no idea of social life, and are more like brutes than men. They came to Frederick Town from all quarters to behold us, as if we had been some strange fight, and were always very liberal of insults and abuse, without the least cause or provocation.*

*On the thirtieth of December, orders were brought from the Congress, that we should be sent to them at Philadelphia; and they were preparing to set out with us next day.*

*It had been preconcerted, that if we should be taken prisoners by the way upon this expedition, we should attempt, either by escape or any other method, to inform the garrison of Detroit of an expedition the rebels intended against them from Pittsburg; and also to bring the garrison of Fort Gage at Kilkulkias Illonois,with the artillery, stores, &c. down the Mississippi to the Gulf of Mexico, and from thence by transports round to join the Earl of Dunmore and the troops Under his command at Norfolk.*

*For this reason I had been long scheming an escape, and had engaged one of the inhabitants named Barclay to accompany me on this hazardous undertaking; and he was to be liberally rewarded for his services.*

*As we were ordered to set out for Philadelphia next morning, there was now no time to be lost in making this attempt.*

*For this purposes watched all this night for the moment that the two centinels might fall asleep on their posts at our door, which they had also locked on the outside; at length the much wished-for period arrived; and that instant unscrewing the lock, I made my escape, with letters, dispatches, and every necessary order, but by an accident was obliged to leave almost all my cloaths behind. After some little difficulty I found Barclay's house, and he getting out of bed, we immediately set out on our journey.*

*There was a deep encrusted snow, and most dreadful roads, so that travelling was beyond expression fatiguing, especially as I went on foot, leaving my horse behind to prevent any suspicion of my route; as no one could imagine that a journey, over the Allegany mountains, to Detroit, and to the Mississippi, would be attempted during that rigorous season of the year, by any person alone, as they must conceive me to be, and on foot.*

*In order to pass on with more privacy, I (endeavoured to cross the Potomack, and travel up on the Virginia side of that river, because so many people from Maryland had seen me while in confinement at Frederick Town and Hagar's Town; but in attempting to go over on the ice, I broke in, and it was with the utmost difficulty my life was saved. Barclay would not venture.*

*It was snowing and freezing at the same time, and I had seven miles over the mountains to go before I came to a house to thaw, dry, and warm myself. At last when I reached a house, there was no fire, the people could not speak nor understand a single word of English, and it was impossible for me to stay; so I travelled on in that wet and frozen condition all day, and at night lay before the fire, at the house of a poor ignorant Dutchman; which I also did did the night before, upon a bear's skin, at the house of a very violent Scotsman, a surveyor, on the side of the Potomack, after having undergone more than can, be expressed in travelling round a town named Sharpsburg, the snow being deep and encrusted over, but not strong enough to support my weight, so that at every step I sunk down almost knee-deep, and cut my legs also by every movement in walking.*

This last description is from the end of December 1775. Another part of Smyth's story begins on January 1, 1776 and is included in the next chapter. Volume 1 of the 1910 book "**History of Frederick County, Maryland**" states the following regarding the November 1775 imprisonment at Hagerstown:

*The following entry relating to these prisoners is found in the proceedings of the Committee of Obserevation at Hagerstown.*

*"At a meeting of the committee on the 20$^{th}$ of November 1775 present, Mr. James Smith, president; Messrs. Stull, Baird, Swearingen, A. Rench, Zwingley, John Rench, and S. Hughes. Doct. John C—— [Connolloy] of Fort Pitt and certain persons called Doctor S—— [Smith] and M. C—— [Cameron]. Were brought before the committee and accused of being inimical to the liberties of America,*

*Resolved, unanimously that the said Doct. C—— (from certain papers produced to this committee and acknowledged to have been written by him) is a dangerous enemy to the colonies and as such shall be sent to the Council of Safety or Convention for further trial.*

*It was also resolved that the aforesaid Doc. S—— and M. C—— being found guilty of many equivocations and coming in the company with the aforesaid Doct. C—— from the dangerous councils of Lord Dunmore, that it is the opinion of this committee that the said S—— and C—— shall be sent to the Council of Safety or Convention for further enquiry."*

# 28. 1776: Independence is declared

### The continuation of Smyth's account takes him past Fort Cumberland twice

Smyth's account continues January 1, 1776, taking him past Fort Cumberland twice, and leaving us with an account of a public house that was located there:

*On the first day of January, 1776, at sun-rise, I came to the mouth of a river named Cunnigocheague, where it enters the Potomack.*

*This river was frozen half-way over, and we were compelled to break the ice, strip, and wade through, with the water up almost to our shoulders.*

*Hearing of a pursuit after me, we struck out of the road into the North Mountain, travelled all day through deep fatiguing encrusted snow, and staid during the night (for I slept not) under a rock in the mountain.*

*On the second of January, we likewise (travelled all day in the mountain, and at night scraped away the snow by the side of a fallen tree, made a fire, and slept a little.*

*On the third of January I directed our course towards the road again, being then behind the pursuit, and staid all night at a miserable hovel by the fire. Here we procured some coarse food, which was extremely acceptable and delicious, having been entirely without any kind of refreshment for the last two days.*

*At this place I heard a thousand falsehoods told concerning me, and was obliged to join in the abuse against myself, which was generally equally groundless and illiberal; several of the people here said they knew me perfectly well, and attributed a multitude of singular actions and exploits to me that I had never before heard of; but they all united in insisting that we ought immediately to have been put to death when taken, to prevent escapes and future mischief.*

*Our journey was somewhat retarded, and rendered extremely disagreeable, by great numbers of large water-courses or rivulets in our way, which we were under the necessity of passing over, all of them being partially or entirely frozen, yet scarcely any able to bear us, so that we had to break the ice on each side, and wade through. Among the multitude of these, I still recoiled the names of the Great Khonholloway and Little Khonholloway.*

*On the fourth of January, being under the necessity of crossing a river that was frozen over, I had three violent falls on the ice, by which I received a deep wound in one of my feet, and a very bad strain in my ancle.*

*This rendered travelling intolerably painful and difficult; however to me there was no alternative, but death to stop, or life to proceed; and I continued to push on, although constantly in extreme torture, until we arrived at a planter's house on the road, about a mile on this side of a large water-course named May's creek; where I was compelled to stop, unable to proceed farther, being absolutely exhausted, and quite overpowered with extreme pain and fatigue.*

*Here Barclay privately made off and left me, after plundering me of what little cloaths I had been able to bring with me, and every valuable article I had secreted from the rebels, viz. some silver and stone buckles, gold rings, and jewels, on which I depended solely for support during this journey; for the* committee, as I have observed before, had only left us a guinea a piece in money, of which one single dollar was all I had remaining.

This fellow surely must have been influenced by the reflection, that in my wretched condition it would be impossible for me to accomplish the hazardous and extensive journey I had undertaken; and that consequently sooner or later must be again apprehended; for which high rewards were offered, and the greatest exertions made by the rebels.

For he never could be tempted by the small booty he obtained to be guilty of such a piece of villainy, after travelling so far, and suffering so much as he had done, along with me. This spoil from me however I presume he thought proper to take to himself when he went off, as satisfaction for his trouble.

No event of my life ever shocked me more than the discovery of this wretch's treachery, when I found he was certainly gone.

A multitude of suspicions crowded in my mind, and a thousand fears alarmed me. Every moment I expected to be seized upon, in consequence of information against me; and I distrusted every person I saw or met.

My mind distracted, my body enfeebled, emaciated, and tormented with excruciating pain, in an enemy's country, destitute of money or resource, and without a single friend, I was in a condition truly to be commiserated, and not to be excelled in distress.

This was a trial the most arduous and severe I ever met with; but still my resolution did not forsake me, and I determined to proceed, notwithstanding every difficulty and danger.

I crossed May's Creek, and Will's Creek, by breaking the ice and wading them, passed by old Fort Cumberland, which is in a beautiful and romantic situation, on the north side of the Potomack, amidst vast mountains and mighty torrents of water that break through the mountains in dreadful and tremendous chasms, appearing very distinctly from this place.

The largest of these breaks in the mountains are those of the river Potomack and of Wills's Creek, which appear from hence superior to the rest in awful grandeur.

There is now only a little public house at Fort Cumberland, where that immense immense ridge particularly named the Allegany Mountains commences.

Here I began to ascend the mighty Allegany, and after travelling all day in an extremity of anguish, pain, and anxiety, after having broken the ice and waded through a black and dismal river named Savage River, and a number, of large and dangerous water-courses besides, I arrived at Gregg's habitation, in the midst of the mountain; where I remained all night amidst the dreadful screamings and howlings of multitudes of every species of wild beasts.

Here I was compelled to break in upon my poor solitary dollar, for, notwithstanding all my intended frugality, nature required support, which money alone could procure.

I set out again next morning, and in this most distressing and wretched condition continued to push forward, until I had got over the Allegany mountains; but, notwithstanding all my circumspection and strenuous exertions, I had the misfortune to be retaken by mere accident on the Yohiogeny River, a branch of the Ohio, on the twelfth of January, by a party of nine ruffians returning from Pittsburg, where they had been dispatched in pursuit of me.

*NOTHING preserved me from immediate death from the hands of these banditti, but the hopes of the reward they should meet with by carrying me to the Congress.*

*However there was no restriction to deter them from exercising the most wanton insult, the highest ignominy, and the most unaccountable cruelties upon me.*

*They set me upon a pack-horse, on a wooden pack-saddle; they tied my arms behind me, and my legs under the horse's belly; they took the bridle off the horse, and fastened a great bell around his neck; and in that condition they drove the horse before them, with me upon his back, along narrow slippery ways covered with ice, and over all the dreadful horrid precipices of the Allegany and Blue Mountains, for a distance little short of three hundred miles.*

*During the first day and night they never halted but for necessary refreshment, of which however they afforded me no share; and every night afterwards compelling me to lie upon the bare ground.*

*Thus travelling in this rapid manner very probably saved my life, as I have been informed since, for another banditti of thirty men from the vicinity of Pittsburg, upon an alarm that a person was taken on his way to raise the Indians against them, had pursued us under oath to kill me, but after following us for a day and a half in vain, despairing to overtake us they returned.*

*I was carried in this inhuman barbarous manner past Tumbleston's, Grigg's,[1538] Fort Cumberland, Cressop's or Old Town, &c. &c. and at several places it was with the utmost difficulty my guard could prevent the ruffian savage inhabitants from murdering me in cold blood: but although they preserved my life, for the sake of the reward they expected for apprehending me, yet they never attempted to protect me from the most cruel and mortifying insults and mal-treatment at every place they halted; and I was frequently even exhibited as a public show, as if of a different shape and appearance from other men.*

*During all this time I tasted nothing but water, excepting one meal of indifferent food; this also contributed in some degree to my recovery, by abating the inflammation of the wound in my foot, and the strain in my ancle, both of which were prodigiously swelled, and so intolerably painful, that, besides entirely depriving me of sleep, I was not able to walk an hundred yards even if it had been to obtain, life and liberty as a reward. I was then delivered up again to the Committee of Hagar's Town; who, after ordering me to be searched four different times in one day, made use of every artifice of promises to delude and threats to intimidate, in order to corrupt my principles, and gain me over to their cause; and when all would not avail they ordered me to be carried to the Congress at Philadelphia in irons. A fresh guard was added to the former, consisting of a Major, and two Captains, the rest being Lieutenants, Ensigns, and Serjeants, amounting to twelve in number, besides the former nine, who would not wait for the irons to be made, but set out with me, bound as before, and my horse tied also with two large ropes, and led by two of the guard, accompanied with fife and drum beating the rogue's march, which which they seemed every where to be particularly fond of.*

*In this manner I was carried to Fredrick Town, and there dragged, bound with cords, before the Committee, which consisted of a taylor, a leather breechesmaker, a shoemaker, a gingerbread-baker, a butcher, and two publicans.*

---

[1538] This account indicates that *"Grigg's"* was between Tomlinson's and Fort Cumberland.

### George Morgan is appointed Agent for Indian affairs in January of 1776

The Continental Congress organized an Indian department in July 1775 to try to maintain peace with the Indians. George Morgan was an honest man, and well respected by the Indians. The Continental Congress appointed him the *"agent for Indian affairs in the middle department"* at Fort Pitt in 1776 and gave him the rank and pay of Colonel on January 8, 1777. In the 1848 book "**Pioneer history: being an account of the first examinations of the Ohio ...**", Hildreth describes Morgan as follows:

> *Colonel Morgan was appointed Indian agent for the middle department, the head quarters of which office were at Pittsburgh, by Congress, in April, 1776. He was a man of unwearied activity, great perserverance, and familiar with the Indian manners and habits, having for several years had charge of a trading post in the Illinois... His frank manners, soldierly bearing, generosity, and, above all, his strict honesty in all his dealings with them, won their fullest confidence...*

### Charles Clinton attempts to patent 'Nicholls Dispute'

Frederick County unpatented certificate 522 relates to the February 5, 1776 survey of the 25¾-acre *"Nicholls Dispute"* for Charles Clinton, which was examined by Francis Deakins.

### Virginia hoped to retrieve cannon from Fort Cumberland in 1776

Volume 8 of the "**Calendar of Virginia State Papers and Other Manuscripts ...**" includes a record from April 1, 1776 that states:

> *Colo. Lewis and Mr. Page are desired to send to Fort Cumberland for any cannon there belonging to this colony, also for one at Col. Cresops and empowered to purchase any other necessaries which may be wanting for the vessels in the Rappahannock river.*

### Thomas Constable obtains property on the waters of Evitts Creek

Thomas Constable appears on Andrew Bruce's 1778 Oath of Fidelity list. A 77-acre tract named Thomas's Choice was surveyed for Robert Constable on April 1, 1776 and patented to Thomas Constable on November 18, 1788 (Frederick County Patent Certificate 4760). The survey begins *"at a bounded White Oak standing about two Per from the head of a large Spring it being a draught of Evits Creek about twenty four Per from where Thomas Constable settled"*. I'm not sure about *"Per"*; which is my interpretation of a highly stylized symbol used in the document.

### Enoch Innes is appointed to dispose of part of the estate of Lord Dunmore

The June 22, 1776 minutes from the "**Proceedings of the Convention of Delegates for the Counties and Corporations in the Colony of Virginia**" include the statement, *"Resolved, That Joseph Neaville and Enoch Innes, gentlemen, be appointed commissioners to dispose of the estate of Lord Dunmore in the county of Hampshire, in the room of John Neaville, and James Innes, gentlemen, who are inconveniently situated for that purpose."*

### The Declaration of Independence

The Declaration of Independence, which was unanimously approved on July 4, 1776, states:

> *IN CONGRESS, July 4, 1776.*
>
> *The unanimous Declaration of the thirteen united States of America,*

*When in the Course of human events, it becomes necessary for one people to dissolve the political bands which have connected them with another, and to assume among the powers of the earth, the separate and equal station to which the Laws of Nature and of Nature's God entitle them, a decent respect to the opinions of mankind requires that they should declare the causes which impel them to the separation.*

*We hold these truths to be self-evident, that all men are created equal, that they are endowed by their Creator with certain unalienable Rights, that among these are Life, Liberty and the pursuit of Happiness. — That to secure these rights, Governments are instituted among Men, deriving their just powers from the consent of the governed, — That whenever any Form of Government becomes destructive of these ends, it is the Right of the People to alter or to abolish it, and to institute new Government, laying its foundation on such principles and organizing its powers in such form, as to them shall seem most likely to effect their Safety and Happiness. Prudence, indeed, will dictate that Governments long established should not be changed for light and transient causes; and accordingly all experience hath shewn, that mankind are more disposed to suffer, while evils are sufferable, than to right themselves by abolishing the forms to which they are accustomed. But when a long train of abuses and usurpations, pursuing invariably the same Object evinces a design to reduce them under absolute Despotism, it is their right, it is their duty, to throw off such Government, and to provide new Guards for their future security. — Such has been the patient sufferance of these Colonies; and such is now the necessity which constrains them to alter their former Systems of Government. The history of the present King of Great Britain is a history of repeated injuries and usurpations, all having in direct object the establishment of an absolute Tyranny over these States. To prove this, let Facts be submitted to a candid world.*

*He has refused his Assent to Laws, the most wholesome and necessary for the public good.*

*He has forbidden his Governors to pass Laws of immediate and pressing importance, unless suspended in their operation till his Assent should be obtained; and when so suspended, he has utterly neglected to attend to them.*

*He has refused to pass other Laws for the accommodation of large districts of people, unless those people would relinquish the right of Representation in the Legislature, a right inestimable to them and formidable to tyrants only.*

*He has called together legislative bodies at places unusual, uncomfortable, and distant from the depository of their public Records, for the sole purpose of fatiguing them into compliance with his measures.*

*He has dissolved Representative Houses repeatedly, for opposing with manly firmness his invasions on the rights of the people.*

*He has refused for a long time, after such dissolutions, to cause others to be elected; whereby the Legislative powers, incapable of Annihilation, have returned to the People at large for their exercise; the State remaining in the mean time exposed to all the dangers of invasion from without, and convulsions within.*

*He has endeavoured to prevent the population of these States; for that purpose obstructing the Laws for Naturalization of Foreigners; refusing to pass others to encourage their migrations hither, and raising the conditions of new Appropriations of Lands.*

*He has obstructed the Administration of Justice, by refusing his Assent to Laws for establishing Judiciary powers.*

*He has made Judges dependent on his Will alone, for the tenure of their offices, and the amount and payment of their salaries.*

*He has erected a multitude of New Offices, and sent hither swarms of Officers to harrass our people, and eat out their substance.*

*He has kept among us, in times of peace, Standing Armies without the Consent of our legislatures.*

*He has affected to render the Military independent of and superior to the Civil power.*

*He has combined with others to subject us to a jurisdiction foreign to our constitution, and unacknowledged by our laws; giving his Assent to their Acts of pretended Legislation:*

*For Quartering large bodies of armed troops among us:*

*For protecting them, by a mock Trial, from punishment for any Murders which they should commit on the Inhabitants of these States:*

*For cutting off our Trade with all parts of the world:*

*For imposing Taxes on us without our Consent:*

*For depriving us in many cases, of the benefits of Trial by Jury:*

*For transporting us beyond Seas to be tried for pretended offences*

*For abolishing the free System of English Laws in a neighbouring Province, establishing therein an Arbitrary government, and enlarging its Boundaries so as to render it at once an example and fit instrument for introducing the same absolute rule into these Colonies:*

*For taking away our Charters, abolishing our most valuable Laws, and altering fundamentally the Forms of our Governments:*

*For suspending our own Legislatures, and declaring themselves invested with power to legislate for us in all cases whatsoever.*

*He has abdicated Government here, by declaring us out of his Protection and waging War against us.*

*He has plundered our seas, ravaged our Coasts, burnt our towns, and destroyed the lives of our people.*

*He is at this time transporting large Armies of foreign Mercenaries to compleat the works of death, desolation and tyranny, already begun with circumstances of Cruelty & perfidy scarcely paralleled in the most barbarous ages, and totally unworthy the Head of a civilized nation.*

*He has constrained our fellow Citizens taken Captive on the high Seas to bear Arms against their Country, to become the executioners of their friends and Brethren, or to fall themselves by their Hands.*

*He has excited domestic insurrections amongst us, and has endeavoured to bring on the inhabitants of our frontiers, the merciless Indian Savages, whose known rule of warfare, is an undistinguished destruction of all ages, sexes and conditions.*

*In every stage of these Oppressions We have Petitioned for Redress in the most humble terms: Our repeated Petitions have been answered only by repeated injury. A Prince whose character is thus marked by every act which may define a Tyrant, is unfit to be the ruler of a free people.*

*Nor have We been wanting in attentions to our Brittish brethren. We have warned them from time to time of attempts by their legislature to extend an unwarrantable jurisdiction over us. We have reminded them of the circumstances of our emigration and settlement here. We have appealed to their native justice and magnanimity, and we have conjured them by the ties of our common kindred to disavow these usurpations, which, would inevitably interrupt our connections and correspondence. They too have been deaf to the voice of justice and of consanguinity. We must, therefore, acquiesce in the necessity, which denounces our Separation, and hold them, as we hold the rest of mankind, Enemies in War, in Peace Friends.*

*We, therefore, the Representatives of the united States of America, in General Congress, Assembled, appealing to the Supreme Judge of the world for the rectitude of our intentions, do, in the Name, and by Authority of the good People of these Colonies, solemnly publish and declare, That these United Colonies are, and of Right ought to be Free and Independent States; that they are Absolved from all Allegiance to the British Crown, and that all political connection between them and the State of Great Britain, is and ought to be totally dissolved; and that as Free and Independent States, they have full Power to levy War, conclude Peace, contract Alliances, establish Commerce, and to do all other Acts and Things which Independent States may of right do. And for the support of this Declaration, with a firm reliance on the protection of divine Providence, we mutually pledge to each other our Lives, our Fortunes and our sacred Honor*

## Lemuel Barret is appointed Captain of a rifle company

The minutes[1539] of the July 16, 1776 meeting of the Maryland Council of Safety include the statement:

*Ordered, That a Warrant be made out, agreeable to a Resolution of Convention, to Lemuel Barret, Esquire, appointed Captain of the Rifle Company to be raised in Frederick County; and that Warrants be made out, agreeable to a recommendation from the Committee of Observation for Frederick County, to Peter Contee Hanson, First Lieutenant; James Lingan, Second Lieutenant; and Richard Dorsey, Third Lieutenant, of said Company.*

## Barret is replaced by Thomas Beal as Captain of the Rifle Company

The minutes[1540] of the July 25, 1776 meeting of the Maryland Council of Safety include the statement:

*Warrant issued to Mr. Thomas Beall, appointed Captain of the Rifle Company to be raised in Frederick County, in the room of Lemuel Barrett, who never acted agreeable to his warrant.*

## Clinton and Cresap are appointed as local Militia Captains in 1776

The minutes[1541] of the July 26, 1776 meeting of the Maryland Council of Safety include the following:

*Ordered That Commissions issue to the following Persons appointed Officers of Militia Companies in Skipton District in Frederick County, to wit.*

---

[1539] **"American Archives"**.

[1540] **"American Archives"**.

[1541] **"Journal and Correspondence of the Maryland Council of Safety, July 7: December 31, 1776"**.

*Dan<sup>l</sup> Cresap, Capt.*   *Andrew Hynes Cap<sup>t</sup>*   *Charles Clinton Cap<sup>t</sup>*
*Sam<sup>l</sup> Hobbs 1 L<sup>t</sup>*   *Isaac Mekrakin 1 L<sup>t</sup>*   *Dickson Simkins 1 L<sup>t</sup>*
*John Henet 2 L<sup>t</sup>*   *Ezekiel Cox 2 L<sup>t</sup>*   *John House 2 L<sup>t</sup>*
  *Rob<sup>t</sup> Floary Ens.*   *John Hays Ens.*

*Jacob Heagle, Ens.*

Clinton's appointment as Captain suggests that he already had a track record of supporting the American cause, which helps to identify him as the individual listed in Scharf's book.

### Washington County is formed

Washington County was formed[1542] from Frederick County at the State Convention on September 6, 1776:

*Whereas, It appears to this convention that the erecting two new counties out of Frederick County will conduce greatly to the ease and convenience of the people thereof;*

*Resolved, That after the first day of October next such part of the said county of Frederick as is contained within the bounds and limits following, to-wit: Beginning at the place where the temporary line crosses South Mountain, and running thence by a line on the ridge of the said mountain to the River Potowmack, .and thence with the lines of said county so as to include all the lands westward of the line running on the ridge of the South Mountain, as aforesaid, to the beginning, shall be and is hereby erected into a new county by the name of Washington County. ...*

*Resolved, That the inhabitants of said county of Washington shall have, hold and enjoy all such rights and privileges as are held and enjoyed by the inhabitants of any county in this State. ...*

Fort Cumberland was now within the bounds of Washington County.

### A newly mapped road to the Casselman River

The October 15, 1776 Sayer and Bennett map of the middle British colonies is a slight variation of the highly schematic and often copied 1755 Lewis Evans map. One difference from the Evans map is a route from Fort Cumberland to the Casselman River that lies north of, and generally parallel to Braddock's road.

### Laying in provisions at Fort Cumberland in 1776

The 1843 book "**American Archives**" includes the *"Plan of General Stephen"*, which includes the following:

*The new recruits of the seven companies to be raised in Youghyougania, Mononolia, and Ohio, to be marched by Fort Cumberland, the nearest way to Lancaster. The Commissaries and men best acquainted with the country to lay in provisions for them at Speirs, Redstone,[1543] The Great Meadows, Great Crossing, and Fort Cumberland.*

---

[1542] "**A History of Washington County, Maryland...**", 1906.

[1543] Redstone is the place now known as Brownsville, Pennsylvania. At some point, Redstone started being used as a departure point for trips downriver by pioneers. For example, Volume 13 of the 1834 "**Hazard's register of Pennsylvania**" describes an iron tablet that had just been cast that stated *"JACOB YODER, Was born in Reading, Pennsylvania, August 11th, 1738: And was a Soldier in the Revolutionary Army in 1777 and 1778. He emigrated to the West in 1780, and in May, 1782, from Fort Redstone, on the Monongahela River, in the FIRST FLAT BOAT that ever descended the Mississippi. He landed at New Orleans with a cargo of produce. He died April 7, 1832, at his Farm in*

This was enclosed with George Washington's December 20, 1776 letter to John Hancock. It suggests that there were structures at Fort Cumberland and the other referenced locations that could be used for storing provisions in 1776.

## A family tradition of a 1776 trail northward from Braddock's road

A 1911 issue of the "**Meyersdale Republican**" includes an article titled "*A Chapter of Early History of Meyersdale*". The article was written by John M. Olinger, who was the grandson of an early pioneer at the site of Meyersdale. According to the article, *"Mr. Olinger's grandfather located here in 1776 and originally owned the land on which the greater portion of the town of Meyersdale is now situated."*

The article states:

> *After he bought this land he returned to his family in York county, gathered his few goods, and started in a two-horse wagon for his new home. He came by the way of Hagerstown and Cumberland, Md, following Gen. Braddock's trail, the route over which the National ____ [1544] was later built. A few miles west of the present site of Frostburg, Md., he left that trail, and struck out for Pocahontas, or a point near that ancient village,[1545] where stood an inhabited hut in which he put up for the night. He tethered his horses out in the open to help themselves with grass and leaves. Next morning, he fed his two horses a loaf of bread, his horse feed having given out. As the country between Pocahontas and Sparta (now Meyersdale) was at that time an almost impenetrable forest, he secured the services of two men of the family whose hospitality he had enjoyed, to help him from there to his new home. It took from early morning until late in the evening to make this last state of the journey. The Pocahontas people who sheltered him and his family were quite poor, yet they gave the best they had and sent the two men along without any pay.*

This Olinger family tradition, if true, indicates the 1776 existence of a road or trail that ran from Braddock's road to the vicinity of the eventual site Pocahontas. Such a route may have included a section of the Turkey Foot Road and is a possible candidate to include the antecedent to Finzel Road.

---

*Spencer County, Kentucky, and lies here interred beneath this tablet."* Thaddeus Harris' 1805 book "**Journal of a Tour...**" describes the flat boats then used by traders heading downriver on the Monongahela as follows, *"These boats are generally called 'Arks;' and are said to have been invented by Mr. Krudger, on the Juniata, about ten years ago. They are square, and flat-bottomed; about forty feet by fifteen, with sides six feet deep; covered with a roof of thin boards, and accommodated with a fire-place. They will hold from 200 to 400 barrels of flour. They require but four hands to navigate them; carry no sail, and are wafted down by the current."*

[1544] My copy of the article is missing a fragment here, but the missing word would obviously be *"road"* or *"highway"*.

[1545] The village of Pocahontas was founded much later than 1776.

# 29. 1777: Lead is delivered to Fort Cumberland

**Robert Gregg is involved in a property transaction on Patterson Creek**

The 1939 book "**Early Records Hampshire County Virginia**" records the following for March 7, 1777, *"GREGG, Robert of Washington Co. (w. Margaret) to Benjamin Parker of Hampshire Co. (lease and release) 100 a. on Patterson Creek; rec. 9-11-1778. Wit.: Sam Dew, Wm. Buffington, Isaac Parsons."*

**A Daniel Cresap land transaction on the South Branch**

The 1939 book "**Early Records Hampshire County Virginia**" records the following for June 9, 1777, *"CRESAP, Daniel Washington Co., Md. (w. Ruth) to Peter Haines Hampshire Co. 180 a. on South Branch; rec. 8-12-1777. Wit.: Sam Dew, Thomas Collins, John Roussaw, Michael Cresap, Wm. Buffington, Enoch Berry."*

**George Morgan's responsibilities grow to include provisioning the western troops**

Part of Morgan's responsibilities included gathering various types of supplies for Indian conferences. This activity snowballed into acquiring provisions for the western forts and expeditions, resulting in the rank of Colonel.

According to Volume 8, "**Journals of the Continental Congress**", page 476, on June 18, 1777, Congress recorded:

*That the commissary general be directed to supply Colonel George Morgan, with five hundred bushels of salt, to be forwarded to Fort Pitt, for curing[1546] the provisions directed by Congress to be stored there.*

According to page 502 of the same book, on June 27, 1777, the Congress recorded:

*That there be advanced to Colonel George Morgan, 20,000 dollars,[1547] for compleating the payment of monies he has engaged for on contracts for provisions, which are directed to be laid up in magazines at Fort Pitt, for the supply of the different garrisons in that quarter; for the expenditure of which, the said Colonel George Morgan is to be accountable.*

*Ordered, That the same be advanced.*

These are a few examples, among many, of Morgan's role in provisioning Fort Pitt.

---

[1546] Salt was used for preserving meat before the advent of refrigeration. My father Roy Dietle indicated that during his Larimer Township, Somerset County, Pennsylvania boyhood, his family made salt pork before the advent of rural electrification allowed the use of refrigerators and freezers. He was describing common knowledge and skills that were being lost to the generations that followed his. His boyhood home was electrified in 1940. Salt became very scarce during the Revolutionary War, which added to Morgan's supply problems.

[1547] During the Revolutionary War, paper currency known as *"Continentals"* was issued by the Continental Congress. Some denominations indicate the value in *"Spanish Milled Dollars"*, while others just reference the *"dollar"*. The *"Continental"* depreciated severely. By 1780, it was only valued at roughly 2.5 percent of its initial face value. Printing was discontinued in 1780. This severe depreciation was a significant problem that Morgan and others reference in correspondence.

### Captain at Cumberland in 1777

Dorman's book "**Virginia Revolutionary pension applications**" indicates that a company of Maryland forces at Cumberland was commanded by Captain Charles Clinton in 1777.

### Delivering a large stock of lead to Fort Cumberland in the summer of 1777

The 1832 pension application of Christopher Hains includes the following:

*That he entered the service of the United States as a regular soldier in June or July 1777 under Captain Samuel Gilkerson in the town of Winchester in the County of Frederick and State of Virginia, for an indefinite term as he supposed, depending for its duration on the will of his officers or during the Revolutionary War. He states that shortly after his enlistment as aforesaid he was one of the guard of about twelve soldiers entrusted with the safe conveyance of five or six wagons loaded with lead from Winchester Virginia to Fort Pitt and proceeded on the way with his said charge as far as Fort Cumberland at or near which place the company met with General McIntosh, by whom they were ordered to deposit the lead at Fort Cumberland, it being unsafe in his opinion as stated to proceed further as many points of the intermediate country were held by hostile Indians who would intercept and take it.*

This deposition suggests that there was at least one building at Fort Cumberland that could be used for storing several wagon loads of lead.

### Two Cresap land transactions in Virginia

The 1939 book "**Early Records Hampshire County Virginia**" records the following for August 8, 1777, *"CRESAP, Thomas of Washington Co. to Jacob Slagle of Hampshire Co. (lease and release) 150 a. on Patterson Creek; rec. 8-12-1777. Wit.: Michael Cresap, James Tarpley, James Dale."* The book also records the following for August 9, 1777, *"CRESAP, Thomas of Washington Co., Md. to James Deale of Hampshire Co. (lease) 100 a. on South Branch; rec. 8-12-1777. Wit.: Michael Cresap, James Tarpley, Jacob Slagle."*

### Brodhead's forces marched to Fort McIntosh via Fort Cumberland in 1777

The 1882 book "**Combined History of Schuyler and Brown Counties, Illinois**" describes the pension application of George Taylor, stating:

*George Taylor, a resident of the county, on the 3d day of September, 1833, made declaration that in September, 1777, in Amherst county, Virginia, he enlisted in the regiment commanded by Col. Broadhead, attached to the command of Gen. McIntosh His regiment marched to Fort Cumberland, thence to the place of Braddock's defeat in Pennsylvania, thence to the Ohio river where a fort called McIntosh was built ... Of those who vouched for Taylor's standing in the community, and avowed their belief in the truth of his statement, are the Rev. Peter Cartwright, the celebrated pioneer Methodist preacher.*

Volume 2 of the 1908 book "**Historical Encyclopedia of Illinois**" states:

*George Taylor enlisted in September, 1777, in Capt. Samuel Schackelford's company, commanded by Col. Broadhead, of Amherst County Va He was first sent to Fort Cumberland and served four months and a half. He Reenlisted four times ... Rev. Peter Cartwright vouched for Mr. Taylor's good character.*

These passages are not documentary evidence; however, it is likely that copies of Taylor's pension papers are available from the National Archives.

## Morgan is relieved of duties during a treason investigation

The Indian situation worsened, despite George Morgan's sincere efforts. People turned against him, and he was falsely accused of treason. The resulting investigation, which exonerated him, also left a record of his accomplishments, which included going beyond his official duties and supplying the western forts so they could remain occupied. During the investigation, Morgan was temporarily relieved of his duties. On October 15, 1777, Congress:

*Resolved, That a deputy commissary general of purchases and a deputy commissary general of issues be appointed for supplying the forts and posts on the western frontiers of Pennsylvania and Virginia. ...*

*That the said deputy commissary general of issues be directed to receive from Colonel George Morgan, all the provisions in his possession belonging to the United States...*

On October 22, 1777, Congress:

*Resolved, That a committee of three be appointed to enquire into the conduct of colonel Morgan; and that he be required forthwith to repair to Congress for that purpose; and that a proper person be appointed to perform the duties entrusted to colonel Morgan until the event of such enquiry...*

Morgan acknowledges this suspension in a November 11, 1777 letter, reproduced in the 1904 "**History of Beaver County...**",[1548] which references *"your Letter of the 30th inclosing a copy of the Resolve of Congress on the 22nd Ulto.,*[1549] *suspending me from my employments in consequence of certain Reports injurious to my Character, representing me as unfriendly to the Cause of America..."*[1550] On November 20, 1777, Congress decided to allow the indefatigable Morgan to continue his work while the treason investigation continued, resolving as follows:

*Resolved, That the case of Colonel G. Morgan be included in the business referred to the consideration of the commissioners who are to be appointed for various purposes on the western frontiers: that, in the mean while, Colonel Morgan be restored to the appointment of agent for Indian affairs, and that he be appointed deputy-commissary general of purchases in the western district.*

## Members of the Coxes Creek settlement retreat via Cumberland circa 1777

Pages 128 and 129 of Volume II of the 1906 book "**History of Bedford and Somerset Counties...**" provide the recollections of Joseph Ankeny, the youngest son of the pioneer Peter Ankeny, concerning the Cox's Creek settlement (now Somerset Pennsylvania). He heard the tales often from his mother, and described them in an 1870 letter to David Husband:

*My uncle, Christian Ankeny,*[1551] *moved to what is now called Somerset county, from Washington county, Maryland, in the spring of 1772 or '73, my father accompanying him, but leaving mother and one child*

---

[1548] This book states, *"General Hand...was constantly hampered by circumstances beyond his control... One difficulty with which he had to contend was the suspicion which arose during the summer of 1777 as to the loyalty of some of the inhabitants of western Pennsylvania and Virginia. Some of the best men in Pittsburg were arrested, among whom was Colonel George Morgan, the United States Indian Agent. Even General Hand himself was suspected".*

[1549] *"Ulto"* means the previous month.

[1550] The letter goes on to list some of his contributions to the American cause, including *"...my having prevented the total Evacuation of the Posts on the Ohio for want of Provisions, through the Neglect or Inability of those instructed to supply them..."*, and requests a speedy hearing.

[1551] Christian Ankeny was taxed in Brothersvalley Township, Bedford County in 1774 (**Pennsylvania Archives**, Third Series, Volume XXII).

*in Maryland. ... My father, Peter Ankeny, commenced his farm[1552] on the Hugus farm, around the spring where the present buildings are now located. He built his log cabin just below the spring, the spring house being the lower story. He cleared several acres where the old orchard now remains, and sowed it in wheat that fall, and returned to Maryland in the spring for his family. He took his wife and only child on horseback, with some pack horses to carry their clothes and bedding, and a ten-plate stove weighing not less than four hundred pounds. With this caravan they took their winding pathway over the Allegheny mountains, full of hope to open a new home in the wilderness for themselves and their posterity. Oh! Here I cannot help but shed tears on reflection of how they must have felt leaving the land of their birth and going to a wilderness of savages. ...*

*Reports of Indian depredations and massacres in Ligonier valley and elsewhere kept the settlement in constant apprehension, and many of them, taking their cattle along, left the country for a time. These were trying times on women and children — at night the cattle bellowing, horses neighing, and the whole neighborhood stock concentrated in one drove, and these crowded and pressed forward on a crooked path, with the fear of an attack in the rear or an ambush in front. Some took the trail by Bedford and McConnell's valley, and others went by Cumberland and Hancock.*

The referenced Indian depredations in the Ligonier valley may be those that occurred during the winter of 1777/1778. A November 4, 1777 letter by Lieutenant Archibald Lochry includes the statement, "...*Eleven other Persons Kill'd and scalped at Palmer's fort Near Loganear amongst which is Ensin Woods at the place where Col Campble was maid prisoner...*"

A November 14, 1777 letter[1553] the Council of Safety wrote to congress describes written complaints of Indian depredations in Westmoreland County, and goes on to state:

*We are further informed by verbal accounts that an extent of 60 miles has been evacuated to the Savages full of Stock Corn, Hoggs & Poultry that they have attacked Palmers Fort about 7 miles from Ligonier without success; and from the information of White Eyes[1554] & other circumstances that Fort Ligonier has been by this time attacked. There is likewise reason to fear the ravages will extend to Bedford & along the frontier.*

The Indian depredations that caused alarm in the Cox's Creek settlement[1555] also could have been those that occurred in the spring of 1778. A May 4, 1778 letter written from Bedford, Pennsylvania by John Piper states:

---

[1552] According to an 1870 letter by Joseph Ankeny that was published in the September 29, 1893 "**Somerset Standard**", his father Peter's house and spring were fortified with *"a stockade of split timber, 15 feet high"*.

[1553] Volume II, page 115 of the 1906 book "**History of Bedford and Somerset Counties...**"

[1554] White Eyes was a Delaware Indian Chief who named one of his sons after George Morgan. The son was educated at Princeton at the expense of the United States (see "**Journals of Congress, 1779**", pages 652 and 656), and along with two other sons, was cared for by George Morgan. In a May 1784 letter to Thomas Mifflin (president of Congress), George Morgan speaks of the youngest son George as follows, *"...the third, who was then in his eighth year, is every way worthy the further patronage of Congress, having now entered Virgil and begun Greek, and being the best scholar in his class, he will be prepared to enter College next Fall. His mildness of disposition is equl to his capacity; and I cannot but take the liberty to entreat a continuance of the patronage of Congress to this worthy orphan, whose father was treacherously put to death at the moment of his greatest exertions to save the United States, in whose service he held the commission of a colonel. His son is now in his thirteenth year. ... I have carefully concealed and shall continue to conceal from young White Eyes the Manner of his Father's death, which I have never mentioned to any one but Mr. Thompson & two or three Members of Congress."*

[1555] For David Husband's circa 1870 published account of Isaac Cox and the Cox's Creek Glades, which is based on the early settler Harmon Husband's journal, see the book "**Recollections of Somerset County's Earliest Years**".

*In the County of Westmoreland, at a little Fort called Fort Wallace within some sixteen or twenty miles of Fort Ligonier, there were nine men killed and one man, their Captn, wounded last week; the Party of Indians was very numerous…*

## Virginia ratifies the Articles of Confederation

On December 16, 1777, Virginia ratified the *"Articles of Confederation and Perpetual Union"*. It was the first state to do so. Maryland was the last of the original 13 states to do so, finally agreeing on March 1, 1781.

## Washington's forces arrive at Valley Forge on December 19, 1777

The following description of Washington's forces at Valley Forge is from Volume 3 of the 1788 book, **"The History of the Rise, Progress, and Establishment, of the Independence of the United States of America…"**:

*The American army marched from White Marsh to Sweed's Ford. The want of clothing was so extreme, that gen. Washington was under the absolute necessity of granting warrants to different officers to impress what the holders would not willingly part with, agreeable to the powers with which congress had invested him, He removed with the troops, on the 19th, to Valley-forge, where they hutted, about sixteen miles from Philadelphia. When the mode of hutting was first proposed, some treated the idea as ridiculous, few thought it practicable, and all were surprised at the facility with which it was executed. It was certainly a considerable exertion for the remnant of an army, exhausted and worn down, by the severity of a long and rather unsuccessful campaign, to sit down in a wood, and in the latter end of December to begin to build themselves huts. Through the want of shoes and stockings, and the hard frozen ground, you might have tracked the army from White Marsh to Valley-forge by the blood of their feet. The taking of this position was highly requisite. Had the army retired to the towns in the interior parts of the state, a large tract of fertile country would have been exposed to ravage and ruin; and they must have distressed in a peculiar manner the virtuous citizens from Philadelphia, who had fled thither for refuge.*

## General Hand writes about Colonel George Morgan

On December 21, 1777 General Edward Hand wrote a letter to Richard Henry Lee, Richard Law, and Daniel Roberdeau from Fort Pitt that includes the following:

*The report of Col. George Morgan's being arrested here was well founded, the Express (a Militia Officer) who brought the enclosed Letter from Col. Zach: Morgan informed some of his Acquaintance in Town, that the principal People here concerned in the Conspiracy, were Col. Geo. Morgan, Col. John Campbell, Capt. Alexr McKee & Simon Girty, and that the Reason they were not pointed out in the Letter was, that, I was myself suspected. From this Information I judged it prudent to secure these Persons to prevent their escaping the Punishment they deserved, if Guilty … Col. Campbell before he had learned my Intention of arresting him, waited on me, and desired Permission to accompany me, which I agreed to, & told Col. George Morgan he might have the same Liberty, which he declined, being then, he said very busie, and remained a Prisoner in his own House. … I was present at the Examination of the greatest Number of the Prisoners, and learned from the Magistrates who examined the whole, that no more than one Man mentioned Col. George Morgan's Name … for this Reason on my Return I took off Col. Morgan's Arrest … I must declare in Justice to him, that every Proceeding of his, that came to my Knowledge, either as Indian Agent, or Commissary, appeared to me, to be that of a Zealous and faithful Servt to the United*

*States. I should have made early mention of his Arrest, but as it is on a groundless Assertion, I wished to have it buried in Oblivion.*[1556]

---

[1556] At least two published versions of this letter exist and vary in small details. One is in the 1912 book "**Frontier defense on the upper Ohio, 1777-1778**", and the other is in the 1919 book "**The Pennsylvania Magazine of History and Biography**".

# 30. 1778: Military activity at Fort Cumberland

### Packing flour from Fort Cumberland to Fort Redstone in 1778

John Bradberry's 1838 pension application includes the statement:

*This next tour of duty in the army of the united states was in the year 1777 or early in the year 1778. He entered said service as a volunteer Twelve mounths more in Captain Mark Harden company of Twelve mounths volunteers unless sooner discharged he entered again in said state of Pennsylvania, but is unable to state the County of said state where said company rendezvoused. he states that he only served Eleven mounths on this tour. during the whole of which time he was engaged in active service as one of a detachment who were employed in packing flour on horses from a place called "old Fort Cumberland" in said state of Pennsylvania to a Fort a short distance below the junction of the Allegany and Monongahelia Rivers called "Fort Red Stick" he believes said last mentioned Fort was also in said state of Pennsylvania, at the expiration of Eleven mounths he was regularly discharged by his Captain Mark Harden which said discharge was destroyed when his house was burnt as above stated.*

The referenced *"Fort Red Stick"* seems to obviously be Fort Redstone. Another deposition, from 1779, describes bringing flour to Fort Cumberland using wagons. These two depositions suggest that there was at least one building at Fort Cumberland that could be used for storing the flour that was brought in on wagons, until such a time it could be loaded onto packhorses.

### A 1778 map shows buildings on both sides of the river

In 1778, Antonio Zatta published a book in Venice, Italy that includes an updated version of a section of John Mitchell's 1755 map that is titled *"Il Maryland, il Jersey Meridionale, la Delaware"*.[1557] While both maps name the New Store at the mouth of Wills Creek, the 1755 map illustrates the fort, while the 1778 map illustrates a building on the Virginia side of the Potomac River, and another building on the Maryland side of the river.[1558] Another update is a completely different route to Bedford. The 1778 route is on the east side of Wills Creek, while part of the route on the 1755 map is on the west side of Wills Creek. The road change suggests the map was revised based on post-1755 information forwarded from North America. Although one should not read too much into what is illustrated on early maps, this map suggests that the new store may have still been operating in the late 1770s, with at least one other building on the Maryland side of the Potomac River.

---

[1557] The map was brought to the attention of the Western Maryland History group by John DeVault.

[1558] The fact that the fort is missing on the map was first noticed by James Conlon. The fact that the map illustrates a building on each side of the Potomac River at Wills Creek was first noticed by Dan Press.

This is the 1778 Italian map *"Il Maryland, il Jersey Meridionale, la Delaware"*, which is an adaptation of John Mitchell's 1755 map. It suggests, but does not prove, that the new store was still open in the late 1770s.

### The United States enters an alliance with France

American and French representatives signed the Treaty of Alliance and the Treaty of Amity and Commerce in Paris on February 6, 1778. On March 17, 1778, a few days after being informed that the United States had been officially recognized as an independent nation by France, Britain declared war on France. Through this chain of events, France became engaged in the American Revolutionary War, and the multifaceted 1778 to 1783 Anglo-French War.

### A new Quartermaster General

General Nathanael Greene was a skilled strategist, and a close confidant and trusted advisor of George Washington. On March 2, 1778, Congress appointed Greene as Quartermaster General, and appointed John Cox and Charles Petit as Greene's Assistant Quartermasters-General. Greene would have preferred a more glorious post but dug into his new responsibilities. In his role as Quartermaster General, he had a significant influence on events in Fort Cumberland that occurred during 1779.

### Andrew Bruce's Oath of Fidelity list from the environs of Fort Cumberland

The 1778 *"Oath of Fidelity and Support"* lists provide some sense of population density in what would become Allegany County. Andrew Bruce's list of men who signed the Maryland Oath of Fidelity, dated March 2, 1778, includes the following names, many of which are recognizable from later records of the Arnold's settlement area:

*Lemuel Barritt; Joshua Luman; Alexander McLoney; William Logsdon;[1559] Barton Luman; Christopher Salmon; John Durbin; Samuel Mackenzie; Thomas Cardry; James Guest; Jacob Tarwalter; Larin Harden; Thomas Warring; Adam Woolback; Daniel Salmon; Joseph Nicholas; Jacob Schultz; John Hanes; George Kelly; Charles Clinton; Godfrey Woolback; Lewis Davison; Thomas Humphry; John*

---

[1559] At the time of Deakins' survey, William Logsdon had lots 3371, 3372, 3381, and 3382.

*Constable; Richard Mattingly; Nicholas Durbin; John Luman; Joshua Davis; Daniel Mackenzie; Moses Luman; Joseph Mattingly; Henry Porter; Isaac Lemaster; Richard Chinoth; Denis Carter; Henry Mattingly; John Tomlinson; Loudon Trotter; Johnse Barkshire; Robert Gregg; Charles Coulson; Thomas Chinoth; John Glasner; Henry Leane; Edward Ward; Samuel Davis; Joseph Lazier; John Plummer; Edward Durbin; John Lazier; Andrew Due; Gabriel Mackenzie; Thomas Plummer; Caleb Luman; Aaron Mackenzie; Andrew Rice; Andrew House; George Richardson; James Hill; Edward Wilson; John Nichole; Frederick Valentine; William Winfield; Stephen Constable; William Durbin; Joseph Workman; Thomas Constable; George Aller; Stephen Workman; Barnet Mattingly; James Haagland; Andrew Workman; Dickinson Simpkins; Samuel Durbin; John Workman; David Swank; John Kennedy; Isaac Workman; Dickenson Simpkins, Sr.; Timothy Connar; Joseph Marsner.*

Along with this list, Andrew Bruce provided the following statement:

*I Certify to the Honorable the Governor and Council, that the Within persons gave their affirmation to and subscribed the Oath of Fidelity to the State of Maryland according to the Act of Assembly and that this is a true Copy of the Book kept by me for that purpose and delivered to the Clerk of this County as ordered.*

### *Analysis of Bruce's list*

This is an important list because it provides a snapshot of local residents in 1778, and it seems useful to investigate these individuals further. Lemuel Barrett is a well-known local resident who is mentioned many times in this book. A Joshua Looman is on the 1783 Upper Old Town and Cumberland hundreds lists. An Alexander Maloney is on the 1783 Upper Old Town Hundred list. A William Logsdon is on Deakins' list of settlers westward of Fort Cumberland. A Barton Looman is on the 1783 Upper Old Town and Cumberland hundreds lists. A John Durbin is on the 1783 Wills Town and Sandy Creek hundreds lists and on Deakins' list. Samuel McKinsey is on the 1783 Wills Town and Sandy Creek hundreds lists and on Deakins' list. A James Guest is on the 1783 Cumberland Hundred list and stated in a 1786 deposition that he had been living on the same property since about 1774. A Thomas Warring and Joseph Nichells are on the 1783 Cumberland Hundred list. A Jacob Shulsa is on the 1783 Wills Town and Sandy Creek hundreds lists and may be Jacob Schultz. A George Kelly is on the 1783 Upper Old Town and Cumberland hundreds lists. Charles Clinton is a well-known local resident and was living on Walnut Bottom in 1782. A Thomas Humphry is on the 1783 Skipton Hundred list. A John Constable and Richard Mattingly are on the 1783 Cumberland Hundred list. A Nicholas Durbin is on Deakins' list. A Joshua Davis is on the 1783 Cumberland Hundred list. A Daniel McKinsey is on the 1783 Wills Town and Sandy Creek hundreds lists. A Moses Lowman and Joseph Mattingly are on the 1783 Cumberland Hundred list. A Henry Porter is on the 1783 Wills Town and Sandy Creek hundreds lists. A Richard Chinoth is on the 1783 Upper Old Town and Cumberland hundreds lists. A Henry Mattingly is on the 1783 Wills Town and Sandy Creek hundreds lists and Deakins' list. John Tomlinson was already a local millwright in 1771, was on the 1783 Wills Town and Sandy Creek hundreds lists and obtained three lots in *"Washington Town"* (Cumberland) in 1785. A Robert Gregg was on the 1783 Skipton and Murleys Run hundreds lists. A Charles Coulson was involved in lawsuits with several local people in 1779. A John Glaisner is on the 1783 Wills Town and Sandy Creek hundreds lists. A Henry Leane witnessed a baptism near Fort Cumberland in 1768. One has to wonder if Edward Ward is Captain Trent's 1754 Ensign. A John Plummer appears in a 1757 court record regarding the theft of livestock from himself and Thomas Cresap. An Edward Durbin appears in the 1783 Wills Town and Sandy Creek hundreds lists and was appointed commissioner of a local road in 1791. Gabriel McKinsay is on the Wills Town and Sandy Creek hundreds lists and on Deakins' list and is a well-known member of Arnold's settlement. A Thomas Plummer and Andrew Rice are on the 1783 Cumberland Hundred list. An Andrew House is on the Upper Old Town Hundred list and on Deakins' list. A George Richardson is on the 1783 Wills Town and Sandy Creek hundreds lists. A James Hill is on the 1783 Cumberland Hundred list. A John Nichells appears in the 1783 Cumberland Hundred list. A Frederick Valentine, Stephan Constable, and William Durbun are on the 1783 Cumberland Hundred list, and William Durbane is on Deakins' list. A Joseph Workman is on the Wills Town and Sandy Creek hundreds lists. A Thomas Constable is on the 1783 Cumberland Hundred list. A Stephen Workman is on the 1783 Wills Town and Sandy Creek hundreds lists and on Deakins' list. A Barnet Mattingly is on the Upper Old Town and Cumberland hundreds lists. An Andrew Workman is on the 1783 Wills Town and Sandy Creek hundreds lists, and on Deakins' list. Although it is difficult to distinguish father from son, a Dickerson Simpkins reported in a deposition that he was already living on Wills Creek by 1771 and was still living there circa 1821. A Samuel Durbin is on the Wills Town and Sandy Creek hundreds lists and on Deakins' list. A John Workman is on the 1783 Wills Town and Sandy Creek hundreds lists and on Deakins' list. A David Swank is on the 1783 Cumberland Hundred list. An Isaac Workman is on the 1783 Wills Town and Sandy Creek hundreds lists and Deakins' list. A Timothy Conner is on the 1783 Wills Town and Sandy Creek hundreds lists.

## Samuel Barrit's list of individuals who signed the 'Oath of Fidelity and Support'

Samuel (probably Lemuel[1560]) Barrit's list, dated March 16, 1778, also includes some names that are easily recognizable as being from the general environs of Fort Cumberland:

*Daniel Cresop; John Maichal; Joshua Stratford; Joseph Cresop; Richard Clark; James Staddert; Henry Gunterman; Tarance Dial; Thomas Cresop; John Ranady; Peter Gunteman; Henry Conrad; William Dorson; Sr.; Robert Gragg, Jr.; John Kimberlan; Martin Dewitt; Moses Ayers, Sr.; Benjamin Power; Jacob Kimbelan; Edward Dawson; Jonathan Clark; William Rashr; Joseph Lee; William Grimes; William Anderson; Peter Dewitt; Joseph Reed; Edward Dorson; Joseph Davies; Thomas Talbard; Samuel Hubbs; Reynon Roman; James Crage; Joseph Callard; Thomas Dawson; Nathaniel Parker; Geo. Hall Ritchards; George Layport; James Prather; Dennis Quick; Allon Dorson; John Scott; Thomas Quick; Edward Dorson; William Posttethwort; Jacob Quick; John King; Jeremiah Allin; Aaron Quick; Samuel Right; John Clark; Moses Munop; Alworth Thornin; Vallentine Horn; Andrew Quick; Zapheniah Ball; William Clouge; Benjamin Quick; Benjamin Hull; Callob Russell; Peter Bonham; Joseph Lee, Jr.; William Cassart; Andrew Breeze; Jeremiah Anderson; James Pairs; Wm. Lee; Jacob Oldwort; Daniel Cassart; James Dorson, Jr.; Joseph Mounts; John Barsman; Nehemiah Martin; Lanord Lethworth; Jacob Flock; James Dorson, Sr.; Michel Heaton; William Lapear; John Lindsey, Sr.; Charles Ranaday; Daniel Pursel; Peter Little; John Coman; Thomas Pursel; Henry Bray; John Coy; Crosteon Bsnedker; Aaron Quick, Jr.; Henry Devitt; Daniel Lovitt; Isaac Fethworth; John Pursel; Britton Lovitt; William Ray; George Focpeh; Philip Crow; George Markwell; Edward Ward; Isaac Laycock; George Swan; John Bell; Henry Gunerman, Jr.; Homes Hartely; Samuel Forgerson; Joseph Inslow; John Hartely; Robert Munroe; Abraham Blew; Isaac Collyer, Jr. Thomas Feaild; David Smith; Isaac Collyer, Sr.; Jonathan Culver; Aaron Atheron, Jr.; Thomas Chinorsath; James Williams; Samuel Lee, Thomas Charrey; William Ogle; John House; John Been; Thos. James Rook; John Hirsh; James Smith; Cosnealve Ward; John Coy, Jr.; John Lindsey, Sr.; Daniel Cresop, Jr.; James Dewitt; Philip Crow; Aaron Atherton; William Gordon; Samuel Claxton; Joshua Atherton; James Wintors; Benj. Johnson, Snr.; Benjamin Atherton; Abraham Petters; Roger Dumeagin; Charles Prather; John Hubart; Barney Dewitt; William Johnson; Jeremiah Willerson; Timothy Tracy; James Fower; Moses Hugham; Aaron*

---

[1560] I have read a good many original Maryland documents where *"Lemuel"* looks like *"Samuel"*. Careful handwriting analysis is necessary to properly interpret such entries.

*Hughnns; Philip Wiggins; David Pursell; Eran James; Robert Flower; William Howell; Moses Ayers, Jr.; Philip Tramell; Isaac Deware; John Atherton; William Moore; Isaac Logston.*

### Analysis of Barrett's list

Some of the names on Barret's are duplicates of those on Bruce's list. Nevertheless, it seems worthwhile to analyze this list in the same manner that Bruce's list was analyzed. Daniel Cresap was a well-known local resident who appears many times in this book. A Joshua Stratford is on the 1783 Skipton Hundred list and was involved in a lawsuit with Thomas Cresap in the 1778/79 timeframe. A Joseph Cresap, Henry Guntryman, Martin Dewitt, Peter Dewitt, Joseph Davis, George Layport, James Prather, Richard Clarke, John Coy, Henry Dewitt, James Dewitt, William Ray, Philip Crow, George Markwell, Robert Munroe, Samuel Ferguson, Aron Atherton, William Ogle, Henry Guntryman, William Johnson, Timothy Tracy, and Daniel Lovett are on the 1783 Upper Old Town Hundred list. A James Stoddert and John Kimberly are on the 1783 Skipton Hundred list. Thomas Cresap is a well-known local area resident. A Henry Conrod was in a lawsuit with Thomas Cresap in 1778. A Robert Gregg is on the Skipton and Murleys Run hundreds lists and was being prosecuted for *"For Selling Liquors above the Rates"* in 1778. Moses Ayres Junior and Senior are on Deakins' list. An Edward Dawson is on the 1783 Upper Old town and Cumberland hundreds lists, and Edward Dawson Junior and Senior are on Deakins' list. A Joseph Lee is on Deakins' list. A William Anderson is on the 1783 Cumberland and Upper Old town Hundreds lists. A James Craig was involved in a lawsuit with Thomas Cresap in 1778. A Thomas Dawson is on Deakins' list. A Nathaniel Parker was involved in a lawsuit with Thomas Cresap in the 1778/79 timeframe. A James Prather was a chain bearer on a local 1762 survey, a James Prather was appointed Captain in 1778, and a James Prather was in a lawsuit with Thomas Cresap in the 1778/79 timeframe. A Dennis and Jacob, Andrew, Benjamin, and Aron Quick are on the 1783 Upper Old Hundred list. A John King is on the 1783 Upper Old Town and Skipton hundreds lists. A John Clarke is on the 1783 Skipton Hundred list. A Moses Munroe is on the 1783 Upper Old Town Hundred list and a Moses Munro is on Deakins' list; this may be *"Moses Munop"*. Valentine Horn is on the 1783 Skipton Hundred list. A Benjamin Hull is on the 1783 Upper Old Town Hundred list and on Deakins' list. A William Lee is on the 1783 Cumberland Hundred list. Joseph Mounts is referenced above, in relation to Bruce's list. Daniel Pursel is referenced above, in regard to Bruce's list. A John Purcell is on the 1783 Skipton Hundred list and a John Pursley is on the 1772 taxables list of Brothersvalley Township, Bedford County, Pennsylvania. A Briton Lovett is on the 1783 Upper Old town and Cumberland hundreds lists. Edward Ward and Isaac Collier are referenced in regard to Bruce's list. A John House is on the 1783 Upper Old Town Hundred list and Deakins' list and was commissioned as a Second Lieutenant in 1778. An Abraham Peter and Charles Prather are on the 1783 Cumberland Hundred list, and a Charles Prather was involved in a lawsuit with Thomas Cresap in 1779. A Barney Dewitt and William Howell are on the 1783 Upper Old Town Hundred list and Deakins' list. Jeremiah Willison is a well-known local resident who is referenced many times in this book. A William Moore is on Deakins' list.

For the individuals who appear on both a hundreds list and Deakins' list, there's a good chance they were living west of Fort Cumberland already in 1783.

### The text of the 'Oath of Fidelity and Support'

The text of the *"Oath of Fidelity and Support"* follows:

*I do sware I do not hold myself bound to yield any Allegience or obedience to the King of Great Britain his heirs or Successors and that I will be true and faithful to the State of Maryland and will to the utmost of my power, Support maintain and defend the Freedom and Independence thereof and the Government as now established against all open enemies and secret and traterous Conspriaces and will use my utmost endeavours to disclose and make known to the Governor or some one of the Judges or Justices thereof all Treasons or Treaterous Consperaces, attempts or Combinations against this State or the Government thereof which may come to my Knowledge so help me God.*

## George Morgan is exonerated and praised

The investigation of George Morgan was completed in March 1778, and a certificate forwarded to Congress included the statement:

*We the commissioners for the western department, acting under authority of Congress, having, in obedience to our instructions, notice being first given to all the neighbouring countries, proceeded to an enquiry into the conduct of colonel George Morgan, agent for Indian affairs ... after the clearest and most satisfactory testimonies, wholly acquit the said colonel George Morgan of the charges against him, of infidelity to his public trust and disaffection to the American cause; and we testify that we are possest of the knowledge of various facts and circumstances evincing not only his attachment to the cause, but also an uncommon degree of diligence in discharging the duties of his employment, and of the attention to the interests of the United States; and therefore are of opinion he ought to be restored to the fullest confidence of his country.*

## Washington County Court, March 1778

In a section titled *"Recognizances Returned to March Court 1778"* in the Washington County Maryland **"March Court Dockett 1778"** [1561], item 11 is an £50 bond of Charles Clinton, in a case of the State of Maryland versus Charles Clinton, for *"Mary Clinton & Christina Simkins to Testify agst Jan° Walker"*.

In a section titled, *"Original Writs to March Court 1778"*, item no. 1 is the case of Nathaniel Parker versus Benjamin Nicholls, and carries the note *"Lanᶦ Barret Security"*. Item 2 is the case of Lamuol Barret versus Thomas Girty. Item 3 is the case of Lamuol Barret versus Charles Colson. Item 4 is the case of Thomas French Esqʳ versus Thomas Lazear and Thomas Plummer. Item 5 is the case of George French Esqʳ versus Peter and Thomas Malott. Item 9 is the case of James Prather versus Thomas Cresap. Item 15 is the case of Thomas Cresap versus Wᵐ Clows. Item 15 is the case of Thomas Cresap versus George Barnhart. Item 16 is the case of Thomas Cresap versus Nathanᶦ Parker. Item 17 is the case of Thomas Cresap versus Henry Conrod. Item 18 is the case of Thomas Cresap versus Joshua Stradford. Item 52 is the case of Majʳ David Rodgers versus Col Thomas Cresap. Item 58 is the trespass case of Thomas Cresap versus James Peares. Item 59 is the case of Thomas Cresap versus James Craig. Item 68 is a case that involved Acquilla White; a man of that name had a 1775 survey in what is now Somerset County, Pennsylvania, (Book D-8, Page 216) that was on the *"old path leading to Turkeyfoot"*. Item 76 is the case of Thomas Warren versus Enoch Innis & Sarah his wife. Item 77 is the case of Thomas Warren versus Thomas Cresap. (The juxtaposition of items 76 and 77 makes them appear to be related.) Item 101 is the case of John Kennedy versus Jacob Cochenour.

In a titled *"Criminal Writs to March Court 1778"*, item 3 is the case of the State of Maryland versus Robert Gregg *"For Selling Liquors above the Rates"* and item 12 is the State of Maryland versus Robert Gregg for *"Bench Warrᵈ on Compaint of Wm Dawson."*

In a section titled *"Continuances to March Court 1778"*, item 2 is the case of *"Anthony Noble for Thoˢ ___ use"* versus Charles Clinton.

---

[1561] MSA CE395-2.

## Coulston's company is divided between Cresap and Clinton

Volume 21 of the "**Journal and Correspondence of the Council of Maryland, April 1, 1778 through October 26, 1779**" includes a letter from the council to Daniel Hughes, Lieutenant of Washington County, that states, "*Capt Charles Coulston has waited on us and tells us that the Company over which he was appointed Captain is, in your now Disposition of the Militia, broke and divided between Daniel Cresap's & Charles Clinton's Companies.*"

## Enoch Innes represents Hampshire County as a Delegate

In May of 1778, an Enoch Innes was one of two Hampshire County Delegates to the Lower House of the General Assembly of Virginia.[1562] Abram Hite was the other Delegate.

## Commissions are issued to members of the Third or Western Battalion of Militia

On May 16, 1778, the following action[1563] was recorded by the Council of Maryland:

*Commissions issued to Lemuel Barritt appointed Colonel, Andrew Bruce Lieut Col° Joseph Inslow Ensign of Capt. Cresaps Company, David Swank Ensign of Capt. Clintons Comp^y also to James Prather Captain Thomas Humphreys first Lieut. Joseph Read second Lieut, Charles Prather Ens. Philip Pindell Capt. Thomas Hynes, first Lieut, Abraham Cox second Lieut and John Webb Ensign belonging to the Third or Western Battalion of Militia in Washington County*

Quite a few of these men are named in the 1778 Oaths of Fidelity lists from the environs of Fort Cumberland.

## The back inhabitants of Maryland need immediate assistance

The following letter[1564] was sent to R. Beatty by the Council of Maryland on May 16, 1778:

*Sir, The distressed and defenceless Situation of the back Inhabitants makes immediate Assistance necessary we are sending off 100 Musketts and 10 Riffles we do not know how the People are off for amunition but by the Express who says they have a good deal of Lead but are bare of Powder we request you'll immediately send off to Col° Hughs two half Barrels of best musket Powder on a Pack Horse and if he should apply to you for Arms Lead or more Powder furnish him without further Orders as far as necessary or as far as you can pray inform us by the first Opportunity what Number of Public Arms fit for use there are in Frederick and be so obliging as to push White and Razor to finish those for which they have Barrels they may probably be soon wanted*

## The Third or Western Battalion of Militia is called into service

The following letter[1565] was sent to Colonel Beatty by the Council of Maryland on May 16, 1778:

*Information being given to this Board that the Indians have commenced Hostilities on the western Frontiers that many Murders have been committed and that great Numbers of the back settlers in this and the Neighbouring States are flying from their Habitations. It is therefore ordered that such and so many of the third or western Battalion of Militia in Washington County as may be judged necessary by the Col° of that Battalion be immediately called into actual Service for the Defence & Protection of the*

---

[1562] "**Biennial report of the Department of Archives and History of the State of West Virginia**", 1908.

[1563] "**Journal and Correspondence of the Council of Maryland, April 1, 1778 through October 26, 1779**", Vol. 21.

[1564] "**Journal and Correspondence of the Council of Maryland, April 1, 1778 through October 26, 1779**", Vol. 21.

[1565] "**Journal and Correspondence of the Council of Maryland, April 1, 1778 through October 26, 1779**", Vol. 21.

*western Frontiers and to act in Concert or if necessary in Conjunction with the Militia of the Adjoining State of Virginia & Pennsylvania against the Enemy and further that in Case the Lieut of Washington County shall judge a greater Force necessary that he call out into the same Service any part of the other Militia of his County in classes, he having regard to the actual service performed already by any of the service classes.*

## Military supplies are being stored at Fort Cumberland in 1778

The following letter[1566] was sent to Daniel Hughes, lieutenant of Washington County, by the Council of Maryland on May 16, 1778:

*We inclose you the Commissions you wrote for, we have done so under a strong Impression of an absolute Necessity of having the back Militia put immediately in the best State of Defence against the Indians. We wish you had sent us a List of all the Officers, that their Commissions might have been issued together. We are packing up and shall send off in the Morning 100 Musquets and 10 Rifles and write Col° Beatty to send you two half Barrels of best musquet Powder The Express thinks it very unsafe to send the Arms and Powder without a good Guard, least the Disaffected and Deserters about Murlie's Branch should seize them: Would it not be well for the Arms and Powder to be sent by you as far as the Tennoloways, giving Notice to a Company or two about old Town to receive them there and to carry them as far as Old Town or Barretts, where they may be put into the Hands of those who are called into service? We are told there's a pretty good Stock of Lead at Fort Cumberland; both Powder and Lead were sent some Time ago into that Part of the Country and we hope it has been taken Care of. We also write to Colo Beatty to furnish you with more Ammunition and what Arms he can, if you judge a further Supply necessary, & apply for it. The Militia to the Westward we hope may be sufficient, if not, you are to assist them with a Company or two from below, and give us Notice by Express, that we may send Assistance from the Counties below you. You will give orders to Col° Barret conformable to the inclosed Order and we flatter ourselves that the People will exert themselves with Alacrity, as the Necessity of exerting themselves at all will probably be of but short continuance. We have given the Express 20 Dollars towards bearing his Expences, of which advise Col° Barrett. We imagine an issuing Commissary & Forage Master can be wanted but a very little while at Hagar's Town; we suppose it must be for the Continental Business, if so, we think you had better employ some Body for the Time such may be wanted, advising the Board of War of it. The Recruits we wish to have sent forward as soon as possible.*

The *"pretty good stock of lead"* statement in this letter helps to prove that there was a military presence at Fort Cumberland in 1778 and seems to be a reference to the lead that Christopher Hains helped to deliver to the fort in 1777.

## Barett is provided with instructions

The following letter[1567] was sent to Colonel Barrett by the Council of Maryland on May 16, 1778:

*We inclose you a Copy of the Order we have passed in Consequence of your Information of the State of the back Country. We much approve your Resolution to spirit up the People to Fort rather than desert the Country. We have ordered 100 good Musquets & 10 Rifles from hence and two half Barrels of Powder from Frederick Town and, if more should be wanted or Arms or Lead, that such be supplied as far as may be from Frederick Town. Col° Hughes has also Directions, if necessary, to send you a Part of the Militia from below and, if more still should be wanted, we shall march them, for if the People behave well in*

---

[1566] "**Journal and Correspondence of the Council of Maryland, April 1, 1778 through October 26, 1779**", Vol. 21.
[1567] "**Journal and Correspondence of the Council of Maryland, April 1, 1778 through October 26, 1779**", Vol. 21.

*defending themselves, they may expect a Powerful and chearful Assistance. Simkins says he thinks there's Danger of the Deserters and Disaffected taking the Arms and Powder, if sent up for Old Town, without a Guard. We have therefore thought it best a Company or two should receive them about the Tennoloways and, considering the Road, we submit to you whether it would not be well for the Arms to be taken out of the Cases at the Tenoloways and the Men carry them up in their Hands. We hope and expect from the great Change in our Affairs, that you will not be long distressed by the Indians, or we on the Water by the British.*

## Commissions for officers of the Western Battalion were issued in June 1778

Volume 21 of the "**Journal and Correspondence of the Council of Maryland, April 1, 1778 through October 26, 1779**" includes a letter that lists commissions issued to various militia companies, including the Western Battalion of Militia in Washington County:

*Monday 22d June 1778.*

*Present as on Saturday, except T. Sim Lee Esqr*

*Edwd Lloyd Esq Attended*

*Commissions issued to…Evan Baker Capt, Josiah Price first Lieut, Thomas Warley second Lieut, Andrew Potters Ens Griffith Johnson Capt. Jeremiah Willison first Lieut Andrew Dew second Lieut William More Ens Charles Clinton Capt, Dickerson Simpkins first Lieut, John House second Lieut Daniel Cresap Capt. Samuel Hubbs first Lieut, John Hench second Lieut belonging to the third or Western Battalion of Militia in Washington County…"*

Charles Clinton, Daniel Cresap, Dickerson Simpkins, Samuel Hubbs, and Jeremiah Willison are readily identifiable as individuals living in the environs of Fort Cumberland. There are also May 1778 references to Captain Clinton's company and Captain Cresap's company.

## 1778 massacres anger Americans

On July 3, 1778, during what became known as the Wyoming Valley Massacre, Iroquois and Tory raiders from New York killed more than 300 Americans in Pennsylvania. On November 11, 1778, another massacre took place at Cherry Valley, New York, where 32 inhabitants were scalped and killed. One popular idea for retaliation was to attack Canada. These events had a significant influence on the logistical contributions to the war effort that were made by Fort Cumberland in 1779.

## Morgan plans to lay in supplies at Skipton and Fort Cumberland

George Morgan's July 31, 1778 *"Estimate of Provisions necessary for 1300 Men from Novr 1ˢᵗ 1778 to August 31ˢᵗ 1779…"* for the western department includes $50,000 for *"Provisions laid in at Skipton, Fort Cumberland, Berkley, Frederick & Connecocheague & others to be laid in for the Militia, Pack Horse Men, Waggoners &c between those Places and Fort Pitt"*.[1568]

---

[1568] **"The Virginia Magazine of History and Biography"**, October, 1915.

**Thomas Plummer is involved in a court matter**

In a section of the August court docket for Washington County, Maryland titled, *"Original Writs to August Courts 1778"*, item 56 is the case of Thomas French versus Thomas Lazoar and Thomas Plummer. A Thomas French was living near Georges Creek in 1769 and appears in the 1783 hundreds list.

**Another Virginian marches through Fort Cumberland on his way to Fort McIntosh**

John C. Clinkenbeard's 1834 pension application includes the statement:

*This affiant then returned to Berkeley County and State of Virginia and entered the service again for a tour of three moths as a private soldier under Captain Josiah Sweringen and served on the campaign under General McIntosh on the Ohio River, that this service was performed in the year 1778 and altho the tour was normally for three months, yet this affiant had to serve from about the last of August until the evening of the 24th of December (4 Months) when he arrived at home in Berkeley County. All this time affiant discharged the duties of a private soldier in said detachment. Our march was from Berkeley to Fort Cumberland thence to Fort Pitt, then down the Ohio to the mouth of Beaver where we built Ft. McIntosh, thence to the forks of the Muskingum and Tuscononay where we built Fort Lawrence in the year 1780.*

**George Morgan is serving as Purchasing Commissary for the Western Department**

An August 14, 1778 War Office document[1569] describes Morgan as the *"purchasing Commissary for the Western department"*, who in that capacity requested 617,500 pounds of fresh beef.

A September 17, 1778 War Office document[1570] states:

*The Board ... are of the opinion that the whole sum asked for by Col. Morgan, vis. Two hundred and four thousand dollars, will be necessary to enable him to lay in the provisions requisite for the troops kept up on the western frontiers, and which must be maintained, to prevent the inhabitants abandoning their extensive settlements.*

On October 24, 1778, an October 16, 1778 War Office document was read to Congress[1571]. It states:

*The Board have considered of Colonel Morgan's letter of the 12th instant referred to them. It appears by the letter of his agent Mr. Shelton, that 1,000 head of cattle have been purchased for the troops at the westward, and by the information of Mr. Gibson, ye express now here from fort Pitt, that several hundred head have actually been delivered, and by that means General McIntosh has been enabled to commence his expedition before the arrival of supplies from Mr. Lockart; and as the cattle were purchased probably at rather high prices, the Board beg leave to report:*

*That sixty thousand dollars be paid to Colonel George Morgan for the purchases of cattle made by his direction for the troops on the western frontiers, and to defray the expence of purchasing and driving the same; he to be accountable for that sum.*

*The Board beg leave to remind Congress that they reported some time since a large sum to be granted to Colonel Morgan to enable him to lay up salt provisions[1572] and flour for next year, for the troops at the*

---

[1569] Volume 12 of the "**Journals of the Continental Congress**", page 869.

[1570] Volume 12 of the "**Journals of the Continental Congress**", page 870.

[1571] Volume 12 of the "**Journals of the Continental Congress**", pages 1059 and 1060.

[1572] The term *"Salt provisions"* means salted meat.

*westward. The forming such magazines is every day growing more difficult and expensive; and in a little time will probably be quite impracticable.*

Although Lockhart was appointed by Congress to procure supplies for McIntosh's campaign against the Detroit garrison, Morgan's supply contribution was significant.

### 500 packhorses were ordered to Fort Cumberland to supply Fort McIntosh in 1778

Large numbers of packhorses were being used on Braddock's road in 1778. On November 5, 1778, Colonel Richard Campbell wrote a letter to Colonel Archibald Steel and Captain Patrick Lockhart from Fort McIntosh that includes the following order:

*You will Immediately prepare and order all the Horses to be Collected that is fit for service. — You are to have 300 taken out of the number that is fit for service kept for Immediate use at this post, five hundred is to be Immediately sent to Fort Cumberland to bring flour and salt to this post under the Care of Mr Brady. The 300 Horses that is left for immediate use at this post is to be employed in bringing forage that is purchased on this side of the Alligany Mountains till they are Called for, if they should be any more Horses fit for service they are to be employed in bringing in forage to this post till further orders. ... and Col Steel will have a Return made of All the Horses fit for service and in what business they are in and what he intends to load on them with from Fort Cumberland...*

### Enoch Innis is involved in a Virginia land transaction

The 1939 book "**Early Records Hampshire County Virginia**" records the following for November 10, 1778, *"INNIS, Enoch (w. Sarah) of Hampshire Co. to Michael Heter of Washington Co. (lease and release) 162 a. on North Branch of Potomac, 128 a. on North Branch of Potomac: rec. 11-11-1778. Wit.: None."*

### The horses will not be able to return more than once

On November 18, 1778, Colonel Richard Campbell wrote a letter from Fort McIntosh to General Lachlan McIntosh that included the following:

*... this is a Certainty, the five hundred Horses that is now gone to Fort Cumberland to bring flour and Salt to this post will not be able to return more than once this Winter...*

### Guarding prisoners at Fort Cumberland in 1778

Basil Shaw's pension application includes the statement:

*it was in 1778 that I Inlisted for the Term of Three years and the first service that I was Directed to attend to, was to Guard British prisoners at fort Cumberland in Maryland and after some _____ months it was ascertained that Col'n. Rawlins's Reg't Could not be reviv'd there being only Two Company's Enlisted one of them was Commanded by Captain Thos. Beale and the other by Capt'n. A. Tannehill, whome I enlisted with and we were ordered to go on to fort pitt & join the Western army in the Indian War. The two Companys that I was attach'd to was called the Maryland Core, and there was no other Maryland Troops there The 8th Pensylvania Reg't Commanded by Col'n. Broadhead and the 9th Virginia Reg't. Commanded by Col'n J. Gibson and the Marryland Core were all the Troops Except the Militia who was Engage in the Indian Warfare at fort pitt after 4 Months service I was appointed a Serjeant, and Continued in the Western at Different Stations untill my 3 years Expri'd & was Discharged by Capt. Tannehill as a Sergeant*

Basil Shaw's pension application suggests that, in addition to one or more buildings at Fort Cumberland for storing lead and provisions, there was also at least one room or building that was suitable for use as a prison. Volume 14 of the 1857 "**Harper's Magazine**" provides a tradition of such a building, stating, *"On Green Street there are two houses — said to have been built by Braddock — constructed of stout timber, heavily ironed and riveted on both sides. One, from the manner in which its doors are made, is supposed to have been a jail; the other — a two-story log and weather-boarded edifice — still goes by the name of Braddock's Court."* Lowdermilk's 1878 "**History of Cumberland**" describes one of these buildings, stating, *"It is thought that a temporary Jail was made of an old log house of very limited dimensions, which stood on the opposite side of the road, a short distance west of the tavern.[1573] This old house was one of the structures supposed to have been built about 1755, and used as a guard house. It had no windows, and the single door was thickly studded with wrought iron nails."*

Basil Shaw's application also places a Captain Thomas Beall at Fort Cumberland in 1778.


## Passing Gwinn's tavern near Fort Cumberland with President Lincoln's grandfather

When Shepard Gum originally filed his Revolutionary War pension application, he mistook his year of enlistment as 1779, but later corrected it to 1778. While under the command of Abraham Lincoln's grandfather, he marched to Fort McIntosh via Gwinn's tavern, which was located near Fort Cumberland. Later, he was in service against Tories in the headwaters of the South Branch of the Potomac River. His original application includes these statements:

> *In the sixth day of August, 1834, personally appeared before the County Court of the County of Howard and state of Missouri, Shepherd Gum, a resident of the County and State aforesaid, aged 73 years, who being first duly sworn according to the Law, doth on his oath, make the following declaration, in order to obtain the benefit of the provision made by the act of Congress passed June 9, 1832. That he entered the military service of the United States in the County of Rockingham, Virginia, under the under the command of Captain Robert Craven in the spring of 1779, and marched under his command to a fort in Tyers Valley for the purpose of guarding the frontiers of Virginia against the incursion of the Indians. In this service I continued three months and was discharged or rather the whole company was disbanded.*

> *In the fall of the year 1779 I again entered the service under the command of Captain Abraham Lincoln, and marched under him to the northwestern part of Pennsylvania, where we formed the army of General McIntosh, at Fort McIntosh, on the north west bank of the Ohio. From thence the whole command of Gen'l McIntosh (except a guard for the garrison) marched to the head waters of the river Muskingum, where we built Fort Lawrence, on the western bank of the Tuscarora, and there met a tribe of Indians with whom we made a verbal treaty & from we procured some supplies of corn. In this term I served three months. ... I also served a term of one month, in an irregular service, against the tories, who were embedded in the mountains on the head waters of the south branch of the Potomac. I do not remember the name of our Captain or whether he was more than a mere leader in this volunteer service. ...*

### Gum corrects his pension application, and adds more detail
Shepherd Gum later provided a correction to his original pension application that stated:

> *In relation to my services as detailed in my original declaration aforesaid, I am now under the impression, from an examination of some of my old papers, and taxing my recollection to its utmost, that I entered the service of the United States under the Command of Captain Robert Cravens in the spring of 1778,*

---

[1573] Faw's Tavern.

*instead of the spring of 1779 as stated in my original declaration, and that, consequently, there is the inaccuracy of one year in the detail of his first, second and third terms of Service.*

*His recollection enables him to state in relation to the second tour of service as detailed in his original declaration, that he was rendesvoused at Harrisonburg, Virginia and marched from thence across the south and north branches of the Potomac; we struck "Braddock's road" at Gwinns Tavern, at the foot of the Allegany mountains, a short distance above Fort Cumberland; we followed "Braddock's road" (a large road cut out by Gen'l Braddock) across the Allegany mountain to the foot of Laurel Hill, passing the camp of Dunbar, where he had once blown up a magazine, as we were given to understand in passing by it. Between "Dunbar's Camp" and "Braddock's old battle ground" we left the road, turning to the left in the direction of Devons old ferry, on the Monogohelia about thirty miles above Fort Pitt – now Pittsburg. From there we struck through the country to Fort McIntosh, on the Ohio, passing Col. Neville's on the head of Shirtee Creek. [1574] ...*

Gwynn's[1575] was a well-known tavern situated between the present-day locations of Cumberland and Frostburg at the intersection of Braddock's road and the Winchester road. According to Patrick H. Stakem's 2011 book "**Cumberland**", Gwynn's tavern was located in LaVale, and was later known as the Six-Mile House. Evan Gwynn owned military lots 3412 to 3415 and the Grove Camp property.

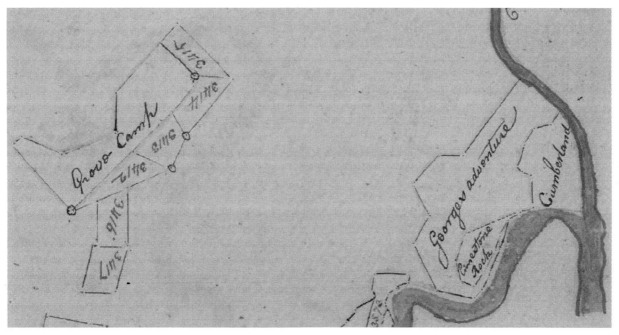

This enlargement of Veatch's map of Deakin's survey of lots westward of Fort Cumberland shows the location of the Grove Camp property.

---

[1574] Chartiers Creek.

[1575] William Brown's 1790 memo book mentions Gwynn's Tavern as follows, *"Gwyns Tavern at the fork, Bradfords old Road"* (Braddock's name was frequently misspelled in the early records). Brown's book also mentions *"Tumblesons Tavern"* (Tomlinson's) and *"Simpkins Tavern"*. In 1806, Gwynn's tavern was referenced by the commissioners Thomas Jefferson appointed to lay out the route of the National Road.

## Congress funds supplies for the west

Because of the hostile Indian tribes, on December 1, 1778, Congress approved new funding for 1,300 men for the western department. The Congressional journal[1576] states:

*A letter of 28 November, from Colonel George Morgan, was read; Whereupon,*

*Congress took into a consideration a report of the Board of War of 14 August last, wherein the Board sets forth,*

*'That Colonel George Morgan, purchasing commissary for the western department, has represented to the Board the necessity of preparing immediately for the laying up of such magazines of provisions as shall be sufficient for the troops maintained for the defence of the western frontiers; that for the supply of 1300 men for ten months, 617,500 lb. of flour, a like quantity of fresh beef, or 494,000 lb. of pork, will be necessary; the cost of which, with 1500 gallons of whiskey, will amount to 204,000 dollars, that on account of hostile Indians to the westward, and the northern tribes, particularly the Senecas, the number of men above stated will be necessary, including 150 for garrisoning Fort Randolph; Whereupon,*

*Resolved, that Colonel George Morgan, commissary of purchases for the western district, be furnished with two hundred and four thousand dollars, to enable him to form magazines of provisions for the use of that department the year ensuing.*

---

[1576] Volume 12 of the "**Journals of the Continental Congress**", page 1181.

# 31. 1779: Morgan's new road

## Morgan cuts a new road from Fort Cumberland to resupply Fort Pitt in 1779

In 1778, Americans were outraged by massacres committed by Tories and British-allied Indians at Wyoming Valley, PA and Cherry Valley, NY. In January 1779, Quartermaster General Nathaniel Greene advised George Washington to respond by launching a two-pronged attack against the food supply of the hostile Indians, with one division marching from a desperately undersupplied Fort Pitt.

In preparation for the attack, Washington asked Greene and Commissary General Wadsworth to improve the transportation of supplies from the *"frontiers of Virginia"* to Fort Pitt. Greene contacted Colonel George Morgan, who was the *"purchasing Commissary for the Western department"*. Morgan assigned Captain Charles Clinton and Colonel Providence Mounts to cut a new, shorter packhorse road from the town of Fort Cumberland to supply Fort Pitt. Clinton lived at Fort Cumberland, and Mounts was a miller and former Cumberland-area resident living at the site of present-day Connellsville, Pennsylvania.

The supply situation was so bleak that Washington cancelled Fort Pitt's role in the campaign. The completion of the new packhorse road changed the supply situation, and Washington's mind.

By putting 1,500 pack horses on the new road, Fort Pitt was adequately supplied by June 24, 1779. Major General John Sullivan led the primary attack from the Wyoming Valley on July 31, 1779, destroying at least 40 Indian villages in New York. Colonel Daniel Brodhead led a successful parallel campaign from Fort Pitt on August 11, 1779, with 605 combatants and 100 escorts for the campaign supplies. Brodhead marched north as far as the upper Seneca towns, destroying a number of Indian villages and over 500 acres of associated crops, and returned to Pittsburgh on September 14, 1779. The twin campaigns were followed by an exceptionally harsh winter, which was devastating to the now under-provisioned hostile Indians. Although the ways of war are cruel, the campaigns provided a new degree of safety for settlers in the western frontier of Pennsylvania.

The new road passed through the southern end of what is now Somerset County, Pennsylvania to take advantage of forage in the *"two plentiful Settlements"* located there. North of Turkey Foot, the route passed through property in the vicinity of Mill Creek reservoir that was surveyed for George Morgan and his brother in 1776. Morgan located his wartime *"bullock Pens"* on this property. The bullock pens were used for holding livestock that was being driven to Fort Pitt. The new road was some 20 to 25 miles shorter than Braddock's road, and dryer, because it remained on the eastern side of the Youghiogheny River.

The military origin of the Turkey Foot Road, briefly summarized here, is proven by detailed military correspondence that is provided in the remainder of this chapter.

## Transporting liquor from Fort Cumberland

A wagoner is described in the February 7, 1829 journal of the Pennsylvania Senate:

*Mr. Leech, from the committee on claims, to whom were referenced the petition and documents of Isaiah Graham, reported,*

*That the petitioner states he is the surviving executor of the last will and testament of James Graham, late of Cumberland county, deceased, that the said James Graham, was on the first day of January, 1779, appointed assistant quarter master of the Pennsylvania line, to raise a brigade of private property teams,* *to transport liquors to fort Cumberland, for the western department; that in pursuance of the said appointment, he did raise a brigade of twelve teams, and performed the said service, for which the petitioner alleges James Graham was never fully paid. It does appear to your committee, from accompanying documents, that James Graham did perform some services, for which the petitioner presents an account of several items, amounting to $85 81, on which he charges about 47 years of interest, amounting to $243 48, making a claim in the whole against the state, of $329.29.*

### A multi-pronged attack is proposed to disrupt the Indian food supply

In a January 5, 1779 letter to Washington, Greene advised against attacking Canada. He recommended moving against the Indian food supply in New York instead, using a multi-pronged attack to include a division from Fort Pitt:

*I think the fact is pretty clearly ascertaind that there is a great scarcity of Provision and Forage.[1577] The Middle and Eastern States have been harassed very greatly for four Campaigns running by means of which the Country has got much exhausted and the People sore with the hardships they have suffer'd, and the state of our currency added to the other two considerations renders a contracted plan and a breathing spell for the People absolutely necessary. No foreign Expedition should be undertaken while the Enemy remains formidable in these States.*

*There is three principal objects to be attended to in the plan of next Campaign. To take a position favorable for subsisting the army with ease and at the least Expence, To scourge the Indians at the proper season, and route the Enemy from N York should the state of the Garrison there render it practicable. ...*

*To scourge the Indians properly there should be considerable bodys of men march into their Country by different routes and at a season when their Corn is about half grown. The month of June will be the most proper time. One division to move from Fort Pitt. One division by way of Wyoming and the other by the Mohawk River. The only object should be that of driving off the Indians and destroying their Grain and as soon as that is completed to return again. This must be done whether the Enemy continues in great or little force in New York.*

*No offensive operations can take place against N York until green forage can be had. ...*

The need for forage is mentioned repeatedly in other correspondence. This need played a significant role in determining the route of the road from Fort Cumberland that became known as the Turkey Foot Road.

### A plan to deliver supplies to Fort Cumberland in the spring of 1779

On January 19, 1779, Abraham Shepherd sent a letter to his brother David Shepherd from Mecklensburg that includes the following statement, which seems to reference a plan to deliver a shipment of salt to Fort Cumberland:

*The articles I have sent you Except the salt and Mohair I shall charge to your private account. I have spoke to Nate Tomson to get a canoe made by spring which will carry forty bushels to Fort Cumberland he assures me of its being done but there is no certainty of his promises.*

Samuel Gordon Smyth's 1909 book "**A Genealogy of the Duke-Shepherd-Van Metre Family**" has an abstract of two letters in the Shepherd manuscripts at the Wisconsin Historical Society that states:

---

[1577] For a detailed look at the severe forage problem and its effect on transportation, and the extreme difficulties faced by those who were charged with provisioning the troops, see Erna Risch's 1981 book "**Supplying Washington's Army**". (Published by the Center of Military History, United States Army.)

*Abraham Shepherd wrote his brother, Col. David Shepherd, 4 Aug., 1778, that the price of salt is £6 per bushel, powder 10 shillings per lb. and blankets sell at £6. On 2 Nov., 1778 he quotes salt at £9 per bushel, and suggests a "corner" in salt.*

## Washington orders pack saddles for the campaign Greene proposed

By January 27, 1779, Washington began preparations for the attack, writing to Greene from Philadelphia:

*You are hereby directed to provide with all convenient dispatch Twenty five hundred pack saddles of the cheapest and strongest kind fit for the purpose of transporting Provisions, Stores and Baggage.*

As will be shown by documentary evidence below, after the Turkey Foot Road was cut, 1,500 packhorses were using the new road later in 1779 to supply Fort Pitt.

## Fort Pitt desperately needs supplies in January 1779

On January 30, 1779, Washington took action to try to obtain supplies for Fort Pitt for the impending attack, writing to the President of Congress from Philadelphia:

*In consequence of the authority vested in me by Congress of 'directing and superintending the military operations in these States,' I was led to make enquiry into the State of the Magazines to the Westward. From a late letter of Genl. McIntosh's to myself, and several to the Board of War, I find that he has been so much distressed for provision, that he has been obliged suddenly to disband all the Militia that were in service, and seems to be very apprehensive that he shall with difficulty subsist the two Continental Regiments and a few Independent Companies, thro' the Winter. I communicated this to the Commissary General of Purchases, and desired him to make an estimate of what Magazines of provisions he could establish at Fort Pitt during the Winter, or time enough in the Spring to commence operations should they be necessary. In answer to this he informed me, that the supply of the Army in the Western department had never been under his direction, and that therefore he did not conceive himself authorized to take any Steps in the matter. I have thought it my duty to represent this to Congress as early as possible that proper enquiries may be made of those who have hitherto had the charge of procuring supplies, whether they have made the necessary arrangements for establishing proper Magazines at Fort Pitt in the Spring, and if they have not, or cannot engage to do it with certainty, it will be necessary without loss of time to authorize the Commissary General of purchases to extend his Commission so as to include the Western operations. He, from transacting his Business upon a very large scale, is more likely to be acquainted with the general Resources of the Country, and consequently more able to supply our wants, than those who have been confined to a particular district. If the Commissary General is to undertake the establishment of the Magazines, he should immediately be made acquainted with it, that he may begin to put matters in a train for moving the provision from below as soon as the State of the Roads will admit, as I take it for granted that none can go farther than the foot of the Mountains during the winter. I fear, notwithstanding our utmost exertions, it will be late before sufficient Magazines can be formed, especially of Flour, the Crops beyond the Allegahany having been generally lost last summer by the evacuation of the Country. The transportation of that Article therefore must be very distant. I hope Congress will view this matter in the same important light that I do, and that whatever their determination may be, it be as speedy as the case will admit. In addition to what I have said, I shall only remark that many good consequences result from having all the Branches of the same department under one head...*

## A plan for an attack from Fort Pitt

On January 31, 1779, Washington wrote to Brigadier General Lachlan McIntosh, commander at Fort Pitt, about the upcoming campaign:

*I make no doubt but you have a sufficiency of difficulties to struggle with, but am glad to find that the steps you have taken have given at least a temporary relief to the Inhabitants upon the frontier, and I hope by pursuing a steady and properly concerted plan next Campaign we may, if we cannot engage the friendship of the savages, reduce them to the necessity of remaining quiet. To effect this, it is determined, at present, to carry the War into the Indian Country next Spring as early as the season and the state of our Magazines will admit. No particular plan is yet fixed, nor are the places which will be the most proper objects of attack yet marked out. But as we may conclude that Fort Pitt will be one of the principal places from whence we shall commence our operations, I must desire you will immediately upon the Rect. of this set about making the following preparations and collecting the necessary intelligence of the state of the Country, Waters &c. over which we shall probably pass.*

*It will in the first place be necessary to provide Batteaus or Canoes, (which-ever may be thought most suitable for the Waters of that Country) for 1000 or 1200 Men, and endeavour to form Magazines sufficient for the same number for three or four months. From your letter to me and those to the Board of War, I imagine you will be able to do little towards the latter, as the provision must chiefly go from below, I shall therefore endeavour to put matters in a proper train for the formation of Magazines as early as possible, before I leave this town.*

Washington goes on to discuss a possible attack against Detroit, and then describes the possibility of an attack against the Seneca Indians:

*But if an expedition against the Indians of the Six Nations should be determined upon in preference to the other, it will be necessary to enquire how far the Force assembled at Pittsburg seemingly with an intent to operate either against the Indians upon the Ohio or agt. Detroit may be turned to a cooperation with other Bodies from Albany from the Susquehannah, or perhaps from both. To form a judgment of the practicability of this, the distance between Fort Pitt and the Country of the six Nations especially the Senecas, who are most numerous, warlike and inimical of the whole, should be exactly ascertained...*

*Persons (either Indians or Whites) of trust should be hired for the several purposes before mentioned; they should not know that we ourselves are undetermined as to the plan of our operations, and then each party will suppose that the Route which they are sent to explore is the one by which we mean to carry on an expedition.*

*If they betray the confidence reposed in them, they will deceive the Enemy in every quarter but that which may happen to be our real object. As the force collected at and the preparations made at Fort Pitt will point equally every way, it will add to the distraction of the enemy should they find out that we are making enquiries concerning the different Routes leading to their posts.*

## Congress responds to George Washington

On February 1, 1779, Congress gave Washington the authority to direct the Commissary and Quartermaster departments:

*Resolved, That the Commander-in-Chief give such directions as he may think proper for arranging the commissry's and quarter master's departments to the westward, any resolutions of Congress notwithstanding; and that for his information the secretary be directed to lay before him the several letters on that subject from Colonel G. Morgan to Congress; and that the Board of War communicate to him all necessary intelligence that may have come to them respecting the same subject.*

## Look into the transportation issue!

On February 14, 1779, Washington wrote to Commissary General Jeremiah Wadsworth from Middle Brook about drawing provisions for Fort Pitt from the surrounding region and from Virginia, and asks him to look into the means of transportation:

*If my order of the _____, respecting the Magazine of Provision at Fort Pitt did not explicitly declare that the quantity there directed to be laid up by the first of May is to be over and above the necessary supplies for the Troops in that Quarter I now inform you that this was my meaning; And I have further to desire that you will form a Magazine under like circumstances, and for the same time (that is four Months) for one thousand Men at Sundbury on Susquehanna.*

*For particular reasons I think it advisable, that the Magazine at Pittsburgh should be drawn from the Frontiers of Virginia, and the parts of Pensylvania contiguous to that Post; and, that the supplies for Sundbury be drawn from the Westside of the Susquehanna. You will consult the Quarter master Genl. on the means of Transportation that no disappointment may take place in either of these cases.*

## Washington writes McIntosh again

On February 15, 1779, Washington again wrote to McIntosh from his headquarters at Middle Brook about launching an attack against the Indians from Fort Pitt, and describes how he is trying to address the dire supply problem at Fort Pitt:

*The more I contemplate on an Expedition from Fort Pitt, the more perswaded I am of the superior advantages that will result from its co-operation with some enterprize from this quarter (if circumstances will permit) but as a measure of this kind depends upon contingencies, no perfect plan can be yet formed; but as there will be little or no difference, in the preparation for an Expedition up the Alligany against the hostile tribes of the Six Nations, and one against the Indians more Westerly and Detroit, I would have you confine your attention more to the first than the latter objects; keeping the design as much as possible an impenetrable secret, under an Idea that you are preparing to prosecute the objects of the last campaign; and to lessen as much as possible the expence of land transportation, you mean to make use of that by Water.*

*The only means that can lead to a discovery of the real design, is the steps which must necessarily be taken to obtain a thorough knowledge of the rout, and other circumstances to form the plan; but this may be covered in a great degree by the adoption of similar measures (which may eventually be equally necessary) the other way. Your oblique enquiries in the first case, should always be accompanied with pointed ones in the second, which will naturally give the bias to that way of thinking.*

Washington goes on to ask McIntosh to investigate the route of attack, then states:

*I have directed the Commissary Genl. of purchases under the inclosed resolve, to lay in four Months provision for 1200 Men, at Pittsburg, by the first of May. He will continue Colo. Morgan in this business, if he chooses it; but as it is necessary to avoid interference in office that all the branches of the same department should be under one general direction, and superintendance, my orders have gone, and must go through him.*

## A tumultuous time in local history due to Indian raids is revealed in a February 1779 letter

Pages 120 and 121, Volume II, of the 1906 book "**History of Bedford and Somerset Counties...**" reveal that 1779 was a tumultuous time in local history. A February 16, 1779 letter to the Pennsylvania General Assembly from various Bedford county and township tax assessors (including Henry Abrams of the Turkeyfoot settlement and Hugh Robinson who lived about two miles south of the present-day site of

Meyersdale) describes a period of Indian depredations within the county that made it impractical to levy taxes. The letter states:

> *To the Honourable the Representatives of the Freemen of the Commonwealth of Pennsylvania in general Assembly met.*
>
> *The Petition of the Board of Commissioners Assessors & Assistant Assessors of Bedford County — Humbly Sheweth: That the Petitioners have met in order to Lay the Taxes directed by Law to be paid by this County, but the situation of the greatest part of the County is such that Humanity forbids them to levy the Same and induces them to apply to the Honourable House for relief and to represent That for eighteen months past the frontier inhabitants have almost entirely been deprived of the fruits of their labor by the incursions of the Indians. Many of them are gone entirely out of the County, and when that part of the Petitioners whose duty it is to take the Returns of Property went to the once Chearful abodes of Humble Industry & content the Inhabitant had fled to preserve his life, and nothing presented to their view but forlorn inhabitations and untilled fields (in several of which the grave of the former owner murdered by the Indians was to be seen) and to levy Taxes off those would be adding distress to the afflicted and taking from the Poor that which he has not to give.*
>
> *That part of the Inhabitants which remained collected into forts — some formed into Companies and Ranged along the Frontiers in order to afford some small Protection to the rest who, at the hazzard of their lives ventured out to save their Scanty harvest and to prepare another but they were so often driven in that it was but little they could do.*
>
> *The Panic occasioned by one incursion was scarcely over till they were alarmed afresh by another. Many were deprived of Sowing & planting & not a few were prevented from reaping that which they had put in-In Consequence of which Famine Stares us in the face. There is not Bread enough amongst us to sustain the Inhabitants till Harvest & were it to be had for Money which it is not. Many of the Poorer sort have not wherewithal to purchase it. The great Plenty of Money that is circulating in other parts of the Country is to them no relief because their Savage Foe has prevented them from having anything to sell to acquire Money and many of them have undergone hardship & distress and suffered such loss that they are really objects of Compassion & if the Times would permit their Situation would strongly Plead for Public assistance to save the helpless families of those to have perished by the Sword, and those who have been deprived of Providing Bread for their families from suffering by Famine. The few who have been permitted to remain at their Habitations, and reap the fruits of their industry will chearfully pay their part of the Taxes according to their circumstances but should the whole Quota laid on this County be levied off them it is so large and their numbers so few that they would be reduced to beggary by it. We therefore intreat the interposition of the Honourable House and that they would grant such an exemption in the premises as to their wisdom shall seem meet & the Petitioners as in duty bound shall pray &c.*

Clearly, the British alliance with Native Americans was impacting the American war effort. As a result of letters such as this one, on March 20, 1780, the Pennsylvania Legislature passed a relief statute[1578] titled *"An act for the relief of the suffering inhabitants of the counties of Northampton, Bedford, Northumberland and Westmoreland."* The act is Chapter DCCXCI of the Statutes at Large of Pennsylvania.

## Washington writes to Greene about transportation

To make doubly sure the problem of transportation to Fort Pitt was addressed, Washington wrote directly to Nathanael Greene from Middle Brook on February 24, 1779:

---

[1578] **"The Statutes at Large of Pennsylvania from 1682-1801..."**, Volume 10.

*I have given the Commissary General orders to lay in a Magazine of four months provisions for Twelve hundred men at Fort Pitt, and another of the like quantity for One thousand men at Sunbury, both to be formed by the first day of May next, and exclusive of the quantities necessary for the subsistence of the troops in these quarters.*

*I have directed him, if possible, to draw his supplies for Pittsburgh from the frontiers of Virginia, and those for Sunbury from the Westside of the Susquehanna. You will consult with him and afford him the necessary aid respecting the transportation.*

At some point, Quartermaster General Greene asked George Morgan to look into the issue of transporting supplies from Virginia. The fact that Greene did so is revealed by a May 2, 1779 letter from Morgan to Greene that is included below.

### Congress asks Washington to act to protect the frontier

On February 25, 1779, Congress passed a resolution asking Washington to chastise the Indians:

*Resolved, That the representation of the circumstances of the western frontiers, communicated by a committee of the general assembly of Pensylvania, and also copies of the memorials and of the letters from the governors of Connecticut and New-York, respecting the depredations on the said frontiers, be transmitted to the commander in chief, who is directed to take effectual measures for the protection of the inhabitants and chastisement of the savages.*

### March 1779 Washington County Maryland court

In a section titled, *"Recognizances Respected to March Court 1779"* in the Washington County, Maryland **"March Court Dockett 1779"**, item 2 is a bond of £300 for Peter Tittle *"For Godfrey Richards App$^e$ to Answer"*. The bond appears to have been collected by L. Barrett.

In a section titled, *"Judicial Dockett to March Court 1779"*, item 6 is the case of Lemuel Barrett versus Charles Coleson, and item 4 is the case of Lemuel Barrett versus *"James Murphy for Cha$^s$ Coleson's use"*. In a section titled, *"Tryal Dockett to March Court 1779"*, item 9 is the case of James Prather versus Thomas Cresap. Item 11 is the case of Thomas Cresap versus George Barnhart. Item 12 is the case of Thomas Cresap versus Nathaniel Parker. Item 13 is the case of Thomas Cresap versus Joshua Stradford. Item 20 is the case of Major David Rogers against Colo Tho$^s$ Cressap. Item 25 is the case of Thomas Warren versus Thomas Cresap. Item 36 is the case of Thomas Warren versus *"Enoch Ennis & wife"*.

In a section titled, *"Continuances to March Court 1779"*, item 11 is the case of Thomas Cresap versus James Craig. Item 22 is the case of Lemuol Barrett versus Charles Coleson. Item 26 is the case of Enoch Enns versus Edward Ward (who appears in local 1778 Oath of Fidelity lists). Item 27 is the case of *"David Rogers & Mary his Wife Ext$^r$ of Mich$^l$ Cresap"* versus Edward Ward. Item 31 is the case of Tyler Waugh versus Thomas Cresap.

In a section titled, *"Imparlances to March Court 1779"*, item 4 is the case of Charles Prather versus Thomas Cresap. Item 17 is the case of Charles Coleson versus Peter Title (Tittle). Item 18 is the case of *"Casper Billager for Charles Coleson's use"* versus Peter Title.

In a section titled, *"Original Writs to March Court 1779"*, item 6 is the case of Thomas Cresap versus *"Thomas Warren & Lidia his wife"*. Item 11 is the case of Thomas Cresap versus James Pearce. Item 19 is the case of Lemuel Barrett versus Thomas Girty. Item 22 is the case of *"Mary Rogers & Michael Cresap Exet$^{rs}$ of Mich$^l$ Cresap"* versus James Elliott. Item 23 is the case of Moses Rawlings versus Thomas Gallium (I am not sure of the spelling of Gallium). Item 63 is the case of John Simpkins versus Joseph Briant; a man by the name of John Simpkins shows up in Deakins list of settlers west of Fort Cumberland, but I don't know if both records pertain to the same individual.

### Washington admonishes Wadsworth

On March 2, 1779, Washington directed Jeremiah Wadsworth to increase the amount of provisions at Sunbury, and included the admonition, *"The Supply for Fort Pitt as mentioned in the above order of the 14th. Ulto. must not be dispensed with either in quantity, or time, under no pretence whatsoever."*

### Washington writes to Governor George Clinton

Washington's March 4, 1779 letter to New York Governor George Clinton describes a plan to take the fight to the Indians in response to the 1778 massacres:

*Dear Sir, The President of Congress has transmitted me your Excellency's letter to the delegates of New York, representing the calamitous situation of the northwestern frontier of that State, accompanied by a similar application from the Pennsilvania Assembly, and a Resolve of the 25th directing me to take the most effectual measures for the protection of the inhabitants and chastisement of the Indians.*

*The Resolve has been in some measure anticipated by my previous dispositions for carrying on offensive operations against the hostile tribes of Savages.*

### McIntosh is replaced by Brodhead

On March 5, 1779, Washington appointed Colonel Daniel Brodhead to replace McIntosh, who had by then requested to be relieved of his command.[1579] In his letter of appointment, Washington emphasizes the need for provisions to support the upcoming attack:

*You will observe by my letter of the 15th. Feby. that I have directed the Commy. General, to endeavour to form his magazines by the 1st. May, by which time I hope the other preparations will be in sufficient forwardness to move. ...*

*The establishment of adequate magazines and the preparation of a sufficient number of Boats, of the kind that may be deemed most proper, are what ought principally to engage your attention. Should the enquiries concerning the Country, the Waters, the distances & ca. be not so compleat as might be wished, we might yet proceed, but without the others we must be intirely at a stand.*

The construction of boats was a continuing problem that is not highlighted in this chapter.

### Morris writes a scathing letter to Washington about McIntosh

A meeting Washington had with George Morgan was the result of a scathing March 14, 1779 letter Gouverneur Morris wrote to Washington about McIntosh. Part of the letter is quoted here:

*You will excuse in me the Liberty I have taken in requesting Colo Morgan to call on you. That Gentleman can give you much and important information relative to the State of our Western Frontiers. From the first View of the Commander of that Department in York Town he struck me as one of those who excel in the Regularity of still Live from the Possession of an indolent uniformity of soul. The little Eagerness he shewed to go thence when every Thing almost depended on Vivacity gave no good omen of his success. ... When I heard of some Proceedings in the Department I ventured to say aloud that no Good would follow from the Exertions of the Army under his Command. Unfortunately I have not been mistaken. I have reason to believe that his Recall hath become necessary from a variety of Causes. ... I believe it is unnecessary for me to say that Colo Morgan is a Man of Honor and Truth as he is of your acquaintance but as you may not know him so well as to know how much he may be relied on permit me to assure you*

---

[1579] **"The Writings of George Washington from the Original Manuscript ..."**, Volume 14, John C. Fitzpatrick, Editor.

*that I have the highest Reason to believe that you cannot derive Information from a more certain source or thro a surer Channell*

## Morgan describes cutting the Turkey Foot Road

Around March 18, 1779, Morgan wrote a letter to Greene regarding the transportation of supplies to Fort Pitt, in which he describes cutting a new road to Fort Pitt. The letter includes the following statements:

*The service has suffer'd from Want of Attention to the Water Carriage on Potomack.*

*Six Batteaux sufficient to carry 100, or 120 Kegs of \_\_\_\_\_ each, and twenty Cannoes capable of carrying 30 Kegs each, should be kept on that River, for the Transportation of Stores to Skipton.*

*One Store House and a Coopers Shop, should be built at the Mouth of Connecocheague, One at _____ Landing on the Virginia Side and One at Skipton. Coopers should be stationd at each of those Places.*

*A Road may be opend from Fort Cumberland to Fort Pitt which will shorten the Distance 22 or 25 Miles in 81. The New Road may easily be made a much better One for Waggons than the old One can be even with the same Labour and it leads through two plentiful Settlements for Forage Vizt [1580] The South End of Brothers Valley and Turkey Foot Settlement. I have directed it to be opend for Pack Horses, and to be surveyd. More than One half is already done.*

Morgan's letter proves that he was responsible for having the Turkey Foot Road cut through the present-day Salisbury, Pennsylvania area, which was then a part of Brothersvalley Township, Bedford County. The road went through that area and the general Turkeyfoot region so the packhorses could draw forage from the plentiful settlements that were already located there in 1779.

## Transportation to the western forts is hazardous

On March 19, 1779, Greene wrote a letter to Wadsworth, which includes the following statement:

*Col Morgan your deputy for the district of Fort Pitt was here to day. He refuses to act upon the usual commission. He says the business is so laborious and risky that he will not engage in it without a larger commission. He has represented the matter to Congress; and they have it now under consideration.*

*The business of that district is so much behind hand, that I am afraid it will be difficult for us to get it forward so as to keep pace with the opening season. However I will try.*

*I like Col Morgan exceedingly; and intend giving him a kind of general superindendance in my department as well as yours. That if the present Agents don't give him the necessary assistance in forwarding the provisions; to empower him to take such further measures as he may think the good of the service may require.*

## Washington wavers about the attack from Fort Pitt

Around the time Morgan wrote to Greene about cutting the new road, he talked to Washington in person. Washington mentions the conversation in a March 20, 1779 letter to a fellow founding father, Gouverneur Morris:

*I have received your favour of the 14th Inst by Colo Morgan, and have a good deal of conversation with him respecting our affairs to the Westward.*

---

[1580] An abbreviation for videlicet. The definition for videlicet in the 1780 book "**A General Dictionary of the English Language**" is *"To wit, that is generally written Viz."*

*I wish matters had been more prosperously conducted under the command of Genl McIntosh. ...[1581] He is now coming away, and the second in command, Brodhead (as there will be no military operation of consequence to be conducted) will succeed him...*

## Brodhead is ordered to plan an attack

On March 22, 1779, Washington wrote a letter to Brodhead that includes the following statement:

*You are to inform me with precision and by a careful Express when you will be ready to begin your movement from Fort Pitt, when you can be at Kittanning, when at Venango, when at the head of the Navigation, how far it is from thence to the nearest Indian Towns, and when you can reach them. In making your estimate of the times, you are to calculate upon moving as light as possible, and with only a few pieces of the lightest Artillery. These are necessary for me to know with as much accuracy as possible, that the plan of co-operation, upon which much depends, may be perfectly formed.*

*I would wish you to pacify and cultivate the friendship of the Western Indians by all the means in your power.*

*When you are ready to move and your probable destination can be no longer concealed, contrive ways to inform them that you are going to meet a large force to fall upon and destroy the whole Country of the Six Nations, and that if they do in the mean time give the least disturbance to the Frontiers, that whole force will be turned against them, and that we will never rest till we have cut them off from the face of the Earth.*

## George Morgan's memorial to the General Assembly of Pennsylvania

George Morgan's March 25, 1779 memorial to the General Assembly of Pennsylvania[1582] describes the reason for cutting the Turkey Foot Road, and describes the route and his desire to upgrade it into a wagon road:

*To the Honble the Representatives of the Freemen of Pennsylvania in General Assembly met —*

*The Memorial of George Morgan.*

*Sheweth,*

*That great impediments have arisen in the Transportation of public stores to the Ohio, from the badness of the Roads leading to Fort Pitt, which have been neglected so much that Carriages pass with the utmost Difficulty —*

*That a New Road may be opend from the Pennsylvania Line near to Fort Cumberland leading through Bedford County into the Old Road in Westmoreland County, which will shorten the Distance from thence to Fort Pitt, at least 22 Miles in 80– Whereby all the Stores procured from Virginia & Maryland for the Army on the Ohio may be transported, with a great Saving of Time & Expence to the United States in general & much Advantage to this State in particular; As the New Road may be opend & made better for Waggons, than what is called the Virginia Road can be at the same Expence —*

---

[1581] The redacted part of this letter describes McIntosh's good qualities that Washington observed at Valley Forge, and McIntosh's neutrality regarding the boundary dispute between Virginia and Pennsylvania, as reasons for having appointed McIntosh to command at Fort Pitt.

[1582] Robert R. Reed collection, University of Illinois at Urbana-Champaign, Urbana, Illinois.

*That the public service on the Frontiers of this State has suffer'd from Pack-Horse-Men, Drovers & other necessary Persons employd by the staff of the Continental Army, being drafted into the Militia, & heavy Fines being levied on those who did not attend the Call of the County Lieutenants —*

*As the Interest of this State in general & of the suffering frontier Inhabitants thereof in particular is deeply concernd in facilitating every Military Operation in that Quarter, Your Memorialist presumes this Representation to the Honourable House, with whom alone the Remedies rest, will not be disagreeable—*

*GM*

*Philada March 25th 1779*

*Memorial–G Morgan To the Assembly of Pennsylvania*

## The missing Morgan letters from March of 1779

A March 25, 1779 letter from George Morgan to Charles Clinton and a March 27, 1779 letter from George Morgan to Zack Connell are described as referencing the new road. Zack Connell evidently is the militia Captain Zachariah Connell[1583], who ultimately owned property on the Turkey Foot Road in Fayette County, Pennsylvania and founded Connellsville. The letters were owned by George Morgan's descendant Mrs. A. G. Happer[1584] circa 1930. The current whereabouts of the letters is unknown.

## Joseph Reed writes to his lieutenants about the planned invasion of Indian country

On March 27, 1779, Joseph Reed, president of the Supreme Executive Council of Pennsylvania, wrote a letter to his lieutenants about steps being taken to defend Bedford and Westmoreland Counties, in which he says, *"It is also a very encouraging Circumstance that Gen. Hand, who is to command on the Frontiers of North[n] & Northumberland, & Col. Broadhead at Fort Pitt, are both Inhabitants of this State, & will have every Inducement & Motive to exert themselves to the utmost. But we are farther to acquaint you, that these are only Parts of the System, for it is fully determined to penetrate into the Indian Country, and by a seasonable, vigorous Stroke make them feel the weight of American Arms."*

## Worrying the campaign logistical details

On April 5, 1779, Washington wrote to Greene about provisions for the campaign:

*I wish to know, how many horns have been delivered to your department in consequence of the general orders for that purpose; and that you would take measures to have a sufficient number of them converted into the common powder flasks for the proposed expedition. And that the whole may be under your view.*

*You will also be pleased to give directions for the necessary complement of shot pouches.*

---

[1583] The 1912 book "**Frontier Defense on the Upper Ohio, 1777-1778**" includes Samuel Murphy's recollection of Zachariah Connell being credited with killing an armed Indian lad during General Hand's winter expedition against the Indians. That expedition, which became known as the Squaw Campaign, consisted mostly of militia from Westmoreland County, Pennsylvania. In 1776, Connell was appointed as a Captain of Yohogania County, which was a Virginia County that overlapped Pennsylvania's Westmoreland County. After Virginia and Pennsylvania agreed to resolve their competing claims, Fayette County, Pennsylvania was formed from Westmoreland County in 1783. According to the "**Pennsylvania Archives**", *"Zacharia Connell"* was a member of Captain William Perry's Westmoreland County militia during some part of the 1778-1783 time period.

[1584] According to the 1893 Beers "**Commemorative Biographical Record of Washington County, Pennsylvania**", Matilda (Morgan) Happer was the great-granddaughter of Colonel George Morgan. According to the "**Pittsburgh Press**", she was the widow of the merchant Andrew G. Happer and died on February 1, 1935 at age 86.

## An April 20, 1779 update on cutting the road

On April 20, 1779, Captain Charles Clinton wrote the following letter to Morgan from Fort Cumberland:

> *Yours of the 25th of March came to hand the 6th instant. I have open'd the Road from this place to Turkey Foot except four or five miles which I expect will be completed this week. I shall be in Want of Money to pay the Hands, which you will please to send by the first Opportunity — I think three thousand five hundred dollars will be sufficient — The Men who are employed are all of Opinion that a good Waggon Road may be made as the whole way is clear of Swamps except about twenty Perches near the little Crossings — The enclosed Survey is laid down by a Scale of 600 equal parts to an Inch –*

The reference to *"little Crossings"* is confusing today; but when Clinton wrote this letter, the entire Casselman River was known as the *"Little Crossings"*.[1585] Clinton's road survey has not been found;[1586] but in the context of Morgan's letters, Clinton's letter clearly describes the Turkey Foot Road.

## Analysis of Clinton's swamp statement

In terms of determining the route east of Turkeyfoot, Clinton's April 20, 1779 reference to 20 perches (110 yards) of swamp near the Little Crossings is not definitive. The term *"swamp"* encompassed more in the 1700s than what it generally brings to mind today.[1587] For example, Heckewelder's 1796 map mentions a *"swamp which will make good meadows"* near present-day Detroit. The July 15, 1760 journal entry of Captain Thomas Hutchins, (later the Geographer General of the United States) reports, *"Marched through very Rich Bottoms, commonly called Swamps, almost all this day."*[1588] He was near French Creek at the time. Wallace quotes Bishop John Ettwein's June 11, 1772 journal entry about the *"Great Swamp"*, and states that the term comprised the majority of the mountains in Sullivan County. The journal[1589] reads, *"After we crossed the Susquehanna at the ford our way led straight to the mountains, and after proceeding two miles, we entered the Great Swamp, where the undergrowth was so dense that oftimes it was impossible to see one another at a distance of six feet."*

Many North American swamps that could be easily drained for fields or pasture were drained long ago. To a certain extent, the swamps that remain today are simply the more intractable ones (or protected, like Finzel Swamp) that survived humankind. Any poorly drained area would have been soft and problematic for a primitive road.[1590]

---

[1585] Clinton's mention of *"Little Crossings"* seems, at first blush, to mean that Clinton's road went through the present-day Grantsville area, where the 1813 Stone Bridge crosses the Casselman River. After all, that place has been referred to as the *"Little Crossings"* since George Washington called it that when crossing it on June 19, 1755 with Braddock's expedition. The complicating factor with that interpretation is that the entire Casselman River was sometimes referred to as *"Little Crossings"*. For example, Doctor James Craig's October 2, 1784 letter to General Washington (quoted at length in the following chapter) mentions *"sixty miles of difficult navigation up the Little Crossing"*. This is a clear reference to a stream, rather than a fording site. For another example, see the 1790 Abrams survey of the present-day location of Confluence. Volume IV of the 1814 book "**The Geographical and Historical Dictionary of America and the West Indies**" also refers to the Casselman River as *"Little Crossings"*, stating, *"TURKEY FOOT, in Youghiogany river, is the point of junction of the great S. Branch, Little Crossings from the s. e. and N. Branch from the n. It is 40 miles from the mouth of the river, 20 miles s.s.w. of Berlin, in Pennsylvania, and 29 n.e. of Morgantown. Lat. 39° 48' n."*

[1586] The survey and original letter are not part of the Morgan Letter Book Collection at the Carnegie Library (Pittsburgh) or the Morgan family papers at the Senator John Heinz History Center (Pittsburgh).

[1587] Wallace expounds on this subject on page 8 of his 1965 book "**Indian Paths of Pennsylvania**".

[1588] *"A Journal of a March from Fort Pitt to Venango, and from thence to Presqué Isle..."* from the 1878 publication "**The Pennsylvania Magazine of History and Biography**", Volume II.

[1589] From the 1901 "**The Pennsylvania Magazine of History and Biography**", Volume XXV.

[1590] A swampy area remains 2.7 miles east of the Casselman River along Route 40 in Maryland, at the old stone bridge across Meadow Run.

*Candidate swamps near the Casselman River*

The ground just west of the Casselman River at Salisbury, Pennsylvania is level and low lying. Another candidate for a colonial *"swamp"* appears to be the Engles Mill area, 2.6 miles east of the Casselman River near Salisbury. Harry Ringler, Senior recalls one small swamp east of Salisbury that was drained (location unreported) and is now used as a field. Although few people today are familiar with beaver dams, they were also a cause of temporary swamps in level areas.

## Steel is exonerated

In an April 21, 1779 letter, Washington approved a January 1, 1779 court martial verdict that found Deputy Quarter Master General Colonel Archibald Steel[1591] innocent of charges leveled against him by General McIntosh, including the charge of *"the delaying the transporting provisions and other stores for the expedition until it was too late"*, even though *"Steel acknowledged that he did not, nor could not, transport the flour &c. over the mountain, which was purchased by Colonel Morgan..."*

## Brodhead's attack is temporarily canceled

On April 21, 1779, Washington wrote to Brodhead from Middle Brook that he decided against using Fort Pitt in the attack against the six nations. One of the reasons was the supply problem:

*Dear Sir: Since my last letter, and upon a further consideration of the subject, I have relinquished the idea of attempting a cooperation between the troops at Fort Pitt and the bodies moving from other quarters against the six nations. The difficulty of providing supplies in time, a want of satisfactory information of the routes and nature of the country up the Alleghany, and between that and the Indian Settlements, and consequently the uncertainty of being able to cooperate to advantage and the hazard which the smaller party might run, for want of a cooperation are principal motives for declining of it. The danger to which the frontier would be exposed, by drawing off the troops from their present position, from the incursions of the more western tribes, is an additional though a less powerful reason. The post at Tuscarowas is therefore to be preserved if, under a full consideration of circumstances it is judged a post of importance and can be maintained without runing too great a risk and the troops in general under your command, disposed in the manner best calculated to cover and protect the country on a defensive plan.*

*As it is my wish however, as soon as it may be in our power to chastize the Western savages by an expedition into their country; you will employ yourself in the mean time in making preparation and forming magazines of Provisions for the purpose. If the expedition against the six nations is successfully ended, a part of the troops employed in this, will probably be sent, in conjunction with those under you to carry on another that way.*

## The Council of Maryland references the forthcoming western expedition

On April 24, 1779, the Council of Maryland sent the following letter[1592] to Daniel Hughes, Lieutenant of Washington County:

*Yesterday Afternoon, after writing the Letter herewith sent you we received yours of the 19ᵗʰ Insᵗ with Colᵒ Barrett's Letter inclosed.*

*We flatter ourselves that if an Expedition goes on the Westward, that Force will necessarily call off the Indians from the Frontiers, but in the mean Time the Inhabitants must be encouraged and protected, or*

---

[1591] On May 22, 1778, Nathanael Greene appointed Colonel Archibald Steel to be the Deputy Quartermaster General *"for the Garrison of Fort Pitt on the Ohio, and the neighboring Country west of the Allogana mountains"*.

[1592] "**Journal and Correspondence of the Council of Maryland, April 1, 1778 through October 26, 1779**", Vol. 21.

*they will leave their Settlements, Col° Barrett has proposed in his Letters, the Building Stockaded Forts at three different Places; he does not mention his Ideas of the Expence or the Number of Men which will be necessary: we should have been Glad of your Sentiments on these Points, as well as the Means of supplying Provisions, as well as the Means of supplying Provisions, Any thing that is done, we imagine, ought to be with a meer Temporary View. You will be frequently advised of the Situation of Things and therefore may, on a Change of Circumstances so likely to happen, be able to do what is proper before you can advise us. As Things now appear to us, we think it would be well for Col° Barrett to draw out a Company, for a Month from his Battalion and that about sixty Men should be drawn out from your County Militia below, for the same Time; Barrett's Battalion renewing their Number from Time to Time, whilst necessary and, if it should be necessary, to replace the sixty Men, then to draw them below: if you think this Number necessary, we desire and empower you to give the necessary Orders accordingly or to order any less Number that you may think sufficient. If from the Situation of Affairs, you should judge it absolutely necessary, that a greater Force should be immediately sent we desire you to send out what you may think necessary to keep the People from deserting their Habitations and advise us by Express that we may exert every Means in our Power to preserve the Settlements and divide the Burthen as equally as may be. You do not mention the Quantity of Powder & Lead that you have or whether you have any; furnish Col° Barrett with what may be necessary, if you have it, if not, order from Frederick Town an ample Supply. We wish you to concert the Means of supplying Provisions on the best Terms and to appoint some Person to conduct that Business whose Activity and Integrity may be relied on.*

## Washington explains the cancelation of the campaign from Fort Pitt

Around April 24, 1779, President Reed wrote a letter to Washington from Philadelphia that includes the statement:

*We have been at a very great Expence in sending Stores of all kinds up to Fort Pitt, & as that Part of the Plan is altered which seemed to require a Collection of Troops there, I hope they may be used in some such Way as to check the temporary Ravages of the Indians – At least affording Westmoreland complete Protection.*

On April 27, 1779, Washington wrote a long letter back to Reed from his headquarters at Middle Brook that includes the following:

*The hurry in which I am often obliged to write letters will sometimes not allow them to be as full and explicit as might be wished. But besides the reasons assigned in my last for relinquishing the idea of a co-operation from Fort Pitt according to the original plan, the uncertainty of timing it well and a want of sufficient information of the country, through which they would have to pass. I might have added another, which had no small influence in the determination. I found, by my accounts from that quarter, that the removal of these troops, would not only uncover the part of the country where they now are; but add confidence to the Western Indians, already too much inclined to hostility, and expose our affairs there to the most disagreeable consequences.*

## Morgan writes to Royal Flint

On April 29, 1779, George Morgan writes to Royal Flint (an assistant commissary of purchases) about his efforts concerning the supply of Fort Pitt. The letter includes the following statement:

*As I have made it a point to employ men of character & influence in their respective counties, I hope very shortly to be able to inform you that all the necessary provisions are laid in at Pittsburgh in spite of the delays of the treasury.*

## Morgan sends another road update

On May 2, 1779, Morgan wrote the following letter to Greene, updating him on the status of the new road, and requesting money to pay the hands. He declines a commission on the road cost, indicating that he is doing his part for the good of the country:

*Although the annexd Extrat of a Letter does not communicate the full Intelligence I could wish, I do myself the pleasure to transmit it to you, that you may see I have not been inattentive to the small matter you were pleased to commit to my charge. I have not yet received advice from the Gentleman I directed to open the Road from Turkey Foot to Fort Pitt; but I doubt not its being speedily done, as he is a Man of Activity, and every way qualified for the Service to complete which I sent him three thousand dollars. I therefore take the liberty to request that you will transmit an Order to me for this Sum and the Amount of Captain Clintons demand, the whole being six thousand five hundred dollars, for which I will Acct. Or, if you please your D Qr Mr Genl for the Department may settle and pay the Acct for I would not wish to interfere with him in any Advantage of Commission. It will be a sufficient recompence to me if I have in this Instance, promoted the public, and render'd you an agreeable Service.*

*In spite of the delays of the Treasury, I have been able to make as ample Provision in the Commissarys Department, as could have been expected; and Colonel Steel tells me he has 600 Horses engaged in transporting Flour from Skipton, to which place it is now carried by water to the great Saving of Time and Expence.*

Clinton's above-quoted April 20, 1779 letter accompanied this May 2, 1779 letter from Morgan to Greene. From these two letters, it is clear that Morgan's road ran from Fort Cumberland to support Fort Pitt, crossed the Casselman River somewhere, and passed through the Turkeyfoot region. The May 2, 1779 letter also shows that Greene assigned the road construction project to Morgan.

## Sullivan is appointed to lead the eastern campaign

In a May 3, 1779 follow-up letter to Brodhead, Washington writes from his headquarters at Middle Brook:

*I have been favoured with your Letter of the 3rd. Ulto., with its several Inclosures. I wrote you on the 21st. of April, some days before the receipt of it, that I had relinquished the idea of attempting a co-operation between the Troops at Fort Pitt and the bodies moving from other Quarters against the Six Nations, and assigned the reasons. Lest this Letter should have miscarried by any accident I now enclose you a Copy, and you will consider it as a Letter of Instructions, as far as it extends.*

*I have written to the Board of War on the subject of Cloathing and Money for the Troops under your command; and I am persuaded they will use their endeavours to furnish such supplies, as may be in their power.*

On May 4, 1779, Washington wrote to Greene that he appointed Major General John Sullivan to command the attack on the Six Nations:

*Having already fully explained to you the plan of the Western expedition against the Indians of the six nations, and the preparations necessary in your department; I am now to inform you that Major General Sullivan is appointed to the command of this expedition, and to desire that you will comply with his immediate requisitions for every thing which falls under the providence of your department so far as is consistent with the general directions, you receive from me, relative to the operations of the army at large.*

## Supplies are moving toward Fort Pitt

On May 8, 1779, Colonel John Cox wrote a letter to Greene that includes the following statement:

*I this moment Received your favor of the 6th Inst, in answer to which I am to inform you that every possible step in my power hath been taken to expedite the necessary preparations as well for the intended Indian Expedition, as for the Army at large, and I flatter myself that most of the Articles ordered to be deposited at Estherton are now their and those for Fort Pitt on their way up.*

On the same day, Reed wrote a letter to Washington to say he understood why the Fort Pitt attack was canceled:

*We are perfectly satisfied with the Motives which have induced your Excelly to lay aside the Cooperation of the Troops from Fort Pitt...*

### A May 17, 1779 letter describes an Indian invasion in Bedford County, Pennsylvania

A May 17, 1779 letter from Bedford states:

*Pursuant to adjournment the subscribers met at George Milligan's with the Intention to assess and lay the Quota of the 62000 Dollars as also the taxes for the current year but the Indians having made a recent and general Invasion into this County the unfortunate Inhabitants have generally been obliged to abandon their Habitations and either fly or collect into Forts to save their lives has made it impossible for the full board to meet.*

### Brodhead reaches out for supplies

On May 17, 1779, Brodhead wrote a letter to Colonel Thomas Smyth that includes the statement:

*The Troops here are in great distress for want of provisions, and I am unable to strike a single stroke until a supply arrives, I am informed that a considerable quantity is arrived at Bedford & must intreat you if possible to send it on immediately.*

On May 22, 1779, Brodhead wrote a letter to Washington that states:

*You can scarcely conceive how difficult it has been for some time past to procure meat for the Troops at this post. I think we have been without that article upwards of Twenty days...*

*In my last I mentioned a Great supply of salt provisions having arrived at Bedford which could not be brought on for want of forage but the information I had then rec'd was wrong and I am informed by the Quartermaster at Carlisle, there is only forty nine barrels of Pork...*

### McIntosh declares against George Morgan

On May 22, 1779, Daniel Brodhead wrote a cordial letter to George Morgan that stated:

*It is a long time since I had the pleasure of hearing from you, I hope you are in perfect health and the full enjoyment of every human felicity.*

*I am told Gen. McIntosh has declared against you a second time, & that a gentlemen with whom he lately smoked the calumet is gone down to support him. We feel the effects of Gen McIntoshes economical plans, & have greatly suffered for want of meat... If there be any worth communicating of news or politics and you can find leisure to write me a very long letter, I shall take great pleasure in reading it...*

### Brodhead continues to write about provisions

On May 26, 1779, Brodhead wrote a letter to Greene that mentions *"... some salt provisions I was under the necessity of drawing from the Magazine at Carlisle, still remains at Bedford, for want of forage to enable teams to bring them on ..."* This shows that not all the supplies intended for Fort Pitt came through

Fort Cumberland. On the same day, Brodhead also wrote a letter to Colonel Stephen Bayard from Pittsburgh that includes the following:

*Doctor Morgan[1593] arrived a few days ago and informed me you was on the road with the Regimental stores, and as a Field officer is and has long been wanting at this place, I sent Captain Moore to take charge of the stores that you might not be longer detained.*

*I am much surprised that no Assi't Deputy Qr. Master is stationed at Old Town or Skipton, a place where I am told most of our stores are loaded and unloaded, and consequently the Brigades Rendezvous, and shall write to Col. Davis on that account, because I believe much more might be done by the Pack horses than what I learn is done.*

*I believe the stores are in no danger from the Enemy, but we must keep a look out against those we esteem our Friends...*

Brodhead's reference to *"Old Town or Skipton"* is a clue that most of the supplies for Fort Pitt were coming out of Virginia, as Washington had directed Wadsworth on February 14, 1779. Since Braddock's road was cut as a wagon road, it may seem surprising that packhorses were still being used in 1779. Jacob Brown's 1896 book "**Brown's Miscellaneous Writings...**" provides insight, indicating that packhorses were the norm on Braddock's road for many years:

*This now historic road, when made, was of sufficient capacity to pass vehicles; with a mere removal of timber and rocks—no engineering, grading, or smoothing. But there was scarcely a wagon passed over it for the first thirty years. Such heavy articles as salt, iron, etc., were carried from the East to the West over the mountains on pack horses. Tradition (the oldest inhabitant cannot reach back) tells how they then went in convoys, single file, in this road.*

### Brodhead takes a swipe at McIntosh

On May 26, 1779, Brodhead took a swipe at McIntosh in a letter to Nathanial Greene which stated:

*I am glad General McIntosh is to go to the Southward, and I really wish him success, but if he is to have the command there we may soon be informed that his temper is disagreeable to the inhabitants and others there, as well as those in this district.*

### Morgan resigns from public service

In a May 28, 1779 letter to Congress, George Morgan tendered his resignation. The ultimate reason was likely due to the irascible McIntosh's continuing animosity toward Morgan. Macintosh was trying to profer charges against Morgan and wrote an angry letter to George Washington on the subject on May 14, 1779.[1594] After passing the letter on to Washington, Alexander Hamilton replied to Macintosh in a May 14, 1779 letter, stating that the proposed court marshal *"would be attended with so many difficulties as to make it utterly inconvenient."* George Washington's correspondence also contains an April 17, 1779 document from McIntosh, listing charges against George Morgan. Washington shelved the charges.

In his resignation letter, Morgan states that:

*...it is his opinion an Agent for Indian Affairs in the Western Department is at present unnecessary further than to act under the sole direction of the Officer commanding in the Department — which, from the*

---

[1593] This appears to be a reference to George Morgan's brother John, who is not to be confused with the Colonel John Morgan of Springhill Township, Fayette County, who is described on page 773 of Ellis' 1882 book "**History of Fayette County**".

[1594] "**Collections of the State Historical Society of Wisconsin**", Volume 23.

*conduct of General McIntosh the late Commandant on most occasions, Colo Morgan begs leave to decline — being fully satisfied, that a perseverance in the late adopted Indian Politics will terminate in a general Indian War, which, by a proper conduct may be avoided. — These are the sentiments Colonel Morgan has held forth to Congress ever since he had the honour of acting under them — They are dictated from honest principles & a sincere desire to serve his Country without injuring the Indians who wish to live in Peace with us. But as Gentlemen of knowledge & superior abilities differ in opinion & as Policy may require a certain conduct toward the Indians which Colo Morgan is not capable of, he most respectfully entreats the favor of Congress to allow him to retire from the employment of Agent for Indian Affairs and more particularly as some Circumstances in his family require his immediate attention. For this reason & others he also most respectfully requests a person may be appointed in his place to act as Deputy Commisary General of Purchases in the Western Department...*

For a summary of the intractable challenges of Indian policy and military supply that Morgan valiantly wrestled with, see the chapters *"Fort Pitt: Indian Affairs 1776-1779"* and *"Fort Pitt: Problems of Supply"* in Max Savelle's 1932 book "**George Morgan Colony Builder**". Also see the article *"George Morgan, Indian Agent Extraordinary, 1776-1779"* in the October 1934 issue of "**Pennsylvania History**". Morgan's mention of *"Circumstances in his family that require his immediate attention"* seems to be a reference to his need to be in the east to devote attention to the land interests of the Indiana Company.[1595] In spite of this resignation, Morgan continued to work on the supply problems of the western department.

## Sullivan's marching orders are to lay waste to the Indian settlements

Washington's May 31, 1779 instructions to Sullivan include this statement:

*The expedition you are appointed to command is to be directed against the hostile tribes of the six nations of Indians, with their associates and adherents. The immediate objects are the total destruction and devastation of their settlements and the capture of as many prisoners of every age and sex as possible. It will be essential to ruin their crops now in the ground and prevent their planting more. ...*

*So soon as your preparations are in sufficient forwardness, you will assemble your main body at Wyoming and proceed thence to Tioga, taking from that place the most direct and practicable route into the heart of the Indian Settlements. ...*

*I would recommend that some post in the center of the Indian Country should be occupied with all expedition, with a sufficient quantity of provisions, whence parties should be detached to lay waste all the settlements around with instructions to do it in the most effectual manner; that the country may not be merely overrun but destroyed.*

*After you have very thoroughly completed the destruction of their settlements; if the Indians should show a disposition for peace, I would have you to negotiate on condition that they will give some decisive evidence of their sincerity by delivering up some of the principle instigators of their past hostility into our hands—Butler, Brandt, & the most mischevious of the tories that have joined them or any other they may have in their power that we are interested to get into ours...*

*But you will not by any means listen to an overture of peace before the total ruin of their settlements is effected ... Peace without this would be fallacious and temporary...*

---

[1595] In 1796 George Morgan moved to his *"Morganza"* farm in Washington County, where he lived out the remainder of his life. A historical marker at Latitude 40.273475°, Longitude -80.158345° along Morganza Road, in Cannonsburg, marks the site of the farm.

## Fort Pitt receives supplies

On June 24, 1779, Brodhead wrote a letter to Reed about actions taken recently against Indians. One part of the letter states:

*I now have a considerable quantity of Provisions, & could make a successful Campaign up the Alleghany, but I am not at Liberty to do it. ...*

*The wicked Waggoners & pack horse drivers have destroyed at least one sixth of our Spirits, &c. In future it had better be cased.*

Since the new road was initially cut as a packer's path, the reference to *"Waggoners"* indictes that not all the supplies were coming by the new road.

On the next day, Brodhead wrote a letter to George Washington that included the statement:

*With great pleasure, I can now inform your excellency, that I have upwards of four hundred head of beef cattle, and near a thousand kegs of flour, with which, had I your permission, I conceive I could make a successful expedition against the Senecas.*

Morgan's November 9, 1779 letters (below) make clear that the new road from Fort Cumberland played a significant role in provisioning Fort Pitt during the summer of 1779, helping to make Brodhead's expedition possible.

## Brodhead plans a diversionary attack

On July 11, 1779, Brodhead wrote a letter indicating that he was going to make a diversionary attack in support of Sullivan. Washington wrote the following to Brodhead on July 13, 1799:

*Yours of the 25th of June was delivered me yesterday. I inclose you a duplicate of mine of the 23d. which gave my consent to an expedition against the Mingoes—I am glad to hear you had received a supply of provisions and only waited my concurrence to make an expedition against the Senecas. I hope by this time you are carrying it into execution.*

Brodhead's July 11, 1779 letter suggests that he had received Washington's June 23, 1779 letter.

## Brodhead chastises Steel

On July 15, 1779, Brodhead strongly chastises Steel:

*It is not a little surprising, that notwithstanding the frequent requisitions I have made, you seem determined not to make me acquainted with ye instructions you have received for supplying this district. If Flour is not transported over the Mountain faster than it has hitherto been, it will not be in my power to employ a single man from the country, however great the demand may be. I assure, Sir, yt I had entertained great hopes of extraordinary exertions from you after the charges yt have been exhibited against you,[1596] and yet I am sorry to say, too little has been effected. Therefore, I am obliged to make a peremptory demand of the copy of your instructions, and return of the Articles you have procured in obedience to your orders. It has been frequently alleged that the Pack horse Drivers are very idle, at and between Old Town and this place, and as they are accountable to you, I expect you will see that abuse corrected.*

---

[1596] An April 21, 1779 general order from George Washington notes that *"The Court do unanimously acquit Colonel Steel of each and every of the charges made against him by General McIntosh...the court are satisfied on the most mature consideration that the general distresses of our country, Colonel Steel's want of money and other causes mentioned by different evidences have been the occasion thereof."*

### Brodhead asks nearby counties for volunteers

On July 17, 1779, Brodhead wrote a letter to the lieutenants of nearby counties asking for volunteers. The letter includes the following:

> *His Excellency, the Commander in Chief, has at length given me a little latitude, and I am determined to strike a blow against one of the most Hostile nations, that in all Probability will effectually secure the tranquility of the Frontiers for years to come.*

### A report of no flour at Fort Cumberland or Old Town

On July 31, 1779, Colonel Daniel Brodhead wrote a letter[1597] to General Washington from Fort Pitt that includes the statement, *"The quantity of flour on hand at these Magazines is very small, and I am informed there is none at Cumberland or Old Town. It would give me great pleasure to co-operate with General Sullivan, but I shall be into the Seneca Towns a long time before he can receive an account of my movement, I shall, however, endeavor to inform him, if a Messenger can be hired to carry a letter."* The letter includes a postscript that states, *"I have just learned that two Soldiers have lately been killed at Fort Lawrens, two boys on Wheeling Creek, two boys taken on Racoon Creek and one man slightly wounded, and a Soldier last evening killed at Fort McIntosh, and a Serjeant slightly wounded. The inhabitants are so intent upon going to Kentuck and the falls of Ohio, that I fear I shall have but few volunteers."*

### Sullivan's successful expedition against the Indian settlements

Sullivan's now famous expedition was significantly delayed due to severe logistical difficulties. His troops finally set forth from the Wyoming Valley on July 31, 1779, destroying at least 40 Indian villages in a wide-ranging, highly successful campaign in New York.

### Brodhead complains to Greene about Colonel Steel

Brodhead's August 2, 1779 letter to Greene includes the following:

> *The Destruction of publick stores for this Department was not confined to Fort Pitt. I rather incline to believe the greater destruction happened before they reached it. I believe much of them were destroyed here too, for want of regularity in the issues…*

> *As to Colo. Steel I have not seen him since April, and but seldom heard from him; I never knew what instructions he received, or what stores I might expect from him until a few days ago. …*

> *I don't know how far Col. Morgan may be culpable, but by a letter I received from him last Summer, at Carlisle, he did not consider himself Comm'y of the Department, but alleged that Mr. Lockart was the proper purchasing Comm'y, and of that I gave Gen'l McIntosh a copy. I believe, as I said before, that the chief misfortunes in this department were owing to the General's haughty insulting temper. …*

> *In a few days more I shall march towards the Seneca towns up the Alleghany, and am much obliged for your good wishes.*

Morgan was correct. Patrick Lockhart was specifically appointed by Congress on June 11, 1778, to *"procure provisions, pack-horses, and other necessaries for the army destined for"* operations against the garrison of Detroit. Nevertheless, as previously quoted, Morgan was lauded in an October 16, 1778 War Office document for delivering several hundred cattle that enabled McIntosh *"to commence his expedition before the arrival of supplies from Mr. Lockart."*

---

[1597] **"Pennsylvania Archives"**.

## Charles Clinton is involved in a property transaction on the North Branch

The 1939 book "**Early Records Hampshire County Virginia**" records the following for August 9, 1779, "*SIMMONDS, Thomas (w. Agnes) of Hampshire Co. to Charles Clinton of Washington Co. (lease and release) 199 a. on North Branch of Potomac; rec 8-10-1779. Wit.: None.*"

## Brodhead's parallel campaign is also successful

Brodhead left Fort Pitt on August 11, 1779 with 605 combatants and 100 escorts for the campaign supplies. According to a letter he wrote to George Washington on September 16, 1779, Brodhead marched north as far as the upper Seneca towns, destroying a number of Indian villages and over 500 acres of associated crops, and returned to Pittsburgh on September 14, 1779. Sullivan's and Brodhead's successful attacks were followed by the exceptionally harsh winter of 1779, which was devastating to the now under-provisioned Indians. The expedition is summarized as follows in Volume 3 of the 1788 book, "**The History of the Rise, Progress, and Establishment, of the Independence of the United States of America…**":

> *Col. Broadhead also engaged in a successful expedition against the Mingo and Munsey Indians, and the Senecas on the Alleghaney river. He left Pittsburgh August the 11th, with 605, rank and file, including militia and volunteers, and did not return till the 14th of September. They went about 200 miles from the fort, destroyed a number of towns, and cornfields to the amount of 500 acres, and made a great deal of plunder in skins and other articles.*

### Brodhead reports to Washington

Brodhead's report[1598] to George Washington states:

> *Pittsburgh, Sep'r 16th 1779. Dear General,*
>
> *I returned from the expedition against the Seneca & Muncy nations the 14th Inst., & now do myself the honor to inform you how far I have succeeded in prosecuting it.*
>
> *I left this place the 11th of last month with six hundred & five Rank & File, including Militia & Volunteers, & one Month's provision which except the live Cattle was transported by water under the escort of one hundred Men to a place called Mahoning, about 15 Miles above Fort Armstrong, where after four days detention by excessive Rains & the straying of some of the Cattle, the Stores were loaded on Pack Horses, and the troops proceeded on the march for Canawago on the path leading to Cuscushing; at ten miles on this side the town, one of the advanced guards consisting of fifteen White men, including the spies & eight Delaware Indians, under the command of Lieut. Hardin of the 8th Penn'a Reg't, whom I have before recommended to your Excellency for his great bravery & skill as a partisan, discovered between thirty & Forty warriors coming down the Allegheny River in seven Canoes. These warriors having likewise discovered some of the Troops, immediately landed stript off their shirts & prepared for action, and the advanced Guard immediately began the attack — All the troops except one column & Flankers being in the narrows between the River and high hill were immediately prepared to receive the enemy, which being done, I went forward to discover the Enemy, & six of them retreating over the River without arms, at the same time the rest ran away leaving their Canoes, Blankets, Shirts, provisions and eight Guns, besides five dead & by the signs of Blood, several went off wounded, only two of my men & one of the Delaware Indians (Nanouland) were wounded & so slightly that they are already recovered & fit for action. — The next morning the Troops proceeded to Buchloons,[1599] where I ordered a small Breastwork to be thrown up of felled Timber & fascines, a Capt. & forty men were left to secure our Baggage & Stores, & the Troops immediately proceeded to Canawago, which I found had been deserted about eighteen months past. Here the Troops seemed much mortified because we had no person to serve as a*

---

[1598] "**Pennsylvania Archives**", 1856.

[1599] The Buckaloons historical marker is in the Allegheny National Forest, between Youngville and Warren, Pennsylvania, 137 miles north-northeast of Fort Pitt, at Latitude 41.835685°, Longitude -79.257407°.

*Guide to the upper Towns, but I ordered them to proceed on a path which appeared to have been travelled on by the Enemy some time past, & we continued marching on it about 20 Miles before any discoveries were made except of a few tracks of their spies. But immediately after ascending a high hill we discovered the Allegheny River & a number of Corn Fields, & descending several towns which the Enemy had deserted on the approach of the Troops. Some of them fled just before the advanced Guards reached the Towns & left several packs of Deer skins. At the upper Seneca Towns we found a painted image or War post, clothed in Dog skin, & John Montour told me this Town was called Yoghroonwago, besides this we found seven other Towns, consisting in the whole of one hundred and thirty Houses, some of which were large enough for the accommodation of three or four Indian families. The Troops remained on the ground three whole days destroying the Towns & Corn Fields. I never saw finer Corn altho' it was planted much thicker than is common with our Farmers. The quantity of Corn and other vegetables destroyed at the several Towns, from the best accounts I can collect from the officers employed to destroy it, must certainly exceed five hundred acres which is the lowest estimate, and the plunder taken is estimated at 30 m. Dollars, I have directed a sale to be made of it for the benefit of the Troops. On my return I preferred the Venango Road, the old towns of Conawago, Buchloons & Mahusquechikoken, about 20 Miles above Venango, on French Creek, consisting of 35 large houses were likewise burnt. — The greatest part of the Indian houses were larger than common, and built of square & round logs & frame work. From the great quantity of Corn in new Ground & the number of new houses Built & Building it appears that the whole Seneca & Muncy nations intended to collect to this settlement which extends about eight Miles on the Allegheny River, between one hundred & seventy & two hundred Miles from hence. the River at the upper Towns is little if any larger than Kiskamanitis Creek. It is remarkable that neither man or Beast has fallen into the Enemies hands on this expedition, & I have a happy presage that the counties of Westmoreland, Bedford & Northumberland, if not the whole western Frontiers will experience the good effect of it.*

*Too much praise cannot be given to both officers and soldiers of every Corps during the whole expedition, their perseverance and zeal during the whole march thro' a Country too inaccessible to be described can scarcely be equalled in history. Notwithstanding many of them returned barefooted and naked they disdained to complain, and to my great mortification I have neither Shoes, Shirts, Blankets, Hats, Stockings nor leggins to relieve their necessities.*

*On my return here I found the Chiefs of the Delawares, the principal Chief of the Hurons, and now the king of the Maquichee tribe of the Shawanese, is likewise come to treat with me; about 30 Delaware warriors are here likewise ready to go to war, but I have nothing to encourage them with, and without the means of paying them I cannot send them out. The Troops here have at least nine Months pay due to them and there is neither money nor Pay Master to discharge the arrearages. A majority of my Regt. are now discharged and the term of the two Ranging Companies of Westmoreland expired, so that I shall be weak in Troops to prosecute an expedition which by your permission I should be happy to make against Detroit, taking the Shawanese in my way. I should be happy to have your permission to make occasional excursions against any of the Indian nations who may hereafter prove inimical to us, as sometimes a favorable opportunity may be lost before I can be favored with your particular orders. Likewise to know your pleasure in regard to the Senecas and Muncies should they in their great distress sue for peace. I have before taken the liberty to give you my opinion respecting them, and the pairings of scalps and the hair of our Countrymen at every Warrior's camp on the path we marched are new inducements for Revenge.*

*I am informed that Col. Clark who took Post St. Vincent, is making peace and war with the natives. I am not instructed how far your Excellency has authorized him to do so and apprehend the worst consequences to this frontier should either Col. Clark or myself enter into a treaty of peace with one of the Indian nations and the other Break it, and by my instructions I am confined to the immediate command of the Troops here, I can take no step to prevent such a probable [event?], but humbly entreat you to do it.*

*The Wyandotts and the Maquichees tribe of the Shawanese promise very fair, and I have promised them peace provided they take as many prisoners and scalps from the Enemy as they have done from us and on every occasion join us against the enemies of America, which they have engaged to do.*

*The two soldiers I sent Express to Genl. Sullivan are not yet returned, and I apprehend they have fallen into the Enemy's hands.*

*A few Indian Goods, Paint and trinkets at this juncture would enable me to engage the Delawares to harrass the enemy frequently.*

*The Bearer, Capt. McIntire, has some private as well as public Business to transact at Philada. I have therefore ordered him to proceed to Head Quarters and he will have the honor to wait on you with this letter.*

*I have the honor to be with the most perfect regard and esteem, your Excellency's most*

> *Obed't H'ble Serv't,*
>
> *D. BRODHEAD. Directed,*
>
> *His Excellency Genl. Washington.*

## A payment to Colonel Lemuel Barrett

On September 1,1779 the Council of Maryland ordered[1600] *"That the said Treasurer pay ... Eight pence and Fifteen Pounds for the use of Col° Lemuel Barret p Acc^ts passed by the Aud. Gen^l"*.

## Brodhead continues to ask Morgan for help with supplies

On September 23, 1779, Brodhead wrote a letter to Reed stating, *"I hope a second supply of Stores is on the road for my Regt..."* Despite George Morgan's May 28, 1779 resignation from his two thankless jobs, it appears that he remained engaged in some capacity. A September 24, 1779 letter that Brodhead wrote to Morgan describing a hoped-for attack against Detroit states, *"My Coffee, Tea and Sugar, is nearly expended, and there is none to be purchased here except at a trible price, if therefore this should reach you whilst you continue in the purchasing Department, you will greatly oblige me by purchasing a Barrel of Coffee, another of sugar and three pounds of Green Tea, besides a few poinds of loaf sugar for my table."* The letter also mentions some documents Brodhead sent to the Board of War, including *"copies of Talks between me and the Savages, which you will doubtless be made acquainted with."*

## Sundry Purchases for the Western Department

A manuscript document with the cover title *"No 7 Sundry Purchases Sept 1779"* was found by Lynn Wright. As best I can determine, the main page of the document states:

*The United States to Charles Clinton for Sundry Purchases for the Department Brigade of Packhorses in the western Department*

*1779 Sep.^t*

| No | | | | £ | S | P |
|----|----|----|----|----|----|----|
| 1 | 1 | to Charles Clinton for Smith work | with Receipt | ~ | 10 | ~ |

---

[1600] **"Archives of Maryland"**, Volume 21.

| | | | | | |
|---|---|---|---|---|---|
| 2 | | to Do[1601] for Do | 11 | 5 | ~ |
| 3 | 2 | to Do for Do | 2 | 10 | ~ |
| 4 | | to Thomas Simons for Riding Express 1 ½ Days | 9 | 7 | 6 |
| 5 | 7 | to M$^r$ Peter Tittle for Portage of Sundry Brigade at His acc.$^l$ and Receipt[1602] | 909 | 7 | 6 |
| 6 | 11 | to Charles Clinton for Porter[1603] | 1 | 2 | 6 |
| 7 | | to Jonathan Irons for Riding Express to Maj$^r$ ___ With Col Davis Letter about March Last | 7 | 10 | ~ |
| 8 | 14 | to Isaac Colliar for Portage of one horse three Day | 1 | 2 | 6 |
| 9 | 14 | to Charles Clinton for Smith Work | 4 | 6 | 9 |
| 10 | 16 | to Lemuel Barrett for taking up and Packing one Continental Horse 20 Days | 12 | ~ | ~ |
| 11 | 19 | to Dickson Simkins for taking up and Bringing to This Place one Con.$^l$ Horse | 9 | 10 | ~ |
| 12 | 29 | to Charles Clinton for Porter ___ ___ Receipt | 10 | 17 | 6 |
| | | ___ ___ ___ ___ Charles Clinton[1604] | 367 | 8 | 9 |

I suspect that the reason this document was found in the Cumberland County, Pennsylvania Archives is because Carlisle was a major manufacturing and supply center.[1605] The familiar names recorded on the document make it abundantly clear that it is a record of expenses incurred by Captain Charles Clinton at Fort Cumberland, Maryland for disbursements he made, and blacksmith work he performed, in support of a packhorse brigade supplying the western department of the Continental Army. Thomas Simons[1606] and Colonel Davis are the only individuals that I do not recognize as definitely being from the Cumberland, Maryland area, but Davis is identified in Brodhead's May 26, 1779 a letter to Colonel Stephen Bayard as being connected with the Quartermaster Department.

The reference to Continental Horses is apparently a reference to the use of government-owned horses, as opposed to privately owned horses.

---

[1601] "Do" means "Ditto".

[1602] I am not entirely sure about the word "Receipt".

[1603] I am not entirely sure about the word "Porter".

[1604] This appears to be a signature, as if Charles Clinton is affirming the validity of the document.

[1605] For example, George Washington's January 17, 1777 letter to John Hancock includes the statement, "By a late Resolve of Congress, the Towns of Carlisle in Pennsylvania and Brookfeild in Massachusets are fixed upon for the proper places to erect Elaboratories and lay up Magazines of military Stores." Also, George Washington's March 20, 1778 letter to Major General Horatio Gates from Valley Forge includes the statement, "The Field Artillery, heavy twelves and the twenty four pounders that were at Albany and such other military Stores as will not be immediately wanted down the River, will be ordered on by General Knox and what are not wanted here sent to Carlisle. That place will then be the grand Arsenal of all Artillery & Stores on this side of Hudsons River as Springfield will be of those on the East side."

[1606] A Thomas Simmons is mentioned in the July 6 to 8, 1756 orders at Fort Cumberland, as follows, "John Leigh and Thomas Simmons—as it is the first offence — and they were ignorant of the consequence of Desertion — two hundred and fifty lashes each."

This is a snippet from the document *"No 7 Sundry Purchases Sept 1779"*.

### Morgan's November 9, 1779 letters about the new Turkey Foot Road

On November 9, 1779, Morgan wrote letters concerning the new road out of Fort Cumberland to Colonel Charles Petite, Assistant Quartermaster General, and Providence Mounts. Copies of the letters were found among Morgan's papers.[1607] The first letter is to Charles Petite:

*Princeton November 9th 1779*

*Dear Sir*

*From the extraordinary Rise of Wages & Produce, I find the new Road will Cost a mutch more Considerable Sum than I thought when I Last Conversed with you The bearer Mr William Wilson[1608] on whom I gave Captin Clinton (one of the undertakers) a Letter of Credit has advanced to him aboute twenty thousand Dollars, the Sum I have received from you, & Providance Mounts Esqr to whome I have advanced Six thousand Dollars has now made application to me for the further Sum of Eight thousand Dollars to enable him to Settle his accts for that part of the Road he undertook to open, and there yet Remains a Number of Rocks to Remove & Sum Bridges to make before the Road will be Compleate for wagons*

*At present it is Constantly traveled by more than 1500 Horses in public Servis, & cuts of twenty two Miles in the Distance from Fort Pitt, to Fort Cumberland — to which if the goodness of the Road be added will make a difference of three days in Everey Trip without making aney Allowance for Detention by the Rise of Waters which frequently happen on the old Road — This has enabled us to keep up a Constant plentifull Supply of Provisions in the western Department the last Season & when the above mentioned Rocks are Removed & Bridges built so as to Compleat the Road for wagons it will Reduce the Expence of Carriage Verey Considerably as well as facilitate the public Servis — For these reasons I must Request the favor of you to pay to the Bearrer Mr William Wilson the Sum of twenty thousand Dollars for Compleating this Business which with the like sum I have formerly Received from you shall be accounted for by Your obedient humble*

*Servant*

---

[1607] Robert R. Reed collection, University of Illinois at Urbana-Champaign, Urbana, Illinois.

[1608] This isn't the first time William Wilson delivered a message for George Morgan. In June of 1776 he was sent to ask the Delaware and Shawnee to wait for George Morgan to arrive before deciding whether to conference with the British at Detroit. See *"Report of William Wilson to the Commissioners for Indian Affairs"*, September 20, 1776 (**"American Archives"**, fifth series, Volume 2, page 514.)

*GM*

*PS*

*Mr. Wilson has Reviewed the Road & Can inform you particularly abouts it —*

*Colonel Charles Petite*

*A. Qr Master Genl*

The statement *"... Detention by the Rise of Waters which frequently happen on the old Road"* is a reference to packhorses on Braddock's road being unable to cross the Youghiogheny River during high water. The Turkey Foot Road was a dryer route because it avoided the Youghiogheny River.

The second November 9, 1779 letter is to Providence Mounts:

*To Providence Mounts Esqr Phila Novr 9th 1779*

*Dear Sir*

*I have Recd your favor of the 20th Ulto by Mr. Wilson to whome I have given orders to answer your Draft for ten thousand Dollars to enable you to Discharge the demands on you to finish the Road Complete for Waggons to pass & Repass without obstructions of Fallen Timber Rocks, Swamps, Trees &c & to bridge wherever wanted — Should you want a further Sum Mr Wilson or Mr Mitchel will Supply you — for which purpose & to enable you to form a perfect Judgement of Mr Clintons part of the Road as well as your own I recommend to you to Ride yourself to Skipton for the money Unless Mr Wilson has a safe opportunity to send it to you with this letter —*

*I incline to sell my interest at Salt Lick & will take £ 12 P acre in hand or Eight Bushels of Indian Corn to be Delivered on the place next october or November & Shall be glad if you can find me a purchaser on Either of these Terms*

*I hope your Family are well I have sent Mr Skelton[1609] a proper Supply of Cash which be pleased to inform Mr Hay of & request him to go to Fort pitt for what he wants*

*I am Sir Your humble*

*Servant*

*Geo. Morgan*

*November 9th 1779 Copies of Letters To Coll Charles Petit & Coll Prov. Mounts.*

These two letters show that the new road was used to support the summer campaign season: Brodhead's campaign that began on August 11, 1779. They also show that Providence Mounts extended the route that Clinton cut to Turkeyfoot and was in the process of upgrading the new road to handle wagons.

## Brodhead asks again for supply help from Morgan, despite Morgan's resignation

Brodhead wrote again to Morgan on November 23, 1779, asking for help with supplies. The letter includes the statement:

*I have heard nothing from you since the arrival of Mr. Boreman, and as it is highly expedient to lay in a greater quantity of meat than is yet purchased, I should be glad to know why no money is sent up to discharge the debts due from your Department and make further purchases. Mr. Boreman assured me*

---

[1609] Joseph Skelton served as the commissary of stores at Fort Pitt as an agent of George Morgan.

*there was a considerable sum ready for you. Should a reinforcement be sent to this District the flour on hand will likewise be deficient. I wrote you some time ago and requested you would purchase some Tea, Sugar & Coffee for me, which I hope you have done. ... I am very anxious to hear from you and hope you will be here very soon.*

## David Blue and James Graham bring military supplies to Fort Cumberland by wagon

The October 15, 1838 pension application[1610] of David Blue tells the story of moving supplies approximately 72 miles from Virginia to Fort Cumberland in the fall of 1779. The relevant portion is quoted here:

*... David Blue, a resident of said County of Union and State of Kentucky aged seventy eight years who being first duly sworn according to law, doth on his oath, make the following declaration in order to obtain the benefit of the act of Congress passed June 7 1832*

*That he entered the service of the United States under the following named officers and served as herein stated —*

*That in the year 1778 & 1779 he resided in Berkley County Virginia that in the fall 1779, he was drafted at Shepherdstown then Berkley County Virginia for a three months tour of militia duty in the service of the United States in the army of the Revolution — that he and a few others who were then drafted (were not marched north as most of the drafted men were then marched) were attached, to waggons and teams, and were employed in hauling flour from Berkley County to Cumberland old fort at or near the foot of the Alleghany mountain for the use of the United States — who ordered the change of service he does not now recollect, but he was put with his waggon & team, (owned by his father Uriah Blue under the command of Capt Duncan Campbell and twenty four waggons & teams & driven were engaged in hauling the flour aforesaid, and he made three trips from Berkley to Cumberland old fort and back and at the end of the third trip received from Capt Campbell a written discharge for a three months tour of militia duty, as had been stipulated when he was transferred from the militia drafted to march, to driving the waggon as aforesaid*

## Thomas Cresap sells Virginia property on the North Branch of the Potomac River

The 1939 book "**Early Records Hampshire County Virginia**" records the following for December 8, 1779, "*CRESAP, Thomas (w. Margaret) of Washington Co. to Michael Cresap of Hampshire Co. 400 a. on North B. Potomac; rec. 8-8-1780. Wit.: Robert Wilson, Lawrence Hass, James Blue, T. Humphrey, Samuel Simeock, Enoch Innis.*"

## Procuring salt from Fort Cumberland when Indians were still active in the area

The December 22, 1864 issue of the Uniontown, Pennsylvania newspaper "**Genius of Liberty**" includes the obituary of Mrs. Hannah Mountain:

*MOUNTAIN — In Addison, Somerset county, Pa., of Friday the 2nd of December, Mrs. Hannah Mountain, in the 93rd year of her age. Another of those loved and venerable links that united us to a past age is broken. One by one they are passing away and soon nothing but kindly memories of friends, or the loving remembrances of closer kindred will be left us. Mother Mountain retained all her faculties to the last and sunk to sleep, from pure physical exhaustion, and not from disease. She had lived in that age when the Red men roamed proudly through his native and scarce broken forests, when the commonest necessaries of life, (salt as an instance) were brought across the mountains from Fort Cumberland; then*

---

[1610] The pension application was found by Barrelville resident Francis Bridges.

*the frontier settlement. Now when the shriek of the locomotive is startling her native vallies, when plenty crowns the labors of the husbandman, where hundreds are hurriedly jostling each other in ....... the race of surrenders her soul to her God, and goeth forth to reap the great reward of a well spent life.*

The obituary appears to reference stories that Hannah Mountain told family members about procuring salt and other necessaries of life from Fort Cumberland, and about Indians still being in the area, during her youth. The previously quoted February 16, 1779 letter to the Pennsylvania General Assembly from various Bedford county and township tax assessors describes a period of Indian depredations within the county that made it impractical to levy taxes. Hannah would have been old enough to remember this tumultuous period of her life. By 1784, numerous property surveys were being made in the part of Bedford County that would become Somerset County, suggesting that the danger from Indians had passed. This suggests that the trips to Fort Cumberland for salt that are described in Hannah Mountain's obituary were made before Fort Cumberland formally became a recognized town. Hannah Mountain is the daughter of Oliver Drake,[1611] who migrated to the Turkeyfoot region circa 1770,[1612] and settled where Draketown is located.[1613] Oliver Drake appears in the list of 1773 Brothersvalley Township, Bedford County taxables.[1614] According to the **"Pennsylvania Archives"**, fifth series, Volume V, *"Muster rolls, etc., 1743-1787"*, on December 10, 1777, Oliver Drake was the First Lieutenant of the Turkey Foot Company of the First Battalion of the Bedford Militia, and was Captain of the company on April 25, 1777. According to Volume 2 of the 1906 book **"History of Bedford and Somerset Counties..."**, Oliver Drake was Captain of the Turkeyfoot company in 1778, 1779, and 1781.

---

[1611] On August 18, 2012, Nancy Becker wrote on the **"Drake Family"** website that one of her cousins had photos of the Mountain family Bible that confirm that Hannah was Oliver Drake's daughter. According to the **"Pennsylvania Archives"**, fifth series, Volume V, *"Muster rolls, etc., 1743-1787"*, on December 10, 1777, Oliver Drake was the First Lieutenant of the Turkey Foot Company of the First Battalion of the Bedford Militia, and was Captain of the company on April 25, 1777. According to Volume 2, pages 240 and 241 of the 1906 book **"History of Bedford and Somerset Counties..."**, Captain Oliver Drake is buried at the Jersey church, and was Captain of the Turkeyfoot company in 1778, 1779, and 1781. Volume 3 of the 1980 book **"Mayflower Families Through Five Generations"** lists an Oliver Drake who was born January 25, 1745. Volume 2 of the 1982 book **"Genealogies of Pennsylvania families: from The Pennsylvania genealogical magazine"** lists Oliver Drake as being born in New Jersey on January 24, 1745, as marrying F. Skinner on August 22, 1770, and as having a gristmill at Draketown, Pennsylvania. These are secondary sources, rather than documentary evidence. Draketown is a small village near Confluence, Pennsylvania that is located at Latitude 39.851643°, Longitude -79.368171°

[1612] The book **"Reflections: Ursina 1787 – 1994"** indicates that the Jersey settlers came into the Turkeyfoot area and settled during the spring of 1770. This may be based on the 1906 book **"The History of Bedford and Somerset Counties..."**, which indicates that Oliver Drake was among the Jersey settlers who came to the Turkeyfoot region in 1770. These are secondary sources, rather than documentary evidence.

[1613] The 1906 book **"The History of Bedford and Somerset Counties..."** states, *"Oliver Drake settled on the land where Draketown now is. He undoubtedly was a leading man in this pioneer settlement. Soon after coming into the country he built a grist mill, which so far as we have able to learn was the first built in these parts."* This is a secondary source, rather than documentary evidence. Draketown is a small village at Latitude 39.851643°, Longitude -79.368171°.

[1614] According to William Henry Egle's 1898 book **"Returns of taxables for the counties of Bedford (1773 to 1784)..."** Oliver Drake appears among the 1773 taxables of Brothersvalley Township, and the 1774 to 1776, 1779, and 1783 taxables of Turkeyfoot Township. For the Bedford County tax lists from 1773 to 1784, see the 1898 book **"Returns of taxables for the counties of Bedford (1773 to 1784..."**. For the tax assessment lists, see Cassaday's 1932 book **"The Somerset County Outline"**.

## Lowdermilk's ancestor served during the Revolutionary War

The book "**Register of the District of Columbia Society of the American Revolution, 1896**" reveals Lowdermilk's ancestral connection to the Revolutionary War, stating:

*Maj. William Harrison Lowdermilk.*

*Publisher and Bookseller. Born, Cumberland, Md., January 7, 1839.*

*Son of Upton Reid Lowdermilk and Eliza (Rizer) Lowdermilk. Grandson of Peter Lowdermilk and Mary (Kershner) Lowdermilk. Great-grandson of Michael Kershner and Mary (Motter) Kershner.*

*Michael Kershner, of Fort Cumberland, Maryland, Private, Captain Philip Grayble's Company, Colonel Honsaker's Maryland Regiment; discharged, 1779.*

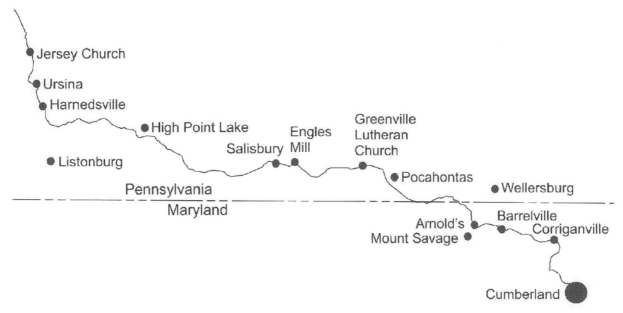

This is a rough schematic of the southern part of the Turkey Foot Road. This map corrects an error near Harnedsville that was included in an earlier version of the map which was published in the November 2011 issue of the "**Laurel Messenger**". The location of the road varied over time, and this is not a depiction of the exact 1779 route. This is included merely to provide a general understanding of the route.

# 32. 1780: The effect of the deep snow

## The impact of Broadhead's campaign, and the deep snow that came afterwards

### The winter of the deep snow

In a February 11, 1780 letter[1615] to President Reed from Pittsburgh, Colonel Brodhead wrote, "*The clothing remains at the foot of the Hill, and the Troops here are suffering for want of many articles, nor do I know that they can be brought 'till some time in the Spring, Captn Finley is arrived and informs me that the Snow is four feet deep upon the Mountains.*"

According to pages 13 and 170 of John Cassaday's 1932 book "**The Somerset County Outline**", the winter of 1779 to 1780 was the "*deep snow*", which gave settlers relief from the Indian raids. The average depth of snow was said to be four to five feet. This heavy snow is described on page 123 of the 1906 book "**History of Bedford and Somerset Counties...**" as follows:

*Early in the winter of 1779-80 there was a very heavy fall of snow. It is said to have been from four to five feet deep on a level, and seems to have lain until very late in the spring of 1780. On February 27, 1780, Colonel Brodhead wrote from Fort Pitt: "I fear the public horses will all perish before grass comes again unless a sum of money can be furnished to purchase forage. The great depth of snow on the Allegheny and Laurel hills has prevented our getting every kind of stores, nor do I expect to get any until the last of April."*

*This great depth of snow for the time isolated the people who still remained in these settlements from their neighbors both to the east and west. In fact, from all accounts, the settlers were largely isolated from each other all of the winter. In a way, this deep snow was really a blessing that brought a feeling of security to the settlers for the time being, for it was not believed that the Indians would attempt any incursion with such a snow covering the earth as this was. But when spring had really come, this blockade of snow soon disappeared under the warmth of the sun, and the fears of Indian invasion were once more renewed.*

Pages 128 and 129 of the book provide the recollections of Joseph Ankeny, a son of the pioneer Peter Ankeny of the Coxes Creek Settlement (now Somerset, Pennsylvania). He heard the tales often from his mother:

*In the fall of 1779 the neighbors were all busy threshing and preparing to go to mill to get their flour ground out. My father had finished his threshing, and intended to go to Jones' mill, which was at the foot of Laurel Hill, about twelve miles, this being the only mill within thirty or forty miles,[1616] but the evening before he*

---

[1615] "**Pennsylvania Archives**", Volume 8, 1853.

[1616] According to Cassaday's 1932 book "**The Somerset County Outline**", Jones' mill may have been the only mill in what is now Somerset County when it was built in 1779. An article in the May 1960 "**Laurel Messenger**" states, "*The JOURNAL of Peter Ankeny reported (1779) a grist mill built on Laurel Creek by William Jones...*", and also states, "*The Husband JOURNAL reported (1779) a tub mill located on the south side of Flaugherty Creek...built by Adam Cook...*" The Jones mill at the foot of Laurel Hill is identified on the 1792 Reading Howell map. Volume I of Boucher's "**Old and New Westmoreland**" provides a succinct description of a tub mill, as follows, "*The first water-power mills were operated by water wheels known as the tub-mill wheel, which gave its name frequently to the stream which turned it. The tub-mill wheel was in a round enclosure that resembled a large tub. The water falling on it made it revolve, and thus the perpendicular shaft to which it was fastened was turned, and by gearing, made the mill stones revolve, or ran a saw, as the occasion might be.*" The tub mill wheel is, in its essence, a water powered turbine. Several tub mills are maintained as tourist attractions in the Great Smokey Mountains National Park. For more information about the Jones Mill on the waters of Laurel Hill Creek, see the May 1968 and August 1976 issues of the "**Laurel Messenger**", which

*was to start it commenced to snow, and by morning the snow was about three feet, and it continued to snow for forty successive days, more or less every day. The snow was from four to five feet average depth. Nobody was able to get to the mill, and they lived on potatoes and boiled wheat in lieu of bread for six weeks, and it made a good substitute, and they never thought of starving. Some time in March, the snow having settled some, all hands turned out to break the path to the mill, and in four days they returned with flour.*

### The campaign, and the deep snow, had a devastating effect on the Indians

Mary Jemison was married to Chief Hiokatoo and was known to the Indians as the *"White Woman"*. Before Sullivan's attack, she lived at Beard's town, the headquarters village of the Senecas, in the Genesee country. In 1823, she described the effect of the harsh winter that followed the destruction of the Indian villages and food supply by Sullivan:

*The succeeding winter was the most severe that I have witnessed since my rememberance. The snow fell about five feet deep, and remained so for a long time; and the weather was extremely cold, so much so, indeed, that almost all of the game upon which the Indians depended on for subsistence perished, and reduced them almost to a state of starvation through that and three or four succeeding years. When the snow melted in the spring, deer were found dead upon the ground in vast numbers; and other animals of various descriptions perished from the cold also, and were found dead in multitudes. Many of our people barely escaped with their lives, and some actually died of hunger and freezing.*

The effect of Brodhead's campaign, combined with the severe winter, would have been similar. In a letter[1617] he wrote to General Sullivan, Brodhead indicates that his forces came relatively close to the Genesee country, stating, *"Yahrungwago is about forty miles on this side Jenesseo, where I should have gone had I not been disappointed in getting a sufficient number of shoes for my men."* (Brodhead's previously quoted letter to George Washington indicates that his forces were at Yoghroonwago.)

The 1838 book **"Sketches of Rochester"** quotes from the book **"Annals of Tyron County"** as follows regarding the Sullivan campaign:

*The country of the Onondagas, the Cayugas, and the Senecas, the three western tribes, was completely overrun and laid waste. To some it may seem that too much severity was exercised in the burning of Indian towns, and that corn, &c., was wantonly destroyed; but it must be borne in mind that this was not a bare retaliatory measure, though as such it might have been justified by the previous conduct of the Indians. Their towns were their retreats, and from thence they made incursions into the settlements: driven back to Niagra, and rendered dependent upon the English for supplies of provisions, they would necessarily be much crippled in their future operations. Though, as we have seen, this campaign did not put a stop to the ravages of the Indians, yet they never recovered from the severe chastisement which they received. A part only of the Indians ever returned to their old settlements from which they were driven. During the following winter, 1779-80, they remained in and about Niagra. Provisions were scarce; those they received were salt; a kind to which the Indians were unaccustomed. They took the scurvy, and died in great numbers. The winter was unusually cold, which increased the difficulties of their situation.*

Gresham's 1891 book **"Biographical and portrait cyclopedia of Chautauqua County, New York"** reports similarly:

*As a result of Sullivan and Broadhead's expeditions against the Indians in 1779, and the destruction of their towns and of the products of their fields which was accomplished as their harvests were ripening, the Indians of the Genesee and Allegheny rivers were without shelter and without food. The winter of 1779 and 1780, was one of unexampled severity. Such deep snows, and such ice, had not been known in*

---

place the mill on Jones Mill Run, and Volume II, page 119 of the 1906 book **"History of Bedford and Somerset Counties..."**

[1617] **"History of Warren County, Pennsylvania..."**, 1887. Also see the **"Pennsylvania Archives"**.

*the memory of the oldest natives. Deer and turkies died in the woods for want of food by hundreds. Great numbers of Indians perished during the winter of cold and starvation. To escape general destruction, the Indians fled to Fort Niagara for shelter and relief. There, to add to their desolation a fatal disease induced by unusual exposure swept them off in great numbers. As the Indians had freely shed their blood during the war, and now had suffered almost annihilation for their faithful adherence to the cause of the king, the British authorities could not without gross ingratitude omit to provide for their relief. Large numbers of Indians had gathered around the fort, and along the river Niagara, and during the winter had fed from the British stores. To relieve themselves from this burden, the British Government encouraged the Indians to establish themselves at convenient places, and obtain support by cultivating the land. Chautauqua County encompasses Jamestown, New York, and is located immediately east of Erie County, Pennsylvania.*

Boucher's 1918 book "**Old and New Westmoreland**" describes the protective benefit afforded to the Pittsburgh area as the result of Brodhead's campaign and the severe winter:

*A campaign of this kind...into the Indian country was at best very destructive to the natives and, as a result, they were forced to seek winter quarters farther west and south, and many of them never returned. But Broadhead's campaign was followed by one of the severest winters in the history of the United States. It set in late in 1779 and lasted until March or April, 1780. The British drove wagons across the harbor between New York and Staten Island on the ice. Around Pittsburgh the winter was equally severe. Snow fell early and accumulated until it was four feet deep in the valleys and on the mountains it was much deeper. All communication with the east ws cut off and all of Westmoreland county suffered for every possible convenience. Scouting parties made up by the soldiers of Fort Pitt, were not only impossible but unnecessary, for the deep snow prevented the Indians from coming here to commit depredations. Many Delawares came to the fort early in the winter and were kept there until spring, thus further depleting their limited stores. The Indians suffered correspondingly and especially those whose crops and houses had been destroyed by Broadhead's troops. These suffered worse than any others. Scores of them starved to death, and, whilst this weakened the enemy, it but increased the hatred and malice of the race for the pioneer settlers and the American army. It reduced the Senecas to such an extent that when spring came they could scarcely renew their depredations, and settlers around Fort Pitt for once were allowed to plant their spring crops in peace so far as their worst enemies in the North and East were concerned.*

Difficult as the ways of war may be to digest, Brodhead's operation was a success, and we are here today to talk about it. Even though war is incomprehensibly cruel, the descendants of the pioneers of western Pennsylvania owe a certain debt of gratitude to Brodhead and his army for protecting the lives of their ancestors. This debt extends to the men who cut the road that made Brodhead's campaign possible, to the packhorse drivers who risked their lives to deliver the precious supplies, and to the settlers who provided forage and other assistance to the packhorse trains.

## Army supplies were being purchased at Fort Cumberland in 1780

According to the 1903 book "**The life and times of Thomas Smith, 1745-1809**", a February 1780 letter from Colonel Thomas Smith, of the Quartermaster's service, includes the statement:

*The Bearer, Mr. Diedier some time ago lent me 3000 Dollars which I expected to have paid him long ago, & am very sorry that his readiness to oblige the Public has been a disadvantage to him; I have bought 73 bushels of corn from him at Fort Cumberland. I have drawn on you for the sum lent, the Price of the Corn & part of what is owing to myself, in the whole D10,000 which I request you will pay immediately as he is obliged on his way to Baltimore to come round by Carlisle, & if he should meet with any delay it will be a loss for him as he has engaged Horses to meet him there a certain day....*

This letter shows that the Quartermaster department was purchasing supplies at Fort Cumberland in 1780.

### Captain Isaac Craig's detachment marched to Fort Pitt via Fort Cumberland in 1780

In 1780, Captain Isaac Craig delivered stores and a detachment of Procter's artillery from Carlisle to Fort Pitt via Fort Cumberland. A memorandum[1618] of his march lists various stops west of Fort Cumberland as follows: June 8, Fort Cumberland; June 9, Halls; June 10, Tittle's, June 11, Tomlinson's; June 12 & 13, Bear Camp; June 14, Rice's; June 15, Big Meadows. These dates indicate that traveling over Braddock's road with artillery was extremely difficult. The letters ordering this march go into the subject of how Craig is to obtain forage and replacement horses during the march. Forage was a huge component of planning any military movement in those days.

### Hunting Tories near Fort Cumberland in 1780

The 1832 pension application of Isaac Linton includes the following statement:

*In the beginning of January in the year 1780, Declarant was again drafted to serve a tour of three months militia duty, and did perform the same under the command of Capt. Moses Chapline & Lieutenant Lemar. At the commencement of this last mentioned service the company was engaged in search of certain Tories, who were inimical to the American Cause. Their leaders or officers were Messrs. Susman, John Flecher and Bainbridge. Our search was in the mountainous parts of Frederick county, westwardly to near Fort Cumberland, our search continued Three weeks and we brought into Frederick town twelve or fourteen Tories. The three above named, viz. Susman, Flecher and Bainbridge were tried at Tories, who had contemplated to destroy the magazine and Barracks and let the prisoners free, and after trial, were condemned to be hung and were hung at Fredericktown. Declarant was one of the Guard over the said three mentioned Tory officers, and was present on guard when they were hung.*

The barbarous death sentence of two of these men (*"Susman"* and *"Flecher"*) is recorded in Volume 1 of the "**History of Western Maryland**" as follows:

*Peter Sueman, Nicholas Andrews, John George Graves, Yost Plecker, Adam Graves, Henry Shett, Casper Fritchie, attend. It has been suggested to the court that notwithstanding your guilt has been ascertained by an impartial jury, you consider the proceedings against you nothing more than solemn mockery, and have adopted a vain idea, propagated by the enemies of this country, that she dare not punish her unnatural subjects for engaging in the service of Great Britain. From the strange insensibility you have heretofore discovered, I was indeed led to conclude that you were under a delusion, which might prove fatal to your prospects of happiness hereafter. I think it is my duty, therefore, to explain to you your real situation. The crime you have been convicted of, upon the fullest and clearest testimony, is of such a nature that you cannot, ought not, to look for a pardon. Had it pleased heaven to permit the full execution of your unnatural designs, the miseries to be experienced by your devoted country would have been dreadful even in the contemplation. The ends of public justice, the dictates of policy, and the feelings of humanity all require that you should exhibit an awful example to your fellow-subjects, and the dignity of the State, with everything that can interest the heart of man, calls aloud for your punishment. If the consideration of approaching fate can inspire proper sentiments, you will pour forth your thanks to that watchful Providence which has arrested you at an early date of your guilt. And you will employ the short time you have to live in endeavoring, by a sincere penitence, to obtain pardon from the Almighty Being, who is to sit in judgment upon you, upon me, and all mankind.*

*I must now perform the terrible task of denouncing the terrible punishment ordained for high treason.*

*You, Peter Sueman, Nicholas Andrews, Yost Plecker, Adam Graves, Henry Shett, John George Graves, and Casper Fritchie, and each of you, attend to your sentence. You shall be carried to the gaol of*

---

[1618] The memorandum is included in Volume 2 of the 1880 book "**Pennsylvania in the War of the Revolution, Battalions and Line…**"

*Fredericktown, and be hanged therein; you shall be cut down to the earth alive, and your entrails shall be taken out and burnt while you are yet alive, your heads shall be cut off, your body shall be divided into four parts, and your heads and quarters shall be placed where his excellency the Governor shall appoint. So Lord have mercy upon your poor souls.*

From the pension application of Isaac Linton, it appears that their sentences may have been commuted to hanging.

### A sale of property on Bird Run

The 1939 book "**Early Records Hampshire County Virginia**" records the following for May 9, 1780, *"HARDIN, John, Sr. (w. Catherine) of Monongala Co. to Joseph House of Hampshire Co. (lease and release) 211 a. on Birds Run, a branch of North Branch of Potomac. Rev. 5-9-1780. Wit.: None."*

### A British plan to attack Fort Pitt and Fort Cumberland in 1780

On July 28, 1780, Captain John Rodgers sent a letter to Lieutenant William Clark[1619] from Cahoes that included the following:

*...the Man I Last Mentioned in M<sup>r</sup> Carnys Letter Brings News in 21 Days from Michelemcanaugh[1620] and says the Governor of that place was then setting of to Destroyt[1621] to fight A Great Man that Was Coming there as he tells the Indians and Informs them at the same time that he shall then Go to the falls of Ohio where he shall Fight a second time from thence to Fort Pitt but shall have a third fight on the way his forth Battle to be at Pitt and his Fifth and Last Battle to be at Fort Cumberland & Garrison that and then return and Go home to his King for a reward by this they may have word of the Col. Marching that way*

It seems that the Governor of Detroit believed there would be a military force to engage at Fort Cumberland once he arrived there.

### William Anderson provided forage and flour to the army during the Revolution

William Anderson lived across the river from Cresaptown, in what is now Hampshire County, West Virginia, at a place known as Anderson's bottom. An April 9, 1796 document associated with proving his will is recorded on page 26 of Will Book 1-22 includes the following statement:

*Support provided by William Anderson to the Revolutionary War per Publick Claims:*

*Wm. Anderson for provisions & forage for cattle drivers £1-5-7.*

*William Anderson 86# flour 8s-7.*

### The original route of the Turkey Foot Road crossed the Glade Road at Ruffs Dale

The 1776 survey of John Amberson (Emerson) and John McClintock (Book U, page 291) describes their 228-acre property as being located on *"Buffelow Lick Run"*. At the time of the survey, The Emerson-McClintock property was nearly surrounded by unclaimed land.

---

[1619] A transcript of this letter is included in Louise Phelps Kellogg's 1917 book "**Frontier Retreat on the Upper Ohio, 1779-1781**". Kellogg reports that *"Clark served until Feb. 15, 1784, in the earlier years at Fort Jefferson, later at Louisville. In 1782 he took part in the Wabash campaign..."*

[1620] Mackinac, Michigan.

[1621] Detroit, Michigan.

An abstract of a November 8, 1780 deed (recorded May 22, 1783) describes John Emerson's sale of property located on Lick Run and the Turkey Foot Road. The property is described as being bounded by the properties of Denis Raixdon, George Fisher, Joseph DeVoss, John Conrad, and Hans Tarr. Lick Run is now known as Buffalo Run, which passes through Ruffs Dale, Pennsylvania.

Somehow, Emerson's 1780 property sale went awry, because Emerson deeded the property to Joseph DeVoss on April 15, 1790. This transaction was recorded on February 10, 1791. Joseph Devoss was one of the property owners adjoining John Emerson's property in 1780, as described above. Devoss's 1793 survey for 371-acres (Book A-16, pages 42 and 43) is located on the Glade Road, just a few yards west of Buffalo Creek, and a bit of it covers the southernmost part of Ruffs Dale. Based on the shape of DeVoss's survey, Devoss's property is clearly a combination of Emerson's 1776 property and another property that bordered Emerson's property on the west.

As described above, the owners of the land that was adjacent to Emerson's property in 1780 were Joseph Devoss, Denis Raixdon, George Fisher, John Conrad, and Hans Tarr. Devoss's survey shows that George Fisher (Book A-59, page 5) and John Conrad (Book C-46, page 31) were still adjoining property owners in 1793. This further substantiates that Devoss's property included the Emerson property. On modern roads, Devoss's property is the same four miles from the Woodrow[1622] property that Dr. Wellford describes in his 1794 journal that describes traveling the Turkey Foot Road.

The reference to the Turkey Foot Road and Lick Run in Emerson's November, 8 1780 deed is significant because the deed was written the year after the northern part of Turkey Foot Road was cut as a military road by Providence Mounts, and it is the most northernmost reference to the Turkey Foot Road I have found. Emerson's deed proves that the military road that was cut from Fort Cumberland in 1779 crossed the Glade Road at Ruffs Dale. Moving from fact to inference, one can infer that the Turkey Foot Road may have merged with Braddock's road in the general vicinity of Hunker. For orientation purposes, Braddock's road was the antecedent to Preacher Street, which runs from Latitude 40.196628°, Longitude -79.610697° to Latitude 40.198107°, Longitude -79.616281°.

### What was the impact of all the Revolutionary War military activity at Fort Cumberland?

When one visualizes the wagon traffic needed to keep all the packhorses loaded, and the men, horses, and cattle fed, Fort Cumberland must have been filled with a tremendous amount of hustle and bustle during the war. One can imagine that there must have been storehouses, men to unload wagons and load packhorses, quarters for men, meadows for cattle being driven through, etc. Surely, the war must have brought economic benefit to farmers in the general region, who would have had an opportunity to sell farm products to the army.

One may reasonably wonder if buildings that may have survived from the last war were sufficient for the Revolutionary War activities, or if new buildings were required — and whether these buildings helped to form the nucleus of the town that was laid out in the mid-1780s. One may also reasonably wonder if the wartime activity helped to precipitate an aggregation of the individuals who would eventually become the first residents of the new town. One thing we do know, from Basil Shaw's pension application, is that Captain Thomas Beall, the eventual founder of the town of Cumberland, was at Fort Cumberland in 1778.

---

[1622] According to Gresham's 1890 book "**Biographical and Historical Cyclopedia of Westmoreland County, Pennsylvania**", John Woodrow *"was a leader in an alarm of Indians in the neighborhood, on account of which they call him 'Colonel.'"* George Dallas Albert's 1882 book "**History of the County of Westmoreland, Pennsylvania**" reports that John Woodrow was *"a farmer, and a descendant of Puritan stock"*. In regard to his will, the 1917 book "**Publications of the Genealogical Society of Pennsylvania**" states, *"John Woodrow of Westmoreland, dated December 25, 1792, proved January 3, 1793; wife Mary; children: William, John, Margaret, Mary and Rachel, all minors; wife, Samuel Cunning, James Woodrow and Robert Newell executors; witnesses, John Hill, William Latta and Henry Evans."*

# 33. 1781: The war is won

## Maryland ratifies the Articles of Confederation
On February 2, 1781, Maryland ratified the *"Articles of Confederation and Perpetual Union"*. It was the last state to do so.

## A reference to Colonel Enoch Innis
A February 22, 1781 letter Colonel Garret Van Meter sent to Governor Thomas Jefferson from Hampshire County, Virginia includes the following:

*I have to acknowledge the receipt of your Excellencys letters of the 24th. December and 19th. January, both of which came to my hand the 13th. Instant. As Colo. Enoch Innis, who has your Excellency's Commission as County Lieutenant, has never qualified himself to act under his Commission, the command has consequently devolved on me; I have also received the Act of Assembly for recruiting this States Quota of Troops to serve in the Continental Army. Likewise Twenty Five Thousand Pounds for procuring provisions and for the Detachment of our Militia who are required to join Colo. Clark.*

*From the late arrival of these important papers Your Excellency will readily suggest that it will be impossible to comply with them, within the limited time, nevertheless, I shall take every prudent step, in order that every part of your Orders may be executed. For this purpose I have given the necessary orders to the Officers, I have likewise appointed a Commissary and Quarter Master, who will procure provisions and means of transportation to Fort Pitt. I have no certain account where Colo. Clark is, nor have I heard from that Gentleman since the receipt of your Excellency's letter. I have complied with your Orders respecting the Proclamations, and in short with every other requisition in both your Excellency's letters so far as time would admit.*

*I enclose you a return of one of the Battalions of this County. The others I have not yet had a proper return of from the Officers, but believe it to be nearly of equal strength with the former.*

## Enoch Innis once again acts as Livingston's attorney
The 1939 book "**Early Records Hampshire County Virginia**" records the following for March 15, 1781, *"INNIS, Enoch (Atty." LIVINGSTON, James of Hampshire Co. to Francis Perpoint of Hampshire Co. 191 a. on North Branch of Potomac: rec. 5-8-1781. Wit.: Sam Dew, James Scott, William Price."* According to Rice's book set, this is the sale of North Branch Lot No. 8 to Francis Pierpont, who was already living on the property.[1623] Livingston had originally received the property from Frederick Ice in 1762.

## There was a farm on Walnut Bottom on May 10, 1781
The November 21, 1782 ejectment lawsuit in Washington County, Maryland titled *"George Mason's Lessee vs. Thomas Troublesome[1624] and Charles Clinton"* documents the presence of a farm on Walnut bottom on May 10, 1781: The day *"Timothy Peaceable"* was ejected from the farm at gunpoint by *"Thomas Troublesome"*. Since the case has special relevance to Cumberland, the following is my amateur attempt at

---

[1623] "**Colonial Records of the Upper Potomac**", Volume 5.
[1624] *"Thomas Troublesome"* is a fictional identity that was once used a legal term of art.

creating a transcript of the case. The transcript is long and redundant but will give any interested reader a good sense of the progression of a lawsuit in the latter part of the 1700s.[1625]

*November Term 1782*

*George Mason's Lessee vˢ Thomas Troublesome & Charles Clinton (Teste)*

*Be it remembered that heretofore to wit on the twentieth day of July in the year of our Lord one thousand Seven hundred and eighty one Timothy Peaceable lessee of George Mason by Edward Scull his Attorney declared in Court here against Thomas Troublesome in a plea of trespass and ejectment, with a notice thereto annexed in manner and form following, to wit: Washington County __ Thomas Troublesome late of the said County Yeoman was attached to answer Timothy Peaceable of a pleas wherefore with force and arms he the said Thomas into one messoage, one stable and two hundred and fifty acres of land lying and being in Washington County aforesaid, being part of a tract of land called Walnut Bottom, which George Mason Esquire in Trust for the Ohio Company, to him the said Timothy did demise for a term of years which is not yet expired did enter and him the said Timothy from his farm aforesaid did eject and other harms to him did to the great damage of the said Timothy, and against the peace, and so forth. And whereupon the said Timothy by Edward Scull his Attorney complains, that whereas the aforesaid George Mason on the tenth day of May in the year of our Lord one thousand seven hundred and eighty one at Washington County aforesaid had demised to him the said Timothy the aforesaid tract of land with the appurtenances to hold to him the said Timothy and assigns from the first day of April then Part fast until the full end and term of ten years then next following and fully to be complete and ended by virtue of which said demise the aforesaid Timothy into the said Tract of land with the appurtenances did enter and was thereof possessed, and the said Timothy, being thereof possessed, the said Thomas afterward, to wit, the same tenth day of May in the year of our Lord one thousand seven hundred and eighty one aforesaid at Washington County aforesaid with force and arms and so forth into the said tract of land with the appurtenances in as aforesaid for the term aforesaid which is not yet expired did enter and him the said Timothy from his farm did eject and other harms to him did to the great damage of the said Timothy and against the Pease &c. Whereof in the said Timothy saith he is ____ and hath damage to the value of two hundred pounds and therefore he brings suit and so forth.*

*E. Scull atty for pett*                    *John Doe |*
                                                          *&    | Pledge &c.*
                                      *Richard Roo |*

*Sir,*

*I am informed that you are in possession of the premises in this declaration of ejectment mentioned or of some part thereof, and being sued in this action as casual ejector and having no claims or title to the same, do advise you to appear to this declaration at the next County Court to be held at Elizabeth Town on the fourth Tuesday of August next by some attorney of that Court, and there aby and of the same court cause yourself to be made defendant in my stead and to confess to the lean, entry and ouster a _____ judgement will be given against me and you will be turned out of possession.*

*(To Mr Charles Clinton Tenant in possession of the premises)*

*I am Yours Thomas Troublesome*

*A copy of which said declaration and notice was made and sent to the Sheriff of Washington County aforesaid, thereon endorsed "to be served on the defendant tenant in possession or set up on the premises at least eight days before Court." At which mentioned fourth Tuesday of August in the year of our Lord one thousand seven hundred and eighty one, and the day of the return of the foregoing declaration on*

---

[1625] MSA CE457-000001.

*ejectment, comes into Court here the said Thomas Troublesome lessee of the said George Mason by Edward Scull his Attorney aforesaid and the Sheriff of Washington County to with S Beall Gentlemen to whom a copy of the said declaration on ejectment and notice as aforesaid was in form aforesaid made and sent as befits(?) his service thereof to the Court here in form following to wit "copy left 1ˢᵗ August 1781 S Beall Shf." —*

*Whereupon the said Timothy Peaceable lessee of the said George Mason by his said Attorney prays that the defendant, the tenant in possession of the premises aforesaid or those under whom he claims to his declaration aforesaid may appear and answer thereupon Charles Clinton the landlord of the premises in question comes here into Court by Baker Johnston his Attorney, therefore on motion of the said Charles Clinton by his said Attorney, it is ordered by the Court here that the said Charles Clinton be joined and made defendant together with Thomas Troublesome tenant in possession of the said premises in common rule by consent in ejectment instead of the casual ejector in case the said Thomas Troublesome shall appear the said Charles Clinton by Baker Johnston his Attorney in pursuance of the notice aforesaid comes into Court here, whereupon it is ruled by the Court here with the consent of the said Timothy Peaceable lessee of the said George Mason by his Attorney aforesaid and the said Charles Clinton who claims the title in question by his Attorney aforesaid that the said Charles Clinton be admitted defendant in the place of the non defendant Thomas Troublesome the casual ejector and that he immediately receive a declaration and plead thereto the general issue, and at the trial thereon to be had the said the said Charles Clinton shall appear in his proper person or by his attorney or counsel and confess to the lease, entry and actual ouster and expulsion of so much of the tenements in the declaration of the said Timothy Peaceable lessee as aforesaid, as in the possession of the said Charles Clinton or his tenant, or of any other person claiming by or under his title, or in default thereof, that judgement be entered against the non defendant Thomas Troublesome the casual ejector but that the prosecution be staid against him until he makes default in any of the premises, and it is further ruled by the Court here with consent of counsel that if by reason of any such default the said Timothy Peaceable lessee as aforesaid shall become nonsuit at the trial that said Charles Clinton shall take no advantage thereof, but shall pay the said Timothy Peaceable Whereas aforesaid his certs &c. and it is further ordered by the Court here that if upon trial of the said issue a verdict shall be given for the said Charles Clinton or if the said Timothy Peaceable lessee as aforesaid shall not prosecute his declaration upon any other cause than for the not nonassessing lease, entry and ouster as aforesaid then the said George Mason lessor of the aforesaid Timothy Peaceable shall pay cost, &c and thereupon the aforesaid Timothy Peaceable lessee as aforesaid by his Attorney aforesaid declared against the said Charles Clinton in the plea aforesaid in a manner and form following, to wit. Washington County to Charles Clinton late of said County Yeoman was attached to answer Timothy Peaceable of a plea wherefore with force and arms he the said Charles Clinton into one messuage, one stable and two hundred and fifty acres of land lying and being in Washington County aforesaid, being part of a tract of land called Walnut Bottom, which George Mason in trust for the Ohio Company to him the said Timothy did demise for a term of years which is not yet expired, did enter and him the said Timothy from his said farm aforesaid did eject, and other harm to him did, to the great damage of the said Timothy and against the Pease and so forth. And whereupon the said Timothy by Edward Scull his Attorney complains that whereas the aforesaid George Mason on the tenth day of May in the year of our Lord one thousand seven hundred and eighty one at Washington County aforesaid had demised to him the said Timothy the aforesaid tract of land with the appurtenances to hold to him the said Timothy and his assigns from the first day of April then last past until the full end and term of ten years then next following and fully to be complete and ended, by virtue of which said demise the aforesaid Timothy into the said tract of land with the appurtenances did enter and was possessed thereof an the said Timothy being thereof possessed the said Thomas afterward to wit the same tenth day of May in the year of our Lord one thousand seven hundred and eighty one aforesaid at Washington County aforesaid with force and arms and so forth into the said tract of land with the appurtenances to as aforesaid demised for the term aforesaid which is not yet expired did enter and him the said Timothy from his farm aforesaid did eject and other harm to him did to the great damage of the said Timothy and against the Peace &c.*

*Wherefore the said Timothy saith he is _____ and hath damage to the value of two hundred pounds and therefore he brings suit &c E Scull atty for plff Thereupon on motion of the said Charles Clinton by his Attorney aforesaid, leave is given by the Court here to the said Charles Clinton to ascertain his defense and answer to the declaration aforesaid of the said Timothy Peaceable before as aforesaid on the plea aforesaid until the fourth Tuesday of November next the same day is given to the said Timothy Peaceable lessee as aforesaid and so forth. At which said forth Tuesday of November in the year of our Lord one thousand seven hundred and eighty one, until which day the said Charles Clinton had leave to ascertain his defense and answer to the declaration aforesaid of the said Timothy Peaceable lessee as aforesaid in the plea aforesaid come again into Court here as will the said Timothy Peaceable lessee as aforesaid by his Attorney aforesaid as the said Charles Clinton by his Attorney aforesaid, and the said Charles Clinton, by his Attorney aforesaid, and the said Charles Clinton by his said Attorney defends the force and injury when and so forth, and says that he is not guilty of the trespass and ejectment aforesaid in the declaration aforesaid mentioned in manner and form as the said Timothy Peaceable lessee as aforesaid above complains against him and of this he puts himself upon the Country, and the said Timothy Peaceable lessee as aforesaid in like manner thereupon further process of and upon the premises aforesaid between the parties aforesaid, by consent of the said parties and their Attornies aforesaid and by order of the Court here thereon is further continued until the fourth Tuesday of March next. At which mentioned fourth Tuesday of March in the year of our Lord one thousand seven hundred and eighty two until which day the said Charles Clinton had leave to ascertain his defense and answer to the declaration aforesaid of the said Timothy Peaceable lessee as aforesaid in the plea aforesaid come again into Court here as well the said Timothy Peaceable lessee as aforesaid by his attorney aforesaid as the said Charles Clinton by his said Attorney, and the said Charles Clinton by his said Attorney defense the force and injury as before, when and so forth: thereupon further process of and upon the premises aforesaid, between the parties aforesaid by consent of the said parties and their Attornies aforesaid and by order of the Court here thereon is further continued until the fourth Tuesday of August next. At which mentioned fourth Tuesday of August in the year of our Lord one thousand seven hundred and eighty two until which day the said Charles Clinton had leave to ascertain his defense and answer to the declaration aforesaid of the said Timothy Peaceable lessee as aforesaid in the plea aforesaid and come again into Court here as will the said Timothy Peaceable lessee as aforesaid by his Attorney aforesaid as the said Charles Clinton by his said Attorney and the said Charles Clinton by his Attorney aforesaid defends the force and injury (as before) when and so forth. Thereupon further process of and upon the premises aforesaid, between the parties aforesaid, by consent of the said parties and their Attornies aforesaid, and by order of the Court here thereon is further continued until the fourth Tuesday of November next. At which mentioned fourth Tuesday of November in the year of our Lord one thousand seven hundred and eighty two until which day the said Charles Clinton had leave to ascertain his defense and answer to the declaration aforesaid of the said Timothy Peaceable lessee as aforesaid in the plea aforesaid, come again into Court here as will the said Timothy Peaceable lessee as aforesaid by his Attorney aforesaid as the said Charles Clinton by his Attorney aforesaid, and the said Charles Clinton by his said Attorney defends the force and injury when and so forth: Whereupon, for trying the issue aforesaid between the parties aforesaid within joined it is ordered that the Sheriff of Washington County cause to come before the Court here, twelve &c by whim &. and who neither so? To recognize &c. because as will so? And thereupon it is ordered by the Court here, that twenty persons from the pannel of petit jurors be drawn by ballot, according to the Act of Assembly in such case made and provided; and thereupon the twenty persons being so drawn by ballot and written upon two lists, one of which said lists is delivered to the counsel for the respective parties, and the counsel for each of the said parties having stricken out four persons from the said list, thereupon the remaining twelve being called come, to wit, William Gordan, Ludwick Young, Thomas Hynds, Joseph Reynolds, Frederick Dashis, John Houscholder, John Knodo, Peter Thompson, George Custard, Jeremiah Lackland, Nathan Petticoat and Dennis Davis who being empannelled and sworn to say the truth in the premises upon their oaths do say that the said Charles Clinton is not guilty of the trespass and ejectment aforesaid as the aforesaid Timothy Peaceable above by pleading hath alleged, therefore it is considered by the Court here that the said Timothy Peaceable lessee as aforesaid take nothing by his declaration aforesaid, but for his false complaint against the said the said (sic) Charles Clinton to be in mercy and so forth, and that the said Charles Clinton go thereof without day &c. and it is further considered by the Court here that the said Charles Clinton recover against the said Timothy Peaceable lessee as aforesaid the sum (blank) dollars and (blank) cents for his cost and charges by him laid out and expended in about his defence in this behalf sustained to the said Timothy Peaceable lessee as aforesaid by the Court here adjudged and so forth and that the said Timothy have execution thereof*

*Test Elie Williams cert*

## The Revolutionary War ended in October 1781
The Revolutionary War was won with the October 19, 1781 surrender of Cornwallis at the Battle of Yorktown. The first article of the *"Articles of Capitulation"* states:

*The Garrisons of York & Gloucester including the Officers and Seamen of his Britannic Majesty's Ships as well as other Mariners, to surrender themselves Prisoners of War to the Combined Forces of America & France — The Land Troops to remain prisoners to the United States. The Navy to the naval Army of his Most Christian Majesty —*

## A 1781 law appropriating the land west of Fort Cumberland for Maryland soldiers
According to "**The Land-holder's Assistant**" (1808), Chapter 20, Section 2, of the Laws of Maryland, passed in November 1781, *"appropriates all vacant lands to the westward of Fort Cumberland to the benefit of the soldiers of the Maryland line."* Another part of the same book states, *"...an ample provision was made by the act of 1781, opening the land office, for fulfilling the engagements, or the intentions, of the state of Maryland towards its officers and soldiers, by the first enacting section of that law, which has been already given at large, and which, in substance, appropriated all the lands westward of Fort Cumberland, reserved or otherwise, except so far as they were fairly covered by warrants and locations in right of American citizens, and actually paid for, to the purpose of discharging the aforesaid engagements."*

## John Jacob marries Michael Cresap's widow
The introduction to John J. Jacob's 1826 book "**A biographical sketch of the life of the late Captain Michael Cresap**" states, *"And I think it was in the Summer or Autumn of this year, 1781, that I was married to Captain Cresap's widow, with whom I lived near forty years."* 1783 tax records show that John Jacob was the executor of Michael Cresap's estate.

## Enoch Innis transfers a Virginia property to John Haynes
The 1939 book "**Early Records Hampshire County Virginia**" records the following for December 27, 1781, *"INNIS, Enoch of Hampshire Co. to John Haynes of Bedford Co. 134 a. on North Branch of Potomac; rec. 5-14-1782, Wit.: John Roussaw, Joseph Haynes, Joseph Williams, Joseph Nicholas."*

# 34. 1782: The names of a few residents

**Charles Clinton was living on Walnut Bottom in 1782, and Wiley was living nearby**

The 1825 court case of *"Bealls Lessee vs. Lynn"* states:

*The plaintiff then offered in evidence, by Benjamin Wiley, a competent witness, that the witness knows the tract of land called The Brothers, and lived on it in 1782. In 1782 The Brothers was all in woods. James Clarke lived in Baltimore, and claimed title to the land as his own, and agreed to lease a part of it to the witness, who went on the land in the summer of 1782, under that agreement, and cleared about an acre, and fenced it in and built a cabin near the lines of Walnut Bottom; but after seeing the lines run, and finding the lines of Walnut Bottom then held by George Mason took in part of the laud he expected to lease, he refused to take the lease, and left the land, and went to Baltimore, after having remained on the land eight or ten months. Witness lived in Baltimore from 1783, at which time he left The Brothers until 1787, when witness again returned with his family. He lived in Virginia, about two and a half miles from Cumberland. In 1782 the witness understood from James Clarke and Charles Clinton, that the latter was agent for Clarke, and had the care of The Brothers as agent of Clarke; at that time Clinton lived on Walnut Bottom, where the Town of Cumberland now stands, and it was Clinton who pointed out to him the land he was to lease from said Clarke, as before stated, and part of which was found on survey to be in Walnut Bottom. In 1785 witness went to Cumberland, Clinton was then gone.[1626]*

Other Maryland records show that Clinton had been somewhere in the general area since at least 1774.

**The estate of Jacob Good sells property on Patterson Creek**

The 1939 book "**Early Records Hampshire County Virginia**" records the following for May 14, 1782, *"GOOD, Jacob, dec'd by PUTMAN, Peter, executor of will Hampshire Co. to Isaac Good of Hampshire Co. 278 a. on Patterson Creek; rec. 5-10-1785. Wit.: Sam Dew."* Jacob Good had Lot no. 13 on Patterson's Creek in 1749.

**Colonel Innes had a plantation at Fort Cumberland in 1782**

According to Volume 1 of the 1916 book "**Manuscripts from the Burton Historical Collection**", on June 27, 1782, David W. Meriwether wrote a letter to his father from the *"Forks of Cheet and Monongalia"* that includes the statement *"I wish much to move from this Quarter as I'm sensible there is, and will be danger every Summer so long as the war continues. I have conditionally rented a plantation of Colo. Innes at Fort Cumberland the particulars Cousin Nicholas will Inform you. We have much talk of peace here, but I fear without foundation."*

**A recorded apology**

The 1939 book "**Early Records Hampshire County Virginia**" records the following for August 13, 1782, *"BURROUGHS, Jeremiah to Col. Michael Cr[e]sap Apologizing to Mr. Cresap for accusing him of a crime, that he did not do. Rec. 8-14-1782. Wit.: None."*

---

[1626] In a May 22, 1784 deed, Henry Beeson sold a lot in Uniontown to Charles Clinton of Washington County, Maryland. This may explain his absence from Cumberland in 1785.

## Another individual who was living in the environs of Cumberland in 1782

According to Volume 6 of "**The Literary Era**", Benjamin Walker's November 10th diary entry regarding a journey to Redstone in 1782 states, "*10th to Gess at fort Cumberland 12 to Wm Lodgstones 12 at yee foot of Alogoney on the New Road by tumilsons mill to Tumilsons. Lodged 12 miles 11th to Coliers 11 to the big Youghiogheny 8 to Daughertys 14…*"

It seems probably that "*Gess*" is a reference to James or Elizabeth Gist, who lived below Fort Cumberland. The February 28, 1786 deposition of James "*Gest*" in the writ of Ejectment concerning the Pleasant Valley tract is included in Alfred Proctor James' Book "**The Ohio Company: Its Inner History**". The deposition states, "*About twelve years ago he moved to the place where he now resides where he has lived ever since as a tenant to the Ohio Company…*" The February 28, 1786 deposition of Elizabeth Gist states, "*on or about the year 1759, Col[o] George Mercer give her former Husband Samuel Plum[1627] Possessn of a tract of Land for which her said Husband was to pay Annually One Ear of Indian Corn, whereon her Husband Erected the House where she now lives, and has lived ever since, as a Tenant to the Ohio Comp[y] (or Col[o] George Mason)*" These depositions show Elizabeth Gist had been living in the general area of Fort Cumberland continuously from at least 1759, and that James Gist had been living in the area continually from at least 1774. Even though they were apparently living on the Pleasant Valley tract some miles from Fort Cumberland, they were still part of the general Cumberland area community. James Guest is listed in the Cumberland hundred list for 1783.

## The Potomac River was considered useful for water transportation in 1782

In 1782 Thomas Jefferson wrote[1628] "*…Fort Cumberland, the head of the navigation on the Patowmac…*" Eventually, this waterway would play a role in the economy of the town of Cumberland.

## Indian depredations in Bedford County, near the Maryland line, in 1782

In 1782 Bernard Dougherty wrote a letter[1629] to the Honorable Dr. Gardner that included the following:

*I beg leave to lay the inclosed through your means before the Honorable Board of Council, as it gives (though imperfectly) some acct of the present Situation of the County of Bedford… Nothing can be more distressing than the present situation of it, for the places said in the inclosed to be broken up, are nearly on the Marrland line…*

## The Husband family retreats to Fort Cumberland in 1782

A circa 1870 article by David Husband, based on his ancestor Herman Husband's journal that was in his possession, was reprinted in the October 13, 1893 "**Somerset Standard**". The article describes the flight of the Cox's Creek Settlement in 1782:

*We shall now give a brief outline of what has been preserved of the facts and incidents connected with the leaving and returning of our ancestors in those days of sorrow and danger. A messenger arrived from the great road, along which the news of the terrible fate of Hannastown was borne eastward. On his arrival at Brown's blockhouse expresses were sent around to notify the remaining settlers to meet and consult on what was to be done. The meeting took place a few days after and resulted in a general conclusion to fly to places of more safety until the storm of savage cruelty abated. …*

---

[1627] A man named Samuel Plumb appears on the 1761 Old Town Hundred list.
[1628] The passage is from Paul Leicester Ford's 1904 book "**The Works of Thomas Jefferson**".
[1629] "**Somerset Standard**", October 13, 1893.

*The families moved off as fast as they could get off, every one directing their course to places of security or to where they had relatives or acquaintances. Some returned to Conocheaeugere, others to York and Cumberland Counties. The Husband family went to the neighborhood of Cumberland, Md. ... The morning that they left several of the families were still not ready to start and several men and women came to bid them a cordial farewell and see them start. They took with them ten head of horses and colts, four cows, and ten head of cattle, including a yoke of oxen. ... they took the trail through Brothersvalley to Cumberland, where they arrived on the evening of the third day. They encamped near the fort until an empty cabin was found about two miles off, into which they moved. The horses and cattle were disposed of as opportunity offered for mere nominal prices, several were given out for their keeping, as were also the oxen and some of the cows. ...*

# 35. 1783: A thriving farming settlement

### A thriving farming settlement existed in the environs of Fort Cumberland in 1783

The *"Cumberland Hundred"* and other local hundreds lists from 1783 help to prove the existence of a thriving agricultural community in the environs of Fort Cumberland, by identifying the acreage of meadows and arable land of various named properties. For example, Waterford in Arnold's settlement had 98 arable acres, John Tomlinson's Wills Town property along Wills Creek had 90 acres of meadow and 80 arable acres, and the Walnut Bottom property at present-day Cumberland had 6 acres of meadow and 30 arable acres. Because it took so long to clear land in those days, the large amount of arable acreage indicates that the community had been in existence for a considerable number of years prior to 1783.

The presence of a substantial agricultural community in the environs of Fort Cumberland helps to explain why the Turkey Foot Road was routed through the area in 1779: The farms would have provided the forage that was needed for the packhorses and livestock traveling between the Skipton (Old Town) and Casselman Creek settlements on their way to Fort Pitt.

### Sugar Bottom, revisited

The 1783 Upper Old Town hundreds list indicates that Joseph Mounts had a mill on the Sugar Bottom property in 1783, and an abnormally large collection of horses (16) — considering that he only had 40 arable acres and 8 acres of pasture. The fact that he had five to eight times more horses than a typical neighbor indicates that he was engaged in some type of horse-related business. The list also indicates that he had five slaves.

The presence of a mill suggests that Joseph Mounts had plenty of neighbors to do business with; because mills are of little use without nearby farmers in need of milling services. Sugar Bottom was located along the Winchester Road, which terminated at Gwynne's tavern on Braddock's road, west of Cumberland. This prime location makes some individuals wonder if Joseph Mounts may have sold services, provender, or other goods to travelers.[1630]

### Residents of the Great Youghiogheny Glades petition for pre-emption

The 1856 "**Index to the Journals of the Senate and House of Delegates of the State of Maryland**" provides the following summary of an item from the April 1783 meeting of the House of Delegates:

> *Petition from sundry inhabitants of Great Yohogany Glades in, setting forth that at the risk of their lives they had settled plantations westward of Fort Cumberland, praying pre-emption, &c., read. 25.*

### A proclamation 'Declaring the cessation of arms' is approved by Congress

The *"***Journals of Congress***"* records that on April 11, 1783, the *"United States of America in Congress assembled"* approved a proclamation *"Declaring the cessation of arms, as well by sea as by land, agreed upon between the United States of America and his Britannic Majesty; and enjoining the observance thereof."* that begins with a preamble stating, *"Whereas provisional articles were signed at Paris on the thirtieth day of November last between the ministers plenipotentiary of the United States of America for*

---

[1630] One currently missing piece of the Joseph Mounts story is the estate inventory his executors were required to prepare.

*treating of peace, and the minister plenipotentiary of his Britannic Majesty..."* Congress approved the preliminary articles of peace on April 15, 1783.

### Evan Gwynn, Deputy Sheriff

The record[1631] of the court case of *"Steuart, et al. Lesses vs. Mason"* includes the following:

> *The defendant at the trial in the general court at October term 1805, offered to read in evidence a paper, purporting to be the deposition of Col. Thomas Cresap, taken on the 29th of April 1783, by and before a certain Evan Gwynn, the deputy of Henry Shryock, then, before and afterwards, sheriff of Washington county. And he proved to the court, that Cresap died after, the taking of the deposition...*

### Generational changes

As an example of generational change that was taking place, on May 27, 1783 Isaac Collyer — an early local settler — deeded his Hart's Delight tract to Joseph and Michael Collyer.[1632]

### A Virginia property sale on the North Branch of the Potomac River

The 1939 book "**Early Records Hampshire County Virginia**" records the following for August 12, 1783, *"FORMAN, John, Jr. FORMAN, Catherine of Hampshire Co. to James Martin of Hampshire Co. 150 a. on North Branch of Potomac; rec 8-12-1783. Wit.: None."*

### Thomas Beall purchases Walnut Bottom on October 25, 1783

Thomas Beal, son of Samuel, purchased the *"Walnut Bottom"* tract from George Mason on October 25, 1783. The deed was recorded on November 9, 1783.[1633]

### The hundreds lists from the environs of Fort Cumberland

The following is an alphabetical list of taxables owning property in the environs of Fort Cumberland, taken from the tax assessment of 1783. The list includes the identity of the hundreds list the landowner is associated with and is presented here to show the extent of the settlement in the environs of Fort Cumberland in 1783. While some of the names, such as David Ross, are those of absentee landowners, many of the properties they owned would have been rented to tenant farmers:

Anthony Able. Wills Town and Sandy Creek ● Adam Acord. Wills Town and Sandy Creek ● George Acord. Wills Town and Sandy Creek ● Archabald Allen. Upper Old Town ● Jonathan Anderson. Upper Old Town and Cumberland ● Josiah Anderson. Upper Old Town ● Mary Anderson. Cumberland ● Samuel Anderson. Upper Old Town and Cumberland ● William Anderson. Cumberland ● William Anderson. Upper Old Town ● William Anderson. Cherry Lick, 32 acres. Cumberland ● Anthony Arnold. Pleasent Levell, 4 acres. Wills Town and Sandy Creek ● Moses Aston. Cumberland ● Aron Atherton. Upper Old Town ● Benjamin Atherton. Upper Old Town ● Peter Atherton. Upper Old Town ● Joseph Augustus. Skipton ● John Backharn. Upper Old Town ● Bethel Bacster. Wills Town and Sandy Creek ● William Barnes. Upper Old Town ● Lambert Barrett. Ash Swamp, 100 acres. Upper Old Town ● Lambert Barrett. Pollys Pleasure, 200 acres. Upper Old Town ● Lambert Barrett. Squerrill Neck, 200 acres. Upper Old Town ● Lambert Barrett. Black Oak Levell, 100 acres. Upper Old Town ● Alexander Beall. Cumberland ● John Beall. Wills Town and Sandy Creek ● Josiah Beall. Cumberland ● Mathew Beall. Upper Old Town ● Thomas Beall. 100 acres. Cumberland ● Thomas Beall. 320 acres. Cumberland ● Zephaniah Beall. Upper Old Town ● Paul Beesy. Cumberland ● James

---

[1631] "**Reports of Cases Argued and Determined in the Court of Appeals, Maryland, In 1810, 1811, 1812, 1813, 1814, & 1815**", Volume III, 1826.

[1632] "**Colonial Records of the Upper Potomac**", Volume 5.

[1633] The original deed was located by Joseph Robertson, who posted it on the timeline of the Western Maryland History Facebook Group on May 1, 2016.

Belbs. Wills Town and Sandy Creek • James Berry. Skipton • Ignatius Bevins. 40 acres. Skipton • Jacob Biglar. Wills Town and Sandy Creek • Zopher Blackley. Wills Town and Sandy Creek • John Blair. Wills Town and Sandy Creek • Isiah Bonham. Upper Old Town • Valentine Bottle. Cumberland • Hezekiah Bound. Upper Old Town • Hezekiah Bound. Upper Old Town and Cumberland • John Bound. Upper Old Town • John Bowman. Upper Old Town • John Bowman. Skipton • Runian Bowman. Upper Old Town • Walter Boyd. Upper Old Town • Charles Bradgett. Upper Old Town • Matthew Branstater. Wills Town and Sandy Creek • John Bray. Upper Old Town • William Brewer. Upper Old Town • John Briggs. Upper Old Town • Daniel Brown. Upper Old Town • William Brown. Cumberland • Andrew Bruce. Mount Pleasant, 440 acres. Wills Town and Sandy Creek • Andrew Bruce. Resurvey on Fertile Valley, 1000 acres. Skipton • Norman Bruce. Pond Lick, 320 acres. Wills Town and Sandy Creek • Norman Bruce. Egypt, 50 acres. Wills Town and Sandy Creek • Norman Bruce. Pumpkin Hall, 120 acres. Wills Town and Sandy Creek • Norman Bruce. Lubberland, 75 acres. Wills Town and Sandy Creek • John Brummage. Upper Old Town • James Burditt. Upper Old Town • William Burgess. Skipton • Valentine Burgett. Wills Town and Sandy Creek • Henry Burriss. Skipton • John Buscraft. Upper Old Town • Collin Campbell. Upper Old Town and Cumberland • William Carr. Upper Old Town • William Caster. Upper Old Town • Anthony Chambers. Upper Old Town • James Chambers. Upper Old Town • William Chapman. Cumberland • Mary Chineworth. Cumberland • Auther Chinoth. Upper Old Town • John Chinoth. Upper Old Town • Richard Chinoth. Upper Old Town and Cumberland • William Chinoth. Upper Old Town and Cumberland • Thomas Cinoth. Upper Old Town and Cumberland • John Clarke. Skipton • Joseph Clarke. The Brothers, 934 acres. Cumberland • Joseph Clarke. 300 acres. Upper Old Town • Richard Clarke. Upper Old Town • John Clem. Wills Town and Sandy Creek • Samuel Clifton. Upper Old Town • Thomas Clifton. Upper Old Town • William Coddington. Wills Town and Sandy Creek • Barnet Cole. Skipton • William Collard. Upper Old Town • Isaac Collier. Hearts Delight, 175 acres. Cumberland • Joseph Collier. Cumberland • Michal Collier. Bear Camp, 90 acres. Wills Town and Sandy Creek • Jacob Conn. Upper Old Town • Timothy Conner. Wills Town and Sandy Creek • John Constable. 84 acres. Cumberland • Stephen Constable. 48 acres. Cumberland • Thomas Constable. 77 acres. Cumberland • Thomas Cordery. Upper Old Town • Thomas Cornett. Upper Old Town • William White. Cotton. Upper Old Town and Cumberland • William Cowen. Cumberland • Abner Cox. Upper Old Town • James Cox. Upper Old Town • John Cox. Upper Old Town • John Coy. Upper Old Town • Daniel Cresap. Indian Purchase, pt, 500 acres. Upper Old Town • Daniel Cresap. Ross' Mistake, 620 acres. Upper Old Town • Daniel Cresap. Indian Purchase, pt, 363 acres. Upper Old Town • Daniel Cresap. Good Will, 100 acres. Upper Old Town • Daniel Cresap. Lime Stone Rock, 63 acres. Upper Old Town • Daniel Cresap. Little Meadow, 50 acres. Upper Old Town • Daniel Cresap. Skipton • Joseph Cresap. Three Springs, 257 acres. Upper Old Town • Michael Cresap. Alder Thickett, 80 acres. Skipton (estate) • Michal Cresap. Addition to Seven Springs, 56 acres. Skipton (estate) • Michal Cresap. Hopewell, 76 acres. Skipton (estate) • Michal Cresap. Deakins' Forgetfullness, 26 acres. Skipton (estate) • Michal Cresap. Cresaps Prospect, 110 acres. Skipton (estate) • Thomas Cresap. Skipton • John Crisman. Wills Town and Sandy Creek • Jacob Criss. Cumberland • John Crofus. Upper Old Town and Cumberland • John Crow. Upper Old Town and Cumberland • Philip Crow. Upper Old Town • Thomas Cummings. Cumberland • Joseph Cunningham. Cumberland • David Cyserd. Skipton • William Cyserd. Skipton • John Dailey. Upper Old Town • David Davis. Cumberland • Ebenezer Davis. Ash Bottom, 30 acres. Upper Old Town • John Davis. Cumberland • Joseph Davis. Upper Old Town • Joshua Davis. Cumberland • Richard Davis. Skipton and Murleys Run • Edward Dawson. Upper Old Town • Edward Dawson. Upper Old Town • Edward Dawson. Upper Old Town and Cumberland • James Dawson. Clover Bottom, 60 acres. Upper Old Town • James Dawson. Upper Old Town and Cumberland • Lewis Dawson. Walnut Valley, 62 acres. Cumberland • William Dawson. Clover Bottom, 60 acres. Upper Old Town • Francis Deakins. 48 acres. Cumberland • Francis Deakins. Skipton • John Deakins. Percie, 87 acres. Skipton • Stephen Deakins. Cumberland • William Deakins. Elbow, 64 acres. Skipton • Daniel Dean. Upper Old Town • Marsham Deane. 52 acres. Skipton • Thomas Detty. Skipton • Forbis Devers. Upper Old Town • David Devore. Wills Town and Sandy Creek • William Devour. Upper Old Town • James Dew. Skipton and Murleys Run • Barney Dewitt. Upper Old Town • Henry Dewitt. Upper Old Town • James Dewitt. Upper Old Town • Martin Dewitt. Upper Old Town • Peter Dewitt. Upper Old Town • Jacob Ditton. Upper Old Town • Isaac Dolson. Upper Old Town and Cumberland • Roger Domiger. Upper Old Town • Nicholas Donovan. Wills Town and Sandy Creek • Samuel Doras. Wills Town and Sandy Creek • Timothy Downing. Cumberland • Jacob Dull. Upper Old Town • Edward Durbin. Wills Town and Sandy Creek • John Durbin. Wills Town and Sandy Creek • Samuel Durbin. Wills Town and Sandy Creek • William Durbun. Cumberland • Enoch Enniss. 164 acres. Cumberland • Michal Esgreg. Wills Town and Sandy Creek • Samuel Ferguson. Upper Old Town • William Finch. Upper Old Town and Cumberland • John Flatt. Upper Old Town and Cumberland • Mary Frazer. Buflow Run, 149 acres. Wills Town and Sandy Creek • Daniel Frazier. Cumberland • Aron Freeland. Venture, 50 acres. Cumberland • Benjamin Freeland. Hazel Grove, 50 acres. Cumberland • Robert Freeland. Cumberland • George French. St. Catharines, 1314 acres. Upper Old Town • George French. Skipton • Josiah Frost. Wills Town and Sandy Creek • John Frund. Wills Town and Sandy Creek • Cornelius Fullen. Upper Old Town • John Fuller. Upper Old Town • John Furman. Upper Old Town • Adam Gardner. Skipton and Murleys Run • Brian Garner. Upper Old Town • George Glaisner. Wills Town and Sandy Creek • John Glaisner. Wills Town and Sandy Creek • George Glen. Cumberland • Jacob Good. Skipton • Aron Gooden.

Cumberland • Peter Grady. Upper Old Town • John Grate. Wills Town and Sandy Creek • Ludwick Greenwalt. Wills Town and Sandy Creek • Robert Gregg. Skipton and Murleys Run • Robert Gregg. Indian Fields, pt, 100 acres. Skipton • Edward Grimes. Wills Town and Sandy Creek • Peter Grimes. Upper Old Town • Paul Grimm. Wills Town and Sandy Creek • John Gross. 33 acres. Skipton • Joseph Groves. 30 acres. Skipton • James Guest. Cumberland • Evan Guinne. Upper Old Town • Henry Guntryman. Upper Old Town • Henry Haines. Upper Old Town • Henry Hall. Wills Town and Sandy Creek • James Hall. Wills Town and Sandy Creek • John Hall. Mill Run, 120 acres. Wills Town and Sandy Creek • Joseph Hall. Cumberland • Richard Hall. Wills Town and Sandy Creek • Thomas Hall. Upper Old Town • Savil Harding. Upper Old Town • Jacob Harmon. 25 acres. Cumberland • Nehemiah Harriss. Upper Old Town • Peter Hartman. Wills Town and Sandy Creek • Jacob Hazlewood. Upper Old Town • Leonard Heartley. Wills Town and Sandy Creek • Thomas Heartley. Skipton • Moses Heirs. Upper Old Town • Moses Heirs. Upper Old Town • William Henderson. Flemons, 100 acres. Cumberland • James Hill. Cumberland • Mary Hinton. Cumberland • Vachel Hinton. Locust Thickett, 100 acres. Cumberland • James Hoglen. Wills Town and Sandy Creek • Hannah Hollett. Cumberland • John Hollett. Cumberland • Thomas Hollett. Cumberland • Valentine Horn. Skipton • Andrew House. Upper Old Town • John House. Upper Old Town • Samuel Howard. Upper Old Town • William Howell. Upper Old Town • Aron Hugham. Upper Old Town • Benjamin Hull. Upper Old Town • Thomas Humphreys. Seven Springs, pt, 4 acres. Skipton • Joseph Ihefs. Upper Old Town • George Inkle. Willitts Choice, 100 acres. Cumberland • Abraham Inlow. Upper Old Town and Cumberland • John Inlow. Upper Old Town • Edward Irons. Cumberland • Jonathan Irons. Cumberland • Rebecca Irons. Cumberland • William Irons. Cumberland • John Jackson. Cumberland • Samuel Jackson. Upper Old Town • John J.. Jacob. Dispute, 286 acres. Cumberland • John J.. Jacob. Butter & Cheese, 340 acres. Cumberland • John J.. Jacob. Seven Springs, 1706 acres. Skipton • John J.. Jacob. Prospect, 53 acres. Skipton • John J.. Jacob. Addition to Seven Springs, 56 acres. Skipton (estate of Michael Cresap) • John J.. Jacob. Hopewell, 76 acres. Skipton (estate of Michael Cresap) • John J.. Jacob. Deakins' Forgetfullness, 26 acres. Skipton (estate of Michael Cresap) • John J.. Jacob. Cresaps Prospect, 110 acres. Skipton (estate of Michael Cresap) • John J.. Jacob. Alder Thickett, 80 acres. Skipton (estate of Michael Cresap) • Denton Jacques. Grove Camp, 397 acres. Upper Old Town • Evan James. Upper Old Town • Isaac James. Upper Old Town • Matthias Jeane. Upper Old Town • Joseph Jhefs Cable?. Upper Old Town • Abraham Johnson. Upper Old Town • Benjamin Johnson. Upper Old Town • John Johnson. Upper Old Town • Thomas Johnson. Cumberland • William Johnson. Upper Old Town • Benjamin Jolly. Skipton • James Jolly. Skipton and Murleys Run • Edward Jones. Wills Town and Sandy Creek • Frances Jones. Upper Old Town • William Jones. Upper Old Town • George Kelly. Upper Old Town and Cumberland • John Kelso. Wills Town and Sandy Creek • Joseph Kelso. Wills Town and Sandy Creek • John Kent. Cumberland • John Key. Walnutt Levell, 440 acres. Upper Old Town • Robert Kiles. Upper Old Town • John Kimberly. Skipton • James King. Skipton and Murleys Run • John King. Upper Old Town • John King. Skipton • Samuel King. Upper Old Town • Thomas King. Skipton • Valentine King. Skipton • Thomas Langton. St. Catharines, 1314 acres. Upper Old Town • George Layport. Upper Old Town • William Lazear. Hyetts Grove, 50 acres. Cumberland • Thomas Lazer. Hyetts Grove, 50 acres. Cumberland • Jacob Lee. Upper Old Town and Cumberland • Josiah Lee. Upper Old Town • Stephen Lee. Upper Old Town • William Lee. 100 acres. Cumberland • Edward Lifton. Upper Old Town • Zachariah Linton. Upper Old Town • James Little. Wills Town and Sandy Creek • James Little. Skipton • William Lockwood. Cumberland • Elisha Logston. Wills Town and Sandy Creek • Thomas Logston. Wills Town and Sandy Creek • William Logston. Waterford, 115 acres. Wills Town and Sandy Creek • Rosamond Long. Upper Old Town • Barton Looman. Upper Old Town and Cumberland • John Looman. Upper Old Town and Cumberland • Joshua Looman. Upper Old Town and Cumberland • Briton Lovett. Upper Old Town and Cumberland • Daniel Lovett. Upper Old Town • Caleb Lowman. Lowmans Ramble, 100 acres. Cumberland • Moses Lowman. Lowmans Ramble, 100 acres. Cumberland • Philip Lucas. Cumberland • John Lyon. Upper Old Town • Jonathan Madden. Cumberland • Richard Madden. Cumberland • Alexander Maloney. Upper Old Town • Joseph Malott. Upper Old Town • George Markwell. Upper Old Town • William Markwell. Upper Old Town • John Marshall. Upper Old Town • George Mason. sundry tracts, 660 acres. Cumberland • George Mason. The Cove, 510 acres. Upper Old Town • Stephen Masters. Wills Town and Sandy Creek • John Mathew. Wills Town and Sandy Creek • Thomas Mathews. Wills Town and Sandy Creek • William Mathews. Skipton • Barnet Mattingly. Upper Old Town and Cumberland • Clement Mattingly. Cumberland • Henry Mattingly. Wills Town and Sandy Creek • Joseph Mattingly. Cumberland • Richard Mattingly. Cumberland • Ovid McCracken. Harmitts Retreat, 344 acres. Skipton • Angus McDonald. Glenco, 500 acres. Skipton (heirs) • Archabal McDonald. Straden, pt, 75 acres. Skipton • James McDonald. Upper Old Town • George McDowell. Upper Old Town and Cumberland • Gabriel McKinsay. Wills Town and Sandy Creek • Aron McKinsey. Wills Town and Sandy Creek • Daniel McKinsey. Wills Town and Sandy Creek • John McKinsey. Wills Town and Sandy Creek • Samuel McKinsey. Wills Town and Sandy Creek • Gabriel McKisay. Wills Town and Sandy Creek • John McNeal. Upper Old Town • William McRoby. Upper Old Town and Cumberland • George Meatheweather. Upper Old Town • Nicholas Meatheweather. Upper Old Town • George Miller. Skipton • Richard Minton. Upper Old Town • David Mitchell. Round Bottom, 96 acres. Skipton • David Mitchell. Good Hope, 50 acres. Skipton • David Mitchell. Betsys Blessing, 70 acres. Skipton • Isaac Mixer. Skipton • Phinchas Mixer. Skipton and Murleys Run • John Montgomery. Upper Old Town •

Alexander More. Upper Old Town • Joseph More. Upper Old Town • William More. Fards Beginning, 61 acres. Cumberland • William More. Wills Town and Sandy Creek • Joseph Mountz. Sugar Bottom, 304 acres. Upper Old Town • Moses Munroe. Upper Old Town • Robert Munroe. Upper Old Town • Solomon Munroe. Upper Old Town • Benjamin Murdock. Bear Camp, 120 acres. Wills Town and Sandy Creek • Christopher Myres. Wills Town and Sandy Creek • Henry Myres. Wills Town and Sandy Creek • Michal Myres. Cumberland • John Nichells. Butter & Cheese, 140 acres. Cumberland • John Nichells. Kindness, 19 1/2 acres. Cumberland • Joseph Nichells. Cumberland • Allen Nickson. Upper Old Town and Cumberland • John Nipton. Upper Old Town • John Nixson. Upper Old Town • William Nixson. Upper Old Town • Laurence O'Neal. Rabets Range, 84 acres. Skipton • Laurence O'Neal. 70 acres. Skipton • Laurence O'Neal. 1100 acres. Skipton • William Ogle. Upper Old Town • Ohio Company. Walnutt Bottom, 517 acres. Wills Town and Sandy Creek • Robert Parker. Wills Town and Sandy Creek • John Patterson. Skipton • James Pearce. Cumberland • John Pecker. Skipton • William Persons. Wills Town and Sandy Creek • Abraham Peter. Cumberland • Henry Peters. Upper Old Town • Henry Pippinger. Wills Town and Sandy Creek • Jerum Plummer. Poplar Valley, 90 acres. Cumberland • Thomas Plummer. Cumberland • Peter Poland. Upper Old Town • Henry Porter. Wills Town and Sandy Creek • Moses Porter. Wills Town and Sandy Creek • Jacob Potts. Wills Town and Sandy Creek • Charles Prather. Friendship, 128 acres. Cumberland • James Prather. 162 acres. Upper Old Town • George Preston. Wills Town and Sandy Creek • Richard Prichard. Upper Old Town • John Pritchett. Cumberland • Richard Pritchett. Upper Old Town and Cumberland • John Purcell. Straden, pt, 121 2/3 acres. Skipton • Andrew Quick. Upper Old Town • Aron Quick. Upper Old Town • Benjamin Quick. Upper Old Town • Dennis Quick. Upper Old Town • Jacob Quick. Upper Old Town • John Randolph. Upper Old Town • John Rausaw. Cumberland • John Rauton. Wills Town and Sandy Creek • Moses Rawlings. Skipton • William Ray. Upper Old Town • Solomon Rees. Cumberland • Elijah Reeves. Upper Old Town • John Rhubert. Upper Old Town • Andrew Rice. Goodness, 53 acres. Cumberland • Frederick Rice. Upper Old Town • John Rice. Wood Cock Valley, 63 acres. Cumberland • Godfrey Richard. Upper Old Town • George Richardson. Wills Town and Sandy Creek • George Riddle. Upper Old Town • Adam Roads. Upper Old Town • Edward Robert. Upper Old Town and Cumberland • Walter Robert. Upper Old Town • David Robertson. Wills Town and Sandy Creek • John Robertson. Skipton • Thomas Rock. Upper Old Town and Cumberland • Ross. 25 acres. Skipton (heirs) • David Ross. Cresaps Kindness, 1425 acres. Cumberland • David Ross. White Oak Levell, 425 acres. Cumberland • David Ross. Bigg Bottom, 197 acres. Cumberland • David Ross. Shoots Request, 160 acres. Cumberland • David Ross. Peavine Bottom, 82 acres. Cumberland • David Ross. Prize, 240 acres. Cumberland • David Ross. Turky Flight, 265 acres. Cumberland • David Ross. Bucks Lodge, 440 acres. Upper Old Town • David Ross. Luck, 212 acres. Upper Old Town • David Ross. Three Springs, 97 acres. Upper Old Town • David Ross. White Oak Levell, 150 acres. Wills Town and Sandy Creek • David Ross. White Oak Point, 125 acres. Wills Town and Sandy Creek • David Ross. Workmans Desire, 75 acres. Wills Town and Sandy Creek • David Ross. Johnsons Fancy, 50 acres. Wills Town and Sandy Creek • Joseph Rowner. Upper Old Town • Andrew Rude. Upper Old Town and Cumberland • Samuel Rugg. Wills Town and Sandy Creek • William Ruggles. Cumberland • Jacob Rush. Skipton • William Rutherford. Upper Old Town • George Sapp. Wills Town and Sandy Creek • Jacob Sapp. Martins Choice, 30 acres. Cumberland • Jacob Sapp. Neglect, 145 acres. Cumberland • Elijah Sarrell. Upper Old Town • William Shaw. Wills Town and Sandy Creek • Elizabeth Shoemaker. Upper Old Town • John Showell. Cropton. Upper Old Town • Jacob Shulsa. Wills Town and Sandy Creek • Samuel Simcock. Skipton • Able Simpkins. Adams Folly, 50 acres. Cumberland • Dickerson Simpkins. Rising Sun, 140 acres. Cumberland • Silas Simpkins. Why Not, 150 acres. Cumberland • John Sinks. Upper Old Town • Garrard Sneadecor. Wills Town and Sandy Creek • Matthias Snuck. Upper Old Town • Joseph Sprigg. Good Hope, 500 acres. Skipton • Joseph Sprigg. Indian Fields, 410 acres. Skipton • John Stagg. Upper Old Town • William Stagg. Upper Old Town • Jacob Starcher. Wills Town and Sandy Creek • James Stoddert. Skipton • Joshua Stratford. Suspence, 156 acres. Skipton • Peter Stuck. Wills Town and Sandy Creek • Henry Stump. Skipton • John Suck. Wills Town and Sandy Creek • David Swank. 50 acres. Cumberland • Leonard Tetoard. Upper Old Town • Peter Tittle. Mount Pleasant, 100 acres. Wills Town and Sandy Creek • Benjamin Tomlinson. Wills Town, 30 acres. Wills Town and Sandy Creek • Jesse Tomlinson. Good Will, 100 acres. Wills Town and Sandy Creek • John Tomlinson. Wills Town, 260 acres. Wills Town and Sandy Creek • Nathaniel Tomlinson. Wills Town, 260 acres. Wills Town and Sandy Creek • Timothy Tracy. Upper Old Town • Samuel Treet. Cumberland • John Trimbell. Wills Town and Sandy Creek • John Trotter. Wills Town and Sandy Creek • Jacob Tuther. Wills Town and Sandy Creek • Thomas Twigg. Skipton • Frederick Valentine. Cumberland • John Ventene. Upper Old Town • George Waddle. Wills Town and Sandy Creek • Robert Wallace. Skipton • Samuel Wallace. Skipton • Thomas Warring. Cumberland • Michal Watson. Skipton • Leonard Weazer. Skipton • Moses Weck or Weeks. Cumberland • Moses Weeks or Wecks. Cumberland • James Welch. Wills Town and Sandy Creek • John Welkey. Skipton • Thomas Welky. Skipton and Murleys Run • William Wentfield. Cumberland • George West. Upper Old Town and Cumberland • Alpheus Wickevere. Wills Town and Sandy Creek • John Wicoff. Wills Town and Sandy Creek • Able Wiley. Cumberland • Benjamin Wiley. Cumberland • Walter Wiley. Upper Old Town and Cumberland • Barnett Williams. Upper Old Town and Cumberland • Joseph Williams. Cumberland • Nathaniel Williams. Upper Old Town and Cumberland • John Williamson. Upper Old Town and Cumberland • Charles Willison. Skipton and Murleys Run •

Adam Wolfhart. Wills Town and Sandy Creek ● Andrew Workman. Wills Town and Sandy Creek ● Isaac Workman. Wills Town and Sandy Creek ● James Workman. Wills Town and Sandy Creek ● John Workman. Wills Town and Sandy Creek ● Joseph Workman. Wills Town and Sandy Creek ● Stephen Workman. Wills Town and Sandy Creek ● George Young. Wills Town and Sandy Creek.

# 36. 1784: Grand schemes for transportation

### The Treaty of Paris is ratified in January of 1784

The United States Congress ratified the Treaty of Paris on January 14, 1784. The ratification begins with the following preamble:

*Whereas definitive articles of peace and friendship between the United States of America and his Britannic majesty, were concluded and signed at Paris on the 3d day of September, 1783, by the plenipotentiaries of the said United States, and of his said Britannic Majesty, duly and respectively authorized for that purpose..."*

### Abraham Johnson sells a tract on Cabbin Run

The 1939 book "**Early Records Hampshire County Virginia**" records the following for January 28, 1784, *"JOHNSON, Abraham, Sr. (w. Rachel) of Hampshire Co. to Jacob Bogard of Hampshire Co. 46 a. on Cabbin Run; rec 3-9-1784. Wit.: Gabriel Wright, William Hough, Abraham Johnson, Jr."*

### Washington writes to Jefferson about transportation in 1784

On March 29, 1784, George Washington wrote a letter[1634] to Thomas Jefferson that included the following:

*My opinion coincides perfectly with yours respecting the practicability of an easy, and short communication between the Waters of the Ohio and Potomac. Of the advantages of that communication, and the preference it has over all others. And of the policy there would be in this State, and Maryland to adopt and render it facile; but I confess to you freely, I have no expectation that the public will adopt the measure; for besides the jealousies wch. prevail, and the difficulty of proportioning such funds as may be allotted for the purposes you have mentioned, there are two others, which, in my opinion, will be yet harder to surmount; these are (if I have not imbibed too unfavourable an opinion of my Countrymen) the impracticability of bringing the great, and truly wise policy of the measure to their view; and the difficulty of drawing money from them, for such a purpose if you could do it. for it appears to me, maugre all the sufferings of the public creditors, breach of public faith, and loss of public reputation, that payment of the taxes which are already laid, will be postponed as long as possible! how then are we to expect new ones, for purposes more remote?*

### Cresap transfers Virginia property to Luther Martin

The 1939 book "**Early Records Hampshire County Virginia**" records the following for May 11, 1784, *"CRESAP, Thomas of Baltimore, Md. to Luther Martin of Baltimore, Md. Parcel of land on South Branch; rec 5-11-1784. Wit.: Michael Cresap, John J. Jacob, Charlotte Storddart."*

### Thomas Cresap transfers Virginia property to Michael Cresap

The 1939 book "**Early Records Hampshire County Virginia**" records the following for June 12, 1784, *"CRESAP, Thomas of Washington Co. to Michael Cresap of Washington Co. 400 a. in Hampshire Co.,*

---

[1634] "**The Writings of George Washington from the Original Manuscript Sources 1745-1799**", Volume 27, 1938.

*near Skipton; rec. 8-10-1784. Wit.: John J. Jacobs, Michael Cresap, Charlotte Stoddard, Elizabeth Cresap."*

### Thomas Cresap transfers Virginia property to William Young

The 1939 book "**Early Records Hampshire County Virginia**" records the following for June 23, 1784, *"CRESAP, Col. Thomas of Washington Co. to William Young of Hampshire Co. Parcel of land on Potomac R; rec. 8-10-1784. Wit.: Joseph Sprigg, Michael Cresap, John J. Jacobs, Elizabeth Cresap."*

### John Jacob purchases Virginia property on the North Branch of Potomac River

The 1939 book "**Early Records Hampshire County Virginia**" records the following for August 10, 1784, *"WALKER, John, Sr. (w. Mary) Hampshire Co. to John Jeremiah Jacob Hampshire Co. Hampshire Co. (bill of sale) 200 a., 150 a., on North Branch; rec. 8-10-1784. Wit.: None."* Also recorded for the same day, *"WALKER, Thomas of Hampshire Co. to James Prather of Washington Co. (bill of sale) 33 a., 62 ½ a on North Branch; rec. 8-10-1784. Wit.: None."*

### Washington's September 10, 1784 journal entry

George Washington's journal entry for September 10, 1784 states:

> *Set off a little after 5 Oclock altho' the morning was very unpromising. Finding from the rains that had fallen, and description of the Roads, part of which between the old Town & this place (old Fort Cumberland) we had passed, that the progress of my Baggage would be tedeous, I resolved (it being Necessary) to leave it to follow; and proceed on myself to Gilbert Simpson's, to prepare for the Sale which I had advertised of my moiety of the property in co-partnership with him and to make arrangements for my trip to the Kanhawa, if the temper & disposition of the Indians should render it advisable to proceed. Accordingly, leaving Doctr. Craik, his Son, and my Nephew with it, I set out with one Servant only. Dined at a Mr. Gwins at the Fork of the Roads leading to Winchester and the old Town, distant from the latter abt. 20 Miles & lodged at Tumbersons at the little Meadows 15 Miles further.*

> *The Road from the Old Town to Fort Cumberland we found tolerably good, as it also was from the latter to Gwins, except the Mountain which was pretty long (tho' not steep) in the assent and discent; but from Gwins to Tumberson's it is intolerably bad — there being many steep pinches of the Mountain — deep & miry places and very stony ground to pass over. After leaving the Waters of Wills Creek which extends up the Mountain (Alligany) two or three Miles as the road goes, we fell next on those of George's Creek, which are small — after them upon Savage River which are more considerable; tho' from the present appearance of them, does not seem capable of Navigation.*

This passage indicates that Gwynn's tavern was located where the Winchester Road via Short Gap and Patterson Creek forked from Braddock's road.

### Tomlinson's, Mount's, and Daugherty's, west of Fort Cumberland in 1784

George Washington's journal entry[1635] for September 11, 1784 states:

---

[1635] A transcript of Washington's 1784 journal is provided in Hulbert's 1905 book "**Washington and the West, Being George Washington's Diary of September, 1784, Kept during his journey into the Ohio Basin in the interest of a commercial union between the Great Lakes and the Potomac River**". One of the purposes of Washington's September 1784 trip was to find trade routes that would tether the western lands to the thin band of civilization on the east coast. Hulbert eloquently states this aspect of Washington's visionary thinking, *" 'There are no Alleghanies in my politics,' said Daniel Webster in the Senate in 1836; that was Washington's political theory in 1784. 'Intercourse between*

*Set out half after 5 o'clock from Tomlinson's, and in about one and a half miles came to what is called the Little Crossing of Youghiogheny. Breakfasted at one Mount's,[1636] on the Mountain 11 miles from Tomlinson's. The road being exceedingly bad, especially through what is called the Shades of Death. Baited[1637] at the Great Crossing of the Yohogheny, on Braddock's Road, which is a large water distance from Mount's 9 miles, and a better road than between that and Tomlinson's. — Lodged at one Daughertys a Mile & half short of the Great Meadows... distant from the crossing 12 Miles.*

### Washington reports that Dr. Craig is taking the new road back from Simpson's place
George Washington's journal entry for September 22, 1784 states:

*... From this information I resolved to return home that way;[1638] & my Baggage under the care of Doct. Craik and Son, having, from Simpsons,[1639] taken the Rout by the New (or Turkey foot) Road as it is called (which is said to be 20 Miles near[er] than Braddocks) with a view to make a more minute enquiry into the Navigation of the Yohiogany Waters...[1640]*

This quote refers to starting Doctor Craig back on the northern part of the road that was cut a few years before by Charles Clinton and Providence Mounts, since it refers to *"...the New (or Turkey foot) Road..."*. This is the earliest usage of the name *"Turkey Foot Road"* that I have found. The specific reason that Washington sent Doctor Craig back that way was *"to make a more minute enquiry into the Navigation of the Yohiogany Waters..."* Washington's mileage savings statement is similar to that in Morgan's March 1779 letter to Greene, which states, *"A Road may be opend from Fort Cumberland to Fort Pitt which will shorten the Distance 22 or 25 Miles..."* Presumably, Washington knew about the Turkey Foot Road as a result of his interactions with Greene and Morgan.

### George Washington meets a youthful Albert Gallatin
Albert Butler Hulbert's 1911 book "**Washington and the West**" gives the following account of the first encounter between George Washington and a youthful Albert Gallatin, who would eventually become known as the *"father of the Cumberland Road"*:

*On the morning of the twenty-fourth the party, including their host, pushed on to the Cheat at its junction with the Monongahela at the present village of Point Marion. ... Following the dividing ridge between the rivers, the home of John Pierpont, grandfather of Francis H. Pierpont, War Governor of West Virginia, was reached, the site of which will be pointed out to the visitor near the present Pierpont M. E. Church, distant four miles from Morgantown, West Virginia, and four miles from Mount Chateau, the Cheat River resort. At the surveyor's office Washington did not find the records desired, save those of*

---

the mighty interior West and the seacoast,' said Edward Everett in Faneuil Hall in 1835, 'is the great principle of our commercial prosperity'; that was Washington's commercial theory in 1784. Far-seeing as were Everett and Webster and Clinton and the Morrises, Washington excelled them all in that he antedated them inrealizing the destinies of America ran east and west."

[1636] Dr. Wellford's October 26, 1794 journal entry refers to the tavern as *"Mountain's Hovel"*. Doctor Wellford was born in England on April 12, 1753.

[1637] According to Sheridan's 1780 "**A General Dictionary of the English Language**", one definition of *"bait"* is *"To stop at any place for refreshment..."*

[1638] The referenced *"that way"* was an exploratory route.

[1639] Gilbert Simpson, at what is now Perryopolis, Pennsylvania. Perryopolis is located on the Youghiogheny River, about 11 miles south of West Newton, and 12.4 miles northwest of Connellsville.

[1640] The contemplated use of the Casselman River as a canal may be why the stone arch on the Little Crossings Bridge near Grantsville is built so unusually high. According to Steve Colby's "**The Cumberland Road Project**" website, a 1963 sesquicentennial document of the Little Crossings Historical Committee quotes an article by Captain Charles E. Hoye from the September 30, 1947 issue of "**The Glades Star**" which indicates that the arch was intended to accommodate a canal.

*lands at the mouth of the Little Kanawha secured by Rutherford and Briscoe, names well known in Wood County and Parkersburg.*

*When Washington brought up the inland navigation problem, Hanway sent to Morgantown for General Zackwell Morgan, the founder of the city which bears his name. From him Washington learned that there were three routes eastward to the Potomac through the rugged region watered by the upper Cheat and Youghiogheny rivers; one was the "New Road" running from Morgantown through the Sandy Creek Glades to Braddock's Road, which it entered a mile west of Jockey Hollow; another branched from the New Road in Sandy Creek Glades and following McCullough's Path came to the North Branch at what is Fort Pendleton; the third ran from the neighborhood of the present Clarksburg, crossed the Cheat at Dunkard's Bottom, one of the earliest clearings west of the Alleghanies made by a family of that name, and also crossed the Potomac at Fort Pendleton. All these paths were deer and buffalo trails to and from the splendid feeding grounds in the Glades; the first pioneers found them roads ready to their feet leading into the Glades from the East and out of them again toward what became "Morgan Town" and "Clarkstown," fifteen miles below the portage to the present Bullstown on the Little Kanawha.*

*The navigation of the Cheat below Horseshoe Bottom was reported adversely; and the only hope of an all-Virginia route from the Potomac to the Little Kanawha was to be secured by improving one of these roads through the Glades to Fort Pendleton — the one through Sandy Creek Glades or the one through Dunkard's Bottom.*

*Here at the Pierpont home occurred that famous interview between the youthful Albert Gallatin and Washington, to which the former frequently referred in after life. We have deferred reference to it till now in order that the picture that Washington so dimly draws may stand complete before this most interesting side-light is thrown upon it. Born in 1761, Gallatin came to America in 1780; during 1782 he was instructor in French at Harvard College, and early in 1784 came westward to lands he had purchased near Washington's in Pennsylvania, at the mouth of George's Creek, of which mention is made in the diary. It is likely that Gallatin was visiting the surveyor with reference to his lands, though on this point we are not made clear by his biographers. "The story of the interview," writes one of them, Stevens, "was first made public by Mr. John Russell Bartlett, who had it from the lips of Mr. Gallatin. The version of the late Hon. William Beach Lawrence . . . differs slightly in immaterial points. Mr. Lawrence says:*

*" 'Among the incidents connected with his (Mr. Gallatin's) earliest explorations was an interview with General Washington, which he repeatedly recounted to me. He had previously observed that of all the inaccessible men he had ever seen, General Washington was the most so. And this remark he made late in life, after having been conversant with most of the sovereigns of Europe and their prime ministers. He said, in connection with his office, he had a cot-bed in the office of the surveyor of the district when Washington, who had lands in the neighborhood, and was desirous of effecting communication between the rivers, came there. Mr. Gallatin's bed was given up to him, — Gallatin lying on the floor, immediately below the table at which Washington was writing [in his diary]. Washington was endeavoring to reduce to paper the calculations of the day. Gallatin, hearing the statement, came at once to the conclusion, and, after waiting some time, he himself gave the answer, which drew from Washington such a look [of rebuke] as he never experienced before or since. On arriving by a slow process at his conclusion, Washington turned to Gallatin and said, "You are right, young man." Bartlett, in his recollection of the anecdote, adds that Washington, about this period, inquired after the forward young man, and urged him to become his land agent, — an offer which Gallatin declined.' "*

*This version of Gallatin's story, looked at from the standpoint of Washington's diary is fairly well authenticated. There can be no doubt that it was at Pierpont's that the interview occurred, though as Freeman had been offered the position of land agent it is difficult to harmonize the detail of the story with Washington's record. Another version of the story is given by Henry Adams, who says: "Mr. Gallatin said he first met General Washington at the office of a land agent near the Kenawha River, in northwestern Virginia, where he [Gallatin] had been engaged in surveying. The office consisted of a log house fourteen feet square, in which was but one room. ... Many of the settlers and hunters familiar with the country had been invited to meet the general. ... On his arrival General Washington took his seat at a pine table in the log cabin, or rather land agent's office, surrounded by the men who had come to meet him. They all stood up, as there was no room for seats. Some of the more fortunate, however, secured quarters on the bed. ... Mr. Gallatin stood among the others in the crowd, though quite near the table, and listened attentively to the numerous queries put by the general, and very soon discovered from the various relations [accounts] which was the only practicable pass through which the road could be made. He felt uneasy at the indecision of the general, when the point was so evident to him, and without reflecting on the impropriety of it, suddenly interrupted him, saying, 'Oh, it is plain enough, such a place [a spot just mentioned by one of the settlers] is the most practicable.' The good people stared at the young surveyor (for they only knew him as such) with surprise, wondering at his boldness in thrusting his opinion unasked upon the general.*

*"The interruption put a sudden stop to General Washington's inquiries. He laid down his pen, raised his eyes from his paper, and cast a stern look at Mr. Gallatin, evidently offended at the intrusion of his opinion, but said not a word.*

*Resuming his former attitude, he continued his interrogations for a few minutes longer, when, suddenly stopping, he threw down his pen, turned to Mr. Gallatin, and said, "You are right, sir.'"*

*The question naturally arises, Why was Gallatin staying at the surveyor's office? Perhaps he was learning the trade. The picture drawn of Washington at the table working the day's sum of information down to brief compass and the young man watching him from the floor is of intense interest; because it was no doubt here and now that the future statesman and champion of internal improvements received his first important inspiration. As is well known, Gallatin's comprehensive scheme as Secretary of the Treasury, less than twenty years later, involved the improvement of the Susquehanna, Potomac, and James rivers up the eastern slopes of the Alleghanies and of the Alleghany, Monongahela and Kanawha rivers down the Western slopes — Washington's identical plan in 1784, when, as a boy, Gallatin watched him from the floor of the surveyor's office and with irrepressible energy made his impromptu answer. In fact, Mr. Adams states that the reason Gallatin selected George's Creek for a base of operations was that he held in his hand the best practical connection between the Ohio and the Potomac "which was their path to Richmond and a market." Local tradition has it in the neighborhood that Gallatin's answer was to the effect that Braddock's Road marked the most feasible route. There was reason enough for Washington's agreeing with him and for giving him a glance!*

Albert Gallatin implemented one of George Washington's dreams in the form of the National Road.

### Canoes reported in use above Fort Cumberland in 1784

George Washington's journal entry for September 26, 1784 includes a statement about information received from Friend and Logston, *"...but in general I could gather from them, especially from Joseph Logston, who has (he says) hunted along the Water course of the River that there is no fall in it — that from Fort Cumberland to the Mouth of Savage River the water being good is frequently made use of in its present State with Canoes..."*

### Washington's visionary thinking concerning western transportation

According to Barrow's 1888 book "**The United States of Yesterday and of To-morrow**", Washington wrote the following[1641] to Governor Benjamin Harrison of Virginia after his 1784 journey:

---

[1641] "**Tracks**", Volume 39, 1954 gives the date of this letter as October 10.

*I need not remark to you that the flank and rear of the United States are possessed by other powers, and formidable ones too. ... If the Spaniards on their right and Great Britain on their left, instead of throwing stumbling-blocks in their way, as they now do, should hold out lures for their trade and alliance! When they gain strength, which will be sooner than most people conceive...The Western States hang upon a pivot; the touch of a feather would turn them any way.*

## Doctor James Craig's October 2, 1784 letter to George Washington

Doctor James Craig's letter to George Washington, written from Mount Vernon and dated October 2, 1784, mentions the Turkey Foot Road from Cumberland. It states:

*I have thought it might be more satisfactory to leave you the different accounts I received respecting the communication between the waters of the Youghiogany and the North Branch of the Potomac, that you might, from a view of the whole, collect an opinion for yourself. It appears to me, that the land carriage from the Fork of Youghiogany to Cumberland, which, from a variety of accounts, will not be more than thirty miles, is to be preferred to sixty miles of difficult navigation up the Little Crossing, and twenty miles land carriage afterwards, which is the distance from the Little Crossing on the Turkey-foot road to Cumberland. If the communication is to be carried on by the Little Crossing, the Turkey-foot road is to be preferred to Braddock's old road, as it is infinitely Better, and above two miles shorter. Indeed I found the whole Turkey-foot road across the mountains much better and nearer than Braddock's road; that if there were good entertainment, no one could hesitate in the choice.*

## A resolution to write to Pennsylvania about laying out a road to the Youghiogheny River

The 1856 "**Index to the Journals of the Senate and House of Delegates of the State of Maryland**" includes the following summary of an item from the November 1784 meeting of the House of Delegates:

*Resolution, requesting the, to write to the legislature of Pennsylvania, to request permission to lay out a road through such part as may be necessary in the best direction from Fort Cumberland to the navigable point of the Youghiogheny, sent to senate 66; returned assented to 67.*

## Ellicott stays at Mounts Tavern in November of 1784

Andrew Ellicott's November 24, 1784 journal entry describes his experience with the road west of Mount's, and with Mount's tavern, as follows:

*Before Day this Morning we eat Brakefast and began our Journey about Sun-Rise – the Weather extreme cold and the Roads bad to a degree before unknown the ground covered with Snow which hid the Mud-Holes and rendered Traveling not only tedious but dangerous ... About 5 OClock P.M. we took up our Quarters at one Mr. Mountains. At 4 OClock we passed the Memorable West Line began by Messrs. Mason & Dixon and compeated by us this Season and verified by the most exact Astronomical Observations — Mr. Mountain has a Sufficiency of Liquors and provisions but falls short in the Article of Bedding — he has but three one Occupied by himself and Wife one by the small Children and the Other by the Bar-Maid — for this last I endeavoured to stipulate for my fellow Traveller and colleague the Revd Doctr Andrews on account of his late ill state of health but she Absolutely refused having any thing to do in a Bargain ... I then requested a part for myself the other she might occupy herself in if she pleased to this she objected I then offered her my Blankets and Sheets to this She agreed with pleasure I then told the Doctr the Bed was his and gave him my title but the Hussey immediately Reniged and reclaimed the Bed — We then concluded to spread our Blankets and Sheets before the Fire – this we performed and lodged amidst an Heteroclite of all the Characters of the Mountains..."*

### Ellicott stays at Tittle's Tavern in November of 1784

Andrew Ellicott's November 25, 1784 journal entry describes staying at Tittle's, as follows, *"... Began our Journey before Day-light ... we passed the highest Ridges of the Allegany about 2 OClock P.M. ... in the Evening we took up our Quarters at one Mr. Tittles and have a large open house to ourselves..."*

### A Simpkins at Old Town in 1784

Andrew Ellicott's November 26, 1784 journal entry describes staying at another Simpkins's, as follows, *"At day light we settled our Bill and mounted our Horses ... about 9 Oclock we made the foot of the Allegany at the Junction of the Maryland and Virginia Roads ... at this Stage we Brakefasted and then my Colleague and self took an Affectionate farewell he goes by the way of Winchester to Williamsburgh — he is a Sensible lively Companion and a good man — about 12 Oclock I got to Wills Creek the Climate is quite altered and I laid aside my cap — In the Evening I made Old-Town and put up at Mr. Simpkins — my Friends in this Place flocked about me as if I had been raised from the Dead ..."*

### A 1784 law voids certain land grants to the westward of Fort Cumberland

According to "**The Land-holder's Assistant**" (1808), Chapter 75, Sections 3 and 6, of the Laws of Maryland, passed in November 1784, *"...enacts, that all grants for land lying within any manor to the westward of Fort Cumberland, and all grants issued, or to be issued, for lands to the westward of Fort Cumberland, on surveys or resurveys, in which vacancy is included made in virtue of warrants granted on or after the sixth day of October 1774, shall be void, and so held, and adjudged, in all courts of law and equity."*

Chapter LXXV[1642] of the Laws of Maryland states:

*An ACT to authorise the issuing grants for the lands therein mentioned.*

*WHEREAS, by the act, entitled, An act to appropriate certain lands to the use of the officers and soldiers of this state, and for the sale of vacant lands, it was enacted, that all the lands within this state in Washington county, westward of Fort Cumberland, and for which located warrants had not issued or surveys been made under common warrants, and were then bonâ fide the property of any subject of this or any of the United States, and on which the money had been actually paid, should be and were thereby appropriated to discharge the engagement of lands thereto made to the officers and soldiers of this state, and the residue to the use of the public, as the general assembly should thereafter direct, and that no grant should issue on any survey made in virtue of such warrants before the order of the general assembly: And whereas divers of the citizens of this state are justly entitled to have their titles perfected in lands lying to the westward of Fort Cumberland, on certificates of survey made before the passing of the said act, in virtue of warrants fairly obtained and duly executed, and the with-holding their patents, is not only prejudicial to them but injurious to the state, in delaying the settlement and improvement of those lands,*

*II. Be it enacted, by the general assembly of Maryland, That at any time after the first day of July next, a grant may issue in the usual mode to any citizen of this or any of the United States, for any land within this state westward of Fort Cumberland, regularly surveyed, by virtue of a special or common warrant obtained between the twenty-second day of March and the sixth day of October, in the year seventeen hundred and seventy-four, and for which the common consideration of one shilling sterling per acre was*

---

[1642] "**Hanson's Laws of Maryland 1763-1784**".

*paid, and which certificates were, at the time of passing the said recited act, bonâ fide the property of any citizen of this or any of the United States.*

*III. And be it enacted, That any grant issued or to be issued for any land lying within any manor to the westward of Fort Cumberland, shall be void, and so shall be held and adjudged in any court of law or equity within this state.*

*IV. And be it enacted, That if any grant hath been obtained, or shall hereafter be obtained, on any certificate returned in virtue of any warrant granted between the twenty-second day of March and the sixth day of October, in the year seventeen hundred and seventy-four, which certificate, at the time of passing the said recited act, was not bonâ fide the property of some citizen of this or some one of the United States, or for which the consideration aforesaid was not paid, such grant shall be void, and so shall be held and adjudged in any court of law or equity within this state; and the chancellor may offer to the person applying for a grant to be examined upon oath or interrogatories touching the matters aforesaid, and to examine witnesses respecting the same, in order that it may be discovered, in a summary manner, whether the certificate was, at the time of passing the above recited act, bonâ fide the property of some citizen of this or some one of the United States, and the consideration was paid as aforesaid; and if the party shall refuse to be examined upon oath or interrogatories, and to have the matter inquired into in a summary manner, then the chancellor may note the same, and give information thereof to the attorney-general, who shall file a bill in chancery against such person for the discovery of the truth of the facts by the regular course of the proceeding in the chancery court; and if it shall appear to the chancellor, either upon examination in a summary way aforesaid, or upon a bill being filed as aforesaid, that the certificate upon which patent shall be applied for was not bonâ fide the property of some citizen of this or some of the United States at the time of passing the above recited act, or that the consideration was not paid as aforesaid, in every such case the chancellor shall not order grant to be issued on such certificates, but shall declare the same void and of none effect; and the register of the land-office shall endorse the chancellor's determination on the certificate, and shall make a note thereof in the margin of the record wherein the warrant upon which such certificate was made hath been recorded.*

*V. And, whereas it is represented to this general assembly, that on sale of lands by the commissioners of the late proprietary to citizens of this state, from the year seventeen hundred and sixty-seven to the year seventeen hundred and seventy-one, grants have not issued in some cases where the whole consideration was satisfied, and in other cases where part of the purchase money remained unpaid; Be it enacted, That where all the purchase money for the sales as aforesaid has been paid, and in case where part only of the purchase money hath been paid, and any purchaser shall pay the balance due to the treasurer of the western shore, that in either case grant shall issue in the usual form to the purchaser and his heirs; and any money which shall be such purchasers be paid to the said treasurer as aforesaid, shall be by him paid to the legal representative of the late proprietary.*

*VI. And be it enacted, That if any grant has or shall hereafter issue for any lands to the westward of Fort Cumberland, on surveys or resurveys, in which vacancy is included, made in virtue of warrants granted on or after the sixth day of October, seventeen hundred and seventy-four, such grants shall be void, and so held and adjudged in all courts of law and equity.*

*VII. And, whereas there may have been surveys to the westward of Fort Cumberland made under warrants granted between the twenty-second day of March and sixth day of October, seventeen hundred and seventy-four, where the quantity expressed in the warrant has been exceeded, Be it enacted, That grants may issue on any survey, where the quantity expressed in the warrant has been exceeded not above one fourth, and such excess shall be paid for to the treasurer of the western shore.*

Clement Dorsey's book "**The general public statutory law and public local law of the state of Maryland...**", Volume 141, includes Chapter 67 of the laws of Maryland, as follows:

*A SUPPLEMENT to the Act, entitled, an act to authorize the issuing grants for the lands therein mentioned.*

*WHEREAS by the last clause in the act, entitled, an act to authorize the issuing grants for the lands therein mentioned, it is enacted, that where surveys have been made to the westward of Fort Cumberland, under warrants granted between the twenty-second day of March and sixth of October, seventeen hundred and seventy-four, and the quantity expressed in the warrant has been exceeded, grants may issue on such surveys, where the quantity expressed in the warrant has not been exceeded above one-fourth, and such excess shall be paid for to the treasurer of the western shore; And whereas surveys have been made to the westward of Fort Cumberland under warrant granted before the sixth of October, seventeen hundred and seventy-four, the quantity expressed in which has been exceeded above one-fourth, and the whole caution money due on the certificates thereof hath been paid to the treasurer, under the act allowing a longer time to compound on old certificates, and making further regulations respecting the sale of vacant lands, on or before the first of November, seventeen hundred and eighty-two, or under the act allowing a longer time to compound on old certificates, on or before the first of July, seventeen hundred and eighty-three, and the proprietors of the said certificates cannot in such cases obtain patents, to the great injury of the said proprietors, and the injury of the state in delaying the settlement and improvement of the lands mentioned in the certificates aforesaid.*

*SEC. 2. Be it enacted by the General Assembly of Maryland, That in all cases where it shall appear to the chancellor, by an examination in the manner prescribed by the first aforesaid act, that the certificate of any survey which hath exceeded the quantity expressed in the warrant more than one-fourth, and which hath been compounded for as aforesaid, was bona fide the property of some citizen of this state, or of some one of the United States, at the time of passing the act, entitled, an act to appropriate certain lands to the use of the officers and soldiers of this state, and for the sale of vacant lands, and that the proprietor of such certificate is, in equity and justice, and agreeably to the rules and practice of the examiner-general under the old government in passing certificates in which the quantity of land expressed in the warrant is exceeded, and of issuing grants on such certificates, entitled to a grant for the same, then and in such case the chancellor may order a grant to issue for the same; but if it shall appear to the chancellor, by an examination in the manner as aforesaid, that any such certificate, at the time of passing the said last aforesaid act, was not bona fide the property of some citizen of this state, or some one of the United States, or that the proprietor of such certificate is not justly and equitably entitled to a grant for the same, in such case he shall endorse on the said certificate his order or decree that the said certificate is void and of no effect; and the intendant, or any other person who shall be authorized to draw on the treasury, shall give the proprietor of such a certificate an order on the treasury of the western shore for the caution or composition money which hath been paid for such certificate, which order shall be discharged out of any money not specially appropriated, and the treasurer shall thereupon retain the said certificate as a voucher.*

The reference to *"the rules and practice of the examiner-general under the old government"* shows a necessary deference to policies established by the preceding British government. Had the new government failed to recognize such precedents, land ownership in Maryland would have been thrown into a state of utter turmoil.

## The December 22, 1784 Report of the Commissioners of Virginia and Maryland
Volume 361 of the book "**Congressional Edition**" includes the following:

*Report of the Commissioners of Virginia and Maryland.*

*At a meeting at the city of Annapolis, on the 22d day of December, 1784, of the commissioners appointed by the commonwealth of Virginia to confer with persons authorized on the part of the State of Maryland, upon the subject of opening and improving the navigation of the river Potomac, and concerting a plan for opening a proper road between the waters of the Potomac and the most convenient western waters, and a committee appointed by the Senate and House of Delegates of Maryland to meet the commissioneis of Virginia for the purpose aforesaid, were present General Washington and General Gates, from Virginia; The Hon. Thomas Stone, Samuel Hughes, and Charles Carroll of Carrollton, Esquires, of the Senate; and John Cadwallader, Samuel Chase, John Debutts, George Digges, Philip Key, Gustavus Scott, and Joseph Dashiell, Esquires, of the House of Delegates.*

*General Washington in the chair; Randolph B. Latimer appointed clerk.*

*The conference proceeded to take the subject-matters to them referred into their consideration, and, thereupon, came to the following resolutions:*

*That it is the opinion of this conference that the removing the obstructions in the river Potomac, and the making the same capable of navigation from tide-water as far up the north branch of the said river as may be convenient aud practicable, will increase the commerce of the commonwealth of Virginia and State of Maryland, and greatly promote the political interests of the United States, by forming a free and easy communication and connexion with the people settled on the western waters, already very considerable in their numbers, and rapidly increasing from the mildness of the climate and the fertility of the soil.*

*That it is the opinion of the conference that the proposal to establish a company for opening the river Potomac, merits the approbation of, and deserves to be patronised by, Virginia and Maryland, and that a similar law ought to be passed by the Legislature of the two Governments to promote and encourage so laudable an undertaking.*

*That it is the opinion of this conference that it would be proper for Virginia and Maryland each to become subscribers to the amount of fifty shares, and that such subscription would evince to the public the opinion of the Legislatures of the practicability and great utility of the plan, and that the example would encourage individuals to embark in the measure, give vigor and security to so important an undertaking, and be a substantial proof to our brethren of the western Territory of our disposition to connect ourselves with them by the strongest bonds of friendship and mutual interest.*

*That it is the opinion of this conference that an act of Assembly of Virginia "for opening and extending the navigation of the river Potomac from Fort Cumberland to tide-water," ought to be repealed.*

*That it is the opinion of this conference, from the best information they have obtained, that a road to begin about the mouth of Stony river may be carried in about twenty or twenty-two miles to the Dunker bottom, on Cheat river; whence this conference are of opinion that batteau navigation may be made, though, perhaps, at considerable expense. That if such navigation cannot be effected by continuing the road about twenty miles farther, it would intersect the Monongahela, where the navigation is good and has been long practised.*

*That a road from Fort Cumberland to Turkey-foot would be about thirty-three miles, whence an improvement of the Youghiogeny river would be necessary, though probably it might be done at less expense than the navigation of the Cheat river could be rendered convenient from the Dunker bottom.*

*That it is a general opinion that the navigation on Potomac may be extended to the most convenient point below, or even above, the mouth of Stony river, whence to set off a road to Cheat river; and this conference is satisfied that that road, from the nature of the country through which it may pass, wholly through Virginia and Maryland, will be much better than a road can be made at any reasonable expense from Fort Cumberland to the Youghiogeny, which must be carried partly through Pennsylvania.*

*That it is the opinion of this conference that, if the navigation on Potomac should be carried to about the mouth of the Stony river, a communication with the western waters, through a road thence, extended even to Monongalia, would be preferable in most points of view to that by a road from Fort Cumberland to Turkey-foot, the only other way practicable and in any great degree useful; that the communication by a road from Fort Cumberland to the present navigable parts of the Youghiogeny, and thence through that river, though in the opinion of this conference a second object only, would facilitate the intercourse with a very respectable number of the western settlers, contribute much to their convenience and accommodation, and that the benefits resulting therefrom to these States would compensate the expense of improving that road.*

*The conference therefore recommended that the Legislatures of Virginia and Maryland appoint skilful persons to view and accurately examine and survey Potomac, from Fort Cumberland to the mouth of Stony river and the river Cheat, from about the Dunker bottom to the present navigable part thereof, and if they judge the navigation can be extended to a convenient distance above Fort Cumberland, that they may thence survey, lay off, and mark, a road to the Cheat river, or continue the same to the navigation, as they may think Will most effectually establish the communication between the said eastern and western waters. And that the said road be cut and cleared not less than eighty feet, and properly improved and maintained in repair, not less than forty nor more than fifty feet wide, at the joint expense of both States; and your conferees beg leave to recommend that each State appropriate three thousand three hundred and thirty-three and one-third dollars for the purpose; and this conference are farther of opinion that the States of Virginia and Maryland request permission of the State of Pennsylvania to lay out and improve a road through such part of that State as may be necessary, in the best and most proper direction from Fort Cumberland to the navigable part of the Youghiogeny; and, on such permission being obtained, that proper persons be appointed to survey, mark, clear, and improve, such road, at the equal expense of Virginia and Maryland.*

*Which are submitted to the consideration of the Legislatures of Virginia and Maryland.*

*By order: R. B. LATIMER, Clerk.*

## The Patowmack Company is approved in 1784

Chapter XXXIII of the Laws of Maryland is titled *"An ACT for establishing a company for opening and extending the navigation of the river Patowmack."* Section XVII of the act includes this statement:

*And it is hereby declared and enacted, That the tolls herein before allowed to be demanded and received at the nearest convenient place below the mouth of the south branch, are granted, and shall be paid on condition only, that the said Patowmack company shall make the river well capable of being navigated, in dry seasons, by vessels drawing one foot water, from the place on the north branch at which a road shall set off to the Cheat river, agreeably to the determination of the assemblies of Virginia and Maryland, to and through the place which may be fixed on below the mouth of the south branch for receipt of the tolls aforesaid; but if the said river is only made navigable as aforesaid...*

Section XVIII of the act states:

*And it is hereby provided and enacted, That in case the said company shall not begin the said work within one year after the company shall be formed, or if the navigation shall not be made and improved between the great falls and Fort Cumberland, in the manner herein before mentioned, within three years after the said company shall be formed, that then the said company shall not be entitled to any benefit, privilege or advantage, under this act...*

Part 2 of the 1915 **"Report of the Chief of Engineers U.S. Army"** summarizes the history of the Patowmack Company as follows:

*In 1785 The "Patowmack Company" was organized under the direction of George Washington, by authority of the States of Virginia and Maryland, for the purpose of making the Potomac navigable from Georgetown to Cumberland, Md., from which point it was expected that a good road would lead to the Ohio River. To this end it did some open-channel work and built five short lengths of canal to surmount the chief obstacles which were found at Little Falls, Great Falls, Seneca Falls, Shenandoah Falls, and House Falls, the latter being about 5 miles above Harpers Ferry. Navigation was opened in 1802, but the facilities afforded were not satisfactory. After an existence of about 35 years and an expenditure of $700,000, the "Patowmack Company" became bankrupt.*

## George Lowdermilk reportedly built a house at Fort Cumberland circa 1784

Although not documentary evidence, Lowdermilk's 1878 book "**History of Cumberland**" reports:

*About 1784 George Lowdermilk built a frame house some fifty yards west of Washington's headquarters, and occupied it for twenty years.*

# 37. 1785: The town begins

**Reportedly, a tavern existed at the site of Cumberland when the town was laid out**

Although not documentary evidence, in his 1878 book "**History of Cumberland...**" Lowdermilk states:

*There was certainly one tavern, and not improbably more than one, on the present site of Cumberland before the establishment of the town, for we know that when Thomas Beal ... laid out the town on the 4th of October, 1784, Dickinson Simkins[1643] was keeping an inn at that point.*

The 1784 date in the quoted passage is on conflict with page 259 of Lowdermilk's book, which states:

*Immediately after purchasing this land, Beall went to work clearing that part of "Walnut Bottom" lying west of Will's creek, and erected several buildings. In 1785 he laid out at a town, which was commonly called Washington Town, and sold a number of lots to settlers.*

**Washington writes to Richard Henry Lee about a new road from Fort Cumberland**

According to the 1825 book "**Memoir of the Life of Richard Henry Lee...**", on February 8, 1785, George Washington wrote to Richard Henry Lee about "*...an application to the state of Pennsylvania, for permission to open another road from fort Cumberland to the Youghioany, at the three forks, or Turkey foot.*" This letter relates to Washington's involvement in the Patowmack Company, and the possibility of improving the Potomac River for navigation. See Corra Bacon-Foster's 1912 book "**Early chapters in the development of the Patomac route to the West**" for more information. According to an article by Rush C. Faris in Volume 13 of "**The Chautauquan**", in 1891, the road westward from Cumberland that Washington envisioned in the 1780s was finally realized when the National Road was built during the first quarter of the nineteenth century, long after Washington's death.

**A law resolving property ownership conflicts with Pennsylvania**

Chapter LXVI of the Laws of Maryland, passed March 11, 1785 and titled *"An ACT ascertaining the mode of granting titles to the purchasers of certain confiscated property"*, contains two sections that are relevant to the history of the Cumberland region:

*VI. And be it enacted, That all reserves made of any land in this state for which no patent ever issued, (except only the reserve to the westward of Fort Cumberland and the reserves of the city of Annapolis and Baltimore-town,) shall be taken off, and any land within the said reserves may be taken up as other vacant land, at the price of seven shillings and six-pence current money per acre, or at such other price as such vacant land hereafter may be directed by the legislature to be taken up at.*

*VII. And, whereas there are sundry citizens of this state who hold lands in virtue of patents granted by the late proprietaries of Pennsylvania, antecedent to the running and settling of the divisional line between the two states: And whereas it was mutually agreed by the two proprietaries, that all inhabitants on either side of the boundary line who obtained patents for their lands in Pennsylvania or Maryland*

---

[1643] William Brown's 1790 memo book mentions *"Simpkins Tavern"*. It also mentions and *"Tumblesons Tavern"* (Tomlinson's), and *"Gwyns Tavern at the fork, Bradfords old Road"* (Braddock's name was frequently misspelled in the early records).

*should have their titles confirmed in which ever they happened to fall; therefore, Be it enacted, That any person or persons holding lands within the limits of this state, granted and patented by the proprietaries of Pennsylvania antecedent to the settlement of the said divisional line, and which were, before the running and settling the divisional line aforesaid, considered as lying within the limits of Pennsylvania, and subject to the jurisdiction thereof, shall be at liberty to take out and receive patents from the land-office of this state; and the register of the land-office of the western shore is hereby empowered and directed, on application of any of the above described landholders, and upon their producing their Pennsylvania patents or authenticated copies, which shall be lodged in the land-office, to grant a patent or patents for the lands expressed in such original grant or grants, and the person or persons thus receiving patents in exchange shall not be liable to pay any purchase or caution money, or be liable to any charge or demand whatsoever,except the common fees of office.*

### Thomas Beall purchases a large Virginia property

The 1939 book "**Early Records Hampshire County Virginia**" records the following for May 11, 1785, *"PEERPOINT, Francis of Hampshire Co. to Thomas Beall of Washington Co. 891 a. on North Branch; rec. 11-9-1785. Wit.: Asa Mounts, Joseph Andersen, Joseph Mounts."*

### Thomas Cresap is blind by 1785

Andrew Ellicott's journal entry[1644] for May 17, 1785 states:

*Left this town after breakfast and rode to Old-Town. At this place disposed of my brother's and servants' horses, and procured others better adapted to the woods. This Evening I spent with the Celebrated Col. Cressap. He is now more than 100 Years Old he lost his eyesight about 18 months ago; but his other faculties are yet unimpaired, his sense Strong and manly and his ideas flow with ease."*

### A considerable number of people are settling at Cumberland

Andrew Ellicott's journal entry for May 18, 1785 states, *"... Rode to Mr. Gwyns. A considerable number of people are settling at Cumberland they expect in a Short Time to rival Hagers-Town in the Back Trade they will fail for want of an Extensive fertile Country Adjoining the place ... at this Stage we found a considerable number of Mountaineers disputing about Religion — they were inclining to Methodistism — O My God! what mischiefs Arise in this Sublunary World among us small and inconsiderable beings about the forms which will best please thee and enable us to reach that bliss promised us both by Reason and Revelation —"*

### Ellicott returns to Mr. Mountains

Andrew Ellicott's journal entry for May 19, 1785 states, *"Rode to M*^r^*. Mountains — From Gwynnes to this place a distance of about 26 Miles the Trees are yet divested of their Various foliage and traces of Winter are yet Visible the Gardens refuse to the Industrious Husbandman the Sweets of a Vegetable Diet —"*

### Andrew Porter describes Oldtown in the spring of 1785

Andrew Porter's journal entry for May 22, 1785 includes the statement, *"Arrived at Old Town. The fore axle tree of our carriage broke coming into the Town. This place consists of about a Dozen houses built*

---

[1644] Most of the 1785 journal entries of Andrew Ellicott are from the book "**Andrew Ellicott: his life and letters**", 1908. This journal entry is from "**The History of the Cresaps**", 1937.

about ¼ *of a mile to the North of the Potomack.*" His May 23 entry states, "*Got our carriage repaired*" and his May 24th entry states, "*Rained Hard last night and the fore part of the day and raised the waters that empty into the Potomack so as to make them impassable.*"

## Virginia proposes a new westerly road from Fort Cumberland

Minutes from the May 24, 1785 meeting of the Supreme Executive Council of Pennsylvania include the following incomplete note:

*A letter from Patrick Henry, Esquire, Governor of the State of Virginia, inclosing a resolution of the Legislature of that Commonwealth, requesting a permission from this State to lay out and improve a road in the best and most proper direction from Fort Cumberland to the navigable part of* [1645]

This seems to be a result of the December 22, 1784 report of the Commissioners of Virginia and Maryland that is quoted above.

## Andrew Porter refers to the town of Fort Cumberland in the spring of 1785

Andrew Porter's journal entry[1646] for May 25, 1785 states:

*Set out on our journey — found some difficulty in crossing the narrows — in this place the mountain approaches so close to the Potomack as to leave a narrow defile for the road which is overflowed in time of freshlet. This defile is about 60 perches in length. Wills Creek was rapid and deep — nothing but a small canoe to put us over — took our carriage to pieces, floated the body over after the canoe. Arrived at Fort Cumberland. This Town is built in the forks of Wills Creek and the Potomack. dist 15 M.*

This shows that Fort Cumberland was considered to be a town before its formal establishment by state law. Andrew Porter's journal entry[1647] for May 26, 1785 states:

*This morning broke the hind axle tree of our Carriage at Mr. Guynes about 5 miles dist. From Fort Cumberland — fell to work and put a new one in; but not without some difficulty for want of proper tools.*

Andrew Porter's journal entry[1648] for May 27, 1785 states:

*This day found the roads bad beyond description — Swamply, rocky & mountainous. Arrived at Mr. Tomblesons. Dist. 20 miles.*

Andrew Porter's journal entry[1649] for May 28, 1785 states:

*The roads much the same as yesterday, lodged at Mrs. Rices. Dist 20 miles.*

Andrew Porter's journal entry[1650] for May 29, 1785 states:

*Crossed the large branch of the Youghogana — the road continued much the same. Few inhabitants on the road — bad entertainment. Our carriage broke down near to Genl. Washington's Meadows where he*

---

[1645] The paragraph ends abruptly; a printing mistake.
[1646] "**The Pennsylvania Magazine of History and Biography**", 1880.
[1647] "**Report of the Secretary of Internal Affairs of the Commonwealth of Pennsylvania**", 1887.
[1648] "**Report of the Secretary of Internal Affairs of the Commonwealth of Pennsylvania**", 1887.
[1649] "**Report of the Secretary of Internal Affairs of the Commonwealth of Pennsylvania**", 1887.
[1650] "**Report of the Secretary of Internal Affairs of the Commonwealth of Pennsylvania**", 1887.

*capitulated to the French and Indians. Got a sledge and carried our baggage and wagon about a mile forward to one Sheppard's. dist. 18 miles.*

*Here we met with Mr Ellicot & Col. Neville, the Virginia Commissioners.*

### The June 10, 1785 survey of Henry West mentions Fort Cumberland

The W.P.A. warrant survey map shows the 310½-acre property of *"Henry West"*. This is actually the property of Henry Wert.[1651] His 1785 survey (Book D-6 Page 254) shows the Turkey Foot Road, and states:

*Situated on the head Waters of Piney Run Flaugherty's Creek adjoining the Turkeyfoot Road leading from Fort Cumberland to Pittsburgh about three quarters of a Mile from the Provencial Line in Brothers Valley Township Bedford County and Surveyed the 10th day of June 1785, in Pursuance of a Warrant dated the 30th day of May 1785*

This survey confirms that the Turkey Foot Road was thought of as connecting Fort Cumberland and Pittsburgh in 1785.

### Pine Tavern, in nearby Pennsylvania, in 1785

The September 2, 1785 survey of James Agin states, *"Situated on the Waters of Flaugherty's Creek on both sides of the Turkey foot Road about two miles North West of the Pine Tavern in Brothers Valley Township Bedford County..."* The 1785 survey of Anthony Haines also references Pine Tavern, stating, *"Situated on the head Waters of Piney Run on both sides of the Turkeyfoot Road about one Mile East of the Pine Tavern in Brothers Valley Township Bedford County..."* The 1785 survey of Henry Haines was just east of that of Anthony Haines, at the state line. It states, *"Situated on the heads of Piney Run on both sides of the Turkey foot Road and Including said Road where it crosses the Provincial Line going to Fort Cumberland..."* The Henry Haines tract was just north of Finzel, Maryland.

These surveys show that there was enough travel out of Fort Cumberland on the Turkey Foot Road in the 1780s to support a tavern in a nearby part of Pennsylvania that is still very rural.

### A 1785 reference to Nemacolin

General Richard Butler's journal describes leaving the site of Marietta, Ohio on October 9, 1785 as follows:

*Sailed at six o'clock, the weather very fine, wind in favor. The climate here is mild and pleasant. I am of opinion this will be found the proper month for seeding the fall grain. Passed Nimach Collins' island and two other small islands, then the mouth of Little Hockhocking, at half-past eight o'clock, A.M."*

Marietta once had a tradition of *"Neal McCollins ghost"*. Volume 8 of **"The National Magazine"** (1888) has a letter from Isaac Craig that states:

*I desire to relieve 'the good denizens of Marietta' from any fright friend Butterfield may have caused them by the Neal McCollins ghost story which he has conjured up. I assure 'the good denizens of Marietta' that they have no cause for alarm — that this Neal McCollins was not a white man, but a*

---

[1651] On the 1876 Beers map, a P. D. Miller residence is shown on the Henry Wert property, on the east side of the Greenville road. This farm is the home of my ancestor Peter D. Miller, who was born on March 10, 1808, died May 28, 1892, and is buried in the Greenville Union Cemetery.

*Delaware Indian, whose name was commonly written Nemacolin; but like most Indian names, not always written the same way.*

The island where Nemacolin lived is believed by some to be Blennerhassett Island, at Parkersburg,[1652] West Virginia.[1653]

## Cumberland was originally called Washington Town

On November 12, 1785 John Tomlinson received a deed for lots 6, 107, and 161 in Washington Town totaling four acres, and located east of Wills Creek.[1654] The deed was recorded on March 30, 1786 and required annual ground rent that was payable the first of January. The amount of the ground rent was one Spanish milled dollar.

## Thomas Beall, of Samuel reportedly built a house at Fort Cumberland circa 1785

Although not documentary evidence, Lowdermilk's book "**History of Cumberland**" reports:

*Thomas Beal, of Samuel, built a house on Liberty street, a short distance below the City Hall, on the opposite side. The date of its erection is uncertain, but it is supposed to have been about 1785. It is still standing.*

Perhaps drawing in part from Lowdermilk, the 1923 book "**History of Allegany County, Maryland**" indicates that Thomas Beall's house on Liberty Street was built before 1787, stating:

*The only other houses known to have been built before Cumberland was erected into a town, were ... a log house[1655] built by Thomas Beall, of Samuel, the proprietor of the town, on Liberty Street, and on the site of the present United States Court House and Post Office.*

According to the 1910 Sanborn Fire Insurance Map of Cumberland, the United States court house and post office building was located at Latitude 39.652483°, Longitude -78.762821°, at the southwestern corner of Liberty Street and Frederick Street. Based on the building outline on the 1910 map, and the description of a stone first story, the same building is still located there. Lowdermilk reports that Thomas Beall was still living on Liberty Street in 1813.

---

[1652] Volume 7782 of the "**Congressional Edition**" (1921) states *"...a marker has been placed to commemorate the spot where the first settlement was made in West Virginia, where the city of Parkersburg now stands. James Neal, the first settler, built a blockhouse which afforded a shelter from the Indians. This was called 'Neal's Station.'"*

[1653] "**Blennerhassett Island**", Swick, et. Al, 2005.

[1654] Washington County Book D, page 707.

[1655] According to Thaddeus Mason Harris' 1805 book "**Journal of a Tour...**", the distinguishing feature between log cabins and log houses was whether the logs were hewn. He states, *"The temporary buildings of the first settlers in the wilds are called Cabins. They are built with unhewn logs, the interstices between which are stopped with rails, calked with moss or straw, and daubed with mud. The roof is covered with a sort of thin staves split out of oak or ash, about four feet long and five inches wide, fastened on by heavy poles being laid upon them. 'If the logs be hewed; if the interstices be stopped with stone, and neatly plastered; and the roof composed of shingles nicely laid on, it is called a log-house.' A loghouse has glass windows and a chimney; a cabin has commonly no window at all, and only a hole at the top for the smoke to escape. After saw mills are erected, and boards can be procured, the settlers provide themselves with more decent houses, with neat floors and ceiling."*

# 38. 1786: An act for 'erecting' the town

**Daniel Cresap is appointed as a Justice of Washington County, Maryland**

The minutes[1656] from a March 9, 1786 meeting of the Council of Maryland include the following:

*John Stull, Joseph Chapline, John Barnes, Richard Davis, Andrew Bruce, John Celler, Charles Prather, Thomas Sprigg, Alexander Clagett, Moses Rawlings, Thomas Henry Hall, John Reid and Daniel Cresap appointed Justices of Washington County.*

**An act for erecting Fort Cumberland into a town passed the legislature in 1786**

Volume 1 of the 1856 "**Index to the journals of the Senate and House of Delegates of the State of Maryland**" provides the following summary of an action taken by the Maryland House of Delegates:

*WASHINGTON COUNTY — Petition from sundry inhabitants of the western part of, and memorial from Samuel Beale, of said county, for act to divide, read 35; committee appointed to report on 36; report 37; read, not concurred with 39. ....*

*Memorial from Thomas Beale, of Samuel, of, praying an act may pass for erecting courts of justice in the western part of said county, also for erecting Fort Cumberland into a town, referred 42; report on, read 46; concurred, and leave to bring in a bill for the better administration of justice in, committee appointed to report 47; reported, read 49; referred to next general assembly 76.*

*On motion, leave given to bring in a bill for the erection of a town near the mouth of Will's creek in 47; bill reported, read, passed 49; sent to senate 50, returned passed 61.*

The words *"for erecting Fort Cumberland into a town"* indicates that an existing community that was commonly called Fort Cumberland was being formally instituted as a town. It seems implausible that the words could possibly mean that the fort structure that was reported as being *"deserted and demolished"* in 1775 and was reported as an earthen fort in 1787 (below), was being turned into a town!

*Names of the petitioners*

According to the "**History of Allegany County, Maryland...**" the persons who signed a petition addressed to the legislature in support of erecting the town were:

*Thomas Beall, George Dent, Andrew Bruce, David Lynn, Even Gwyne, George Lowdermilk, Michael Kershner, George Calmes, Benjamin Wiley, Peter D'Evecmon, Dickeson Simkins, William Hoye, Charles F. Broadhag, John Graham, Charles Clinton, George Hoffman, David Watkins, James McCoy, Jacob Lowry, Jonothan Cox, Thomas Stewart, David Hoffman, John S. Hook, George Payne, Robert Clark, John Lynn, Jeremiah Wilson, John C. Beatty, George Simmons, James Slicer, David Harvey, Eli Williams, John Mustard, George Blocher and Henry Wineow.*

---

[1656] "**Journal of the State Council, 1784-1789**".

### *The text of the act erecting Fort Cumberland into a town*

Lowdermilk's book "**History of Cumberland**" provides the text of the act, but erroneously states that the legislature passed it on January 20, 1787. That date may, instead, be the day it was signed into law by the Governor,[1657] but this hasn't been confirmed. Here, from Lowdermilk, is the text of the act:

*An Act for erecting a town at or near the mouth of Will's Creek, in Washington County.*

*Whereas, It is represented to this general assembly by Thomas Beall, Son of Samuel, that he is possessed of a tract of land called Walnut Bottom, contiguous to the mouth of Will's creek, in Washington county, whereon, at the instance of many of the inhabitants of said county, he hath been induced to lay out ground for a town: and the said Thomas Beall hath prayed a law to appoint commissioners to lay out and erect a town on the said land and to secure the purchasers of lots therein, reserving the right of the proprietors and their interest in the said land; and this general assembly are of opinion that the erecting of a town at the mouth of the said creek may be convenient and beneficial to the public.*

*II. Be it enacted by the General Assembly of Maryland, That Andrew Bruce, Daniel Cresap, George Dent, John Lynn and Evan Gwynn, or any three or more of them, be and are hereby appointed commissioners to survey a quantity of land not exceeding two hundred acres, being part of the said tract of land called Walnut Bottom, contiguous to the mouth of Will's creek, in Washington county, and the same, when surveyed, to lay out into lots, streets, lanes and alleys, (the main streets running in the direction of Patowmack river, not to be less than eighty feet wide: and the streets crossing the said main streets not to be less than sixty feet wide,) to be erected into a town, and to be called and known by the name of Cumberland; and a correct and accurate certificate and plot thereof returned to the clerk of Washington county court, who is hereby required to record the same among the Land Records of the said county, and to keep the original plot in his office, and a copy from the original or the record thereof shall be conclusive evidence as to the bounds and lines of the lots of the said town, and of the streets, lanes and alleys thereof.*

*III. And be it enacted, That the said commissioners, or a major part of them, shall cause the said lots in the said town to be substantially and fairly bounded and numbered, and they and their successors are hereby required, from time to time, to take care that the said boundaries be constantly kept up and preserved.*

*IV. And be it enacted, That on the death, removal or resignation, of any of the said commissioners, the major part of the remaining commissioners shall appoint another to serve in the stead of such commissioner so dying, removing or resigning.*

*V. And be it enacted, That the said commissioners of the said town, or a major part of them, shall have full power to employ a clerk, who shall be under oath, fairly and honestly to enter into a book to be kept for that purpose, all the proceedings of the said commissioners relating to the said town, in which book, among other things, shall be entered a copy of the plot and certificate of the said town, describing every lot by its number, and who the taker up, or purchaser was or shall be; and the said book shall always be open to the inspection and examination of the said commissioners.*

*VI. And be it enacted, That the said commissioners, or a major part of them, are empowered to levy, assess and take, by way of distress, if needful, from the inhabitants of the town, by even and equal proportion, a sum not exceeding ten pounds current money yearly, to be paid to their clerk: and they shall have power to remove or displace their clerk as often as they shall think fit.*

---

[1657] This possible explanation of the date discrepancy was provided to the author by Dan Press.

*VII. And be it enacted, That every purchaser of any of the lots of the said town in fee, and every lessee thereof, for years, or rent reserved, shall hold and possess the same against any person hereafter claiming title to the same, and shall not be disturbed in their possession; and if any person shall hereafter make claim to the land, or any part thereof laid off in virtue of this act, and shall, by due course of law, make good title thereto, such person shall be entitled to recover from the said Thomas Beall, his heirs, devisee, executors or administrators any purchase money or rents by him received from any of the purchasers or lessees of any of the said lots, and, upon any such recovery the tenants holding under the said Thomas Beall shall thereafter hold under pay the rent reserved to the person making title to and recovering the same land.*

*VIII- And be it enacted, That if any of the buildings already built on the land so as aforesaid to be laid out by the said commissioners, and erected into a town, should happen to interfere with, or stand on any of the streets laid off in virtue of this act the same shall be permitted to continue, but shall not at any time hereafter be repaired or rebuilt.*

## Washington advises Mr. Lear to take the new road

In a November 30, 1786 letter to Mr. Tobias Lear, George Washington wrote *"You will proceed to Pittsburgh by the following route. Leesburgh, Keyes' ferry, Bath, Old Town and Fort Cumberland. From the latter pursue the New road by the Turkey foot to Colo. Jno. Stephensons, whh. is in the Road to Pittsburgh"*. According to the 1912 book "**Frontier defense on the upper Ohio, 1777-1778**", John Stephenson lived in Fayette County on Jacob's Creek circa 1768 to 1790. Stephenson's survey (Book C-207, Page 25) indicates that he settled there in 1769.

# 39. After the founding of the town

## Introduction

Although the focus of this book is a compilation of records before the founding of the town of Fort Cumberland, the items in this chapter hopefully add to the understanding of the Cumberland region. This chapter is not intended to be a comprehensive study of the environs of Cumberland in the post-1786 timeframe. Instead, it merely presents a few things I happen to be aware of from previous research. For a more comprehensive account, see Lowdermilk's 1878 book "**History of Cumberland**".

## A postal route is established

The 1898 book "**Standard History of Pittsburg, Pennsylvania**" states:

*In March, 1787, a post route was established from Alexandria, Virginia, to Pittsburg, via Newgate, Leesburg, Winchester, Fort Cumberland, and Bedford, to be weekly from May 1ˢᵗ to November 1ˢᵗ, and fortnightly the rest of the year.*

Although not documentary evidence, the 1884 book "**History of Bedford, Somerset, and Fulton Counties, Pennsylvania…**" states the following in a section about the Cumberland Valley:

*Thomas Coulter was one of the pioneers, and came to the valley before the revolution. For a time he acted as mail-carrier, carrying the mail on his back between Fort Bedford and Fort Cumberland. He was one of the early justices of the peace of Bedford county.*

## The resolves of 1787

The following resolutions are recorded in the *"Resolutions assented to April Session, 1787"* section of the book "**Laws of Maryland 1785-1791**", Volume 204:

*RESOLVED, That the governor and council be requested to appoint and employ some skilful person to lay out the manors, and such parts of the reserves and vacant lands, belonging to this state, lying to the westward of Fort Cumberland, as he may think fit and capable of being settled and improved, in lots of fifty acres each, bounded by a fixed beginning and four lines only, unless on the sides adjoining elder surveys; that the beginning of each lot be marked with marking irons, or otherwise, with the number thereof, and that a fair book of such surveys, describing the beginning of each lot by its situation, as well as number, be returned and laid before the next general assembly; that a brief note of the improvements which may happen to be on any lot, and the name of the person, if any settled thereon, be inserted at the foot of the certificate of survey thereof, and that the reasonable expence of such surveys be paid by this state.*

*RESOLVED, That the governor and council be requested to cause the auditor-general, or other proper officer, to make out an accurate and fair list of the officers and soldiers who are entitled to counties of land under the promises of this state, and to lay the same before the next general assembly.*

According to "**The Land-holder's Assistant**" (1808):

*The resolves of April session 1787 direct the executive to appoint a person to lay down into lots the manors, and such parts of the reserves, and vacant lands, lying to the westward of Fort Cumberland, as he may think capable of improvement: — Under this act Francis Deakins was appointed; and he accordingly laid down the lots, and returned a plat, which is deposited in the land office.*

Another part of the same book states:

*... the session of April 1787, when a resolution was passed authorising the governor and council to appoint and employ some skilful person to lay out the manors, and such parts of the reserves and vacant lands, belonging to the state, lying to the westward of Fort Cumberland, as he might think fit, and capable of being improved, in lots of fifty acres each. In virtue of this resolution Mr. Francis Deakins was appointed for the purpose therein mentioned, who, before the fall session of 1788, had finished the survey, and had returned a general plot of the country westward of Fort Cumberland, on which four thousand one hundred and sixty-five lots of fifty acres each were laid off, besides sundry tracts which had been patented, with a distinction, on the plot, of the kinds which had been settled and improved, from those that remained uncultivated; and had also returned in two books, certificates of all the lots beforementioned.*

## Over 300 families are living west of Fort Cumberland

According to Lowdermilk's "**History of Cumberland**", Deakins documented that 323 families were living west of Fort Cumberland at the time of the survey. This large number of families, which doesn't count families east of Fort Cumberland, and doesn't count families in nearby Pennsylvania and Virginia, helps to illustrate the sheer magnitude of the agricultural settlement in the environs of Fort Cumberland around the time of the founding of the town of Cumberland. The names of the settlers on Deakins' list, taken from Scharf's 1882 book "**History of Western Maryland**", are:

William Ashby, Anthony Able, George Anderson, Patrick Burges, Charles Boyles, Thomas Baker, Philip Bray, Mallner Burnstredder, John Beall, John Blair, John Brendage, Peter Bonham, Norman Bruce,[1658] Daniel Cresap, Sr., Daniel Cresap, John Durbin, Aaron Duckworth, Nicholas Durbin, William Durbane, John Doomer, Joseph Davis, Steven Davis, Levi Davis, Samuel Dawson, Sr., Samuel Elliott, Adam Eckhart, John Ervin, Herman Frazee, Joseph Frost, George Fegenbaker, Briant Gaines, Edward Grimes, Paul Grim, John Groat, Benjamin Green, Sam. Humphreys, Edward Huston, James Henderson, John House, Ralph Adams, John Arnold of A.,[1659] John Arnold of John,[1660] Andrew Bruce, William Barnes, Michael Beeme, Benjamin Brady, John Buhman, Ben. John Biggs, Frederic Bray, Thomas Barkus, George Barkus, Samuel Barrell, William Coddington, Peter Crawl, Thomas Cordray, Henry Crosley, John Cruise, Samuel Dawson, Jr., William Dawson, Sr., William Dawson, Jr., Edward Dawson, Sr., Edward Dawson, Jr., Thomas Dawson, Joseph Dye, Barney Dewitt, Terence Dyal, John Elbin Samuel Ellison, John Eckhart, John Firman, John Friend, Gabriel Friend, Richard Green, Daniel Green, Thomas Greenwade, Salathiel Goff, John T. Goff, Andrew House, Elisha Hall, John Harshan, Moses Hall, Anthony Arnold, Moses Ayres, Sr., Moses Ayres, Jr., Robert Boyd, Matthew Ball, Frederick Burgett, Josiah Bonham, Micijah Burnham, Amariah Bonham, John Brady, John Buckholder, Jacob Beall, Nathan Corey, Godfrey Corbus, Edmund Cutler, Ely

---

[1658] The Bear Camp tract above the village of Mount Savage was originally surveyed for Normand Bruce on April 3, 1767 and patented to him on November 1, 1768 (patented certificate 432).

[1659] The Land Office Military Lots Ledger indicates that John Arnold, of Anthony was located on lot 3364.

[1660] This is confusing, because the Land Office "**Lots Westward of Fort Cumberland**" list indicates that *"Jn Arnold son of Joseph"* was the settler who was found on lots 3373 and 3374 in 1787 during Deakins' survey. The same list shows that the lots were patented to John Mattingly on September 20, 1819. Amanda Paul's present-day farm is on lots 3373 and 3374. According to AL-V-B-066, John Mattingly received the property from Andrew Bruce (or his estate) on April 10, 1804 for $40.00. Thomas A. Stobie of Overland Park Kansas has written on his genealogy website that John Mattingly, born 1773, was the husband of Onea Honor (Arnold) Mattingly who died in 1823, and was the son of Henry Mattingly, born 1751. According to the 1787 Deakins' list, a Henry Mattingly owned lots 3366 and 3367, which were along the present-day Bald Knob Road.

Clark, Michael Corn,[1661] Benjamin Coddington, Samuel Durbin, James Denison, Peter Doogan, Samuel Durbin, Edward Davis, Jacob Duttro, Sr., Jacob Duttro, Jr., Peter Devecmon, David Eaton, George Eckhart, Charles Friend, Hezekiah Frazier, Joseph Friend, Harry Franks, George Fiddler, James O. Goff, Evan Gwynn, John Glasman, John Garey, John Glase, Nicholas Holsbury, Charles Huddy, Richard Hall, George Harness, George Haver, William Howell, Paul Hoye, Robert Johnston, Evan James, Conrad Joleman, John Keyser, Henry Kite, John Lowdermilk, William Logsdon, Daniel Levit, Jacob Lower, Rosemond Long, Joseph Lee, Stephen Masters, Gabriel McKinsy[1662], John Matthews, Sr., John Magomery, Christopher Myer, James McMullen, Nathaniel Magruder, Josiah Magruder, Samuel McKinsy, Peter Nimirck, George Paine, Henry Porter, Moses Porter, George Preston, Henry Peters, John Purguson, Peter Puling, Stephen Pierson, Godfrey Richards, William Rideford, John Richards, John Rubast, Daniel Recknor, John Simpkins,[1663] Jacob Storm, George Sapp, John Steyer, Garrett Snedeger, John Strickler, Matthew Singleman, John Stuck, John Trotter, David Troxell, Peter Tittle, Sr., Ezekiel Totter, James Utter, Sr., James Utter, Jr., John Vanbuskirk, Moses Williams, Adam Hicksenbaugh, Benjamin Hull, Richard Harcourt, William Jones, John Jones, William Jacobs, Jacob Koonts, Henry Kemp, George Laporte, William Logsden, Ralph Logsden, Elisha Logsden, John Lynn, Zachariah Linton, Henry Mattingly, Henry Myers, Philip Michael, Moses Munro, Josiah McKinsy, John Mets, James McPipe, Thomas Matthew, John Neff, Johannes Paugh, Robert Parker, Gabriel Powell, Martin Poling, Sr., John Price, John Ryan, John Rhoads, John Ratton, David Robertson, Adam Rhoads, Peter Stuck, William Show, Joseph Scott, Simon Speed, Matthew Snooke, John Seyler, William Stagg, James Schimer, Peter Tittle, Jr., Michael Tedrick, Jesse Tomlinson, John Trimble, William Utter, Thomas Umbertson, David Vansickle, William Wells, Samuel Hatton, Abraham Hite, Jacob Hazlewood, Samuel Jackson, William Jones, Jacob Kerger, John Kelly, Leonard Stimble, David Lee, John Liptz , Breton Levit, Jacob Lee, James Montain, William Moore, John Matthews, Jr., Jacob Miller, Alexander Moore, Daniel Moore, Moses McKinsy, Daniel McKinsy, Conrad Millen, Elias Majors, John Nepton, Samuel Postlewait, Michael Paugh, Margaret Poling, John Porter, Samuel Poling, Martin Poling, Richard Poling, Charles Queen, Benjamin Rush, Enoch Read, Roger Robertson, Aaron Rice, Michael Raway, John Ragan, John Streets, Moses Spleer, Abel Serjeant, Adam Seigler, Jacob Seigler, Jacob Scutchfield, John Siblely, Frederick Thoxter, John Tomlinson, Jacob Trullinger, Moses Tilsonel, Richard Tilton, Charles Uhl, John Vincent, Henry Woodger, John Workman, Archibald White, Arthur Watson, Jesse Walter, John Wikoff, Alexander Wilhelm, George Wilhelm, Peter Wikoff, Jacob Wikoff, James Woodringer, Alpheus Wigwire, George Waddle, Isaac Workman, Joseph Warnick, William Workman, James Wells, Peter Wells, Samuel Wikoff, George Winters, Andrew Workman, Jacob Workman, Stephan Workman, Thomas Williams, and John Whiteman.

---

[1661] Michael Korn, Sr. is my fifth great grandfather. He eventually moved slightly north of the Mason-Dixon line. The items sold at his December 8, 1824 estate sale show that he was engaged in commercial activity that allowed him to generate locally significant wealth and show that he had access to various commercially manufactured goods. His estate sale is documented in the 1949 book "**The Genealogy of Michael Korns, Sr. of Somerset County Pennsylvania**".

[1662] Gabriel McKinsy (McKenzie) was located in Arnold's settlement. According to Deakins' list, Gabriel McKinsy (Mckenzie) had lot number 3365 at the time of the 1787 Deakins survey. On the Maryland inventory of historic properties, the AL-V-A-222 property is identified as a Logsdon property that was partially on lot 3365. I do not know when ownership transferred to a Logsdon. The earliest Logsdon reference I have seen regarding lot 3365 is the year 1896. Peter Mayors owned lot 2265 after Gabriel McKinsy. Gabriel McKinsey sold lot number 3365 to Peter Majors in 1792. Majors patented it in 1803 (Patented Certificate 1478).

[1663] John Simpkins had a tavern at Bear Camp, as confirmed by a 1796 obituary that reads, *"Alligany County, Marriland July the 14th 1796 died John P. Allen at the house of John Simkins at atherwayes bear camplain brod dags old road half way between fort Cumberland & Union town."* The location of Simpson's Inn is identified on the 1794 Dennis Griffith map as *"Simkin's"*, and is illustrated as being along Braddock's road southeast of Mear's tavern, at the intersection with the Morgantown Road. The Morgantown Road is identified as starting at Simpson's Tavern in the article *"Our history begins on the Youghiogheny"* in a 1956 issue of "**Woodland Trails**".

### The death of Colonel Thomas Cresap

Colonel Thomas Cresap, Sr. died sometime in 1787, and on May 9, 1788 the administrator of his estate was Daniel Cresap.[1664]

### The convening of the Constitutional Convention

On May 25, 1787 the first meeting of the Constitutional Convention was held at Philadelphia, with George Washington presiding.

### Only the remains of the earthen ramparts of the Fort survived in 1787

Thomas Barton's 1758 description of large earth-filled reinforcements helps to explain Samuel Vaughan's July 13, 1787 description of an earthen fort at Cumberland:

> *...when came to Fort Cumberland where are 13 or 14 good framed houses & thought will rapidly increase as being at the head of the North branch of the Patomack 100 or 120 yards over*

> *The remains of the Earth fort is upon the hill commanding the turn of the River & the Creek which is formed thus here ends the Allagany Mountain.*

Vaughan visited Cumberland 29 years after Barton, and apparently all that was left of the fort was the remains of the 20-foot-thick reinforcement Barton described. Vaughan's statement does not provide information regarding whether any buildings from the old fort had survived.

Vaughan's statement *"where are 13 or 14 good framed houses"* shouldn't be interpreted as meaning that there was only a total of 13 or 14 houses in the town. Instead, Vaughan is simply identifying the number of houses that have a more refined type of construction, compared to log houses. The frame houses prove the existence of a sawmill somewhere within the environs of Fort Cumberland.

Vaughn's entire journal entry for July 13, 1787, which mentions 500 families living in the area, reads:

> *July 13*

> *To Tickles farm & tavern, after a descent of a mile & a half good land but stony, came to a Creek a small rising. longer descent when came to waving good land at 5-1/2 miles near a spring is the half way house & here begins Savage Mountain, a small gradual rising & descent then a spring from whence a rising for a mile all good land 1/4 of a mile hilly & very stony, then a gradual descent when came into a fine bottom where is a small farm, here ends savage mountain the residue in hard stones in white freestone sand & then in Brick mould, in a Bottom where is Tickles & another farm, the farmer raises Tobacco & Indian corn has 25 head Cattle & wheat weighs 67 lb the bushel on each side of Tickles are many farms & 500 families.*

> *The Methodists preach every day in different places, Men Women & Children going 7 or 8 miles on week days, neglecting their Families & farms & which is the only religeous sect in the back country through which I passed.*

> *To Gwins farm & tavern, crossed a spring or Creek then 3-miles waving land, some part stony, some a red soil like New Jersey, generally descend then 2-1/2 miles stony still descending some part clear of stone, crossed Braddocks Run, a River 60 yards over when came to Gwins in a bottom Off Braddocks*

---

[1664] **"Colonial Records of the Upper Potomac"**, Volume 6.

*Run is a rocky hill 60 or 70 feet high, a kind of Slate the highest rock hitherto seen here were to be seen several large tracts of land, on which the trees had been burned, by accidental fires as before related.*

*To Fort Cumberland. one mile level 1/2 mile Stony having passed Braddocks run twice, ascended a steep hill, stony, then a white gritt or sand then a red soil, here picked up Iron ore, one mile good land, when came to Fort Cumberland where are 13 or 14 good framed houses & thought will rapidly encrease as being at the head of the North branch of the Patomack 100 or 120 yards over*

*The remains of the Earth fort is upon the hill commanding the turn of the River & the Creek which is formed thus here ends the Allagany Mountain*

## The new Constitution of the United States goes into effect

On September 13, 1788, the Continental Congress passed a resolution putting the new Constitution into operation. By that time, 11 of the 13 states had ratified the document.

## A petition to form a new county and open courts at Fort Cumberland fails in 1788

In Volume 1 of the 1856 "**Index to the journals of the Senate and House of Delegates of the State of Maryland**", a summary of a November 1788 action of the Maryland House of Delegates states:

*WASHINGTON COUNTY — Petition from inhabitants of, referred from last session, referred 14, 19; bill reported for the division of, read 77; on second reading the question was put that the blank be filled with the name of "Smallwood,"[1665] resolved in the affirmative; on progression in reading, the question was put that the county and orphans' courts be held at Fort Cumberland, resolved in the affirmative; the bill being read throughout, the question was put that said bill do pass, determined in the negative 96, 97.*

## An act allowing settlers to purchase land west of Fort Cumberland passed in 1788

As documented beginning near the bottom of page 350 of Volume 204 of the "**Laws of Maryland 1785-1791**", an act was passed on December 23, 1788 that allowed settlers already living on the land to purchase it. The act, Chapter XLIV, is titled *"An act to dispose of the reserved lands westward of Fort Cumberland, in Washington county, and to fulfill the engagements made by this state to the officers and soldiers of the Maryland line in the service of the United States."* Chapter XLIV was passed on December 23, 1788; see pages 350 to 354, "**Laws of Maryland 1785-1791**", Volume 204.

The following summary is provided in "**The Land-holder's Assistant**" (1808):

*The legislature, being now possessed of the necessary information, passed an act (November 1788 ch. 44) to "dispose of the reserved lands westward of Fort Cumberland, in Washington county, and to fulfil the engagements made by this state to the officers and soldiers of the Maryland line in the service of the United States," in which, after reciting the acts by which bounties of land had been promised for military service, the appropriation of 1781, the appointment of Mr. Deakins, and all the facts above stated; and adding that it appeared there were three hundred and twenty three families settled on six hundred and thirty six of the aforesaid lots, which those people had improved and cultivated, they ordained as follows, viz. that whereas, according to the most accurate account that could then be rendered by the auditor general, it appeared that there had been about the number of two thousand four hundred and seventy-five soldiers entitled under the several acts of the legislature to the bounty of lands, and that there ought to be about one hundred lots set apart to fulfil the engagements of lands to recruiting officers,—the*

---

[1665] Major General William Smallwood was elected as the Governor of Maryland on November 17, 1785, and his replacement, Colonel John Eager Howard, was elected on November 21, 1788.

*quantity of two thousand five hundred and seventy-five of the aforesaid lots, (lying in the most fertile part of the county, and contained in the following limits, to wit, beginning at the mouth of Savage river, and running with the north branch of Patowmack river to the head thereof, then north with the ("present") supposed boundary line of Maryland until the intersection of an east line, to be drawn from the said boundary line with a north course from the mouth of Savage river, would include the number of lots aforesaid,) should be distributed by lot among the said soldiers and recruiting officers, and their legal representatives, by a commissioner or commissioners, not exceeding three, to be appointed by the governor and council for that and other purposes presently to be noticed.*

*This provision went to the fulfillment of all the engagements acknowledged and recited by the act: but the legislature thought proper to go further, and proceeded to direct that, part of the remaining lots should be distributed, by lottery, among the officers, and the representatives of the officers of the Maryland line who served to the end of the war, who were deranged by any of the reforms of the army, who were killed, or died of their wounds received in battle, those who were disabled from further service by wounds received, and in consequence thereof retired, and those who died a natural death while in the service with the army; each officer, or his representative, to have four lots: that the lots so granted should be adjacent to those directed to be distributed among the soldiers, and should be contained within the following limits, viz. by extending the aforesaid north course from the mouth of Savage river until its intersection with an east line to be drawn from the aforesaid supposed boundary of Maryland would include the requisite number, allowing to each officer four lots as aforesaid; and that the said lots should be distributed, by lot, among the said officers, and their representatives, by the aforesaid commissioners, each ticket to contain four lots, contiguous to each other, or as nearly so as might be.*

*The act directed further that the auditor-general should furnish the said commissioners with a list of the officers and soldiers entitled as aforesaid, and that no draught should be made for any officer or soldier whose name was not on that list; that after the draught (or lottery) the name of each officer and soldier should be endorsed on the ticket containing the number or numbers (written at length) which had been drawn by or for such officer or soldier, who (or his representative) should thereupon have an estate in fee simple in the lot or lots so drawn and endorsed, without any patent, deed, or grant, to be issued for that purpose.*

*In order to shew in one view all the provisions of this act relative to the military claims, (in virtue of which provisions it is proper here to observe that the distribution of lands, as directed, shortly after took place) I have postponed noticing those which regard the families reported by Mr. Deakins to be settled on a part of the lots laid off as aforesaid, as well as some important general directions which will presently be brought into view. By the first enacting clauses following the recital which has been mentioned, it was directed that a preference should be given to those settlers to purchase the six hundred and thirty six lots by them respectively settled, not exceeding the quantities registered and noted by the surveyor in the books aforesaid, and at not less than five nor more than twenty shillings per acre, to be discharged in three equal payments, on the first of September in the years 1789, 1790, and 1791: in default of any of which payments the land in respect to which such default occurred should be liable to proclamation, in the usual manner, by any citizen of the state of Maryland, and that for the ease and convenience of the people, a proper person or persons, not exceeding three, should be appointed by the governor and council, who should go into the neighborhood, and have power to decide all disputes which might arise concerning preemption, and should value the said lands, those of the best quality at not more than twenty shillings per acre, those of the worst at not less than five shillings, and those of an intermediate kind according to their quality, having regard to the extreme prices aforesaid:—by other sections it was provided that, on payment of the valuation by any person admitted by the commissioners to be entitled to a preemption, patent should issue to such settler, or his representatives, he or they paying the usual fees of office; that, after satisfying the claims aforesaid, as well of settlers as of officers and soldiers, the remainder of the said lots westward of Fort Cumberland should be sold for any kind of specie certificates of the state, and that the purchasers, after payment of the purchase money, should be entitled to patents from the register of the land office, on paying the usual fees; that the aforesaid general plot and books of certificates should be lodged in the land office, and that the said books of certificates of the four thousand one hundred and sixty five lots aforesaid should be considered to all intents and purposes as record books of the land office; and it was further directed that the commissioner or commissioners before mentioned should make a record of all valuations by them made, and of all the lots distributed among the officers and soldiers aforesaid, and of all lots sold by them in virtue of this act, and return the same to the register of the land office, to be by him safely kept. These, which as well as the plot and books of Mr. Deakins were returned agreeable to this direction, are also considered and used, in some sort as record books of the office. But they have not been so denominated by law.*

*It was further provided that the privilege of roads and waters through all the aforesaid lands should be reserved to the public, and the act contained two remarkable suspending clauses, by one of which were noticed certain lands "patented or taken up within the manors and the reserves aforesaid in respect to which the general assembly declined to give orders for any disposition thereof," but directed or recommended that the cases of each kind should be stated by the governor and council, and the attorney general's opinion taken, so that the claim of the state might be prosecuted or relinquished, as law and justice might require. The other had reference to the line by which Mr. Deakins had bounded his aforesaid general survey, which was declared to be, in the opinion of the general assembly, far within that line to which the state of Maryland might rightfully claim as its western boundary, with a further declaration that, at a time of more leisure, the consideration of the legislature ought to be drawn to the western boundaries of the state, as objects of very great importance.*

*The only further provisions of this act which require to be noticed are those by which all remaining reserves were taken off, and all the vacant land in the state made liable to be taken up in the usual manner by warrant, at the rate of three shillings and nine pence instead of the former price of seven shillings and six pence per acre, which as they must be spoken of in another place, I shall not here dwell upon, but shall proceed with what further concerns the settlers westward of Fort Cumberland.*

The *"many farms & 500 families"* statement that Vaughn made on July 13, 1787 shows that there were plenty of families living west of Fort Cumberland when this act was passed on December 23, 1788. Not all the settlers patented their numbered lots promptly; my ancestor Michael Corn didn't patent his lot 3356 until 1802.

### Washington's inauguration as President in 1789
George Washington took the oath of office as the first President of the United States on April 30, 1789.

### Sale of 1,000 lots west of Fort Cumberland is announced in 1789
Volume 2 of the 1883 book "**History of Western Maryland**" states:

*The following is from the Maryland Journal of Friday, July 3, 1789:*

*Notice is hereby given to the officers and soldiers of the Maryland Line, that a distribution of land will be made to them at Upper Marlborough, in Prince George's County, on the 1st and 2d of August next, agreeably to an act of Assembly, and at the same time and place will be offered at public sale about one thousand lots of land, of fifty acres each, for ready money, or specie certificates of the State of Maryland. This land lies to the westward of Fort Cumberland. For a particular description thereof, apply to Capt. Daniel Cresap or Mr. John Tomlinson, who lives near the same.*

*David Linn,*

*Daniel Cresap,*

*Benjamin Brookes,*

*Commissioners.*

## The deadline for payment is extended in 1789

Chapter XLVIII[1666] of the Laws of Maryland, passed on December 25, 1789 and titled *"An ACT respecting the settlers on the reserved lands westward of Fort Cumberland"*, states:

*WHEREAS it is represented, by sundry settlers westward of Fort Cumberland, that the time fixed for them to make their annual payments is at an inconvenient season of the year;*

*II. Be it therefore enacted, by the General Assembly of Maryland, That the time allotted for payment for the lands sold to settlers westward of Fort Cumberland, shall be extended to the first day of May in each year; and the said settlers shall be allowed until the first of May next to make their first payment; provided that nothing in this clause contained shall be construed to affect the rights of any other person or persons, acquired since the first day of September last, to any of the said lots: And provided also, that any person or persons who have already, or may hereafter, proclamate any of the said lots, shall pay such composition money thereon as the original settlers were to pay for the same.*

## Allegany County was formed in 1789

Allegany County was formed from Washington County on December 25, 1789. For the text of the act, see page 1344 of the book "**History of Western Maryland**", Volume 2.

## Reverend Morse mentions roads from Wills Creek to the Youghiogheny

The 1789 book "**Political opinions, particularly respecting the seat of federal empire…**" includes a quote by American geographer Reverend Morse that states:

*From Fort Cumberland, or Will's-Creek, one or two wagon roads may be had (where the distance is said by some to be thirty-five miles; and by others, to be forty, to the Yohogany, a large and navigable branch of the Monongahela…*

Morse was wrong in stating that the Youghiogheny was navigable from a place 35 to 40 miles from Fort Cumberland, but it is still interesting that he describes one or two wagon roads that went there. In 1782, Thomas Jefferson wrote[1667] about the waterfall on the Youghiogeny River that obstructed navigation:

*In its passage through the mountain it makes very great falls, admitting no navigation for ten miles to the Turkey foot. … From the falls, where it intersects the Laurel mountain, to Fort Cumberland, the head of the navigation on the Patowmac, is 40 miles of very mountainous road. Wills Creek, at the mouth of which was Fort Cumberland,[1668] is 30 or 40 yards wide, but affords no navigation as yet.*

---

[1666] "**Laws of Maryland 1785-1791**".

[1667] This is from Thomas Jefferson's 1787 book "**Notes on the State of Virginia**", which was written in 1781 and *"corrected and enlarged"* in 1782, in response to questions Jefferson received from *"a Foreigner of Distinction"*.

[1668] Here, in 1782, Jefferson mentions Fort Cumberland in the past tense.

The *"very great falls"* Jefferson mentioned are the Ohiopyle Falls on the Youghiogheny River, northwest of the present-day town of Confluence, Pennsylvania.

## Population of Allegany County in 1790
According to the 1852 book "**Gazetteer of the State of Maryland**", Allegany County had a population of 4,809 in 1790.

## Disposing of Michael Cresap's real estate
The 1939 book "**Early Records Hampshire County Virginia**" records the following for May 21, 1791, *"JACOB, John Jeremiah (w. Mary) (Executrix of Michael Cresap, dec'd) to Luther Martin of Frederick Co. Ozburn Sprigg of Hampshire Co. Lennox Martin of Frederick Co. All lands and tenements and real property of every kind in Hampshire Co. and Alleghany Co. Rec. 6-16-1791. Wit.: John Mitchell, James Prather, Daniel Cresap, Jr."*

## A circa 1791 description of the fledgling town
Page 19 of Meshach Browning's 1859 book "**Forty-four years of the life of a hunter**" provides an eyewitness impression of Cumberland circa 1791[1669], as follows:

> *On we went, without noise, over the mountains towards Cumberland; and, as the sun began to show its beautiful reflection on the high top of the Dan Mountain, westward of the town, we arrived in sight of the valley in which the town was situated. Here was a new scene to me entirely. The whole valley was covered with a dense fog — nothing was to be seen but the high tops of the western mountains, with here and there stripes of sun-light; whilst all around was in uproar, with cows bellowing, calves bleating, dogs barking, cocks crowing, and, in short, all sorts of noises. The fog was so heavy that I could not see any object until within a few paces of it. Here we halted for our breakfast. By that time the sun had driven away all the misty clouds, and the town was in plain view; and I think that there were not more than twenty or thirty houses, and they mostly cabins, surrounded by large corn-fields, containing heavy crops of corn.*

## A 1791 petition from the purchasers of lots westward of Fort Cumberland
The 1856 "**Index to the Journals of the Senate and House of Delegates of the State of Maryland**" provides the following summary of an item from the November 1791 session of the House of Delegates:

> *FORT CUMBERLAND — Petition from the purchasers of lots westward of, for time to complete their payments, and that one patent may issue for several lots where they belong to one person, referred 23; report on petition, &c., concurred with; leave to bring in a bill 59; a supplement to the act reported*

---

[1669] The date estimate is based on a reference to General St. Clair's November 4, 1791 defeat. Although Mr. Browning's description of Cumberland seems credible, some of the things he wrote seem to be yarns spun from whole cloth, which has caused at least one esteemed local historian to discredit Browning's book. For example, Browning reports on a rattlesnake encountered on the Youghiogheny River as follows, *"It coiled itself up on the water, inflated its body with air, and there laid, as light as a bubble, holding its rattles high up from, the water, and rattling as well as if it had been on land."* However incredible as this statement may seem, the exact same thing is illustrated in a BassFan TV video that shows a large rattlesnake swimming up to a bass boat, and then coiling up after being struck with a fishing rod. The coiled snake appears to be floating on top of the water like a bubble, just as Browning described. A careful evaluation of the video reveals that it is the buoyancy of submerged, water-obscured lower coils that causes the illusion that the snake is floating like a bubble.

*respecting the settlers on the reserved lands to westward of, &c., passed 125; sent to senate 125; returned passed, with amendments, amendments agreed to 129.*

## The Bill of Rights is ratified in 1791

The Bill of Rights was ratified on December 15, 1791, as the first ten amendments to the Constitution.

## Mounts Ford and Ferry at Sugar Bottom

According to Horton's 2000 book "**Hampshire County Minute Book Abstracts 1788-1802**", page 76 of the 1788 to 1791 minutes book mentions *"Mountz's Ford"* on the North Branch, and page 352 references *"Mounts's Ferry"* on the North Branch. An 1831 newspaper article, quoted later herein, connects the ferry to Sugar Bottom. The inset on John Payne's 1799 map "**The States of Maryland and Delaware from the Latest Surveys**" shows the probable site of Mounts's ferry.

Horton provides the information about the ferry in an abstract of an order for road reviewers to view and report on the road that ran from the Short Gap mountain pass, across from Mounts Ferry, to the north branch of the Potomac River. I haven't been able to find a copy of the 1788 to 1791 minutes book, to confirm the exact year of the references to the ford and ferry, but they were obviously no later than 1791.

### *Speculating on the location of Mountz's ford*

Horton provides the information about Mountz's ford in an abstract of an order appointing Thomas Anderson to survey a road from David Neal's old property to Mountz's Ford on the North Branch of the Potomac River. I believe that I have identified the most likely location of the Mountz's ford with a high degree of probability. The logic is presented below.

From February 7, 1775 and March 21, 1775 correspondence between George Washington and Thomas Cresap (included elsewhere herein), and from George Washington's October 26, 1778 letter to his brother John Augustine Washington (included elsewhere herein), it is clear that George Washington knew that his brother owned Northern Branch lots 9 and 10, which were originally surveyed for Garrett Pendergrass and Thomas Cresap, respectively. Lawrence Washington received grants for both properties in 1752, and bequeathed them to his brother Augustine in his June 20, 1752 will. Lawrence's will includes the statement, *"First I give and Bequeath unto my Loveing Brother Augustine Washington and his heirs for ever ... two Tracts of Land lying and being in Frederick County which I Purchased of Colo Cresap [and] Jerrard Pendergrass..."*

On October 11, 1770, Washington recorded in his diary that he crossed the P*otomac "at the lower end of my deceased brother Augustine's land, known by the name of Pendergrass's."* The lower end of Cresap's lot, which was part of Augustine Washington's land, is located approximately at Latitude 39.560541°, -78.822055°, which is also the most likely fording site from a river depth standpoint. There is an island at that location, and such islands are sometimes the result of the river slowing down due to a locally wider flow channel. At the projected fording site, the combined width of the river on both sides of the island is relatively wide, indicating shallow water.

A 1949 aerial photo[1670] of Sugar Bottom shows traces of roads at the widest spot on the river south of the island, and at the widest part of the river north of the island. I've studied enough known fording sites to know what they look like on old aerial photos, and this sure looks like one, with ruts on both sides of the river going to the most likely (widest and shallowest) parts of the river. For example, many of the old fording sites in Pennsylvania are clearly visible on 1939 aerial photos. Two of them (Salisbury and Stewarts) even have wagon ruts across the river bottom that can be seen on 1939 aerial photos. I believe

---

[1670] Photo identified by Julia Jackson.

the reason the old fords show up on early aerial photos is because the old fords were still used by horses and droves into the early 1900s.[1671] When we talked to the farmer who was living on Sugar Bottom in 2016, we learned that he forded over to the island with his tractor.

## An improved road to present-day Corriganville is commissioned in 1791

The following act is recorded in the 1791 book "**Laws of Maryland...**":

*IX. And be it enacted, That one road leading from Hancock-Town, on the nearest direction, to Cumberland-town, in Allegany county; one other road from the Cumberland-town to the Turkey Foot road on the Pennsylvania line; and one other road from Knipton's mill, on Georges creek, to intersect the state road at Savage river, shall or may be opened, straightened, marked and bounded, in the same manner as the public roads are to be done; and that John Denovan, George Robinet, Thomas Beall, of Samuel, Benjamin Tomlinson, [1672] be and are hereby appointed commissioners on the first road; and that Andrew Bruce, Edward Durbin, John Tomlinson, Benjamin Tomlinson, be and are hereby appointed commissioners on the second road; and that John Knipton, Matthew Ball, John Siglar, Mark Poland, senior, be and are hereby appointed commissioners on the third road aforesaid; provided, that the said three last roads shall be opened, straightened, and amended and kept, at the expense of those persons who are interested therein, by subscription or otherwise, and not at the expense of Washington and Allegany counties; and that the commissioners appointed on the said three roads be subject to, and act solely under, the directions of the persons so interested as aforesaid.*

The 1794 Dennis Griffith map shows both a path and a road on the west side of Wills Creek, north of Cumberland, and shows the location of Tomlinson's mill. The road may be the route described above, by the 1791 law book.

## An example of a family migrating westward via Cumberland in 1792

While not documentary evidence, Ruth E. Manley Miller's 1978 publication "**Leonard History**"[1673] contains information about a typical pioneer family migrating westward via Cumberland. The information was collected by descendant Reverend Amos Leonard (a minister in Fayette and Westmoreland counties), who was born circa 1835 and died circa 1890.

According to Miller, Constantine Leonard intended to build a flat boat to take his family down the Ohio River, but died at Connellsville in 1792, while getting his flat boat ready. Leonard's family traveled Braddock's road from Fort Cumberland, using a wagon pulled by a pair of oxen. At Turkeyfoot, they took a shorter route to Connellsville that took them across Laurel Hill, through the Indian Creek Valley, and past the place where Normalville is located (the article refers to the Normalville location as Springfield). These references indicate that part of their journey north of Braddock's road followed the Turkey Foot Road.

---

[1671] My own grandfather, Irvin Dietle, was still farming with horses when I was young, in the 1950s.

[1672] Men named Andrew Bruce, John Tomlinson, and Benjamin Tomlinson are mentioned in Lowdermilk's 1878 book **"History of Cumberland"**. Andrew Bruce was one of the commissioners appointed by the general assembly to lay out the town of Cumberland, and he already had a house there at the time. Benjamin Tomlinson reportedly built a house along Wills Creek about five miles from Cumberland in 1789. John Tomlinson was one of the settlers found living west of Fort Cumberland in 1787.

[1673] Miller's publication is available at the Somerset County Historical Center, Somerset, Pennsylvania.

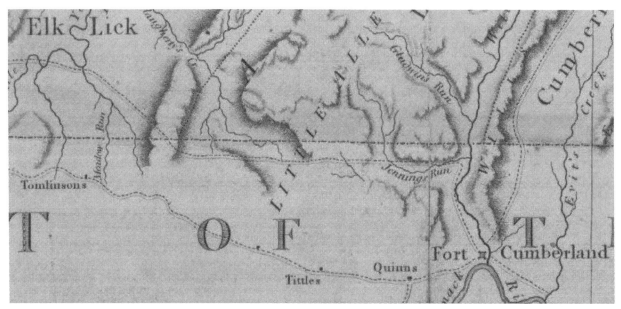

This image is taken from the 1792 Reading Howell map of Pennsylvania. It shows several roads, albiet schematically, radiating outward from the town of Fort Cumberland, and also shows the Winchester road heading southward from Gwynn's tavern at the present-day site of LaVale.

## A road between present-day Barrelville and Frostburg is made public

A law in the 1793 "**Laws of Maryland**" titled *"An Act to establish the road from the Turkey Foot Road towards Braddock's road as a public road, and for other purposes therein mentioned."* states:

*WHEREAS Sundry inhabitants of Allegany county, by their petition to this general assembly have set forth, that there hath been a road from the Turkey Foot road, above the fork of Jenning's Run, leading up the said run by Oswalt's saw-mill to the foot of Mount-Pleasant, and from thence until it intersects Bradock's road at a tract of land called The Mountain, and that, it never having been made a public road by law, they are deprived of the benefit and utility of the same...*

## Westerly road improvements continue after the founding of the town of Cumberland

Chapter LXX of the 1793 Acts of Maryland states:

*WHEREAS the state of Pennsylvania hath laid out, opened and amended, a road from Uniontown, in Fayette county, to the division line:*

*And whereas the said road will be of no benefit unless this state straighten and amend the road from the town of Cumberland to intersect the said road at the Winding-Ridge; and it appearing to this general assembly that the same will be of considerable advantage to this state, by opening a better communication with the Western country; therefore, Be it enacted, by the General Assembly of Maryland, That George Dent, William M'Mahon and Evan Gwynne, or any two of them, be and they are hereby appointed commissioners, to survey, straighten and amend, at the expence of those who have or may subscribe to the same, a road not exceeding forty feet in width, in the best and most convenient direction from the town of Cumberland, in Allegany county, to a tract of land called Good Will, and from thence to intersect the main road from Union-town, in the state of Pennsylvania, where the said road enters this state at the Winding-Ridge; and the said road, when so opened at the expence of the persons aforesaid, and the valuation herein after directed to be made shall be paid, or secured to be paid, to the individuals concerned, shall be recorded among the records of Allegany county, and be thereafter deemed and taken to be a public road for ever.*

### The Potomac is being used for water transportation
Thomas Cooper's 1794 book "**Some Information Respecting America**" quotes a 1793 letter from Reverend Toulmin that describes the use of the Potomac River from Cumberland:

*At present, many boats come down from Fort Cumberland to the Great falls, about ten miles above George Town.*

### John Jacob frees three slaves
The 1939 book "**Early Records Hampshire County Virginia**" records the following for January 1, 1794, "*JACOB, John Jeremiah of Hampshire Co. to Slaves Freeing of three negro children from his services. Rec. 4-9-1994. Wit.: Thomas Cresap, Benj. Foste, Benj. Whitehead.*"

### The militia are to unite at Fort Cumberland
On September 15, 1794, Hamilton wrote a letter to Governor Lee regarding suppression of the Whiskey Rebellion that includes the following:

*It is the President's desire, that no time should be lost in uniting the whole of the militia of Maryland at Fort Cumberland. If the commanding officer has not already taken the field, it is desirable that he should do it without delay, in order to combine, arrange and accelerate the ulterior movements.*

### Providing houses for the sick at Fort Cumberland during the Whiskey Rebellion
An October 13, 1794 order[1674] issued by General Henry Lee at Fort Cumberland includes the statement, "*The Quarter Master General will be pleased to provide proper houses, for the reception of the sick, together with all stores necessary for their accommodation and comfort*".

### Washington reviews the troops at Cumberland during the Whiskey Rebellion
One of the treasured anecdotes of Cumberland is Washington reviewing the troops at Fort Cumberland during the Whiskey Rebellion. Washington's journal entry for October 16, 1794[1675] states:

*16th. After an early breakfast we set out for Cumberland — and about 11 Oclock arrived there.*

*Three miles from the Town I was met by a party of Horse under the command of Major Lewis (my Nephew) and by Brigr. Genl. Smith of the Maryland line, who Escorted me to the Camp; where, finding all the Troops under Arms, I passed along the line of the Army; & was conducted to a house the residence of Major Lynn of the Maryland line (an old Continental Officer) where I was well lodged, & civilly entertained.*

### Identifying Major Lynn
The 1923 book "**History of Allegany County**" by Williams and Thomas states:

*Captain David Lynn, the subject of this sketch, entered the Continental Army as Ensign of the First Battalion of the Flying Camp, in 1776. On March 27, 1777, he was made Lieutenant of the Seventh*

---

[1674] "**The Western Pennsylvania Historical Magazine**", June 1936.

[1675] In his book "**History of Cumberland...**", Lowdermilk indicates that Washington's review of the troops took place on October 19, 1794. This date seems to be off by three days, based on the contemporary evidence I could find. Date-related mistakes are very easy to make when writing a history book, and very difficult to identify and correct before publication. I've made my share.

*Battalion of Maryland Regulars, and on May 22, 1779, he became Captain of the same regiment, and in that capacity he continued to serve until the close of the American Revolution. Among the engagements in which he took a conspicuous part were Germantown and Monmouth, Cowpens and Yorktown. He was a member of the Society of Cincinnati, of Maryland.*

*His brother, John Lynn, also entered the Continental service at an early age. He was made Lieutenant of the First Maryland Regiment, and served with distinction throughout the entire war. He is generally referred to as Colonel John Lynn, and that is the title inscribed on his tombstone in Mount Olivet Cemetery, in Frederick county; and Washington, at whose house he was entertained during, his last visit to Cumberland, speaks of him as Major Lynn, which title was conferred upon him in the spring of 1790 by Gov. Howard of Maryland.*

*Shortly after the close of the American Revolution, Captain David Lynn and big brother John both located in Cumberland, Maryland, and the latter became the first Clerk of the Circuit Court for Allegany county, serving from 1790 until 1801, when he removed from his Cumberland residence, on the northwest corner of Washington and Prospect streets, on Lot No. 66 (where the Richmond, Blackiston and Bretz residences now stand) the deed for which, it is worthy of note, being the first deed recorded after Allegany county became erected. Major Lynn was in the Legislature of Maryland as a representative from Washington when Allegany county was erected in 1789. He married Miss Eleanor Edelyn, and, two years before his death, moved to his estate known as Wild Cherrytree Meadows, at McHenry, then in Allegany, but now in Garrett county. He left two daughters, Jane and Eleanor, the latter of whom married Davis Richardson, and they were the ancestors of the Richardsons now of Charleston, West Virginia.*

This contains an error. The first deed recorded in Allegany County was not for Lot 66. Instead, the first deed recorded in Allegany County was for part of lot 96, which is at the location Williams and Thomas describe.[1676] This is an important detail, because Major Lynn's lot was just across the street from lot 65, the earliest known location of the cabin known as Washington's headquarters. Captain Jonathan Morris sold a portion of lot 96 to Captain John Lynn on August 8, 1788, and the December 4, 1790 indenture was recorded January 1, 1791 in Allegany County Liber A Folio 1. John Lynn sold lot no. 96 to John Johnson for 100 pounds on July 13, 1796, [1677] which means that John Lynn still owned lot 96 when George Washington lodged with him in 1794.

## Wellford's journal entry for October 16, 1794

Doctor Wellford's journal entry for October 16, 1794 states:

*Between eleven & twelve o'clock this day arrived the President of the United States escorted into the town & to Head Quarters near the Fort by three troops of light dragoons, every man of whom cheerfully left ye encampment to pay the President a compliment, every regiment was drawn up in excellent order to receive him, & as he passed the line of Infantry he deliberately bowed to every officer individually. The Artillery at the same time announced his arrival*

## The Washington's headquarters tradition

An article in an 1857 issue of "**Harper's Magazine**" states:

*Until 1846 or 1847, the weather-beaten hovel which Washington occupied as his quarters more than a hundred years ago, still stood behind the fort ... but it has been removed to make way for a modern dwelling.*

---

[1676] This error was identified by Dave Williams.
[1677] The 1796 sale was found by Dave Williams.

A drawing that accompanied the 1857 article illustrates Washington's headquarters. One half of the structure in the drawing is a clear match to the structure known as Washington's headquarters that is now located in Riverside Park. The building was returned to Cumberland in 1921.

Lowdermilk's 1878 book "**History of Cumberland**" states:

> *To designate the houses that are oldest is equally difficult. Certainly the most venerable of them was that known as "Washington's headquarters," which occupied the ground on which Mr. O. C. Gephart's residence now stands, and which is well remembered by hundreds of citizens, as it was not removed until about the year 1844. It was contemporary with Fort Cumberland, and stood but a short distance from the parade ground. This old house was occupied at one time by Mrs. Bridenhart, a daughter of Michael Kershner, and she entertained several students there as boarders for some years. It was also occupied for several years by David Lynn as a residence, afterwards by George Bruce, and finally by John Kane.*

> *In 1844 it was bought by George Blocher,[1678] who moved it to a lot on the Bedford road, a mile distant, where it was repaired and occupied for twenty-two years by John Baker. It still stands, on the ground of Christian Eichner, a short distance from Cumberland.*

The Mr. O. C. Gephart that Lowdermilk references is Judge Oliver Cromwell Gephart, who in 1875 purchased the home that is now known as the C. William Gilchrist Museum of Art. This home is at 104 Washington Street, and is on lot no. 65. This lot is about 212 feet west of lot 66, where the fort was located, and is just across the street from John Lynn's portion of Lot 96.

Thomas Beall of Samuel sold Cumberland lots 33, 41, and 65 *"in the Town of Washington"* to John Lynn on September 9, 1785 (Liber D, Folio 488).[1679] John Lynn sold lot 33 to William Lamar in 1792 (Liber A Page 197) and sold lot 41 to William Robertson in 1792 (Liber A Page 200). The handwritten 1793 tax list for *"3 Distr The Town of Cumberland"* shows John Lynn owning *"1 Lott"* and *"1/3 of a Lott"*. By analysis of the deeds involving John Lynn prior to 1795, it is possible to say with complete confidence that the full lot he owned in 1793 was lot 65, and the 1/3 lot he owned in 1793 was part of lot 96, and he didn't sell either one of them in 1794.

William Lamar is listed as the owner of lot 65 on the 1801[1680] and 1810[1681] tax lists, and the 1810 tax list identifies a house on the lot. Despite a vigorous deed search by Dave Williams, Julia Jackson, and me, neither John Lynn's sale of Lot 65 nor William Lamar's purchase of Lot 65 have been found.[1682] William Lamar sold Lot 65 to his daughter Sarah Lamar on March 1, 1832 (Liber P, Folio 496), and Sarah Lamar sold Lot 65 to Andrew Bruce on September 1, 1838 (Liber W, Folio 172). John Pickell purchased Lot 65 from the estate of Andrew Bruce in June of 1839 (Liber BB, Folio 199), and sold it to George Bruce on June 12, 1842 (Liber CC, Folio 442). George Bruce sold Lot 65 to Thomas Perry on June 11, 1844 (Liber

---

[1678] Julia Jackson found a 1796 deed (Liber B Folio 136) from Thomas Beall of Samuel to Jacob Blocher for a portion of Walnut Bottom on the Bedford road that connects with *"the seventeenth line of Walnut Bottom"*. She also found information indicating that George Blocher sold the property at the corner of Bedford and Columbia streets for the church that is located there. Putting these two things together, this could possibly be the area where the log cabin known as Washington's headquarters was moved in the 1840s.

[1679] This deed was identified by Dave Williams.

[1680] The 1810 tax list was identified by Don Hammon.

[1681] "**Early Allegany County Records, 1788-1812**", Volume II, The Cresap Society.

[1682] Our three-person search for the sale of Lot 65 by John Lynn and its purchase by William Lamar included the exhaustive use of the online deed indexes for Washington and Allegany counties to find potentially relevant deeds using the names of the variety of individuals historians associate with the lot. It also included the use of the *"Abstract of Land Records - Deed Book A 1788-1795"* in Volume II of "**Early Allegany County Records, 1788-1812**".

EE, Folio 269).[1683] According to historian James W. Thomas (see below) George Blocher obtained the Washington Headquarters building from Thomas Perry and moved it to his own farm.

The 1813 section of Lowdermilk's book states:[1684]

*Washington street was then a very steep and rough road. There were but four houses on the south side, one built by Mr. Deakins, and afterwards bought by John Hoye; the old Washington headquarters; a frame house a few yards west of it, and a brick house on the site now occupied by Hon. William Walsh's residence. On the north side were the Court House and jail, the Clerks' office, and the house built by Roger Perry.*

An article in the August 20, 1887 issue of the "**Cumberland Daily Times**" has a section titled *"Old Washington Street"* that states:[1685]

*Here Washington street began to climb its steep ascent, a mere wide country road without pavement or sidewalks. On the right side as you ascend was a large vegetable garden, futher on stood a small one-story building, the office of John L. McMahon, Esq., and afterwards used by Lawyers Buskirk and Samuel M. Semmes. Opposite stood a large brick house with a porch and benches on each side of the door, the dwelling of John Hoye, Esq., afterwards torn down and the present modern building erected by his widow. Further on the right stood a one-story brick, with two rooms, paved with brick, one the county clerk's office and the other the register of wills — the site of the present Allegany academy. Adjoining was a ball alley. There in an open space stood the court house and jail under one roof. Next a two story frame, with one story wings, surrounded by a grass yard and garden with fruit and shade trees, the residence and law office of Roger Perry, Esq., and stands to-day with a few alterations as it did seventy-odd years ago.*

*Nearly opposite stood a small house in imitation of a Swiss chalet, famous as the headquarters of President Washington when he visited Cumberland as commander-in-chief of the army in 1793 (sic). West of this were two frame houses, one built by George Lowdermilk, the other by Jonathan Bradley, and for thirty odd years these comprised all the buildings that stood on Washington street.*

An article by James W. Thomas titled, *"Cumberland Historian Enters Warm Defense of Washington Headquarters"* in the March 20, 1921 issue of the "**Baltimore Sun**" states:

*In your news column of Tuesday last appeared a dispatch from this city containing a letter to the Mayor and City Council at its meeting on Monday, questioning the authenticity of the Washington Headquarters Building now erected here, which letter the Council refused to receive and place upon the record. It was written by T. A. K. Hummelshime, a City Commissioner, and has received but scant notice in the community where the history of this building is so well known, this communication being written because the dispatch may be widely read by persons not familiar with the facts in the case.*

*This building was not reconstructed "from plans that came from the British Museum," as the dispatch alleges, because no such plans ever existed. It was first erected by General Braddock's men on the lot adjoining the present Allegany County Courthouse. Many years later, when Cumberland became a town, a one and a half story addition was added to it and it was used as a residence in 1844, when the lot was purchased by Judge Tomas Perry, for so many years Judge of the Circuit Court of this county, and who was the father of the late Mrs. H. Crawford Black, of Baltimore, for the purpose of erecting thereon a residence, now the pretentious Gephart home. To make room for this edifice, Judge Perry had his friend,*

---

[1683] Information provided by Dave Williams.
[1684] This passage was identified by Dave Williams.
[1685] This article was provided by Julia Jackson.

*George Blocher, move the building to his farm on the Bedford road, knowing the historic value of the headquarters, and hoping thereby to preserve it. Later on it was weather-boarded and has several times been re-roofed, the last time with slate, to more fully preserve it. For more than twenty-five years the writer has been familiar with it and has made repeated efforts to obtain it, but only recently succeeded in doing so, for the purpose to which it is now to be dedicated — a Washington memorial in the city of Cumberland.*

*City Provides Site.*

*After procuring it the writer was requested by the Mayor and City Council to donate it to the city of Cumberland and to erect it in Riverside Park in view of the site of old Fort Cumberland, with which it had been so closely associated. This request was acceded to in July last, on the condition that it would be properly preserved, and upon receiving such assurances the building was erected on the site designated by the Mayor and City Council.*

*The restoration of it was put in the hands of William J. Morley, the contractor who restored the Washington headquarters at Valley Force and who needed no "specifications," it being only necessary to relay the sills, plates and joists of the old building to accurately determine its dimensions, and replace the rafters to give the pitch and shape of the roof. The entire groundwork as it stood when occupied by Washington was intact and was used, as were the rafters, plates and binders, and nothing new has been added, except that the best tile roof obtainable has been placed upon it to insure preservation of its priceless parts, tile being the most ancient as well as the most durable of all roofing materials, and some other stones used for the outside chimney. Where the logs on the sides of the building were too far decayed to be replaced, those from the next oldest house in Cumberland were substituted. Therefore, as it stands today, it contains all of the original material available for the purposes, reconstructed in exactly the same form, and is of the same size and design as the original.*

*Early Records Quoted*

*Of this ancient memorial, Lowdermilk, in his history of Cumberland, 1878, and whose veracity is not in question, in speaking of the older buildings of Cumberland, says: "Certainly the most venerable of them all was that known as Washington's Headquarters, which occupied the ground on which the old Gephart residence now stands, and which is well remembered by hundreds of citizens, as it was not removed until 1844. It was contemporary with Fort Cumberland, and stood but a short distance from the parade grounds. In 1844 it was bought by George Blocher, who moved it to a lot on the Bedford road, where it was repaired and occupied for 22 years by John Baker, and where it still stands." This is corroborated by "Old Squire" Strong in a typewritten interview for the late Governor Lowndes, still preserved, and who had lived in Cumberland from 1810 to the time of his death at a very advanced age: by Mrs. Nancy Miller, who lived in Cumberland from 1883 to the time of her death at the age of 107 years, and whose father, John Rafter, had the distinction of furnishing the little building the last time it was used by Washington: by interviews with a large number of old citizens, who well remembered all about it, including Mr. John Weibel, who took it down and moved it to the Bedford road, and Mr. Christopher Eicher, who at one time owned and lived in it, and from whom efforts, from time to time, were made to obtain it. It is also referred to in an interesting letter, still extant, writing many years ago by Mr. H. D. Black, the father of Mr. H. Crawford Black, of Baltimore, who, writing of Cumberland in "**Ye Olden Times**" and who well remembered the building, says: "It was an imitation of a Swiss chalet and famous as Washington's Headquarters."*

*And thus it is. If the ravages of time had left only a small part of the original structure that housed Washington during the eventful period in which he occupied it, it would have been worthy of preservation and veneration: but as nature and care have dealt so generously with it, today it is the most historic building, perhaps, in the United States, having been Washington's headquarters during the French and Indian war, 1755 to 1758, and again his headquarters in 1794, when in Cumberland as Commander-in-Chief of the American Army, and when for the last time he officially donned his military uniform and regimentals. It should, therefore, occupy a high place in the esteem and in the affection and pride of every American patriot, and should be revered as a hallowed and sacred shrine, standing as it does, as the immortal Washington stood — for victory with glory, peace with honor and liberty with justice.*

*Cumberland, Md., March 16, 1921.*

## The size of the army at Cumberland

Washington's journal entry for October 17-18, 1794[1686] states:

*17th. & 18th. Remained at Cumberland, in order to acquire a true knowledge of the strength — condition — &ca. of the Troops; and to see how they were provided, and when they could be got in readiness to proceed. I found upwards of 3200 Men (Officers included) in this Encampment; Understood that about 500 more were at a little Village on the Virginia side, 11 Miles distant, called Frankfort, under the command of Majr. Genl. Morgan; that 700 more had arrived at that place the evening of the 18th. undr. Brigr. Mathews and 500 more were expected in the course of a few days under Colo. Page and That the whole were well supplied with Provns., Forage & Straw. Having requested that every thing might be speedily arranged for a forward movement, and a light Corps to be organized for the advance under the command of Major Genl. Morgan, I resolved to proceed to Bedford next Morng. ...*

## The probable origin of the Washington's headquarters tradition

The origin of the Washington's headquarters tradition seems to be lost to time. Washington would have needed office space to work out of during the days he stayed in Cumberland in 1794, and a building near the home of his host John Lynn would have been convenient.[1687] The President and a visiting army of 3,200 men would have been a huge event for the little village of Cumberland — and in my opinion, this event is the most likely origin of the Washington's headquarters tradition. There would have been enough residents living in Cumberland at the time of Washington's visit — including Nancy Miller — to ensure that the building he used in 1794 became a part of the local oral history of Cumberland.[1688] Since there were fewer families from the 1750s who remained in the area, it's more difficult to imagine that the tradition survived from that time[1689] — unless Washington told a 1794 Cumberland resident that he had previously used the same building. It seems unlikely that Washington even had a building as a headquarters in 1755, given that contemporaneous records show that General Braddock's headquarters was a tent.[1690] The suspicion that the headquarters tradition originated in 1794 is harmonious with the fact that the building known as Washington's headquarters was on one of the two lots John Lynn was assessed for in Cumberland in 1793 — lot 65 — and was located across the street from the other lot John Lynn was assessed for in Cumberland in 1793 — lot 96 — where one historian thought John Lynn's residence was located in 1794. There is no record that John Lynn made any purchases or sales of lots in Cumberland in 1793 or 1794. Based on this, it seems reasonable to believe that at the time of Washington's visit in 1794, he still owned both of the lots he was assessed for in 1793.

---

[1686] This passage was identified by Dave Williams.
[1687] This observation was made by Robert Bantz.
[1688] This observation was made by Dan Press.
[1689] This observation was made by Dave Williams.
[1690] This observation was made by Dan Press.

*My piece of the 'Washington's headquarters' building*

On March 30, 2016 I gave a presentation for the Allegany County Historical Society titled, *"Things you weren't taught about Fort Cumberland"*, followed by a presentation by Dave Williams about the origin of the Washington Headquarters tradition titled *"The mystery of Washington's headquarters"*. After these presentations, Roland Cradle of Village Restorations presented me with a notched piece of a log that had been salvaged from Washington's headquarters.

Mr. Cradle was tasked with replacing the chinking on Washington's headquarters, and found that the chink (chinking filler material) was made from split and shortened pieces of old decayed building logs. Rather than throwing this chink away, he saved it, knowing that it was from the professional 1921 restoration, and as such, was either from the headquarters building or from the Black Horse Tavern. I wanted to document the story of this log fragment for posterity.

They style of notching on the log fragment matches Washington's headquarters perfectly and is consistent with being the lowermost log. I was able to find a photograph of the Black Horse Tavern and confirm that the notch style on the decayed log fragment I received has nothing in common with that of the Black Horse Tavern. The large hewn timbers forming the walls of the Black Horse Tavern were notched so that the logs laid on top of one another, which requires a much different type of notching than used on Washington's headquarters.

We do not know if George Blocher replaced any logs when the headquarters building was dismantled and erected on his property in the 1840s. We do know that when the building was dismantled and moved back to Cumberland in 1921, Mr. Morley had to replace a few decayed logs. Rather than use new logs, he made replacement logs from the second-oldest building in town, which would have been the Black Horse Tavern.[1691] In this same spirit, it seems clear that Mr. Morley split some of the decayed logs and used them as chink, in order to use as much original building material as possible in the 1921 restoration.

This image shows my fragment of a bottom log from Washington's headquarters.

## The route of the army west of Fort Cumberland

During the westward portion of his Whiskey Rebellion journey, Doctor Wellford's October 24, 1794 journal entry states:

> *From Strickers the Army proceeded this day to Tomlinson's, at the little Meadows, 11 miles. the course of this day's march led the Army over a thousand times ten thousand rocks, thro' a dark, dreary part of the Mountains called the "Shades of Death," & by an almost continued ascent to that rugged and elevated part of the Alleghany Mountains known by the epithet of the "back bone of America.[1692]*

---

[1691] The March 19, 1920 issue of the "**Cumberland Evening Times**" states that the Black Horse Tavern was about to be razed. (Article found by Julia Jackson.)

[1692] In Maryland, Meadow Mountain was known as the backbone. See page 361 of Meshach Browning's 1859 book "**Forty four years of the life of a hunter**", which states, *"This delightful valley lies between the great Back-Bone*

The October 23rd journal entry describes Strickers as being 11 miles from Cumberland:

*The left wing of the Army, with the Commander in Chief, marched from Fort Cumberland to Strickers, 11 miles, & encamped in a meadow; the conduct of this man betrayed the utmost dissatisfaction on the approach of the Army, & his behavior to individuals on their arrival evidently discovered his insurgent disposition.*

### Dining at Beatty's tavern in 1794, and lodging at Captain Thomas Beall's

Doctor Wellford's journal entry for November 27, 1794 covers his trip eastward from Michael Engle's place, near the present-day location of Salisbury, Pennsylvania, to Cumberland, Maryland via the Turkey Foot Road. The journal entry states:

*Thursday, 27th. Left Ingles & crossed the last of the Western Waters, & then ascended the Savage Mtn, went forward to the Alleghany,[1693] cros't the back bone on this Turkey foot road, & breakfasted at Logsdon's, 14 miles, from thence proceeded to Cumberland, 9 miles, crossed Ye Eastern waters on uppermost branch of Potowmac, this day passed thro' a Vale a few miles from Cumberland called the narrows of Mill's (sic) Creek, here a view of a stupendous Mt'n, varied at every step, possessing grandeur, sublimity of object, & everything great to attract the atten'n of those who delight in natural curiosities. 25 miles. Immediately on descending the Eastern side of the Alleghany, discovered the snow leaving us, & on arriving at the foot of the Mountains no snow to be seen, & the weather warmer by several degrees. Dined at Beatty's Tavern in Cumberland, & slept at Capt. Beall's.*

The Narrows is a distinctive water gap defined by the south end of Wills Mountain and the north end of Haystack Mountain. The reference to Captain Beall is clear; it is a reference to Captain Thomas Beall, of Samuel, who founded the town of Cumberland. John C. Beatty was already a resident of Cumberland in 1787. This makes him the likely candidate to be the owner of Beatty's tavern at the time of Doctor Wellford's trip.

### Another adjustment to the land payment schedule is made in 1794

Chapter XXX[1694] of the Session Laws, passed in 1794 and titled *"A Further supplement to an act respecting the settlers on the reserved lands westward of Fort Cumberland"*, states:

*WHEREAS by an act of November session, seventeen hundred and ninety-two, the settlers were authorised to pay one third of the balances due this state on or before the first day of May, seventeen hundred and ninety-three, one third on or before the first day of May, seventeen hundred and ninety-four, and the remaining third on or before the first day of May, seventeen hundred and ninety-five: And whereas at the passage of said law a number of the lots westward of Fort Cumberland were proclamated, but for the use of the original settlers, who were precluded from the benefit of the said law: And whereas by the act of November session, seventeen hundred and ninety-three, the treasurer was authorised to receive the one half of the balances due from the said settlers to this state on or before the first day of May, seventeen hundred and ninety-four, and the remaining half on or before the first day of May, seventeen hundred and ninety-five, provided it appeared by an endorsement on the said warrants they were assigned to the original settler: And whereas the settlers apprehending the treasurer, by the said last recited act, was authorised to receive the one half of the balances due from them at any time before the proclamation*

---

*Mountain and the western hills of the Youghiogheny River, and covers an area of ten or twelve miles. This mountain commences at the Savage River, one of the tributaries of the Potomac, and runs from north-east to south-west ... All the waters on the eastern side of this mountain fall into the Potomac, and all those on the western side into the Youghiogheny, which empties into the Ohio River."* The drainage description fits Meadow Mountain near the state line.

[1693] Wellford's references to the mountain names are obviously mixed up.

[1694] **"Session Laws, 1794"**.

*warrants were out of date, omitted to pay the same on the first day of May last, but made a tender thereof before the said warrants were out of date, when the treasurer would not receive it: And whereas in consequence thereof they again were obliged to proclamate the lots returned to them; and it appearing reasonable to this general assembly to allow to the said persons the benefit of the payments they have made; therefore,*

*II. Be it enacted, by the General Assembly of Maryland, That the treasurer of the western shore shall and he is hereby directed, in all cases where warrants of proclamation have issued to affect any land of the description aforesaid, to receive the balance due this state for any of the said lands at any time before the operation of the said warrants shall cease, provided it shall appear, by an endorsement on the said warrant or warrants, that the same is or are assigned to the original settler; and also to receive, from any of the said settlers whole lands are not proclamated, the balance due this state for the same, at any time before the same shall be proclamated,*

*III. And be it enacted, That the register of the land-office be and he is hereby authorised and directed to issue a patent to any of the said settlers who may comply with this act, as if the whole money had been paid under the said warrant or warrants, any law to the contrary notwithstanding.*

## A house is built on the site of Fort Cumberland

An assessment of the location of Fort Cumberland puts at least part of the bastioned part of the fort on Cumberland lot 66, where the historic Hoye mansion stands on Prospect Square.

Thomas Beall sold Lot 66 *"in the town of Washington"* to Samuel Duvall on June 25, 1785 (Liber D Page 374); there is no reference to the fort.[1695] Lot 66 was sold to George Dent on November 27, 1795 (Liber B Folio 100), and he sold it to Charles F. Broadhag on December 5, 1796. On March 9, 1805, Broadhag transferred the lot to John Hoye, *"it being the lot on which the brick house built by George Dent stands together with said Brick House and all the improvements..."* This indicates that a house was built on the lot in 1796, which means the bastioned part of the fort was gone by then.[1696]

## Cumberland gets a new bridge in 1796

According to a 1974 issue of the "**Heritage Press**" newsletter, the following was the bond contract for replacing a bridge at Cumberland:

*Pursuant to an order of the Levy Court the following bond as recorded this 2nd August 1796: Know all men by these presents that we, William Logsdon, John Logsdon, Ralph Logsdon and Daniel McKinzy are bound unto David Huffman, John Graham and Patrick Murdock for 747 pounds current money of the State. The condition: William Logsdon shall do and will and truly build and finish on or before 1st September, next, a good and sufficient wagon bridge over will's Creek—town of Cumberland at the place where the bridge lately stood, the said Bridge to be at least five feet higher than the late bridge, 16 feet wide with railing three feet high; he also to keep the same in good and sufficient repair for term of seven years and to rebuilt the same if carried away or destroyed, at his own cost — except he not to replace, if the water rises over the bridge."*

Daniel McKinzy was a son of Gabriel McKensey, according to Gabriel's descendant Michael McKenzie.

---

[1695] This deed was identified by Julia Jackson.

[1696] This line of reasoning was provided to the author by Dave Williams.

### Military stores remaining at Fort Cumberland in 1796

In an October 7, 1796 letter[1697] to Samuel Hodgdon, Isaac Craig reports that the militia left military stores at Fort Cumberland, Maryland. To the best I can decipher the faded handwriting, the letter includes the following statement:

*With respect to Evidence of Stores Public property being at Fort Cumberland Gen Neville and others who came over the Mountains with the Militia Army say that at the time the Army advanced __ Fort Cumberland by want of Waggons to transport provisions several That carried Military Stores were unloaded at that place and loaded from thence with Provisions, their former Loads were therefore Deposited at that place, and it is presumed are still there The Distance from Pittsburgh to Fort Cumberland is one hundred and ten miles, Major ____ Lynn[1698] of that place is a proper person to make Enquiry and give full information on this Subject.*

### A petition for a road mentions a store at the site of present day Corriganville in 1797

According to Volume 652, page 8, of the 1797 "**Laws of Maryland**", Ninian Cochran[1699] had a store at the mouth of Jennings Run, where Corrgianville, Maryland is located today. The book references a law that was passed on January 20, 1797 that includes the following:

*WHEREAS sundry inhabitants of Allegany county, by their petition to this general assembly, have represented, that there has been a private road for twenty-seven years past, leading from Cockran's store, at Genning's run on the Turkey Foot road, up Will's creek by Tomlinson's mill to the Pennsylvania line, which intersects a public road leading from the town of Bedford...*

This petition appears to be related to the creation of the new road between Somerset, Pennsylvania and Cumberland, Maryland that is described below.

### Pennsylvania builds a new road to Cumberland

While not documentary evidence, the 1906 "**History of Bedford and Somerset Counties...**" draws from early records to describe a 1797 survey for the Pennsylvania portion of what would become known as the Cumberland road:

*What is known as the old Cumberland road was a road that in some form or another, whether as a packer's trail, a bridle path or a wagon road, may be said to date back to the earliest days of the settlement of Somerset County. It is entirely within the bounds of possibility that it could have been an Indian trail long before the coming of the white man. It certainly is mentioned in the earliest accounts of the Cox's Creek Glades, or Somerset settlement. The road crossed the Allegheny mountain and came by*

---

[1697] Papers of the War Department. Letter identified by Dave Williams.

[1698] The name is deduced from a fragment of the third-to-last letter of the last name, and the clear ending letters *"nn"* of the last name. The third-to-last letter of the last name has to be *"y"* or *"g"*.

[1699] Documentary evidence indicates that Ninian Cochran was also a surveyor, and jointly owned a piece of property with my ancestor Michael Korn. (See the 1796 plat of *"Brodhegs Coal Bank"*, which Michael Korn and Ninian Cochran purchased from Cumberland Postmaster Charles F. Broadhag. Michael Korn sold his share of *"Brodhegs Coal Bank"* to Ninian Cochran on November 5, 1800.) One road survey that Ninian Cochran executed was performed on August 4, 1804 and depicts substantially the same course as present-day Route 47, which extends northward from Barrelville, Maryland. According to Storey's 1907 book "**History of Cambria County, Pennsylvania**", Mary Park emigrated from Ireland with her family in 1794, and *"married Ninian Cochran, a surveyor of Cumberland, Maryland, and in 1827 returned to Johnstown...."* According to Swank's 1910 book "**Cambria County Pioneers**", *"Mary Park, who married Ninian Cochran, removed to Johnstown about 1827, after the death of her husband. ... Mrs. Cochran died at Johnstown in 1834."* According to Scharf's "**History of Western Maryland**", a Ninian Cochran was the Allegany County surveyor from 1813 to 1821 and from 1823 to 1843. Any attempt to reconcile the seemingly conflicting information in these secondary sources would require additional research. One has to wonder if there were father and son surveyors with the same first name.

*where Simon Hay afterwards built his mill; from there it reached the Somerset settlement by way of the locality known as Break Neck, coming in near where Ankeny's mill was built. Just when and under what circumstances this trail or path was made into a road that became passable for wagons, we have no account. It is not marked on the Howell map, elsewhere referred to. This road, in the vicinity of Somerset at least, is abandoned.*

*In 1797 David Wright, Cornelius Hanlin, Jacob Smucker, John Burger, George Shanafelt and Jacob Hochstetter were appointed to view and lay out a road in the direction of Cumberland, Maryland. As there can be no reasonable doubt of the existence of such a road at that time, we can only look on this as an order to review and make such changes as might be needed in the existing road. There seems to have been considerable contention over the matter, which lagged for several years, and in different parts of the proceedings the term "old road" is used. These viewers, starting in the center of the public square in the town of Somerset, went south in the direction of Ankeny's mill by way of Main Cross street, turning to the southeast somewhere near the mill. They passed through Brothers Valley township by way of Hay's mill, reaching or crossing Mason and Dixon's line about seventy-five rods west of the one hundred and sixty-fifth milestone,[1700] which is not far from what in those days was known as Korn's mill, in Southampton township.[1701] This was near where Wellersburg now is. Their report not being satisfactory to all interests, Charles Boyle, John McLean, Henry Hartzell, James Lennehill, John Reed and David King were appointed to review their work. These viewers also started in the center of the public square, but they followed Main street east, apparently getting on what we now know as the Berlin road; but several miles out they turned to the left again and went in the direction of Hay's mill, and while some other changes were made in the road as located by the first viewers, in the main they concurred with them. The people of Berlin wanted the road so laid out that it would pass through that town, and this final report leaving Berlin to the north of it, the people from there came into court and resisted its confirmation. The matter being in the hands of the grand jury, they went so far as to have a paper drawn up setting aside the report of the viewers so far as they had ignored the claims of Berlin, which in some manner they placed in the hands of the grand jury. But the grand jury turned the paper over to the court, which, looking on this proceeding as being highly improper, caused an investigation to be made as to who the author of the paper really was. The report of the last viewers was finally confirmed.*

The antecedent to at least part of this road, now known as the Hays Mill path, is presented in detail in the fourth edition of the book "**In Search of the Turkey Foot Road**". The route of the Cumberland road is illustrated on the 1826 Melish state map of Pennsylvania. The construction of this new road highlights the

---

[1700] The quoted material states that the Cumberland Road surveyors crossed the Mason-Dixon line about 75 rods west of the 165th milestone. According to a study I performed by overlaying Veatch's survey of lots westward of Fort Cumberland onto a modern plat map, the 165th milestone would be about where the present-day Maryland Route 47 (Pennsylvania Route 160) crosses the Mason-Dixon line. Do not be misled by present-day Mason-Dixon line monuments. The original monument numbers are no longer used, and the monuments have not been evenly spaced for many years. For example, in 1917, monument 174 was recorded as being alongside Pennsylvania Route 160. Mason and Dixon's June 10, 1766 letter to Governor Sharpe indicates that surveying stopped at mile 165 at the foot of Savage Mountain in 1766, stating, *"We have continued the line 165, which reaches to the Foot of Savage-Mountain, one of the Ridges of the Allegany Mountains: here we set up the Sector (yesterday,) and intend to begin to return when we have finish'd our observations."*

[1701] Page 683 of the 1906 book is in tension with this passage, *"Southampton township was organized in 1801.",* and and this passage, *"The first gristmill in Southampton township was built near Wellersburg, by Jacob Korns, in 1809."* If the Jacob Korns grist mill even existed in 1797, it would have been located in Bedford County, because the area it was in did not become Southampton Township, Somerset County until 1800 ("**Pennsylvania Statutes at Large**", Chapter MMCXI, *"An act to annex part of Bedford County to the County of Somerset"*, passed March 1, 1800). Extensive research Michael McKenzie and I performed regarding the gristmill indicates that it was located just west of Mutt Witt's small Wellersburg-area brick store, in Richard Witt's present-day yard, at Latitude 39.728043°, Longitude -78.849129°.

contemporaneous commercial importance of the towns of Somerset, Pennsylvania and Cumberland, Maryland.

**Another reference to using the Potomac River for water transportation**
Volume 1 of Isaac Weld's 1799 book "**Travels through the states of North America...**" describes observations made during the 1795 to 1797 time period. One sentence describes transportation on the Potomac River:

> *From hence to Fort Cumberland, one hundred and ninety-one miles above the federal city, there is a free navigation, and boats are continually passing up and down.*

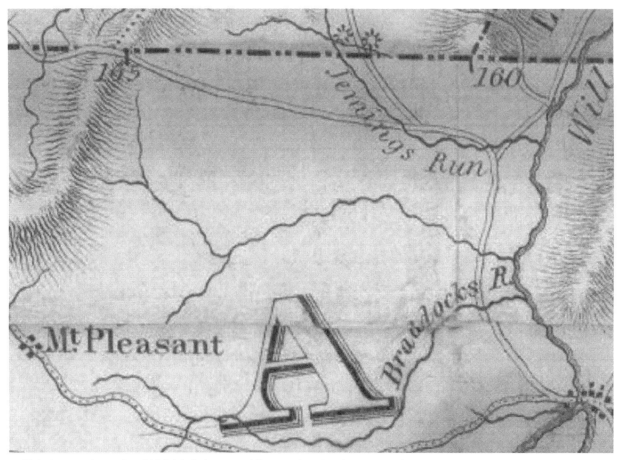

This image from the 1826 Melish map of Pennsylvania shows the Cumberland Road, from Somerset.

**The Sugar Bottom tract is divided among Joseph Mounts' three sons**
We have been following the Sugar Bottom tract from 1746 onward. In his November 1797 will, Joseph Mounts divides Sugar Bottom between his son Jesse, his son Asa, and his *"idiot"* son Providence, leaving Providence in the care of his wife Eleanor, with Eleanor in effective possession of Providence's share, and Jesse and Asa receiving Providence's share after the decease of Eleanor and Providence. The will mentions dwelling houses, barns stables, buildings, orchards, and commodities. The will was proved on December 28, 1797. One of the witnesses to the will was Evan Gwynne.[1702]

---

[1702] The will was located by Scott Williams.

### An 1801 petition to complete a Maryland portion of the Cumberland Road

A petition regarding the completion of part of the Cumberland Road was considered by the November 1801 session of the Maryland Legislature. The legislature left the following record:

*A petition from sundry inhabitants of Allegany county, praying an act may pass to lay off a public road from the Turkeyfoot road, at Robert Parker's, to the Pennsylvania line, to intersect the road leading from Somerset, was preferred, read and referred to Mr. Cresap, Mr. Simkins and Mr. J. Tomlinson to consider and report thereon.*

This explains an August 4, 1804 road survey plat, described below, that was prepared by surveyor Ninian Cochran. Robert Parker lived at the present-day site of Barrelville.[1703]

### Another 1801 petition, interpreted as being related to the new Cumberland Road

The November 1801 session of the Maryland Legislature also recorded the following:

*A petition from sundry inhabitants of Allegany county, praying an act may pass to establish the road laid out from the town of Cumberland to the Pennsylvania line, was preferred, read, and referred to Mr. Cresap, Mr. Simkins and Mr. J. Tomlinson to consider and report thereon.*

The petition[1704] does not say which valley the road was to follow, and it could be referring to a valley located east or west of Wills Mountain. Since the 1797 Sotzmann map clearly shows a road going up the valley east of Wills Mountain (i.e., on the Sotzmann map, the *"Cumberland Valley"*[1705]), the petition is more likely referring to the valley west of the mountain, along Wills Creek. Another factor pointing to the Wills Creek valley is that the 1801 petition relating to the antecedent to Barrelville's Route 47 was referred to three of the same individuals for consideration.

### Maryland Route 47 is laid out in 1804, as part of the new Cumberland Road

An August 4, 1804 plat that was prepared by surveyor Ninian Cochran depicts a road survey that clearly represents the antecedent to the present-day Route 47 (Barrelville Road NW) that extends from the Mason-Dixon line to the Turkey Foot Road (now Route 36) at the location of present-day Barrelville. The plat indicates that the sketched road path intersects a then-existing road from Somerset to Cumberland, as follows:

*By virtue of an order from the Levy Court of Allegany County at their august Session 1803 to Charles Uhl Daniel Logue and John Grate, as commissioners to lay out a road from the Turkey foot road near the fording a Robert Parkers on the north fork of Jennins run Intersect a road at the Pennsylvania [line] leading from the Town of Somersett in Pennsylvania to the Town of Cumberland in said county, I therefore certify that I have carefully surveyed and laid down the aforesaid Road under the direction of the commissioners as the above Plat and table of courses*

---

[1703] Robert Parker is identified as a settler on lot 3350 at the time of Deakins' 1787 survey of lots westward of Fort Cumberland. The 1793 to 1903 Land Office list of*"Lots West of Fort Cumberland"* states that Robert Parker patented lot 3350 from Deakins' survey 30 years later in 1817. Lot 3350 is located at the site of present-day Barrelville, and the 1804 road survey described in this chapter shows that Robert Parker's residence was near the present-day intersection of Routes 47 and 36.

[1704] I didn't recognize the relevance of this petition to the other contemporaneous activity relating to the Cumberland Road when the fourth edition of "**In Search of the Turkey Foot Road**" was written. In the course of writing this book, it became clear when I organized the material in chronological order.

[1705] Now at least part of the valley is commonly referred to as *"Bedford Valley"*. It is not clear to me, studying this from afar, if the *"Bedford Valley"* name is applied to the entire valley between Wills Mountain and Evitts Mountain, or if it is only applied to the part of the valley that is west of the valley ridge that is known as *"Shriver Ridge"*.

*will show, Beginning at A and running with the Black Plain lines shaded with yellow No 1, 2, 3, 4, 5, 6, 7, 8, 9, 10, 11 12, 13, 14, 15, 16, 17, 18, 19, 20, 21 B at the Pennsylvania line near Thos Elwells dwelling house at the road leading from Somersett to cumberland surveyed the 4th day of August 1804.*

This photo from the 1897 book "**Artwork of Allegany County Maryland**" shows the Cumberland Road, formerly the Turkey Foot Road, between Corriganville and Barrelville, in the Jennings Run water gap.

### A description of the town of Cumberland from 1804

In regard to Cumberland, Morse's 1804 book "**The American Gazetteer**" states, *"It Contains about 100 houses, a court house, a gaol, market house, and 3 churches, one for Roman Catholics, one for Methodists, and one for German Lutherans."*

### The National Road is authorized westward of Cumberland in 1807

Chapter MMDCCCXLV of the book "**Pennsylvania Statutes at Large**" is *"An act authorizing the President of the United States to open a road through that part of the state lying between Cumberland, in the State of Maryland, and the Ohio River"* that was approved on April 9, 1807.

### Albert Gallatin mentions the Great Road leading from Mounts ferry to Gwynne's tavern

In a July 13, 1807 letter to Thomas Jefferson about the forthcoming National Road, Albert Gallatin describes Gwynne's tavern as being at the intersection of two great roads, one of which goes by Mounts' ferry to Winchester, and the other connecting with Baltimore and Philadelphia. This letter helps to highlight the importance of the Winchester Road, and the prime location of the Sugar Bottom and Indian Purchase properties.

## The significant economic advantage of boating goods to Fort Cumberland

An article[1706] in an 1808 issue of the Pittsburgh "**Navigator**" includes the following:

*It is matter of much importance that an easy and short portage could be had to connect the waters of the Potomac with those of the Monongahela. The head waters of Cheat and the Potomac come together within about thirty miles, to which portage, however, the navigation of both rivers is difficult, but might be rendered much better by clearing them out. Goods are at this time frequently boated up from Alexandria, Georgetown, etc., as high as Fort Cumberland, whence they are taken in wagons to Brownsville, a distance of about eighty miles. By this route it costs about two dollars and fifty cents per hundred pounds, from Alexandria to Brownsville, which is a saving of about two dollars and fifty cents in the one hundred pounds when brought all the way by land.*

## Local taverns, including Arnold's hotel

Traditions of Arnold's Hotel survive in the Arnold's Settlement area near Mount Savage. Proof survives in the form of an 1809 document that shows payments of tobacco by Peter Bugh, Peter Lowdermilk, Michael Kershner, Archibald Arnold, George Rizer, and Benjamin Tomlinson for *"Complying with the acts of assembly in Keeping ordinary until April Term 1809. —"[1707]*

## The War of 1812

According to the 1913 book "**The British Invasion of Maryland, 1812-1815**", America declared war on Great Britian on June 18, 1812. The Treaty of Ghent was unanimously ratified by the U.S. Senate on February 18, 1815, officially ending the war.

## The earthworks of Fort Cumberland were still identifiable in 1816

Lowdermilk's book indicates that earthworks from the fort survived into the 19th century, and suggests that some form of earthworks extended far enough east to encompass the barracks portion of the fort:

*The fortifications were drawn to a scale, but the proportions were not preserved in mapping out the river, creek, and surrounding grounds. This fact made it somewhat difficult to establish the exact lines of the work, and compelled a resort to the memory of our oldest inhabitants. Mr. Jesse Korns has a distinct recollection of climbing over the remaining earth-works when a boy, and he fixes the easterly lines of the fort — that portion of it which runs to a point nearest Wills Creek — some forty feet east of Emmanuel Church. The conformation of the ground at that spot is strongly confirmatory of his opinion…*

According to Page 254 of the 1949 book "**The Genealogy of Michael Korns, Sr. of Somerset County Pennsylvania**", Jesse Korns[1708] was born 1809, and died 1888. Jesse Korns' description of where easterly

---

[1706] The article is reprinted in the 1879 book "**Oddities of colonial legislation in America...**"

[1707] If memory serves, this record was identified by Scott Williams.

[1708] I am a distant cousin of Jesse Korns. Mr. Korns' obituary in an 1888 issue of the "**Cumberland Times**" states, "*Mr Jesse Korns died this morning at his residence 64 Bedford Street after an illness of 6 months; aged 78 years. He was the eldest son of Capt. Henry Korns who came to Cumberland from Germany in the later part of the last century, settling on Mechanic Street above the Blue Springs in a house opposite Rabold's Tannery. He began work as a boat builder on Hoblitzell's, now known as Henderson's Island. In 1866, he established a brick yard until 1869, when he formed a partnership with William Landwehr until 1874. He married in 1831 to Miss Ruth Plank and had 1 son and 3 daughters; Mrs. M. C. Little of Cumberland; Mrs. William Price of Pittsburgh; Miss Hester Korns, deceased; and Mr. C. H. Korns of Allegany City PA. The funeral is from the Centre Street ME Church and the remains placed in the Korn's vault at Rose Hill Cemetery.*"

lines of the earthworks were located informs us that the far eastern end of the fort was reinforced with earthworks. Lowdermilk also states:[1709]

> ... *in 1817 an effort was made by subscription to build a church in Cumberland "for the joint use of the Presbyterian and Episcopalian churches of the town." For this purpose $2,122 in money was subscribed, besides the donation of Thomas J. Perry's "lot No. 68, in the fort," then valued at $100, on which the present Emmanuel Episcopal church stands.*

This suggests that in 1817, at least part of lot 68 was flanked by earthworks. In other words, it suggests that the barracks part of the fortification was surrounded by earthworks.

Lowdermilk provides one other clue concerning earthworks, stating, *"The ground to the North-west was somewhat higher, but a small earthwork of a temporary character was constructed on the crest, on the site of the residence of the late James W. Jones, Esq."*

Uria Brown's 1816 journal, which is reproduced in Volume X of the 1915 "**Maryland Historical Magazine**", substantiates Lowdermilk's description the survival of earthworks into the nineteenth century, and provides a description of the town, stating:

> *The Town of Cumberland is a handsome little place with many good brick buildings in the same, it is situated on the North Branch of the River Potomac, Wills Creek a large Stream of Water running through the Town (directly emptying itself in the River) affords an opportunity for the erection of several Merchant Mills, One large New Brick Mill looks well is an acquisition to the place, is bounded in the front by Spurs of the Alegany Mountain, on the rear, the right & the Left by those Little Bull dog Mountains, the whole Afford when on the neighboring hills a pleasant lively romantick appearance (no scarcity of Romanticks in this world).*

> *There is a handsome Bridge hung upon Chains[1710] which carry over Wills Creek into the other part of Town, directly ascending the Hill after crossing bridge on an high yes very high Emminance stand the ruins of the old fort (which takes the mind to Braddocks War) it has full command of the river Down the same for a mile & up about ½ a Mile, the river here makes a very quick short Bend in the form of a horse Shoe, the fort directly standing on the out side of the Shoe at the Toe of the same, which gives comand on both sides of the Shoe, or other wise both up & down the River;*

> *directly opposite this Fort over the River in Virginia Hampshire County, within the Shoe or in the Bend of the River on an high Eminance was erected another Fort which had good command of the River up & down where this fort was, now, stands a large & spacious Brick Dwelling...*

The large brick home that Brown describes at the site of the blockhouse is the circa 1794 Calmes mansion. For a circa 1870 photo of the mansion, see the article *"The Ridgeley Triangle"* in the 2012 issue of the "**Journal of the Alleghenies**".

## A resurvey of the town of Cumberland is ordered by the legislature in 1817

According to the 1817 book "**Laws of the State of Maryland**", the following legislation passed on January 17, 1817:

---

[1709] This passage was identified by Dave Williams.

[1710] For more information on the Cumberland chain bridge, see pages 285, 305, and 342 of Lowdermilk's 1878 book "**History of Cumberland**". The bridge was based on the design of Findly's 1801 bridge across Jacobs Creek. The June 1810 issue of "**The Port Folio**" contains Findly's detailed technical description of his bridge design and describes where such bridges had been built. The article includes the statement, *"There is also one at Cumberland (Maryland) supported by two chains of inch and a quarter bar, span 130, width 15 feet."*

*CHAPTER 92.*

*An act appointing Commissioners to Revise and Correct the Original Plot of the Town of Cumberland, in Allegany County.*

*WHEREAS it is represented to this general assembly, by petition of Thomas Beall, of Samuel, proprietor of the town of Cumberland, in Allegany county, that by virtue of an act of assembly, passed at November session, eighteen hundred and five, appointing Roger Perry, George Hoffman, Jonathan Cox, Evan Gwynn and Upton Bruce, commissioners to mark and bound the said town, in the execution of the powers vested in them by virtue of said act, the surveyor employed by the said commissioners has made some errors that cannot be corrected without legislative interference; Therefore,*

*Sec. 1. Be it enacted by the General Assembly of Maryland, That Roger Perry, George Hoofman, Jonathan Cox, Evan Gwynn and Adam Segur, senior, be and the same are hereby appointed commissioners, with full power and authority, with the assistance of the surveyor of said county, to revise and correct any errors appearing in the original plot of said town, with as full and ample powers as were vested in the commissioners appointed by the aforesaid act of 1805.*

*2. ...And be it enacted, That the said commissioners shall receive one hundred and fifty cents for each and every day they may be employed in the same, to be paid by the said Thomas Beall, of Samuel, but in case of a refusal to pay, the same may be collected before a single justice of the peace in a summary Way.*

## The new National Road is open for travel in 1818

According to the 1904 book "**Hart's history and directory of the three towns...**", the August 8, 1818 issue of the Uniontown, Pennsylvania "**Genius of Liberty**" states:

*The stages have commenced running from Frederick Town, Maryland, to Wheeling, in Virginia, following the course of the National Road westward from Cumberland. This great road, truly an honor to the United States, will be finished from Cumberland to this place in a few months (some of the heavy masonry was not yet finished southeast of Uniontown) and from Brownsville to Wheeling, it is expected, in the course of next summer, leaving only a distance of 12 miles from Uniontown to Brownsville.*

## The Impact of the new National Road on regional commerce

Volume II, pages 212 to 214 of the 1906 "**History of Bedford and Somerset Counties...**" describes the impact of the National Road on residents of Somerset County, Pennsylvania. The impact would have been the same in Allegany County, Maryland. The book states:

*While but a few miles of this one-time great thoroughfare are within Somerset County...it is not probable that the road is anywhere as much as three miles distant from the southern boundary of the county. It was, therefore, the outlet for our southern townships, both to the east and the west. Their produce found its way eastward to Baltimore over this great highway and all goods and merchandise that were brought into that part of the county came over the same route... Almost every mile of the road had its tavern, or public house. ... There were also some taverns that were both tavern and drove stands, for the feeding of the multitudes of animals of all kinds that were on the road at all times, vast quantities of hay, oats and corn were required. In those days not very much corn was raised in Somerset county, but oats was a staple crop, and because of the ready market for it that was found all the way from the Great Crossing at Somerfield to Cumberland, most of the farms in Addison, the two Turkeyfoots, Elk Lick, Summit, Brothersvalley and other townships were devoted to the raising of it. It brought ready money...*

## A massive westward migration between 1790 and 1820

In 1790, the center of the United States population of 3.9 million was about 25 miles east of Baltimore. By 1820, the United States population had grown to 9.6 million, and about half of the people had moved west of Cumberland.[1711] It isn't too difficult to imagine that his migration provided a ready market for people living in the environs of Cumberland.

## A description of Cumberland

In his 1821 book "**A Visit to North America**", Adlard Welby describes Cumberland as follows:

*Of the few picturesque stations it has been our lot to see, Fort Cumberland stands first; it is not in itself a town of any importance or containing many good buildings, but surrounded as it is by mountains covered with beautiful foliage, and its stream winding through the vale, it forms a whole worth of the pencil of a master: at the distance of about six miles are some natural curiosities of rock, cave, and waterfall, which, owing to the lateness of the season, I did not chuse to lose a day in viewing though invited to it by the respectable old Patriarch of the settlement,[1712] who in his ninetieth year yet offered to walk and accompany us to the scene.*

This depiction of Cumberland, Maryland is from Adlard Welby's 1821 book "**A Visit to North America**".

---

[1711] The census information is from the 1901 book "**The Leading Facts of American History**" by D. H. Montgomery.

[1712] This apparent reference to the age of Thomas Beall of Samuel, proprietor of the town of Cumberland, cannot be reconciled with the 1744 birth date, apparently taken from a family Bible, that is provided in the book "**The ancestry and descendants of Gustavus Beall and Thomas Heugh Beall**" (book identified by John DeVault).

## Thomas Beal, of Samuel, proprietor of the town of Cumberland, died in 1823

An 1823 issue of the "**Maryland Advocate**" identifies Captain Thomas Beal as a Revolutionary War soldier, stating:

*Died on Tuesday the 25th, Captain Thomas Beall of Samuel, at an advanced age. He was a participator in the struggles of the Revolution and proprietor of the town of Cumberland.*

## Ground Breaking for the Chesapeake and Ohio Canal

The 1848 book "**A Discourse Delivered in Quincy, March 11, 1848, at the Interment of John Quincy Adams…**" states, *"On the 4ᵗʰ of July, 1828, he helped break ground for the Chesapeake and Ohio Canal, thinking it an important event in his life."* The ground-breaking event, which took place near Georgetown, is covered in detail in the 1849 book "**Life and public services of John Quincy Adams, sixth president of the United States…**"

## The National Road is in bad condition by 1828, and is repaired in 1835

According to a May 1, 1828 resolution recorded in Volume 168 of the "**Congressional Edition**", the National Road was then in a *"dilapidated condition"*. The National Road was repaired with stone in 1835, according to the October 17, 1835 issue of "**Nile's Register**", which states, *"…the covering of stone lately put on the Cumberland road, is understood to be sufficiently packed to admit of traveling upon it at the ordinary speed—and that the road will every day become better."* Jacob Brown's 1896 book "**Brown's Miscellaneous Writings…**" describes the stone that was put on the road in the 1830s as macadamizing, and describes the process as follows:

*Limestone was quarried…then reduced by sledgehammers to the size of about three or four pounds, and after that broken down to an egg size by small round hammers in the hands of the laborers in sitting position… When the stone was thus broken…they were then spread with a horse rake over the whole bed. I believe the depth or thickness was nine inches… the road in time became packed and solidified…*

## The 'place long known by the name of Mountz's Ferry'

Circling back once again to the Sugar Bottom tract, the February 10, 1831 issue of Hagerstown's "**The Torch Light and Public Advertiser**" indicates that Sugar Bottom was still known as Mounts Ferry, stating:[1713]

*A Tract of LAND, called "SUGAR BOTTOM," Containing 304 acres of Bottom Land of a superior quality, lying on the Potomac River, about 8 miles above Cumberland, including the place long known by the name of Mountz's Ferry. This last place will be laid off into two Farms, with a suitable quantity of wood land and water…"*

---

[1713] This reference to Sugar Bottom was found by Julia Jackson. This reference suggests that a road that branched from or at one time served as the Winchester Road crossed Sugar Bottom. No map that illustrates such a road has been found, but prior to the discovery of this article, Bruce D. Carter presented the hypothesis that just such a road could have come through Sugar Bottom from the mountain pass known as Short Gap, by turning right after the road passed through Short Gap. An inset on John Payne's 1799 map **"The States of Maryland and Delaware from the Latest Surveys"** shows the Winchester Road crossing the Potomac River just west of the horseshoe bend of the Potomac River, which forms three sides of Sugar Bottom (map found by Robert L. Bantz). This is the same general area where the Winchester Road crosses the Potomac River on the 1897 topographical map of the area. Payne's map refers to the Winchester Road as the *"Great Road"*.

## A turnpike company is incorporated in Pennsylvania and Maryland

Pages 7,628 to 7,631 of the 1874 volumes of the "**Pennsylvania Archives**" include the August 23, 1832 charter of the Somerset and Cumberland Turnpike Road Company. The introduction begins with the statement *"The Governor this day issued his letters patent under the Great Seal of the State incorporating the suscribers to the stock of the Somerset and Cumberland Turnpike Road Company..."* Page 8,340 includes text from the January 10, 1837 *"Executive Minutes of Governor Joseph Ritner"* which states:

> *Upon the application of the President of the Somerset and Cumberland turnpike road Company, the Governor this day appointed George Tile, Peter Putman and Michael Rheem Esquires, of the County of Somerset, Commissioners to view and examine twenty miles of the said road, and to report to him in writing ... whether the said twenty miles of the said road, are made and perfected in a complete and workmanlike manner, according to the true intent and meaning of the acts of the General Assembly, passed March 18th 1816, and April 5th 1832, which authorize the making of the same turnpike road.*

Although not documentary evidence, Volume II, page 208 of the 1906 "**History of Bedford and Somerset Counties...**" states:

> *In the year 1832 a charter was granted for the incorporating of the Somerset and Cumberland Turnpike Company. The commissioners were Charles Ogle, George Chorpening, Frederick Gebhart, George Weller, Jacob G. Miller, John Brubaker, Jacob Kennell, James Platt and Henry Fuller. The patent was to issue when twenty or more persons would subscribe for two hundred shares of the stock. The road was to be not less than forty and not more than fifty feet wide, with a twenty foot bed. It was to be two feet high in the centre, well ditched, and constructed of substantial material—wood, gravel, slate, stone or other hard substances. This turnpike was speedily constructed, and it passed form Somerset, through Berlin and Wellersburg, reaching the National Road about three miles west of Cumberland. It had the usual fortune of such improvements.*

Although not documentary evidence, Lowdermilk's "**History of Cumberland**" states that on October 18, 1832, *"A meeting was held at Jacob Fechtig's tavern in Cumberland, with a view to securing the construction of a turnpike from Cumberland to intersect the Cumberland and Somerset Road at the Pennsylvania line. A number of persons from Somerset were present, and a committee was appointed to draft a petition to the Legislature asking authority for the construction of the road."*

The "**Journal of the Proceedings of the Senate of the State of Maryland**" indicates that on March 15, 1833, the governor signed *"An act entitled, an act to incorporate a company to made (sic) a turnpike road from such point as the Somerset and Cumborland Turnpike Company of Pennsylvania shall fix upon at the Pennsylvania line, to the public square in the town of Cumberland, or to intersect the United States road, commonly called the National road, at such point as may be most convenient and practicable."*

Scharf's 1882 book "**History of Western Maryland**" reports that:

> *In compliance with an act of the Legislature incorporating a company to make a turnpike road from the Pennsylvania line, to intersect the road then making by the Somerset and Cumberland turnpike company, and thence in the direction of Cumberland, to intersect the National Road, subscription books were opened at Slicer's hotel, in Cumberland, on the first Monday in August, 1833 by the commissioners,—Bene S. Pigman, William McMahon, Jacob Snyder, Gustavus Beall, John M. Buchanan, Joseph Everstine, George Blocher, Martin Rizer, Jacob Tomlinson.*

## The earthworks of Fort Cumberland were still traceable circa 1833

In his 1833 book "**A History of the Valley of Virginia**", Samuel Kercheval reports being informed by John Tomlinson that the remains of Fort Cumberland could still be seen, although *"On the ancient site of the fort there are several dwelling houses, and a new brick Episcopal church."*

## A Somerset County portion of the turnpike was mentioned in 1834

The 1834 "**Annual Report of the Geologist of Maryland**" mentions *"crossing the Savage, over the Somerset turnpike in Pennsylvania, no outcroppings of the millstone grit are met with..."*, proving that this Pennsylvania section of the turnpike was already open in 1834.

## Toll gates are authorized on the new Somerset and Cumberland Turnpike in 1837

Page 8,387 of the 1874 volume of the "**Pennsylvania Archives**" includes text from the May 10, 1837 *"Executive Minutes of Governor Joseph Ritner"* that states:

> *A License to erect gates and turnpikes and to receive the tolls authorized by law was this day granted by the Governor, and issued under the lesser seal of the State to the President managers and company of the Somerset and Cumberland turnpike road for the distance of twenty miles of said road, agreeably to the acts of the General Assembly of March 18th 1816 and April 5th 1832.*

## One last look at Sugar Bottom, and the ferry there

A January 20, 1838 deed[1714] includes the statement:

> *...Pigman having taken upon himself the said tract afterwards to wit. Appeared at public Sale at the tavern of James Black in the town of Cumberland on the fourteenth day of October, eighteen hundred and thirty one, the real estate of the Said James _eatt, when the said Charles _ Cresap was the highest bidder and purchaser for two hundred and Seventy five acres, and three quarters of an acre, more or less, of the Said real estate, bordering on and including the ferry on the North branch of the Potomac river at Six dollars per acre, on the terms and conditions mentioned in the decree, amouting to the Sum of Sixteen hundred and fifty four dolllars fifty cents, Consisting of part of the tract of land Called "Sugar Bottom" part of the tract of land called "Mounts Neglect" and part of the tract of land called "Spear" the whole of the tract of land called "Cedar Hill" and lot number thirty five hundred and Seventy one lying westward of Fort Cumberland....*

This is our last glimpse of Mountz's ferry, which had been in operation since at least 1791.

## The iron works at Mount Savage

Although not documentary evidence, the 1923 book "**History of Allegany County, Maryland**" states the following in regard to Mount Savage, Maryland:

> *The real life of the place began in 1839, when the Mount Savage Iron Works were erected. Two years later, two blast furnaces were added to the works, coal mines had been opened to supply the furnaces, which required as much as 150 tons a day. In order to transport its products to Cumberland, a macadam road was constructed.*

---

[1714] Allegany County Land Records, Liber T, Folio 471 to 473. Deed identified by Julia Jackson.

### An outsider purchases a large tract of land for mineral development in 1840

Samuel B. Barrell purchased a significant amount of property in the Barrelville[1715] area, including lot 3350. This purchase became known as *"Barrells Purchase"*, and is illustrated on Allegany County, Maryland Patented Certificate 212 (MSA S1188-234), which documents the 1418-and-five-eighths-acre, May 16, 1840 resurvey of *"...Samuel B. Barrell of the City of Boston in the Commonwealth of Massachusetts..."*

This depiction of the Mount Savage Iron Works is from the April 1857 issue of "**Harper's New Monthly Magazine**".

### The Baltimore and Ohio Railroad reaches Cumberland in 1842

The Baltimore and Ohio Railroad was opened to Cumberland on November 1, 1842. While not documentary evidence, Lowdermilk's 1878 book "**History of Cumberland**" states:

*November 1. — The Baltimore and Ohio Railroad was on this date opened to Cumberland, and the wonderful locomotive made its first appearance here. No other event has ever transpired in the history*

---

[1715] Barrelville is a former mining town that is named for Bostonian Samuel B. Barrell, who was the son of Joseph Barrell (See Benjamin Joy's 1816 pamphlet "**A True Statement of Facts, in Reply to a Pamphlet lately Published, by Messrs. Charles Barrell, Henry F. Barrell, George Barrell, and Samuel B. Barrell**"...) Chapter 272 of the 1844 book "**Laws Made and Passed by the General Assembly of the State of Maryland...**" indicates that *"An act to incorporate the Barrellville Mining Company"* was passed on March 7, 1844. The act identifies Samuel B. Barrell, William Ridgely, and John Pickell as being involved in the company. An 1852 "**New York Times**" article states, *"The first mines reached are those of the Parker Vein Coal Company, at Barrallville, on the north fork of Jennon's run, under the management of M. P. O'Hern, Esq. A Railroad, three quarters of a mile in length, and spanning Jennon's run by an elegant Viaduct forty feet in height and three hundred in length, connects them with the main road, while their little mining village, with its clean and pretty cottages, presents a picturesque appearance. The Parker Vein was the first discovered and earliest mined in the Coal field, and was boated down the Potomac for use in the Government Arsenal at Harper's Ferry, long before the iron age of Railroads had commenced."* This article proves that Barrelville was already in existence in 1852. An 1856 issue of the "**Mining Magazine**" states, *"The village of Barrallville, containing tenements for about forty families, a school-house, store, tavern, barns, stables and outbuildings..."*

*of the place which created so much pleasurable excitement. Business was entirely suspended, and men, women and children gathered about the terminus of the road to witness the arrival of the trains. From the mountain tops, and valleys, throughout the adjoining country, the people came in crowds, and the town was in a fever of excitement for many days.*

## An 1842 article mentions the completion of a Maryland section of the turnpike

A November 19, 1842 fluff article in Volume 63 of the "**Niles National Register**" describes the completion of a Maryland section of the turnpike that included the Turkey Foot Road:

*In connection with the improvements of Cumberland, it deserves to be mentioned that a turnpike road of about six miles has just been finished, along the valley of Wills creek and the north branch of Jennings' run, to the Pennsylvania line — which gives a continuous turnpike road from Cumberland to Pittsburg, but ninety-eight miles long. The portion of this road, thirty-four or thirty-five miles between the Pennsylvania Line and the town of Somerset, in the county of that name, was constructed by the United States Bank of Pennsylvania, and was a part of the consideration, or bonus paid it ... The road, though rough, is judiciously ... upon easy grades, and as materials for improve ... road abound upon its line, the objective, on the ... of its roughness, will be obviated as soon as its importance is developed. It is now the shortest, and will be rendered the most certain route of travel between Pittsburg and the Atlantic. It will, I should suppose, be constituted the great post route, as it will assuredly give the greatest dispatch to the mails; and as I see, has already attracted the attention of the Pittsburgers for this purpose. It has also attracted the notice of the stage proprietors, an active and sagacious class of citizens, who are quick to discern the course of travel, and prompt in providing for its accommodation.*

*This road is, as I have stated, the shortest turnpike road from Cumberland to Pittsburg. It passes through the towns of Berlin and Somerset, in Somerset county, and Mount Pleasant, in Westmoreland county, Penn. ...*

*Nor can this road to Somerset fail to draw an extensive trade to Cumberland — penetrating, as it does, the heart of Somerset, one of the most fertile and best cultivated counties in Pennsylvania. The industrious farmers of that county will now enjoy a convenient market for their surplus productions, an advantage of which they have hitherto been measurably deprived, by their remote position, in the midst of the mountains. The extensively and favorably known glades butter is chiefly the production of Somerset county, and is destined to reach your market by a new and speedier route than that over which it has been transported in years past.*

The article was written by *"S. J. A"* of Frostburg. One significant aspect of the article is that it reveals that the Maryland section of the turnpike, which was authorized by law in 1833, was not completed until late 1842. Although some aspects of the article are clearly promotional in nature, many of the things the author predicted did indeed come true. The road did become a mail and stage route, and the current embodiment continues to promote commercial intercourse between Somerset County and Cumberland.

## The Somerset and Cumberland Turnpike facilitated development of mineral resources

The Somerset and Cumberland Turnpike was important to the communities it passed through and facilitated the development of mineral resources in the area. As an example of the commercial influence of the road, Scharf's 1882 book "**History of Western Maryland**" states:

*Samuel B. Barrelville (founder of the village of this name) advertised in January, 1843, to deliver coal from his mines, which were situated near the forks of Jennings Run,[1716] only seven miles from Cumberland. He had opened two veins of coal upon his lands, – one the old Parker vein, the other the Bluebaugh vein.*

*He sold the former at five cents per bushel at the mouth of the mine, and the latter at four. David Percy was superintendent of his mines. The coal was transported five miles over the Cumberland and Somerset turnpike to its intersection with the National road, two miles from Cumberland.*

The above quote (which mangles Samuel Barrell's last name) shows the importance of the road before the circa 1845 advent of the Mount Savage Railroad,[1717] and helps to reveal the burgeoning influence of outside investment in the environs of Cumberland.

### A reference to the Mount Savage Iron Works in 1843

According to the book "**Session Laws, 1842**", an act that was passed on March 1, 1843 states:

*Be it enacted by the General Assembly of Maryland, That the president and directors of the Maryland and New York Iron and Coal Company, be and they are hereby authorized and empowered to lay out and construct a turnpike road from a point at or near the works of said company, known as the Mount Savage Iron Works, to intersect with the road recently laid out and constructed along the valley of Jenning's Run within the limits of Maryland, by the Cumberland and Somerset Turnpike Road Company, incorporated by an act of the general assembly of Maryland, passed December session eighteen hundred and forty-one, chapter sixty, and that for the purpose of enabling the said Maryland and New York Iron and Coal Company to lay out and construct the turnpike road as aforesaid, the president and directors thereof are hereby invested with all and singular the rights and powers as to the condemnation of lands through which it may be necessary for said road to pass, the size of the road, the construction of the necessary bridges and viaducts, and the erection of toll gates and the collection of tolls thereon, as are vested in the said Cumberland and Somerset Turnpike Road Company...*

This act is included here because it shows that the iron works at Mount Savage was in existence in 1843, and because it gave a private company the right to condemn property for a road. The *"Mount Savage Furnace"* is shown on an 1842 manuscript map of the area. According to the same book quoted above, an act that was passed on March 3, 1843 indicates that the Mount Savage Iron Works turnpike had already been built when the act authorizing it was passed. The book states:

*An act to incorporate a Company to construct a Turnpike Road from Frostburg, Allegany County, down the valley of Jenning's Run, to intersect the Turnpike recently constructed by the Maryland and New York Iron and Coal Company, at or near the Mount Savage Iron Works.*

---

[1716] The 1834 "**Annual Report of the Geologist of Maryland**" refers to the North Branch of Jennings Run as the *"Wellers' branch of Jennings' run"*.

[1717] Perhaps relying on Scharf's 1882 book, the 1893 book "**Maryland, Its Resources, Industries and Institutions**" states that *"Coal was at first hauled by wagon from Mt. Savage to Cumberland, but in 1844 the Mt. Savage railroad was constructed along Jennings Run."*

## An 1844 description of Cumberland

The 1844 book "**The Central Traveller**" describes Cumberland as follows:

*Cumberland, a large and well built town, and seat of justice of Allegany county. It is beautifully situated on the north bank of the Potomac, at the mouth of Wills creek, and contains, besides the court-house, &.c., upwards of 130 dwellings, with stores, taverns, shops, &c. The State road from Baltimore, terminates, and the National or Cumberland road, commences, here. The line of the Chesapeake and Ohio Canal, as located, passes through the town, which is now in a flourishing condition.*

## An 1844 long haul mail route

The February 19, 1844 issue of the Pittsburgh "**Daily Morning Post**" solicits a proposal for carrying the mail northwest from Cumberland via the Somerset and Cumberland Turnpike, as follows:

*1609 From Cumberland, Md., by Wellersburg Pa, Berlin, Somerset, Donnegal, Mount Pleasant New Staunton, Madison and Fulton's, to Tinker's Run, 85 miles and back, in two horse coaches, with a tri-weekly branch in two horse coaches from Somerset to Stoystown, 10 miles and back, to be __ in due connection.*

## The Chesapeake and Ohio Canal is completed to Cumberland in 1850

In regard to the Chesapeake and Ohio Canal, Volume 1 of the 1853 "**Mining Magazine...**" states that it, *"was begun during the administration of John Quincy Adams, as President of the United States, who dug the first spadeful of earth on the 4th of July, 1828, but was not completed and opened to Cumberland until the 10th day of October, 1850. It cost upwards of $15,000,000, and was originally intended to connect the waters of the Chesapeake Bay and Ohio River. This design was long since abandoned, its friends being content to reach the mineral riches of the Cumberland region."*

## The plank road from Cumberland to West Newton

The Plank Road is described in Volume II, pages 208 to 210 of the 1906 "**History of Bedford and Somerset Counties...**" While the description in the book may include some speculation, it still provides pertinent information:

*About 1850 many people took to the notion that the making of good roads by macadamizing with stone was a mistake. At that period many parts of Somerset county were still covered with dense forests of the best of white pine timber. About the only market for lumber, aside for the limited local demand was to be found at Cumberland. The owner of a county sawmill was glad to haul his product to Cumberland, some twenty or more miles away, and sell it for a dollar, or perhaps less, per hundred feet. The question was asked, why not use this cheap lumber in making a first-class road? By laying of plank a solid and smooth roadway would be secured.*

*It was proposed to convert the road the entire distance from Cumberland to West Newton, in Westmoreland county, into a plank road. Gen. Thomas Shiver, of Cumberland, Maryland became interested, and, taking up the project, handled it so successfully that it was carried through. Among a lot of other plank road legislation, a sort of an omnibus bill of the session of 1850, there was a section for the incorporation of the Wellersburg & West Newton Plank Road Company, with Joseph Markle, John Lansold, James W. Jones, Henry Baker, David Lavan, Andrew J. Ogle, Isaac Ankeny, John Brubaker, David Lepley, George Klingaman[1718], James Gardner, John C. Plummer, Rudolph Boose, John R. Brenham, Thomas Benford, Soloman Baer, Michael A. Sanner, Henry Little, William Colvin, C.P.*

---

[1718] George Klingaman is one of my ancestors.

*Markle, William Hitchman, Doctor John Cover and Samuel Philson, or any five of them, as incorporators. There was to be four thousand shares of stock of the par value of twenty-five dollars each. The road was to be commenced within three years and completed in four years. It was to be laid on the beds of the existing roads from Wellersburg to West Newton.*

*The two old turnpike companies still held their franchises and occupied the route. The question was, how to dispossess them. There were smart people in those days, as well as in these later days of our own time. There always are such, and the promoters of this scheme were equal to the occasion. Like many people, these old turnpike companies had managed to get into debt. A section has been smuggled into the act of incorporation permitting any one to whom they happened to owe anything to obtain judgment and have them sold out by the sheriff. We presume this was done. At any rate, they were made give way, and the plank road was speedily built. As a general thing, the planks were only eight or nine feet long, and were laid close together on the ground, a level bed having been prepared for them. This made a good road for the time being, but it soon wore out. In most places it was only a trifle more than a single track, and the wheels of all wagons having to run pretty much over the same part of the road, the plank soon wore thin. Then too, some plank wore away sooner than others, and it speedily became a very rough road, as any one yet living who ever drove over it can testify to. While the middle of the plank were still good, it became the custom, whenever it was possible to do so, to drive with one wheel in the middle of the track and the other on the outside. This prolonged the life of the road for some years.*

*Financially, the road proved a disappointment, and it never brought in enough in the way of tolls to keep it in anything like decent repair. Yet, as Johnstown on the north, and Cumberland on the east, were the only two railroad points that the people of Somerset county could reach, this road enjoyed a considerable amount of local traffic, which continued up to the time of the completion of the Pittsburgh & Connellsville railroad, in 1871. After that, it's existence was a very sickly one, and in a few years it was abandoned, and has become a township road.*

Because the road was only one track wide, whenever two wagons met, one had to temporarily get off onto the side of the road. To facilitate getting the wagon wheels back onto the plank road surface, it was common practice to leave a few of the planks longer than the others. If all the planks were the same length, then the wheels would tend to simply skid along the edge of the road, rather than ride up onto it. Because some of the planks were longer, the wheels would contact them at nearly right angles, and roll up to the level of the road.

The 1850 section of Lowdermilk's "**History of Cumberland**" states, *"A plank road was built from Cumberland to West Newton, Pa., at the head of steamboat navigation on the Youghiogheny."* This reference to river transportation helps to explain the importance of the road.

## A description of Cumberland in the mid-1800s

The 1857 book "**A new and complete statistical gazetteer of the United States of America founded on and compiled from official federal and state returns and the census of 1850**" states:

*Cumberland, p. v.,[1719] and cap. Alleghany co., Md.: on the N. bank of the Potomac r., at the mouth of Wills' cr., 146 m. W. N. W. Annapolis, and by R. R. from Baltimore, 179 m. It is the centre of the vast mining region of Alleghany county, and an entrepot on the great line of travel from the Atlantic to the Western States. The Baltimore and Ohio R. R. passes through it, and here commences the great National Road leading to the Mississippi river. The Chesapeake and Ohio Canal also terminates here. Besides these great works of internal improvement, there are diverging from Cumberland several lines of railroads connecting with the various mines of the Cumberland Coal and Iron Companies. The village contains a court-house, the county prison, a market-house, two banks, and several fine buildings,*

---

[1719] Postal village.

*workshops, etc., connected with the public works; also, several handsome church edifices. Three newspapers are published here weekly, the "C. Civilian" (whig), the "Alleghanian" (dem.), and the "Unionist" (neutral)—each circulating from 400 to 500 copies of each issue. In 1850, the population of Cumberland was 6,067,[1720] of which 5,576 were white persons, 267 free colored persons, and 224 slaves, and hence it is the second town of Maryland in respect of population. In 1840, the population was only 2,428, the increase in the subsequent decade having been 149.8 per centum. The coal of this region is semi-bituminous, of excellent quality, and suitable for ocean steamships and a variety of other purposes to which the anthracite has hitherto been applied; it is brought to the markets of the East on the railroad and canal to Baltimore, and thence Is tugged through the Chesapeake and Delaware Canal, and the Delaware and Raritan Canal, to the harbor of New York. The quantity of this mineral delivered in Baltimore In 1850 was 146,645 tons, and about 80,000 tons were deposited at Alexandria. ...*

## Almost every trace of Fort Cumberland is gone

An article in the July 4, 1861 issue of Cumberland's "**Civilian & Telegraph**" states:[1721]

*The old Fort is now gone — almost every trace of it has been obliterated. — But its memories remain. From it radiated the forces of civilization that reared a mighty empire in the rich and fertile valley of the Mississippi. Here Briton and American, Marylander and Virginian, Pennsylvanian and Carolinian stood side by side in defending a nation's march to populate and civilize the unbroken wilderness of the West. — Here Washington learned the arts of the camp, and the tactics of war, and laid the foundation of that military character that gave freedom to a continent and the watchword of Liberty to a world.*

---

[1720] Lowdermilk's 1878 book "**History of Cumberland...**" reports the 1850 population of Cumberland as 6,105.

[1721] This passage was identified by Andy Petenbrink.

This 1898 drawing (MSA C1741 2367), which is the last page of Allegany County Liber E, shows the general location of Fort Cumberland relative to town streets and lots.

# 40. The town was still called 'Fort Cumberland' long after it was founded

## Introduction

Various surveys from what is now Somerset County, Pennsylvania refer to Cumberland, Maryland as *"Fort Cumberland"* long after the fort was reported as being *"demolished"* in 1775 and demonstrate that the town itself was for a time known as *"Fort Cumberland"*. The 1811 Reading Howell map is the first Reading Howell map to use *"Cumberland"* instead of *"Fort Cumberland"*.

## Surveys along the Hays mill path

John Well's 1794 survey refers to what we now call the Hayes mill path as *"the Road from Berlin to Fort Cumberland"*. The 1794 survey of George Cook refers to the route as *"the road leading from Simon Hays Mill[1722] to Cumberland"*. The 1794 survey of George Hafner refers to the route as *"the Path leading from Fort Cumberland to Simon Hays Mill"*. The 1794 survey of Mary Simpson identifies the route as *"the path leading from Simon Hays Mill to Fort Cumberland"*. The 1794 survey of Samuel Dunlap identifies the route as *"the path leading from Simon Hays Mill to Fort Cumberland"*. (The present-day Mount Carmel Lutheran Church at White Oaks is situated on Dunlap's property.) The 1794 survey of Samuel Gillard shows what appears to be a switchback across a minor branch of Laurel Run and identifies the route as *"the path leading from Simon Hays Mill to Fort Cumberland"*. The George Wyman property in the vicinity of present-day Pleasant Union, surveyed in 1794, describes the route as *"the road leading from Hays Mill to Fort Cumberland"*.

### A survey along the Turkey Foot Road

The 1795 Leonard March survey states that the property is *"situate on the Waters of Elklick Creek on both sides of the Turkeyfoot Road leading to Fort Cumberland in Elklick Township Somerset formerly Bedford County…"*

---

[1722] Simon Hay's mill is the origin of the name of the little village of Hays Mill (Latitude 39.850985°, Longitude -78.973855°). Simon appears in the list of 1779 Brothersvalley Township property holders with 300 acres. According to the February 1960 "**Laurel Messenger**", the June 26, 1779 birth of Simon's son Valentine is listed in the records of the Berlin Reformed Church, and Valentine's elder brothers were born at Conocochegue in 1775 and 1777. An article about Simon Hay in Volume 3 of the 1906 "**History of Bedford and Somerset Counties…**" indicates that two of his children, Jacob and Elizabeth, lived on a farm that became the site of Wellersburg — which helps to explain the Hayes mill at Wellersburg that is illustrated on the 1818 Melish manuscript map of Somerset County. Jacob owned the farm first, and then sold it to George Weller, who was or became Elizabeth's husband. For detailed information on the Hayes Mill at Wellersburg, see the 2012 issue of the "**Journal of the Alleghanies**". For more information on Simon Hay, see Page 552A of the 1884 book "**History of Bedford, Somerset and Fulton Counties…**", which mentions trips to Wills Creek. For information about the Simon Hay farm, see the February 1979 issue of the "**Laurel Messenger**". The article makes clear, based on federal direct tax records, that Simon Hay's house was one of the finest in Somerset County in the year 1798. Only three other houses in the county were assessed at a higher value.

### An 1801 reference to the town of Fort Cumberland

Chapter XLV of the Laws of Maryland references Cumberland as *"Fort Cumberland"*, stating:

> *... and John Lynn and Thomas Cresap, who will meet such persons as are or may be appointed for the same purpose by the state of Virginia, at Fort Cumberland, on the said first Monday in March...*

This is not a reference to Colonel Thomas Cresap, Sr., who was long dead by 1801.

### An 1805 reference to the 'town of Fort Cumberland'

Volume 2 of the 1805 book "**Philadelphia Medical and Physical Journal**" states:

> *The Editor is informed, that several cases of the disease of Bronchocele, or Goitre, have, within the last four or five years, occurred, especially among females, at, and in the vicinity of, the town of Fort-Cumberland, in Maryland.*

### An 1817 reference to the town of Fort Cumberland

The 1817 book "**Acts and Joint Resolutions of the General Assembly of the Commonwealth of Virginia**" includes a resolution that passed both houses of the general assembly of Virginia on February 22, 1817 that states the following:

> *Resolved by the general assembly, That the Executive be, and they are hereby requested, in pursuance of the recommendation of the board of public works, to open a correspondence with the governments of the United States, and of the states of Ohio, Indiana, and Kentucky, for the purpose of obtaining their cooperation, in effecting an extension of the national road from the Ohio to Fort Cumberland, as far as Winchester...*

Clearly, the town of Cumberland was referred to as Fort Cumberland long after the palisades were gone.

*— finis. —*